# Readings in

# **Juvenile Delinquency**

EDITED BY

RUTH SHONLE CAVAN

Rockford College

J. B. LIPPINCOTT COMPANY

PHILADELPHIA AND NEW YORK

*[handwritten notes at top:]* This book is a collection of a number of articles & or selections written by professionals who deal directly w/ delinquents. The readings give a comprehensive view of juv Delinq. as a field of study. The book is divided into sections which deal with Theories, patterns & influences in which Juv. Del. ~~Prog~~ Prev. Prog &

# Preface

THIS COLLECTION of readings brings together in one volume a number *the* of articles or sections of books that together give a comprehensive *J.S.* view of the status of juvenile delinquency as a field of study. The *are* thirty-six selections are organized into nine sections, which may be *also* grouped loosely into five subdivisions of the field of study of delin- *discussed* quency. Section I throws open the question of what is meant by juvenile delinquency and how its frequency may best be measured. Sections II, III, and IV review current theories of social and indi- vidual causative factors, with special attention to the interweaving of delinquent behavior with family and school influences. Section V comprises six articles on specific patterns of delinquent behavior. Sections VI, VII, and VIII turn to a different phase of the subject— the many institutions of prevention, control, and treatment of de- linquents. A final section reviews attempts to predict future delin- quency in young children and presents a study that traces the progress through thirty years of children who were known delin- quents.

A major purpose of this book is to place in the hands of college students a collection of original writings of professional people, both theoreticians and those who deal directly with delinquents. The col- lection may be used to illuminate and supplement college textbooks or, with supporting lectures, may become the chief textbook. In com- parison with a book written by one author, a book of readings has both advantages and disadvantages. It lacks the continuity of a book written by one author, but it has the inestimable advantage of placing

v

before the reader exactly what an author had to say on his subject, in his own phrases and with the overtones of author-personality that creep into professional articles.

A book of readings serves another purpose. It prolongs the time during which worthwhile articles are saved from the obscurity of the bound volumes of periodicals shelved in dark recesses in the library. It brings to the reader material that he might never discover or would not take the trouble to locate in its original form.

Certain principles guided the selection of the thirty-six articles from the vast number in the bibliography with which the editor started. The articles delve at critical points into the fields of study usually included in textbooks on juvenile delinquency. They are current; therefore, purely historical articles have been avoided, although introductory notes are included where needed to give the background of some current theory or practice. For the most part, simply descriptive articles have been omitted in favor of articles that deal with controversial aspects of the field—and of these there are many. Controversies indicate the growing edge of the subject where thinking is needed. In order to reach a wide range of readers, articles phrased in highly technical terms have been bypassed, although the articles selected rest firmly on sound theoretical thinking or research. Articles dealing primarily with research methods are not included; however, many of the articles detail the methods used in a specific piece of research. The book therefore has been planned to stir the reader's critical thinking on the current situation without diverting him into historical or technical bypaths.

Since a major purpose is to supplement textbooks, a chart has been included listing the chief texts in juvenile delinquency by chapter and citing appropriate readings by number. This device will facilitate quick coordination of textbook and readings.

The editor thanks the many authors and publishers who consented to the reprinting of the material in this book.

RUTH SHONLE CAVAN

*Rockford, Illinois*
*October, 1963*

# Contents

Patterns, & Influenced ~ in. 19
theories
as well as
to

Contents    ix

# Delinquency—
# What and How Much?

THE THREE articles in this section are attempts to answer two perennial questions: What kinds of behavior constitute juvenile delinquency? How many juvenile delinquents are there in a given country? The first article, by Teeters and Matza, tackles the problem for the United States. It is actually less concerned with the number of delinquents (which changes somewhat from year to year) than with the basic difficulties of defining delinquency and computing rates.

In the second article, Cavan conceives of all behavior as constituting a continuum, one in which delinquent behavior is ranked as a type of nonconformity that is beyond the tolerance of the community.

The third article, by Lejins, carries the problem of definition and rates into the international field. It opposes the assertion of a delegate to the Second United Nations Congress on the Prevention of Crime and the Treatment of Offenders who said that juvenile delinquency is a symptom of the decadence of a nation.

# 1.    The Extent of Delinquency in the United States

## Negley K. Teeters and David Matza

Dr. Teeters, who holds the Ph.D. degree from Ohio State University, is Chairman of the Department of Sociology and Anthropology at Temple University. He is the author or co-author of books on penology in Europe and South America, *The Cradle of the Penitentiary, The Prison at Philadelphia, Public Executions in Pennsylvania, New Horizons in Criminology*, and others. He has also written numerous articles in the fields of criminology and penology.

David Matza has the Ph.D. degree from Princeton University and is Assistant Professor of Sociology at the Berkeley campus of the University of California. He has had his writings appear in various professional publications.

During this year when preparations are being made for the Sixth White House Conference on Children and Youth, it is not out of place, in assaying the extent of delinquency, to quote from the third conference held in 1930: "There exists no accurate statement as to the amount of delinquency in this country, nor whether it is increasing or decreasing." And again: "There is no accurate conception as to what actually constitutes delinquency." [1] These same words might well be stated at the White House Conference in 1960.

The term "juvenile delinquency" does not appear in the literature until 1823 when a New York philanthropic society changed its name from the *Society for the Prevention of Pauperism* to the *Society for the Reformation of Juvenile Delinquents*. But there can be little doubt that there have always been juvenile delinquents. But as to "how many" we cannot know. They were referred to through the years as "wayward," "depraved," "unfortunate," "wild," "headstrong," "willful," or "handicapped." The first special institutions for delinquents in this country were the early Houses of Refuge established in New York in 1824, in Boston in 1826, and in Philadelphia in 1828. The first institution in the world for the treatment of delinquent youth was the *Hospice of San Michael* in Rome in 1704.

Negley K. Teeters and David Matza, "The Extent of Delinquency in the United States," *Journal of Negro Education*, 28 (Summer, 1959), 200-213 with certain omissions. Reprinted with permission of the publisher of the *Journal* and the authors.

[1] *The Delinquent Child*, New York: Century, 1932, p. 23.

It has always been difficult—even impossible—to compute the extent of delinquency. It has always been popular for each generation to believe its children were the worst, the most lawless, and the most unruly. Sir Walter Scott, writing in 1812, deplored the insecurity of Edinburgh where groups of boys between 12 and 20 scoured the streets at night and knocked down and robbed all who came in their way. In an article in the *Atlantic Monthly* for December, 1926 and bearing the intriguing title "The Habit of Going to the Devil," Archer Butler Hulbert presents an array of diatribes against youth, as culled from the press during the early part of the nineteenth century. He found that in 1827 "a glance at our country and its moral conditions fills the mind with alarming apprehension; the moral desolation and flood tides of wickedness threaten to sweep away not only the blessings of religion, but the boasted freedom of our republican institutions as well." In 1828 he found: "No virtuous public sentiment frowns down upon the criminal to shame him into secrecy" and a year later, "And what of our youth? The lamentable extent of dishonesty, fraud, and other wickedness among our boys and girls shocks the nation." He found that in 1831, "Half the number of persons actually convicted of crime are youths who have not yet reached the age of discretion (how familiar that sounds in 1959)." He further finds that in 1830 "The army of youthful criminals from the slums are augmented by children abandoned by the shiftless of the working classes, by families wrecked by living beyond their means, and by wayward unfortunates from reputable families. Large numbers of these youngsters belong to organized gangs of thieves and cutthroats . . . Of 256 convicts in the Massachusetts State Prison, forty-five were thieves at 16 and 127, had at that age, become habitual drinkers." [2]

A century later, in 1930, we find the oft-quoted statement of the Wickersham Commission of the prison population of that year—54.8 per cent had been less than 21 years of age when convicted. In 1938 Harrison & Grant, in their startling study of young offenders in New York City, stated that of those persons arrested for lesser offenses, minors were responsible for only 4.5 per cent of the total, whereas of the more serious crimes, the arrest rates of those under 21 were many times higher. [3]

It was the startling data presented in this work that galvanized into motion the American Law Institute to draw up the Youth Correction Authority Model Act of 1940, which subsequently was adopted in modified form in California and a few other states. Almost twenty years ago

[2] The *Atlantic Monthly*, 138:804-6, December, 1926.
[3] Leonard V. Harrison & Pryor M. Grant, *Youth in the Toils*. New York: Macmillan, 1939, pp. 44-45.

we found the following sober analysis of youthful delinquency and crime to substantiate the findings of Harrison & Grant; it could well have been written in 1959:

> Youthful offenders are an especially serious factor in the crime problem. Young people between 15 and 21 constitute only 13 per cent of the population above 15, but their share in the total amount of serious crime committed far exceeds their proportionate representation. They are responsible for approximately 26 per cent of the robberies and thefts; they constitute some 40 per cent of our apprehended burglars and nearly half of our automobile thieves. Boys from 17 to 21 are arrested for major crimes in greater numbers than persons of any other four year group. They come into court, not for petty offenses but for serious crimes, twice as often as adults of 35 and 39; three times as often as those of 45 and 49; five times as often as men of 50 to 59. Nineteen year olds offend more frequently than persons of any other age, with 18 year olds next. Moreover, the proportion of youths less than 21 in the whole number arrested, has increased 15 per cent during the past three years; 108,857 not yet old enough to vote were arrested and fingerprinted last year.[4]

Such was the situation as reported in 1940.

Before analyzing the extent of delinquency, let us set down some data from the Uniform Crime Reports for 1957. Taking the serious categories of crime we find that arrests for all crimes reported (by the police in 1,473 cities of over 2,500 representing a population of 40,176,369 based on the 1950 census) 19.3 per cent were of persons under 21 years of age. Of the arrests for the serious categories, 14.5 per cent of all for homicides were of those under 21; 44.7 per cent of the robberies; 16.9 per cent for all aggravated assaults; 44.1 per cent for the rapes; 68.0 per cent of all the burglaries; 62.4 per cent of all larcenies; and 80.6 per cent of all auto thefts.

At first glance and without interpretation this is indeed an alarming picture. But like all statistics, they do need considerable interpretation. We quote in this connection, the former F.B.I. affiliate and presently operating Director of the Chicago Crime Commission, Mr. Virgil Peterson:

> A few years ago the Attorney General of the United States . . . informed the people: "I have been asked to bring you the facts and the figures, the tragic evidence of juvenile crime . . . Here are some . . . of the figures chargeable to some of our youth . . . 51 per

---

[4] Digested in the *Prison Journal*, April-July, 1940, pp. 57-8, from a pamphlet *The American Law Institute*. See also, Thorsten Sellin, "The Criminality of Youth," Philadelphia: *The American Law Institute*, October, 1940.

cent of all burglaries, over half of them; 36 per cent of all robberies . . ." Naturally; these figures given by the highest law enforcement official of the land were widely quoted in the press, over the radio, from speakers' platforms, and by crime prevention groups. Actually, the figures were based only on the available fingerprint cards of persons arrested and charged with burglary and robbery— a small sample from a huge army of burglars and robbers.[5]

Mr. Peterson points out that of all burglaries reported, only 31.3 per cent were cleared by arrest; and that of each ten burglaries reported no one knows who committed seven of them; and of the vast number arrested, the majority were youth. He continues:

> Their youthful recklessness and inexperience in crime make it relatively easy to apprehend them. The professional criminal is more difficult to detect and apprehend. And it is reasonable to assume that he is responsible for a large percentage of our unsolved crimes. At any rate, the Attorney General's flat statement that over half of the burglaries were attributable to youth was little more than an opinion— an opinion that may be far from the truth.

Further along in his article Mr. Peterson adds this startling remark: "During the five year period from 1947 through 1951 over a million burglaries were reported to the police in about 2,200 cities . . . No one knows who committed over 800,000 of them." But the bulk of those arrested were youth under 21 years of age. The same can be stated of practically all categories. The monetary value of articles stolen by youth is generally quite small. Lumped into these "burglaries" are thefts of hub caps or tire gauges from filling stations, or other objects of trifling value. It is important to note that the Federal Bureau of Investigation's definitions of robbery and burglary include "attempts" as well as the actual commission of these acts. The arrest rate also includes many instances of mistaken identity at the scene of the crime.

In order to present a picture of national delinquency trends between 1940 and 1957 it is necessary to use a number of different sources of information.[6] The reason for this is that prior to 1952 it is not possible to convert Uniform Crime Report data into rates since there is no base population reported. Therefore, we shall infer the trends between 1940 and 1952 from the Juvenile Court Statistics. While this may be questioned, there seems to be good reason to believe there is considerable similarity between the direction or changes indicated by both collecting systems. As I. Richard Perlman of the Children's Bureau, states:

[5] *Atlantic Monthly*, "Crime Does Pay," pp. 38-42, Fe 1953.
[6] Figures for 1958 will not be available until autumn, 1959.

We find that despite the fact that neither of these series (Juvenile Court Cases and Police Arrest data from the Uniform Crime Reports between 1938 and 1947) represents a completely accurate measurement of juvenile delinquency and despite the differences in the unit of count, the extent of coverage and geographical representation, nevertheless there is remarkable similarity between the direction of changes indicated by the two lines. Both increased sharply from 1942 to 1943, both decreased between 1943 and 1944, both increased again in 1945 to the ten year peak and both showed sharp decreases in 1946 and 1947.[7]

If Perlman is right we are able to increase greatly the length of time subsumed by our descriptive series. Table I below shows the increase in juvenile delinquency rates between 1940 and 1952 as indicated by the Juvenile Court Statistics. Table II shows the increase in juvenile delin-

## TABLE I

JUVENILE DELINQUENCY CASES (AGES 10-17) 1940-1952
JUVENILE COURT STATISTICS *

| Year | Per Cent (1940 as 100) | Child Population of United States Per Cent (1940 as 100) |
|------|------|------|
| 1940 | 100 | 100 |
| 1941 | 112 | 99 |
| 1942 | 125 | 98 |
| 1943 | 172 | 97 |
| 1944 | 165 | 96 |
| 1945 | 172 | 95 |
| 1946 | 148 | 94 |
| 1947 | 131 | 93 |
| 1948 | 128 | 93 |
| 1949 | 135 | 92 |
| 1950 | 141 | 91 |
| 1951 | 149 | 93 |
| 1952 | 165 | 95 |

* Herbert A. Bloch and Frank T. Flynn, *Delinquency, The Juvenile Offender in America Today*. New York: Random House, 1956, p. 27.

quency rates between 1952 and 1956 as supplied by the Uniform Crime Reports.

[7] "The Meaning of Juvenile Delinquency Statistics," *Federal Probation*, pp. 63-67.

We may infer from Tables I and II the following tendencies: A gradual increase between 1940 and 1942, a marked increase in delinquency beginning in 1943 and lasting through 1945 with a slight dip in 1944, a gradual decrease beginning in 1946 and continuing through 1948, a grad-

## TABLE II

INCREASE IN DELINQUENCY RATES BETWEEN 1952 AND 1956 *

| Year | Per Cent (1952 as 100) |
|------|------------------------|
| 1952 | 100.0 |
| 1953 | 107.7 |
| 1954 | 111.6 |
| 1955 | 121.3 |
| 1956 | 147.9 |

* Rates computed from Uniform Crime Report data using estimated number of children (0-18) in reporting areas as base population.

ual increase from 1949 to 1951, a more marked increase between 1951 and 1952, a continuing gradual increase from 1952 to 1954, and finally another marked increase beginning in 1955 and lasting at least until 1957. Except for the period 1946 to 1948 and except for a slight dip in a high plateau in 1944, the picture revealed by official national statistics is one of continuous increase, sometimes gradual, sometimes rather rapid.

For the years between 1952 and 1957, we have computed delinquency rates by specific offense categories in order to obtain a more concise understanding of trends during this period. In Table III we present the delinquency rates per 100,000 persons using the number of persons in the Populations represented in the Uniform Crime Reports as the base population. [Tables III and IV, giving details of trends from 1952 to 1956, have been omitted, inasmuch as they are discussed below and analyzed in Table V. Ed.] In Table IV we present the delinquency rates per 100,000 children (0-18) using the estimated number of children in the Populations represented in the Uniform Crime Reports as a base population.[8] We see in Tables III and IV that there is considerable

[8] The base population in Table III is the number of persons residing in the cities included in the Uniform Crime Reports as of the 1950 Census. The base populations for Table IV were computed by first correcting the total populations for increases that had taken place since 1950, and then applying the proportion of children for each year to the corrected total population. We are indebted to the Population Reference Bureau for the estimates of total population (1950-1958) and the estimates of youthful population (1950-1956).

variation by offense in the shifting delinquency rates experienced during this period. In a few offenses, Embezzlement and Fraud, Prostitution and Offenses Against the Family, we observe decreasing rates of delinquency. These, however, are the exceptions. In all other offense categories we see varying degrees of increase in the delinquency rates. In Table V, we have classified the offenses according to the magnitude of the increase.

This series of tables represents the basis upon which we shall continue in this paper. The problem is obviously one of interpretation. What do the figures tell us?

The fundamental question is whether this increase in delinquency is apparent or real. There are three positions that may be taken in attempting to come to any conclusion: First, that the data accurately reflect a real increase; second, that the increases are due to artifacts of data-collecting methods; and finally that the official statistics overrate the increase but that there has been some real increase.

The official description of delinquency trends is not readily accepted by the academician. The point of departure for the theoretical criminologists has been the insistence that the official increase represents, not a reflection of real increases, but rather they are due to a number of diverse artifacts inherent in the subtle processes involved in the collection of the data.

The academicians—who may be referred to here as skeptics—possess an antipathy to "alarmist" tendencies in the interpretation of delinquency statistics; furthermore, they are concerned with distortions and error usually inherent in any system of collecting information.

The strength of the "alarmist" point of view exists, for the most part, outside the university. It is found most frequently among spokesmen of mass media, law-enforcement officials, serious citizens, and practitioners who are face to face with the delinquent, especially juvenile court jurists. The public has aligned itself with this "alarmist" point of view, especially since its "common-sense" impression of the problem supports it. Thus, it is not surprising that many informed and most uninformed Americans are disturbed by the "rising tide" of juvenile delinquency during the past twenty years.

The academic intellectual finds it impossible to accept the obviousness of the "common-sense" approach. His skepticism sometimes manifests itself in a rather charming—even if irritating—"hide-bound conservatism." Yet, the reluctance to accept new ideas is simply a form of skepticism that is necessary in any scientific endeavor. Scholars or academicians are, by definition, endowed, rightly or wrongly, with a near-monopoly of

## TABLE V

CLASSIFICATION OF OFFENSES BY AMOUNT OF INCREASE: 1952-1956

(Estimated Youthful Population
Used as Base Population)—Ratio of 1956 Rates to 1952 Rates

### HIGH INCREASE OFFENSES

|                              | (160 and above) |
| ---------------------------- | --------------- |
| Receiving Stolen Property    | 415             |
| Liquor Laws                  | 288             |
| Weapons                      | 213             |
| Other Assaults               | 187             |
| Larceny                      | 172             |
| Aggravated Assault           | 167             |
| Narcotics                    | 165             |

### MEDIUM INCREASE OFFENSES

|                              | (Between 136 & 160) |
| ---------------------------- | ------------------- |
| Auto-Theft                   | 160                 |
| Driving while Intoxicated    | 160                 |
| Rape                         | 154                 |
| Suspicion                    | 151                 |
| Murder and Manslaughter      | 147                 |
| All Other Offenses           | 141                 |
| Disorderly Conduct           | 137                 |

### LOW INCREASE OFFENSES

|                              | (Between 100 & 139) |
| ---------------------------- | ------------------- |
| Other Sex Offenses           | 135                 |
| Forgery and Counterfeiting   | 130                 |
| Drunkenness                  | 129                 |
| Burglary                     | 125                 |
| Vagrancy                     | 119                 |
| Robbery                      | 115                 |
| Murder by Negligence         | 113                 |
| Gambling                     | 107                 |

### DECREASE OFFENSES

|                              | (Below 100) |
| ---------------------------- | ----------- |
| Embezzlement and Fraud       | 87          |
| Prostitution and Vice        | 56          |
| Offenses Against Family      | 20          |

expertness. Thus they are in the intellectually impossible situation of being the judges and the judged. Therefore, we must bend over backward to be certain that we consider carefully the "alarmist" point of view, precisely because our first impulse is to dismiss it. More important, we must sometimes supply the opposition point of view with the sophistication that it, unfortunately, so often lacks. In reality, the "alarmists" are not the best spokesmen for their own position. They often lack the technical skills necessary to support their position and thus become vulnerable to those trained in the arts of logic, argumentation and scientific methodology.

There are a number of methods used by the "skeptics" in minimizing the apparent increases in delinquency. One is the thesis of the "expanding denominator" which contends that the growth of child population offsets the increase in delinquency rates. Empirically this argument has some validity but not too much. Thus, if we compare Table III with Table IV we see that the delinquency rate of 1956 was 54 per cent higher than that of 1952 if we *do not* take into consideration the expanding youthful population for that period; but if we *do* take the growth into consideration we find the increase in delinquency about 48 per cent. Thus, while we may contend that the "expanding denominator" may reduce the cause for alarm, it by no means completely disarms the vocal proponents of common sense.

The second argument of the skeptics is more sophisticated. It may well be asserted that the legal definition of delinquency throughout the nation has become less precise, more confused and vague. Stated another way, there is more delinquency because more and more overt acts—as well as covert—are being defined or considered delinquent. In addition, too, more and more minors are being counted for the same act, e.g., "57 youths charged with homicide" with one murder tabulated; "20 youths charged with carrying firearms" when only one of the group possessed a pistol. The skeptics contend that it is official policy in administering justice that has changed rather than the actual content and substance of juvenile behavior. We should also add that quite frequently it is the same child who is arrested over and over again and thus increases the delinquency rate.

This argument is often coupled with the assertion that norms in urban communities become increasingly formalized. This results in certain types of youthful behavior being officially dealt with rather than being handled through unofficial or informal forces of control such as parents, storekeepers, and neighbors. In many cities, the agents of formal control usually have a penchant for "recording" and "bookkeeping" and "referring" which usually results in an almost insatiable hoarding of a wide variety of records and statistics. The norms of bureaucratic management therefore impel the recording of many trivial deviant acts rather than of disposing of such cases on a personal and informal level. Thus, in many of our large cities, we find records of cases labeled with the vague nomenclature, "adjusted" or "unofficially handled."

What empirical evidence is there that the changes in methods of law-enforcement are responsible for the alleged increase in delinquency? The available evidence leads us to believe that some, but by no means all, can be explained by these changes. For instance, if we examine the data between 1952 and 1956, there is little evidence that the bulk of the increase can be attributed to vague and diffuse definitions. This is admittedly a short period of time but it is a period within which the data seem roughly comparable and it is, furthermore, a period during which a significant increase in delinquency rates took place.

In Table V above, we divided the various offense categories into (a) High Increase Offenses; (b) Medium Increase Offenses; (c) Low Increase Offenses, and (d) Decrease Offenses. The four best examples of vaguely defined offenses which appear in the Uniform Crime Reports are "Suspicion," "Disorderly Conduct," "Vagrancy" and "All Other Offenses." Three of these are "Medium Increase" offenses. This means that the rates of increase for these offense categories was about the same as that for total delinquency. The fourth, "Vagrancy," was a "Low Increase" offense. The vaguely defined offenses, therefore, contributed *slightly less* than their share to the increases that had taken place in delinquency within this five year period.

Another factor involves wider definitions of delinquency related to technological innovations. Traffic violations and the casual sale and use of guns are examples of anti-social behavior which parents and grand-

*TABLE VI*

PERCENTAGE INCREASE IN DELINQUENCY
RATES BETWEEN 1952 AND 1956

Total Delinquency vs. Diffusely Defined Offense Categories

|  | *Per Cent* |
| --- | --- |
| Total Delinquency | 48 |
| Suspicion | 51 |
| All Other Offenses | 41 |
| Disorderly Conduct | 37 |
| Vagrancy | 19 |

parents of modern youth could not have easily committed. Therefore, in some states—Utah for example—traffic offenses comprise more than half of all delinquencies. In the period between 1954 and 1956, traffic violations in Utah constituted 58.4 per cent of all delinquencies. In that state traffic violations rose from 1 per 1,000 of school age children in 1935 to 40 per 1,000 in 1955. It must be pointed out, however, that in Utah, conventional delinquency followed the national pattern. For example, out of each 1,000 school age children, there were 12 delinquents in 1935, 18 in 1940, 41 in 1943, 27 in 1945, 16 in 1950 and 30 in 1955.[9]

A final argument used by the skeptics pertains to the improvements in techniques of apprehending and recording delinquents. We have more delinquents simply because we are better able to capture and count them. Such improvements have taken place but it is doubtful that a significant proportion of increased rates can be attributed to these improvements.

In discussing improved methods of collecting statistics, it must be remembered that every additional reporting area brings with it not only an additional number of recorded delinquents (the numerator) but also an increase in the base population (the denominator). With each increase in the numerator, there is an increase in the denominator. The question is whether the increase in the denominator is proportionate or disproportionate to increases in the numerator.

Let us assume that City X reports for the first time in 1954. If its rate of delinquency has been higher through the years than the average of cities reporting prior to 1954, then all previous rates were underestimated because City X, a high delinquency city, was not included in previous compilations. On the other hand if City X has traditionally been a low delinquency area then all previous rates have been overestimated because it was not included in previous compilations. The answer to our question, therefore, depends on whether or not the cities that have only recently begun to report are relatively high or low delinquency areas. One may suggest that generally the larger cities tend to report first and smaller communities later. If delinquency is more concentrated in the large cities, as sociologists have traditionally held, then it may well be that we have *overestimated* the national rates of delinquency in the past and therefore *underrated* the differences between the rates of from 1940 to 1956.

While all of the above is quite conjectural, it can be stated that a major innovation in reporting that took place in 1953 was coupled with an increase that was rather "average" in all respects. We see in Table VII

---

[9] Biennial Report of the Director, Bureau of Services for Children, State Department of Public Welfare, Utah, Juvenile Courts, Ja 1, 1954 to Je 30, 1956.

below that the Uniform Crime Reports in 1952 were based on data compiled from 232 cities with population over 25,000. Starting in 1953, there are a great many cities reporting, ranging from 1,174 in 1953 to a maximum of 1,551 in 1956 (all over 2,500). The increase in delinquency rates between 1952 and 1953, the year of the major innovation in the number and type of cities included in the compilation, was 7.7 per cent. Between 1953 and 1954 the increase was 3.9 per cent. Between 1954 and 1955 there was a 9.7 per cent increase. Between 1955 and 1956 there was a 26.6 per cent increase. Thus it would seem that there is no striking relationship between major changes in the system of data-gathering and the official increases in delinquency.

## TABLE VII

### POPULATION REPRESENTED IN UNIFORM CRIME REPORTS 1952-57

| 1952 | 23,344,305 | (232 cities over 25,000) |
|------|------------|--------------------------|
| 1953 | 37,255,808 | (1174 cities over 2,500) |
| 1954 | 38,642,183 | (1389 cities over 2,500) |
| 1955 | 41,792,800 | (1477 cities over 2,500) |
| 1956 | 41,219,052 | (1551 cities over 2,500) |
| 1957 | 40,176,369 | (1473 cities over 2,500) |

There remains the question of improved methods of apprehension. Once again our belief is that we cannot attribute much of the increase to this, important though it may be. If we did make this contention, we would be obliged to answer some knotty questions as, for example, how account for the decreased rates between 1946 and 1948? Was there a decrease in police effectiveness during those years? If there are any years during which a realistic decrease in police effectiveness might be assumed, it would be the wartime period 1942 through 1945 when there was a critical manpower shortage; yet in this period we find an extremely high rate of delinquency. The inescapable fact is that delinquency rates are highly fluctuating in character, whereas there is every reason to assume that methods of apprehension and police efficiency have constantly improved. We do not intend to dismiss completely the role played by increasing police effectiveness in artificially raising the official rates. We merely wish to point out that its importance can, like all other phases of the problem, be overemphasized.

Thus far our position has been somewhere between that of the "alarmist" and the "skeptic." For the years between 1940 and 1957 our belief is that although the official statistics perhaps overrate the increase in the delinquency rates, there has, nevertheless, been some real increase. However, we do not believe that one may assume lower and lower rates for years previous to 1940.

As we stated above, delinquency rates are highly fluctuating. They are not stable, nor theoretically should we expect them to be. Juveniles by their nature should be expected to respond quickly to abrupt changes in the social structure. Delinquency rates should be diagnostic of various forms of social disorganization and social reconstruction. This means that unless we adhere to the fashionable but superficial view that modern times are decadent and that some unspecified era in past history is the repository of all things good, there is reason to suppose that delinquency rates were high in other periods—perhaps as high as those currently experienced. The early years of nineteenth century England immediately come to mind.

We argued earlier that there is nothing drastically new about the content or substance of delinquency. It has always been a feature of human existence—a part of the "backwash" of our culture. But one may ask, is it not true that there is a great deal more delinquency among modern youth? The answer depends a good deal on how far back one wishes to go for comparisons. It is often assumed that if the present rates are really higher than those of let us say, 1935, then they are *ipso facto* higher than the rates experienced in all years prior to 1935. There takes place, unconsciously to be sure, that curious reversal of the "evolutionary" mentality, the mentality of the "golden age." Just as the gloomy demographers of the thirties erred in extrapolating short-run tendencies into the future, so a disgruntled and neo-traditionalist public errs in simply extrapolating short-run tendencies back into the dark and unknown recesses of history.

There is one obvious reason why both predictions of the future and assessments of the past can be treated in so cavalier a fashion. We know little that is measurable about either. It is highly probable that the rates of delinquency of the late fifties seem dramatically high only because we have been forced by the data to choose a slice of history that *accidentally* begins with relatively low rates and culminates in relatively high rates. The fact that we happen to be "cheek to jowl" with them gives us no little concern. Put another way, the delinquency rates of today (the late fifties) may be "very high" only when we compare them to the "very low" rates of the late thirties.

We may see some scant evidence for this point if we turn to scattered local statistics that go back beyond the middle thirties. Table VIII shows the number of delinquency complaints and the rates for Cuyahoga County, Ohio for the years between 1918 and 1957. [Table VIII has been omitted, since its contents are summarized in the text. Ed.] The city of Cleveland is located within Cuyahoga County.[10]

We may make two inferences from this table. First, the pattern of fluctuation between 1932 and 1957 is roughly similar to that experienced by the nation as a whole. Second, and more important, we note that the rates in Cleveland and the rest of the county were twice as high in the period during and after World War I than the rates experienced during the early and late fifties. The delinquency rate was 65.9 per 1,000 children (12-17) in 1918, 63.2 in 1919 and 52.0 in 1920. In 1925 the rate was 41.5; in 1932 it was 35.8; in 1939 it was 21; in 1943 it was 31.7; in 1945 it was 34.7; in 1950 it was 25.2; and in 1957 it was 33.5.

What was the rate before World War I? We do not know. We can say, however, that despite the better reporting, despite the better detection, the delinquency rates of at least one large metropolitan area were twice as high in World War I than in World War II. Of course, this does not prove too much, if anything. We have no idea how typical the experience of this one large urban county is. We cite it in order to suggest the intriguing possibility that the extent of delinquency, as well as its character, was just as serious, if not more so, in the dark and unknown recesses of history.

[10] Statistics from Mr. John J. Alden, Chief of Probation Services for the Juvenile Court of Cuyahoga County, Cleveland, Ohio. Population based on resident births (uncorrected for deaths, in-migration, out-migration). Source: A Sheet-a-Week, prepared by Howard Whipple Green, Mr 5, 1953.

## 2.   The Concepts of Tolerance and Contraculture as Applied to Delinquency

### Ruth Shonle Cavan

The author holds the degree of Doctor of Philosophy from the University of Chicago and is Professor Emeritus of Sociology at Rockford College. She is the author of research reports and textbooks on the family and criminology, including *Juvenile Delinquency* and *Criminology*. This article was her Presidential Address to the Midwest Sociological Society in 1961.

In defining juvenile delinquency, laws are of little use. Usually laws are specific only in relation to serious adult offenses such as murder, assault, robbery, burglary, and so forth. Children are delinquent if they

Ruth Shonle Cavan, "The Concepts of Tolerance and Contraculture as Applied to Delinquency," *Sociological Quarterly*, 2 (1961), 243-258. Reprinted with permission of the editor of the *Quarterly*.

are found guilty in court of breaking any of the federal, state, or local laws designed to control adult behavior. Delinquency statistics, however, indicate that these serious offenses account for only a small proportion of the delinquencies of children. Most of the behavior that gets a child into trouble with the police and courts comes under a much less definite part of the law on juvenile delinquency. Examples are easy to find. The Illinois law defines as delinquent a child who is incorrigible or who is growing up in idleness, one who wanders about the streets in the nighttime without being on any lawful business, or one who is guilty of indecent or lascivious conduct. Laws in some other states are still more vague. New Mexico rests its definition on the word habitual. A delinquent child is one who, by habitually refusing to obey the reasonable and lawful commands of his parents or other persons of lawful authority, is deemed to be habitually uncontrolled, habitually disobedient, or habitually wayward; or who habitually is a truant from home or school; or who habitually so deports himself as to injure or endanger the morals, health, or welfare of himself or others. In these laws there is no definition of such words or phrases as incorrigible, habitual, indecent conduct, or in the nighttime. How much disobedience constitutes incorrigibility? How often may a child perform an act before it is considered habitual?

The federal Children's Bureau dodges all this by stating flatly that juvenile delinquency cases are those referred to courts for certain violations of laws or for conduct so seriously antisocial as to interfere with the rights of others or to menace the welfare of the delinquent himself or of the community.[1] This approach does not help much. Someone has to decide when the child has violated a law or when his conduct is antisocial. Parents, teachers, and police make the decisions. What guides them in deciding when a child's behavior justifies a court hearing? Is a court hearing the only measure of delinquency? Or are there gradations in delinquency? If so, where along the line of gradation does a child become so out of line that his behavior merits calling him a delinquent? If delinquent behavior has gradations, does good behavior also have gradations?

This paper is an attempt to assign misbehavior to a place in the total social structure, and to determine when misbehavior should be termed delinquency. The Children's Bureau definition is tentatively used: behavior that interferes with the rights of others, or menaces the welfare of the delinquent or the welfare of the community. I am concerned chiefly with the last, construed to mean the effective functioning of the social organization.

[1] *Juvenile Court Statistics, 1957*, Statistical Series No. 52 (Washington, D.C.: Children's Bureau, 1959), p. 4.

## The Behavior Continuum

A word now about Figure 1. The figure represents the social structure, the framework of which consists of the institutions and less formal but fairly permanent organizations that, operating together, carry on the functions of the society. Area *D* represents the central or dominant part of the social structure, where institutions are found that set the formal standards for behavior and exert the formal means of control. The base line represents the extent of deviations from the central social norms. According to this hypothetical formulation, behavior falls into a continuum from condemnable behavior (area *A*) through decreasing degrees of disapproved behavior to the central area *D* and then through increasing degrees of good behavior to near perfection in area *G*.

The area above the line represents the volume of behavior—or more concretely the number of people—that falls into the area controlled by

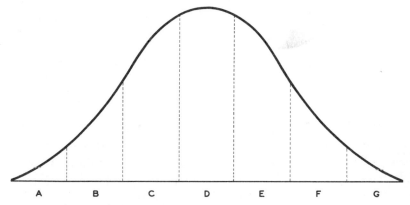

|   |   |   |   |   |   |   |
|---|---|---|---|---|---|---|
| A | B | C | D | E | F | G |

FIGURE 1. Hypothetical formulation of behavior continuum

A. Underconforming
   contraculture
B. Extreme under-
   conformity

C. Minor under
   conformity
D. Normal
   conformity
E. Minor over-
   conformity

F. Extreme over-
   conformity
G. Over conforming
   contraculture

the norms and into successive segments of deviation. There is sufficient evidence, that I will not quote, to support a bell-shaped curve.[2]

[2] Floyd H. Allport, "The J-Curve Hypothesis of Conforming Behavior," *Journal of Social Psychology*, 5:141-83 (1934); R. T. LaPiere, and P. R. Farnsworth, *Social Psychology* (McGraw-Hill: New York, 1936), p. 400.

Even though we know that behavior falls into a continuum, nevertheless we tend to think in terms of dichotomies. We have the sinner and the saint, the devil and the angel, the alcoholic and the teetotaller, the criminal and the upright citizen, the juvenile delinquent and the model child. We tend to think in terms of black and white, whereas between these two rare extremes are many shades of gray. For instance, one might set up such a series as pitch black, charcoal gray, slate gray, tattletale gray, dingy white, off white, and lily white. In this series of seven, the modal term (area $D$) is not white but tattletale gray. (This term is borrowed from the advertisements of a few years ago in which the sheets flapping on the line were tattletale gray because the housewife had not used the right kind of laundry soap.) Observed behavior falls into similar gradations. The child may break into a store at night and steal (black); deliberately pick up valuables during store hours; occasionally pick up things as opportunity arises; pilfer small objects (tattletale gray); be meticulous about not taking things; remonstrate with others who steal; or report other children to teachers or police for even minor pilfering (lily white).

## Social Norms and Modal Behavior

To avoid confusion, certain terms require clarification. The formal standards that dominate area $D$ are social norms. They are related to but not identical with values. Values are ideals or ultimate goals, perhaps never attained. They are abstractions. Social norms are the specific formulations to implement the values in practical, attainable form. They constitute the expectations of society and often are stated in terms implying that exact conformity is expected. However, a third level may be identified, the working plans or modal behavior of the majority of people.

For adequate functioning of society a balance must be maintained between the rigid social norms and the more flexible modal behavior. Complete conformity to the social norms, always, by everyone, is rarely demanded. A concession is made to human nature itself—to the difficulty of always observing rules, or always suppressing impulses, or always standing at attention. Some of these concessions have been institutionalized in the familiar swing back and forth between consecration and carnival. After the religious rites at Christmas we have our modern New Year's Eve; and Mardi Gras precedes Lenten abstinence. Concessions are often made in areas of behavior not vital to the main social functions. Other concessions are made to certain groups, especially the young and the very old. The behavior in the central area $D$ therefore is not strict conformity to social norms, but permits some deviations. $D$ is an area of flexibility or tolerance, but only to the extent that the social organization itself is not threatened.

Normally, children are taught to accept the social norms and to confine their behavior to the area of tolerance. Most people find in this area a satisfactory way of life. Their behavior is reasonably well restrained and predictable. The society functions adequately.

## Underconformity and Overconformity

In the illustration of the continuum given above, pilfering of small objects was given as the modal type of behavior falling within the area of tolerance although not rigidly conforming to the social norm of honesty. With this formulation, both more serious forms of stealing and meticulous avoidance of taking things are deviations from the social norms and the modal behavior. There is deviation in the nature of underconformity to the social norms, shown to the left on Figure 1, and deviation in the nature of overconformity to the social norms, shown to the right. Underconformity is an exaggeration of the tolerance allowed by the modal norms; for example, if the modal behavior permits a small amount of pilfering of candy and comic books in the corner store, the underconformer expands the tolerance to include stealing of more valuable objects. Overconformity is an exaggeration of the strict observance of formal social norms. Honesty may be exaggerated to the point where a person would not keep even a pencil that he found nor use an article belonging to someone else even in an emergency.

Either underconformity or overconformity that exceeds the limits of tolerance poses a threat to the operation of the social organization. Overconformity, as a threatening type of deviation, has often been omitted from the formulations of sociologists or has been only casually mentioned. It is true that overconformity usually does not constitute delinquency or crime in the same degree as underconformity. However, it should be included in any discussion providing a complete picture of the social structure, of which delinquency and crime are one kind of deviation and overconformity the opposite kind.

The issue with reference to overconformity has sometimes been obscured by the tendency to think of the social norms not as our workable expectations of behavior but as ideal or perfect standards. An example may be drawn from the introductory text by Lundberg, Schrag, and

## TABLE 1

### CHARACTERISTICS OF STAGES OF CONTINUITY IN BEHAVIOR

| | A Delinquent Contraculture | B Extreme Under-conformity | C Minor Under-conformity | D Normal Conformity | E Minor Over-conformity | F Extreme Over-conformity | G Overconforming Contraculture |
|---|---|---|---|---|---|---|---|
| Public attitude | Condemnation; "hard core" | Disapproval | Toleration without approval | Tolerance with approval | Toleration without approval | Disapproval | Condemnation |
| Public reaction | Rejection; school expulsion; commitment to correctional school | Police warnings; school suspension; referral to social agency | Disciplinary action by school or parent | Indifference; acceptance; mild reproofs | Ignoring | Ostracizing | Rejection |
| Child's attitude toward public | Rejection of values of D | Wavering between acceptance and rejection of D values | Acceptance of values of D; feelings of guilt | Acceptance of values of D; no guilt feelings | No deviation in personal conduct | Criticism of D behavior in others | Rejection of D values |
| Child's self-concept | As delinquent, outlaw | Confused, marginal to C and A | As misbehaving nondelinquent | As a conforming nondelinquent | As a true conformer | Better than others | His way is the only right way |
| Examples | Armed robbery; burglary | Larceny of valuables | "Borrowing" and keeping; pilfering | Minor pilfering; unauthorized borrowing | Borrowing only with permission | Extreme care not to use other's possessions; criticism of others | Report even minor pilfering to teacher or police |
| | Rape; serious sex deviations | Promiscuity; minor sex deviations | Extensive normal sex relations | Minor normal sex relations; petting | Normal, only in marriage; no petting | Restrained, even in marriage | Celibacy as a philosophy |
| | Drug addiction | Occasional use of drugs | Smoking of marihuana | Smoking tobacco | No smoking; use coffee or tea | No stimulating drinks, even though mild | Opposition to use by others |

Larsen.[3] These authors establish the institutional expectations and the area of tolerance in the middle, with most people fitting their behavior into this area. They also show disapproved behavior to the left, as is done in Figure 1. However, to the right they show approved deviations, whereas Figure 1 and Table 1 define these deviations as disapproved and a threat to area D. According to Lundberg, *et al.*, approved deviations exceed the standard set by the group, and include at the extreme some 2 or 3 per cent of people who are given public recognition for their overconformity. According to this formulation, the ideal standards for behavior would be at the extreme right, would constitute virtual perfection, and, practically, would be attained by almost no one. Everyone except the 2 or 3 per cent would be deviants.

Research studies of juvenile delinquents sometimes ignore the central area of modal behavior and compare delinquent children (area A) with near-perfect children (area G). Sheldon and Eleanor Glueck in their much discussed book, *Unraveling Juvenile Delinquency*, make such a comparison.[4] They matched each of 500 correctional-school boys with a boy of the same age, intelligence, and social background, whose behavior was exemplary. Not only were these control boys without any police, court, or correctional-school record, but 74 per cent were without any known delinquency of even a minor nature. The Gluecks had difficulty in finding 500 such overly good boys, and eventually had to include a few boys guilty of such misbehavior as smoking in their early years, hopping trucks, once or twice swiping much desired articles in five-and-ten-cent stores, crap shooting, sneaking into movies, occasional truancy, being stubborn to their mothers, and a very occasional occurrence of staying out late at night, using vile language, drinking, running away from home, and bunking out. Some of the deficiences were very trivial and had occurred when the boy was seven or eight years old. The Gluecks then were comparing boys from area A—the most seriously underconforming—with boys from area G—the most seriously overconforming. This selection may account for the fact that, whereas the delinquents tended to be active, aggressive, impulsive, and rebellious, the control group tended to be neurotic, fearful of failure or defeat, and submissive to authority. The middle group of boys with normal conformity or D-type behavior, who live within the tolerance limits of the community, is completely ignored. In the Glueck study the control group is fully as deviant as the delinquent group, but in the opposite direction.

[3] George A. Lundberg, Clarence C. Schrag, and Otto N. Larsen, *Sociology*, rev. ed. (Harper: New York, 1958), p. 349.

[4] Sheldon and Eleanor Glueck, *Unraveling Juvenile Delinquency* (Cambridge, Mass.: Harvard University Press, 1950), pp. 23-39, Chap. 21.

Actually, it seems very doubtful whether so much admiration is really accorded the overconforming group as some sociologists and researchers state or imply. The good behavior and achievements that are rewarded by society seem much more likely to be in area *D* or *E* than in area *F* or *G*. For example, consider the descriptive terms and epithets that are applied to youths whose behavior falls into the different areas. Boys in area *A* are often referred to as little savages, hoodlums, punks, bums, or gangsters—not very complimentary terms. But boys in area *G* also are not complimented; they are often referred to as sissies, goody-goods, teacher's pet, drips, brains, fraidy-cats, wet blankets, or squares. Adults and youth alike admire the boys in area *D*, who are essentially conforming but not rigidly so. The area *D* youth is "all boy," or the all-American boy; he can take care of himself; he is ambitious; he can hold his own with the best of them; he is a good sport. A little later, in college, he makes a "gentleman's C." He may occasionally borrow small things that he needs and forget to return them, truant off and on but not enough to damage his school record, cheat on tests in subjects that he doesn't like, mark up the walks and walls of a rival high school, do some property damage under the stress of excitement, outwork and outsmart his rivals, lie for his own advantage, and occasionally sass his parents and neglect his home chores. But he stays within the tolerance limits; he is developing, even in misbehavior, traits that will help him fit into the adult competitive *D* pattern of behavior; he is moving toward the social expectations for his future as an adult.

## Areas *C* and *E*

Let us look at areas *C* and *E*, representing minor deviations from the social norms and the modal behavior of area *D*. Minor deviations only are involved, whether they are under- or overconforming. Parents, teachers, employers, and other adults keep a wary eye out for these deviations. They are not a serious threat to the social organization but might become so if they increased in frequency or seriousness. The general attitude is toleration without approval, as indicated in Table 1 after "public attitude." Efforts to rectify or prevent these deviations usually are handled by parents or school officials. More attention is given to the underconformers than the overconformers. However, overconformers are admonished not to interfere with other people's fun, and are urged to get into the swing of things, to enjoy themselves, and to let themselves go in normal fashion.

The youth who falls into one of these two areas is regarded as a member of the social institutions and groups that control area *D*. He is "one of ours," erring a little, but to be brought back into the groups, disciplined if need be, and forgiven.[5]

The youth in areas *C* and *E* accepts the standards of area *D*. He identifies himself with groups in area *D*, and would be lost without them. He feels guilty about not meeting the expectations of groups in area *D* and tends to rationalize his shortcomings. In the *C* area the boy agrees that stealing is wrong and insists he meant to return the property he took; he is contrite and filled with good intentions. He thinks of himself as nondelinquent.[6] The overly conscientious youth in area *E* also feels guilty because he is not measuring up to the expectations of area *D*. He also rationalizes: he doesn't join the boys on Saturday night because he doesn't want to worry his parents; he needs the time to study, and so on.

## Areas *B* and *F*

Behavior in areas *B* and *F* is definitely disapproved according to the social norms and the modal behavior patterns of area *D*. *B*- and *F*-type behaviors are a threat to the smooth operation of the social organization. The chronic truant of area *B* interferes with the effective operation of the school; but the boy who always is perfectly prepared or who is always on hand after school to do the schoolroom chores is also a hindrance in a school that wishes to draw all boys into participation. He may of course be temporarily rewarded by appreciation from an overworked teacher who welcomes his help even though it is at the expense of the boy's participation with other boys in nonschool activities.

The underconformers in area *B* are made to feel that they are violators of the social norms; but they are not abandoned by representatives of area *D*.[7] Police warn or arrest but do not necessarily refer boys to the

[5] This analysis was drawn from Solomon Kobrin, "Problems in the Development of the Image of the Delinquent in Mass Society," paper presented at the annual meeting of the Illinois Academy of Criminology, Chicago, May 6, 1960.

[6] William W. Wattenberg, "Ten-Year-Old Boys in Trouble," *Child Development*, 28:43-46 (1957); Wattenberg and F. Quiroz, "Follow-up Study of Ten-Year-Old Boys with Police Records," *Journal of Consulting Psychology*, 17:309-13 (1953); Wattenberg, "Eleven-Year-Old Boys in Trouble," *Journal of Educational Psychology*, 44:409-17 (1953); Wattenberg, "Normal Rebellion—or Real Delinquency?" *Child Study*, 34:15-20 (Fall, 1957).

[7] Stanley Schachter, "Deviation, Rejection, and Communication," *Journal of Abnormal and Social Psychology*, 46:190-207 (April, 1951). In an experiment with small groups, the dissenter at first is the object of increased interaction in the effort to restore him to consensus; when this fails, he is rejected.

juvenile court. The school may suspend disorderly boys but does not expel them. Parents inflict severe penalties. These disapproved underconformers are made to feel that they are on the outer margin of area C and in danger of losing their membership in conforming groups. One more misstep and they are out.

Youth in overconforming area F are handled somewhat differently. The attitude toward them is one of impatience, sometimes of scorn. They too are made to feel that they are on the outer margin of acceptability. They are socially ostracized, ignored in invitations to parties, and excluded by youth from membership in many groups because they would hamper activities. If adults take any action it is in the nature of trying to stimulate them to normal youth activities, or in some cases referring them to psychiatric clinics for diagnosis and treatment of their extremely overconforming behavior.

Youth themselves in either area B or F feel themselves to be in a marginal position, neither in nor out of the normal social organization. They waver between accepting and adjusting to modal behavior and social norms of the D area, and abandoning these norms altogether. They are in contrast to youth in areas C and E with slightly deviating behavior who feel that they are wanted by groups in area D. The more seriously nonconforming youth in areas B and F feel alternately wanted and rejected by the conforming groups in area D. The youth is in an anomalous position and often feels isolated from all groups. He may become involved in a spiral type of interaction in which each move on the part of the representative of area D calls for a countermove on his part. If the youth perceives the approach to him as friendly he may respond with friendliness and a spiral will be set up that carries him back into conforming groups. But if he perceives the approach of conforming groups as hostile and rejective, he will respond in kind and the process of alienation will increase until he breaks off all contacts with the various conforming groups. Underconformers show their hostility by stealing, vandalism, and attacks of various sorts. Overconformers show hostility by vociferous criticism of conforming groups.

Areas B and F are the ones where reclamation of youth must occur if it is to take place at all. Much of what is done with nonconformers is punitive and tends to push a youth further along in the process of alienation from conforming groups. The reverse process might pull him back into conformity. He should be made to feel that he is not a threat to society or permanently outside the approved area of behavior, unworthy of association, even though he has seriously transgressed the codes or social norms.

## Areas A and G

Areas A and G differ from the ones already considered in that they do not represent simply deviation from the central modal behavior and social norms, but rather detachment from social norms and opposition to them. In full development, areas A and G are *contracultures,* one of which is built up around disregard for the social norms, the other around overcompliance with the norms.

The term "contraculture" is new in sociology and calls for clarification. It is a replacement for the term subculture when applied to sharply deviating types of behavior. The term subculture refers to a body of beliefs and behavior that differs to some extent from the main culture but is not in conflict with it in destructive fashion. The term contraculture has been proposed by J. Milton Yinger to signify certain qualities of detached groups.[8] According to Yinger's analysis, the contraculture has developed values and modes of behavior that are in conflict with the prevailing social norms (area D). The values and behavior of the contraculture are not only different from but are opposed to the social norms.

The logical end result is that people who accept the contraculture tend to organize into small contra-organizations with their own social norms, hierarchy of status positions, roles, and methods of control. A contracultural organization is not only a threat to the social norms but an active disintegrative element in the total social structure. Youth in areas B and F who are rejected by socially conforming groups may in turn reject these groups and pass into the appropriate contraculture. They are then no longer responsive to either the social norms or the efforts of members of area D to reclaim them.

Let us consider area A, extreme underconformity. Youth in this area are condemned not only in terms of their behavior but as persons. They are referred to as the "hard core" or "real" delinquents. They are physically exiled at least for a period of time. The school may expel them permanently, the judge may commit them to a correctional school or a prison. Occasionally such a youth may receive the death sentence.

The delinquent youth in the delinquent contraculture for his part rejects the conforming groups of society. He no longer measures his behavior against the expectations of area D. His standard of measure-

[8] J. Milton Yinger, "Contraculture and Subculture," *American Sociological Review,* 25:625-35 (1960). Albert K. Cohen used the term "delinquent subculture" for essentially the same type of behavior as found in a contraculture.—*Delinquent Boy* (Glencoe, Ill.: Free Press, 1955).

ment is the small, more restricted, less demanding standard of the delinquent contraculture. Here he may be applauded for stealing, chronic
truancy, or fighting. Toward groups in area D he is indifferent, hostile,
or vengeful.

The effort to draw members of the delinquent contraculture back into
area D is often doomed to failure. The street workers in New York City
and other large cities, who have been successful in re-establishing approved social behavior in many street clubs or gangs, note that they
cannot influence the hard-core delinquents who are thoroughly incorporated into a delinquent or youthful criminal gang. The street workers,
who represent the values and norms of area D, are to the members of
the contraculture outsiders and enemies who threaten the little structure
of the contraculture.[9] If the street workers or other adults were able to
influence individual members of the contraculture, the youth would again
have to traverse the disorganizing experiences of area B before he could
reach the relative security of area C. He would meet the scorn and rejection of his own gang-mates without having assurance that members
of area C or D would accept him.

What of the overconforming contraculture? Criticism, ostracism, and
rejection of youth in area F also drive many of them into withdrawal
into small closed groups with their own social organization. Many enter
already formed adult contracultures that have values and customs opposed to those of the central culture. As examples we have conscientious
objection to war, refusal to salute the flag, rejection of medical care
when ill or for ill children, refusal to have children vaccinated, refusal
to send children to school for the number of years required by law,
celibacy, and community ownership of property. Each of these practices
is an exaggeration of some value or social norm contained in the general culture. Each is socially disapproved according to the norms of area
D or is illegal. They are attacks on the general social values and norms,
and if they were to spread throughout the nation they would undermine
the social structure seriously. Some overconforming contracultures are
content to withdraw into isolation; some attack the general social norms
through propaganda or legislation. Others, however, are more militant
and occasionally some members physically attack members or symbols
of the general culture. (Carrie Nation, smashing the windows of saloons,
might be an example of a member of a militant overconforming contraculture.)

[9] *Reaching the Fighting Gang* (New York: New York City Youth Board, 1960).

## Further Applications to Juvenile Delinquency

This analysis of deviancy in the social organization clarifies several problems connected with juvenile delinquency. Three of these will be discussed.

1. The relation of public attitudes to social class.[10] Each social class or other large subcultural group has its own definition of what behavior falls into the area of tolerance, what is disapproved mildly or seriously, and what is condemned. Even when these groups share a basic culture and verbally accept the social norms, their concepts of approved and disapproved behavior may differ. The difference between middle- and lower-class definitions of behavior is especially pertinent, since most school officers and judges represent the middle class and most seriously misbehaving youth come from the lower class. Figure 2 is an attempt to indicate the difference between lower-class and middle-class judgments of what may and may not be tolerated. The behavior that the lower class would regard as falling in area *D*, to be accepted with tolerance, might be placed by the middle class in area *C* (barely tolerated behavior), or even in area *B*. Lower-class parents, other adults, and children might regard certain behavior as acceptable, whereas teachers and judges might regard it as unacceptable or reprehensible. An example is the case of the father whose son was in a correctional school for taking a car

Lower-class evaluation of behavior

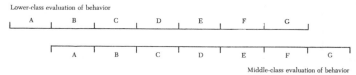

Middle-class evaluation of behavior

FIGURE 2. Discrepancies between lower-class and middle-class evaluations of identical behavior

for joy riding. The father said, "Of course, he took a few cars, but he did not strip them; he just wanted to use them. He is not a bad boy." But in the eyes of the judge, the boy had stolen the cars. This shifting of the class judgments on behavior is especially interesting at the left-hand extreme. The middle class tends to regard certain acts as type *A*, condemned behavior, that the lower class would regard as either *B* or *A*. This gives a wide range of everyday lower-class behavior that receives middle-class condemnation.

[10] Marshall Clinard, "Areas for Research in Deviant Behavior," *Sociology and Social Research*, 42:415-19 (1958). Among areas for research, Clinard suggests differences among social classes.

At the overconforming end of the scale the situation is reversed. Behavior that the middle class regards as acceptable and approved (type *D*), the lower class might regard as overconforming type *E* behavior. The lower class would perhaps regard behavior that is either *F* or *G* by middle-class standards as all extremely overconforming.

These shifts can be illustrated briefly by sexual attitudes and behavior in the two social classes. The casual sex relations of boys and girls that are regarded as natural and normal in some lower-class groups are regarded as underconformity and delinquency by middle-class standards. On the other hand the petting that some middle-class groups regard as an acceptable substitute for intercourse, the lower class would regard as prudish overconformity. At the extreme left, however, the two classes would tend to agree in condemning serious sex deviations, forcible rape, incest, exploitation of little children, and prostitution. At the extreme right, also, there would tend to be agreement, since both classes would probably look with disfavor on universal advocacy of celibacy, for example, as practiced by the Shakers. The argument would not apply to religious organizations where celibacy affects only a small portion of the total religious subculture. Such differences in attitudes of the two social classes lead to misunderstandings. Mishandling of the deviants of one social class by authorities in the other class almost automatically follows from such differences in judgment of the same behavior.

2. The evaluation of the behavior continuum is important in the expectations of behavior for delinquent youth on probation or parole. Usually probation or parole entails laying upon the youth a number of stringent restrictions on behavior. The penalty for disobedience often is commitment or return to correctional school. Such conditions as the following are typical: obedience to parents; regular school attendance; return home at an early hour of the evening, sometimes with the hour specified; and avoidance of disreputable companions and places. At least some of these requirements are overconforming by lower-class standards and virtually impossible for the youth to follow if he is to remain in the lower-class community and not be isolated from his natural social groups. The result is disregard for the requirements and deception on the part of the youth. Probation and parole might more often be successful if the youth were required to meet reasonably conforming lower-class standards.

3. The third point that may be clarified by the behavior continuum is the often repeated statement that all boys are delinquent but only poor boys are pulled into court or committed to correctional schools. It is true, according to several studies, that much delinquent behavior is overlooked and that most middle-class boys and girls at some time have behaved in such a way that they might have been brought into juvenile

court. A recent study by Short and Nye compares misbehavior of high-school students with that of correctional school students.[11] Some boys and girls in both groups had committed each of a long list of delinquencies. But it was apparent that the correctional-school boys and girls far outstripped the high-school students in the seriousness of their acts and the frequency with which they had committed them. For example, half of high-school boys but almost 100 per cent of correctional-school boys had skipped school; a fourth of high-school boys but 85 per cent of correctional-school boys had skipped school more than once or twice. Or, take a more serious offense, the theft of something worth fifty dollars or more. Five per cent of high-school boys compared with 90 per cent of correctional-school boys had taken things of this value. Almost no high-school boys compared with almost half of the correctional-school boys had committed this offense more than once or twice. An examination of the entire set of data leads to the conclusion that the high-school students had confined their delinquencies to acts within the area of tolerance of the community, whereas the correctional-school boys were guilty of behavior of types *B* or *A*, highly disapproved and regarded as threatening to the social organization.

In conclusion, this paper has attempted to state a hypothesis whereby behavior may be placed in a continuum running from an underconforming contraculture through various degrees of disapproved behavior to normal conformity and then through stages of overconforming behavior to an overconforming contraculture. The reaction of the normally conforming segment of the population to deviations varies in severity according to the threat posed to the social norms by either under- or overconformity. Minor deviants usually are drawn back into conformity. Serious deviants often are treated so severely that they are alienated and withdraw into a contraculture.[12]

[11] James F. Short, Jr., and F. Ivan Nye, "Extent of Unrecorded Juvenile Delinquency, Tentative Conclusions," *Journal of Criminal Law, Criminology and Police Science,* 49:296-309 (1958).

[12] In addition to the titles cited in the notes, the reader's attention is directed to the following general references:

Marshall Clinard, *Sociology of Deviant Behavior* (New York: Rinehart, 1957), Chap. 1; Richard A. Cloward, "Illegitimate means, Anomie, and Deviant Behavior," *American Sociological Review,* 24:164-76 (1959); Albert K. Cohen, "The Study of Social Disorganization and Deviant Behavior," in Robert K. Merton, Leonard Broom, and Leonard S. Cottrell (eds.), *Sociology Today: Problems and Prospects* (New York: Basic Books, 1959) Chap. 21; Robert Dubin, "Deviant Behavior and Social Structure: Continuities in Social Theory," *American Sociological Review,* 24:147-76 (1959); Robert K. Merton, "Social Conformity, Deviation, and Opportunity Structures: A Comment on the Contributions of Dubin and Cloward," *American Sociological Review,* 24:177-89 (1959); Robert K. Merton, *Social Theory and Social Structure* (rev. ed., Glencoe, Ill.: Free Press, 1957); Talcott Parsons, *The Social System* (Glencoe, Ill.: Free Press, 1951).

## 3. American Data on Juvenile Delinquency in an International Forum

Peter P. Lejins

The author received his Ph.D. degree from the University of Chicago, and is now Professor of Sociology at the University of Maryland. Some of his other activities include serving as Chairman and Consultant of the Committee on Uniform Crime Reports for the F.B.I., doing research on the experiences of former juvenile delinquents in military service, serving as a delegate to two United Nations Congresses on Prevention of Crime and Treatment of Offenders, publishing articles and reports, and leading citizens' groups devoted to the prevention of delinquency.

The following statement is the result of this writer's experience as a member of the United States Delegation to the Second United Nations Congress on the Prevention of Crime and the Treatment of Offenders which took place in London in August 1960. The writer was assigned to the section of the Congress which dealt with the problems of juvenile delinquency. Although the Congress was meant, of course, to be a purely professional undertaking, possibly because of the extremely sensitive international situation, it developed into something like the United Nations in miniature. Perhaps the fact that the Soviet Union was participating in such a Congress for the first time had something to do with it. There were moments when the 85 participant countries and territories aligned themselves as the Iron Curtain camp on the one hand, and the supporters of the Western democracies on the other.

Matters of crime and delinquency as presumable indices of the quality and effectiveness of the competing social orders suddenly acquired new significance in the current international battle of ideologies. The emphasis on this role of juvenile delinquency reached its climax in a statement by a representative of an international organization who said, in paraphrase: "Juvenile delinquency is a symptom of the decadence of a nation." Coming from a country where juvenile delinquency is given serious attention and is freely discussed, and where the statistical figures on delinquency being compiled by federal and local governmental agen-

Peter P. Lejins, "American Data on Juvenile Delinquency in an International Forum," *Federal Probation*, 25 (June, 1961), 18-21. Reprinted with permission of the publisher.

cies are ever increasing, the American delegates suddenly found them-selves confronted with this startling interpretation given in an interna-tional forum to "bigger and better" juvenile delinquency.

The importance of an accurate interpretation of the meaning of de-linquency data for the purpose of international comparison thus was forcefully brought to the fore. Suddenly it became very obvious how important it is to understand correctly what one's own delinquency control system consists of specifically and how it is reflected in the statis-tical figures, and to understand at the same time how delinquency is being controlled in other countries and how it is reported there. It goes without saying that these are proper issues for the consideration of the scientist and the professional without any prodding by political exigen-cies, but the political implications gave new emphasis to them.

From a wide variety of significant points which suggest themselves in this general context, three of the more important ones will be dis-cussed: First, the difference in the operational concepts of delinquency used in the United States and in the majority of the other countries; second, the transfer to such public agencies as the juvenile court, pro-bation departments, police, etc., the functions with regard to the control of juvenile behavior formerly performed by such conventional social-izing institutions as the family, school, church, and neighborhood; and thirdly, the degree to which the public control of juvenile behavior problems is developed in different countries, for example, the avail-ability of personnel, facilities, etc.

## American Concept of Juvenile Delinquency

The current separation of juvenile delinquency control from the con-trol of adult criminality started in this country around the turn of the century. From the very beginning the position generally advocated in the United States has been that juvenile delinquency should be con-sidered as something essentially different from adult crime: The purpose of public action in the case of a juvenile offender is primarily the welfare of the child rather than his punishment. It is felt there should not be too much emphasis on the responsibility of the child, since often his parents or his community are as much or even more responsible for his misbehavior than he himself. Also, the particular offense committed by the child is not considered especially important as such—its real meaning is that of a symptom of an underlying problem, and therefore it is preferred to adjudicate a juvenile as a juvenile delinquent without making reference to a particular offense. Gradually there has been developed in the United States a list of acts or of patterns of behavior which—while not criminal code offenses—nevertheless serve as a valid reason for adjudicating a juvenile as a delinquent. The statutes defining juvenile delinquency often expressly list such behavior as being disobedient or ungovernable, running away from home, or absence from school.

As the result of the above the practices pertaining to the referral of juveniles for juvenile court action are quite different from those obtaining in the case of adult crime. In some ways they are more lenient, in the sense that they may keep a child from being referred for court action in cases where an adult would definitely be referred. In some ways they are more severe, because a juvenile may be referred for acts which would not be made the basis for bringing an adult before the criminal court. Moreover, there is a great deal of difference in the considerations leading to adjudication in the adult and the juvenile court. Juvenile delinquency statistics in the United States reflect the adjudications before the juvenile courts of the country in terms of the concept of juvenile delinquency outlined above.

The situation is quite different in most other countries. As a rule they have no special concept of juvenile delinquency in the sense in which it exists in the United States; rather, juvenile delinquency in those countries is understood to cover criminal code offenses committed by persons below a certain age. While, in addition, there is really no lower age limit for juvenile delinquency in the United States—because there is no reason why even a very young child could not be handled by public authority for his own benefit—other countries usually completely exclude the younger age brackets from any action by public law-enforcement agencies. Moreover, even older children, in cases which in the United States would be considered delinquency, are frequently handled in other countries under the heading of educational measures. Many other countries, therefore, would consider as juvenile delinquency only criminal code offenses committed by juveniles in the upper age brackets, and only these are accordingly reflected in the juvenile delinquency statistics.

Thus when American statistics on juvenile delinquency are compared with similarly labelled statistics from another country, adjustments with regard to the definition may well be necessary because of the following factors: (1) the lower age groups may be completely excluded from the statistics of the foreign country while they are included in the United States statistics; (2) the somewhat older age groups which present behavior problems, while handled as delinquents in the United States, are very likely handled through special educational measures in the other country and therefore are not included in the delinquency statistics; (3) only criminal code offenses committed by juveniles are in all probability recorded abroad, while also the special juvenile offenses are included in the U.S. statistics; and (4) the general philosophy of adjudication for the welfare of the child probably results in more adjudications in the United States than does the much more punitive philosophy of the court proceedings in other countries.

## Transfer of Control to Public Agencies

There were no juvenile courts in the United States prior to 1899; there were no separate public institutions for juvenile offenders prior to 1853; there were no separate private institutions for juvenile offenders prior to 1825. But what about juvenile delinquency prior to these dates? Juvenile offenders were handled by the criminal courts and sent to penal institutions together with adults. Studies show there were not too many juveniles in the criminal courts and the penal institutions of those early days, certainly nothing like today, even when an adjustment is made for the general increase in population figures. The answer is very clear. Very many of the cases which today are referred to the juvenile court were formerly handled by the traditional institutions for socializing the young—in other words, the family, the community, the church, and the school.

This analytical observation leads to a statement, the full meaning of which is unfortunately grasped only infrequently: When reference is made to a juvenile behavior problem as an act of juvenile delinquency, it really means that this problem is being handled formally by a special public agency rather than informally by an institution which, in the given society, is normally responsible for bringing up children. It follows that an increase in juvenile delinquency reflects not only the behavior of juveniles, but also the policy of handling delinquents in the respective society—specifically the extent to which control has been transferred from the family, home, school, and neighborhood to the formal law-enforcement agencies such as the juvenile court, probation departments, and police. Hence, a country which has transferred more such control to the public law-enforcement agencies will appear to have more delinquency than a country which has not yet reached the stage of development that leads to such a transfer. Thus, higher statistics of juvenile delinquency need not reflect the volume of behavior problems among juveniles, but rather the type of control pattern used with regard to such problems.

It will be noticed what a difference in the interpretation of the statistical figures on juvenile delinquency the above analysis brings about. On the basis of the conventional interpretation of such statistics a high delinquency rate means a serious danger signal. On the basis of the above analysis, a low delinquency rate may reflect a pattern of delinquency control that is typical of an "underdeveloped country" which still relies on the patriarchal methods of social control which are not necessarily the best nor the most suitable for the modern urbanized and industrialized community. In other words, the rate of juvenile delinquency may have no relation to the scope of behavior problems of the young but, instead, may reflect adherence to either the old or the new systems of control.

Variations in the reported amounts of juvenile delinquency in different countries need not necessarily place these countries in relation to each other on the basis of the amounts of juvenile misbehavior, but rather locate them along a developmental continuum of gradual social change in the methods of handling the socialization of their young.

Professor Manuel López-Rey, representative of the Secretary-General of the United Nations to the Congress, and at that time chief of the Social Defense Section of the United Nations, did not speak in vain when he, in introducing the Secretariat report at the opening session of the Section on The New Forms of Juvenile Delinquency, stated that studies show that juvenile delinquency is higher and is on the increase in "the so-called highly developed countries" as compared with the less advanced countries. Professor López-Rey also noted that a certain positive correlation exists between the extent of reported delinquency and the available welfare services in the countries under comparison, although he cautioned that this does not mean that welfare services are a criminogenic factor.[1] This observation fits very well into the frame of reference used by this writer in the analysis of juvenile delinquency. The greater availability of welfare services, while not a cause of juvenile problems, means more frequent action by the public authorities with regard to juvenile behavior problems, especially in the United States, and hence is reflected in increased statistics of delinquency.

Of course, this analysis does not mean that greater or lesser amounts of juvenile misbehavior may not cause respectively higher or lower statistics of juvenile delinquency. It simply means that the variations in the rates of delinquency are not a function of only one variable, as the

---

[1] See report by the Secretariat: *The New Forms of Delinquency, Origin, Prevention and Treatment,* United Nations document A/CONF 17/17, 1960; also Manuel López-Rey, "Some Misconceptions in Contemporary Criminology" in *Essays in Criminal Science,* Sweet and Maxwell, Ltd., London, 1960.

current simplicist interpretation usually assumes, but are rather a function of at least two variables, the second one being the policies and methods of control.

## Degree of Development of Special Agencies

The degree to which the given society has transferred the control of juvenile behavior from the conventional socializing institutions as the home, school, and church to public agencies as the juvenile court, probation departments, and police is expressed not only in the adoption of the principle as such, but also in the practical availability of the services of the public facility. This availability means primarily the size of the staff to carry out the functions of the court. Thus a community may establish a juvenile court and by statute transfer to it the functions of control in certain cases, e.g., in the case of a run-away child, an ungovernable child, or in the case of truancy, but the staff of the juvenile court may be so small that only a fraction of the actual cases can possibly be handled by it. One juvenile court judge with a small staff will handle fewer cases than several juvenile court judges with extensive probation departments at their disposal. This, in turn, will influence the statistics of juvenile delinquency: the gradual increase in the number of cases handled by the juvenile courts being a function at least in part of the gradual expansion of the personnel. A comparison between two countries, one of which has a juvenile court and a judge for every 100,000 inhabitants, and a country which has a similar law on paper but has only one juvenile court judge and a comparable number of probation officers for a population of 5 million, may be completely misleading if the number of cases handled is interpreted as an index of juvenile misbehavior only. In reality, it is at least in part also a function of the degree of development of the special public agencies for handling delinquent children.

The same applies not only to the juvenile court and the probation facilities, but also, for example, to institutional facilities if statistics of children committed to institutions are used as an index of the extent of delinquency. If a community does not build additional institutions, an increase of committed children can be expressed only in terms of overcrowding of the existing institution, and it will exercise a discouraging influence on committing children if it is generally known that the facilities are overcrowded. The opening of an additional institution may have the effect of increasing the number of committed children, with a resultant reflection in the respective statistics.

## In Lieu of a Summary

For the purpose of pulling together the foregoing discussion, perhaps an example will serve in lieu of a formal summary. Let us return to the meeting of the United Nations Congress which was mentioned at the beginning of this article.

On the one hand the United States statistics of juvenile delinquency presented there include such juvenile court cases as "glue sniffing" by boys 10 years old and under.

On the other hand the representative of one of the larger nations of the world stated on the floor of the Congress, in response to a direct question (in paraphrase): "But of course we record as juvenile delinquencies only the serious criminal code acts of the older juveniles; after all we have special educational programs for the younger children who misbehave and for the older children who are not too criminalistic. We would not dream of branding these as criminals and delinquents."

A third party voices the observation, previously stated, about delinquency being a symptom of a society's decadence, while the representatives of 85 nations are the listeners and onlookers in this discussion. Some of them do not quite see what the problem is, because their own country may still be dealing with juvenile behavior problems in the accustomed way of a preindustrial society, does not have too much official public-agency action and therefore no alarming figures, and is perhaps only slightly concerned about some juvenile disorganization in its developing urban centers. Others may have accepted the modern delinquency control patterns which they know are being used in the industrial and urban societies. But they really have only token facilities which could not possibly produce alarming "delinquency statistics," because of the small volume of business which the limited facilities and small staffs can handle. Many of the representatives of the younger members of the international community are not sufficiently versed in the intricacies of this complicated matter and cannot penetrate through the surface language of figures to the true meaning. Misunderstandings and misinterpretations easily occur.

These misinterpretations, if allowed to stand, may well become one of the component elements in an attitude leading to the rejection of the social order which displays such "symptoms of decadence." At the same time it must be admitted that United States criminologists and correctional personnel are not too concerned about the situation, nor are they particularly prepared to give the proper interpretations since they are engrossed in the promotion of their delinquency control programs back home. In this context they do not feel there is an immediate need for a broader perspective and perhaps sense that the analysis of juvenile delinquency statistics such as is made here might even detract from the immediate goal. And yet, not only international relations, but also a sound scientific approach and the long-run needs of practice require a broader look at what is actually happening. It would appear that we need to develop within the field a "specialty" of comparative study of the patterns of social control as they apply to juvenile delinquency, and also develop a cadre of professional personnel who will maintain an interest in the issues of this type, develop better insight, and be available to render interpretations on occasions similar to the one that gave rise to this paper.

# Theories of Delinquency
# as a Social Product

T HE SEARCH for basic theories to bring different types of delinquency.into a common framework goes on unceasingly. Specialists from many different disciplines formulate theories with or without supporting evidence from empirical research and often without any effort being made toward coordinating the various disciplines. Article 4 reviews some of the obstacles to the development of a scientific analysis of delinquency that would be more than a patchwork of theories borrowed from different disciplines.

Many theories have evolved from the findings that show that official delinquency of a serious nature is concentrated in certain areas of cities. The basis for present studies lies in the careful analysis that Clifford R. Shaw and his associates made in the 1920's and 1930's, showing that the highest rates of juvenile arrests, juvenile court hearings, and correctional school commitments were in the lower-class areas of large cities.[1] These areas were called delinquency areas. The first interest of sociologists was in the dilapidated physi-

---

[1] The outstanding studies were: Clifford R. Shaw and associates, *Delinquency Areas*, University of Chicago Press, Chicago, 1929; Shaw, Henry McKay, and associates, *Juvenile Delinquency and Urban Areas*, University of Chicago Press, Chicago, 1942; and Shaw and McKay, *Social Factors in Juvenile Delinquency*, A Study . . . for the National Commission on Law Observance and Enforcement, Number 13, volume 2, Washington, D.C., U.S. Government Printing Office, 1931.

cal characteristics of these slum areas and in the symptoms of gross social disorganization and cultural conflict. Later sociologists, perhaps studying a later phase of community development in the slum areas, turned their attention to indigenous social organizations and to the development of lower-class culture. At the height of the interest in studies of delinquency areas, a note of caution was introduced by Sophia Robison and researchers who followed her lead. When their studies showed that a widespread net of delinquency lay over all areas of a city they suggested that the variation in official rates was perhaps a reflection of the way in which delinquents were handled in different areas rather than an indication of the amount of delinquency that occurred.[2] While the emphasis of research still tends to be on the slum areas, a beginning has been made to widen the base of research and to bring all delinquency, whether of the poor or of the rich, into a general framework.

One line of research that has grown out of these early studies is the analysis of delinquency as an integral part of different social-class cultures.

Article 5 (Kvaraceus and Miller) presents much delinquency as a natural outgrowth of lower-class culture—as an attempt on the part of lower-class children and adolescents to conform to patterns of behavior and achieve standards of value that are an accepted part of lower-class culture, regardless of how abhorrent the behavior may seem to members of higher social classes.

In Article 6, England takes a similar approach, seeking the origins of the delinquency of middle-class children (which differs from that of lower-class children) in middle-class culture itself. According to his analysis, middle-class culture rejects the teenager from adult roles and fosters the growth of a teenage culture that meets many of the needs of this group, although not always in ways approved by adults.

Articles 7 and 8 also are concerned with lower-class culture. The authors do not envision delinquency as an outgrowth of lower-class standards and values, but as a protest of lower-class youth who are

[2] Sophia Moses Robison, *Can Delinquency Be Measured?* Columbia University Press, New York, 1936.

discontented and frustrated because they cannot move into middle-class positions and claim the advantages of middle-class culture.

In Article 7, Cohen separates from the general lower-class culture certain features which he terms the delinquent subculture. This subculture, according to Cohen, has developed among boys' gangs, whose members are denied by circumstances the opportunity to advance into middle-class status. Cohen does not claim that his theory of a delinquent subculture will account for all types of delinquency, even in the lower class. His theory has aroused criticism and controversy and has stimulated new thinking on the subject of delinquency, although it was not supported by empirical research.

In Article 8, further analysis has been carried out by Cloward and Ohlin; first, to ferret out factors in the neighborhood milieu that further the development of delinquent subcultures and second, to distinguish between types of delinquent subcultures and the conditions under which each type arises. As with Cohen's analysis, the theory was logically developed but was not validated by empirical research.

In Article 9, Matza and Sykes review the characteristics of the delinquent subculture as set forth by various writers, and then propose a new interpretation. The values of the delinquent are not profoundly different from many of those of conventional middle-class society, although they may be expressed differently and are not counterbalanced by conventional values. Many of the values that play a large part in the delinquent's scheme of life are identical with or similar to the leisure values of the middle class; for example, excitement or adventure. In the middle class, these values are overlaid with other values; in delinquent groups they come to the surface. The authors suggest the value of studying the similarities between the delinquent society and the larger society instead of emphasizing the differences.

Finally, in Article 10, a generalization is made as to the process whereby delinquent behavior develops. The articles numbered 5, 6, 7, and 8 have all linked juvenile delinquency with specific types of groups or communities. The same research that shows high rates of delinquency in certain areas of a city also shows that many—

usually most—boys in these areas do not have delinquency records. Why do not all boys become delinquent in communities where a delinquent subculture seems to flourish? In Article 10, Haskell makes a close analysis of the conditions under which boys identify with or reject the delinquent subculture, and suggests ways to reduce delinquent behavior.

## 4.  Toward a Science of Delinquency Analysis

### Charles J. Browning

> The author, who is Associate Professor of Sociology at Whittier College, received the degree of Doctor of Philosophy from the University of Southern California. He typically spends the summer as a Deputy Probation Officer, working in the probation camps of the Los Angeles County Probation Department. He has contributed to professional journals.

A common thread running through the critical literature on juvenile delinquency is the conclusion that the accumulating researches are inadequate. Periodically, inventories and evaluations of both old and new studies are undertaken, indicating that little advance has been made in the scientific understanding and control of delinquency.[1] It is now represented as a "baffling problem" of overwhelming complexity.[2] Some suggest that a science of delinquency analysis may not be possible because of the unyielding difficulties encountered when trying to discover and develop a body of causal and etiological theory.[3]

This paper proposes that (1) research in delinquency need not con-

Charles J. Browning, "Toward a Science of Delinquency Analysis," *Sociology and Social Research*, 46 (1961-62), 61-74. Reprinted with permission of the publisher and author.

[1] Jerome Michael and Mortimer Adler, *Crime, Law, and Social Science* (New York: Harcourt-Brace, 1933); Barbara Wootton, *Social Science and Social Pathology* (New York: The Macmillan Company, 1959); Helen L. Witmer and Ruth Kotinsky, "New Perspectives for Research on Juvenile Delinquency" (Washington, D.C.: U.S. Children's Bureau, 1956); Sophia Robison, *Juvenile Delinquency* (New York: Holt, Rinehart and Winston, 1960); and others.

[2] Negley Teeters in the Foreword to Clyde B. Vedder, *The Juvenile Offender* (New York: Random House, 1954), v, vi.

[3] See Peter Lejins, "Pragmatic Etiology of Delinquent Behavior," *Social Forces*, 29 (March, 1951), 317-20.

tinue indefinitely to be impotent, (2) certain necessary conditions for the development of a science have not yet been met in delinquency analysis, (3) there are a number of unresolved theoretical issues that retard the development of bodies of integrated theory, and (4) elementary analysis of the term "juvenile delinquency" indicates that the various parts of it are not equally difficult to explain and understand. In order to support these propositions, the following problems have been selected for examination: (a) the lack of a clear conception of what juvenile delinquency means and includes, or the neglect of what has been called qualitative analysis in some sciences; (b) the prolonged lack of consensus as to what constitutes the theoretical foundations of a science of delinquency analysis; and (c) the argument that delinquency analysis like criminology is a dependent science.

## What Is Juvenile Delinquency?

Social and behavioral scientists have frequently found a pressing social problem—or the phenomenon giving rise to the social problem—to be the subject of their research. The burden of the researcher's task in this setting tends to bear upon etiological and causal analysis, especially when the research is sponsored by an agency primarily concerned with checking and controlling the problem. Matters of definition, conceptualization, and classification of delinquency itself, *the dependent variable,* are quickly passed over in order to identify possible causes, such as slum housing, broken homes, and gang membership, *the independent variables.* Research in delinquency has been handicapped by the lack of careful descriptive analysis of what juvenile delinquency includes and means.

The term "juvenile delinquency" was coined in the community, probably by reporters, social workers, humanitarians, or educators; and it was intended to designate a phenomenon which they continuously observed and knew could not be easily explained. As it came to be generally used, an implication that the phenomenon was somewhat unitary if not homogeneous developed. Cohen has observed that delinquency, like measles, seems to have been regarded as a homogeneous something which people have or have not, and that it is thought sufficient, therefore, to simply note that a person is or is not a "delinquent."[4] But, today, the phenomenon has become so complex in character that it

[4] Albert K. Cohen, *Delinquent Boys: The Culture of the Gang* (Glencoe, Ill.: The Free Press, 1955), 172.

subsumes a variety of meanings, dimensions, and definitions. Identified as a "blanket concept" [5] and an "umbrella term," [6] its present content hardly allows for unitary theoretical explication. One is tempted to abandon such an ambiguous, catchall term, but that might only result in the admission of another term just as indiscriminate. A more promising alternative is to identify the distinct, if overlapping or related, meanings or dimensions of the generic term or the multiple phenomena that the term may now subsume, and then go on to deal with each of them definitively.

A survey of the scholarly literature on juvenile delinquency reveals at least four distinct uses of the term. These are: (1) delinquency as deviant behavior, (2) delinquency as distinct legal and/or social status, (3) delinquency as a subculture trait, and (4) delinquency as a social problem. Deviant behavior occurs as individual acts of behavior, but often these acts combine to form behavior patterns, deviant personality organizations, and finally careers in a deviant way of life. Delinquency as a distinct legal and social status may include predelinquency, proto-delinquency (unofficial), real delinquency (adjudicated), and confirmed delinquency (recidivistic). Delinquency as a form of subculture generally refers to juvenile "gangland," but "teen-age" subculture in general now seems to be generating some middle and upper class delinquency not directly associated with "gangland." Delinquency as a social problem has its social class and local, regional, and national characteristics and dimensions. All of these appear to be elemental and must be reckoned with. Generalizations about delinquency may be confusing, misleading, or false unless the usage or meaning for which they hold is specified.

Nye and others have called attention to the critical methodological and theoretical problems that arise when studies confuse or equate delinquent behavior with official delinquency.[7] Legally adjudicated delinquency is held to be unrepresentative of delinquent behavior in general. In addition, delinquency depends in many cases on other things than delinquent behavior, such as community practices, court standards, and concentration of preventive efforts on predelinquency; and in other cases it is largely independent of delinquent behavior, e.g., adjudication on the basis of attitude or social situation. Tappan has identified the

---

[5] Robert K. Merton in Witmer and Kotinsky, op. cit., 27.

[6] Earl Raab and Gertrude Selznick, Major Social Problems (Evanston, Ill.: Row, Peterson and Co., 1959), 60.

[7] F. Ivan Nye, Family Relationships and Delinquent Behavior (New York: John Wiley and Sons, 1958), 24; Cohen, op. cit., 170-71; Merton in Witmer and Kotinsky, op. cit., 27-28. Nye actually demonstrated in a field study that this problem has a basis in experience, that findings are different when official and unofficial delinquent populations are compared.

difficulties inherent in trying to define delinquency in terms of behavior, has developed a strong case for proving delinquency in court, and has definitively analyzed delinquency as a distinct legal and social status.[8]

Cohen has questioned whether all juvenile delinquent behavior can be fitted to a single descriptive theoretical concept or frame of reference, has emphasized the danger of assuming that delinquent and criminal behavior represent different degrees of development of a common dimension, and has presented a strong case for equating some juvenile delinquency with a delinquency subculture rather than with adjudicable behavior as such. "The delinquent's conduct is right, by the standards of his subculture, precisely *because* it is wrong by the norms of the larger culture." [9]

Little attention seems to have been given to the difficulties that arise when delinquency as a social problem is equated with the generic term or when it is not specifically differentiated from other uses or meanings included in the generic term. Textbooks which affirm that delinquency is a social problem tend to focus their analysis on problems of determining what delinquency is and who delinquents are legally and behaviorally. Analysis of the nature of delinquency consistently ends with admittedly indefinite and unsatisfying definitions of delinquency. Delinquency as a social problem is confused with delinquency as a legal, behavioral, or methodological problem. These problems may be related, but they are not the same problem. Fuller and Myers conceive of social problems as behavior patterns or conditions that are considered undesirable and in need of correction by many members of a society.[10] The use of the concept in this paper is intended to be consistent with theirs. A behavioral problem may or may not be a social problem. And the analysis of delinquency as a social problem does not necessarily give rise to the same theoretical or empirical points of dispute that analysis of delinquency as a legal term or behavioral concept does.

Examination of the following descriptive statements indicates some of the difficulties which arise when generalizations are attempted without considering adequately the specific dimensions and meanings of the generic term:

It [juvenile delinquency] is distinctly a phenomenon of the modern world.[11]

[8] Paul W. Tappan, *Juvenile Delinquency* (New York: McGraw-Hill Book Company, 1949), 4-30.

[9] Cohen, *op. cit.*, 28.

[10] Richard C. Fuller and R. C. Myers, "The Natural History of Social Problems," *American Sociological Review*, 6 (June, 1941), 320-29.

[11] Henry M. Shulman, *Juvenile Delinquency in American Society* (New York: Harper and Brothers, 1961), 1.

Delinquency is a world wide phenomenon and is not peculiar to any one nation.[12]

Such a phenomenon [juvenile delinquency] is unknown among primitives and has been relatively unknown among most of the great cultural systems of the world. Asiatic countries, the Middle East, and Africa are only beginning to experience it in a serious way.[13]

Juvenile delinquency is an urban and/or industrial phenomenon.[14]

For delinquency is not . . . a property of individuals or even of subsubcultures; it is a property of the social systems in which these individuals and groups are enmeshed.[15]

Generally speaking, delinquency is a function of social marginality.[16]

In the first place, delinquency *in general* is mostly male delinquency.[17]

When each of the four usages is substituted for the generic term in these statements, it becomes evident that the accuracy of the statements is affected. Delinquency as deviant behavior is not distinctly a phenomenon of the modern world. Delinquency as a distinct legal and social status and delinquency as a subculture are not yet world-wide phenomena. Delinquency as anti-social deviant behavior did not begin in, nor is it limited to, urban and/or industrial societies; it has and does exist among preliterates. Delinquency as deviant behavior is a property of social systems but also of individuals—at least, individuals-as-group-members. Delinquency as legal status (official rates) may suggest that delinquency in general has its locus in marginal groups, but it is doubtful whether the same can be said for antisocial behavior in general. The same predicament arises when generalizations on the basis of sex are attempted. Only some of the more gross instances of equivocation or ambiguity can be presented here; there are many others of lesser degree in the learned as well as the popular literature on the subject.

The above statements are obviously presented out of context, but examination of the context will reveal that the issue in point cannot be explained away on that basis. It also amounts to more than a semantic

[12] Martin H. Neumeyer, *Juvenile Delinquency* (New York: D. Van Nostrand Company, Inc., 1961), v.

[13] Paul H. Landis, *Social Problems* (Chicago: Lippincott, 1959), 345.

[14] Shulman, *op. cit.*, 158-60; Frank Tannenbaum, "Social Forces in the Development of Crime," in Clyde B. Vedder, Samuel Koenig, and Robert E. Clark, *Criminology: A Book of Readings* (New York: Dryden Press, 1953), 220-23.

[15] Richard A. Cloward and Lloyd E. Ohlin, *Delinquency and Opportunity: A Theory of Delinquent Gangs* (Glencoe, Ill.: The Free Press, 1960), 211.

[16] Herbert A. Bloch and Frank Flynn, *Delinquency: The Juvenile Offender in American Today* (New York: Random House, 1956), 44.

[17] Cohen, *op. cit.*, 44.

problem, of oversights on the part of those who write about delinquency. And, changing from one umbrella or blanket term to another hardly resolves the issue. It is no longer defensible to simply list and decry the variety of ways in which the term has been used throughout the community, or to simply catalogue the obstacles confronted when trying to define it, or even to conclude that the only alternative is "to define the reference that it shall carry within the framework of a given discussion." [18] Nothing short of careful and systematic identification, conceptualization, and delineation of the several valid meanings of delinquency (the dependent variable in most studies) and their several dimensions will be sufficient. The failure of students of delinquency to do this kind of sound exploratory and "qualitative" analysis is substantially responsible for the slow development of a science of delinquency. Superficial analysis at this level frustrates the identification and formulation of the most significant etiological and causal hypotheses in the beginning, and ends by impeding the communication lines on which social workers, public officials, and citizens depend for reliable knowledge about delinquency.

## Theoretical Foundations for a Science of Delinquency

There is increasing agreement among social scientists that research must be guided by the most rigorous available theory if it is to be fruitful. But this continuing emphasis on theory is generating fundamental questions about the nature of theory and how bodies of theory are developed in an emerging science. It is also focusing attention on a number of unsettled issues whose resolution might well stimulate the development of theoretical foundations for a science of delinquency. There is rather complete agreement that neither a single-factor nor a unitary theory that is capable of explaining all delinquency in space and time is likely to be discovered; but beyond that, researchers and writers are saying a variety of things about what is required if a science of delinquency analysis is to be forthcoming.

Of the several meanings and dimensions of delinquency which have been identified, it is delinquency as deviant behavior that seems to be the hard, tough core of the total problem. There are theoretical implications for each of the other meanings also, but the discussion that follows bears upon the behavioral meaning and dimensions for the most part.

[18] L. J. Carr, *Delinquency Control* (New York: Harper & Brothers, 1950), 90.

One of the most subtle of the theoretical issues involved in the development of a science of delinquency analysis is whether or not descriptive knowledge is scientific knowledge. Robison seems to agree with Michael and Adler that it is not.[19] Tappan declares that the study of delinquency "must go beyond a merely descriptive level of conduct and personality analysis to discover the inter-relationships and dynamics of elements that determine conduct." [20] But, what science is without its descriptive knowledge—its "qualitative" as well as its "quantitative" analysis? And, what rigorous and fruitful hypotheses of etiological and causal inter-relationships in any science do not depend upon painstaking descriptive analysis? While there is some validity to this general position, it is premature and overdone. Valid descriptive knowledge is a property of a science, and students of delinquency would be better advised to systematically analyze delinquent action itself; the central concepts of the subject matter; variations of delinquency in individual, group, and collective situations; and the social and cultural context of specific patterns of delinquency. Critics have been prone to assume that, because the allegedly vast number of studies which have been done have not produced reliable and valid etiological and causal theories, they have *ipso facto* exhaustively and satisfactorily dealt with all matters short of etiological and causal analysis. The assumption is not sound, but its continued use by implication may have contributed to the widespread pessimism that an etiological and causal science of delinquency is not possible.

Growing partly out of these circumstances has been the resistance or reluctance of researchers to study limited and more homogeneous categories of delinquents—a procedure that might have given us some rigorous special theories of delinquency, if not an all-embracing unitary, general theory. It is special or limited theories at this stage of development that seem to offer the greatest hope for the accumulation of a body of integrated theory, but there is yet substantial difference of opinion among mature scholars on this point. The Gluecks, for example, in their most recent major research effort, state:

> . . . in the present volume we view delinquents as well as non-delinquents as a unitary class. This does not mean that we fail to recognize that there may be clearly definable subgroups among both delinquents and non-delinquents. However, *the first and basic step is to discover similarities and differences in the mass*, in order to arrive eventually at factors in the background and make-up of the delin-

[19] Robison, *op. cit.*, 191, 192. Interpreting Michael and Adler, *op. cit.*
[20] *Op. cit.*, 56.

quents which most markedly differentiate them from non-delinquents, and to construct prognostic tables based on such differentiation by means of which the probability of delinquency in certain children may be early and meaningfully determined without waiting for the actual appearance of delinquent behavior.[21]

Most research studies and theoretical writings, like theirs, while directed toward representative cross-sections of delinquents in the mass and general theories of delinquency, have not turned out to be exhaustively or convincingly general. Students are urged to embrace the eclectic, multiple-factor, interdisciplinary approaches—presumably to arrive at a causal formula which accommodates all levels of analysis, channels of influence, and their dynamic interplay. The heterogeneous samples (however well matched or representative) sought for studies of this kind have not given us a verifiable all-embracing causal or etiological theory, and emphasis on this methodology has probably diverted or held up research based on reliable subcategories of delinquents which are capable of giving us testable hypotheses of limited range.

It hardly seems necessary that issues of this kind should continue retarding the development of a science of delinquency analysis. Sciences approaching the complexity of human behavior in their subject matter develop bodies of theory. "General theory" and "special theory" are relative terms and both appear to be common to the development of bodies of theory. Sometimes the discovery of special theories has led to the discovery of more general unifying theories, and sometimes general theories have been able to predict special theories yet undiscovered or unconceived. What Merton has said so well for sociology as a whole is applicable to the emerging science of delinquency analysis:

. . . sociology will advance in the degree that its major concern is with developing theories of the middle range and will be frustrated if attention centers on theory in the large. I believe that our major task *today* is to develop special theories applicable to limited ranges of data—theories, for example, of class dynamics, of conflicting group pressures, of the flow of power and the exercise of interpersonal influence—rather than to seek at once the "integrated" conceptual structure adequate to derive these and all other theories . . . To say that both general and special theories are needed is to be correct and banal: the problem is one of allocating our scant resources. I am suggesting that the road to effective conceptual schemes in sociology will be the more effectively built through work on special theories, and

[21] Sheldon and Eleanor Glueck, *Unraveling Juvenile Delinquency* (Cambridge: Harvard University Press, 1950), 15.

that it will remain a largely unfulfilled plan, if one seeks to build it directly at this time.[22]

Applied specifically to the problem of developing an adequate body of delinquency theory, this is a suggestion that theories be tested first which are designed to relate empirical uniformities and segregated hypotheses in relatively limited areas, e.g., the subcultural theory advanced by Cohen that explains at the same time why most delinquency committed by juvenile gangs is male delinquency and is located in the working class (two of the most persistent findings in delinquency studies), or the formulation of a theory that will explain simultaneously the unlawful sexual behavior of male and female juveniles in upper, lower, and middle social classes.

Another set of detracting issues revolves around the nature of delinquency as human behavior. Is it normal or abnormal? Is it necessary to create a pathology to explain it? Is delinquent behavior symptom or syndrome, sickness or disease? Is it a positive thing that can be explained as one of the products of socialization or a negative thing that comes with the failure of social controls to restrain it? Does delinquent behavior constitute a single or more than one dimension? These are only a part of a perplexing array of points of dispute that confront those who seek to understand delinquent behavior.

The work of Porterfield, Robison, Short, and Nye with general populations of juveniles, adolescents, or college students has demonstrated that most young people commit delinquencies of one kind or another even though they vary in frequency according to sex, social class, and other criteria.[23] That is to say, a normal child engages in some delinquent behavior sometime during the process of becoming an adult. Tappan, Merrill, and others also regard delinquent behavior as normal when viewed etiologically.[24] They see it as the expected response to disorganized family life, for example, just as socially approved and nondelinquent behavior is the expected response to organized and supervised family life. If, also, it is assumed that every child has a delinquency potential, that no child is born with built-in adjustments to the

[22] Robert K. Merton, *Social Theory and Social Structure* (Glencoe, Ill.: The Free Press, 1957), 9.

[23] Austin L. Porterfield, *Youth in Trouble* (Austin: Leo Potishman Foundation, 1946); Robison, *op. cit.*, Chap. 4; Nye, *op. cit.*; James F. Short, Jr., and F. Ivan Nye, "Extent of Unrecorded Juvenile Delinquency: Tentative Conclusions," *Journal of Criminal Law, Criminology, and Police Science*, 29 (November-December, 1958), 296-302.

[24] Tappan, *op. cit.*, 65; Maud A. Merrill, *Problems of Child Delinquency* (Boston: Houghton-Mifflin Company, 1947), Chap. 1; Hertha Tarrasch, *Focus*, 29 (July, 1950), 97-101.

standards imposed by an adult external world, and that socially acceptable, alternative behavior patterns are not always live options, then this provides additional support for interpreting delinquent behavior as normal behavior. And, of course, delinquent behavior which can be equated with a subculture that is delinquent is normal to that culture. Delinquent behavior is abnormal when it violates the limits of established conduct norms and is committed or practiced by a minority of the members of a community; it becomes statistically, if not substantively, normal when committed or practiced by the majority. It is also abnormal when it is not prescribed by one's own reference groups and when it is neurotic or psychotic—i.e., when it is the type of behavior with which practicing psychiatrists are ordinarily concerned.[25] But, in the latter case, if it can be substantially demonstrated that the mental illness or handicap preceded the delinquent act(s), even the courts are now inclined to regard those acts as normal functions of an abnormal $x$ factor that gives rise to deviant behavior. Present knowledge, therefore, seems to indicate that a pathology is not necessary to explain most delinquent behavior; and that a minority of persons and acts that seem to require it appears to be as reliably accounted for as other categories of deviants and deviant behavior by theories currently used by psychologists and psychiatrists studying abnormal behavior.

The conception of delinquency as a disease has been generally discounted for some time, but "symptomology" still persists. Truancy, possession of alcoholic beverages, and forcible rape are all held to be only or merely symptomatic of "complex interrelated causes,"[26] "the essential elements,"[27] or "maladjustment"[28]—presumably some basic, underlying $x$ factor. Delinquencies, in the plural, refers to a variety of acts in violation of the juvenile code; in the singular, the term connotes an $x$ factor that gives rise to full range of symptomatic acts. It is probable that legal persons have tended to make too much of behavioral acts and that clinically oriented persons have tended to regard them too lightly. Cohen has observed that the analogy of delinquency to a symptom meriting little investigation in its own right has been overworked;[29] but, allowing that it may still have some validity, this $x$ factor must be regarded as a hypothesis—not as a postulate or as a verified theoretical fact—until it is identified and substantiated.

[25] Alfred R. Lindesmith and Anselm L. Strauss, *Social Psychology* (New York: Dryden Press, 1956), 663-67.
[26] William C. Kvaraceus, *Juvenile Delinquency and the School* (Yonkers-on-Hudson: World Book Company, 1945), 53.
[27] Tappan, *op. cit.*, 56.
[28] Merrill, *op. cit.*, 19.
[29] Cohen, *op. cit.*, 172.

Whether delinquent behavior is a negative thing resulting from a failure of controls or a positive thing that can be explained as a product of socialization, depends in part upon what assumptions are made about the nature of human beings. Is it conformity to the regulations of society which must be learned, or deviations from those regulations? Is delinquency caused or prevented? Does a juvenile learn to become a delinquent, or is he a delinquent until he has learned to observe the regulations of his society? The alternatives suggested in these questions are not necessarily inconsistent and may even be complementary. Reiss and Nye have conducted studies using failure of controls as a frame of reference. They allow for the successful operation of controls in delinquent gangs or subcultures at the same time they propose that most delinquency can be explained as a failure of controls in the larger society and the dominant culture.[30] It is probable, taken case by case, that delinquents vary from those whose deviant behavior is natural or normal (least learned) and controls have been most adequate to those where controls have failed and delinquency has been most learned. The identification of distinct types and dimensions of delinquent behavior should resolve most of the disagreements associated with this issue.

Does delinquent behavior constitute a single or more than one dimension? Nye and Short observe that delinquency has generally been treated as an attribute—not as a variable. Their research showed that as many as eleven different acts occur along a single dimension.[31] Scott, however, obtained some evidence for at least two dimensions: (1) acts affecting anonymous persons or impersonal property and (2) acts that introduce conflict and injury into interpersonal relations.[32] These dimensions derive from the dichotomous character of the *objects* of delinquents' behavior. Other possibilities for multiple dimensions inhere in the primary sources of the behavior itself (e.g., individual, group, institutional, collective) and the levels of organization of behavior (e.g., isolated acts, patterns of acts, deviant personality organization, and careers in a deviant way of life). While this point is not so controversial and depends more upon further research, it illustrates the kind of fundamental descriptive analysis which remains to be done in order to test theories of the middle range.

[30] Albert J. Reiss, "Delinquency as the Failure of Personal and Social Controls," *American Sociological Review*, 16 (April, 1951), 196-208; Nye, *op. cit.*

[31] F. Ivan Nye and James F. Short, Jr., "Scaling Delinquent Behavior," *op. cit.*, 22 (June, 1957), 326-31.

[32] John Finley Scott, "Two Dimensions of Delinquent Behavior," *American Sociological Review*, 24 (April, 1959), 240-43.

## Is Criminology a Dependent Science?

A number of writers who maintain that criminology may become a science propose that it is a highly synthetic and/or a dependent science. "It receives its contributions from experts in such disciplines as biology, anthropology, physiology, medicine, psychiatry, psychology, social administration, sociology, economics, law, political science, and penology and corrections."[33] "An empirical science of criminology is not at present possible because no empirical sciences of psychology and sociology now exist."[34] "Criminology is a dependent discipline. When the sciences on which criminology depends have progressed further, solutions of the problems of 'character disease' will become more likely."[35]

"It is not to be expected that criminological theory will develop wholly adequate and acceptable explanations of behavior until the whole group of 'the behavior sciences' reaches a corresponding adequacy of theoretical explanation of human behavior in general."[36] "The point has been well taken that a science of normal behavior is prerequisite to the scientific analysis of problem conduct . . . man does not yet possess a well-systematized science of human behavior."[37]

This argument loses part of its force when it fails to distinguish between criminology and the applied disciplines of penology and corrections. It leads to the same kind of disorder which earlier grew out of the failure to distinguish between sociology as a basic social science and social work as an art or applied science. And, in the main, medicine (including psychiatry) and social administration are not disciplines given over to the pursuit of scientific knowledge; they generally gather it from the basic sciences. Sellin has recommended that the term "criminology" be used to designate only the body of scientific knowledge about crime and the pursuit of such knowledge.[38]

Sellin goes on to observe, however, that ". . . the 'criminologist' . . . actually remains a psychologist, a sociologist, a psychiatrist, a jurist, or a political scientist, with a specialized concern in a question which

---

[33] Walter C. Reckless, *The Crime Problem* (New York: Appleton-Century-Crofts, 1955), 7.

[34] Michael and Adler, *op. cit.*, 85.

[35] Gluecks, *op. cit.*, 4, 289.

[36] George B. Vold, *Theoretical Criminology* (New York: Oxford, 1958), 314.

[37] Tappan, *op. cit.*, 56.

[38] Thorsten Sellin, *Culture Conflict and Crime* (New York: Social Science Research Council, Bulletin 41, 1938).

impinges on his broader interests. The 'criminologist' does not exist who is an expert in all the disciplines which converge in the study of crime."[39] Robison, interpreting Sellin in her recent textbook on delinquency, concludes from this remark that ". . . lacking these prerequisites one cannot arrive at valid generalizations, principles, or laws which have predictive values."[40] The conclusion, as interpreted, is untenable. It may become necessary to use terms like "sociological criminologist" or "psychological criminologist," but it is difficult to see why any science must stand or fall on the condition of any one person (or any group of persons trained in a common discipline) being able to master all the disciplines converging upon it. The theoretical model implied in this conclusion is not a body of special and more general theories consistent with one another yet capable of standing alone; but an all-embracing, unitary theory that includes the concepts and contributions of all relevant disciplines and which stands or falls as a whole. A sociology of crime and delinquency is possible apart from equivalent developments in related disciplines, and it is capable of developing valid special theories (if not some of the more general ones) that are necessary to an integrated body of theory. Sociological analysis cannot explain all the data of delinquency and it shares with other disciplines in the emerging body of theory; but this relationship does not constitute dependency to the extent that the theories of any one discipline are invalid or inadequate because they do not embrace and reconcile the contributions of every other relevant discipline.

This reduces the issue to the relation of the behavioral sciences to one another, and, more particularly, to the relation of the general sciences like sociology, psychology, and anthropology to special sciences like criminology and delinquency. The existence of disciplines like social psychology and social anthropology bears witness to the overlapping subject matter of the general behavioral sciences. To say that they are dependent upon one another is not so accurate as to say that they are interdependent. Few scholars would hold that any given social or behavioral discipline could not become a science until some or all of the others did. The case appears to be somewhat the same for general as related to special disciplines or sciences. They, too, are interdependent, and it is not easy to demonstrate that the dependency is great from special to general and small from general to special. A sociologist specializing in the study of a particular range of human behavior, i.e., deviant behavior which violates the delinquency or criminal code,

[39] *Ibid.*, 3, 4.
[40] Robison, *op. cit.*, 192.

may be just as able to contribute to the total body of theory on human behavior as the psychologist who starts by constructing a general theory of human behavior and then proceeds to test it exhaustively in selected ranges or dimensions of that behavior. The position that criminology is necessarily dependent upon any one or all of the general behavioral sciences; (a) can be reduced to a division-of-labor judgment, (b) assumes that the organization of knowledge has been accomplished and that the boundaries have been rather permanently established, (c) assumes that the phenomenon, crime, consists essentially or exhaustively of the deviant behavior of individual criminals, and (d) ignores the fact that bodies of theory which have become established in the mature sciences have accumulated piece-meal, i.e., from delimited or special problems or ranges of subject matter, until more general theories capable of organizing them consistently and parsimoniously were discovered.

In what way is a science of normal conduct prerequisite to the scientific analysis of problem conduct? Obviously, this question is irrelevant if one accepts the proposition that problem conduct is normal conduct. It is also irrelevant in a multicultural setting where conduct is problematic primarily because one culture does not accept the normal behavior of another culture or subculture. It probably has its greatest force where the problem conduct is pathological and severe, e.g., psychotic conduct.

## Conclusions

Each of the basic sciences involved in delinquency analysis can proceed to work on theory that comes within the segment of human experience for which it is ordinarily responsible in the academic division of labor. A reasonable goal for a science of delinquency analysis is a body of theory built up from the smaller bodies or ranges of theory contributed by the interdependent basic sciences. Theoretical issues that have become stumbling blocks in delinquency analysis stand to be substantially resolved if both theorists and empiricists will give the necessary attention to systematic and definitive qualitative or descriptive analysis. And the several phenomena that have been identified as constituent parts of the generic concept, juvenile delinquency, call for individual assessment with regard to their complexity, resistance to understanding and explanation, and susceptibility to intelligent control. In addition, the possible dimensions of each one deserve to be explored. If these tasks are undertaken with reasonable rigor, delinquency research will not continue to be unconvincing, and a science of delinquency analysis will at least have moved beyond some of the necessary conditions for its establishment.

## 5.   Norm-Violating Behavior and Lower-Class Culture

## William C. Kvaraceus and Walter B. Miller

Dr. Kvaraceus, Professor of Education at Boston University, has acted as consultant on various projects concerned with delinquency and was Director of the National Education Association Project on Juvenile Delinquency. He is the author of numerous publications in the field of delinquency, including *The Community and the Delinquent, Juvenile Delinquency and the School, The KD Proneness Scale and Check List,* and the co-author of two publications from the National Education Association Project—*Delinquent Behavior, Culture and the Individual* and *Delinquent Behavior, Principles and Practices.*

Dr. Miller holds the Ph.D. degree in Social Anthropology from Harvard University. His professional affiliations include the Graduate School of Education at Harvard University, Boston University, and the directorship of the Research Program of the Boston Delinquency Project. His published articles include a number in the field of juvenile delinquency.

A bunch of street-corner youngsters are hanging around a variety store. Someone says, "Gee, it's dull around here. What a dead neighborhood. There's never anything to do. Nothing ever happens."

Someone else comes along and says, "Hey, Paul has some cans of beer." The group goes off, starts drinking beer, and becomes engaged in discussion of feats of daring and danger. Then someone says, "Gee, it's dead around here. Let's go and find something to do. Let's pick up a car somewhere and go for a ride." The group agrees, off they go, and the groundwork for a night of "trouble" has been prepared.

The terms "lower class" and "middle class" are used here to refer to systems of behavior and concerns rather than groups defined in conventional economic terms. There are "rich" and "poor" in the lower class as well as in the middle and upper classes. Owning an automobile, even a Buick or a station wagon, is no longer in itself a sufficient symbol

William C. Kvaraceus and Walter B. Miller, *Delinquent Behavior, Culture and the Individual* (National Education Association of the United States, Washington, D.C., 1959), Chapter 9. Reprinted with permission of the publisher.

or criterion of class status. Wealth, as evidenced by personal possessions or bank books, is becoming less useful as a primary determinant of family status. What are some of the patterned forms of behavior and focal concerns which characterize the culture of the lower class, and how are these related to norm-violating behavior of lower-class adolescents? [1]

A large proportion of delinquency today has its origins in the streetcorner subculture of lower-class society. A close look is needed at the forces in this milieu which often tend to generate norm-violating behavior for a large segment of the delinquent population.

Lower-class culture [2] refers specifically to a way of life which is followed by a large segment of the present-day population of this country, whose concerns, values, and characteristic patterns of behavior are the product of a well-formed cultural system. Preliminary evidence indicates that somewhere between 40 and 60 per cent of the total population of the United States share or are significantly influenced by the major outlines of the lower-class cultural system.[3] In this report attention is directed chiefly to this cultural system in an urban setting. In its most representative form, it reveals a distinctive patterning which differs significantly from that of middle-class culture.

Much of the delinquency of lower-class youngsters may be seen as an attempt by the acting individual to adhere to forms of behavior and to achieve standards of value as they are defined within this type of community.

## Lower-Class Focal Concerns

The behavior of those involved in a given cultural system may be said to be motivated by a set of "focal concerns," which receive special emphasis within that culture.[4] "Achievement," for example, is a gen-

[1] The presentation and description of focal concerns of lower-class culture as well as the discussion of how these concerns influence delinquent behavior are adapted from: Walter B. Miller. "Lower Class Culture as a Generating Milieu of Gang Delinquency." *Journal of Social Issues* 14: April 1959.

[2] The criteria here pertain particularly to large urban communities and are less applicable to certain ethnic groups, such as the Italians and Chinese.

[3] Statistics as to the prevalence of lower-class culture, using educational, occupational and economic indexes, are presented by Walter B. Miller in "Cultural Features of an Urban Lower Class Community," reproduced by Community Services Branch, National Institutes of Health, March 1959.

[4] The "focal concern" as a concept for describing and analyzing subcultural groups in the United States is introduced and discussed in: Miller, *Journal of Social Issues* 14: April 1959, *op. cit.*

erally recognized concern of most members of the middle class. In lower-class culture, similarly, certain focal concerns are dominant; these include: *trouble, toughness, smartness, excitement, fate,* and *autonomy.* In relating these concerns to the behavior of lower-class youngsters, each concern must be considered as a *dimension* within which a fairly wide range of alternative behavior patterns may be followed by different individuals in different situations. At the same time, it will be necessary to relate the influence of these concerns to the motivation of delinquent behavior by specifying the nature of behavioral orientation in each instance. How concealed (covert) and how direct (overt) is the influence of each of these concerns? Does the individual's behavioral adjustment to his culture stem from a positive orientation toward the particular concern (does he appear to seek out the aspect) or from a negative orientation toward it (does he reject it)?

Norm-violating behavior in this subculture is not to be simply explained on the basis of direct imitative behavior, nor is it solely the outgrowth of a so-called delinquent subculture which arises from conflict with middle-class values which are misunderstood, rejected, and scorned by the delinquent.

## TROUBLE

"Getting into trouble" and "staying out of trouble" represent dominant concerns for lower-class individuals. Prestige may often attend a boy or girl's success in achieving or avoiding involvement with authorities of official agencies. "Trouble" is a word that constantly occurs in lower-class conversation: A mother may express relief that her daughter is going steady with a boy "who has never been in trouble"; an unmarried daughter who becomes pregnant is described as having "got in trouble with a man." In spite of the greater prevalence of both official and unofficial norm-violating behavior in lower-class communities, there still remains much leeway in the choices to be made by the adolescent who is raised in this type of environment. Although individuals are often motivated in the direction of getting into trouble, the choice frequently favors staying out of trouble.

Some writers, in referring to the lower-class youngster's propensity for trouble, have said, "These street-corner kids don't know right from wrong." This is far from true. Lower-class adolescents are very conscious of what the official rules of society are. At the actual point of being impelled or motivated to engage in given types of delinquent activity—getting into a gang fight, picking up a hot car, getting drunk, gambling, "hooking" school, all of which may be legally defined as delinquencies—their perception of the potential gains to themselves in terms of prestige, group status, and appropriate or demanded behavior outweighs their perception of the sanctions that can be directed against them for the specific delinquent act. For the youngster born and bred in this cultural milieu the total dynamics underlying choice of alternative forms of behavior, including the individual's perception of potential gains to himself, frequently throws the weight of decision on the side of norm-violating behavior. Other aspects of the dynamics and direction of choice will be discussed later.

## TOUGHNESS

Physical prowess, "masculinity," endurance, athletic ability, strength, all rank high in the concerns of lower-class adolescents and are evident in the kinds of heroes they select. The tough guy, the gangster, the pugilist, the tough cop, the combat infantryman and the "hard" teacher are heroic models.

Feats of toughness and exploits requiring physical and mental endurance are constant conversation pieces in street-corner society. Anything that smacks of the effeminate and the soft is scorned and ridiculed. The street-corner boy will say, "Man, I ain't been home or ain't slept for two nights. I've been on the prowl." Or: "They grilled me and beat me with a hose but I didn't admit nothin." Similarly: "My old man and me had one helluva fight. Man, he beat me up good." Some aspects of this type of masculine behavior may be explained as attempts by the street-corner boy to accommodate to certain fears relating to "masculine" identity acquired as the result of his early relations with his parents.

## SMARTNESS

Skill in duping and outsmarting the other guy as well as the ability to avoid being duped by others indicate a lower-class concern with "smartness." Although the "IQ" of the lower-class adolescent—as measured by school-administered intelligence tests, which entail certain types of verbal and academic aptitudes—is almost invariably low, his "duplicity" quotient must be high if he is to operate effectively in the world of the street corner.

In this world the lower-class adolescent will most likely disdain the "academic" wisdom of the teacher. Instead of seeing the teacher as a "person who knows," the lower-class boy may regard him as someone who knows very little about what really goes on in the streets and alleys, the flats and tenements, the street corners and backyards of the city. The models of estimable achievement in the area of "smartness" are the con man, the fast-man-with-a-buck, and the bunco operator, whose victims are seen as suckers and dupes.

## EXCITEMENT

The search for thrill and stimulation is a major concern in the lower-class community, where life often involves monotonous and dull routines in the home, on the job, and in just "hanging around." Frequent complaints about boredom and monotony are related to a recurrent quest for excitement and stimulation. The desire for excitement is reflected in prevalent patterns involving drinking, gambling and playing the numbers, goading ("testing") official authorities such as teachers and policemen, picking up girls, going out on the town, participating in a "rumble," destroying public property, stealing a car, and joy riding. All these acts involve risk, and their perpetrators court "trouble." Much of the delinquency related to this cultural concern involves the quality of high adventure. Although aggression against persons and property may figure in many of these acts, such behavior, from the actor's point of view, cannot be interpreted simply as "antisocial"; the aggressive component is one by-product of a complex of motives which includes the quest for "excitement."

## FATE

Lady Luck is a reigning goddess of lower-class society: "I was unlucky, I was caught" and "He's lucky, the police didn't catch up with him." Every boy hopes that his luck will change and that his number will come up soon. Any evil that befalls him can be explained away by evoking an ill-fated destiny. The prevailing philosophy of Kismet in lower-class culture operates to inhibit directed seeking after certain goals and provides a handy excuse for misadventures. Gambling in its many forms—numbers, pool, cards, dice and horses—nicely combines the element of thrill with that of luck.

## AUTONOMY

Many lower-class youngsters indicate in no uncertain terms, "No one is going to boss me, but nobody." Yet lower-class delinquents frequently seek out, through norm-violating behavior, situations in which they will be told what to do, when to do it, how to do it, and whether it is right when done. Overt expression of dislike, disdain, and resentment of external control over behavior apparently runs counter to an implicit seeking out of highly restrictive social environments where rules, regulations, and edicts exert close control over all behavior. The large percentage of lower-class youth in such institutions as the armed forces, the disciplinary school, and the state training school casts doubt on the reliability of their overt complaints against dominant authority. The common use of the term "boss" for landlord, first-line supervisor, or local politician also reflects the pattern of seeking of stable sources of dependency accompanied by verbal protest against these same restricting and controlling authorities.

Norm-violating behavior by lower-class pupils which serves to "test" the firmness of school authority may represent an expression of the need for "being controlled," which is often equated with "being cared for" by superordinate authority. If kicking up, talking back, truanting, or running from an institution are dealt with severely, firmly, and quickly, the pupil is reassured, although he may complain bitterly about his "unfair" and "tough" punishment or the "bad luck" of being caught. Moreover, studies of street-corner society indicate that certain restrictive social environments such as the school, after being tested by the norm-violating youngsters, may be rejected for failing to be *strict enough rather than for being too strict*. The problem presented to public schools enrolling many lower-class youngsters is how to preserve and use the coercive controls that are implicitly sought by the very same individuals who elude authority and complain most loudly about being pushed around by the principal and attendance officer. The tough "independence" of many youngsters from this subculture presents a neat exterior camouflage for strong dependency needs and cravings implicit in the recurring lower-class complaint against unjust, coercive, and arbitrary authority.

## The Interplay Among Focal Concerns

How does their cultural milieu contribute to the lower-class youngster's involvement in delinquent behavior? Three general processes may be cited. *First,* engaging in certain cultural practices which comprise essential elements of the total life pattern of lower-class culture automatically violates certain legal norms. Examples of this may be seen in the use of profanity, in hanging around or loitering, and in the serial-mating pattern characteristic of many homes.[5] *Second,* in certain instances where alternative avenues to valued objectives are available to the youngster, the law-violating route frequently entails a relatively smaller investment of energy and effort than the law-abiding route. *Third,* the *demanded* response to certain situations recurrently engendered within lower-class culture may call for the commission of illegal acts. For many youngsters the bases of prestige are to be found in toughness, physical prowess, skill, fearlessness, bravery, ability to con people, gaining money by wits, shrewdness, adroitness, smart repartee, seeking and finding thrills, risk, danger, freedom from external constraint, and freedom from superordinate authority. These are the explicit values of the most important and essential reference group of many delinquent youngsters. These are the things he respects and strives to attain. The lower-class youngster who engages in a long and recurrent series of delinquent behaviors that are sanctioned by his peer group is acting so as to achieve prestige within this reference system.

Adjustment to street-corner living is not, by any means, easy. Members of lower-class street-corner groups are often the most fit and the most able youngsters in their community, for this is a tough league in which to make the grade. One must possess both stamina and perseverance as well as the capacity to interact and to subordinate self to the over-all needs of the group. These same qualities, directed to different ends, are often cited as important ingredients for success in school and on the job. Similar skills and drives in the case of the middle-class boy are often directed toward the Eagle Scout badge. It is these motives and qualities of the lower-class boy which may, under the proper circumstances, be channeled into law-abiding activities.

Can a street-corner youngster who is able to adapt effectively to his primary neighborhood reference groups also adapt himself to the classroom? Many of the prestige factors in his peer group have been enumerated. When the same child comes to school, the whole set of definitions as to the basis of prestige is shifted. Now the capacity to apply oneself assiduously and conscientiously to intellectual tasks is of prime importance. To gain status within the academic frame of reference, one must achieve in "book learning" and acquire certain linguistic patterns. But a young male who engages successfully in these types of behavior runs a serious risk of being tagged as effeminate by his neighborhood peers. To the extent that the youngster, thus in conflict, continues to take his peer group as his primary object of reference, to that extent he

[5] For a fuller discussion of serial mating in lower-class culture, see Chapter 11 [of source of this chapter].

will be impeded in making an easy or ready adjustment to the scho. situation. As the schools are discovering, there are a great many youngsters for whom their peer group remains as the reference group of highest priority. The measure of the students' "adjustment" must always depend on the extent to which the other groupings of which the youngsters form an effective part have systems of values resembling those of the groupings in which they receive their early learning experiences.

Some school-connected experiences such as football—with its long, tedious practice periods and drills, interspersed with a weekly battle that calls for a sharp focus of all physical skills and strength in concentrated measure and for a short duration—find analogies in lower-class life and in certain kinds of lower-class occupational roles. A dull, slow, and typical week in this subculture frequently culminates in a "night out on the town" and by "hanging one on." It should also be noted that a substantial portion of the labor force today (about 50 per cent) still consists of laborers, unskilled workers, and routine factory operatives. Most of these jobs are filled by lower-class individuals. Graduates of the street corner, as they grow and assume their roles in the world of work, have been prepared to operate within these interactional milieus, for their street-corner and occupational groups share similar sets of ideas, principles, and values. The job routines of the fireman, trucker, soldier, sailor, logger, and policeman reflect the occupational rhythmic pattern characteristic of lower-class community living, street-corner activity, and football—long periods of routine activity broken by intense action and excitement. As one views occupational needs of the future and, at the same time, analyzes the prevailing features of street-corner society, the following conclusion emerges: *The essential outlines, values, and language patterns; the emphasis on "smartness"; the regard for strength and physical prowess, all appear to remain functional, adjustive, and adaptive for these youngsters.*[6]

There are many nondelinquent lower-class youngsters. The same neighborhoods produce cops and crooks, pimps and priests. What factors make the difference between quitting school and going on to college or in becoming a fireman rather than a firebug? The next section presents a hypothesis that may suggest an answer to this question, one of particular importance to the school.

[6] This position is developed and the following typology included in Walter B. Miller's "Implications of Lower Class Culture for Social Work," to be published in *The Social Service Review* XXXIII: No. 3, September 1959.

erns of Adaptation to Social Class Movement

as of adaptation to the problems of aspiration and class
~~~~~~~~ be identified within the adolescent lower-class community. These may be delineated in terms of two major factors: first, the extent to which the individual youngster manifests a realistic desire for upward social movement—which involves the actual adaptation of a different set of class-related behavior patterns, and not merely symbols of status such as cars and big houses—and, second, the extent to which such upward aspirations are actually feasible in light of the youngster's early family training and his resultant personality characteristics. On this basis, three patterns of adaptation can be distinguished:

1. *"Stable" lower class.* This group consists of youngsters who, for all practical purposes, do not aspire to higher status or who have no realistic possibility of achieving such aspirations.
2. *Aspiring but conflicted lower class.* This group represents those for whom family or other community influences have produced a desire to elevate their status, but who lack the necessary personal attributes or cultural "equipment" to make the grade, or for whom cultural pressures effectively inhibit aspiration.
3. *Successfully aspiring lower class.* This group, popularly assumed to be most prevalent, includes those who have both the will and the capacity to elevate their status. The familiar educational success story involved here is in the best tradition of the Horatio Alger "rags to riches" dream of American folklore. Moreover, when these cases do appear, they are dramatized and, by implication, presented as the norm. Cases of this type were more frequent during the late nineteenth and early twentieth centuries and were related to the epic migrations from the "old country." As this migration has ebbed and as many of those with upward aspiration have achieved their objective, the number of persons in this category has diminished considerably. At present, the highest untapped potential is probably in the Negro group, most of whom are still in the lower class and thus represent a vast reservoir of potentially upwardly mobile individuals.

At present there is little reliable research evidence as to the relative prevalence of these three types. However, it should be noted that there is evidence that Type 1, the "nonaspiring" lower-class youngster, is far more common than generally supposed, and that this group does not seem to be getting smaller, and may be getting larger. Type 2, the group that is being "stalled," is particularly significant in any consideration of delinquency because of the inevitable frustrations and conflicts associated with this position. Frictions arising when the youngster's levels of aspiration exceed his realistic potential or when serious obstacles thwart realistic levels of aspiration may contribute to the motivation of much delinquent behavior. Here is an important and profitable area for further research and for special attention by the schools.

The factor of aspiration level also relates significantly to the problem of the school drop-out. Usually the youngster who drops out of school as soon as it is legally possible is culturally lower class. The fact that approximately 45 per cent of those youngsters completing the fifth grade do not graduate from high school [7] is a good indication of the size of the lower-class adolescent population and indicates clearly that the "drop-out" is not merely a relatively isolated "learning problem," but, in fact, represents a highly prevalent social class group. "Dropping out" is a recurring, standard practice and derives support from the whole cultural system. This often creates a difficult situation for youngsters of Type 2. For example, an adolescent boy may evidence a desire to continue in school, but his older brother will say, "For cripes sake, you still going to school? What do you want to go to school for, you can drop out now? You're old enough." "I never went to school," adds the old man. "Go get a job. Be something beside a book reader."

To the negative pressure that this youngster gets from his family is added the taunts of his peer group who see him carrying his books home for study. They yell at him, "Hey, you still going to school? What kind of a fairy are you?" In such cases where certain influences have caused the adolescent to consider continuing in high school and going on to college as a desirable course of action, the basic definitions of his own cultural environment operate to block and stall him. This youngster must be tough indeed to move out and up. There is always conflict in such a situation. It is perhaps this group that is most likely to strike out in aggressive or norm-violating fashion against school and family.

For the youngsters in Type 1, experience in school is generally regarded as meaningless and useless. They may sit out the school in relatively passive compliance but not without considerable annoyance to school authorities. Their problems and the school's problem end on their sixteenth birthday. School becomes for members of this group another arena in which to demonstrate their toughness, their smartness, their

---

[7] U.S. Department of Health, Education, and Welfare, Office of Education. "Statistical Summary of Education." *Biennial Survey of Education in the United States, 1952-54*. Washington, D.C.: Superintendent of Documents, 1957. Chapter 1, p. 10.

autonomy, their daring—to the great discomfort of the school. To them, most school teachers are "a bunch of real squares."

Many of those lower-class youngsters who are in the "stable" group and even some who are upwardly mobile to a slight degree, in terms of both aspiration and potential, can manage to live out their adolescence as relatively law-abiding youngsters who get into little serious trouble with the law. Many school people tend to see the future lives of these youngsters in terms of only two major alternatives—an essentially lower-class or an essentially middle-class way of life. A third alternative—and one which is far more feasible in a large proportion of cases—is to train and prepare the youngster for a *law-abiding lower-class way of life.*

For that segment of law-abiding lower-class youngsters for whom the commission of a delinquent act is relatively rare or infrequent, the school and other community agencies should make every effort to recognize and exploit those elements in their cultural environment and personalities which provide support for a pattern of law-abiding behavior.

# 6.   A Theory of Middle Class Juvenile Delinquency

## Ralph W. England, Jr.

The author received the degree of Doctor of Philosophy from the University of Pennsylvania, and has taught at that institution, the University of Illinois, and the University of Rhode Island. He has been a consultant on prison labor for the United Nations and prepared that organization's publication, *Prison Labor*, in 1955. His articles in the field of criminology have appeared in a number of professional journals.

Since 1948 the number of children aged ten to seventeen coming before juvenile court authorities has more than doubled, while the number of children within these ages in the total population has increased by only 19 per cent.[1] Despite the caution with which one must regard juvenile court data, police arrest statistics and the testimony of numerous

Ralph W. England, Jr., "A Theory of Middle Class Juvenile Delinquency," *Journal of Criminal Law, Criminology and Police Science*, 50 (March-April, 1960), 535-540. Reprinted with permission of the publishers of the *Journal*.

[1] JUVENILE COURT STATISTICS: 1956, Children's Bureau Statistical Series, No. 47, U.S. Children's Bureau, Washington, D.C., 1958.

persons working with youth support the Children's Bureau figures.[2] There exists non-statistical evidence that an unprecedented share of the apparent increase in delinquency is being contributed by "normal" youngsters from middle class families in communities and neighborhoods lacking previous experience with serious misbehavior among their children. Rowdiness in and out of school, abuse of driving privileges, joy-riding, thefts, excessive drinking, vandalism and sexual misconduct are among the principal forms of disapproved acts seemingly becoming more frequent among teenagers from "better" backgrounds. And the problem is not merely a phenomenon of metropolitan areas: towns and smaller cities in which delinquency of any kind was nearly non-existent before the war are reporting similar difficulties.

A number of researches have shown the existence of considerable unrecorded delinquency among socially advantaged youths,[3] but few theoretical attempts have been made to explain such behavior. In an article published in 1942 Talcott Parsons touched briefly upon the existence and nature of a "youth culture": [4]

> Perhaps the best single point of reference for characterizing the youth culture lies in its contrast with the dominant pattern of the adult male role. By contrast with the emphasis on responsibility in this role, the orientation of the youth culture is more or less specifically irresponsible. One of its dominant notes is "having a good time" in relation to which there is a particularly strong emphasis on social activities with the opposite sex (pp. 606-607).
>
> . . . it is notable that the youth culture has a strong tendency to develop in directions which are either on the borderline of parental approval or beyond the pale, in such matters as sex behavior, drinking and various forms of frivolous and irresponsible behavior (p. 608).
>
> [The youth culture] shows strong signs of being a product of tensions in the relationships of younger people and adults (p. 608).

The last sentence foreshadows his later theory that in the process of acquiring a masculine role-identity middle class boys react against the feminine identification of their childhoods by engaging in "masculine protest" behavior of a rough, destructive kind. The relative inability of youths today to observe directly their fathers' occupational roles, coupled with the ubiquity of feminine roles in the home, forces an eventual re-

---

[2] HERBERT A. BLOCH AND FRANK T. FLYNN, DELINQUENCY: THE JUVENILE OFFENDER IN AMERICA TODAY, Random House, New York, 1956, p. 29.

[3] F. IVAN NYE, JAMES F. SHORT, JR. AND VIRGIL J. OLSON, Socioeconomic Status and Delinquent Behavior, AMER. JOUR. OF SOC., 63:381-389 (Jan., 1958), note 3; FRANK E. HARTUNG, A Critique of the Sociological Approach to Crime and Correction, LAW AND CONTEMP. PROB., 23:703-734 (Autumn, 1958), p. 730.

[4] TALCOTT PARSONS, Age and Sex in the Social Structure of the United States, AMER. SOC. REV., 7:604-616 (Oct., 1942).

bellion not only against "feminineness" but against the "goodness" which seems to the child an integral part of femininity.[5]

A number of objections to this theory can be raised. (a) In the process of "protesting masculinity" why is the trait of adult male responsibility shunned while other presumed traits of the male (loud, aggressive, rambunctious behavior) are adopted? (b) One can imagine middle class boys who live in dormitory suburbs and large cities having some difficulty picturing their fathers' occupational roles, but this may not be true in smaller cities and in towns where the fathers' places of work are more readily accessible for visits, and where their roles are less likely to be obscured by employment in bureaucratic organizations. (c) How can the participation of girls in the youth culture be explained by Parson's theory? (d) Are mothers' roles especially ubiquitous in communities where commuting time for the father is not so great that he cannot be with his family meaningfully except on weekends? "Catching the 7:05" each morning before the children are up and returning in the evening shortly before their bedtime is a pattern found only in our largest cities. (e) Is it to be assumed that the seeming increase in middle class delinquency since the Second World War is the result of a postwar increase in sons' difficulties in identifying with their fathers' roles, in the absence of basic post-war changes in our society's occupation structure?

The present paper begins with a backtrack on Parson's thinking to his idea that hedonistic irresponsibility characterizes the youth culture of the United States, and a departure from this in another direction from that taken by him. The theory to be presented here is that some middle class delinquency is the result of an interaction between certain aspects of our general cultural system and an emerging teenage system, producing norms entirely functional to the latter but not to the former.

## The Teenage System

The groundwork for the emergence of a teenage culture in our society was laid a century and more ago when youngsters were gradually removed from functional roles in the economy through restrictive apprenticeship codes, protective labor legislation, the compulsory education movement, and the withdrawal of children from agricultural activities attendant upon urbanization. However diverse the forces were which

[5] Talcott Parsons, "Certain Primary Sources and Patterns of Aggression in the Social Structure of the Western World," *Psychiatry*, 10:167-181 (May, 1947).

led to this removal from productive roles, the result was that for probably the first time a major society deactivated a large and energetic segment of its population without clearly redefining the status and function of that segment. The resulting ambiguity of status, the blurring of the lines separating childhood from youth and youth from adulthood, has been commented upon by many observers; the middle class teenager, with his typically lengthened period of ambiguous status compared with working class youngsters, is faced with contradictory expectations. He is not expected to engage in productive labor, but neither is he encouraged to loaf; he is discouraged from early marriage, but is allowed to engage in proto-courtship; he cannot vote, hold public office, or serve on a jury, but is expected to be civic-minded; he is given many privileges and a large measure of individual freedom, but without the obligatory ties to significant others which, for the adult, help keep privilege and freedom from deteriorating into license.

Bloch and Niederhoffer [6] have recently suggested that certain attributes of adolescent life (tattooing, hazing, the adoption of nicknames, etc.) serve as latter-day rites of passage into adolescence to lessen the anxiety-producing absence of adult-sponsored rites. For several generations the teen years have been a singularly faddist time of life, and peculiarities of dress, speech, values and interests are increasingly conspicuous among this population group. It seems reasonable to presume, as have Bloch and others, that these widely-shared peculiarities are highly functional to teenagers, and are not simply youthful fancies. Some might, indeed, be the equivalent of primitive rites of passage; others might serve to maintain the new status; still others might be the ordinary *impedimenta* of a burgeoning youth cultural system.

It is the writer's contention that certain post-World War II changes—mainly in communications—have speeded the development of long-nascent tendencies arising from the ambiguous status of our teenage population. These changes have had the general, if inadvertent, effect of making teenagers newly aware of themselves as a nation-wide segment of our society by fostering communication within this population group. Probably none of these changes singly could have produced this effect, but their conjuncture following the war provided means for teenagers to enter into at least secondary contact far beyond the pre-war confines of their respective communities.

1. Perhaps basic is the exploitation of an enlarged market for teenage goods and services following our post-war rise in living standards and the consequent possession of large amounts of spending money by young-

[6] Herbert A. Bloch and Arthur Niederhoffer, *The Gang*, Philosophical Library, New York, 1958, Ch. 5.

sters. An estimated nine billion dollars are spent annually by teenagers.[7] National advertising campaigns, many found only in the new teen magazines, publicize products tailored to the interests and needs of this age group: motor scooters, acne creams, portable phonographs and radios, western and rock-and-roll movies, auto accessories, hot-rod conversion kits, unusual clothing, mail-order dance lessons, etc. The wide distribution of these items is contributing to the growth of a nationally shared but age-restricted material culture.

2. Post-war changes in local radio broadcasting with increased reliance on canned material, particularly popular music, has brought into prominence the disc jockey, whose seeming chumminess with entertainers gives him some of the glamour of show business. Despite competition from television the number of operating commercial broadcasting stations increased from 890 to 3,680 between 1945 and 1958,[8] many of them being located in smaller communities throughout the country. The number of disc jockeys has been estimated at 2,500,[9] compared to a handful before the war, and their audiences, apparently are drawn mainly from among persons in their teens and early twenties. The recent disturbance in Boston where a disc jockey was accused of inciting his young followers to riot, and the power of these men to stimulate teenage interest in charity drives, contests and the like, are suggestive of their role in teenage communications.

3. Similar to the above, but with the added element of visual impact, is TV programming of teen dance shows, from Dick Clark's nationally broadcast AMERICAN BANDSTAND to the one-channel town's airing of the local equivalent with a lone disc jockey providing the recorded music. The particular image of teenage life thus promulgated by many of the country's 544 operating commercial television stations (contrasted with six in 1945 [10]) probably reaches a large audience.

4. Young people's magazines have been published for many decades in the United States. With few exceptions, their common stamp was one of staid, moralistic conservatism which viewed adolescence as a period of preparation for an adulthood of similar qualities. Since 1944, however, when SEVENTEEN began publication, a number of magazines have appeared whose kinship to the older YOUTH's COMPANION and AMERICAN BOY is only faintly discernible. At least eleven of these are currently in the market, led by SEVENTEEN, whose monthly circulation is slightly

---

[7] CONSUMER REPORTS, *Teen-age Consumers*, 22:139-142 (March, 1957).
[8] STATISTICAL ABSTRACT OF THE UNITED STATES: 1958, U.S. Bureau of the Census, Washington, D.C., p. 519.
[9] NEWSWEEK, 49:104-105 (April 1, 1957).
[10] STATISTICAL ABSTRACT, *op. cit.*, p. 519.

over one million copies. Co-Ed, 'Teen, Cool, Hep Cats, Modern Teen, Ingenue and Dig have combined circulations of about 1,500,000.[11] These publications are similar in format to movie and TV magazines read by many adults, but their picture stories emphasize younger personnel from the entertainment industry, and they contain a thin scattering of teenage love stories, youth "forums," puzzles and articles on automobiles and high school sports. In sharp contrast with the moralistic flavor of earlier youth magazines, the post-war group is distinguished by its portrayal of hedonistic values within an essentially amoral setting: the teen years are not ones of preparation for responsible adulthood, but of play and diversion.

5. A final influence contributing to the teenagers' awareness of themselves as a distinct population group may be the very fact that the post-war years have seen public attention directed increasingly toward our youth because of the apparent increase in juvenile problems. Teenagers seem very much aware that such problems exist, even if their outlines are not clear to the youngsters.[12]

Given the existence of a large population segment permeated with anxiety arising from its ill-defined status, and communicating, however imperfectly, on a national scale, one observes elements necessary for the development of something akin to a minority group psychology: a shared sense of grievance and alienation among substantial numbers of persons readily identifiable by some conspicuous trait—in this case, being in the teen years. Listing further points of similarity between minority groups and today's teenagers, one could mention *leaders and spokesmen* in the persons of disc jockeys, young entertainers and some educationists; a distinctive set of material and nonmaterial *culture traits; sentiments of exclusiveness* toward most adults and toward "square" (i.e., adult-oriented) youngsters; and *culture heroes*, selected mainly from among entertainers and athletes.

While the theory being presented here does not hinge on teenagers constituting a true minority group, it does assume that on a national scale there is evolving a complex of attitudes and values tending to control and motivate teenagers in ways consonant with the role implied

---

[11] Consumer Magazine and Farm Publication Rates and Data for May 27, 1959, pp. 400, 411-419. Circulation figures for Datebook, Teens Today and *16* are not currently listed in Rates and Data. A "Teensters' Union" has recently been organized by Modern Teens magazine, ostensibly "for the improvement of teen-age society."

[12] A crude measure of the increased public attention to our youth can be obtained by a count of Readers' Guide to Periodical Literature entries under *Youth— United States*. For the respective two-year periods of May, 1945 to April, 1947; April, 1951 to March, 1953; and March, 1957 to February, 1959 the number of entries was 24, 42 and 60.

by their position as a youthful group having leisure, relatively ample spending money and few responsibilities. The theme of this emerging culture seems to be one of an increasingly institutionalized but immature and irresponsible hedonism, as Parsons suggested.

It is evident that not all teenagers behave as if they were participants in such a culture. The degree to which any particular youth is controlled and motivated by the norms of the teenage system may be a function of the extent and intensity of his affiliation with youthful autonomous cliques, for these, rather than individuals, appear to be the social units of the teenage world. The relative importance of clique-membership may in turn be inversely related to a teenager's commitment to groups—usually adult-dominated—which purvey conventional normative systems, and which have the inherent disadvantage, in competing for teenagers' loyalties, of requiring accommodation to adult demands.

While strong peer-group appeal is exhibited among both working class and middle class youngsters, there may exist class differences both in the content of the youth culture shared by teenagers from the two strata, and in the duration of the culture's importance in the lives of its followers. Those teenagers currently labeled "hoods" by other youngsters are marked by levis and leather jackets, motorcycles and jalopies, frankly promiscuous girl friends, truculent, aggressive behavior in school, and a sneering avoidance of extracurricular school social activities. For these youngsters delinquent motivations may indeed stem from their experiences with snobbish discrimination within the high school social structure, as Cohen maintains.[13] But their earlier entrance into the labor market and their lower age at marriage enable them to acquire adult roles—and to become saddled with adult responsibilities—sooner than middle class teenagers. By contrast, the middle class "social crowd"—more seemly and fashionably dressed, smoother mannered, driving late-model cars, peopling the parties and proms in their communities, and indulged by their prosperous and permissive parents—constitute the spending market alluded to earlier, and may be proportionately greater participants in the teenage communications network and in that part of the teenage culture depicted in it.

## Delinquency and the Teenage Culture

An ethos of irresponsible hedonism is not in itself productive of delinquent motivations, and I am not suggesting that middle class delinquency is simply a manifestation of unchecked impulses, as the term "irrespon-

[13] Albert K. Cohen, *Delinquent Boys: Culture of the Gang*, Free Press, Glencoe, Ill., 1955.

sible hedonism" connotes. The relationship between this ethos and delinquency is more complex. If the teenager's urgent need for status affirmation is met by the teenage culture, then it becomes necessary for him to reject influences from the adult world which threaten it, and to accept only those giving it support. The threatening influences are attitudes and values running counter to short-run, irresponsible hedonism, such as hard work, thrift, study, self-denial, etc., while those supportive of it are cultural elements adaptable to it. It is the writer's contention that delinquent motivations among middle class teenagers arise from this adaptive process, in which the teenage world, peopled by immature and inexperienced persons, extracts from the adult world those values having strong hedonistic possibilities, with the result that the values of the teenage culture consist mainly of distorted and caricatured fragments from the adult culture. These highly selected and altered values then serve to motivate and give direction to members of the youth world, sometimes in ways adults define as delinquent. Some examples of such value transformation will make my meaning clear.

1. Abuse of driving privileges by some teenagers is a persisting problem in most communities. Open mufflers, drag-racing, speeding, playing "chicken," or just aimlessly driving about constitute nuisances and sometimes dangers on public streets and highways. To emotionally mature adults automobiles primarily represent—and are operated as—means of transportation, but in the process of adaptation to the adolescent ethos they are redefined as playthings whose important qualities are less those pertaining to getting from place to place than to glitter, power and speed, and teenagers tend to operate them in ways appropriate to these qualities. Youth's intense interest in cars is reflected in the current number of magazines (twenty-one) devoted to the automobile. Eighteen of these were founded since 1945, and fourteen since 1950. Their reported combined monthly circulation is about 2,300,000. Hot Rod Magazine leads this group, with about 490,000 paid monthly circulation.[14] Some 2,000 so-called "speed shops" supplied by 100 manufacturers distribute parts and accessories for youthful car enthusiasts.[15]

A more serious problem with respect to automobiles is the increasing number of cars "borrowed" for joy rides by middle class (or at least "favored group") teenagers.[16] Larceny is customarily defined as taking

---

[14] Rates and Data, op. cit., pp. 65-74.

[15] Consumer Reports, op. cit., p. 139.

[16] William A. Wattenberg and James T. Balistrieri, Automobile Theft: A "Favored Group" Delinquency, Amer. Jour. of Soc., 57:575-579 (May, 1952). In studying 3,900 cases of juvenile auto theft in Detroit, the authors observed that not only were the boys from somewhat better neighborhoods than other delinquents, but were well socialized in their peer-group relationships. The "favored group" characteristic has reportedly been observed also in Britain. See, T. C. N. Gibbens, Car Thieves, Brit. Jour. of Delinquency (April, 1958).

another's property with intent to deprive the owner permanently of its use; joyride thievery seldom involves this criminal intention, and apprehended youngsters are quick to point out—quite accurately—that they were "merely having a little fun." (It is worth noting that cars borrowed for joy rides almost invariably embody qualities extraneous to mere transportation. Flashy convertibles are especially vulnerable.)

2. The competitive spirit, valued in our larger society as a spur to achievement, but hedged about with customary and legal restrictions, becomes productive of bitter and childish rivalries when it is applied to high school intermural contests. The youngsters, aroused by pep committees, coaches and alumni, transform competition into a hedonistic travesty: witness the growing problem of fights, car chases and vandalism attendant on important games.

3. Whether or not we are a sex-obsessed society, as European observers sometimes contend, the meaning of sex to our teenagers is confused and contradictory. On the one hand, pre-marital chastity and forebearance are upheld as prime moral values. On the other, sex is heavily exploited in most of the popular media of entertainment. The image of sex, love and romance presented by these media is one rejected by most adults whose views have been tempered by the realities of life, but the middle class youngsters of the teenage world, bemused by their burgeoning sex drives in the prolonged and presumably chaste interval between puberty and marriage, and betrayed by their inexperience, are inclined to accept this image as valid. More importantly, this image is considerably more congenial to their ethos than one conveying restraint and self-control; sex and love are redefined as ends in themselves, and have acquired sufficient preeminence in the teenage system since 1945 to motivate youngsters of twelve to begin "going steady," and of sixteen to contemplate marriage seriously.

4. Among the adult values attractive to the teenage ethos, the use of alcoholic beverages is perhaps the one most readily lending itself to distortion, for the temperate use of alcohol by adults themselves requires a degree of restraint seldom found in youngsters. Normatively, alcohol is utilized by the middle class as a social lubricant and as an adjunct to food, and strong social pressures help limit its use to those functions. By custom (as well as by law) teenagers are forbidden generally to use alcoholic beverages on their own for any purpose. But its fundamental hedonistic quality—its capacity to intoxicate—makes it so highly adaptable to the teenage ethos that when alcohol is used, this quality is emphasized, and drinking to excess becomes the norm. A further difficulty arises from the obligatory secretiveness of teenage middle class drinking: it must be done quite apart from adult eyes in auto-

mobiles, public parks, rented cottages and motels where drinking parties can easily get out of hand.

## Summary

Post-war changes in communications processes are heightening in-group feelings within a large population segment which, during the last one hundred years, has experienced increased status ambiguity as the productive roles of this group have diminished. The intensive pre-occupation with play among today's teenagers results from the circumstance that hedonistic pursuits, evoked by the youngsters' present position in the social structure, are becoming the status-defining "function" of this emerging national interest group. In order to retain the need-satisfactions produced by this new status clarification, the group's values and norms must support its play function by constituting a hedonistic ethos, and must neutralize non-hedonistic pressures from the adult world either by denigrating them entirely or by altering them to conform with the teenage culture. Once incorporated into that culture, they become controlling and motivating forces for those teenagers sharing the system but in directions sometimes inconsistent with adult norms.

## 7.  The Delinquent Subculture

## Albert K. Cohen

The author, who holds the degree of Doctor of Philosophy from Harvard University, is Professor of Sociology at Indiana University. He is co-editor of *The Sutherland Papers*, and has published numerous articles on juvenile delinquency.

## The Content of the Delinquent Subculture

The common expression, "juvenile crime," has unfortunate and misleading connotations. It suggests that we have two kinds of criminals, young and old, but only one kind of crime. It suggests that crime has its meanings and its motives which are much the same for young and old; that the young differ from the old as the apprentice and the master differ at the same trade; that we distinguish the young from the old only because the young are less "set in their ways," less "confirmed" in the same criminal habits, more amenable to treatment and more deserving, because of their tender age, of special consideration.

The problem of the relationship between juvenile delinquency and adult crime has many facets. To what extent are the offenses of children and adults distributed among the same legal categories, "burglary," "larceny," "vehicle-taking," and so forth? To what extent, even when the offenses are legally identical, do these acts have the same meaning for children and adults? To what extent are the careers of adult criminals continuations of careers of juvenile delinquency? We cannot solve these problems here, but we want to emphasize the danger of making facile and unproven assumptions. If we assume that "crime is crime," that child and adult criminals are practitioners of the same trade, and if our assumptions are false, then the road to error is wide and clear. Easily and unconsciously, we may impute a whole host of notions concerning the nature of crime and its causes, derived from our knowledge and fancies about adult crime, to a large realm of behavior to which these notions are irrelevant. It is better to make no such assumptions; it is better to look at juvenile delinquency with a fresh eye and try to explain what we see.

What we see when we look at the delinquent subculture (and we must not even assume that this describes *all juvenile* crime) is that it is *non-utilitarian, malicious* and *negativistic*.

We usually assume that when people steal things, they steal because they want them. They may want them because they can eat them, wear them or otherwise use them; or because they can sell them; or even— if we are given to a psychoanalytic turn of mind—because on some deep symbolic level they substitute or stand for something unconsciously desired but forbidden. All of these explanations have this in common, that they assume that the stealing is a means to an end, namely, the possession of some object of value, and that it is, in this sense, rational and "utilitarian." However, the fact cannot be blinked—and this fact is of crucial importance in defining our problem—that much gang stealing has no such motivation at all. Even where the value of the object stolen is itself a motivating consideration, the stolen sweets are often sweeter than those acquired by more legitimate and prosaic means. In homelier language, stealing "for the hell of it" and apart from considerations of gain and profit is a valued activity to which attaches glory, prowess and profound satisfaction. There is no accounting in rational and utilitarian terms for the effort expended and the danger run in stealing things which are often discarded, destroyed or casually given away. A group of boys enters a store where each takes a hat, a ball or a light bulb. They then move on to another store where these things are covertly exchanged for like articles. Then they move on to other stores to continue the game indefinitely. They steal a basket of peaches, desultorily munch on a few of them and leave the rest to spoil. They steal clothes they cannot wear and toys they will not use. Unquestionably, most delinquents are from the more "needy" and "underprivileged" classes, and unquestionably many things are stolen because they are intrinsically valued. However, a humane and compassionate regard for their economic disabilities should not blind us to the fact that stealing is not merely an alternative means to the acquisition of objects otherwise difficult of attainment.[1]

Can we then account for this stealing by simply describing it as another form of recreation, play or sport? Surely it is that, but why is this form of play so attractive to some and so unappealing to others? Mountain climbing, chess, pinball, number pools and bingo are also different kinds of recreation. Each of us, child or adult, can choose from a host of alternative means for satisfying our common "need" for recreation. But every choice expresses a preference, and every preference reflects something about the chooser or his circumstances that endows the object of his choice with some special quality or virtue. The choice is not self-explanatory nor is it arbitrary or random. Each form of recreation is distributed in a characteristic way among the age, sex and social class sectors of our population. The explanation of these distributions and of the way they change is often puzzling, sometimes fascinating and rarely platitudinous.

By the same logic, it is an imperfect answer to our problem to say: "Stealing is but another way of satisfying the universal desire for status." Nothing is more obvious from numberless case histories of subcultural delinquents that they steal to achieve recognition and to avoid isolation or opprobrium. This is an important insight and part of the foundation on which we shall build. But the question still haunts us: "Why is stealing a claim to status in one group and a degrading blot in another?"

If stealing itself is not motivated by rational, utilitarian considerations, still less are the manifold other activities which constitute the delinquent's repertoire. Throughout there is a kind of *malice* apparent, an enjoyment in the discomfiture of others, a delight in the defiance of taboos itself. Thrasher quotes one gang delinquent:

[¹ Footnote omitted. Ed.]

We did all kinds of dirty tricks for fun. We'd see a sign, "Please keep the streets clean," but we'd tear it down and say, "We don't feel like keeping it clean." One day we put a can of glue in the engine of a man's car. We would always tear things down. That would make us laugh and feel good, to have so many jokes.*

The gang exhibits this gratuitous hostility toward non-gang peers as well as adults. Apart from its more dramatic manifestations in the form of gang wars, there is keen delight in terrorizing "good" children, in driving them from playgrounds and gyms for which the gang itself may have little use, and in general in making themselves obnoxious to the virtuous. The same spirit is evident in playing hookey and in misbehavior in school. The teacher and her rules are not merely something onerous to be evaded. They are to be *flouted*. There is an element of active spite and malice, contempt and ridicule, challenge and defiance, exquisitely symbolized, in an incident described to the writer by Mr. Henry D. McKay, of defecating on the teacher's desk.[2]

All this suggests also the intention of our term "negativistic." The delinquent subculture is not only a set of rules, a design for living which is different from or indifferent to or even in conflict with the norms of the "respectable" adult society. It would appear at least plausible that it is defined by its "negative polarity" to those norms. That is, the delinquent subculture takes its norms from the larger culture but turns them upside down. The delinquent's conduct is right, by the standards of his subculture, precisely *because* it is wrong by the norms of the larger culture.[3] "Malicious" and "negativistic" are foreign to the delinquent's vocabulary but he will often assure us, sometimes ruefully, sometimes with a touch of glee or even pride, that he is "just plain mean."

In describing what might be called the "spirit" of the delinquent culture, we have suggested also its *versatility*. Of the "antisocial" activities of the delinquent gangs, stealing, of course, looms largest. Stealing itself can be, and for the gang usually is, a diversified occupation. It may steal milk bottles, candy, fruit, pencils, sports equipment and cars; it may steal from drunks, homes, stores, schools and filling stations. No gang runs the whole gamut but neither is it likely to "specialize" as do many adult criminal gangs and "solitary" delinquents. More to our point, however, is the fact that stealing tends to go hand-in-hand with "other property offenses," "malicious mischief," "vandalism," "trespass," and

*Frederic M. Thrasher, *The Gang* (Chicago: University of Chicago Press, 1936), pp. 94-95.
[2 Footnote omitted. Ed.]
[3 Footnote omitted. Ed.]

truancy. This quality of versatility and the fusion of versatility and malice are manifest in the following quotation:

> We would get some milk bottles in front of the grocery store and break them in somebody's hallway. Then we would break windows or get some garbage cans and throw them down someone's front stairs. After doing all this dirty work and running through alleys and yards, we'd go over to a grocery store. There, some of the boys would hide in a hallway while I would get a basket of grapes. When the man came after me, why the boys would jump out of their places and each grab a basket of grapes.[*]

Dozens of young offenders, after relating to the writer this delinquent episode and that, have summarized: "I guess we was just ornery." A generalized, diversified, protean "orneriness," not this or that specialized delinquent pursuit seems best to describe the vocation of the delinquent gang.[4]

Another characteristic of the subculture of the delinquent gang is *short-run hedonism*. There is little interest in long-run goals, in planning activities and budgeting time, or in activities involving knowledge and skills to be acquired only through practice, deliberation and study. The members of the gang typically congregate, with no specific activity in mind, at some street corner, candy store or other regular rendezvous. They "hang around," "roughhousing," "chewing the fat," and "waiting for something to turn up." They may respond impulsively to somebody's suggestion to play ball, go swimming, engage in some sort of mischief, or do something else that offers excitement. They do not take kindly to organized and supervised recreation, which subjects them to a regime of schedules and impersonal rules. They are impatient, impetuous and out for "fun," with little heed to the remoter gains and costs. It is to be noted that this short-run hedonism is not inherently delinquent and indeed it would be a serious error to think of the delinquent gang as dedicated solely to the cultivation of juvenile crime. Even in the most seriously delinquent gang only a small fraction of the "fun" is specifically and intrinsically delinquent. Furthermore, short-run hedonism is not characteristic of delinquent groups alone. On the contrary, it is common throughout the social class from which delinquents characteristically come. However, in the delinquent gang it reaches its finest flower. It is

[*] Clifford R. Shaw and Henry D. McKay, *Social Factors in Juvenile Delinquency*, Vol. II of National Commission on Law Observance and Enforcement, *Report on the Causes of Crime* (Washington: U.S. Government Printing Office, 1931), p. 18.
[4 Footnote omitted. Ed.]

the fabric, as it were, of which delinquency is the most brilliant and spectacular thread.[5]

Another characteristic not peculiar to the delinquent gang but a conspicuous ingredient of its culture is an emphasis on *group autonomy*, or intolerance of restraint except from the informal pressures within the group itself. Relations with gang members tend to be intensely solidary and imperious. Relations with other groups tend to be indifferent, hostile or rebellious. Gang members are unusually resistant to the efforts of home, school and other agencies to regulate, not only their delinquent activities, but any activities carried on within the group, and to efforts to compete with the gang for the time and other resources of its members. It may be argued that the resistance of gang members to the authority of the home may not be a result of their membership in gangs but that membership in gangs, on the contrary, is a result of ineffective family supervision, the breakdown of parental authority and the hostility of the child toward the parents; in short, that the delinquent gang recruits members who have already achieved autonomy. Certainly a previous breakdown in family controls facilitates recruitment into delinquent gangs. But we are not speaking of the autonomy, the emancipation of *individuals*. It is not the individual delinquent but the gang that is autonomous. For many of our subcultural delinquents the claims of the home are very real and very compelling. The point is that the gang is a separate, distinct and often irresistible focus of attraction, loyalty and solidarity. The claims of the home versus the claims of the gang may present a real dilemma, and in such cases the breakdown of family controls is as much a casualty as a cause of gang membership.[6]

## What the Delinquent Subculture Has to Offer

The delinquent subculture, we suggest, is a way of dealing with the problems of adjustment we have described. These problems are chiefly status problems: certain children are denied status in the respectable society because they cannot meet the criteria of the respectable status system. The delinquent subculture deals with these problems by providing criteria of status which these children *can* meet.

This statement is highly elliptical and is based upon a number of assumptions whose truth is by no means self-evident. It is not, for example, self-evident that people whose status positions are low must necessarily feel deprived, injured or ego-involved in that low status. Whether they will or not depends upon several considerations.

[5, 6 Footnotes omitted. Ed.]

We remarked earlier that our ego-involvement in a given comparison with others depends upon our "status universe." "Whom do we measure ourselves against?" is the crucial question. In some other societies virtue may consist in willing acceptance of the role of peasant, low-born commoner or member of an inferior caste and in conformity to the expectations of that role. If others are richer, more nobly-born or more able than oneself, it is by the will of an inscrutable Providence and not to be imputed to one's own moral defect. The sting of status inferiority is thereby removed or mitigated; one measures himself only against those of like social position. We have suggested, however, that an important feature of American "democracy," perhaps of the Western European tradition in general, is the tendency to measure oneself against "all comers." This means that, for children as for adults, one's sense of personal worth is at stake in status comparisons with all other persons, at least of one's own age and sex, whatever their family background or material circumstances. It means that, in the lower levels of our status hierarchies, whether adult or juvenile, there is a chronic fund of motivation, conscious or repressed, to elevate one's status position, either by striving to climb within the established status system or by redefining the criteria of status so that one's present attributes become status-giving assets. It has been suggested, for example, that such typically working-class forms of Protestantism as the Holiness sects owe their appeal to the fact that they reverse the respectable status system; it is the humble, the simple and the dispossessed who sit at the right hand of God, whereas worldly goods, power and knowledge are as nothing in His eyes. In like manner, we offer the view that the delinquent subculture is one solution to a kindred problem on the juvenile level.

Another consideration affecting the degree of privation experienced in a given status position is the "status source." A person's status, after all, is how he stands in somebody's eyes. Status, then, is not a fixed property of the person but varies with the point of view of whoever is doing the judging. I may be revered by some and despised by others. A crucial question then becomes: "Whose respect or admiration do I value?" That *you* think well or ill of me may or may not *matter* to me.

It may be argued that the working-class boy does not *care* what middle-class people think of him, that he is ego-involved only in the opinions of his family, his friends, his working-class neighbors. A definitive answer to this argument can come only from research designed to get at the facts. This research, in our opinion, is yet to be done. There is, however, reason to believe that most children are sensitive *to some degree* about the attitudes of *any persons* with whom they are thrown into more than the most superficial kind of contact. The contempt or indifference of others, particularly of those like schoolmates and teachers, with whom we are constrained to associate for long hours every day, is difficult, we suggest, to shrug off. It poses a problem with which one may conceivably attempt to cope in a variety of ways. One may make an active effort to change himself in conformity with the expectations of others; one may attempt to justify or explain away his inferiority in terms which will exculpate him; one may tell oneself that he really doesn't care what these people think; one may react with anger and aggression. But the least probable response is simple, uncomplicated, honest indifference. If we grant the probable truth of the claim that most American working-class children are most sensitive to status sources on their own level, it does not follow that they take lightly rejection, disparagement and censure from other status sources.

Even on their "own" social level, the situation is far from simple. The "working class," we have repeatedly emphasized, is not culturally homogeneous. Not only is there much diversity in the cultural standards applied by one's own working-class neighbors and kin so that it is difficult to find a "working-class" milieu in which "middle-class" standards are not important. In addition, the "working-class" culture we have described is, after all, an ideal type; most working-class *people* are culturally ambivalent. Due to lack of capacity, of the requisite "character structure" or of "luck," they may be working-class in terms of job and income; they may have accepted this status with resignation and rationalized it to their satisfaction; and by example, by class-linked techniques of child training and by failure to support the middle-class agencies of socialization they may have produced children deficient in the attributes that make for status in middle-class terms. Nevertheless, all their lives, through all the major media of mass indoctrination—the schools, the movies, the radio, the newspapers and the magazines—the middle-class powers-that-be that manipulate these media have been trying to "sell" them on middle-class values and the middle-class standard of living. Then there is the "propaganda of the deed," the fact that they have seen with their own eyes working-class contemporaries "get ahead" and "make the grade" in a middle-class world. In consequence of all this, we suspect that few working-class parents unequivocally repudiate as intrinsically worthless middle-class objectives. There is good reason to believe that the modesty of working-class aspirations is partly a matter of trimming one's sails to the available opportunities and resources and partly a matter of unwillingness to accept the discipline which upward striving entails.

However complete and successful one's accommodation to an humble status, the vitality of middle-class goals, of the "American dream," is nonetheless likely to manifest itself in his aspirations for his children. His expectations may not be grandiose, but he will want his children to be "better off" than he. Whatever his own work history and social reputation may be, he will want his children to be "steady" and "respectable." He may exert few positive pressures to "succeed" and the experiences he provides his children may even incapacitate them for success; he may be puzzled at the way they "turn out." But whatever the measure of his own responsibility in accounting for the product, he is not likely to judge that product by unadulterated "corner-boy" standards. Even "corner-boy" parents, although they may value in their children such corner-boy virtues as generosity to friends, personal loyalty and physical prowess, are likely also to be gratified by recognition by middle-class representatives and by the kinds of achievement for which the college-boy way of life is a prerequisite. Even in the working-class milieu from which he acquired his incapacity for middle-class achievement, the working-class corner-boy may find himself at a status disadvantage as against his more upwardly mobile peers.

Lastly, of course, is that most ubiquitous and inescapable of status sources, oneself. Technically, we do not call the person's attitudes towards himself "status" but rather "self-esteem," or, when the quality of the self-attitude is specifically moral, "conscience" or "superego." The important question for us is this: To what extent, if at all, do boys who are typically "working-class" and "corner-boy" in their overt behavior evaluate themselves by "middle-class," "college-boy" standards? For our overt behavior, however closely it conforms to one set of norms, need not argue against the existence or effectiveness of alternative and conflicting norms. The failure of our own behavior to conform to our own expectations is an elementary and commonplace fact which gives rise to the tremendously important consequences of guilt, self-recrimination, anxiety and self-hatred. The reasons for the failure of self-expectations and overt conduct to agree are complex. One reason is that we often internalize more than one set of norms, each of which would dictate a different course of action in a given life-situation; since we can only *do* one thing at a time, however, we are forced to choose between them or somehow to compromise. In either case, we fall short of the full realization of our own expectations and must somehow cope with the residual discrepancy between those expectations and our overt behavior.

We have suggested that corner-boy children (like their working-class parents) internalize middle-class standards to a sufficient degree to create a fundamental ambivalence towards their own corner-boy behavior. Again, we are on somewhat speculative ground where fundamental research remains to be done. The coexistence within the same personality of a corner-boy and a college-boy morality may appear more plausible, however, if we recognize that they are not simple antitheses of one another and that parents and others may in all sincerity attempt to indoctrinate both. For example, the goals upon which the college-boy places such great value, such as intellectual and occupational achievement, and the college-boy virtues of ambitiousness and pride in self-sufficiency are not as such disparaged by the corner-boy culture. The meritoriousness of standing by one's friends and the desire to have a good time here and now do not by definition preclude the desire to help oneself and to provide for the future. It is no doubt the rule, rather than the exception, that most children, college-boy and corner-boy alike, would like to enjoy the best of both worlds. *In practice,* however, the substance that is consumed in the pursuit of one set of values is not available for the pursuit of the other. The sharpness of the dilemma and the degree of the residual discontent depend upon a number of things, notably, the intensity with which both sets of norms have been internalized, the extent to which the life-situations which one encounters compel a choice between them, and the abundance and appropriateness of the skills and resources at one's disposal. The child of superior intelligence, for example, may find it easier than his less gifted peers to meet the demands of the college-boy standards without failing his obligations to his corner-boy associates.

It is a plausible assumption, then, that the working-class boy whose status is low in middle-class terms *cares* about that status, that this status confronts him with a genuine problem of adjustment. To this problem of adjustment there are a variety of conceivable responses, of which participation in the creation and the maintenance of the delinquent subculture is one. Each mode of response entails costs and yields gratifications of its own. The circumstances which tip the balance in favor of the one or the other are obscure. One mode of response is to desert the corner-boy for the college-boy way of life. To the reader of Whyte's *Street Corner Society* the costs are manifest. It is hard, at best, to be a college-boy and to run with the corner-boys. It entails great effort and sacrifice to the degree that one has been indoctrinated in what we have described as the working-class socialization process; its rewards are frequently long-deferred; and for many working-class boys it makes demands which they are, in consequence of their inferior linguistic, academic and "social" skills, not likely ever to meet. Nevertheless, a certain proportion of working-class boys accept the challenge of the middle-class status system and play the status game by the middle-class rules.

Another response, perhaps the most common, is what we may call the "stable corner-boy response." It represents an acceptance of the corner-boy way of life and an effort to make the best of a situation. If our reasoning is correct, it does not resolve the dilemmas we have described as inherent in the corner-boy position in a largely middle-class world, although these dilemmas may be mitigated by an effort to disengage oneself from dependence upon middle-class status-sources and by withdrawing, as far as possible, into a sheltering community of like-minded working-class children. Unlike the delinquent response, it avoids the radical rupture of good relations with even working-class adults and does not represent as irretrievable a renunciation of upward mobility. It does not incur the active hostility of middle-class persons and therefore leaves the way open to the pursuit of some values, such as jobs, which these people control. It represents a preference for the familiar, with its known satisfactions and its known imperfections, over the risks and the uncertainties as well as the moral costs of the college-boy response, on the one hand, and the delinquent response on the other.

What does the delinquent response have to offer? Let us be clear, first, about what this response is and how it differs from the stable corner-boy response. The hallmark of the delinquent subculture is the explicit and wholesale repudiation of middle-class standards and the adoption of their very antithesis. *The corner-boy culture is not specifically delinquent.* Where it leads to behavior which may be defined as delinquent, e.g., truancy, it does so not because nonconformity to middle-class norms *defines* conformity to corner-boy norms but because conformity to middle-class norms *interferes with* conformity to corner-boy norms. The corner-boy plays truant because he does not like school, because he wishes to escape from a dull and unrewarding and perhaps humiliating situation. But truancy is not defined as intrinsically valuable and status-giving. The member of the delinquent subculture plays truant because "good" middle-class (and working-class) children do not play truant. Corner-boy resistance to being herded and marshalled by middle-class figures is not the same as the delinquent's flouting and jeering of those middle-class figures and active ridicule of those who submit. The corner-boy's ethic of reciprocity, his quasi-communal attitude toward the property of in-group members, is shared by the delinquent. But this ethic of reciprocity does not sanction the deliberate and "malicious" violation of the property rights of persons outside the in-group. We have observed that the differences between the corner-boy and the college-boy or middle-class culture are profound but that in many ways they are profound differences in emphasis. We have remarked that the corner-boy culture does not so much repudiate the value of many middle-class achievements as it emphasizes certain other values which make such achievements improbable. In short, the corner-boy culture temporizes with middle-class morality; the full-fledged delinquent subculture does not.

It is precisely here, we suggest, in the refusal to temporize, that the appeal of the delinquent subculture lies. Let us recall that it is characteristically American, not specifically working-class or middle-class, to measure oneself against the widest possible status universe, to seek status against "all comers," to be "as good as" or "better than" anybody—anybody, that is, within one's own age and sex category. As long as the working-class corner-boy clings to a version, however attenuated and adulterated, of the middle-class culture, he must recognize his inferiority to working-class and middle-class college-boys. The delinquent subculture, on the other hand, permits no ambiguity of the status of the delinquent relative to that of anybody else. In terms of the norms of the delinquent subculture, defined by its negative polarity to the respectable status system, the delinquent's very nonconformity to middle-class standards sets him above the most exemplary college boy.

Another important function of the delinquent subculture is the legitimation of aggression. We surmise that a certain amount of hostility is generated among working-class children against middle-class persons, with their airs of superiority, disdain or condescension and against middle-class norms, which are, in a sense, the cause of their status-frustration. To infer inclinations to aggression from the existence of frustration is hazardous; we know that aggression is not an inevitable and not the only consequence of frustration. So here too we must feel our way with caution. Ideally, we should like to see systematic research, probably employing "depth interview" and "projective" techniques, to get at the relationship between status position and aggressive dispositions toward the rules which determine status and toward persons variously distributed in the status hierarchy. Nevertheless, despite our imperfect knowledge of these things, we would be blind if we failed to recognize that bitterness, hostility and jealousy and all sorts of retributive fantasies are among the most common and typically human responses to public humiliation. However, for the child who temporizes with middle-class morality, overt aggression and even the conscious recognition of his own hostile impulses are inhibited, for he acknowledges the *legitimacy* of the rules in terms of which he is stigmatized. For the child who breaks clean with middle-class morality, on the other hand, there are no moral inhibitions on the free expression of aggression against the sources of his frustration. Moreover, the connection we suggest between status-frustration and the aggressiveness of the delinquent subculture seems to us more plausible than many frustration-aggression hypotheses because it involves no assumptions about obscure and dubious "displacement" of aggression against "substitute" targets. The target in this case is the manifest cause of the status problem.

It seems to us that the mechanism of "reaction-formation" should also play a part here. We have made much of the corner-boy's basic ambivalence, his uneasy acknowledgement, while he lives by the standards of his corner-boy culture, of the legitimacy of college-boy standards. May we assume that when the delinquent seeks to obtain unequivocal status by repudiating, once and for all, the norms of the college-boy culture, these norms really undergo total extinction? Or do they, perhaps, linger on, underground, as it were, repressed, unacknowledged but an ever-present threat to the adjustment which has been achieved at no small cost? There is much evidence from clinical psychology that moral norms, once effectively internalized, are not lightly thrust aside or extinguished. If a new moral order is evolved which offers a more satisfactory solution to one's life problems, the old order usually continues to press for recognition, but if this recognition is granted, the applecart is upset. The symptom of this obscurely felt, ever-present threat is clinically known as "anxiety," and the literature of psychiatry is rich with devices for combatting this anxiety, this threat to a hard-won victory. One such device is reaction-formation. Its hallmark is an "exaggerated," "disproportionate," "abnormal" intensity of response, "inappropriate" to the stimulus which seems to elicit it. The unintelligibility of the response, the "over-reaction," becomes intelligible when we see that it has the function of reassuring the actor against an *inner* threat to his defenses as well as the function of meeting an external situation on its own terms. Thus we have the mother who "compulsively" showers "inordinate" affection upon a child to reassure herself against her latent hostility and we have the male adolescent whose awkward and immoderate masculinity reflects a basic insecurity about his own sex-role. In like manner, we would expect the delinquent boy who, after all, has been socialized in a society dominated by a middle-class morality and who can never quite escape the blandishments of middle-class society, to seek to maintain his safeguards against seduction. Reaction-formation, in his case, should take the form of an "irrational," "malicious," "unaccountable" hostility to the enemy within the gates as well as without: the norms of the respectable middle-class society.[1]

If our reasoning is correct, it should throw some light upon the peculiar quality of "property delinquency" in the delinquent subculture. We have already seen how the rewardingness of a college-boy and middle-class way of life depends, to a great extent, upon general respect for property rights. In an urban society, in particular, the possession and

[1 Footnote omitted. Ed.]

display of property are the most ready and public badges of reputable social class status and are, for that reason, extraordinarily ego-involved. That property actually is a reward for middle-class morality is in part only a plausible fiction, but in general there is certainly a relationship between the practice of that morality and the possession of property. The middle-classes have, then, a strong interest in scrupulous regard for property rights, not only because property is "intrinsically" valuable but because the full enjoyment of their status requires that that status be readily recognizable and therefore that property adhere to those who earn it. The cavalier misappropriation or destruction of property, therefore, is not only a diversion or diminution of wealth; it is an attack on the middle-class where their egos are most vulnerable. Group stealing, institutionalized in the delinquent subculture, is not just a way of *getting* something. It is a means that is the antithesis of sober and diligent "labour in a calling." It expresses contempt for a way of life by making its opposite a criterion of status. Money and other valuables are not, as such, despised by the delinquent. For the delinquent and the nondelinquent alike, money is a most glamorous and efficient means to a variety of ends and one cannot have too much of it. But, in the delinquent subculture, the stolen dollar has an odor of sanctity that does not attach to the dollar saved or the dollar earned.

This delinquent system of values and way of life does its job of problem-solving most effectively when it is adopted as a group solution. We have stressed in our chapter on the general theory of subcultures that the efficacy of a given change in values as a solution and therefore the motivation to such a change depends heavily upon the availability of "reference groups" within which the "deviant values" are already institutionalized, or whose members would stand to profit from such a system of deviant values if each were assured of the support and concurrence of the others. So it is with delinquency. We do not suggest that joining in the creation or perpetuation of a delinquent subculture is the only road to delinquency. We do believe, however, that for most delinquents delinquency would not be available as a response were it not socially legitimized and given a kind of respectability, albeit by a restricted community of fellow-adventurers. In this respect, the adoption of delinquency is like the adoption of the practice of appearing at the office in open-collar and shirt sleeves. Is it much more comfortable, is it more sensible than the full regalia? Is it neat? Is it dignified? The arguments in the affirmative will appear much more forceful if the practice is already established in one's milieu or if one senses that others are prepared to go along if someone makes the first tentative gestures. Indeed, to many of those who sweat and chafe in ties and jackets, the possibility of an alternative may not even occur until they discover that it has been adopted by their colleagues.

This way of looking at delinquency suggests an answer to a certain paradox. Countless mothers have protested that their "Johnny" was a good boy until he fell in with a certain bunch. But the mothers of each of Johnny's companions hold the same view with respect to their own offspring. It is conceivable and even probable that some of these mothers are naive, that one or more of these youngsters are "rotten apples" who infected the others. We suggest, however, that all of the mothers may be right, that there is a certain chemistry in the group situation itself which engenders that which was not there before, that group interaction is a sort of catalyst which releases potentialities not otherwise visible. This is especially true when we are dealing with a problem of status-frustration. Status, by definition, is a grant of respect from others. A new system of norms, which measures status by criteria which one can meet, is of no value unless others are prepared to apply those criteria, and others are not likely to do so unless one is prepared to reciprocate.[2]

We have referred to a lingering ambivalence in the delinquent's own value system, an ambivalence which threatens the adjustment he has achieved and which is met through the mechanism of reaction-formation. The delinquent may have to contend with another ambivalence, in the area of his status sources. The delinquent subculture offers him status *as against* other children of whatever social level, but it offers him this status *in the eyes of* his fellow delinquents only. To the extent that there remains a desire for recognition from groups whose respect has been forfeited by commitment to a new subculture, his satisfaction in his solution is imperfect and adulterated. He can perfect his solution only by rejecting as status sources those who reject him. This too may require a certain measure of reaction-formation, going beyond indifference to active hostility and contempt for all those who do not share his subculture. He becomes all the more dependent upon his delinquent gang. Outside that gang his status position is now weaker than ever. The gang itself tends toward a kind of sectarian solidarity, because the benefits of membership can only be realized in active face-to-face relationships with group members.

This interpretation of the delinquent subculture has important implications for the "sociology of social problems." People are prone to assume that those things which we define as evil and those which we define as good have their origins in separate and distinct features of our society. Evil flows from poisoned wells; good flows from pure and crystal fountains. The same source cannot feed both. Our view is different. It holds

[2 Footnote omitted. Ed.]

that those values which are at the core of "the American way of life," which help to motivate the behavior which we most esteem as "typically American," are among the major determinants of that which we stigmatize as "pathological." More specifically, it holds that the problems of adjustment to which the delinquent subculture is a response are determined, in part, by those very values which respectable society holds most sacred. The same value system, impinging upon children differently equipped to meet it, is instrumental in generating both delinquency and respectability.

# 8.  Types of Delinquent Subcultures

## Richard A. Cloward and Lloyd E. Ohlin

> Both authors hold the degree of Doctor of Philosophy from the University of Chicago and both are on the faculty of the New York School of Social Work of Columbia University. Both have participated in various studies of delinquency. Cloward is co-author of *Social Perspectives on Behavior* and *Theoretical Studies in Social Organization of the Prison.* Ohlin's writings include *Selection for Parole* and *Sociology and the Field of Corrections.*

We come now to the question of the specific social conditions that make for the emergence of distinctive delinquent subcultures. Throughout this analysis, we shall make extensive use of the concepts of social organization developed in the preceding chapter: namely, integration of different age-levels of offenders, and integration of carriers of conventional and deviant values. Delinquent responses vary from one neighborhood to another, we believe, according to the articulation of these structures in the neighborhood. Our object here is to show more precisely how various forms of neighborhood integration affect the development of subcultural content.

## The Criminal Subculture

The criminal subculture, like the conflict and retreatist adaptations, requires a specialized environment if it is to flourish. Among the en-

Reprinted with permission of the publisher from *Delinquency and Opportunity*, by Richard A. Cloward and Lloyd E. Ohlin, Chapter 7, "Subcultural Differentiation." Copyright 1960 by The Free Press, a corporation.

vironmental supports of a criminal style of life are integration of offenders at various age-levels and close integration of the carriers of conventional and illegitimate values.

## INTEGRATION OF AGE-LEVELS

Nowhere in the criminological literature is the concept of integration between different age-levels of offender made more explicit than in discussions of criminal learning. Most criminologists agree that criminal behavior presupposes patterned sets of relationships through which the requisite values and skills are communicated or transmitted from one age-level to another. What, then, are some of the specific components of systems organized for the socialization of potential criminals?

*Criminal Role-Models*—The lower class is not without its own distinctive and indigenous illegitimate success-models. Many accounts in the literature suggest that lower-class adults who have achieved success by illegitimate means not only are highly visible to young people in slum areas but often are willing to establish intimate relationships with these youth.

> Every boy has some ideal he looks up to and admires. His ideal may be Babe Ruth, Jack Dempsey, or Al Capone. When I was twelve, we moved into a neighborhood with a lot of gangsters. They were all swell dressers and had big cars and carried "gats." Us kids saw these swell guys and mingled with them in the cigar store on the corner. Jack Gurney was the one in the mob that I had a fancy to. He used to take my sis out and that way I saw him often. He was in the stick-up rackets before he was in the beer rackets, and he was a swell dresser and had lots of dough. . . . I liked to be near him and felt stuck up over the other guys because he came to my home to see my sis.[1]

Just as the middle-class youth, as a consequence of intimate relationships with, say, a banker or a businessman, may aspire to *become* a banker or a businessman, so the lower-class youth may be associated with and aspire to become a "policy king": " 'I want to be a big shot. . . . Have all the guys look up to me. Have a couple of Lincolns, lots of broads, and all the coppers licking my shoes.' " [2] The crucial point here is that success-goals are not equally available to persons in different positions in the social structure. To the extent that social-class lines act as barriers to interaction between persons in different social strata, conventional success-models may not be salient for lower-class youth.

[1] C. R. Shaw, "Juvenile Delinquency—A Group Tradition," *Bulletin of the State University of Iowa*, No. 23, N. S. No. 700, 1933, p. 8.

[2] *Ibid.*, p. 9.

The successful criminal, on the other hand, may be an intimate, personal figure in the fabric of the lower-class area. Hence one of the forces leading to rational, disciplined, crime-oriented delinquency may be the availability of criminal success-models.

*Age-Grading of Criminal Learning and Performance*—The process by which the young acquire the values and skills prerequisite for a stable criminal career has been described in many studies. The central mechanism in the learning process is integration of different age-levels of offender. In an extensive study of a criminal gang on the Lower East Side of New York City, Bloch and Niederhoffer found that

> . . . the Pirates [a group of young adults] was actually the central organizing committee, the party headquarters for the youthful delinquents in the area. They held regular conferences with the delegates from outlying districts to outline strategy. . . . The younger Corner Boys [a gang of adolescents in the same vicinity] who . . . were trying to join with the older Pirates . . . were on a probationary status. If they showed signs of promise, a couple of them were allowed to accompany the Pirates on tours of exploration to look over the terrain around the next "job." [3]

At the pinnacle of this age-graded system stood an adult, Paulie.

> Paulie had real prestige in the gang. His was the final say in all important decisions. Older than the other members [of the Pirates] by seven or eight years, he maintained a certain air of mystery. . . . From talks with more garrulous members, it was learned that Paulie was the mastermind behind some of the gang's most impressive coups.[4]

The basis of Paulie's prestige in the gang is apparent in the following account of his relationship with the full-fledged adult criminal world:

> From his contacts, information was obtained as to the most inviting locations to burglarize. It was he who developed the strategy and outlined the major stages of each campaign of burglary or robbery. . . . Another vital duty which he performed was to get rid of the considerable loot, which might consist of jewelry, clothing, tools, or currency in large denominations. His contact with professional gangsters, fences, bookies, made him an ideal choice for this function.[5]

Learning alone, as we have said, does not ensure that the individual can or will perform the role for which he has been prepared. The social

[3] H. H. Bloch and Arthur Niederhoffer, *The Gang: A Study in Adolescent Behavior* (New York: Philosophical Library, 1958), pp. 198-99.
[4] *Ibid.*, p. 201.
[5] *Ibid.*

structure must also support the actual performance of the role. To say that the individual must have the opportunity to discharge a stable criminal role as well as to prepare for it does not mean that role-preparation necessarily takes place in one stage and role-performance in a succeeding stage. The apprentice may be afforded opportunities to play out a particular role at various points in the learning process.

> When we were shoplifting we always made a game of it. For example, we might gamble on who could steal the most caps in a day, or who could steal in the presence of a detective and then get away. This was the best part of the game. I would go into a store to steal a cap, by trying one on when the clerk was not watching, walk out of the store, leaving the old cap. With the new cap on my head I would go into another store, do the same thing as in the other store, getting a new hat and leaving the one I had taken from the other place. I might do this all day. . . . It was the fun I wanted, not the hat. I kept this up for months and *then began to sell the things to a man on the West Side. It was at this time that I began to steal for gain.*[6]

This quotation illustrates how delinquent role-preparation and role-performance may be integrated even at the "play-group" stage of illegitimate learning. The child has an opportunity to actually perform illegitimate roles because such activity finds support in his immediate neighborhood milieu. The rewards—monetary and other—of successful learning and performance are immediate and gratifying at each age level.

INTEGRATION OF VALUES

Unless the carriers of criminal and conventional values are closely bound to one another, stable criminal roles cannot develop. The criminal, like the occupant of a conventional role, must establish relationships with other categories of persons, all of whom contribute in one way or another to the successful performance of criminal activity. As Tannenbaum says, "the development of the criminal career requires and finds in the immediate environment other supporting elements in addition to the active 'criminal gangs'; to develop the career requires the support of middlemen. These may be junk men, fences, lawyers, bondsmen, 'backers,' as they are called."[7] The intricate systems of relationship between these legitimate and illegitimate persons constitute the type of

---

[6] Shaw, *op. cit.*, p. 3. Emphasis added.

[7] Frank Tannenbaum, *Crime and the Community* (New York: Columbia University Press, 1938), p. 60.

environment in which the juvenile criminal subculture can come into being.[8]

An excellent example of the way in which the content of a delinquent subculture is affected by its location in a particular milieu is afforded by the "fence," a dealer in stolen goods who is found in some but not all lower-class neighborhoods. Relationships between such middlemen and criminals are not confined to adult offenders; numerous accounts of lower-class life suggest not only that relationships form between fences and youngsters but also that the fence is a crucial element in the structure of illegitimate opportunity. He often caters to and encourages delinquent activities among the young. He may even exert controls leading the young to orient their stealing in the most lucrative and least risky directions. The same point may be made of junk dealers in some areas, racketeers who permit minors to run errands, and other occupants of illegitimate or semilegitimate roles.

As the apprentice criminal passes from one status to another in the illegitimate opportunity system, we should expect him to develop an ever-widening set of relationships with members of the semilegitimate and legitimate world. For example, a delinquent who is rising in the structure might begin to come into contact with mature criminals, law-enforcement officials, politicians, bail bondsmen, "fixers," and the like. As his activities become integrated with the activities of these persons, his knowledge of the illegitimate world is deepened, new skills are acquired, and the opportunity to engage in new types of illegitimate activity is enhanced. Unless he can form these relationships, the possibility of a stable, protected criminal style of life is effectively precluded.

The type of environment that encourages a criminal orientation among delinquents is, then, characterized by close integration of the carriers of conventional and illegitimate values. The *content* of the delinquent subculture is a more or less direct response to the local milieu in which it emerges. And it is the "integrated" neighborhood, we suggest, that produces the criminal type of delinquent subculture.

STRUCTURAL INTEGRATION AND SOCIAL CONTROL

Delinquent behavior generally exhibits a component of aggressiveness. Even youth in neighborhoods that are favorable learning environments for criminal careers are likely to engage in some "bopping" and

[8] In this connection, see R. A. Cloward, "Social Control in the Prison," *Theoretical Studies of the Social Organization of the Prison*, Bulletin No. 15 (New York: Social Science Research Council, March 1960), pp. 20-48, which illustrates similar forms of integration in a penal setting.

other forms of violence. Hence one feature of delinquency that must be explained is its tendency toward aggressive behavior. However, aggressiveness is not the primary component of all delinquent behavior; it is much more characteristic of some delinquent groups than of others. Therefore, we must also concern ourselves with the conditions under which the aggressive component becomes ascendant.

The importance of assessing the relative dominance of expressive and instrumental components in delinquent patterns is often overlooked. Cohen, for example, stresses the aggressive or expressive aspect of delinquent behavior, remarking that "it is non-utilitarian, malicious and negativistic," although he also asserts that these traits may not characterize all delinquency. Cohen's tendency to neglect relatively nonaggressive aspects of delinquency is related to his failure to take into account the relationships between delinquent behavior and adult criminality. However, *depending upon the presence or absence of those integrative relationships,* behavior that appears to be "non-utilitarian" in achieving access to conventional roles may possess considerable utility for securing access to criminal roles. Furthermore, these integrated systems may have important consequences for social control.

To the extent that delinquents take as their primary reference group older and more sophisticated gang boys, or even fully acculturated criminals or racketeers, dramatic instances of "malicious, negativistic" behavior may represent efforts to express solidarity with the norms of the criminal world. Delinquents who so behave in an attempt to win acceptance by older criminals may be engaging in a familiar sociological process; namely, overconformity to the norms of a group to which they aspire but do not belong. By such overconformity to the norms of the criminal world, delinquents seek to dramatize their eligibility for membership. To an observer oriented toward conventional values, aggressive behavior of this kind might appear to be purposeless. However, from the perspective of the carriers of deviant values, conspicuous defiance of conventional values may validate the "rightness" of the aspirant. Once he has been defined as "right," he may then be selected for further socialization and preparation for mature criminal activity.

Once the delinquent has successfully demonstrated his eligibility for acceptance by persons higher in the criminal structure, social controls are exerted to suppress undisciplined, expressive behavior; there is no place in organized crime for the impulsive, unpredictable individual. A dramatic illustration of the emphasis upon instrumental performance is offered by the case of Murder, Inc. Abe Reles, a former member of the syndicate, who turned state's evidence, made certain comments about Murder, Inc. which illustrate perfectly Max Weber's famous characterization of the norms governing role performance and interpersonal relationships in bureaucratic organizations: *"Sine ira et studio"* ("without anger or passion").

The crime trust, Reles insists, never commits murder out of passion, excitement, jealousy, personal revenge, or any of the usual motives which prompt private, unorganized murder. It kills impersonally, and solely for business considerations. Even business rivalry, he adds, is not the usual motive, unless "somebody gets too balky or somebody steps right on top of you." No gangster may kill on his own initiative; every murder must be ordered by the leaders at the top, and it must serve the welfare of the organization. . . . The crime trust insists that that murder must be a business matter, organized by the chiefs in conference and carried out in a disciplined way. "It's a real business all the way through," Reles explains. "It just happens to be that kind of business, but nobody is allowed to kill from personal grievance. There's got to be a good business reason, and top men of the combination must give their okay." [9]

The pressure for rational role performance in the adult criminal world is exerted downward, we suggest, through interconnected systems of age-graded statuses. At each point in this illegitimate hierarchy, instrumental rather than expressive behavior is emphasized. In their description of the Pirates, for example, Bloch and Niederhoffer observe that Paulie, the adult mastermind of the gang, avoided expressive behavior: "The younger Pirates might indulge in wild adolescent antics. Paulie remained aloof." [10] Paulie symbolized a mode of life in which reason, discipline, and foresight were uppermost. To the extent that younger members of the gang identified with him, they were constrained to adopt a similar posture. Rico, the leader of a gang described in a recent book by Harrison Salisbury, can be characterized in much the same way:

This youngster was the most successful kid in the neighborhood. He was a dope pusher. Some weeks he made as much as $200. He used his influence in some surprising ways. He persuaded the gang members to stop bopping because he was afraid it would bring on police intervention and interfere with his drug sales. He flatly refused to sell dope to boys and kicked out of the gang any kid who started to use drugs. He sold only to adults. With his money he bought jackets for the gang, took care of the hospital bills of members, paid for the rent on his mother's flat, paid most of the family expenses and some-

[9] Joseph Freeman, "Murder Monopoly: The Inside Story of a Crime Trust," *The Nation*, Vol. 150, No. 21 (May 25, 1940), p. 648. This is but one of many sources in which the bureaucratization of crime is discussed.

[10] Bloch and Niederhoffer, *op. cit.*, p. 201.

times spent sixty dollars to buy a coat as a present for one of his boys.[11]

The same analysis helps to explain a puzzling aspect of delinquent behavior; namely, the apparent disregard delinquents sometimes exhibit for stolen objects. Some theorists have concluded from this that the ends of stealing are not utilitarian, that delinquents do not steal because they need or want the objects in question or for any other rational reason. Cohen, for example, asserts that "were the participant in the delinquent subculture merely employing illicit means to the end of acquiring economic goods, he would show more respect for the goods he has thus acquired." [12] Hence, Cohen concludes, the bulk of stealing among delinquents is "for the hell of it" rather than for economic gain. Whether stealing is expressive or instrumental may depend, however, on the social context in which it occurs. Where criminal opportunities exist, it may be argued that stealing is a way of expressing solidarity with the carriers of criminal values and, further, that it is a way of acquiring the various concrete skills necessary before the potential criminal can gain full acceptance in the group to which he aspires. That is, a certain amount of stealing may be motivated less by immediate need for the objects in question than by a need to acquire skill in the arts of theft. When practice in theft is the implicit purpose, the manner of disposing of stolen goods is unimportant. Similarly, the status accruing to the pickpocket who can negotiate a "left-front-breech" derives not so much from the immediate profit attaching to this maneuver as from the fact that it marks the individual as a master craftsman. In other words, where criminal learning environments and opportunity structures exist, stealing beyond immediate economic needs may constitute anticipatory socialization. But where these structures do not exist, such stealing may be simply an expressive act in defiance of conventional values.

Shaw pointed to a related aspect of the social control of delinquent behavior. Noting the prestige ordering of criminal activities, he commented on the way in which such definitions, once internalized, tend to regulate the behavior of delinquents:

> It is a matter of significance to note . . . that there is a general tendency among older delinquents and criminals to look with contempt upon the person who specializes in any form of petty stealing. The common thief is not distinguished for manual dexterity and accomplishment, like the pickpocket or mobsman, nor for courage,

[11] H. E. Salisbury, *The Shook-up Generation* (New York: Harper & Bros., 1958), p. 176.

[12] A. K. Cohen, *Delinquent Boys: The Culture of the Gang* (Glencoe, Ill.: Free Press, 1955), p. 36.

ingenuity and skill, like the burglar, but is characterized by low cunning and stealth—hence the term "sneak thief." . . . It is possible that the stigma attaching to petty stealing among members of older delinquent groups is one factor which gives impetus to the young delinquent's desire to abandon such forms of petty delinquency as stealing junk, vegetables, breaking into freight cars . . . and to become identified with older groups engaged in such crimes as larceny of automobiles and robbery with a gun, both of which are accredited "rackets" among older delinquents. . . .[13]

To the extent that an area has an age-graded criminal structure in which juvenile delinquents can become enmeshed, we suggest that the norms governing adult criminal-role performance filter down, becoming significant principles in the life-organization of the young. The youngster who has come into contact with such an age-graded structure and who has won initial acceptance by older and more sophisticated delinquents will be less likely to engage in malicious, destructive behavior than in disciplined, instrumental, career-oriented behavior. In this way the adult criminal system exerts controls over the behavior of delinquents. Referring to urban areas characterized by integration of different age-levels of offender, Kobrin makes an observation that tends to bear out our theoretical scheme:

. . . delinquency tends to occur within a partial framework of social controls, insofar as delinquent activity in these areas represents a tolerated means for the acquisition of an approved role and status. Thus, while delinquent activity here possesses the usual characteristics of violence and destructiveness, there tend to develop effective limits of permissible activity in this direction. Delinquency is, in other words, encompassed and contained within a local social structure, and is marginally but palpably related to that structure.[14]

In summary, the criminal subculture is likely to arise in a neighborhood milieu characterized by close bonds between different age-levels of offender, and between criminal and conventional elements. As a consequence of these integrative relationships, a new opportunity structure emerges which provides alternative avenues to success-goals. Hence the pressures generated by restrictions on legitimate access to success-goals are drained off. Social controls over the conduct of the young are effectively exercised, limiting expressive behavior and constraining the discontented to adopt instrumental, if criminalistic, styles of life.

[13] Shaw, *op. cit.*, p. 10.
[14] Solomon Kobrin, "The Conflict of Values in Delinquency Areas," *American Sociological Review*, Vol. 16 (Oct. 1951), p. 657.

## The Conflict Subculture

Because youngsters caught up in the conflict subculture often endanger their own lives and the lives of others and cause considerable property damage, the conflict form of delinquency is a source of great public concern. Its prevalence, therefore, is probably exaggerated. There is no evidence to suggest that the conflict subculture is more widespread than the other subcultures, but the nature of its activities makes it more visible and thus attracts public attention. As a consequence, many people erroneously equate "delinquency" and "conflict behavior." But whatever its prevalence, the conflict subculture is of both theoretical and social importance, and calls for explanation.

Earlier in this book, we questioned the common belief that slum areas, because they are slums, are necessarily disorganized. We pointed to forms of integration which give some slum areas unity and cohesion. Areas in which these integrative structures are found, we suggested, tend to be characterized by criminal rather than conflict or retreatist subcultures. But not all slums are integrated. Some lower-class urban neighborhoods lack unity and cohesiveness. Because the prerequisites for the emergence of stable systems of social relations are not present, a state of social disorganization prevails.

The many forces making for instability in the social organization of some slum areas include high rates of vertical and geographic mobility; massive housing projects in which "site tenants" are not accorded priority in occupancy, so that traditional residents are dispersed and "strangers" re-assembled; and changing land use, as in the case of residential areas that are encroached upon by the expansion of adjacent commercial or industrial areas. Forces of this kind keep a community off balance, for tentative efforts to develop social organization are quickly checked. Transiency and instability become the overriding features of social life.

Transiency and instability, in combination, produce powerful pressures for violent behavior among the young in these areas. First, an unorganized community cannot provide access to legitimate channels to success-goals, and thus discontent among the young with their life-chances is heightened. Secondly, access to stable criminal opportunity systems is also restricted, for disorganized neighborhoods do not develop integration of different age-levels of offender or integration of carriers of criminal and conventional values. The young, in short, are relatively deprived of *both* conventional and criminal opportunity. Finally, social controls are weak in such communities. These conditions, we believe, lead to the emergence of conflict subcultures.

SOCIAL DISORGANIZATION AND OPPORTUNITY

Communities that are unable to develop conventional forms of social organization are also unable to provide legitimate modes of access to culturally valued success-goals. The disorganized slum is a world populated with failures, with the outcasts of the larger society. Here families orient themselves not toward the future but toward the present, not toward social advancement but toward survival. The adult community, being disorganized, cannot provide the resources and opportunities that are required if the young are to move upward in the social order.

Just as the unintegrated slum cannot mobilize legitimate resources for the young, neither can it provide them with access to stable criminal careers, for illegitimate learning and opportunity structures do not develop. The disorganized slum, populated in part by failures in the conventional world, also contains the outcasts of the criminal world. This is not to say that crime is nonexistent in such areas, but what crime there is tends to be individualistic, unorganized, petty, poorly paid, and unprotected. This is the haunt of the small-time thief, the grifter, the pimp, the jackroller, the unsophisticated "con" man, the pickpocket who is all thumbs, and others who cannot graduate beyond "heisting" candy stores or "busting" gas stations. Since they are unorganized and without financial resources, criminals in these areas cannot purchase immunity from prosecution; they have neither the money nor the political contacts to "put in the fix." Hence they are harassed by the police, and many of them spend the better part of their lives in prison. The organized criminal world is generally able to protect itself against such harassment, prosecution, and imprisonment. But professional crime and organized rackets, like any business enterprise, can thrive only in a stable, predictable, and integrated environment. In this sense, then, the unintegrated area does not constitute a promising launching site for lucrative and protected criminal careers. Because such areas fail to develop criminal learning environments and opportunity structures, stable criminal subcultures cannot emerge.

SOCIAL DISORGANIZATION AND SOCIAL CONTROL

As we have noted, social controls originate in both the conventional and the illegitimate sectors of the stable slum area. But this is apparently not the case in the disorganized slum. The basic disorganization of the conventional institutional structure makes it impossible for controls to originate there. At the same time, Kobrin asserts, "Because adult crime in this type of area is itself unorganized, its value system remains implicit and hence incapable of generating norms which function effectively on a groupwide basis." Hence "juvenile violators readily escape not merely the controls of conventional persons in the community but those of adult violators as well." Under such conditions,

> . . . [the] delinquencies of juveniles tend to acquire a wild, un-trammelled character. Delinquents in this kind of situation more fre-quently exhibit the personality traits of the social type sometimes referred to as the hoodlum. Both individually and in groups, violent physical combat is engaged in for its own sake, almost as a form of recreation. Here groups of delinquents may be seen as excluded, isolated conflict groups dedicated to an unending battle against all forms of constraint. The escape from controls originating in any social structure, other than that provided by unstable groupings of the de-linquents themselves, is here complete.[15]

Unlike Kobrin, we do not attribute conflict behavior in unorganized urban areas to the absence of controls alone. The young in such areas are also exposed to acute frustrations, arising from conditions in which access to success-goals is blocked by the absence of any institutionalized channels, legitimate or illegitimate. They are deprived not only of con-ventional opportunity but also of criminal routes to the "big money." In other words, precisely when frustrations are maximized, social con-trols are weakened. Social controls and channels to success-goals are gen-erally related: where opportunities exist, patterns of control will be found; where opportunities are absent, patterns of social control are likely to be absent too. The association of these two features of social organization is a logical implication of our theory.

SOCIAL DISORGANIZATION AND VIOLENCE

Those adolescents in disorganized urban areas who are oriented toward achieving higher position but are cut off from institutionalized channels, criminal as well as legitimate, must rely upon their own resources for solving this problem of adjustment. Under these conditions, tendencies toward aberrant behavior become intensified and magnified. These ado-lescents seize upon the manipulation of violence as a route to status not only because it provides a way of expressing pent-up angers and frustra-tions but also because they are not cut off from access to violent means by vicissitudes of birth. In the world of violence, such attributes as race, socioeconomic position, age, and the like are irrelevant; personal

15 *Ibid.*, p. 658.

worth is judged on the basis of qualities that are available to all who would cultivate them. The principal prerequisites for success are "guts" and the capacity to endure pain. One doesn't need "connections," "pull," or elaborate technical skills in order to achieve "rep." The essence of the warrior adjustment is an expressed feeling-state: "heart." The acquisition of status is not simply a consequence of skill in the use of violence or of physical strength but depends, rather, on one's willingness to risk injury or death in the search for "rep." A physically immature boy may find a place among the warrior elite if, when provoked, he will run such risks, thus demonstrating "heart."

As long as conventional and criminal opportunity structures remain closed, violence continues unchecked. The bulk of aggressive behavior appears to be channeled into gang warfare; success in street combat assures the group that its "turf" will not be invaded, that its girls will not be molested, that its members will otherwise be treated deferentially by young and old in the local community. *If new opportunity structures are opened, however, violence tends to be relinquished.* Indeed, the success of certain efforts to discourage violent, aggressive behavior among warrior gangs has resulted precisely from the fact that some powerful group has responded deferentially to these gangs. (The group is powerful because it can provide, or at least hold out the promise of providing, channels to higher position, such as jobs, education, and the like.) The most dramatic illustration of this process may be seen in programs conducted by social group workers who attach themselves to street gangs. Several points should be noted about the results of these programs.

First, violent behavior among street gangs appears to diminish rapidly once a social worker establishes liaison with them. Reporting on the outcome of detached-worker programs in Boston, for example, Miller notes, "One of the earliest and most evident changes . . . was that groups worked with directly [by social workers] relinquished active participation in the [established] network of conflict groups. . . ." [16] The reduction in conflict may reflect the skill of the social workers, but another explanation may be that *the advent of the street-gang worker symbolized the end of social rejection and the beginning of social accommodation.* To the extent that violence represents an effort to win deference, one would logically expect it to diminish once that end has been achieved.

Secondly, a detached-worker program, once initiated, tends to give rise to increased violence among groups to which workers have *not*

<hr/>

[16] This quotation and those that follow are from W. B. Miller, "The Impact of a Community Group Work Program on Delinquent Corner Groups," *Social Service Review*, Vol. 31, No. 4 (Dec. 1957), pp. 390-406.

been provided. In the Boston experience, to the extent that they interpreted having a street-club worker as an act of social deference, gangs came to compete for this prestigeful symbol. As Miller notes, "During later phases of the Program [there was] an upsurge in gang fights involving Program groups. . . . These conflicts did not involve Program groups fighting one another but represented for the most part attacks on Program groups by corner groups in adjacent areas which did not have an area worker." Miller suggests that such attacks took place in part because "the outside groups knew that Program groups were given a social worker in the first place because they were troublesome; so they reasoned, 'They were bad, and they got a social worker; if we're bad enough now, we'll get a social worker, too.'" An attack by an outside gang on a Program gang was not, therefore, simply an expression of the traditional hostility of one gang toward another but an attempt on the part of the non-Program gang to win "rep." Thus Miller is led to observe, "A program aiming to 'clean up' the gang situation in a single section of the city cannot count on limiting its influence to that section but must anticipate the fact that its very successes in its home district may increase difficulties in adjacent areas." This suggests that programs aimed at curbing violence constitute a new opportunity structure in which gangs compete for social deference from the conventional world.

Finally, a resurgence of violent behavior may be observed when the liaison between the street worker and the gang is terminated if the members of the gang have not been successfully incorporated in a conventional opportunity system. Continuing to lack conventional economic opportunity, the gang fears the loss of the one form of recognition it has achieved from conventional society, symbolized by the street worker. Hence the group may reassert the old patterns of violence in order to retain the social worker. Under these conditions, the conventional society will continue to accommodate to the group for fear that to do otherwise would result in renewed violence, as indeed it so often does. A successful street-gang program, in short, is one in which detached workers can create channels to legitimate opportunity; where such channels cannot be opened up, the gang will temporize with violence only as long as a street worker maintains liaison with them.

In summary, severe limitations on both conventional and criminal opportunity intensify frustrations and position discontent. Discontent is heightened further under conditions in which social control is relaxed, for the area lacking integration between age-levels of offender and between carriers of conventional and criminal values cannot generate pressures to contain frustrations among the young. These are the circumstances, we suggest, in which adolescents turn to violence in search of status. Violence comes to be ascendant, in short, under conditions of relative detachment from all institutionalized systems of opportunity and social control.

## The Retreatist Subculture

The consumption of drugs—one of the most serious forms of retreatist behavior—has become a severe problem among adolescents and young adults, particularly in lower-class urban areas. By and large, drug use in these areas has been attributed to rapid geographic mobility, inadequate social controls, and other manifestations of social disorganization. In this section, we shall suggest a hypothesis that may open up new avenues of inquiry in regard to the growing problem of drug use among the young.

### PRESSURES LEADING TO RETREATIST SUBCULTURES

Retreatism is often conceived as an isolated adaptation, characterized by a breakdown in relationships with other persons. Indeed, this is frequently true, as in the case of psychotics. The drug-user, however, must become affiliated with others, if only to secure access to a steady supply of drugs. Just as stable criminal activity cannot be explained by reference to motivation alone, neither can stable drug use be fully explained in this way. Opportunity to use drugs must also be present. But such opportunities are restricted. As Becker notes, the illegal distribution of drugs is limited to "sources which are not available to the ordinary person. In order for a person to begin marihuana use, he must begin participation in some group through which these sources of supply become available to him." [17]

Because of these restrictions on the availability of drugs, new users must become affiliated with old users. They must learn the lore of drug use, the skills required in making appropriate "connections," the controls which govern the purchase of drugs (e.g., drugs will not generally be made available to anyone until he is "defined as a person who can safely be trusted to buy drugs without endangering anyone else"), and the like. As this process of socialization proceeds, the individual "is considered more trustworthy, [and] the necessary knowledge and intro-

[17] H. S. Becker, "Marihuana Use and Social Control," *Social Problems*, Vol. 3, No. 1 (July 1955), pp. 36-37.

ductions to dealers [then become] available to him." According to Becker, the "processes by which people are emancipated from the larger set of controls *and become responsive to those of the subculture*" are "important factors in the genesis of deviant behavior." [18] The drug-user, in other words, must be understood not only in terms of his personality and the social structure, which create a readiness to engage in drug use, but also in terms of the new patterns of associations and values to which he is exposed as he seeks access to drugs. The more the individual is caught in this web of associations, the more likely that he will persist in drug use, for he has become incorporated in a subculture that exerts control over his behavior.

Despite these pressures toward subcultural formation, it is probably also true that the resulting ties among addicts are not so solidary as those among participants in criminal and conflict subcultures. Addiction is in many ways an individualistic adaptation, for the "kick" is essentially a private experience. The compelling need for the drug is also a divisive force, for it leads to intense competition among addicts for money. Forces of this kind thus limit the relative cohesion which can develop among users.

## "DOUBLE FAILURE" AND DRUG USE

We turn now to a discussion of the social conditions which give rise to retreatist reactions such as drug use among adolescents. According to Merton,

> Retreatism arises from continued failure to near the goal by legitimate measures and from an inability to use the illegitimate route because of internalized prohibitions, this process occurring while the supreme value of the success-goal has not yet been renounced. The conflict is resolved by abandoning both precipitating elements, the goals and the norms. The escape is complete, the conflict is eliminated and the individual is asocialized.[19]

[18] *Ibid.*, p. 35. Emphasis added.

[19] R. K. Merton, *Social Theory and Social Structure*, Rev. and Enl. Ed. (Glencoe, Ill.: Free Press, 1957), pp. 153-54. For discussions of drug use among juveniles, see D. L. Gerard and Conon Kornetsky, "Adolescent Opiate Addiction—A Study of Control and Addict Subjects," *Psychiatric Quarterly*, Vol. 29 (April 1955), pp. 457-86; Isidor Chein *et al.*, *Studies of Narcotics Use Among Juveniles* (New York University, Research Center for Human Relations, mimeographed, Jan. 1956); Harold Finestone, "Cats, Kicks, and Color," *Social Problems*, Vol. 5, No. 1 (July 1957), pp. 3-13; and D. M. Wilmer, Eva Rosenfeld, R. S. Lee, D. L. Gerard, and Isidor Chein, "Heroin Use and Street Gangs," *Criminal Law, Criminology and Police Science*, Vol. 48, No. 4 (Nov.-Dec. 1957), pp. 399-409.

Thus he identifies two principal factors in the emergence of retreatist adaptations: (1) continued failure to reach culturally approved goals by legitimate means, and (2) inability to employ illegitimate alternatives because of internalized prohibitions. We take it that "internalized prohibitions" have to do with the individual's attitudes toward norms. Retreatists, according to Merton, do not call into question the legitimacy of existing institutional arrangements—a process which might then be followed by the use of illegitimate alternatives. Rather, they call into question their own adequacy, locating blame for their dilemma in personal deficiencies. One way of resolving the intense anxiety and guilt which ensue is to withdraw, to retreat, to abandon the struggle.

This definition of the processes giving rise to retreatist behavior is useful in connection with some types of retreatism, but it does not, we believe, fit the facts of drug use among lower-class adolescents. It is true that some youthful addicts appear to experience strong constraints on the use of illegitimate means; the great majority of drug-users, however, had a history of delinquency before becoming addicted. In these cases, unfavorable attitudes toward conventional norms are evident. Hence we conclude that internalized prohibitions, or favorable attitudes toward conventional norms, may not be a necessary condition for the emergence of retreatist behavior.

If internalized prohibitions are not a necessary component of the process by which retreatism is generated, then how are we to account for such behavior? We have noted that there are differentials in access both to illegitimate and to legitimate means; not all of those who seek to attain success-goals by prohibited routes are permitted to proceed. There are probably many lower-class adolescents oriented toward success in the criminal world who fail; similarly, many who would like to acquire proficiency in the use of violence also fail. We might ask, therefore, what the response would be among those faced with failure in the use of *both* legitimate and illegitimate means. We suggest that persons who experience this "double failure" are likely to move into a retreatist pattern of behavior. That is, retreatist behavior may arise as a consequence of limitations on the use of illegitimate means, whether the limitations are internalized prohibitions or socially structured barriers. For our purpose, the two types of restriction are functional equivalents. Thus we may amend Merton's statement as follows:

> Retreatism arises from continued failure to near the goal by legitimate measures and from an inability to use the illegitimate route because of internalized prohibitions *or socially structured barriers,* this process occurring while the supreme value of the success-goal has not yet been renounced.

This hypothesis permits us to define two general classes of retreatist: those who are subject to internalized prohibitions on the use of illegitimate means, and those who seek success-goals by prohibited routes but do not succeed. If we now introduce a distinction between illegitimate opportunity structures based on the manipulative use of violence and those based on essentially criminal means, such as fraud, theft, and extortion, we can identify four classes of retreatist.

Types I and II both arise in the manner described by Merton—that is, as a consequence of internalized restrictions on the use of illegitimate means. The two types differ only with respect to the content of the internalized restraints. In type II, it is the use of criminal means that is precluded; in type I, it is the use of violence. Resort to illegitimate means, violent or criminal, apparently evokes extreme guilt and anxiety among persons in these categories; such persons are therefore effectively cut off from criminal or violent routes to higher status. For persons of types III and IV, access to illegitimate routes is limited by socially structured barriers. They are not restrained by internal prohibitions; they would employ illegitimate means if these were available to them.

### Retreatist Adaptations

| Basis of Illegitimate Opportunity Structure | Restrictions on Use of Illegitimate Means | |
| --- | --- | --- |
| | Internalized Prohibitions | Socially Structured Barriers |
| Violence | I | III |
| Criminal Means | II | IV |

Generally speaking, it has been found that most drug addicts have a history of delinquent activity prior to becoming addicted. In Kobrin's research, conducted in Chicago, "Persons who become heroin users were found to have engaged in delinquency *in a group-supported and habitual form* either prior to their use of drugs or simultaneously with their developing interest in drugs." [20] And from a study of drug addicts in

[20] Solomon Kobrin, *Drug Addiction Among Young Persons in Chicago* (Illinois Institute for Juvenile Research, Oct. 1953), p. 6. Harold Finestone, in a study of the relationship between addicts and criminal status, comments: "The impression gained from interviewing . . . was that these addicts were petty thieves and petty 'operators' who, status-wise, were at the bottom of the criminal population of the underworld" ("Narcotics and Criminality," *Law and Contemporary Problems*, Vol. 22, No. 1 [Winter 1957], pp. 69-85).

California, "A very significant tentative conclusion [was reached]: namely, that the use of drugs follows criminal activity and criminal association rather than the other way around, which is often thought to be the case." [21] In other words, adolescents who are engaged in group-supported delinquency of the criminal or conflict type may eventually turn to drug use. Indeed, entire gangs sometimes shift from either criminal or conflict to retreatist adaptations.

We view these shifts in adaptation as responses to restrictions on the use of illegitimate means. Such restrictions, as we have seen, are always operative; not all who would acquire success by violence or criminal means are permitted to do so. It is our contention that retreatist behavior emerges among some lower-class adolescents because they have failed to find a place for themselves in criminal or conflict subcultures. Consider the case of competition for membership in conflict gangs. To the extent that conflict activity—"bopping," street-fighting, "rumbling," and the like—is tolerated, it represents an alternative means by which adolescents in many relatively disorganized urban areas may acquire status. Those who excel in the manipulation of violence may acquire "rep" within the group to which they belong and respect from other adolescent groups in the vicinity and from the adult world. In areas which do not offer criminal opportunities, the use of violence may be the only available avenue to prestige. But prestige is, by definition, scarce—just as scarce among adolescents who seek to acquire it by violence as it is elsewhere in the society. Not only do juvenile gangs compete vigorously with one another, but within each gang there is a continual struggle for prestigeful positions. Thus some gangs will acquire "rep" and others will fail; some persons will become upwardly mobile in conflict groups and others will remain on the periphery.

If the adolescent "failure" then turns to drugs as a solution to his status dilemma, his relationships with his peers become all the more attenuated. Habitual drug use is not generally a valued activity among juvenile gangs. Ordinarily the drug-user, if he persists in such behavior, tends to become completely disassociated from the group. Once disassociated, he may develop an even greater reliance upon drugs as a solution to status deprivations. Thus adolescent drug-users may be "double failures" who are restrained from participating in other delinquent modes of adaptation because access to these illegitimate structures is limited.

Our hypothesis states that adolescents who are double failures are more vulnerable than others to retreatist behavior; it does not imply that

[21] *Narcotics in California* (Board of Corrections, State of California, Feb. 18, 1959), p. 9.

*all* double failures will subsequently become retreatists. Some will respond to failure by adopting a law-abiding lower-class style of life—the "corner boy" adaptation. It may be that those who become retreatists are incapable of revising their aspirations downward to correspond to reality. Some of those who shift to a corner-boy adaptation may not have held high aspirations initially. It has frequently been observed that some adolescents affiliate with delinquent groups simply for protection in gang-ridden areas; they are motivated not by frustration so much as by the "instinct of self-preservation." In a less hostile environment, they might simply have made a corner-boy adjustment in the first place. But for those who continue to exhibit high aspirations under conditions of double failure, retreatism is the expected result.

SEQUENCES OF ADAPTATION

Access to success-goals by illegitimate means diminishes as the lower-class adolescent approaches adulthood. Illegitimate avenues to higher status that were available during early adolescence become more restricted in later adolescence. These new limitations intensify frustration and so create pressures toward withdrawal or retreatist reactions.

With regard to criminal means, late adolescence is a crucial turning point, for it is during this period that the selection of candidates for stable adult criminal roles takes place. It is probably true that more youngsters are exposed to criminal learning environments during adolescence than can possibly be absorbed by the adult criminal structure. Because of variations in personality characteristics, criminal proficiency, and capacity to make "the right connections," or simply because of luck, some persons will find this avenue to higher status open and some will find it closed off. In effect, the latter face a dead end. Some delinquents, therefore, must cope with abrupt discontinuity in role-preparation and role-performance which may lead to retreatist responses.

In the case of conflict patterns, a similar process takes place. As adolescents near adulthood, excellence in the manipulation of violence no longer brings high status. Quite the contrary, it generally evokes extreme negative sanctions. What was defined as permissible or tolerable behavior during adolescence tends to be sharply proscribed in adulthood. New expectations are imposed, expectations of "growing up," of taking on adult responsibilities in the economic, familial, and community spheres. The effectiveness with which these definitions are imposed is attested by the tendency among fighting gangs to decide that conflict is, in the final analysis, simply "kid stuff": "As the group grows older, two things happen. Sports, hell raising, and gang fights become 'kid stuff' and are given up. In the normal course of events, the youthful preoccupations are replaced with the more individual concerns about work, future, a 'steady' girl, and the like." [22] In other words, powerful community expectations emerge which have the consequence of closing off access to previously useful means of overcoming status deprivations. Strains are experienced, and retreatist behavior may result.

As we have noted, adolescents who experience pressures leading to retreatist reactions are often restrained by their peers. Adolescent gangs usually devalue drug use (except on an experimental basis or for the sake of novelty) and impose negative sanctions upon those who become "hooked." The very existence of the gang discourages the potential user:

> The activities of the gang offer a measure of shared status, a measure of security and a sense of belonging. The boys do not have to face life alone—the group protects them. Escape into drugs is not necessary as yet.[23]

In the post-adolescent period, however, the cohesiveness of the peer group usually weakens. Those who have the requisite skills and opportunities begin to make the transition to adulthood, assuming conventional occupational and kinship roles. As the solidarity of the group declines, it can no longer satisfy the needs or control the behavior of those who continue to rely upon it. These members may try to reverse the trend toward disintegration and, failing this, turn to drugs:

> This group organized five years ago for self-protection against other fighting groups in the area. Recently, as the majority grew cool to bopping, a group of three boys broke off in open conflict with the president; *soon after, these three started using heroin and acting "down with the cats."* They continue making efforts to get the gang back to fights. . . . The three users are still out and it is unlikely that they will be readmitted.[24]

For some adolescents, the peer group is the primary avenue to status as well as the primary source of constraints on behavior. For these youngsters, the post-adolescent period, during which the group may disintegrate or shift its orientation, is one in which social controls are weakened precisely when tensions are heightened.

Whether the sequence of adaptations is from criminal to retreatist or from conflict to retreatist, we suggest that limitations on legitimate and illegitimate opportunity combine to produce intense pressures toward retreatist behavior. When both systems of means are simultaneously

[22] Wilmer *et al., op. cit.,* p. 409.
[23] *Ibid.*
[24] *Ibid.,* p. 405. Emphasis added.

restricted, it is not strange that some persons become detached from the social structure, abandoning cultural goals and efforts to achieve them by any means.

## 9.  Juvenile Delinquency and Subterranean Values

David Matza and Gresham M. Sykes

> Matza's record has been given with Article 1.
> Sykes, who holds the Ph.D. degree from Northwestern University, is Professor of Sociology and Chairman of the Department of Sociology and Anthropology at Dartmouth College. His published writings include *Crime and Society, The Society of Captives,* and various articles.

Current explanations of juvenile delinquency can be divided roughly into two major types. On the one hand, juvenile delinquency is seen as a product of personality disturbances or emotional conflicts within the individual; on the other hand, delinquency is viewed as a result of relatively normal personalities exposed to a "disturbed" social environment—particularly in the form of a deviant sub-culture in which the individual learns to be delinquent as others learn to conform to the law. The theoretical conflict between these two positions has been intensified, unfortunately, by the fact that professional pride sometimes leads psychologists and sociologists to define the issue as a conflict between disciplines and to rally behind their respective academic banners.

Despite many disagreements between these two points of view, one assumption is apt to elicit common support. The delinquent, it is asserted, is deviant; not only does his behavior run counter to the law but his underlying norms, attitudes, and values also stand opposed to those of the dominant social order. And the dominant social order, more often than not, turns out to be the world of the middle class.

We have suggested in a previous article that this image of delinquents and the larger society as antagonists can be misleading.[1] Many delinquents, we argued, are essentially in agreement with the larger society,

David Matza and Gresham M. Sykes, "Juvenile Delinquency and Subterranean Values," *American Sociological Review,* 26 (1961), 712-719. Reprinted with permission of the American Sociological Association and the authors.

[1] Gresham M. Sykes and David Matza, "Techniques of Neutralization," *American Sociological Review,* 22 (December, 1957), pp. 664-670.

at least with regard to the evaluation of delinquent behavior as "wrong." Rather than standing in opposition to conventional ideas of good conduct, the delinquent is likely to adhere to the dominant norms in belief but render them ineffective in practice by holding various attitudes and perceptions which serve to neutralize the norms as checks on behavior. "Techniques of neutralization," such as the denial of responsibility or the definition of injury as rightful revenge, free the individual from a large measure of social control.

This approach to delinquency centers its attention on how an impetus to engage in delinquent behavior is translated into action. But it leaves unanswered a serious question: What makes delinquency attractive in the first place? Even if it is granted that techniques of neutralization or some similar evasions of social controls pave the way for overt delinquency, there remains the problem of the values or ends underlying delinquency and the relationship of these values to those of the larger society. Briefly stated, this paper argues that (a) the values behind much juvenile delinquency are far less deviant than they are commonly portrayed; and (b) the faulty picture is due to a gross over-simplification of the middle-class value system.

## The Values of Delinquency

There are many perceptive accounts describing the behavior of juvenile delinquents and their underlying values, using methods ranging from participant observation to projective tests.[2] Although there are some

[2] Frederic M. Thrasher, *The Gang,* Chicago: University of Chicago Press, 1936; Clifford R. Shaw and Maurice E. Moore, *The Natural History of a Delinquent Career,* Chicago: University of Chicago Press, 1931; Albert K. Cohen, *Delinquent Boys: The Culture of the Gang,* Glencoe, Ill.: The Free Press, 1955; Albert K. Cohen and James F. Short, "Research in Delinquent Subcultures," *Journal of Social Issues,* 14 (1958), pp. 20-37; Walter B. Miller, "Lower Class Culture as a Generating Milieu of Gang Delinquents," *Journal of Social Issues,* 14 (1958), pp. 5-19; Harold Finestone, "Cats, Kicks, and Color," *Social Problems,* 5 (July, 1957), pp. 3-13; Solomon Kobrin, "The Conflict of Values in Delinquent Areas," *American Sociological Review,* 16 (October, 1951), pp. 653-661; Richard Cloward and Lloyd Ohlin, "New Perspectives on Juvenile Delinquency" (unpublished manuscript); Dale Kramer and Madeline Karr, *Teen-Age Gangs,* New York: Henry Holt, 1953; Stacey V. Jones, "The Cougars—Life with a Delinquent Gang," *Harper Magazine* (November, 1954); Harrison E. Salisbury, *The Shook-Up Generation,* New York: Harper and Brothers, 1958; William C. Kvaraceus and Walter B. Miller, editors, *Delinquent Behavior: Culture and the Individual,* National Education Association of the United States, 1959; Herbert A. Bloch and Arthur Niederhoffer, *The Gang,* New York: Philosophical Library, 1958; Beatrice Griffith, *American Me,* Boston: Houghton Mifflin, 1948; Sheldon Glueck and Eleanor Glueck, *Unraveling Juvenile Delinquency,* New York: Commonwealth Fund, 1950.

important differences of opinion in the interpretation of this material, there exists a striking consensus on actual substance. Many divisions and sub-divisions are possible, of course, in classifying these behavior patterns and the values on which they are based, but three major themes emerge with marked regularity.

First, many observers have noted that delinquents are deeply immersed in a restless search for excitement, "thrills," or "kicks." The approved style of life, for many delinquents, is an adventurous one. Activities pervaded by displays of daring and charged with danger are highly valued in comparison with more mundane and routine patterns of behavior. This search for excitement is not easily satisfied in legitimate outlets such as organized recreation, as Tappan has indicated. The fact that an activity involves breaking the law is precisely the fact that often infuses it with an air of excitement.[3] In fact, excitement or "kicks" may come to be defined with clear awareness as "any act tabooed by 'squares' that heightens and intensifies the present moment of experience and differentiates it as much as possible from the humdrum routines of daily life." [4] But in any event, the delinquent way of life is frequently a way of life shot through with adventurous exploits that are valued for the stimulation they provide.

It should be noted that in courting physical danger, experimenting with the forbidden, provoking the authorities, and so on, the delinquent is not simply enduring hazards; he is also creating hazards in a deliberate attempt to manufacture excitement. As Miller has noted, for example, in his study of Roxbury, for many delinquents "the rhythm of life fluctuates between periods of relatively routine and repetitive activities and sought situations of greater emotional stimulation." [5] The excitement, then, that flows from gang rumbles, games of "chicken" played with cars, or the use of drugs is not merely an incidental by-product but may instead serve as a major motivating force.

Second, juvenile delinquents commonly exhibit a disdain for "getting on" in the realm of work. Occupational goals involving a steady job or careful advancement are apt to be lacking, and in their place we find a sort of aimless drifting or grandiose dreams of quick success. Now it takes a very deep faith in the maxims of Benjamin Franklin—or a certain naiveté, perhaps—to believe that hard work at the lower ranges of the occupational hierarchy is a sure path to worldly achievement. The delinquent is typically described as choosing another course, rationally or irrationally. Chicanery or manipulation, which may take the form of

---

[3] Paul Tappan, *Juvenile Delinquency*, New York: McGraw-Hill, 1949, pp. 148-154.
[4] Finestone, *op. cit.*
[5] Miller, *op. cit.*

borrowing from social workers or more elaborate modes of "hustling"; an emphasis on "pull," frequently with reference to obtaining a soft job which is assumed to be available only to those with influential connections: all are seen as methods of exploiting the social environment without drudgery, and are accorded a high value. Simple expropriation should be included, of course, in the form of theft, robbery, and the rest; but it is only one of a variety of ways of "scoring" and does not necessarily carry great prestige in the eyes of the delinquent. In fact, there is some evidence that, among certain delinquents, theft and robbery may actually be looked down upon as pointing to a lack of wit or skill. A life of ease based on pimping or the numbers game may be held out as a far more admirable goal.[6] In any event, the delinquent is frequently convinced that only suckers work and he avoids, if he can, the regimen of the factory, store, and office.

Some writers have coupled the delinquent's disdain of work with a disdain of money. Much delinquent activity, it is said, is non-utilitarian in character and the delinquent disavows the material aspirations of the larger society, thus protecting himself against inevitable frustration. Now it is true that the delinquent's attacks against property are often a form of play, as Cohen has pointed out, rather than a means to a material end.[7] It is also true that the delinquent often shows little liking for the slow accumulation of financial resources. Yet rather than saying that the delinquent disdains money, it would seem more accurate to say that the delinquent is deeply and constantly concerned with the problem of money in his own way. The delinquent wants money, probably no less than the law-abiding, but not for the purposes of a careful series of expenditures or some long-range objective. Rather, money is frequently desired as something to be squandered in gestures of largesse, in patterns of conspicuous consumption. The sudden acquisition of large sums of money is his goal—the "big score"—and he will employ legal means if possible and illegal means if necessary. Since legal means are likely to be thought of as ineffective, it is far from accidental that "smartness" is such an important feature of the delinquent's view of life: "Smartness involves the capacity to outsmart, outfox, outwit, dupe . . ."[8]

A third theme running through accounts of juvenile delinquency centers on aggression. This theme is most likely to be selected as pointing to the delinquent's alienation from the larger society. Verbal and physical as-

6 Finestone, op. cit.
7 Cohen, op. cit.
8 Miller, op. cit.

saults are a commonplace, and frequent reference is made to the delinquent's basic hostility, his hatred, and his urge to injure and destroy.

The delinquent's readiness for aggression is particularly emphasized in the analysis of juvenile gangs found in the slum areas of large cities. In such gangs we find the struggles for "turf," the beatings, and the violent feuds which form such distinctive elements in the portrayal of delinquency. As Cloward and Ohlin have pointed out, we can be led into error by viewing these gang delinquents as typical of all delinquents.[9] And Bloch and Niederhoffer have indicated that many current notions of the delinquent gang are quite worn out and require reappraisal.[10] Yet the gang delinquent's use of violence for the maintenance of "rep," the proof of "heart," and so on, seems to express in extreme form the idea that aggression is a demonstration of toughness and thus of masculinity. This idea runs through much delinquent activity. The concept of *machismo,* of the path to manhood through the ability to take it and hand it out, is foreign to the average delinquent only in name.

In short, juvenile delinquency appears to be permeated by a cluster of values that can be characterized as the search for kicks, the disdain of work and a desire for the big score, and the acceptance of aggressive toughness as proof of masculinity. Whether these values are seen as pathological expressions of a distorted personality or as the traits of a delinquent sub-culture, they are taken as indicative of the delinquent's deviation from the dominant society. The delinquent, it is said, stands apart from the dominant society not only in terms of his illegal behavior but in terms of his basic values as well.

## Delinquency and Leisure

The deviant nature of the delinquent's values might pass unquestioned at first glance. Yet when we examine these values a bit more closely, we must be struck by their similarity to the components of the code of the "gentleman of leisure" depicted by Thorstein Veblen. The emphasis on daring and adventure; the rejection of the prosaic discipline of work; the taste for luxury and conspicuous consumption; and the respect paid to manhood demonstrated through force—all find a prototype in that sardonic picture of a leisured elite. What is *not* familiar is the mode of expression of these values, namely, delinquency. The quality of the values is obscured by their context. When "daring" turns out to be acts of daring by adolescents directed against adult figures of accepted

---

[9] Cloward and Ohlin, *op. cit.*
[10] Bloch and Niederhoffer, *op. cit.*

authority, for example, we are apt to see only the flouting of authority and not the courage that may be involved. We suspect that if juvenile delinquency were highly valued by the dominant society—as is the case, let us say, in the deviance of prisoners of war or resistance fighters rebelling against the rules of their oppressors—the interpretation of the nature of delinquency and the delinquent might be far different.[11]

In any event, the values of a leisure class seem to lie behind much delinquent activity, however brutalized or perverted their expression may be accounted by the dominant social order. Interestingly enough, Veblen himself saw a similarity between the pecuniary man, the embodiment of the leisure class, and the delinquent. "The ideal pecuniary man is like the ideal delinquent," said Veblen, "in his unscrupulous conversion of goods and services to his own ends, and in a callous disregard for the feelings and wishes of others and of the remoter effects of his actions." [12] For Veblen this comparison was probably no more than an aside, a part of polemical attack on the irresponsibility and pretentions of an industrial society's rulers. And it is far from clear what Veblen meant by delinquency. Nonetheless, his barbed comparison points to an important idea. We have too easily assumed that the delinquent is deviant in his values, opposed to the larger society. This is due, in part, to the fact that we have taken an overly simple view of the value system of the supposedly law-abiding. In our haste to create a standard from which deviance can be measured, we have reduced the value system of the whole society to that of the middle class. We have ignored both the fact that society is not composed exclusively of the middle class and that the middle class itself is far from homogeneous.[13]

[11] Merton's comments on in-group virtues and out-group vices are particularly germane. The moral alchemy cited by Merton might be paraphrased to read:

> I am daring
> You are reckless
> He is delinquent

Cf. Robert K. Merton, *Social Theory and Social Structure*, Glencoe, Ill.: The Free Press, 1957, pp. 426-430.

[12] T. Veblen, *The Theory of the Leisure Class*, The Modern Library, 1934, pp. 237-238.

[13] Much of the current sociological analysis of the value systems of the different social classes would seem to be based on a model which is closely akin to an outmoded portrayal of race. Just as racial groups were once viewed as a clustering of physical traits with no overlapping of traits from one group to the next (e.g., Caucasians are straight-haired, light-skinned, etc., whereas Negroes are kinky-haired, dark-skinned, etc.), so now are the value systems of social classes apt to be seen as a distinct grouping of specific values which are unique to the social class in which they are found. The model of the value systems of the different social classes we are using in this paper is more closely allied to the treatment of race presently used in anthro-

In reality, of course, the value system of any society is exceedingly complex and we cannot solve our problems in the analysis of deviance by taking as a baseline a simplicity which does not exist in fact. Not only do different social classes differ in their values, but there are also significant variations within a class based on ethnic origins, upward and downward mobility, region, age, etc. Perhaps even more important, however, is the existence of subterranean values—values, that is to say, which are in conflict or in competition with other deeply held values but which are still recognized and accepted by many.[14] It is crucial to note that these contradictions in values are not necessarily the opposing viewpoints of two different groups. They may also exist within a single individual and give rise to profound feelings of ambivalence in many areas of life. In this sense, subterranean values are akin to private as opposed to public morality. They are values that the individual holds to and believes in but that are also recognized as being not quite *comme il faut.* The easier task of analysis is to call such values deviant and to charge the individual with hypocrisy when he acts on them. Social reality, however, is somewhat more intricate than that and we cannot take the black and white world of McGuffey's Readers as an accurate model of the values by which men live.

Now the value of adventure certainly does not provide the major organizing principle of the dominant social order in modern, industrial society. This is especially true in the work-a-day world where so much activity is founded on bureaucratization and all that it implies with regard to routinization, standardization, and so on. But this is not to say that the element of adventure is completely rejected by the society at large or never appears in the motivational structure of the law-abiding. Instead, it would appear that adventure, i.e., displays of daring and the search for excitement, are acceptable and desirable but only when confined to certain circumstances such as sports, recreation, and holidays. The last has been frequently noted in the observation that conventions are often viewed as social events in which conventional canons of conduct are interpreted rather loosely. In fact, most societies seem to provide room for Saturnalias in one form or another, a sort of periodic anomie in which thrill-seeking is allowed to emerge.

In other words, the middle class citizen may seem like a far cry from the delinquent on the prowl for "thrills," but they both recognize and

---

pology, i.e., a distribution of frequencies. Most values, we argue, appear in most social classes; the social classes differ, however, in the frequency with which the values appear.

[14] Robert S. Lynd, *Knowledge for What,* Princeton: Princeton University Press, 1948.

share the idea that "thrills" are worth pursuing and often with the same connotation of throwing over the traces, of opposing "fun" to the routine. As members of the middle class—and other classes—seek their "kicks" in gambling, nightclubbing, the big night on the town, etc., we can neither ignore their use of leisure nor claim that it is based on a markedly deviant value. Leisure class values have come increasingly to color the activities of many individuals in the dominant society, although they may limit their expression more sharply than does the delinquent. The search for adventure, excitement, and thrills, then, is a subterranean value that now often exists side by side with the values of security, routinization, and the rest. It is not a deviant value, in any full sense, but it must be held in abeyance until the proper moment and circumstances for its expression arrive. It is obvious that something more than the delinquent's sense of appropriateness is involved, but it is also clear that in many cases the delinquent suffers from bad timing.

Similarly, to characterize the dominant society as being fully and unquestioningly attached to the virtue of hard work and careful saving is to distort reality. Notions of "pull" and the soft job are far from uncommon and the individual who entertains such notions cannot be thrust beyond the pale merely because some sociologists have found it convenient to erect a simplified conception of *the* work values of society. As Chinoy and Bell, and a host of other writers have pointed out, the conditions of work in modern society have broken down earlier conceptions of work as a calling and there are strong pressures to define the job as a place where one earns money as quickly and painlessly as possible.[15] If the delinquent carries this idea further than many of society's members might be willing to do, he has not necessarily moved into a new realm of values. In the same vein it can be argued that the delinquent's attachment to conspicuous consumption hardly makes him a stranger to the dominant society. Just as Riesman's "inside dopester," Whyte's "organization man," and Mills' "fixer" have a more authentic ring than an obsolete Weberian image in many instances, the picture of the delinquent as a spender seems more valid than a picture of him as an adolescent who has renounced material aspirations. The delinquent, we suggest, is much more in step with his times. Perhaps it is too extreme to say with Lowenthal [16] that "the idols of work have been replaced by the idols of leisure," but it appears unquestionable that we are

[15] Daniel Bell, *Work and Its Discontents,* Boston: Beacon Press, 1956. Ely Chinoy, *Automobile Workers and the American Dream,* Garden City, N.Y.: Doubleday and Company, 1955.

[16] Leo Lowenthal, "Historical Perspectives of Popular Culture," in Bernard Rosenberg and David M. White, editors, *Mass Culture: The Popular Arts in America,* Glencoe, Ill.: The Free Press, 1957.

witnessing a compromise between the Protestant Ethic and a Leisure Ethic. The delinquent conforms to society, rather than deviates from it, when he incorporates "big money" into his value system.[17]

Finally, we would do well to question prevalent views about society's attitudes toward violence and aggression. It could be argued, for one thing, that the dominant society exhibits a widespread taste for violence, since fantasies of violence in books, magazines, movies, and television are everywhere at hand. The delinquent simply translates into behavior those values that the majority are usually too timid to express. Furthermore, disclaimers of violence are suspect not simply because fantasies of violence are widely consumed, but also because of the actual use of aggression and violence in war, race riots, industrial conflicts, and the treatment of delinquents themselves by police. There are numerous examples of the acceptance of aggression and violence on the part of the dominant social order.

Perhaps it is more important, however, to recognize that the crucial idea of aggression as a proof of toughness and masculinity is widely accepted at many points in the social system. The ability to take it and hand it out, to defend one's rights and one's reputation with force, to prove one's manhood by hardness and physical courage—all are widespread in American culture. They cannot be dismissed by noting the equally valid observation that many people will declare that "nice children do not fight." The use of aggression to demonstrate masculinity is, of course, restricted by numerous prohibitions against instigating violence, "dirty" fighting, bullying, blustering, and so on. Yet even if the show of violence is carefully hedged in by both children and adults throughout our society, there is a persistent support for aggression which manifests itself in the derogatory connotations of labels such as "sissy" or "fag." [18]

In short, we are arguing that the delinquent may not stand as an alien in the body of society but may represent instead a disturbing reflection or a caricature. His vocabulary is different, to be sure, but kicks, big-time spending, and rep have immediate counterparts in the value system of the law-abiding. The delinquent has picked up and emphasized one part of the dominant value system, namely, the subterranean values that coexist with other, publicly proclaimed values possessing a more respectable air. These subterranean values, similar in many ways to the values Veblen ascribed to a leisure class, bind the delinquent to the

[17] Arthur K. Davis, "Veblen on the Decline of the Protestant Ethic," *Social Forces*, 22 (March, 1944), pp. 282-286.

[18] Albert Bandura and Richard Haig Walters, *Adolescent Aggression*, New York: Ronald Press, 1959, ch. 3.

society whose laws he violates. And we suspect that this sharing of values, this bond with the larger social order, facilitates the frequently observed "reformation" of delinquents with the coming of adult status.[19] To the objection that much juvenile behavior other than simply delinquent behavior would then be analyzed as an extension of the adult world rather than as a product of a distinct adolescent subculture we can only answer that this is precisely our thesis.

## Delinquency and Social Class

The persistence of the assumption that the juvenile delinquent must deviate from the law-abiding in his values as well as in his behavior can be traced in part, we suspect, to the large number of studies that have indicated that delinquents are disproportionately represented in the lower classes. In earlier years it was not too difficult to believe that the lower classes were set off from their social superiors in most attributes, including "immorality," and that this taint produced delinquent behavior. Writers of more recent vintage have avoided this reassuring error, but, still holding to the belief that delinquency is predominantly a lower class phenomenon, have continued to look for features peculiar to certain segments of the lower class that would create values at variance with those of the rest of society and which would foster delinquency.

Some criminologists, however, have long expressed doubts about the validity of the statistics on delinquency and have suggested that if all the facts were at hand the delinquency rate of the lower classes and the classes above them would be found to be far less divergent than they now appear.[20] Preferential treatment by the police and the courts and better and more varied means for handling the offender may have led us to underestimate seriously the extent to which juvenile delinquency crops up in what are euphemistically termed "relatively privileged homes."

Given the present state of data in this field, it is probably impossible to come to any firm conclusion on this issue. One thing, however, seems fairly clear: juvenile delinquency does occur frequently in the middle and upper classes and recent studies show more delinquency in these groups than have studies in the past. We might interpret this as showing

---

[19] See, for example, William McCord, Joan McCord and Irving K. Zola, *Origins of Crime*, New York: Columbia University Press, 1959, p. 21.

[20] Milton L. Barron, *The Juvenile in Delinquent Society*, New York: Alfred A. Knopf, 1954.

that our research methods have improved or that "white-collar" delinquency is increasing—or possibly both. But in any event, the existence of juvenile delinquency in the middle and upper classes poses a serious problem for theories which depend on status deprivation, social disorganization, and similar explanatory variables. One solution has been to change horses in the middle of the stratification system, as it were, shifting from social environment to personality disturbances as the causative factor as one moves up the social ladder. Future research may prove that this shift is necessary. Since juvenile delinquency does not appear to be a unitary phenomenon we might expect that no one theoretical approach will be adequate. To speak of juvenile delinquency in general, as we have done in this paper, should not obscure the fact that there are different types of delinquency and the differences among them cannot be ignored. Yet it seems worthwhile to pursue the idea that some forms of juvenile delinquency—and possibly the most frequent—have a common sociological basis regardless of the class level at which they appear.

One such basis is offered, we believe, by our argument that the values lying behind much delinquent behavior are the values of a leisure class. All adolescents at all class levels are to some extent members of a leisure class, for they move in a limbo between earlier parental domination and future integration with the social structure through the bonds of work and marriage.[21] Theirs is an anticipatory leisure, it is true, a period of freedom from the demands for self-support which allows room for the schooling enabling them to enter the world of work. They thus enjoy a temporary leisure by sufferance rather than by virtue of a permanent aristocratic right. Yet the leisure status of adolescents, modified though it may be by the discipline of school and the lack of wealth, places them in relationship to the social structure in a manner similar to that of an elite which consumes without producing. In this situation, disdain of work, an emphasis on personal qualities rather than technical skills, and a stress on the manner and extent of consumption all can flourish. Insofar, then, as these values do lie behind delinquency, we could expect delinquent behavior to be prevalent among all adolescents rather than confined to the lower class.

[21] Reuel Denney, *The Astonished Muse,* Chicago: University of Chicago Press, 1957. See also Barbara Wootton, *Social Science and Social Pathology,* New York: Macmillan, 1959; Austin L. Porterfield, *Youth in Trouble,* Austin, Tex.: Leo Potishman Foundation, 1946.

## Conclusion

This theory concerning the role of leisure in juvenile delinquency leaves unsolved, of course, a number of problems. First, there is the question why some adolescents convert subterranean values into seriously deviant behavior while others do not. Even if it is granted that many adolescents are far more deviant in their behavior than official records would indicate, it is clear that there are degrees of delinquency and types of delinquency. This variation cannot be explained simply on the basis of exposure to leisure. It is possible that leisure values are typically converted into delinquent behavior when such values are coupled with frustrations and resentments. (This is more than a matter of being deprived in socio-economic terms.) If this is so, if the delinquent is a sort of soured sportsman, neither leisure nor deprivation will be sufficient by itself as an explanatory variable. This would appear to be in accordance with the present empirical observations in the field. Second, we need to know a good deal more about the distribution of leisure among adolescents and its impact on their value systems. We have assumed that adolescents are in general leisured, i.e., free from the demands for self-support, but school drop-outs, the conversion of school into a tightly disciplined and time-consuming preparation for a career, the facilities for leisure as opposed to mere idleness will all probably have their effect. We suspect that two variables are of vital importance in this area: (a) the extent of identification with adult symbols of work, such as the father; and (b) the extent to which the school is seen as providing roles to enhance the ego, both now and in the future, rather than as an oppressive and dreary marking of time.

We conclude that the explanation of juvenile delinquency may be clarified by exploring the delinquent's similarity to the society that produced him rather than his dissimilarity. If his values are the subterranean values of a society that is placing increasing emphasis on leisure, we may throw new light on Taft's comment that the basic values in our culture are accepted by both the delinquent and the larger society of which he is a part.[22]

[22] Donald R. Taft, *Criminology*, New York: Macmillan, 1950.

## 10.   Toward a Reference Group Theory of Juvenile Delinquency

## Martin R. Haskell

The author received the degree of Doctor of Philosophy from New York University and is on the faculty of City University of New York, Baruch School. For three years he was placement director of the Berkshire Farm for Boys and was in charge of the after-care program in New York City. For the article reprinted here he shared in the sixth Helen L. DeRoy Award, presented by the Society for the Study of Social Problems. Some of his other articles dealing with delinquency have also appeared in professional journals.

In recent years, the perpetration of many serious crimes by adolescents has served to focus attention on the problem of juvenile delinquency and methods of dealing with that problem. Despite a considerable advance in sociological theory in this area, most of the action recommended is not based on current theory and is largely punitive in character. It is the purpose of the writer, in this paper, to contribute to a theoretical formulation that will provide testable hypotheses and suggest action that should lead to a reversal of the trend toward increased juvenile delinquency. Since, from the point of view of society, juvenile delinquency is a form of deviant behavior, theory dealing with deviance and conformity will be briefly considered.

Merton's typology of modes of individual adaptation (9) and Dubin's extension of it (4) furnish us with a comprehensive outline of the forms that deviant behavior can take. Cloward contributes toward an extension of the theory of social structure and anomie by emphasizing the existence of differential systems of opportunity and of variations in access to them (1).

Shaw and McKay, reporting on a study which covered twenty cities and tens of thousands of juvenile delinquents found that delinquency rates were highest in the slum areas of every city studied (10). Cohen provides a partial explanation of this phenomenon by demonstrating the existence of a delinquent sub-culture in the slum areas of a big city (2). In his more recent work on deviant-behavior as interaction

Martin R. Haskell, "Toward a Reference Group Theory of Juvenile Delinquency," *Social Problems*, 8 (Winter, 1960-61), 220-230. Reprinted with permission of the Society for the Study of Social Problems and the author.

process, Cohen makes a further contribution toward a general theory of deviance-conformity by analyzing the choices available to the individual confronted with socially structured strain (3).

We know, then, that the highest delinquency rates are found in the slums of our big cities and that a delinquent sub-culture is found in the same slums. The probability is, however, that a majority of the boys in those areas do not participate in delinquent acts. In most families of delinquent boys in these areas there are non-delinquent siblings. How can we account for this differential response? Furthermore, juvenile delinquency occurs in middle class areas relatively free of the delinquent sub-culture described by Cohen and on occasion sons of middle class parents participate in delinquent behavior. How can we account for delinquency in middle class areas? How can we account for differential response in middle class families?

In this paper an attempt will be made to formulate a reference group theory which will provide answers to these questions. The participation in a delinquent act will be explained in terms of the identification of the actor with some group and the application of the norms of that group in a given situation. How this formulation can be subsumed under a more general theory of behavior will not be discussed.

The author of this paper was placement director of Berkshire Farm for Boys, a residential treatment school for adolescent delinquent boys for three years ending July 1, 1960. In charge of the after-care program in New York City, he had access to case histories including data obtained prior to institutionalization, institutional history and experiences upon return to New York City. His duties involved him in group therapy and role training sessions with boys and members of their families (6). There were seventy boys given after-care supervision during the three year period.

Observations and insights derived from working with these boys and their families provide support for a reference group theory of delinquent behavior. The case histories cited by Shaw also tend to support such a formulation (11). Because of the author's greater familiarity with the Berkshire Farm boys in New York City, illustrative material will be drawn from their experiences.

The reference group theory of delinquent behavior, presently in a developmental stage, will be stated as a series of seven statements or propositions in an effort to answer the question: how does the individual become committed to delinquency?

*Proposition 1. The family is the first personal reference group of the child.* The concept personal reference group is borrowed from Jennings (7). In her terms, a psyche group is one in which the individual as a person receives sustenance, recognition, approval, and appreciation for just being "himself." It consists of those persons with whom the individual wants to associate in a person to person way and with whom he values emotional relationships. A socio group is one in which the individual's efforts and ideals are focused toward objectives which are not his alone. Concerns must be shared and obligations held in common. It is a psyche group that is the personal reference group of the individual. The family is the first such group of which he is a member. How long it remains his personal reference group may depend on how well it performs the functions referred to above.

*Proposition 2. The family is a normative reference group.* By normative group we mean one whose norms conform to those of the larger society. A reference group is a group in which the individual is motivated to gain or maintain membership. The individual therefore holds attitudes to conform with his perception of consensus. When a membership group becomes a reference group it performs a normative function and may also perform a comparison function (8).

A normative reference group as used in this paper is a reference group whose norms conform to those of the larger society. The family is such a group. It is generally ranged on the side of order and the parents function as agents of society in transmitting the culture to the child. Even in families with criminal parents the child is encouraged by the parents to conform to the norms of the society and is punished for deviation.

Many writers have discussed the relationship between social class and delinquency. Delinquency rates in lower class families are found to be higher than those in middle class families and the following explanations are usually offered to account for this fact:

1. Differences in family structure. There are more one-parent families in the lower class because there are more unmarried mothers, more divorces and more separations. Such families often have a woman at the head of them and lack a father image. In those families that are not on relief, the mother goes to work leaving the children with an aged grandmother, other relatives, or neighbors. The families are for large parts of the day, "no parent" families.

2. Differences in values. Middle class families place greater emphasis on educational and occupational goals and reward achievement in these areas. Differences in sex norms, attitudes toward property and fighting are also frequently mentioned.

Less than twenty-five per cent of the Berkshire Farm boys on after-care in New York City were members of families which included a father. All but one or two of the families would be classified as lower class, applying the usual objective criteria. Depth interviews with parents of Berkshire Farm boys on after-care revealed that unpleasant contacts with police, truant officers, schools and courts were commonly experienced. Parents repeatedly referred to the inconveniences and hardships they suffered as a result of the delinquency of their sons. Disciplinary action they had taken to get boys to go to school, stay away from gangs, and obey various laws including beatings, withholding of privileges, restriction of movement, and complaints to police and children's court. In only one instance did a parent express approval of a delinquent act of a boy or defend his delinquent behavior.

In group and individual sessions boys spontaneously identified the views of parents as opposed to truancy, fighting, stealing, destruction and other forms of delinquent behavior. Each reported some punitive action taken by parents when delinquent behavior came to their attention. Diagnoses of family difficulties led to the therapeutic objective of making parents less punitive.

It is generally recognized that in the middle class family parents exert pressure on their children to conform to the norms of the larger society. With respect to the legal norms of the larger society the lower class families of Berkshire Farm boys also apply sanctions to enforce conformity. The difference, if any, is probably one of degree. The family, middle class or lower class is a normative group and as long as it remains a reference group of the boy it is a normative reference group.

*Proposition 3. Prior to his participation in a delinquent act a street group has become a personal reference group of the delinquent boy.* The term "street group" is used instead of "gang" to indicate amorphous character, lack of structure, and the fact that the group need *not* be committed to a delinquent sub-culture. Berkshire Farm boys trace their earliest meaningful peer group relationships to street groups, ranging from three to 12 in number, with which they identified from the time they were nine to 11 years of age. It was in concert with one or more boys from such a street group that each participated in his first delinquent act. The case histories presented by Shaw tend to support this proposition.

*Proposition 4. The street group that becomes the personal reference group of the lower class boy in New York City has a delinquent sub-culture.* The lower class boys in the Berkshire Farm after-care program expressed attitudes and values similar to those described by Cohen in *Delinquent Boys.* Two boys from middle class neighborhoods, while associated with street groups, did not express such attitudes toward property, stealing or truancy.

*Proposition 5. A boy, for whom a street group is a personal reference group is likely, in the dynamic assessment preceding a delinquent act, to decide in favor of the delinquent act.* The street group, whether or not it has a delinquent sub-culture, has no clearly defined objectives and engages in a considerable amount of experimental behavior some of which is delinquent. Once the street group has become his personal reference group a boy needs the approval of the others. The boys in his personal reference group who are with him at the time of the act will exercise an important influence upon the outcome of his assessment. He cannot afford to have them regard him as "punking out" or "chicken." In all probability he will participate in the delinquent act.

*Proposition 6. The individual tends as a member of a personal reference group to import into its context attitudes and ways of behaving which he is currently holding in socio group life.* Important studies of intergenerational conflict in families of immigrants illustrate the fact that children acquire attitudes and ways of behaving in school and in other socio groups and bring these attitudes into the home. The result in immigrant families has been the rejection of parental norms and values (12). The same process appears to be operating in our lower class families. Applying the standards learned in school the lower class boy will find his parents on the low end of the scale in education, occupation, and morals. Importing these attitudes into the home leads him to reject his parents and tends to neutralize the normative influence which they exercise.

An illustration in terms of Merton's modes of individual adaptation may clarify the process. In our society money and success are culture goals. Institutionalized means for attaining them are education, work, and thrift. In the family, a normative group, the boy will learn both the culture goals and the institutionalized means. The family is his personal reference group and his initial adaptation is conformity. If, in socio groups, he learns that the culture goals are unattainable and the institutionalized means available to him are unacceptable he may choose the adaptation of "rebellion." Delinquent boys who chose this form of adaptation are probably the core members and leaders of gangs. If, in socio groups the culture goals are reinforced and the institutionalized means are found to be unacceptable, the boy may choose the adaptation of "innovation." Delinquent boys who chose this form of adaptation are probably peripheral members of gangs.

Innovators and rebels bring attitudes and ways of behaving into the home which cause conflict with normative members of their families. Their newly acquired attitudes cause them to reject the goals and means advocated by their parents and their deviations meet with disapproval. We can see how this can lead the boy to the street and to delinquency.

The same process may lead away from delinquency. The gang member who is an "innovator" accepts the culture goals of money and success. He rejects the institutionalized means of the larger society and substitutes means institutionalized in his delinquent personal reference group, the gang. These approved means may include stealing, gambling, and fighting. Satisfying relationships in a work group, a normative socio group, may influence the development of new attitudes and ways of behaving. As he desires acceptance in the work group he tends to assimilate the sentiments and values of the prestigeful stratum. These sentiments and values oppose stealing, gambling and fighting, the means approved in his gang. He may carry back to the gang the new attitudes and ways of behaving.

Thomas and Znaniecki and others have demonstrated that this process operates when the family is the personal reference group and the school is the normative socio group (12). Case histories of Berkshire Farm boys on after-care indicate that this process operates when a street group is the personal reference group and a work group or some other group is the normative socio group. Boys who were successful in such socio groups as work or school groups resisted participation in delinquent acts even when in the company of members of their street groups. They tended more and more to apply attitudes developed in the work group. Although virtually every boy had a truancy record before being sent to Berkshire Farm for Boys, 14 of the 39 boys on after-care who were employed attended evening high schools. School was accepted as a means of upward mobility and attitudes favorable to school attendance had been reinforced in the work group. Attitudes unfavorable to stealing were also carried from the work group to the street group. The cases of Jerry, and Lefty cited below illustrate the application of this proposition.

*Proposition 7. In a situation where the individual is a member of a normative personal reference group and of a delinquent personal reference group satisfying relationships in normative socio groups will exercise a decisive influence against participation in a delinquent act.* Forty-six of the Berkshire Farm boys on after-care in New York City were living with their immediate families. The families for these boys are here considered normative personal reference groups. Twenty-two of these boys were known to be members of gangs, street groups with delinquent sub-cultures. These boys will be considered members of both delinquent personal reference groups and normative personal reference groups.

Defining a failure as a boy who has been reinstitutionalized by a court, Berkshire Farm has had ten failures in New York City during the three year period from July, 1957 to July, 1960. Nine of the ten failures were members of both normative personal reference groups (families) and delinquent personal reference groups (gangs). A comparison of the functioning in some normative socio groups of the nine gang boys who were failures with the thirteen who were not follows:

1A. Not one of the nine failures was employed at the time of his offense. Seven of them were unemployed more than half the year, preceding the offenses and were not attending school.

1B. Of the 13 non-failures, 11 expressed satisfaction with their jobs and had excellent work records. None of the 11 had been unemployed more than two months of the year and six of them had been on the same jobs for more than a year.

2A. Two of the nine failures were attending school and were subjects of repeated disciplinary action for truancy and bad conduct at school.

2B. One of the two non-failures who attended school had an excellent school record and was working part time. The other had a poor record and was a frequent truant. Three of those working were attending evening schools.

3A. None of the nine failures reported attendance at church or membership in a church group.

3B. Four of the non-failures reported church attendance and two reported membership in church groups.

4A. Four of the nine failures were repeatedly running away from home. Parents of the other five complained about them for staying out late at night, stealing from other members of the family and negativism.

4B. Parents of three of the non-failures complained about them for staying out late and negativism. There were no complaints alleging theft. The parents of seven of the non-failures praised them for honesty, cleanliness, material contributions to the family, and exerting a positive influence on younger siblings.

One may conclude from the above that the non-failures had more satisfying relationships in work groups than the failures. They expressed greater job satisfaction and had far better work records. The number involved in school and church groups was too small for generalization, however, more non-failures than failures participated in these groups. The more favorable attitudes of parents may reflect the fact that behavioral norms were carried from the work group to the home and were reflected in behavioral changes that met with parental approval.

An examination of the case histories of the nine failures and the 13 non-failures compared above reveals no significant differences in race, age, intelligence, family composition, or offenses leading to institutionalization. Two of the non-failures and one of the failures were core members of gangs. The membership of the others was peripheral, involving limited identification and occasional participation in gang activities. Members of both groups had countless opportunities to participate in delinquent acts. An important difference between the failures and non-failures is found in the more satisfying relationships in normative socio groups experienced by the non-failures. This would indicate that satisfying relationships in normative socio groups exercised the decisive influence against participation in delinquent acts. The cases of Teddy and Pedro cited below illustrate the application of this proposition.

Jerry—talking about a projected purse snatching.

> I looked around for a week and couldn't find another job. I was ashamed to come and tell you because I promised not to quit the other job you got me. I had no money and I had nothing to eat that day. I waited for Phil and asked him for two dollars. We were walking along the park on 59th street. Phil said: "Two dollars are not going to help you. Look at those two handbags on the bench. Let's grab them and run for it. The two old ladies won't know what happened." I said no—I don't know why. It just didn't make sense. Here I have only two more years to finish high school. Things are "cool." I like things the way they are. I liked my old job. Maybe I'll get another one like it.
>
> I went to see Jimmy. He bought me a meal and sent me down to see you this morning.

Teddy, who had been a war lord of a Brooklyn gang, discussing plans for a robbery.

> The four of us were walking down the street and we started talking about robbing the candy store. Joe thought it was a good idea and they started to make plans. I told them I had to go and left. I knew they were going to rob the store and I wanted no part of it. I like my job—things are much better at home since I'm working. Why should I take a chance on something like that?

Pedro—describing a projected robbery.

> We were just talking—when someone said: "This bookie that lives here has a lot of dough—a thousand dollars maybe. We can knock him over as he comes out of the house." I didn't like the idea. I'm working and doing all right. What would happen if I get caught. What would my girl say? I was scared. The cops were sure to pick me up for questioning if the robbery happened. I couldn't just take off and let them pull it. I said: "This guy won't have more than a

few dollars. There are too many of us." My friend Louis took my side. We started to argue. There were 7 of us arguing. This bookie walked out, right between us and no one laid a hand on him.

Lefty—discussing the projected stealing of a car.

They wanted a car to go to Rockaway. Whenever they used to ask me if I was with them on something I always said yes. This time I said count me out. I'm doing all right on my job. I've only got two years to finish evening High School. Taking a car is crazy. If they get sore at me over this, the hell with them. I've got other friends.

In each of the situations described above, association with the street group had become less important to the boy. He was reluctant to jeopardize satisfying relationships in normative socio groups. Attitudes and behaviors developed in those groups were carried over to the street group.

The family is almost universally opposed to a boy's affiliation with a street group. How then does a boy who is a member of a normative personal reference group, his family, become a member of a delinquent personal reference group, a street group with a delinquent sub-culture?

The following constitutes an attempt to explain this phenomenon:

1. The lower class boy, a few years after he enters the school system, usually before he is ten years of age, becomes aware of the fact that, applying the standards of the educational system, his parents are failures. Their occupations are rated low, education considered poor, residence depreciated, and habits of dress, eating, and personal cleanliness portrayed as subnormal. The boy's resentment toward his parents grows. A father of one of the boys, a steamfitter, stated that his sons are ashamed of him. They consider his work dirty. Where and why, he asked, have they been taught to look down upon him? And by whom? It is no coincidence that virtually every boy in the program looks down upon the occupation of his father or mother. The two exceptions are from middle class families.

2. The lower class boy perceives of himself as unlikely to succeed at school. This confirms his feelings of inferiority and inadequacy. He accepts the vague success goal imparted to him at school and correctly appraises the likelihood of his failure.

3. Other than the "success" goal, the lower class boy acquires no realistic goal of any kind. It is amazing how many will reply "I don't know" to the question, "What do you want to be?" Each boy knows that he is not likely to become president, governor, an industrialist or a member of any of the professions or occupations viewed with favor in his class room or in his text books. He knows that he can become a

worker of some sort, but finds this sort of endeavor viewed as inferior by his middle class school system.

4. The boy in the lower class family perceives of himself as viewed with disfavor at home because he consumes without contributing. Time and again boys say that they are accused of eating too much, being too hard on clothes, spending too much, etc.

5. The boy, whether in a lower class or middle class family, is objectively inferior to the adults in the family in earnings, skills, and prestige. As a result he tends to perceive himself as generally inferior. He acquires feelings of social competence only as a result of experiences in which he has produced intended effects on other people; making them respond, obtaining expressions of affection, having expressions of affection accepted and giving advice which is accepted. Failing to experience feelings of social competence in the family confirms feelings of inferiority and leads the individual to seek other groups in which he can succeed.

6. The boy, lower class or middle class, who fails to acquire feelings of social competence in the family and does not derive satisfactions in normative socio groups such as work or school groups, gravitates to the street for a great deal of his social life.

7. On the street he finds others who, like himself, have been unsuccessful in experiencing social competence in the family or anywhere else. These boys usually lack any relationships in normative socio groups. If a street group is already in existence the boy we have described tries to join it. If he is accepted; if he wins recognition, approval and appreciation; if here he can make others respond and occasionally have his advice accepted; the group becomes his personal reference group. If the group has a delinquent sub-culture he has become a member of a delinquent personal reference group.

How can we arrest or reverse this trend which seems inexorably to lead to delinquency? We have, by implication, provided a partial answer to the question of why some boys exposed to delinquent norms participate in delinquent acts and others do not. Those who choose conformity refuse to risk the loss of love, the deprivation, or denial that would accompany action disapproved of by their families. The family group as a personal reference group is sufficiently satisfying to deter the boy from going elsewhere. Thus, one method of reversing the trend toward delinquency would be to increase the opportunities for satisfying response in the family group. The emphasis of social case work in this area has been to help members of families to better understand the delinquent. If our analysis is correct, encouraging satisfying participation in normative socio groups should reinforce the family as a normative personal reference group. If the boy could earn money in part time employment or through scholastic subsidy he would meet with much more favorable response in the family. He would also win greater approval in the family by carrying into the home normative patterns of behavior acquired in normative socio groups.

Our educational system can influence adherence to normative reference groups by:

1. Providing classes organized around the problem of developing realistic goals prior to age eleven. Qualifications, opportunities, salaries and training requirements can be stressed.

2. Supplying psychological counseling to boys before their eleventh year to assist them in deciding upon appropriate occupational and social goals. In a society in which upward social mobility for members of the lower class depends to so great an extent on educational achievement we cannot rely on duress alone to encourage scholastic effort. The lower class boy who does not develop any realistic goals attends school because he is compelled to do so, puts forth a minimum of effort, and drops out at the first opportunity. Relating education to an attainable goal makes it more acceptable to the boy. The cases of Len and Carl, cited below, while not typical, illustrate the relationship of goal acquisition to social mobility. Twelve other boys were attending evening high schools, each with an attainable goal.

3. Encouraging respect for skilled and semi-skilled workers and their crafts and occupations by field trips to watch such persons at work, by films emphasizing their contribution to society and lectures by members of labor organizations. Failure to do this has contributed to the present situation in which boys display contempt for the occupations of their parents, view their parents as failures, and perceive all occupational opportunities available to them as undesirable.

4. Stimulating the organization of normative socio groups in the school based on occupational choice, recreational choice, or educational interest. Carpentry clubs, mechanical clubs, radio repair clubs, are of the first type; dramatic clubs, art clubs, music clubs or clubs devoted to a particular sporting activity are of the second type; and French clubs, math clubs, physics clubs are of the third variety.

### THE CASE OF LEN

Len was sent to Berkshire Farm for Boys after several involvements with the law for stealing and truancy. When he returned to New York City on after-care he was seventeen years old. His father had died in a mental institution and his mother was then a patient in a mental institution. One brother was in a reformatory, a sister in a home for retarded girls and two younger siblings in an orphanage. Len, while on after-care, lived in a furnished room in Manhattan. At Berkshire Farm he had decided upon house painting as his career. He found, upon his return to New York City, that he did not like house painting. In the course of counseling sessions he expressed an interest in being an architect or an engineer. Before entering Berkshire Farm for Boys and while at the farm, the scores he attained on I.Q. tests placed him in the low normal range. The meaning of these test scores was explained to him. He felt that they did not accurately reflect his ability. He was told that he could not begin to study for a professional career without first completing high school. That would require four years of attendance. A professional education in evening colleges would require an additional six years. Len was anxious to try. He went to work as a messenger, an occupation he had previously rejected, in order to attend evening high school. His grades have been excellent and he will be graduated in June, 1961, and enter evening college in September. Retests indicate an increase in I.Q. scores have placed him in the above average range. At work he has been promoted several times and is now head of a shipping department.

## THE CASE OF CARL

Before Carl was sent to Berkshire Farm for Boys he had been a truant, been involved in stealing and had run away from home. When he returned to New York City he was sixteen years of age. He is above average in intelligence but saw no reason to finish high school. He went to work as a messenger. In counseling sessions it developed that he wanted to be a psychologist, sociologist or social worker and did not consider it possible to attain any of these professional goals. When the possibilities were made clear to him, he entered evening high school. His present goal is to become a sociologist. He is presently working as a library page and appears to be doing well.

We should also assist the adolescent who is not attending school and who desires and needs employment to find and hold satisfactory employment. In this connection, a review of all discriminatory legislation aimed at restricting work opportunities for adolescents is indicated. Continuation school requirements which have no other objective than keeping young people out of the labor market should be abolished. In lieu of complicated working paper requirements, a document should be issued to every boy fourteen years of age and over attending school, authorizing part time work without red tape in specified occupations during specified hours. At present our laws make it extremely difficult for a boy under sixteen to obtain part time work. Frequently, the earnings derived from part time work supply the financial support necessary to finance higher education. Boys between the ages of sixteen and seventeen are handicapped by the continuation school requirement referred to above. They have already terminated their education and any statute that prevents them from assuming occupational roles should be repealed. Instead of permitting boys to do something constructive in a normative socio group, we leave them on the street with no money, no place to go, and nothing to do but mischief.

In New York City and other urban centers an approach to dealing with gangs is to place a professionally trained group worker with the gang in an effort to substitute non-delinquent for delinquent activity. The manual of the New York City Youth Board, quoted below, presents the rationale for the approach (5, p. 107):

> Participation in a street gang or club, like participation in any natural group, is a part of the growing-up process of adolescence. Such primary group associations possess potentialities for positive growth and development. Through such a group, the individual can gain security and develop positive ways of living with other individuals. Within the structure of his group the individual can develop such characteristics as loyalty, leadership, and community responsibility.

If our analysis is correct, participation in a street group leads to delinquent acts because:

1. Either the street group has a delinquent sub-culture which defines such acts as appropriate (the gangs to which Youth Board workers are assigned are street groups with such delinquent sub-cultures), or

2. The street group is by definition non-normative. It is comprised of young people on the streets with no defined objectives. Such a group engages in a great deal of experimental behavior some of which is likely to violate the legal norms of the larger society. A boys club organized around a socially approved objective would not be classified as a street group.

To give a street group structure and permanence reinforces it as a personal reference group and may actually contribute to delinquency. Yablonsky, based on his study of thirty gangs in New York City, found three characteristic levels of membership organization. In the center, on the first level, are the leaders, youths always working to keep the gang together and in action, drafting, plotting and talking gang warfare. At a second level are youths who claim affiliation but limit their participation. At a third level are peripheral members who participate on occasion and do not specifically identify as members (13). A group so constituted becomes a delinquent personal reference group. The Youth

Board worker cannot effectively oppose the leadership nor can he redirect it. Furthermore, as Merton demonstrates, insofar as subordinate or prospective group members are motivated to affiliate with a group, they tend to assimilate the sentiments and values of the prestigeful stratum in the group (9). In the gang, the significant others are the gang leaders with delinquent values.

Our theoretical orientation would require us to discourage membership in any street group, and most particularly, in any gang, by substituting and supporting normative socio groups. The Youth Board worker could be employed to good advantage organizing boys clubs around constructive leadership and socially acceptable objectives. In such a setting he could become what Merton calls a "reference individual" as distinguished from a "role model." The Heckscher Foundation settlement house in New York City sponsored such boys clubs in the 1920's. They were organized as athletic clubs, attractions including an excellent gymnasium, a swimming pool and a large variety of supervised social events. Delinquent boys did not set the norms for these clubs. A known delinquent was immediately expelled and had to earn his way back by good behavior.

While it may prove difficult and expensive to move those presently in street groups with delinquent sub-cultures into normative socio groups this would contribute greatly toward a reduction in delinquency. It could be accomplished in the following manner:

1. By making available employment opportunities for those not attending school.

2. By facilitating the process of obtaining part time jobs for those attending school.

3. By providing role training to help the boys relate satisfactorily to employers, foremen and fellow workers.

4. By providing normative socio groups as described above.

5. By providing group psychotherapy and role training for those who do not accept work or school groups. As boys learn occupational, family and community roles they become more secure in these roles and their spontaneity and creativity is enhanced. Spontaneity in a role about which one knows little is likely to be pathological spontaneity.

6. By removing from the community those boys who cannot or will not accept any of the above alternatives. After a period at a residential treatment center the boy can be returned to the community with a far better chance of success.

## Summary

In an attempt to answer the question: "How does the individual become committed to delinquency?", a tentative reference group theory is advanced.

An explanation is offered to account for the fact that an individual who is a member of a normative personal reference group, a family, later becomes a member of a delinquent personal reference group, a street group or gang.

Based on the theoretical propositions advanced, recommendations are made which should reverse the trend to increases in delinquency.

Finally, a method of moving those presently in street groups or gangs into normative socio groups is proposed.

## References

1. Cloward, Richard A., "Illegitimate Means, Anomie, and Deviant Behavior," *American Sociological Review*, 24 (April, 1959), 164-176.
2. Cohen, Albert K., *Delinquent Boys; The Culture of the Gang* (Glencoe, Ill., Free Press, 1955).
3. ———, "The Study of Social Disorganization and Deviant Behavior," in R. K. Merton, L. Broom, and L. S. Cottrell (eds.), *Sociology Today* (New York: Basic Books, 1959), 461-484.
4. Dubin, Robert, "Deviant Behavior and Social Structure; Continuities in Social Theory," *American Sociological Review*, 24 (April, 1959), 147-164.
5. Furman, Sylvan S., *Reaching the Unreached* (New York: Youth Board, 1952).
6. Haskell, Martin R., "Role Training and Job Placement of Adolescent Delinquents. The Berkshire Farm After-Care Program," *Group Psychotherapy* (September, 1959), 250-257.
7. Jennings, Helen H., "Sociometric Structure in Personality and Group Formation," in Muzafer Sherif and M. O. Wilson (eds.), *Group Relation at the Crossroads* (New York: Harper, 1953), 332-363.
8. Kelley, Harold H., "Two Functions of Reference Groups," in G. E. Swanson, T. M. Newcomb and E. L. Hartley (eds.), *Readings in Social Psychology* (New York: Henry Holt, 1952), 410-414.
9. Merton, Robert K., *Social Theory and Social Structure* (Glencoe, Ill.: Free Press, 1957).
10. Shaw, Clifford R., and Henry D. McKay, *Juvenile Delinquency and Urban Areas* (Chicago: University of Chicago Press, 1942).
11. Shaw, Clifford R., *The Natural History of a Delinquent Career* (Chicago: University of Chicago Press, 1931).
12. Thomas, William I., and Florian Znaniecki, *The Polish Peasant in Europe and American* (New York: Knopf, 1927).
13. Yablonsky, Lewis, "The Delinquent Gang as a Near Group," *Social Problems*, 7 (Fall, 1959), 108-117.

# Individual Factors in Delinquency

THE PRECEDING section presented several different theories of delinquency as an outgrowth of cultural and social factors. Other writers view delinquency as closely related to innate individual drives, with cultural and social factors playing a secondary role. The general theory that underlies the individual approach states that each baby is born with an array of primitive, aggressive, destructive drives; the baby is at war with the world from the moment of birth. The destructive drives can be tamed by love and understanding in infancy and early childhood. Otherwise, they continue to function and may form the basis for delinquency and crime. According to this point of view, the child does not learn the values and behavior patterns of a delinquent subculture by normal psychological and sociological processes of learning, but on the contrary is born a delinquent and must learn how to be nondelinquent.

In Article 11, a psychiatrist links up the intrapsychic factors of the disturbed or delinquent child with his early parental relationships. Neglect, rejection, and cruelty are viewed as the basis of the child's continued hostility, which may eventually express itself as delinquent behavior. The psychological processes are analyzed.

Article 12, by three sociologists, approaches the individual aspects of delinquent behavior in terms, not of untamed innate aggressive drives, but of socially acquired self-concepts. Reckless has been deeply concerned with identifying factors that cause some boys in high delinquency areas to become delinquent while others follow conventional patterns of behavior. The general neighborhood influences and conditions are the same for both groups. Reckless and his associates therefore turned their attention to personal-social factors, seeking their answer in differences in self-concept. A series of published papers, listed in the first footnote to Article 12, traced the successive stages and findings of a comparative study of "good" and "bad" boys. These papers may be summarized as follows: The two groups of boys, as designated by their teachers, had the same socio-economic status, but the potentially delinquent boys more often came from unstable homes. More subtle differences were revealed. The nondelinquent boys more often than the delinquency-prone felt that their parents were concerned about them and were fair with them; they felt that their families were equal or superior to any other family, and that family relationships were harmonious. Interviews with parents of the two groups of boys showed that parents of nondelinquent boys supervised their sons' activities, were interested in them, and felt that their sons were good and had friends who were good. They did not expect their sons ever to have trouble with the police. Finally, nondelinquent boys regarded themselves as "good"; they avoided trouble and did not anticipate any future trouble with police. Their close friends also were never in trouble.

Reckless and his associates concluded that the "good" boys had been so defined by teachers, parents, and friends; they sought friends who were similarly defined as "good." The boys accepted the self-concept of good and played roles in harmony with this concept. The "bad" boys were defined and treated as "bad" and acted this role.

This finding of the circular process of social definition and role-playing in developing a self-concept was not the end of the research. After four years, when the boys were sixteen (the peak age for delinquency), they were again studied, the results of which study being given in Article 12. Apparently, childhood self-concepts and behavior sets carry over into adolescence. This research does not rule out the existence of a delinquency subculture, but seeks to penetrate the early processes by which boys build up personal self-concepts that will either insulate them against the impact of a delinquency subculture or that will make them vulnerable to the subculture.

In Article 13, Reckless presents his containment theory, which is an effort to integrate individual and social theories of delinquency. He excludes crime and delinquency that emerge from strong inner impulses of an abnormal nature, such as compulsions or phobias; from organic impairment, such as brain damage; or from neurotic mechanisms, such as exhibitionism. None of these accounts for more than a minute proportion of delinquent acts. Reckless first critically reviews more particularistic theories, some of which have been presented in previous articles. He then formulates a theory that coordinates inner controls of behavior, lodged in the personality itself, and outer controls of behavior, exerted on the individual by society. The article therefore may be regarded as a concluding statement to Sections II and III.

# 11.   Antisocial Character Disorder

## Sidney Berman

The author is Associate Clinical Professor of Psychiatry at the George Washington University School of Medicine in Washington, D.C. The article was presented at the 1958 Annual Meeting of the American Orthopsychiatric Association.

After painful attempts to treat delinquent children in clinics and private practice, I found it necessary critically to re-evaluate current theories as they apply to the treatment of this group of behavior disorders. These theories did not explain the phenomena observed in clinical

Sidney Berman, "Antisocial Character Disorder: Its Etiology and Relationship to Delinquency," *American Journal of Orthopsychiatry*, 29 (1959), 612-621. Reprinted by permission of the American Orthopsychiatric Association, Inc. and the author.

cases studied over an extended period of time. Either they were too general or too incompletely structured to permit meaningful application to psychotherapy. This paper presents a theoretical reformulation of certain types of delinquent behavior by the reconstruction process since the behavioral phenomena were less well accounted for by other suppositions.

An inherent technical problem in such a study is the difficulty in treating the delinquent child and his family and therefore the difficulty in obtaining valid data. The unconscious genetic and dynamic material is hard to come by, not only because the parents are elusive and difficult to relate to, but also because they have a problem in recalling forgotten early events which influenced the child's psychological development. These children similarly pose a problem in obtaining data because they relate to treatment with violent opposition, or after showing an early interest in it they quickly attempt to defeat the therapeutic process.

Not until circumstances permitted the treatment of several families over a long period of time was it possible to construct a more complete historical development of the process and to understand the significance of the transference reactions of the child in relation to his past life experiences. In other words, the delinquent behavior here considered could be meaningfully understood only by evaluating the intrapsychic organization of the child in relation to the transactional patterns of the family life to which the child had been subjected.

The concept "juvenile delinquency" is used loosely in reference to a wide disparity of syndromes and symptomatic patterns of behavior. A small group of children with such behavioral disturbances suffer from organic familial, congenital, or acquired defects, low mental endowment or neurotic or psychotic illness. However, most of the children so labeled show a primary need to act in a manner unacceptable to society, because of a characteristic disorganization of function of the psychic processes. This implies that these children have reacted adversely to certain early life experiences which other children have been guided through more adequately. The concern, therefore, is with the psychological factors which structure this morbid behavior.

The diagnostic characteristics of this disturbance warrant its classification as "Antisocial Character Disorder," a terminology which has heretofore been used sparingly and inconsistently. The specific use of this terminology where indicated should result in a more perceptive awareness of the intrapsychic factors which give rise to this behavior, as well as of the basic parental relationships which occur in these families. Regardless of the economic or social status of the family, the psychopathology appears to be the same although the severity and frequency are greater at the lower-class level.

The term antisocial implies that there has been a basic disturbance in the process of socialization of these children. Character disorder refers to the manner in which the maldevelopment is expressed, essentially as socially conditioned derivatives of this disturbance. Instead of primary neurotic or psychotic manifestations, the child defends himself from insoluble conflict with maladaptive behavior. The disturbing experiences of early childhood have not been adequately mastered, and the defective adaptational patterns established at that time eventually become manifest as serious social conflict.

In general, the child's behavior is in the form of uncontrollable, hostile, aggressive acts toward the property or person of others as an attempt to get rid of tension or anxiety. Such adaptational patterns are characteristically in conflict with social values. These children show an aversion to becoming a part of social institutions. They possess a self-centered concern for their own needs, which are impulsively responded to regardless of the consequences. They have essentially no feeling of guilt or remorse about their antisocial behavior. This deviant behavior becomes more manifest as the child gets older, especially when he is confronted with the demands for social adaptation at the time he begins school. Then the well-known symptoms of truancy, defiance of teachers, unlawful acts such as stealing and fire-setting, fights with other children, staying away from home, untruthfulness, irresponsibility and the like are observed. These children also show an unusually high incidence of enuresis, which is of relevance to the nature of the underlying psychopathology.

However, there is a period before the predatory symptoms become overt. Aichhorn [1] described it as the period of "latent delinquency." During this early phase the child most commonly shows an inability to postpone immediate gratification, a tendency to react with uncontrollable behavior, belligerence or defiance if he is not permitted to have his way, an intense disregard for the property rights of other children and a strong resentment of his siblings.

There is no decisive evidence that the children here considered are victims of a constitutional or hereditary defect. Aichhorn (1) felt that general defects in child development, both oedipal and preoedipal, were implicated. Eissler [2] speculated that these patients had a disastrous ex-

---

[1] Aichhorn, A. *Wayward Youth*. New York: Viking Press, 1935.

[2] Eissler, K. R. "Ego-Psychological Implications of the Psychoanalytic Treatment of Delinquents," in *The Psychoanalytic Study of the Child*, Vol. V. New York: Internat. Univ. Press, 1950.

perience in a situation where they expected protection, help or love at a time when the child's early feelings of omnipotence were one of his main tools in dealing with reality. A. Freud [3] described the failure of the delinquent to build up identifications which guide the instinctual behavior in accordance with social standards. She considered the first year of life as a crucial phase, with the mother's absence or neglect or emotional instability causing the destructive urges to remain isolated.

Szurek [4] stressed delinquent behavior as having its origin in the personality organization as a form of defect in "conscience." The more important parent, usually the mother, unconsciously encouraged the antisocial behavior. From these observations, Johnson [5] described superego lacunae in which parents unconsciously condone the acting out of the child. Her cases were reported as "simple cases of superego-defect," that is, a "lack of superego in certain circumscribed areas of behavior."

Van Ophuijsen,[6] Friedlander,[7] Bender,[8] and Bowlby [9] observed very early defects in the relationship of the child to the mother. The child's gratifications were insignificant or unpleasant, resulting in the absence of a functioning superego required to regulate behavior. Kaufman and Heims [10] described the crucial determinant of the delinquency pattern as an unresolved depression, with the depressive nucleus caused by a loss of the parental figure through repeated actual or psychological separations. The child feels these losses or separations as a sadistic act by his parents, and restitution occurs by his going from the frightening passive-receptive state to the active attacking role which may become delinquent. Greenacre [11] felt that the main source of the difficulty probably was with the preoedipal conscience, and her emphasis was on the problem of delayed separation from the mother.

[3] Freud, A. "Certain Types and Stages of Social Maladjustment," in *Searchlights on Delinquency* ( K. R. Eissler, Ed. ). New York: Internat. Univ. Press, 1949.

[4] Szurek, S. A. *Geneses of Psychopathic Personality Trends.* Psychiatry, 5:1, 1942.

[5] Johnson, A. M. "Sanctions for Superego Lacunae of Adolescents," in *Searchlights on Delinquency* ( K. R. Eissler, Ed. ). New York: Internat. Univ. Press, 1949.

[6] van Ophuijsen, J. H. W. "Primary Conduct Disorders," in *Modern Trends in Child Psychiatry* ( N. D. C. Lewis and B. L. Pacella, Eds. ). New York: Internat. Univ. Press, 1945.

[7] Friedlander, K. "Latent Delinquency and Ego Development," in *Searchlights on Delinquency* ( K. R. Eissler, Ed. ). New York: Internat. Univ. Press, 1949.

[8] Bender, L. "Psychopathic Behavior Disorders in Children," in *Handbook of Correctional Psychology* ( R. M. Lindner and R. V. Seliger, Eds. ). New York: Philosophical Lib., 1947.

[9] Bowlby, J. *Forty-four Juvenile Thieves: Their Characters and Home-Life.* London: Baillière, Tindall and Cox, 1946.

[10] Kaufman, I., and L. Heims. *The Body Image of the Juvenile Delinquent.* Am. J. Orthopsychiatry, 28:146-159, 1958.

[11] Greenacre, P. *Conscience in the Psychopath.* Am. J. Orthopsychiatry, 15:495-509, 1945.

Most studies, therefore, stress the early mother-child relationship, with the mother's rejection and hostility or inconsistency resulting in the child's emotional deprivation. Such observations, however, are not exactly specific for this type of pathological process, or they explain only partial aspects of the problem.

Where circumstances permit the study of the family over an extended period of time, the child will exhibit consistent adaptational patterns which are used to cope with the most violent impulses and with overwhelming anxiety to frustration. The intensity of this response is impossible to comprehend unless one has been in intimate contact with it. The reconstruction of the transactional processes in the families making up this study points to certain early life experiences of the child which create in him enduring maladaptational patterns of an antisocial character. These patterns are the result of a specific traumatic concatenation of events occurring approximately at the end of the first year of life and beginning of the second year. The origin is in a defective mother-child relationship which is uniquely pathological. This is, of course, contingent upon the personality characteristics parents bring to their marriage.

In families with a low socioeconomic level, the actual mother often worked, not necessarily because she had to, or she was absent from the home. In her place was a grandmother, aunt, sister or anyone else, including a neighbor. Frequently the father was not present. When he was in the home he was indifferent and detached or harsh and cruel. In families with an average or high economic level, the mother often abdicated her position to a domestic or series of domestics, who cared for the child. The father in these homes either avoided the child or was violent or dictatorial toward him.

During the first 12 months or so of the child's life, that is, as long as the infant was passive, dependent and receptive, the earliest requirements of life appeared to be sufficiently met by someone functioning in the mothering role. Occasionally the mothering process was activated in an overdetermined way because the child had an operation, serious illness or feeding problem. Frequently the mothering-one bestowed upon the child that which she wished for in terms of her own oral dependency desires. This mother-child relationship appeared to be the prevailing one until the child began to develop increased physical activity. Compared to that which follows in the lives of these children, this period of life probably seemed to them to be the phase of seduction.

Normally as an infant becomes active toward the end of the first year of life, motor patterns begin to dominate his behavior. His oral aggressive activity also reaches its height. In addition, there is the capacity for a clearer differentiation of self from others. Now the infant requires more help, care, support, and supervision from the mothering-one to satisfy, contain and direct these impulses into meaningful adaptive patterns. When the child experiences such a relationship, the response to the actual mothering-one and the introjected image of her has the affective quality of love, of trust and of confidence in her as the one who cares for him. And for this love, the infant's oral sadistic impulses and motor patterns are directed in accordance with the mother's standards of behavior. Also, since the child's perceptual acuity is sufficiently developed so that he is able to see his mothering-one as a whole object who may love him or hate him, his response toward her may range from complete love to complete hate.

The children under discussion seem to be subject at this phase of their development to undue stress which establishes the basis of the psychopathology. The demands of the child, which may have the quality of greed because of the nature of the earlier period, clash with the mothering-one's inability to meet adequately and regulate his needs. The relationship of the child to the mothering-one, whether it is the actual mother or the substitute mother, is transformed into one in which he feels unmitigated hatred toward her. If both the mother and the substitute are present, this feeling is primarily directed toward the actual mother, who on the one hand appears available to him but on the other hand repudiates his needs. It does not matter if the mother substitute or the real mother is ineffective, indifferent or cruel. He sees her as one who rejects his needs and he responds to her as the one who hates him. He hates in return, and it is this hatred toward the introjected and real object which becomes the prevailing affective response to the world about him.

The child appears to conceptualize this period of his life as a phase of rejection, since this type of mother now expects the child to take care of himself. Her own dependency needs are such that she finds the infant's demands intolerable. The child may be looked upon by the mother as evil, a nuisance, or an inconvenience. The absence of love thereby creates a vacuum which is filled with this most intense hate, and this conflict has dire consequences for the child's future development.

This presentation to the child of one set of feelings by the one who cares for him and then a reaction toward him with another set of attitudes heightens his hostile oral aggressive feelings and intensifies his motor adaptive responses to such frustration. This frustration is felt in relation to his mother, and the internalized image of her. Love and hate are not strongly bound together in this type of child. The good suddenly becomes deflated and the bad becomes gruesome and overwhelming. There is not the fusion of good and bad as in the manic-depressive position. Rather, the child responds with hatred toward the mother as he feels her to be, that is, as an internalized object. In turn he conceives of his mother as hating him and fears that the introjected mother may act toward him as he feels toward her. Therefore, his feelings are projected back onto the mother as a most violent person. Since the child's hatred is so intense toward both the internalized image of mother and mother as he relates to her, this must be denied and he uses projection to defend himself from his self-consuming rage and despair. He thereby attempts to protect himself as he turns his hatred onto others who he feels may hate him or deny him his desires. The defect which results in the archaic superego of these children is the basis upon which the later defect in conscience and defective social values are structured. One does not develop a conscience if one feels only unmitigated hate. This also accounts for the fact that symptom formation is not prominent in these children, for in order to have symptom formation, one must have strong ambivalent feelings.

Actually this type of mother most often is helpless, confused, disorganized and dependent. She feels there is no one to satisfy her dependency needs and therefore feels unable to care for the needs of her children. She reveals, in time, past serious conflict in relation to her own early life and in addition suffers from current problems, especially with her husband. The father also poses a serious problem to the child, since he may either ignore the child or belittle him and be harsh or cruel. This father is devoid of or lacking in his capacity to give love or tender interest to the family. The mother often motivates the child to act out her own hostile feelings toward the husband by getting the child to defy or provoke him. This only causes the child to feel further exploited and embittered.

The later phases of development are not supported favorably, because of the earlier basic disturbance in development as well as the continuing problems of adjustment. The mother's inability to institute controls frequently is carried over to the toilet training period. Because of the child's intense hostility toward the mother, whom he feels he has lost as a love object, sphincter control on mother's terms may be repudiated. Michaels [12] also describes the high incidence of enuresis accompanying juvenile delinquency as the expression of deficient inhibitory tendencies, and feels that the behavior pattern was the result of the libido's remaining pregenital. As is often the case with enuretic children, their

[12] Michaels, J. J. *Disorders of Character*, Springfield, Ill.: Charles C Thomas, 1955.

parents frequently had the same childhood problem, indicating a disturbance in their early parental relationships.

These basic difficulties are carried over to the oedipal period. Fear of father results in a distorted identification with him as the aggressor or in a reaction toward him as one to be avoided or dreaded. However, it is particularly the relationship to the hated mother which causes the child to associate sex with horror, violence and confusion. The result is a serious defect in the child's ability to work out his own sexual identity. Perverse sexual experiences often occur early in the lives of these children as they attempt to find substitute love objects. The continuation of these distorted relationships to both parents, when present, seriously impairs the child's ability to establish controls which will permit him to adjust to the problems of socialization as he begins to expand his contact with the outside world.

In the meantime, the moral and ethical values of the parents at both the verbal and nonverbal levels have a delinquent orientation and thereby implicitly provide approved ways for the child to use projection and denial as a defense. In that sense, the parents may unconsciously direct the child to act out their own unresolved emotional conflicts, in which they, too, felt denied, neglected and hostile.

Owing to the nature of the superego conflict in which the child's relationship to the internalized parental figures is completely devoid of love, the latency period becomes a turbulent experience for the child. Since the controls from within are defective, the child is ill prepared to cope with the problems of socialization once he begins school. Because of the child's basic hostile orientation, there is no capacity for sublimation. This conflict is projected onto certain teachers, who often are selected as representative of the maternal figure. It is as difficult for him to assimilate the educational experience as it is for him to accept food on the basis of mutual love with the mother. This type of child quickly falls behind in his studies, and truancy and defiance of the school authorities create serious problems.

When adolescence is reached, the defenses centered around the basic problems and oedipal difficulties collapse under the onslaught of bodily sexual changes. The fantasies of sex have a hostile, greedy quality. There also are anxieties about entrapment by the female when the adolescent is a male. Therefore these youngsters either try to exploit the relationship with a unilateral orientation structured solely in terms of what they can get out of it, devoid of any tenderness, or they try to avoid what they feel would be an entrapment. Controls, defective to begin with, may disintegrate completely with an intensification of the antisocial behavior. Under the stress of adolescence, psychosis may occur as a regression to a more primitive level of adjustment. Some of these youngsters also may go on to become criminals, alcoholics and drug addicts. The majority gradually contain the behavior in the form of serious character defects when adulthood is reached and are able to achieve a marginal social adjustment.

It is extremely difficult to get a detailed history of the early life of these children because their mothers are vague concerning the events of the period. This also is carried over into the current life, indicating the parents' lack of perception of the child's problems and their helplessness or neglect in providing the child with stable parental support. Only gradually, after many months of treatment, one sporadically obtains a report of significant information. Two brief case histories are selected to demonstrate the type of child studied.

Case 1. A boy of 16, with a Wechsler-Bellevue IQ of 129, was referred for treatment, after being released on probation for housebreaking. He truanted from school, lied, was a feeding problem at home and had enuresis. His mother avoided her domestic responsibilities and his father was critical and cruel. The patient had transfusions at birth, and was cared for by a maid until he was one year old. After this the mother was lacking in her ability to care for him. She felt overwhelmed, helpless in the management of his behavior, and incapable of meeting his needs. His eating habits were sloppy. He became hyperactive and unmanageable. Toilet training was ineffective. He almost killed his younger brother in a fight over a stick, and he hit other children or destroyed their toys. Impulsive behavior, stealing, and quarrels with teachers caused his parents to send him from one school to another.

He resisted treatment and was almost uncommunicative. The violence of his anger at times reached a high pitch as he tried to provoke the therapist. The orientation in treatment with his mother was non-critical, supportive and educational in order to meet her dependency needs and help with the mothering process. The boy attempted to avoid his problems, used pseudo logic to defend his actions, and attempted to play the therapist against others. He defended himself from an enormous wish to be dependent and be cared for. Only one dream was reported, in which he was out in the rain alone. Treatment was overwhelmingly charged with anxiety, and only after it had continued for two years did his schoolwork improve, his hostility at home lessen, and his closeness to mother find expression. Now, after four years, he occasionally sees the therapist for advice about educational plans and urgent problems, especially centered around his adjustment to the opposite sex.

Case 2. This youngster was admitted to a resident treatment center at the age of nine for serious fire-setting. At school he was violent, restless, and incorrigible. Enuresis also was a problem. Five older brothers had been committed to a training school. His mother was irresponsible, warm but undependable, or cold and distant. The father was unreliable, shifted from job to job, used vile language and drank to excess. At four weeks of age the patient had an operation for intestinal obstruction. He was cared for mostly by the maternal grandmother, who spoiled him. No one remembered him as a problem during his first year. Toilet training was neglected. When he started to walk and showed increased physical activity the grandmother was unable to manage him. The mother was not consistently around and there was no regulation of his life from this time on. At four he began to run away from home and at six years he started to set serious fires following quarrels with his mother. From the day he started school he could not get along with the teachers or his peers. His mother protected him and placed the blame on others. His IQ on the Stanford-Binet was 104. In treatment he was seen four times a week. His behavior was violent and destructive beyond description. Symbolic oral activity was intense and at times associated with anal sadistic and castration patterns. Once in anger there was a fantasy of swallowing glue, then a match, following which he spit out fire. He wanted to swallow the therapist yet he feared the consequences of getting close. After Herculean effort on the part of the therapist the material gradually changed from primary hostile acting-out behavior to symbolic play patterns, and ever so slowly there developed a capacity for verbal communication of his problems.

The incidence of an isolated antisocial act in childhood does not warrant the diagnosis of antisocial character disorder. Indeed the genesis of such sporadic delinquent acts differs sharply from the more serious forms of antisocial behavior.

Also, if treatment of the cases herein considered is centered solely around oedipal material, it becomes meaningless and actually may tend to aggravate the condition. The seemingly obvious inference that the psychopathology is primarily oedipal is not supported by clinical investigation. One may avoid the basic problems if this line of reasoning is followed. In fact, especially this type of mother often rationalizes her difficulties with the child on this basis. A therapy so oriented would only support the defense.

The antisocial character disorder evolves as a result of a series of unique experiences in which the child is often but not necessarily cared for in an overdetermined way for about the first year of life. Then, as intense oral sadism and motor patterns of behavior require integration, the disjunctive mother-child relationship fails the child. There is no one for the child to feel secure with. Object relations are confused. Frustration, distrust, and the most intense hate is directed at the real and the internalized conception of mother. It is this hate essentially devoid of guilt which presents such a difficult problem in treatment. It has no ambivalent quality and is directed totally at the object, that is, the mother, but is defended against by denial and projection. The characteristics of these infantile experiences have a much more sizable part than we think in terms of the child's future development. The impact of this disturbance on subsequent stages of development creates serious problems in addition to those which later occur.

There is no short or easy road to the therapeutic goal, the socialization of these children. The therapist should accept the responsibility for treatment, dedicated to the fact that this type of family may need to use his skills for a long period of time, and that many crises will arise. Treatment implies the participation of the parents, especially the mother. Psychotherapy with the mother requires more active and direct collaboration on the part of the therapist, and therefore it is different from the technique customarily used in child guidance clinics. Since the child reacts toward the therapist with hostile, destructive behavior, the intensity of which may incapacitate the therapist, only gradually is it possible for the child to trust the ego-syntonic support of the therapist. The correction of distorted object relations and the establishment of new identifications for the child can occur only when the therapist is neither seductive nor rejecting. This places a burden on the therapist's own conscious and unconscious responses to the child's hostile provocative behavior. It requires a benevolent, objective, incorruptible relationship in which the child gradually feels he has support and understanding. All too often, the intensity of the child's hate and deviousness may cause the therapist to become ineffective, because it threatens the defenses which the therapist has erected against his own hostile impulses. Thus, there may be the fear that he will assault or be assaulted by the child.

Effective methods of detection and prevention as well as new educational techniques need to be developed. They require an orientation based on the nature of the psychopathology, with assistance provided for the parents as well as the child. This implies the evolution of a social psychiatry which brings guidance and treatment principles into the homes of these parents where indicated, and supports them, especially the mother, in the process of socialization of the children. Not until such an attempt to treat the family meets with failure, should resident treatment be recommended. Even when this is necessary the goals are directed toward the treatment of the child and the parents so that when the child is ready to return home, the home is able to meet the child's psychological needs. To return a child to a home where there have been no significant psychological changes is to invite further difficulties. The educational program also requires a specific orientation toward overcoming this type of child's refractory reaction to the school experience, and the degree of success appears to be directly related to the degree of collaboration which can be achieved between the school and the child's parents.

## 12.  Delinquency Vulnerability: A Cross Group and Longitudinal Analysis

Simon Dinitz, Frank R. Scarpitti, and Walter C. Reckless

Dinitz (Ph.D. University of Wisconsin), is Associate Professor of Sociology at Ohio State University; Scarpitti is a Research Associate at the same institution; and Reckless (Ph.D. University of Chicago) holds the rank of Professor. Reckless' professional experience also includes membership on the Advisory Council of the Division of Corrections, State of Ohio, and on the Scientific Advisory Committee of the International Criminological Society. He is the author of many articles and books on criminology, including *Etiology of Delinquent and Criminal Behavior*, *Vice in Chicago*, *Jail Administration in India*, and *The Crime Problem*.

The research for this and earlier related articles was made possible by grants from the Development Fund of the Ohio State University.

We report here the terminal part of a research project concerned with the attempt to discover what insulates early adolescent boys in high delinquency areas against delinquency. More particularly it deals with the assessments of a group of 70 white boys, currently 16 years of age, who were part of a cohort of 101 twelve-year old white boys, nominated four years previously by their sixth-grade teachers in elementary schools of Columbus (Ohio) high delinquency areas as headed for trouble with the law. Euphemistically, we have referred to them as the "bad" or the "vulnerable" boys. Four years after initial contact, 70 of the original 101 "bad" boys could be located in Columbus, so that re-assessment could be made.

The original group of 101 "bad" boys, of which 70 were located for

Simon Dinitz, Frank R. Scarpitti, and Walter C. Reckless, "Delinquency Vulnerability: A Cross Group and Longitudinal Analysis," *American Sociological Review*, 27 (August, 1962), 515-517. Reprinted by permission of the American Sociological Association and the authors.

re-assessment, constitutes the second of two complementary cohorts. The first cohort is made up of a group of 125 twelve-year old white boys who had been nominated by their sixth-grade teachers in the same elementary schools of Columbus, Ohio as likely to stay out of trouble with the law. We have referred to this cohort as the "good" boys or the boys insulated against delinquency. Four years after initial assessment, 103 of this cohort of 125 good boys were located and re-assessed.

## Method

The methods utilized in this project have been described extensively in other papers and require only brief mention here.[1] In the Spring of 1955, all sixth-grade teachers in selected elementary schools in the high delinquency areas of Columbus, Ohio were asked to nominate the white boys in their classes, who were unlikely to experience contact with the law. A cohort of 125 twelve-year old white boys was thus constituted. Their cases were officially established as "good" by clearance through the files of the police juvenile bureau and the juvenile court. In other words, they as well as their siblings had not had contact with police and court. These 125 boys were then contacted at home. Our field worker administered a research schedule which assessed whether the boy was veering toward good or poor socialization and whether he had a good or poor image of himself and others. Four years later, 103 of these 125 good boys could be located in Columbus, Ohio and a re-assessment of them was made. In the Spring of 1956, the sixth-grade teachers in the same schools were asked to nominate the white boys in their rooms who were (in their judgment) headed for trouble with the law. A cohort of 101 was constituted. These boys were contacted in their homes and were administered a schedule getting at socialization and concept of self. Four years later, 70 of this cohort of 101 could be located in Columbus and were re-assessed.

[1] Walter C. Reckless, Simon Dinitz, and Ellen Murray, "Self Concept as an Insulator Against Delinquency," *American Sociological Review*, 21 (December, 1956), pp. 744-746; Walter C. Reckless, Simon Dinitz, and Barbara Kay, "The Self Component in Potential Delinquency and Potential Non-Delinquency," *American Sociological Review*, 22 (October, 1957), pp. 566-570; Simon Dinitz, Barbara Ann Kay, and Walter C. Reckless, "Group Gradients in Delinquency Potential and Achievement Scores of Sixth Graders," *American Journal of Orthopsychiatry*, 28 (July, 1958), pp. 588-605; Jon E. Simpson, Simon Dinitz, Barbara Kay, and Walter C. Reckless, "Delinquency Potential of Pre-Adolescents in High Delinquency Areas," *British Journal of Delinquency*, 10 (January, 1960), pp. 211-215; Frank R. Scarpitti, Ellen Murray, Simon Dinitz, and Walter C. Reckless, "The 'Good' Boy in a High Delinquency Area: Four Years Later," *American Sociological Review*, 25 (August, 1960), pp. 555-558.

The findings from the assessments of the two complementary cohorts can be separated into two parts: (1) a comparison of the 70 from the 101 bad boys cohort with the 103 from the 125 good boys cohort; (2) a comparison of the assessments of the 70 bad boys at 16 years of age with themselves four years earlier at 12 years of age as well as with the total of the original cohort of 101 bad boys. Number 1 is a cross group comparison; number 2, a longitudinal comparison.

## Cross Group Comparison

At sixteen years of age, four years after original assessment, four of the 103 insulated ("good") boys in the slums had had one minor complaint for delinquency each. One of these was taken to court and placed on probation, while three were settled in the field by a warning from the juvenile bureau. On the other hand, 27 of the 70 vulnerable boys ("bad") from the same slum neighborhoods had had serious and frequent contact with the court, during the four-year interlude between initial assessment at 12 years of age and the assessment at 16 years of age. These 27 boys averaged three plus contacts with the court, involving separate complaints for delinquency.

On a seven-item delinquency check list (taken from a larger list devised by James F. Short)[2] which specifies frequency of acts, the 103 insulated slum boys at 16 showed an average score of 1.3 admitted delinquencies during their lifetime, while the vulnerable group of 70 slum boys had a mean frequency score of 3.1. (Each delinquency item was scored 0 to 2; 0 equalling never; 1, once or twice; 2, several times. The maximum frequency score on all seven items would be 14.)

On a nine-item quasi-scale or inventory, which measures the boy's favorable or unfavorable projections of self in reference to getting into trouble with the law, the cohort of 103 sixteen-year old insulated slum boys showed an average score of 15.8. In this instance, the inventory was scored from 10 for the most favorable answers to 19 for the most unfavorable answers on all nine items. The 70 vulnerable 16-year old slum boys scored on an average of 18.9 on this quasi-scale.

The mean score of the insulated cohort on the De scale of the California Personality Inventory [3] was 13.6, while the mean score of the

[2] F. Ivan Nye and James F. Short, Jr., "Scaling Delinquent Behavior," *American Sociological Review*, 22 (June, 1957), p. 328.

[3] Soc scale (formerly De) is part of the California Personality Inventory, devised by Harrison J. Gough, Department of Psychology, University of California (Berkeley). The CPI is conceived as a substitute for the Minnesota Multiphasic Personality Inventory. However, the scoring on the De is the reverse of what it is on the Soc.

vulnerable cohort on the De scale was 23.4. The De scale (now called Socialization scale) measures a veering toward delinquency or poor socialization or a veering toward non-delinquency or good socialization. A score of 13 for the insulated cohort was in line with the average scores of criterion groups of "good citizens," according to the norms of the scale. The average score of 23 was up close to the mean scores for delinquent groups, court martial cases, and prisoners in the national norms.

Not only had the vulnerable cohort become involved in delinquency very much more than the insulated cohort, but also on the three mentioned supplementary measures, the vulnerable cohort stood in marked, unfavorable contrast with the insulated cohort.

## Longitudinal Comparisons

Here the interest is in comparing the assessments of the 103 "good" boys at 16 years of age with the assessments of the same boys at 12 years of age and the assessments of the 70 "bad" boys at 16 with the assessments of the same boys at 12 years of age. On the De scale, which measures veering toward or away from delinquency or toward poor or good socialization, the 103 good boys had, at 12, a mean score of 14.2; at 16, 13.6. The 70 bad boys at 12 had a mean score on the De scale of 23.6, while at 16 their mean score was 23.4. This is notable cohort stability in self orientation over time.

The individual scores of the 70 "bad" boys on the De scale at 16 correlated with their scores at 12 years of age to the extent of r = .78, which shows a high degree of individual stability in direction of poor socialization over time. However, the coefficient of correlation (r) of the De scores for the boys in the "good" cohort at 16 and at 12 years of age was only .15, which of course does not show individual stability longitudinally.[4]

---

Low score on De, that is down around 14, corresponds to a high score on the Soc, up around 40, and vice versa. We are calling the Soc scale the De scale and scoring it reversely, because we started this way in 1955 before Gough re-named the De scale and reversed the scoring. We used 46 out of the total of 54 items on the De scale, eliminating 8 which were too adult oriented for 12 year old children, and we used a correction factor, approved by Gough, to equate the score on the 46 items with the score on the total of 54 items.

[4] Examination of the scores of 100 boys (the schedules of 3 of the 103 were incompletely filled in) of the good cohort at 12 and at 16 reveal a tendency of the boys at 16 to gravitate toward the mean. Fifty of the 100 scored on an average of 6.28 lower at 16 than at 12 which is in the direction of improvement; 44, an average of 5.64 higher at 16 than at 12; 6, no change. Hence, the best of the good cohort moved from scores of 6 to 14 up toward the mean and beyond the mean, while the poorest of the good cohort moved down toward the mean or slightly below the

Eighty-eight per cent of the cohort of good slum boys at 12 years of age professed that their close friends had not been in trouble with the law. Of the same 103 boys at 16 years of age, 91 per cent said that their close friends had not been in trouble with the law. In contrast, 35 per cent of the 70 boys from the vulnerable cohort claimed at 12 years of age that their close friends had been in trouble with the law; four years later the same 70 boys claimed 34 per cent.

Regarding favorable or unfavorable concepts of self as measured by responses to questions such as "up to now, do you think things have gone your way," "do you feel that grown ups are usually against you," "do you expect to get an even break from people in the future?," there was no major change in the percentage distribution of the responses of the two cohorts at 12 and at 16. The good cohort had a very high percentage of favorable responses and the bad cohort a low percentage of favorable responses. On all three questions listed above, the percentage of favorable responses for the 103 good boys at 16 was 90. For the 70 bad boys at 16 the percentage of favorable responses on the first of the above listed questions was 50; on the second, 29; and on the third, 30.

One is struck with the fact that there is a notable cohort stability of responses of the two groups of slum boys over a critical four year period, namely from 12 to 16 years of age. We feel that this cohort stability is not due to the memorization by the boys of the answers to the same questions administered four years apart.

## Conclusion

In our quest to discover what insulates a boy against delinquency in a high delinquency area, we believe we have some tangible evidence that a good self concept, undoubtedly a product of favorable socialization, veers slum boys away from delinquency, while a poor self concept, a product of unfavorable socialization, gives the slum boy no resistance to deviancy, delinquent companions, or delinquent sub-culture. We feel that components of the self strength, such as a favorable concept of self, act as an inner buffer or inner containment against deviancy, distraction, lure, and pressures. Our operational assumptions are that a good self concept is indicative of a residual favorable socialization and a strong inner self, which in turn steers the person away from bad companions

---

mean. The SD for the mean (14.2) of the 100 boys of the good at age 12 (on the De scale) was 6.2; the SD for the mean (13.6) at age 16 was 4.7, which shows less variation at 16 than at 12. The corresponding figures for the boys of the bad cohort were: at age 12, M = 23.6, SD = 6.9; at age 16, M = 23.4, SD = 6.1.

and street corner society, toward middle class values, and to awareness of possibility of upward movement in the opportunity structure. Conversely, the poor concept of self is indicative of a residual unfavorable socialization (by 12 years of age probably not the result of participation in delinquency sub-culture) and indicative of weak inner direction (self or ego), which in turn does not deflect the boy from bad companions and street corner society, does not enable him to embrace middle class values, and gives him an awareness of being cut off from upward movement in the legitimate opportunity system.

We feel that the selective operation of the self element is not specified in the response to the models of behavior presented to the person by his associates in differential association theory (Sutherland) [5] and is even less specified in delinquency sub-culture theory (Cohen, et al.) [6] as well as "opportunity structure" theory (limited access to legitimate means, alienation, neutralization, etc., according to Cloward, Sykes, et al.).[7] We feel that a self factor in these theories is missing; this self factor can explain selective resistance to deviant patterns or veering away from the street corner and delinquency. On the other hand, we think that the research findings of Albert Reiss [8] and F. Ivan Nye [9] definitely point to this overlooked self-containment factor when they called attention to the operation of personal controls (Reiss) and internalized indirect controls (Nye), in accounting for the veering away from delinquency.

[5] Edwin H. Sutherland, *Principles of Criminology*, 4th ed., Philadelphia: J. B. Lippincott Company, 1947, pp. 6-7.

[6] Albert K. Cohen, *Delinquent Boys: The Culture of the Gang*, Glencoe, Ill.: The Free Press, 1955.

[7] Richard A. Cloward and Lloyd E. Ohlin, *Delinquency and Opportunity*, Glencoe, Ill.: The Free Press, 1960, p. 150; Gresham M. Sykes and David Matza, "Techniques of Neutralization: A Theory of Delinquency," *American Sociological Review*, 22 (December, 1957), p. 665.

[8] Albert J. Reiss, Jr., "Delinquency as the Failure of Personal and Social Controls," *American Sociological Review*, 16 (April, 1951), pp. 196-206.

[9] F. Ivan Nye, *Family Relationships and Delinquent Behavior*, New York: John Wiley & Sons, Inc., 1958, pp. 3-4.

## 13.   A New Theory of Delinquency and Crime

Walter C. Reckless

The author's profile is given with Article 12.

Containment theory is an explanation of conforming behavior as well as deviancy.[1] It has two reinforcing aspects: an inner control system and an outer control system. Are there elements within the self and within the person's immediate world that enable him to hold the line against deviancy or to hew to the line of social expectations? The assumption is that strong inner and reinforcing outer containment constitutes an insulation against normative deviancy (not constitutional or psychological deviancy), that is, violation of the sociolegal conduct norms.

### A Middle Range Theory

Containment theory does not explain the entire spectrum of delinquency and crime. It does not explain crime or delinquency which emerges from strong inner pushes, such as compulsions, anxieties, phobias, hallucinations, personality disorders (including inadequate, unstable, antisocial personalities, etc.), from organic impairments such as brain damage and epilepsy, or from neurotic mechanisms (exhibitionists, peepers, fire setters, compulsive shop lifters). All told these cases are minimal. And containment theory does not explain criminal or delinquent activity which is a part of "normal" and "expected" roles and activities in families and communities, such as the criminal tribes of India, Gypsy vocations and trades (very similar to the former), begging families, and certain phases of delinquency subculture and organized crime. Between these two extremes in the spectrum of crime and delinquency is a very large middle range of norm violation, perhaps as big as two thirds to three quarters of officially reported cases as well as the unreported cases of delinquency and crime. Containment theory seeks to explain this large middle range of offenders. According

Walter C. Reckless, "A New Theory of Delinquency and Crime," *Federal Probation*, 25 (December 1961), 42-46. Reprinted with permission of the publisher.

[1] For the complete statement on Containment Theory, see Walter C. Reckless, *The Crime Problem*, 3rd Ed. New York: Appleton-Century-Crofts, 1961, pp. 335-359.

to its place on the spectrum of delinquency and crime, one might say that it occupies the middle position.

## A Quick Review of Criminological Theories

Before proceeding further, it might be a good idea to see in what directions theory in criminology is pointing at present. Since the early 19th century we have had a long succession of theories, most of which have not stood the test of time. It is possible to assemble these theories into three main camps of schools: (1) biological and constitutional theory —often called the school of criminal biology—in which the mainsprings of deviancy are sought in the inherited physical and mental makeup of man; (2) psychogenic theory, in which the formation of antisocial character is traced to faulty relationships within the family in the first few years of life; and (3) sociological theory, in which the pressures and pulls of the social milieu produce delinquent and criminal behavior.

Mention should be made of some of the specific theories. The dominating theory in Europe today is still the all-inclusive one which falls into the school of criminal biology. It points to the inheritance of weaknesses or pronenesses toward crime and delinquency (plus pressure from a bad environment).[2] Many variants of this theory have shown up in recent years: The attempt to prove inheritance of proneness through the method of studying criminal twins (Lange);[3] the attempt to identify body-mind types (Kretschmer);[4] the general acceptance throughout Europe in the past 25 years of several criminally-oriented types of psychopaths, based on inherited proneness (according to Kurt Schneider);[5] the attempt to identify and explain habitual (serious) offenders as contrasted with occasional offenders or offenders of opportunity, according to early onset which in turn points to inheritance of proneness (Irwin Frey);[6] the specification of the mesomorphic somatotype (muscular) as the type of constitution which is most usually related to delinquency (first according to William Sheldon [7] and later to the Gluecks).[8]

[2] Franz Exner, *Kriminologie.* Berlin, 1949, pp. 115-120.

[3] Johannes Lange, *Crime and Destiny,* translated by Charlotte Haldane. New York: C. Boni, 1930.

[4] E. Kretschmer, *Physique and Character,* translated by W. I. H. Sprott. New York: Harcourt, Brace & Co., 1925.

[5] Kurt Schneider, *Psychopathische Persönlichkeiten,* 6th Ed. Berlin, 1943.

[6] Irwin Frey, *Die Frühkriminelle Rückfallsverbrecher.* Basel, 1951, pp. 95-98, 103, 253.

[7] William H. Sheldon, *Varieties of Delinquent Youth.* New York: Harper and Brothers, 1949, p. 727.

[8] Sheldon and Eleanor Glueck, *Physique and Delinquency.* New York: Harper and Brothers, 1956, p. 219.

The psychogenic school probably claims August Aichhorn as its foun-tainhead. According to Aichhorn,[9] faulty development in the first few years of life makes it impossible for the child to control his impulses. The child lingers on as a sort of aggrandizing infant, living in the pleasure principle and failing to develop the reality principle in life. Friedlander [10] indicates that this faulty development in the first few years of life adds up to an antisocial character structure, incapable of handling reality properly. Redl,[11] who is also a disciple of Aichhorn, calls attention to the failure of the child to develop a management system over his im-pulsivity; that is, fails to develop a good ego and super ego.

The sociologists, ever since Ferri [12] (Italy, c. 1885), have been calling attention to bad environmental conditions. This was echoed by Bonger,[13] who placed the blame for disproportional crime and delinquency among the proletariat on the pressures of the capitalistic system. However, the American sociologists in the twenties pointed to conditions of social or community disorganization, rather than factors related to poverty. They became engrossed with identifying the location and characteristics of high delinquency areas of the city, specifying family disruption and conflict instead of broken home, and calling attention to the modal im-portance of companionship in delinquency.

It was not until around 1940 that a basic American sociological theory of delinquency and criminal behavior was propounded. This was done by Sutherland and it was called differential association.[14] According to this theory, delinquent or criminal behavior is learned as is most other kinds of behavior—learned in association with others, according to the frequency, intensity, priority, and duration of contacts. Suther-land's theory really is not basically different from the one announced by Tarde [15] 50 years earlier, which regarded criminal behavior as a product of imitation of circulating patterns. Glaser [16] fairly recently proposed differential identification as a substitute for differential association. One takes over the models of behavior from those (reference) groups with

---

[9] August Aichhorn, *Wayward Youth*. New York, 1936.

[10] Kate Friedlander, *The Psycho-Analytic Approach to Delinquency*. New York: International Universities Press, 1947.

[11] Fritz Redl and David Wineman, *Children Who Hate*. Glencoe, Illinois: The Free Press, 1951.

[12] Enrico Ferri, *Criminal Sociology*. New York: Appleton and Co., 1896.

[13] W. G. Bonger, *Criminality and Economic Conditions*, translated by H. P. Horton. Boston: Little, Brown and Co., 1916.

[14] Edwin H. Sutherland, *Principles of Criminology*, 4th Ed. Philadelphia: J. B. Lippincott Co., 1947, pp. 6-7.

[15] Gabriel Tarde, *Penal Philosophy*, translated by R. Howell. Boston: Little, Brown and Co., 1912.

[16] Daniel Glaser, "Criminality Theories and Behavioral Images," *American Journal of Sociology*, Vol. 61, 1956, p. 440.

which one identifies. But this does not have to be a face-to-face or person-to-person identification. (One can identify with the Beatniks without having actual physical contact with them.)

Still more recently Albert Cohen,[17] picking up the lead from Whyte's *Street-Corner Society,* contended that working class boys who turned their backs on middle class virtues and values, found the solution for their status problems in the delinquency subculture of the gang. And most recently of all is the theory propounded by Cloward and Ohlin [18] that urban slum boys gravitate to delinquency subculture when they discover they do not have access to legitimate avenues of success.

## Comment on the Theories

Working backward in commenting on these theories, one might say that Cloward's theory only applies to those forms of delinquency which are part and parcel of the role structure of delinquency subculture. Jackson Toby [19] makes the estimate that this might only be 10 per cent of the whole spectrum of delinquency. Assuming that Cloward's focus is very restricted, his theory does not account for the boys who do not gravitate toward the fighting gang, the criminal gang, and the retreatist groups (drugs). It does not specify that the ones who do gravitate to the three types of subculture have internalized an awareness of inaccessibility to legitimate success goals. It does not indicate that there are degrees of participation in gangs and that delinquency involvement of some members might be nil.

Cohen's theory has somewhat more merit. Somewhere and somehow in the growing-up process, slum boys turn their backs on middle-class values and look to street-corner groups to come to their aid. But Cohen is not able to specify the boys who do or do not turn their back on middle-class virtues and opportunities and gravitate to the street corner. He does not indicate whether only some of the boys in the street corner get involved in delinquent acts, as Shaw and Thrasher did a generation ago. So we have two interesting sociological formulations here, but not much realistic applicability.

Sutherland's differential association theory was meant to be a general theory, applying to the entire spectrum of delinquency and crime, from

[17] Albert K. Cohen, *Delinquent Boys: The Culture of the Gang.* Glencoe, Illinois: The Free Press, 1955, pp. 128-133.
[18] R. A. Cloward and Lloyd Ohlin, *Delinquency and Opportunity.* Glencoe, Illinois: The Free Press, 1960.
[19] Private circulated comment on the Cloward and Ohlin book, 1961.

low to high in the class structure and across the board in personality. The trouble with Sutherland's theory (as well as Tarde's and Glaser's) is that it does not explain who *does* and who *does not* take up with carriers of delinquent patterns or who internalizes and who does not internalize delinquent models of behavior.

Coming now to the contributors to theory in the psychogenic school (Aichhorn, Redl, *et al.*), one should observe that at the most they only occupy a small end of the total spectrum of delinquency and crime. It is granted that there are some individuals whose ego and superego development is too weak or poor to control impulses and to handle ordinary expectancies. But it is not at all clear just which children succumb to or are recipients of faulty socialization in the first few years of life. And it is not clear just which of the children, teenagers, late adolescents, and adults who are supposed to have little control over their impulse system run afoul the laws and regulations of society and those who do not.

One certainly finds it difficult to specify just exactly what the proneness is that is supposed to be the mainspring of serious, habitual, and early-starting offenders (criminal biology). It seems to be a sort of weakness in character. The evidence for the inheritance of proneness is very skimpy and most unimpressive, a sort of unreliable family-tree assessment by clinicians.

William Sheldon was able to specify the different kinds of somatotypes, much more definitely than Kretschmer was able to specify his body-mind types. A group of 200 problem youth in a Boston hostel, according to Sheldon, tended to have mesomorphic (athletic) body types along with several related forms of mental deviancy. The Gluecks discovered that among 500 delinquent and 500 nondelinquent boys the delinquents showed up very much more mesomorphic than the nondelinquents. The mesomorphs were found by the Gluecks to have a higher delinquency potential than other body types. Associated with mesomorphy were strength, social assertiveness, uninhibited motor responses, less submissiveness to authority. While mesomorphy does not explain all of delinquent behavior in the Gluecks' sample, it is certainly associated with a large segment of it and seems to reinforce many of the mental, emotional, and family traits connected with delinquency. Future studies will have to confirm the mesomorphic potential in delinquency.

## Gluecks: 4 to 1 Causal Law

Out of their research on 500 delinquent and 500 nondelinquent boys, the Gluecks [20] proposed a five point causal law. According to this formulation, delinquents are distinguishable from nondelinquents (1) physically, in being essentially mesomorphic; (2) temperamentally, in being restless, impulsive, aggressive, destructive; (3) emotionally, in being hostile, defiant, resentful, assertive, nonsubmissive; (4) psychologically, in being direct, concrete learners; (5) socioculturally, in being reared by unfit parents. This might be looked upon as a 4 to 1 law: four parts individual and one part situational. Items 2, 3, and 5 were chosen from among more than 100 overlapping traits, which distinguished delinquents from nondelinquents. The use of more sophisticated statistical methods would have enabled the Gluecks to find the two or three components within this maze of overlapping items which basically differentiate the delinquents from the nondelinquents. Nevertheless, the 4 to 1 causal law still stands as one of the few formulations which is worth attempting to confirm, qualify, or disprove by more rigorous research methods in the future. The law covers most of the spectrum of juvenile delinquency as we know it in the United States, certainly insofar as the full spectrum is represented by 500 boys from Boston who had been committed by juvenile courts to state schools in Massachusetts for delinquency.

## Ingredients of Inner and Outer Containment

In contrast to the buck-shot approach of the Gluecks, that is shooting out in all directions to explore and discover, containment theory seeks to ferret out more specifically the inner and outer controls over normative behavior. It is attempting to get closer on the target of delinquency and crime by getting at the components which regulate conduct.

Inner containment consists mainly of self components, such as self-control, good self-concept, ego strength, well-developed superego, high frustration tolerance, high resistance to diversions, high sense of responsibility, goal orientation, ability to find substitute satisfactions, tension-reducing rationalizations, and so on. These are the inner regulators.

Outer containment represents the structural buffer in the person's immediate social world which is able to hold him within bounds. It consists

[20] Sheldon and Eleanor Glueck, *Unraveling Juvenile Delinquency.* New York: The Commonwealth Fund, 1950, pp. 281-282.

of such items as a presentation of a consistent moral front to the person, institutional reinforcement of his norms, goals, and expectations, the existence of a reasonable set of social expectations, effective supervision and discipline (social controls), provision for reasonable scope of activity (including limits and responsibilities) as well as for alternatives and safety-valves, opportunity for acceptance, identity, and belongingness. Such structural ingredients help the family and other supportive groups contain the individual.

Research will have to ferret out the one or two elements in inner and outer containment which are the basic regulators of normative behavior. Undoubtedly in the lists cited above there are items which, if present, determine the existence of other items and cause most of the regulation of conduct. Likewise, research must indicate the way in which the inner and outer regulatory systems operate conjointly. How much self-strength must be present in a fluid world with very little external buffer? How much weakness in self-components is an effective external buffer able to manage?

## Supporting Research

The research and observations so far which give support to containment theory are the following:

1. According to Albert J. Reiss,[21] as a result of a study of Chicago delinquents who failed and succeeded on probation, the relative weakness of personal and social controls accounts for most cases of delinquency. Reiss found, however, that the personal controls had more predictive efficiency than the social controls as far as recidivism was concerned.

2. Nye [22] presented evidence to the effect that trends toward delinquent behavior are related to four control factors: (a) direct control which comes from discipline, restrictions, punishments; (b) internalized control which is the inner control of conscience; (c) indirect control which is exerted by not wanting to hurt or go against the wishes of parents or other individuals with whom the person identifies, and (d) the availability of alternative means to goals. Nye contends that his social control theory should not be applied to compulsive behavior or the behavior influenced by delinquency subcultures. He feels that the more indirect control is effective, the less

---

[21] Albert J. Reiss, Jr., "Delinquency as the Failure of Personal and Social Controls," *American Sociological Review*, Vol. 16, 1951, pp. 196-206.

[22] F. Ivan Nye, *Family Relationships and Delinquent Behavior*. New York: John Wiley and Sons, Inc., 1958, pp. 3-4.

need for direct control; the more internalized control is effective, the less need for any other type of control.

3. Reckless and Dinitz [23] found that a favorable concept of self insulated 12-year-old boys in the slum against delinquency, including perceptions about self, companions, home, and school. A poor concept of self, including perceptions that one is likely to get into trouble, his friends are in trouble, his family and home are unsatisfactory, that he will not finish school, and so on, was associated with delinquency vulnerability in 12-year-old slum boys. Four years later, followup contact revealed that the good self-concept group had pretty much held the line and the favorable direction, while the poor self-concept group had gravitated in unfavorable directions, 35 per cent being involved with the law three times on an average. Reckless and Dinitz look upon a good or poor self-concept as an internalization of favorable or unfavorable socialization.

4. As a result of his observations on hyperaggressive, hostile children, Redl [24] identifies 22 functions of the ego in managing life situations. He conceives of the ego as the manager in the behavior control system, while the superego is looked upon as the system which gives the signals to the ego. Redl, as is true of Aichhorn disciples, recognizes, particularly at the extremes, ego shortage and ego strength as well as a sick conscience and a healthy one.

Containment theory points to the regulation of normative behavior, through resistance to deviancy as well as through direction toward legitimate social expectations. It may very well be that most of the regulation is in terms of a defense or buffer against deflection. At any rate, it appears as if inner and outer containment occupies a central or core position in between the pressures and pulls of the external environment and the inner drives or pushes. Environmental pressures may be looked upon as condition associated with poverty or deprivation, conflict and discord, external restraint, minority group status, limited access to success in an opportunity structure. The pulls of the environment represent the distractions, attractions, temptations, patterns of deviancy, advertising, propaganda, carriers of delinquent and criminal patterns (including pushers), delinquency subculture, and so forth. The ordinary pushes are

[23] Walter C. Reckless, Simon Dinitz, and Ellen Murray, "Self Concept as an Insulator against Delinquency," American Sociological Review, Vol. 21, 1956, p. 745; "The Self Component in Potential Delinquency and Potential Non-Delinquency," Ibid., Vol. 22, 1957, p. 569; Simon Dinitz, Barbara Ann Kay, and Walter C. Reckless, "Group Gradients in Delinquency Potential and Achievement Score of Sixth Graders," American Journal of Orthopsychiatry, Vol. 28, 1958, pp. 598-605; Frank Scarpitti, et al., "The 'Good' Boy in a High Delinquency Area: Four Years Later," American Sociological Review, Vol. 25, 1960, pp. 555-558.

[24] Fritz Redl and David Wineman, Children Who Hate. Glencoe, Illinois: The Free Press, 1951, pp. 74-140.

the drives, motives, frustrations, restlessness, disappointments, rebellion, hostility, feelings of inferiority, and so forth. One notices at once that Bonger as well as Cloward fall into pressure theory, while Tarde, Sutherland, and Glaser fall into pull theory.

In a vertical order, the pressures and pulls of the environment are at the top or the side of containing structure, while the pushes are below the inner containment. If the individual has a weak outer containment, the pressures and pulls will then have to be handled by the inner control system. If the outer buffer of the individual is relatively strong and effective, the individual's inner defense does not have to play such a critical role. Likewise, if the person's inner controls are not equal to the ordinary pushes, an effective outer defense may help hold him within bounds. If the inner defenses are of good working order, the outer structure does not have to come to the rescue of the person. Mention has already been made of the fact that there are some extraordinary pushes, such as compulsions, which cannot be contained. The inner and outer control system is usually not equal to the task of containing the abnormal pushes. They are uncontainable, by ordinary controls.

## Seven Tests of Validity

1. Containment theory is proposed as the theory of best fit for the large middle range of cases of delinquency and crime. It fits the middle range cases better than any other theory.

2. It explains crimes against the person as well as the crimes against property, that is the mine run of murder, assault, and rape, as well as theft, robbery, and burglary.

3. It represents a formulation which psychiatrists, psychologists, and sociologists, as well as practitioners, can use equally well. All of these experts look for dimensions of inner and outer strength and can specify these strengths in their terms. Differential association and/or pressure of the environment leave most psychiatrists and psychologists cold and an emphasis on push theory leaves the sociologists for the most part cold. But all of the experts can rally around inner and outer weakness and strengths.

4. Inner and outer containment can be discovered in individual case studies. Weaknesses and strengths are observable. Containment theory is one of the few theories in which the microcosm (the individual case history) mirrors the ingredients of the macrocosm (the general formulation).

5. Containment theory is a valid operational theory for treatment of

offenders: for restructuring the milieu of a person or beefing up his self. The most knowledgeable probation workers, parole workers, and institutional staff are already focusing to some extent on helping the juvenile or adult offender build up ego strength, develop new goals, internalize new models of behavior. They are also working on social ties, anchors, supportive relationships, limits, and alternative opportunities in helping to refashion a new containing world for the person.

6. Containment theory is also an effective operational theory for prevention. Children with poor containment can be spotted early. Programs to help insulate vulnerable children against delinquency must operate on internalization of stronger self components and the strengthening of containing structure around the child.

7. Internal and external containment can be assessed and approximated. Its strengths and weaknesses can be specified for research. There is good promise that such assessments can be measured in a standard way.

Finally, it is probable that the theory which will best supplement containment theory in the future will be "damage theory," according to which a light to dark spectrum of damage produces maladjustment and deviancy. The problem here is to find measures to isolate the less serious and less obvious damage cases and to estimate how far into the middle range of delinquency and crime the lighter impairments go.

SECTION IV

# Family and School Influences
# in Delinquency

PRECEDING articles have emphasized the importance of the family in transmitting values and in shaping the expression of innate drives among young children. The effect of role models that parents consciously or unconsciously place before their children does not end with early childhood. There are deep-seated and continuing results, as Article 14 demonstrates. This careful piece of research analyzes family relationships from five-year records made when certain groups of boys were between the average ages of seven and twelve. Years later, when the boys were adults, their records in crime (or lack of such records) were studied with reference to the parental role models of the early years. A clear picture is achieved of the types of parents whose sons later have a high probability of becoming criminals and of the way in which the influence of one parent may offset the influence of the other.

Somewhat in contrast to Article 14 is number 15, which descriptively comments on the effect of broken homes. Since children usually remain with their mothers if parents are unmarried or separated after marriage, the pertinent broken home is the "female-based household." The need for a parental model of the same sex places the boy in such a household in a peculiarly vulnerable position.

The school is an institution with which all normal children have

169

experience. Its impact on the pre-teen age child is second only to that of the family. As is true of the family, the influence may lead the child into adjustment with social values and expectations, or it may alienate the child. Article 16 reviews current research and opinions of educational leaders that point up both the strengths and weaknesses of public schools with relation to the development of delinquent behavior.

## 14.  The Effects of Parental Role Model on Criminality

Joan and William McCord

Joan McCord is a Research Associate at Stanford University and previously held research positions at Boston University School of Social Work and the Laboratory of Human Development and Laboratory of Social Relations at Harvard University. William McCord (Ph.D. Harvard University) is Associate Professor of Sociology and Assistant Dean of Humanities and Sciences at Stanford University. The McCords are joint authors of articles and of three books: *Psychopathy and Delinquency, Origins of Crime*, and *Origins of Alcoholism*.

Those who are at all familiar with criminology no longer question the importance of the family environment in the causation of crime. Among the many factors in the home which are known to be related to crime are the parents' attitudes toward their children, their methods of discipline, and their attitudes toward society. This last factor, the parental role model—the behavior and attitudes of the parents—is the focus of this paper. Many criminologists have emphasized the importance of the paternal role model in the making of criminals.[1] The aim of this paper is a more detailed investigation of the ways in which paternal role models affect criminality.

The present research is an outgrowth of the Cambridge-Somerville Youth Study, designed by Dr. Richard Clark Cabot for the prevention of

Joan and William McCord, "The Effects of Parental Role Model on Criminality," *Journal of Social Issues*, 14, No. 3 (1958), 66-75. Reprinted with permission of the publisher.

[1] See for example: Healy, William, and Augusta F. Bronner. *Delinquents and Criminals*. New York: Macmillan, 1926; and Glueck, Sheldon, and Eleanor T. Glueck. *Unraveling Juvenile Delinquency*. New York: The Commonwealth Fund, 1950.

delinquency. In 1935, Dr. Cabot and his staff selected 650 lower- and lower-middle-class boys from Cambridge and Somerville, Massachusetts, as participants in the project. Half of these boys were referred to Dr. Cabot as pre-delinquents, and the other half (added to avoid stigmatizing the group) were considered "normal" by their teachers and community officers. The average age of these boys was seven. After interviews, physical examinations, and psychological testing, each boy was matched to another as nearly similar in background and personality as possible. One from each pair (determined by toss of a coin) was placed in a treatment group; the remaining boys constituted the control group.

The treatment program began in 1939 and continued (on the average) for five years. Counselors gathered information from teachers, ministers, parents, and neighbors detailing the backgrounds of each of their boys. More importantly, the counselors repeatedly visited the boys and their families. Although two books have been written which point to the failure of this treatment as a preventive to crime,[2] the comprehensive reports written by the counselors provide a fund of information on the backgrounds of these boys who are now men.

Seventy-two boys who died, moved away from the area, or were dropped from the project near its beginning have been omitted from the present study. For the remaining 253 boys, running records had been kept which depicted each boy as he acted in his family and among his peers. The records describe conversations overheard by the counselors and discussions with the counselors; they report casual and formal interviews with or about the boys and their families.

In 1955 a staff of trained workers read these voluminous case records and recorded data pertaining to the behavior of each boy's parents. Thus, information on family background was based on direct, repeated observations by a variety of investigators, over an extended period of time.

Also in 1955, the names of the subjects and their parents were sent through the Massachusetts Board of Probation. In this way, we learned which of our subjects and which of their parents had acquired criminal records either in Massachusetts or Federal courts. For the purpose of this study, we defined as criminal anyone who had been convicted at least once for a crime involving violence, theft, drunkenness, or sexual violations. We recognize, of course, the deficiencies in this standard: some criminals may escape detection, and a number of cultural variables

[2] Edwin Powers, and Helen Witmer. *An Experiment in the Prevention of Delinquency.* New York: Columbia University Press, 1951; William McCord, and Joan McCord, with Irving Zola. *Origins of Crime,* New York: Columbia University Press, 1959.

intercede between the committing of a crime and subsequent conviction. Nevertheless, as we have argued elsewhere in more detail, we believe that this is the most objective standard available.

The information produced by the Cambridge-Somerville Youth Study enabled a unique longitudinal analysis of the causes of crime: the boys averaged seven years of age when the data were first collected, while their average age was twenty-seven when their criminal records were gathered. Moreover, since all of the boys came from the relatively lower-class, disorganized urban areas, they were all exposed to the delinquent sub-culture described by James Short and Albert Cohen elsewhere in this issue. Since this factor was held constant, we could concentrate our attention on those variables which differentiate among boys living in transitional areas.

In the study of the relation between role models and crime, we focused on three interacting variables in the familial environment of the boys: the role model of the parents, the attitudes of the parents toward the child, and the methods of discipline used by the parents.

The *parental role model* was, of course, our basic variable. Information about this factor was ascertained from two sources. First, the verbatim records kept by the observers contained direct evidence of the everyday behavior of the parents. Second, reports from the Boston Social Service Index and the Massachusetts Board of Probation reported all contacts between the parents and community agencies. We classified each parent into one of three groups: (1) those who had been convicted by the courts for theft or assault or who had spent time in a state or Federal prison; (2) those who, though they were non-criminal by our definition, were known to be alcoholic (many had records for repeated drunkenness) or were sexually promiscuous in a blatant fashion; and (3) those who were neither criminal nor alcoholic nor sexually unfaithful. These we considered as non-deviant. Two raters independently checking the same randomly selected cases agreed on 90 per cent.

In addition, information was gathered concerning the *attitudes of each parent toward the subject*. Previous research has linked parental rejection and crime; consequently, we expected that the influence of the parental role model might well depend on the emotional relation between the child and his parents. A parent was considered "warm" if he or she generally enjoyed the child and showed affectionate concern for him. A parent was considered "passive" if he or she had very little to do with the child. And a parent was considered "rejecting" if he or she gave primarily negative attention to the child. Finally, of course, there were a number of absent parents. (We rated step-parents in families where they had replaced the natural parents.) Using these classifications, three judges agreed in their ratings on 84 per cent of the fathers and on 92 per cent of the mothers in the cases selected at random from the sample.

*Disciplinary methods*, as well as parental attitudes, have often been cited as an important variable in the causation of crime. Since discipline can be regarded as the mediator between parental values and the child's learned behavior, we naturally wished to investigate the importance of this factor. The classification of discipline rested upon a theoretical division between techniques which depended upon the physical strength of the parent for effectiveness, and those techniques which utilized withdrawal of love. Verbal or physical attacks upon the child—beatings, displays of violent anger, and aggressive threats—constituted our "punitive discipline" category. Use of approval and verbal disapproval, reasoning, and withholding privileges were considered "love-oriented" discipline. If both parents regularly used one or the other of these basic methods, we classified the discipline as consistent. If one or both parents were erratic in their discipline or if they disagreed in their techniques, we considered the discipline inconsistent. Only if there was evidence that almost no restraints of any kind were used by the family did we consider the discipline to be "lax." Thus we arrived at five classifications of discipline: 1) consistently punitive, 2) consistently love-oriented, 3) erratically punitive, 4) erratically love-oriented, and 5) lax. Three raters agreed in the classification of 88 per cent of the cases they read.

In our sample of 253 subjects, we found that 45 boys had been raised by criminal fathers, and of these boys 56 per cent had themselves been convicted of crimes. Sixty-nine boys had alcoholic or sexually promiscuous fathers, and of these boys 43 per cent had themselves been convicted of crimes. Of the remaining 139 boys, only 35 per cent had received criminal convictions. These differences are significant at the .05 level.

Clearly, paternal deviance tends to be reflected in criminality among the sons. As a next step, we wished to determine whether paternal rejection of the son aggravated or hindered the boy's tendency to imitate the father. Two conflicting hypotheses appeared reasonable. One might hypothesize that boys would be more likely to imitate or "identify" with their fathers if these fathers were affectionate towards them. (If this were true, the highest criminal rates would appear among boys having criminal, but "warm" fathers.) On the other hand, one could hypothesize that criminality is primarily an aggressive response to emotional deprivation—and that a criminal model serves to channel aggression against society. (If this second hypothesis were true, one would expect the highest criminal rates among boys having criminal, rejecting fathers.) To check which hypothesis was more adequate, we held constant the fathers' attitudes toward their sons and found the following pattern:

## TABLE 1

### PER CENT CONVICTED OF CRIMES

| Father's Attitude Toward Boy | Father's Role Model | | |
| | Criminal | Alcoholic or Promiscuous | Non-deviant |
| --- | --- | --- | --- |
| Warm | (N: 13) 46 | (N: 15) 27 | (N: 67) 33 |
| Passive | (N: 6) 50 | (N: 15) 40 | (N: 16) 13 |
| Rejecting | (N: 13) 85 | (N: 25) 60 | (N: 30) 40 |

(Absent fathers and 8 about whom there was inadequate information are omitted.)

This analysis suggests that *both* paternal rejection and a deviant paternal model tend to lead to criminality. Holding constant rejection by the father, sons of criminals had a significantly [3] higher incidence of criminality than did sons of non-deviants. Holding constant paternal criminality, subjects raised by rejecting fathers had a signficantly higher rate of criminality than did those raised by warm or passive fathers. *Criminal rates were highest among paternally rejected boys whose fathers were criminal.*

What effect does the mother's attitude have on the boy's tendency to imitate his father's behavior? One would naturally assume that rejecting mothers would have a relatively high proportion of criminal sons. Two theories might account for this expected result: either maternal rejection tends to "push" a boy toward greater closeness with his father, or maternal rejection increases aggression and a criminal role model channels aggression against society. Because the criminal rates for sons of passive women approximated those for maternally rejecting women, the second explanation seems more adequate:

## TABLE 2

### PER CENT CONVICTED OF CRIMES

| Mother's Attitude Toward Boy | Father's Role Model | | |
| | Criminal | Alcoholic or Promiscuous | Non-deviant |
| --- | --- | --- | --- |
| Warm | (N: 27) 41 | (N: 45) 42 | (N: 102) 28 |
| Passive | (N: 6) 83 | (N: 4) 25 | (N: 12) 50 |
| Rejecting | (N: 9) 89 | (N: 19) 53 | (N: 19) 53 |

(Absent mothers and 2 about whom there was inadequate information are omitted.)

[3] Tests of significance were two-tailed, using P < .05 as the minimum standard for asserting significance.

The importance of maternal warmth to the process of gaining acceptance of the rules of society can be seen in Table 2. Even among boys whose fathers presented non-deviant role models, absence of maternal warmth resulted in significantly higher criminal rates.

From this analysis we conclude: (1) Maternal affection decreases criminality, while maternal rejection or passivity increases criminal tendencies. (2) The criminal-producing effect of a criminal role model is aggravated by absence of maternal warmth. The combination of a criminal father and a passive or rejecting mother is strongly criminogenic.

Next, we investigated the effects of disciplinary methods upon the child's tendency to imitate his father's behavior. One of the questions we had in mind concerned the conscious values of criminal fathers. Assuming that discipline accorded with conscious values, we could test the nature of these values through analysis of the interrelationship of discipline and role model. If the conscious values of criminals supported criminality, one would anticipate that the highest criminal rates would occur among sons of criminals who were disciplined consistently. If the conscious values of criminals supported the non-criminal values of society, however, one would expect relatively low criminality among this group.

A second question we hoped to answer dealt with the relative effectiveness of punitive as opposed to love-oriented techniques in the prevention of criminality. While the evidence generally supports the theory that love-oriented techniques have superior effectiveness in transmitting the values of society, we wished to check the relationship of disciplinary technique to criminality among our sample of (largely) lower-class subjects who were exposed to a deviant subculture.

The figures which help to answer both of these questions are presented in Table 3.

### TABLE 3

#### PER CENT CONVICTED OF CRIMES

| | Father's Role Model | | |
|---|---|---|---|
| Discipline | Criminal | Alcoholic or Promiscuous | Non-deviant |
| Consistent: | | | |
| Punitive | (N: 2) 0 | (N: 1) 100 | (N: 11) 18 |
| Love-oriented | (N: 11) 18 | (N: 8) 25 | (N: 41) 29 |
| Erratic: | | | |
| Punitive | (N: 17) 76 | (N: 26) 54 | (N: 41) 44 |
| Love-oriented | (N: 3) 67 | (N: 14) 43 | (N: 23) 26 |
| Lax | (N: 12) 75 | (N: 20) 35 | (N: 20) 50 |

Quite clearly, this analysis indicates that the conscious values of criminals support the non-criminal values of society. Of those boys raised by criminal fathers, a significantly *lower* proportion whose discipline had been consistent became criminal. This agrees with the findings of Maccoby, Johnson, and Church reported elsewhere in this issue.

Unfortunately, the distribution according to techniques of discipline permits only very tentative answers to our second question. Although there is a tendency, holding constant erratic administration, for punitive techniques to correspond with higher criminal rates, the difference is not statistically significant. Comparing criminal rates between the two techniques in instances where these were administered consistently, we find a tendency for punitiveness to result in lower criminal rates (though this difference, too, is not statistically significant). The relationship between techniques of discipline and consistency is, however, very strong and may, perhaps, account for some previous findings which have indicated that love-oriented discipline tends to deter criminality.

Our results suggest: (1) Conscious values, even within a deviant sub-culture, support the non-criminal values of general society. (2) Consistent discipline effectively counteracts the influence of a criminal father. (3) Consistency of discipline is more strongly related to transmission of values than is the technique of discipline.

In these analyses of the effect of the paternal role model in the causation of crime, we have seen that the father's criminal behavior, paternal rejection, absence of maternal warmth, and absence of consistent discipline are significantly related to high crime rates. To ascertain the interrelationship among these factors, we computed the criminal rates for each category of familial environment:

## TABLE 4

### PER CENT CONVICTED OF CRIMES

| Father's Role Model | Two Loving Parents, Discipline | | One Loving Parent, Discipline | | No Loving Parent, Discipline | |
|---|---|---|---|---|---|---|
| | Consistent | Erratic or Lax | Consistent | Erratic or Lax | Consistent | Erratic or Lax |
| Criminal | (N: 5) 40 | (N: 8) 38 | (N: 8) 0 | (N: 9) 100 | .......... | (N: 12) 92 |
| Alcoholic or Promiscuous | (N: 5) 40 | (N: 16) 38 | (N: 5) 20 | (N: 28) 43 | .......... | (N: 15) 60 |
| Non-deviant | (N: 29) 28 | (N: 37) 30 | (N: 18) 13 | (N: 30) 37 | (N: 3) 33 | (N: 16) 75 |

(Passive fathers were considered as "loving"; passive mothers were grouped with absent and rejecting women.)

Several interesting relationships emerge from this chart:

1. Boys reared by parents both of whom were loving were generally

not criminal. In this group of boys, neither the paternal role model nor disciplinary methods bore a significant relation to crime.

2. Boys reared in families where only one parent was loving were strongly affected both by methods of discipline and by the paternal role model.

3. In families where neither parent was loving, the crime rate reached a high level regardless of the paternal model.

4. Among subjects whose discipline had not been consistent, parental affection seemed to have a stronger influence on criminality than the paternal model. Holding constant paternal criminality, crime rates among sons of two loving parents were significantly lower than for those who had only one or neither parent loving.

Thus, we see that consistent discipline or love from both parents mediates against criminality, whereas absence of parental love tends to result in crime. The paternal role model seems to be most crucial for boys who are raised by only one loving parent and whose discipline is not consistent.

Theoretically, one might assume that the father's role model would be more important than the mother's in determining the criminal behavior of the sons. In the above analyses, we have not considered the influence of the mother's role model. Yet criminal rates, computed on the basis of the mother's role model, indicated that this might be a critical variable.

Fifteen of our subjects had mothers who were criminal, by our definition, and of these boys 60 per cent had themselves been convicted of crimes. Thirty boys had mothers who were alcoholic or promiscuous, and 67 per cent of these boys had received criminal convictions. Of the remaining 208 boys, only 36 per cent had criminal convictions. These differences are significant at the .01 level.

The interaction of the mother's and father's role model can be seen clearly in Table 5. In this table mothers who were criminal, alcoholic, or promiscuous are grouped together as "deviant."

### TABLE 5

#### PER CENT CONVICTED OF CRIMES

| Mother's Role Model | Father's Role Model | | |
|---|---|---|---|
| | Criminal | Alcoholic or Promiscuous | Non-deviant |
| Deviant | (N: 16) 88 | (N: 17) 59 | (N: 12) 42 |
| Non-deviant | (N: 29) 31 | (N: 52) 42 | (N: 127) 34 |

If either the mother or the father was non-deviant, crime rates were not significantly related to the role model of the other parent. Yet, if the mother was deviant, crime rates varied significantly according to the father's role model; and if the father was criminal, the mother's role model seemed to be strongly influential in determining the behavior of the son.

As a summary of these many factors which mediate between the parental role model and criminality, let us see in Table 6 the interrelationships of these variables as they affect criminality:

## TABLE 6

### PER CENT CONVICTED OF CRIMES

| Parental Role Model | Two Loving Parents, Discipline | | One Loving Parent, Discipline | | No Loving Parent, Discipline | |
|---|---|---|---|---|---|---|
| | Consistent | Erratic or Lax | Consistent | Erratic or Lax | Consistent | Erratic or Lax |
| Father Criminal; Mother Deviant | (N: 1) 100 | (N: 3) 100 | (N: 1) 0 | (N: 4) 100 | .......... | (N: 7) 86 |
| Father Criminal; Mother Non-deviant | (N: 4) 25 | (N: 5) 0 | (N: 7) 0 | (N: 5) 100 | .......... | (N: 5) 100 |
| Father Alcoholic or Promiscuous; Mother Deviant | (N: 1) 0 | (N: 1) 0 | (N: 1) 0 | (N: 5) 60 | .......... | (N: 9) 78 |
| Father Alcoholic or Promiscuous; Mother Non-deviant | (N: 4) 50 | (N: 15) 40 | (N: 4) 25 | (N: 23) 39 | .......... | (N: 6) 33 |
| Father Non-deviant Mother Deviant | (N: 3) 33 | (N: 4) 25 | (N: 1) 0 | (N: 2) 50 | .......... | (N: 2) 100 |
| Father Non-deviant; Mother Non-deviant | (N: 26) 27 | (N: 33) 30 | (N: 17) 18 | (N: 28) 36 | (N: 3) 33 | (N: 14) 71 |

This final analysis regarding the relationship of the paternal role model to criminality suggests several conclusions:

1. If the father is criminal and the mother is also a deviant model, criminality generally results regardless of parental affection.

2. If the father is criminal but the mother is non-deviant, and only one parent is loving, consistent discipline apparently deters the son from becoming criminal.

3. If the father is criminal but the mother is non-deviant (holding discipline constant), parental affection seems to be crucial: two loving parents apparently counteract the criminogenic force of a criminal father.

4. If the father is criminal and both parents are loving, the mother's deviance greatly increases the likelihood of criminality.

To put these conclusions regarding the influence of a criminal father in another form, one could say that the son is extremely likely to become criminal unless either (a) both parents are loving and the mother is non-deviant, or (b) parental discipline is consistent and one parent is loving. *Twenty-four of the twenty-five boys whose fathers were criminal and whose backgrounds evidenced neither of these mitigating circumstances had criminal records as adults.*[4]

## Summary

This paper, an outgrowth of a larger longitudinal study of the causes of crime, has been concerned with the effects of the parental role model on crime. Over a five year period, observations were made of the day-to-day behavior of 253 boys and their families. These observations are relatively valid, for the investigators had no chance of learning the eventual outcome of their subjects' lives. Twenty years later, the criminal records of these boys, now adults, were examined. The backgrounds of the men were independently categorized and compared to their rates of crime. All of the men came from relatively lower-class, urban areas; thus one major factor in the causation of crime, the influence of a delinquent sub-culture or tradition, was held constant.

The following conclusions emerge from this paper:

1. The effect of a criminal father on criminality in the son is largely dependent upon other factors within the family.

---

[4] Although the distribution of other factors among alcoholic or promiscuous fathers is quite poor, we may perhaps stretch the evidence to suggest that paternal alcoholism and promiscuity are not nearly so criminogenic as popular literature would have us believe.

2. If paternal rejection, absence of maternal warmth, or maternal deviance is coupled with a criminal role model, the son is extremely likely to become criminal.

3. Consistent discipline in combination with love from at least one parent seems to offset the criminogenic influence of a criminal father.

4. The conscious values, even among criminals, seem to support the non-criminal norms of society. These conscious values are transmitted through consistent discipline.

More generally, we conclude:

First, the old adage, "like father, like son," must be greatly qualified —at least when one is talking about criminality. Children imitate their father's criminality when other environmental conditions (rejection, maternal deviance, erratic discipline) tend to produce an unstable, aggressive personality.

Second, in terms of crime, it seems fallacious to assume that sons imitate their criminal fathers because they have established an affectionate bond with the fathers and "identify" with them. Rather, it would appear that rejection by the father creates aggressive tendencies in the child who, having witnessed a criminal model in childhood, tends to channel aggression into criminal activities.

Third, again in terms of crime, the parents' conscious values can affect the child's behavior if these values are impressed upon the child by consistent discipline. Even though the actual behavior of the parent contradicted his conscious values, the consistently disciplined son tended more often to follow the expressed values, instead of the behavior, of the parent. This finding opposes those who maintain that children will follow their parents' values only if the parents' actions reinforce their values.

Thus, this study casts serious doubt on some of the more popular opinions concerning the causes of crime.

# 15.  The Broken Home

## William C. Kvaraceus

The records of the author and of Miller, who is cited in the article, are given with Article 5.

*Female-based Household.* Walter B. Miller [1] has identified a prevalent type of household unit in lower-class communities that frequently takes the form of a female-based household. This type of family unit has been described as "one in which a male acting in the 'father' role is either absent from the home; only sporadically present; or, when present, only minimally or inconsistently involved in the support and raising of children." In this type of household one frequently finds a grandmother (or other female relatives) and one or more daughters who are child bearing. Frequently associated with this type of household is the "serial monogomy" mating pattern in which the child-bearing female lives with a succession of mates or temporary "husbands." This type of female-based household represents a fairly stabilized form of household in many societies. It is much more common in large urban centers than most people suspect. Miller has estimated that between 25 and 50 per cent of all household units in lower class urban neighborhoods, particularly in and around the larger housing projects, fall into this category. This household pattern is prominent in the lower-class Negro urban community. It has many implications for the psychological and social growth and development of youngsters who are reared in such a home setting.

The psycho-social implications of the female-based household point to a number of hazards to healthy growth and development of children and youth. Lacking a positive father figure, a young son living in such a family may experience more than the ordinary amount of difficulty in personality growth, especially when trying to resolve the Oedipal phase of the growth process. At the same time the presence or the shadow of an inadequate, negative, or unsuccessful father figure may constantly beam the conflicting messages: "Don't be a bum like your father"; "All

William C. Kvaraceus, "The Nature of the Problem of Juvenile Delinquency in the United States," *Journal of Negro Education*, 28 (Summer, 1959), excerpt from pp. 195-196. Reprinted with permission of the publishers of the *Journal*.

[1] Walter B. Miller. "Implications of Lower Class Culture for Social Work," *The Social Service Review*, 33: No. 3, September, 1959.

men are no good." What is presented here is a model for non-identifica-
tion with the attendant problem of overt rejection or disassociation of the
male-parent figure. This is particularly true of Negro households as the
Elmira report[2] points out. In the dearth of positive male figures as
found in older brothers or male kin, the Negro boy (or white lower-class
youngster) may not be adequately sustained even by the traditional
matriarchal family in which the mother plays the male role as well
as she can. He may need to turn to his street-corner group and seek
his male identification through this association. In testing and proving
his maleness he may engage in feats and episodes that involve norm-
violating behavior that brings him to the attention of an official agency or
authority. Since personality formation rests heavily upon identification
with the appropriate parental figure, the preponderance of the female-
based household, as Miller has pointed out, may have special significance
in the higher delinquency rates of lower-class culture.

# 16. The Schools and the Problems of Delinquency: Research Studies and Findings[1]

## Bernice Milburn Moore

The author, who holds the degree of Doctor of Philosophy from
the University of North Carolina, is Assistant to the Director, The
Hogg Foundation for Mental Health, University of Texas. She also
holds the position of Consultant in Home and Family Education,
Texas Education Agency. She is the author of *Our Concern—Children
and Youth.*

The existence of juvenile delinquency, says Samuel Miller Brownell,
former commissioner for the United States Office of Education and now

Bernice Milburn Moore, *Crime and Delinquency,* 7 (March, 1961), 201-212. Reprinted with the permission of the National Council on Crime and Delinquency.

[2 Aaron Antonovsky and Melvin J. Lerner, "Negro and White High School Youth
in Elmira," *The Elmira Study,* State Commission Against Discrimination of New
York, 1957. Mimeographed, 65 pp.]
    1 Most of this article was adapted from Chapter 5, *Juvenile Delinquency: Re-
search, Theory and Comment,* published (1958) by the Association for Supervision
and Curriculum Development, National Education Association, and was reprinted
by the gracious permission of Robert E. Leeper, editor of publications.
    For an excellent theoretical orientation to juvenile delinquency, see *New Perspec-
tives for Research on Juvenile Delinquency,* 1955, and *Juvenile Delinquency, Facts
and Facets,* 1960, U.S. Children's Bureau.

superintendent of schools in Detroit, proves, in a broad
tion has not been fully successful. He states that edu
for children—the home, school, and church, as well
groups—even in combination have not been able to
in delinquency.[2]

Harrison E. Salisbury, New York *Times* journalist, wrote in his
of articles on "The Shook-Up Generation" that "ever since the novel and
film *Blackboard Jungle,* New Yorkers have been increasingly aware of
the impact of teen-age violence on the educational system."[3]

From an educator of note comes this statement:

> With the rise in juvenile delinquency, the medicine men are once
> again prescribing their favorite panacea. For prevention and cure of
> delinquency, we are advised to "get tough," "go back to the wood-
> shed," "apply the nightstick. . . ." Naturally, the advocates of the
> return to the woodshed are among the severest critics of modern
> programs of education. Their editorial spokesmen satirically deride
> "the bleeding hearts who say education is the answer."[4]

Still another comment is worthy of attention since it comes from Jes-
sie C. Binford, social worker at Hull House for more than thirty years:

> The sad fact is that some of our juvenile court judges and many
> educators agree . . . that the only solution to juvenile delinquency
> is work for our children.
> It does not seem to occur to these that we owe our children an
> education—which is all too little now—and that we must adapt our
> curriculum to the needs of children so that they will *want* to remain
> in school at least until they are 16 years of age.[5]

Available facts, however, have shown that between 95 and 98 per cent
of school-age children are normal personalities, reasonably healthy, and
law-abiding. Of the less than 5 per cent who express their deviation in
delinquency, 95 per cent of the seventeen-year-olds, 85 per cent of the
sixteen-year-olds, and 50 per cent of the fifteen-year-olds are not in
school. In fact, approximately 61 per cent of the delinquents between

[2] Samuel Miller Brownell, "Delinquency—An Important Problem in Education,"
*School Life,* Jan., 1954, pp. 52-53.

[3] Harrison E. Salisbury, reprint from the New York *Times,* March 23-30, 1958, p. 8;
also, New York, Harper, 1958.

[4] William Van Til, "Combating Juvenile Delinquency Through Schools," *Educa-
cational Leadership,* March, 1956, pp. 362-363.

[5] Letter, May 3, 1956. (Letters quoted throughout this article were answers to a
request addressed by the author to members of Discussion Group 57, Tenth Annual
Conference of the Association for Supervision and Curriculum Development, 1955.)

ages of eight and seventeen are out of school.[6] This close relationship etween teen-age youth who are out of school and juvenile delinquency was noted at the May, 1961, conference sponsored by the National Committee on Children and Youth, a follow-up committee established by the 1960 White House Conference. Under a special grant from the Ford Foundation, public school educators and other leaders from fifteen cities were called together to discuss public school dropouts as they affect rates of deviant behavior, unemployment, and other social problems for this age group.

Delinquency, then, according to Brownell, is related to public schools in three ways:

1. Schools may produce delinquency.
2. Schools may help prevent delinquency.
3. Schools may help deal with delinquency through curriculum and activities.[7]

## The Schools as Producers of Behavior Problems

The most startling of these three statements is that the school may contribute to the development of delinquency through offering frustrating experiences, by not maintaining interest, by not releasing tensions built up in other relationships, and by not developing a feeling of satisfaction among youngsters that will keep them from, or move them out of, delinquent behavior.[8]

As factors creating this school failure, Brownell cites poor preparation of teachers for detecting the special needs of children, lack of time for teachers to really know the children they teach, and failure to provide teachers with special assistance in dealing with severe behavior problems.[9]

Howard W. Lane, in remarks made on a symposium of the American Orthopsychiatric Association in 1956, said he had "made a little survey out on Long Island to see what it means to a school child to live in the suburbs." He discovered "five important hazards to a child." The most serious, he indicated, is to be a slow reader. The second is to be a boy, to whom many more symptoms of poor mental health were attributed than to girls. Girls, he said, mature earlier and are easier to have around. The third hazard is to be left-handed, and Lane stated there is no doubt

[6] Brownell, *op. cit.*, p. 52.
[7] *Ibid.*
[8] *Ibid.*
[9] Brownell, *op. cit.*, p. 53.

that "the attention and the little discriminations a 'lefty' experiences chip away at mental health." He admitted reluctance to list the two more "little hazards": a mother being *away from home* a good deal and a father being *at home* a good deal! [10] Lane made the plea that schools must be built and organized to accommodate childlike behavior, and that too few places, including homes, are now available for children to be and to act like children.

In his *Juvenile Delinquency and the School,*[11] William C. Kvaraceus described the Passaic, N.J., child welfare experiment of cooperative action among the school system, the police department, and other agencies dealing with children. He quoted Arthur C. Johnson as having remarked that the delinquent child may be an inescapable headache for the schools, but the schools may be an even greater headache for the deviant child! [12] Moreover, he added that "much of the school data points to a multiplicity of unwholesome, unsatisfactory, unhappy, and frustrating situations in which delinquents are enmeshed. Some schools appear to furnish experiences which are predisposing to aggressive behavior." [13]

Among these experiences is retardation. In reference to this, Kvaraceus stated that one great difference between the general youth population in school and the delinquent is the "rejection and condemnation" of the delinquent because he so often fails to be promoted.[14] Habits of failure and feelings of inferiority are characteristic of delinquency, Kvaraceus continues, and it is no wonder these youth resort to rebellion and flight from the classroom. Truancy and vandalism, too, are more than likely direct protests against defeating experiences in school.[15]

In addition, delinquents themselves gave these reasons for disliking school: clothes which were not as good as those of the other children; being made fun of by the teacher; inability to get along "with the crowd"; being in class with "a lot of dumb clucks"; and discipline for tardiness.[16]

Finally, in a discussion section on juvenile delinquency at the Tenth Annual Conference of the Association for Supervision and Curriculum Development in 1955, a group of school administrators, teachers, social

[10] Howard Lane, "Educational Aspects of Prevention," *American Journal of Orthopsychiatry,* April, 1957, pp. 246-251.
[11] William C. Kvaraceus, *Juvenile Delinquency and the School,* New York, World Book Co., 1945.
[12] *Ibid.,* p. 156.
[13] *Ibid.,* p. 135. See his positive appraisal of these same forces later in this article.
[14] *Ibid.,* p. 140.
[15] *Ibid.,* p. 144.
[16] *Ibid.,* p. 50.

workers, and others added several items to this list of negative forces in the schools: textbooks often too difficult for use or understanding by children from underprivileged families and areas; the problem of keeping in school those children whose parents have no interest in school attendance; the stereotyped subject matter of many high schools; teachers excessively permissive or excessively rigid in control or inconsistent in discipline; and careless gossip among teachers about children who have been in trouble or whose families are in difficulty.[17]

Donald H. Goff, chief, Bureau of Classification and Education, New Jersey Department of Institutions and Agencies, added a different dimension to this discussion. Primarily concerned with "fundamental attitudes of youngsters toward behavior norms," he indicated that if there were one clearly defined set of such norms, the whole problem would be simplified. However, great heterogeneity of population and the impersonality and high mobility of urban living tend to bring about wide differences in what is considered acceptable behavior.

Schools, Goff believes, attempt to teach a single standard of normative values, which brings about a rigidity in what is accepted as normal behavior by children. This creates confusion, because many children or youth are confronted with unreal behavior standards as far as their own home and neighborhood experiences are concerned.[18]

Harry Estill Moore discussed this at some length when he wrote:

> There is, it seems, a double code of morality—one for natives and one for the school people. Just here, it may be speculated, may be a fertile source of rejection of the teacher as "impractical" by youth and adults. Having imposed an abnormal behavior code on the teachers, the community then brands them as abnormal, and views them with suspicion, relegating them to the role of "stranger." [19]

Goff verified this point of view when he wrote that delinquents in training schools seem to tie in the stereotype of "schoolmarm" with the rigidity of middle-class mores as imposed in school. He concluded that the schools are confronted with the problem of consensus "in order to allow for group living," but that this consensus can best be reached through interpersonal relations which are grounded in the recognition of human worth and dignity and not through basing "wrong" or "right" behavior on one particular act. In fact, Goff would like to see how effective a rigidly subject-centered high school program can be in developing appreciation for human worth when compared with a similar

[17] Mimeographed notes, Discussion Group 57, *op. cit.*, p. 2.
[18] Goff, letter, May 4, 1956.
[19] Harry Estill Moore, *Nine Help Themselves*, Austin, University of Texas, 1955, p. 61.

attempt on the part of a school with a modified subject-centered program where interest in the human personality is the core of the whole curriculum.[20]

## School and the Social Delinquent

Bertram M. Beck points out that the "social delinquent" will and can respond to a curriculum especially designed to enrich his experiences and serve as a supplement in cases where there is neighborhood and family deprivation.[21] A telling example of this approach was described by Salisbury in "Operation More."[22] Mrs. Cecile Sands, a member of the Board of Education, insisted that a school especially designed for difficult behavior problems would succeed if it had additional appropriations to get what it really needed in such areas as guidance, psychiatric aid, and afterschool programs. At one such school—an "exceptional 600" school located in Brooklyn—youngsters who normally would be dismissed at 3 p.m. stay under supervision until five o'clock. Average afterschool attendance is about thirty-five—all of them gang members unacceptable to neighborhood community centers. Sidney I. Lipsyte, the principal, says of his school: "Too often it is pictured as a holding operation. We see it as a therapeutic operation." He believes about 90 per cent of his boys become useful citizens, and he refuses to judge their behavior by the standards of the middle-class world.[23]

All-day schools,[24] Beck indicates, are of tremendous importance to the social delinquent since the school furnishes him a "protected environment" for his own safety as well as for his development. Expert male supervision, he points out, is imperative, and the school board has to be ready to accept disruption, property damage, and "different" behavior—as Lipsyte does.

Furthermore, Beck continues, curriculum has to meet cultural differences and class differences, even while teaching values of a larger society. The best teachers of social delinquents, he believes, are men who have grown up in the neighborhood. Therefore, he advocates re-

[20] Goff, letter, op. cit.
[21] Bertram M. Beck, "The School and Delinquency Control," *Annals of the American Academy of Political and Social Science*, Nov., 1955, pp. 60-61.
[22] Salisbury, op. cit., p. 10.
[23] Ibid., p. 10.
[24] See "All-Day Neighborhood Schools," Interim Report No. 13, and "600 Day-Schools" (Proceedings), Interim Report No. 3, New York City Public Schools; Robert M. MacIver, "Juvenile Delinquency," *The Nation's Children* (Eli Ginzberg, ed.), Vol. 3, New York, Columbia University Press, 1960, pp. 88-119.

cruiting potential teachers from high schools located in gang areas and, with scholarships as incentives, training them to teach youth with the same background of social inequities that they themselves had experienced. In addition, teachers in these schools should be paid a premium since this type of teaching takes dedication to a cause as well as to a profession.[25]

Early detection of social delinquents, according to Beck, comes from among those who are truant and those who are retarded in reading. Schools in areas of high delinquency require an extra supply of remedial reading teachers as well as qualified social workers, psychologists, and psychiatrists. When truancy occurs among too many too frequently, the curriculum should be changed forthwith. Schools can do little for the social delinquent without these resources and without working with parents who have no concern about their children's dropping out of school.[26]

A number of years ago Detroit Public Schools tried an experiment which may prove of interest to schools located near colleges and universities. It was part of a larger attempt called "The Detroit School and Community Pilot Project for Reducing Delinquent Behavior," directed by Paul E. Johnson. Among other important phases of this program was the unique effort to bring remedial assistance to a larger number of children in a school where intensive help was already being given to problem youngsters. Nine student teachers from the College of Education of Wayne University served as special tutors for fifth- and sixth-grade children with academic difficulties. One of these teachers worked with children from the first through the fourth grades and gave tutorial aid in penmanship, vocabulary and reading, and arithmetic. Besides these benefits of this "100-hour program" of special help, there were others: the possibility for children with numerous absences to catch up with the class; the concrete aid and personal attention given to "problem children"; the discovery of weaknesses in children's problem-solving abilities; and the provision of remedial help to more children than would have been possible any other way.[27]

Harry Estill Moore has pointed out that delinquents are often exceedingly limited in total experiences available for children and youth in communities. This lack contributes not only to retardation in school

25 Beck, op. cit., p. 62; cf. article by McCandlish Phillips, New York Times, May 22, 1961, p. 33, on a "600" school for delinquent girls: "Its twelve teachers are paid $600 a year above their regular salaries as a kind of academic hazard pay. But, as one of them said, . . . 'only a fool would do it for the money.'"

26 Beck, op. cit., p. 63.

27 A progress report on "The Detroit School and Community Pilot Project for Reducing Juvenile Delinquency" (First Year, p. 16).

but to inadequate socialization in culture as a whole.[28] Schools, therefore, find themselves having to make up for inadequacies in social experience as well as in academic achievement. By this he means that very often, poverty of opportunity on one front or the other will preclude a child's accomplishment of developmental tasks (as Havighurst uses the term).[29]

Notable among the schools which offer special help is the M. Gertrude Godvin School, in Boston. This school proudly reported that, of the 6,000 unmanageable or chronically truant boys sent there over the past twenty years, 84 per cent are now living normal lives as responsible citizens.[30] These boys, under the intelligent principalship of Agnes Lavery, are in a "disciplinary school" where their treatment is not "soft" and where they, with their parents, are taken before the juvenile court judge for a hearing if the rules of the school are repeatedly broken.[31]

Curriculum runs the gamut of needs at Godvin School, from tailoring classes where boys learn to make their own clothes, to preparation of "the best school lunches in Boston" where they learn to cook, to academic subjects where they are brought up to age-grade levels by special assistance in classes with boys of their own age and development. Because the relationship between school truancy and adult crime is exceedingly high (one Massachusetts prison head estimated that 75 per cent of his inmates had been truants), every effort is made to hold the interest of Godvin boys through the curriculum and through a humane and warm approach to their problems.[32]

In 1958, a group of fifty California high-school principals were asked to describe programs in their schools which were related to meeting delinquency problems. As Robert D. Morgans reported, a wide variety of activities was described around the premises that delinquency and lack of success are correlates; that youth in trouble with no strong adult to whom they may turn are apt to become delinquent; and that lack of activities and standards of recognized worth to one's self and one's society may lead to antisocial and delinquent behavior.[33]

Schools reported they were attacking problems of failure by revising their curriculum, providing work experience programs and special

[28] Harry Estill Moore, "Definition of Conditioned Participation" in *Dictionary of Sociology* (Henry Pratt Fairchild, ed.), New York, Philosophical Society Library, 1944, p. 57.

[29] Robert J. Havighurst, *Human Development and Education*, New York, Longmans, Green, 1953.

[30] Mary Handy, "Willingly—to School," *NEA Journal*, Dec., 1955, pp. 544-545.

[31] *Ibid.*, p. 545.

[32] *Ibid.*

[33] Robert D. Morgans, "What California High Schools Are Doing about Juvenile Delinquency," *California Journal of Secondary Education*, Dec., 1958, pp. 461-465.

classes for children of both low and high abilities, by developing faculty attitudes on the importance of success to these youngsters, by praising youth when they succeeded, and by letting the public know of their accomplishments. Effective youth counseling and work with parents were major approaches to meeting youngsters' needs for a strong adult figure. Special emphasis was placed upon attendance counseling and follow-up on absence, youth guidance clinics, youth problem councils of different agency personnel, more use of case conferences, and inservice education of teachers for their own counseling role. Work with parents took the form of discussion groups with trained consultants, and conferences to help strengthen parental relationships with their children.

To combat the feeling of worthlessness, youngsters were offered opportunities to serve their schools and communities through projects of recognized value and dignity; and, through a shift from entertainment programs to those of community welfare, youth could give of their own talents to meet school and community needs. Strong school clubs were formed where everybody had an opportunity for membership. Student government, school committees on "problems" with "problem youth" as members, intramural athletic teams to include all interested boys, community recreation projects, and community-wide youth councils were also reported as school aids.

To develop acceptable standards, high school youth themselves were involved in establishing codes of conduct. Classroom discussions of values were followed up by "character propaganda" campaigns with youth using slogans they had developed. Similar suggestions were offered by Clare C. Walker in her article, "A Positive Approach to Delinquency." [34]

Needless to say, these are but a few examples of school programs effectively meeting problems of delinquents, but they indicate a variety of approaches that seem to have merit.

## The Asocial Delinquent and the School

Teachers, Beck says, must give up their sentimental notions concerning "keeping children out of court" when they come up against the asocial delinquent. Youngsters devoid of conscience are dangerous whether they are victims of *anomie* (normless behavior), are "psychopathic personalities," or have "character disorders." From these youth come criminals who murder wantonly, who, without reason or provocation, attack to maim and mutilate, who seem to be without feelings and

[34] *NEA Journal*, Oct., 1958, pp. 466-468.

conscience. Delay in dealing with them is a hazard, Beck reiterates, and "permissiveness only makes them worse." He feels these deviants should be brought to the attention of official agencies immediately before "tragic delinquency" occurs.

For them, the prognosis is not good. Beck makes it clear that these youth need a highly controlled environment or institutional care both for their own safety as well as for the protection of others. These delinquents, he believes, are in the main too damaged to be allowed to stay in school.[35]

Although criticism was leveled at William Jansen, the former superintendent of schools in New York City, for suspending more than 900 youths during February, 1958, many schoolteachers and administrators reported that it improved conditions in their schools "immeasurably." But others, like Joseph C. Noethen, a district superintendent, indicated that "society is only deferring the payment of its debt" and is "going to have to pay a high interest on it. Kicking the kids into the streets creates wolf packs. Suspension is supposed to have a therapeutic effect. Mass action destroys the therapeutic value." [36]


## Prevention of Delinquency

Robert M. MacIver, director of New York's Juvenile Delinquency Evaluation Project, notes that schools are the most stable social institutions many children ever encounter and the only one which can help them. "Bad as the adolescent may be in school," MacIver points out, "he is better behaved, a better member of society, in school than anywhere else." [37]

From this it would appear that the more children and youth who do stay in school for more years, the greater will be the opportunity to assist the delinquents toward responsible maturity and to contribute to the prevention of delinquent behavior. This, of course, must be within the limits of safety, as pointed out by Beck.

William C. Kvaraceus came up with an unusual approach in a recent article on "The School as a Catalyst in Precipitating Delinquency." [38] He contended that because schools have the longest and closest contact with children, they have an unusual and strategic opportunity to prevent and control delinquency. In contrast to some subcultural settings,

[35] Beck, op. cit., p. 63.
[36] Salisbury, op. cit., p. 9.
[37] Ibid., p. 9.
[38] Elementary School Journal, Jan., 1959, pp. 211-214.

schools are ordered, precise in their demands upon children, and regulated toward "the hard work of learning." They force postponement of goal satisfactions and demand frustration tolerance, self-control, and self-denial with long-run satisfactions in mind. But delinquents or pre-delinquents reach a "near-boiling point" in such an atmosphere, for such "good schools" tend to "bring out or precipitate" aggressive behavior in youngsters whose personal backgrounds in home, family, and community are "negatively charged." Because they do, schools are in the position of being able to locate those who need help, can set up programs of assistance through both their own and community resources, and thereby help prevent or control delinquent behavior. Here, Kvaraceus asserts, the schools, rather than cause delinquent behavior, function as catalysts which serve to locate children in trouble.

Brownell points out that schools also prevent delinquency when they teach each child according to his own abilities.[39] Schools with this approach can find out what sort of person each child is and handle him accordingly. Every child, he stresses, is an important human being and should be treated as such. Brownell believes that schools, because they compensate for home and neighborhood deficiencies, should *strive to keep their students in school.*

Detailing these two statements, Brownell offers four recommendations: 1. Each teacher must have a small enough group of children so he can know and teach them as individuals. 2. Teachers need adequate preparation and must be interested in working with children and youth. 3. Staffs of psychologists, school physicians, and social workers should be on hand in schools to work with special problems. 4. School programs and procedures must be supported by parents and other community leaders if they are to be effective. School programs, out of necessity, should adapt to the differences between fast and slow learners, between shy and aggressive children, and between groups vastly different in experiences, background, and culture. Delinquents are made, not born, Brownell adds. People have to understand the needs of children and spend money to meet them.[40]

Though he approaches his discussion from the opposite pole—the problems of the gifted child—James B. Conant (former president of Harvard) arrives at almost the same conclusion as Brownell. After a study of about fifty high schools "East, West, North and South," [41] Conant wrote:

[39] Brownell, *op. cit.*, p. 53.
[40] *Ibid.*, p. 64.
[41] Carnegie Corporation of New York, *Quarterly*, April, 1959, pp. 1-4.

I am convinced that a satisfactory course of study for the bright boy or girl (the academically talented) can be offered in the public high school which is of a general or comprehensive type. . . . I am further convinced that the students in the comprehensive school derive certain advantages from their school years which are denied to their contemporaries in special schools.[42]

A good guidance system is "the keystone of the arch of public education," he points out, since it is here that aspirations, hopes, abilities, and capacities can be determined and channeled into flexible areas of study to meet the needs and vast differences of young persons. One of the beauties of the comprehensive school, Conant states, is that "late bloomers" may be shifted from one course of study to another. In these schools are opportunities for the intellectually gifted and for the average; for those who wish to pursue academic training to the peak of proficiency and for those who would complete their formal education at the end of high school; for those who will go into business and for those who will become skilled artisans in industry. In certain situations, all youth should share common experiences for the mutual benefit of each.[43]

Public schools of the United States, Bertrand Russell once stated, are the single most powerful agent for "transforming a heterogeneous selection of mankind into a homogeneous nation." This belief that public schools can serve basic democratic principles without slighting individual goals should, Conant says, "hearten a people who care about both the minds and the hearts of their children."[44] And, it might well be added, a people who care even about their delinquents.

To achieve the aims of Brownell and Conant, schools do have special needs. Garry Cleveland Myers points up a human aspect of the problem when he writes that research is needed on "how to establish wholesome restraint or how to balance restraint and love effectively—both at home and at school. Practically all of us agree on the value of love. . . . But love without restraint seems to commit suicide while restraint without love also fails."[45]

Approaching this same problem of the schools and delinquency prevention from an entirely different point of view, F. V. Lehn, principal of the Waukegan Township Secondary Schools, asked his teachers to fill out a simple questionnaire concerning major problems of juvenile

---

[42] *Ibid.*, p. 2. Dr. Conant was chosen to undertake the study of dropouts discussed at the May, 1961, conference of the National Committee on Children and Youth (see p. 202 above).

[43] *Ibid.*, p. 3.

[44] *Ibid.*, p. 4.

[45] Letter, March 15, 1956.

delinquency as they are directly related to the school's educational program. His teachers listed the following: [46]

1. Parental indifference and lack of discipline in the home.

2. Inadequate community recreational facilities and lack of motivation to participate in group activities.

3. Too few high school courses designed for those not academically inclined and in which slow learners may remain interested and succeed.

4. Lack of teachers who have special training and who have the personality to deal successfully with delinquent students.

5. Inadequate foster homes.

6. Lack of training for young people before and after marriage as to their responsibilities—all of which would lead to a better home environment.

7. The bad effect that behavior of delinquents and predelinquents has on other student associates.

8. The disrupting influence of the juvenile "sophisticate" who is allowed to remain in school because he is not a delinquent.

9. Indifference and neglect of spiritual obligations by parents, and the fact that delinquency flourishes even among church youth groups.

10. Violations of the law by adults, which lead to lawlessness among children.

11. Too free use of automobiles by students.

Teachers in secondary schools agree with the findings of researchers and school administrators in regard to delinquency and its related problems. In fact, Beck believes that the only hope of alleviating future social delinquency and neurosis is to educate young persons in high schools in child development, family living, and homemaking, as the teachers of Waukegan have stressed in Point 6 above.[47]

These presentations by American educators state in slightly different terms what Kvaraceus has written of delinquency and the schools in his article, "Preventing and Treating Juvenile Delinquency—Some Basic Approaches," [48] and in his book, *The Community and the Delinquent*.[49] It is becoming possible, he said, to spot delinquency earlier; referral to proper sources of treatment and help contributes greatly to prevention. He insists, as do Beck, Brownell, and Robert L. Sutherland,[50]

---

[46] Letter, April 23, 1956.

[47] Beck, *op. cit.*, p. 64.

[48] William C. Kvaraceus, "Preventing and Treating Juvenile Delinquency—Some Basic Approaches," *The School Review*, Dec., 1955, pp. 477-479.

[49] William C. Kvaraceus, *The Community and the Delinquent*, New York, World Book Co., 1954.

[50] Robert L. Sutherland, *Delinquency and Mental Health*, Austin, Texas, Hogg Foundation for Mental Health, 1959, pp. 1-7.

that child study is an essential for teachers if they are to perform their diagnostic functions successfully and to assist with treatment of youngsters with special problems. He is convinced that no hope exists for the delinquent unless guidance personnel, psychologists, psychiatrists, and psychiatric social workers can be made easily accessible to the individual child through the school and the community. Treatment must be specifically designed to meet *personal, social,* and *environmental* needs of the deviant child—what Kvaraceus calls the community aspect of child study.

As corollaries to the above basic principles, Kvaraceus lists coordination of all community resources for children and money to develop intensive child study and diagnostic programs based on proven scientific knowledge.[51]

## Education in the Home

Salisbury, in his description of home and community situations out of which delinquency grows, discusses the inadequate preparation of parents for homemaking ·and child-rearing.[52] He states that thousands of families were moved into housing projects in New York City without preparation for living in these new kinds of quarters. Moreover, the families who were in the neighborhood prior to the advent of the newcomers were ill-prepared to receive and live with them.

The Dallas Public Schools, in cooperation with the Dallas Housing Authority and the Home and Family Life Division, Texas State Department of Education, have met these two problems by an intensive homemaking education program for adults with many of the education centers located in the housing projects themselves. At these study centers, home economics teachers have developed everything from rudimentary instruction in housekeeping, child care, basic nutrition, sewing, and care of clothing to family and community interpersonal relations. Work has been done with family groups on their own problems as well as with groups of homemakers. This is one excellent example of the coordination of community resources through leadership of the school's home and family life education division.

Kvaraceus stresses that to bridge the gap between home and school, parent education is of paramount importance, not only in the study of children's behavior but also in the total processes of homemaking and

[51] Kvaraceus, *op. cit.* note 48, pp. 478-479.
[52] Salisbury, *op. cit.,* pp. 6-7.

family living. Moreover, parent education includes of necessity actual participation in the learning processes rather than simply listening to "guest speakers." [53]

Robert L. Sutherland, too, writes of the "parent education" teacher:

> This teacher, employed by the public schools, devotes his full time to organizing discussion groups with parents and, through other educational methods, helping parents join with teachers in basing their work with children upon scientific knowledge of the processes of human growth and development.[54]

## Summary

Let us summarize by listing some important areas of school life in which schools play an important role in preventing and handling delinquency: [55]

1. School superintendents can stimulate an interrelationship between the school and the community and can improve the overall school setting and educational program for *all* children, deviant and normal alike.

2. Through teachers, special school services, and administrators, schools must develop competence in evaluating the effectiveness of their own programs by the control of undesirable behavior as well as by grades and promotions.

3. Schools must make every effort to select better-trained school personnel from the school custodian through teachers to the top administrator, persons who are interested in and know how to work with children and youth.

4. Child study by teachers should be a continuing part of their in-service education toward effectively diagnosing behavior problems and making appropriate treatment referrals.

5. An effective guidance program is as necessary to preventing and controlling delinquency as it is to giving maximum opportunity for the "gifted" and average child.

6. The case conference should be more extensively used in the study and treatment of individual children with problems—as demonstrated by the Philadelphia Case Study Committee.

[53] Kvaraceus, *op. cit.* note 49, pp. 252-259.
[54] Sutherland, *op. cit.*, p. 4.
[55] Based on and paraphrased from Kvaraceus, "The Central Role of the Schools," *The Community and the Delinquent,* Chapter 10, pp. 265-317. See also Kvaraceus et al., *Delinquent Behavior—Culture and the Individual* and *Delinquent Behavior— Principles and Practices,* Washington, D.C., National Education Association, 1959.

7. Flexible curriculum and teaching methods are especially necessary in order to maintain interest of and offer satisfaction to youth whose experiences and background are limited by deficiencies in the home and neighborhood.

8. Policies of promotion, grading, discipline, and handling truancy need to be improved to prevent youngsters from developing intense feelings of defeat and inferiority with consequent hostility toward the schools.

9. Cooperation with the home should be continued and expanded through the use of school social workers, through welcoming parents to school for conferences and participation, and through home and family life education programs for parents.

10. Finally, the school has the major responsibility of interpreting its role in delinquency prevention and control to both the board of education and the community, stressing its need of funds to enrich the total school program and to make possible special flexibility of curriculum and service.

SECTION V

# Patterns of Delinquent Behavior

A NUMBER of types of delinquent behavior have been studied to obtain a general picture of the interrelated events that make up the pattern of a specific type. Among adults a given criminal pattern may be highly systematized, with each event falling into order and leading into the next event. Delinquences of juveniles are not so closely organized; nevertheless, chains or webs of events can be found that tend to control behavior once the juvenile has taken the first step. Personal qualities and motivations usually are omitted from the studies, which are of types of delinquency, not of delinquents as persons.

Theories of gang delinquency have been presented in Section II, Articles 7 and 8. In Article 17, the juvenile gang is seen through the eyes of the New York City Youth Board, whose staff has had intensive experience of a practical nature with gangs. It is well known from many studies that children and adolescents much more frequently engage in delinquent behavior in groups than alone. These delinquent groups fall into the general classification of peer groups, generally accepted as normal and valuable types of association for children and adolescents. The problem is not why boys and girls form into peer groups or gangs, but why some peer groups organize their behavior around delinquency.

Article 18 is a careful analysis of car-theft. It distinguishes be-tween two types of car-theft and also makes use of a control group of non-car-stealing delinquents. Article 19 concentrates on van-dalism; Article 20 deals with adolescent sex offenders; and 21 analyzes the use of narcotics among youth. In Article 22, Hill presents juvenile delinquency as a "way of life," closely inter-woven with cultural and social conditions. His analysis brings de-linquency of minority groups, especially Negroes, into the general framework of delinquency causation and dispels any misconception that special racial factors are operative.

## 17.    Peer Group Turned Gang

## Staff of the New York City Youth Board

> The book from which this excerpt is drawn was a cooperative effort of certain staff members of the New York City Youth Board. The direction and preparation of the text were in the hands of Arthur J. Rogers, Deputy Commissioner of Youth Services and Director of Social and Athletic Clubs, assisted by Hugh K. Johnson, Chief, Coun-cil of Social and Athletic Clubs, and Aaron Schmais, Supervisor of this Council. The editor was Donald J. Merwin, Director of Com-munity Relations of the Youth Board.

## Genesis of Peer Groups in the Urban Setting

There is striking variety and much overlapping in the types of peer groupings found in New York City. Often it is difficult to differentiate the delinquent from the non-delinquent group. However, it is possible to place the potentially or actually delinquent group in four major cate-gories.

The first type develops from a particular spot, usually a street corner or a candy store. Here there is a group of friends who have usually grown up together and have been playmates when they were younger. It is a group that will usually hang around, talking, occasionally be-coming engaged in some joint activity. As a rule, this type of group's members are not extremely close to each other, although individuals

*Reaching the Fighting Gang,* New York City Youth Board, New York, 1960, pp. 14-21. Reprinted with permission of New York City Youth Board.

within the group may be good friends. They owe their association primarily to the common use of the corner or store and to their earlier associational relations. As a group, they manifest very little serious anti-social behavior. Their involvement in conflict is rare and in almost all instances is defensive, occurring only after a series of harassments which serve to mobilize them for protection.

A second type of peer group is the club. It is almost always organized around some common interest of the group. It may be a basketball or baseball team that has expanded into a social-athletic club. Usually it is a group, which, in addition to the qualities of the corner peer group, has a common interest in which most of the membership is engaged. While the peer group which remains primarily on the street corner seldom, if ever, uses a social agency, the interest or club-type peer group may do so, depending solely on what the agency can offer. The club type of peer formation may also exist when a conflict group has renounced conflict and has embarked on becoming a social club. The interest in this situation is somewhat differentiated and to a greater degree the members are bound by former ties. These types of peer groups are likewise seldom involved in any serious anti-social acts, although as individuals and sub-groups they do become involved. The possibilities for this type of group to be involved in conflict are more pronounced since they come into contact with organized groups much more. They are not, however, as noted above, organized with a conflict orientation.

A third type is the group in conflict. It is referred to throughout this book as the gang or the street club. This is a peer group which, starting out as either one of the types above or a combination of both, has—due either to considerations of protection or aggression—become involved in conflict with other groups. As a rule it has weapons and an organization designed to carry out its conflict orientation. Anti-social acts are common and are of an individual and group nature. It is important to reiterate that it has as its origin a basic primary peer group formation.

The fourth type is the thoroughly delinquent and pathological grouping. This type of totally committed group is rare and when found is almost impossible to work with. Such a group is usually small in number, four to six, and is frequently located within a conflict group as a clique. Due to its group ties and relationships with the overall gang, some beginning work has been attempted with this type.

In a group where the average membership was 15-16, Ruben was twenty-six, Tong, twenty-four, Bop, twenty-three, and Johnny, nineteen. Ruben the leader of this sub-group, was a young man with extremely sadistic impulses which he vented by spur of the moment initiation rites. Almost any young member was likely to find himself suddenly the victim of an extemporaneous initiation. These took the form of Ruben playing the role of a detective and the youngster playing the role of victim apprehended during a rumble. This provided Ruben with an opportunity of interrogating the victim around imaginary situations with wrong answers, which he alone determined, subjecting the victim to harsh and brutal beatings with his belt. Tong, an extremely disturbed young man, acted as an informer, and while providing guns and ammunition for the gang, would unbeknownst to the group continually alert the Police Department to their activities. His closest associate was Johnny, recently returned from a state mental hospital. Johnny played the role of constantly exhorting the younger group members to defend the honor of the overall gang and was continually berating the group for their sloppy appearance. He himself was very fastidious. However, at parties given by the group extreme care had to be taken not to put Johnny to work in the coat room. Invariably when Johnny worked in the coat room, coats were cut, buttons disappeared, etc. Bop, the fourth member of this group, was a young man who related to all people on an infantile level. He was continually demanding food and drink. If these were not provided with due deference, he frequently passed into uncontrollable fits of rage. As abnormal as was the individual behavior of these members, even more disturbed were their contacts with each other which were filled with betrayals, conspiracy, plots, deceptions, etc.

# High Hazard Neighborhoods

If teenage peer associations are both natural and have very real constructive potentialities, why do some street clubs develop anti-social behavioral patterns? Since anti-social behavior and delinquency have multiple causation, and since each street club is different in a variety of ways, we can at best present a broad statement regarding those factors which have had influence on street clubs.

Negative socio-economic environmental influences, such as overcrowded and inadequate housing, slum dwellings, economic deprivation, lack of adequate recreational facilities, discriminatory practices, parental rejection, adult hostility, community and neighborhood rejection, family and personal disorganization, do much to cause aggressive, hostile behavior on the part of the street club member. He lives in a sub-culture which evidences violence day in and day out. Even though this violence provokes anxiety, fear, and insecurity and represents a personal threat to the individual, he nevertheless accepts it as a standard mode of behavior. Any rejection of this pattern results in a loss of status and accusations of "punking out." In the sub-culture of the street club member, there is an emphasis on gross material values as opposed to moral and spiritual values. Many street club boys look upon the narcotics seller, the pimp, and the local racketeer as idols, and consider as evidence of their success, their big cars, flashy clothes, and ability to spend large amounts of money, to make quick deals, exert power and heap abuse upon persons less powerful than themselves.

The neighborhoods in which these boys grow up are those where not only is adult crime prevalent, but delinquency is presented very early as a norm. They are, in many instances, neighborhoods where these patterns have been handed down from generation to generation. Likewise these are the neighborhoods that, in addition to being mobile with diverse ethnic composition, have become economically depressed and subject to great and serious change. Residents, and particularly youth, in their drive for status in neighborhoods where legitimate means are circumscribed, turn more and more to acquiring status symbolically, in the forms of material and economic goods, and very often illegally.

The street club, which has organized itself out of a sense of dealing with these factors, is particularly susceptible to all these influences. It is through the group that the street club member reacts to the environment in which he lives and finds support for his feelings of anger and frustration. It is within this structure that it is possible for him to gain a sense of identity which is so important. He needs it to avoid overtaxing his limited amount of ego strength. To develop insight or to deal with his personal problems exceeds his feelings of self-esteem and self worth. He rebels through the group against the feeling of nothingness, and through his gang activities employs the mode of behavior accepted in his sub-culture to seek recognition and status though they be negative in substance. Alone he is insecure, frightened and immobilized by anxiety and uncertainty. He is overwhelmed by his own problems. The welfare agencies, schools, and recreation centers occasionally may accept, then reject him because of overt, aggressive behavior.

More and more he turns to the organized conflict group. This is not necessarily done as a pursuit of anti-social behavior, but as a means of dealing with his total environment, in what many times is the only available means.

## Needs That Gang Fulfills

There is a need for further clarification of what belonging to a gang means to a member. Were it solely a matter of protection, or the only grouping available, it would hardly account for the intensity that is characteristic of gang membership. Admittedly there are a host of needs that membership in any such group provides the member. Among these are:

1. His need to convince himself that he is a person of worth;
2. His need for acceptance, belonging and recognition;
3. His need for new experiences, shared interests and ideals;
4. The need for a common support on a peer level in a sub-culture of society toward which tremendous punitiveness, hostility and conflict is directed;
5. The need to possess, to own and control;
6. The need for status in the neighborhood and community in which he lives;
7. The need to identify with something in the sub-culture which symbolizes power, authority and prestige;
8. The need to have an impersonal medium through which he can rebel against environment, both physically and socially; to deal with and express his fears, anxieties, insecurities, as well as those feelings of hostility, aggression and anger;
9. The need for protection from real or fantasized threat;
10. The need for opportunity for sublimating and expressing basic drives;
11. The need for peer group-evolved concepts of equality, justice and control; and
12. The teenage need for symbolic group ceremonies and activities.

## Emergence of the Conflict Group

The great majority of street clubs begin when their members are still very young, perhaps between the ages of nine and eleven, or even younger. Although at this point the groups are still embryonic, the solid base for what becomes the full-fledged gang is being formed. At this age level we find members of the group gathered together naturally in a play group relationship. They come together in the playground, the school, on the stoop, in the cellar, on the sidewalks, and in vacant lots, where they can best meet their associational and recreational needs. In the slum areas from which the majority of our street clubs stem, the members of these play groups may all be residents of the same apartment building, or at least of the same city block. Almost invariably these groups evolve from a common location which historically becomes incorporated as "their block," "their candy store," "their stoop," or "their playground."

It is at this level that the formation of psychic ties begins. These same ties will develop later in the street club, and serve to form the essential core group's relationship to one another. At this stage there are no formal requisites to membership in the play groups above and beyond the need to be accepted, liked, and be alike. These boys are usually from, or identified with, the same class, race, age, and social milieu. Their development is natural and universal at this stage and they are not organized as a group. There are no leadership hierarchies and their activities revolve around common and natural interests and needs of youngsters. These associations with one another are reinforced by the ongoing contact they have with each other in school, in recreation, in the street, through their parents, in the hallways, going to the store, and in all the facets of daily living. As these groups grow older there is considerable movement into and away from the group. The essential membership which will later go on to become the core group of the street club remains intact with continuous contact. As the group members grow and mature, the form of their group association may itself change and transform many times, taking on new interests, falling under the sway of new individuals who move into positions of popularity and leadership.

It is at the age level of ten to fifteen that the environment makes itself intensely felt in these groups. Particular mention must be made of the impingement and influence that the older organized groups in the neighborhood have on these younger natural groups. Like all adolescents, some of these boys are establishing their independence of grownups and are inclined to seek models among the older boys in the neighborhood. Others, because of inappropriate models in their immediate family, seek them outside among older gang members and other neighborhood figures. Here many times they find these older boys organized into conflict groups. This, then, becomes the behavior which the younger boys seek to emulate and from which they derive status. On the other hand, the younger group fulfills the older gang's need to seek out younger natural formations and to enlist them in their own structure as the means of swelling their ranks and increasing their influence in the neighborhoods. They use these boys exploitively as runners, provocateurs, or scouts, perhaps looking towards the future to make certain that these younger groups follow existing patterns. The younger pre-gang groups, faced as they are with the neighborhood influences, struggling for recognition and status, and a means for dealing with a society that they have interpreted as being hostile and rejecting, many times readily adopt the delinquent sub-cultural standards as epitomized by conflict gang groups. As a result, these younger groups may bind themselves into a structured relationship with the older organized gangs as a younger division or as a sphere of influence. They may not make any formalized contract with the older group, and yet form such ties so as to be looked upon favorably by and receive some status from this older group. This younger element will in certain instances, where prestige and status is desired, choose to use the name of the older group. In fact, many incidents of conflict are caused by just such a situation. Whether or not the younger group joins forces in a structured or unstructured way is ultimately unimportant; even if they are not joined, the influence of the older groups in the neighborhood will be felt and have its meaning for younger natural ones. This may be through direct intervention, harassment, protection or the overall climate of gang life in the street.

As the younger group enters into middle adolescence and their world begins to broaden, here again the older groups make a great impact in terms of their seeming mastery over the perplexing problems facing these growing boys. The type of neighborhoods from which they come literally teem with clubs, pre-gang and gang groups. They become a way of life and very few boys, if any, remain outside of the organized clubs' influence. Given so many groups in one area or so many different groups coming together in schools, dances, leagues, or night centers, there are bound to occur differences and conflicts. Many times these are the kind that would occur anywhere in any community, at any level. The difference, however, is that these groups have heard about and witnessed the ways in which countless gangs have resolved their differences. They are well-versed in the folklore of the neighborhood; that is, which group did what, what is the damage, etc., and they take great pride and find satisfaction in relating these episodes. Younger groups that have already become attached in one way or another with dominant conflict gangs meet these disputes in the same way that the older boys have done, advised, helped or taught them. Those natural groups which have remained without direct gang affiliation are often faced with a choice, when they come into contact with a sub-group of a conflict gang; either to protect themselves or to be harassed, bullied, or otherwise abused. Often the choice made is to defend themselves. In forming a conflict group the impetus is usually given by a relatively small number of boys, who, because of the need for protection, influence, and power, accept the fact that these can only be met and realized through the medium of the formal gang structure.

/ In summary, there are a number of bases for the group, gang or street club formation. These are ecological, associational, recreational, historical, and reflect needs for pleasure, power, influence, protection and status. These occur in various combinations depending on the unique environmental, social and cultural conditions at a particular time in relation to a particular place. The nature and function of the street club varies with internal and external needs, as well as with the pressures brought to bear upon the group and individual members. )

## 18.  Boys Who Steal Cars

### Erwin Schepses

> The author has had a long experience with delinquent boys, as Director of Social Service, New York State Training School for Boys at Warwick, and as Director of Social Services, Boys' Training Schools Home Service Bureau, New York State Department of Social Welfare. He has published other articles in the field of delinquency.

The growing motorization of the countries of the Western world has led to an increase of car thefts. This has been observed in this country, Great Britain, France, Sweden, West Germany, to name only a few countries for which figures are readily available.

To give a few examples, the annual crime figures of the Police Department of the City of New York for 1958, as reported by the New York *Times* of February 2, 1959, show that in that year there were 13,718 complaints of auto theft. This figure represented 14 per cent of all complaints of felony-type offenses. Dr. Gibbens gives the figures of car thefts per 100,000 population for London and several Scandinavian cities for the years from 1950-54.[1] The increase, particularly in Swedish cities where it amounts to more than 100 per cent during the period indicated, is quite striking.

Erwin Schepses, "Boys Who Steal Cars," *Federal Probation*, 25 (March, 1961), 56-62. Reprinted with permission of the publisher.

[1] "Car Thieves," *British Journal of Delinquency*, 1958, Vol. VIII, No. 4, p. 258.

What is perhaps even more significant and disturbing is the extent to which young people are involved in car thefts. Our sources of material, unfortunately, operate with various age groups. The New York City police report for 1958 lists arrests of young people under 16 years of age. There were 1,011 arrests for car thefts in this age group. Since total arrests for offenses, which would have been felonies if committed by an adult, amounted to 5,836, arrests for car thefts contributed 17.3 per cent of the total. It may be interesting to note that from 1957 to 1958 arrests of offenders under 16 for car theft increased by 24.8 per cent and total arrests by 25.1 per cent. In 1954, Bloch and Flynn [2] reported 57.6 per cent of all persons arrested for car thefts were under 18. The *Uniform Crime Reports* of the Federal Bureau of Investigation for 1958 state that in that year, 30,240 persons were arrested in the United States for car theft. Of these, 5,308 (17.6 per cent) were 16 years old; 5,666 (18.7 per cent), 15 years old; and 5,018 (16.6 per cent), under 15. [3]

In European countries, too, the very large number of adolescents involved in car thefts has caused alarm. [4]

For our purpose, it suffices to say that car thefts present a grave problem quantitatively, and that the problem is even more serious because of the large number of young people participating in this activity.

The question we are trying to answer is this: What kind of a person is the boy involved in auto theft? Does he differ from other young delinquents who have committed antisocial acts of a different nature, and if so, in what respect? Does he come from a different environment —cultural, economic, familial? What are the chances of his rehabilitation?

Our investigation is based on record material of the New York State Training School for Boys at Warwick, New York, generally known as Warwick. At the time of this study—the 3 years from January 1, 1952 to December 31, 1954—this institution admitted boys on court commitment from New York City and from rural Orange county where the school is located. These boys were 12 to 16 years old on admission with the exception of a few who were over 16. [5]

---

[2] Herbert A. Bloch and Frank T. Flynn, *Delinquency*, Random House, New York, 1956, p. 43.

[3] *Loc. cit.*, p. 93.

[4] For Germany: Franz Exner, *Kriminologie*, 3rd edition, 1949, p. 98. For France: Dr. P. Parrott, J. Ribettes, and Mlle. A. M. Mabille, "Le Vol de Voiture Chez l'Adolescent," *Sauvegarde de l'Enfance*, May 1957, p. 665 seq., 669. Neither source gives statistical material.

[5] This was technically possible since under New York State Law a delinquent child may be committed to a training school after he has reached his 16th birthday,

The primary group studied consisted of all boys—81 in number—who came to the Training School from January 1952 to December 1954 with a history of involvement in one or more car thefts. We selected this period because this gave us an opportunity to evaluate the boys' adjustment under aftercare, which, at that time, was handled by a department under the supervision of the Training School,[6] and the reasons for their ultimate discharge from aftercare. None of the boys of the car-theft group and only 8 boys of the control group are still on parole.

In addition to the car-theft group, we have studied a control group of 81 boys, the same number who did *nct* have a record of stealing automobiles. These boys were selected at random from the total number admitted to the institution in 1952, 1953, and 1954, with one important qualification. Since the racial affiliation emerged as an important distinguishing quality between the two groups,[7] it was necessary to let the control group reflect the racial composition of the total admissions during the 3-year period of the study. In 1952, 1953, and 1954, Warwick admitted 1,408 boys. A total of 572 were white (40.6 per cent), 630 were Negro (44.8 per cent), and 206 were Puerto Ricans (14.6 per cent). The control group, accordingly, was divided in the same proportion, with 33 whites, 36 Negroes, and 12 Puerto Ricans. Apart from this, there has been no further manipulation of the control group sample.

It may also be helpful to point out that at Warwick, Puerto Ricans are counted as a group, separately from either whites or Negroes. They are different culturally; many of them have only a limited command of the English language, and their adjustment difficulties are reflected in their specific delinquency histories.[8]

The records used by us for our investigation contain court material

---

provided the offense was committed prior to the 16th birthday. One boy in the control sample who was over 16 came to Warwick from a correctional institution for which he was considered to be too immature. There were no children under 12 in our samples who, technically, could have been committed to the Training School under certain conditions.

[6] Since January 16, 1956, parole supervision is administered by the Home Service Bureau, an independent agency, under the New York State Department of Social Welfare. It serves not only Warwick, but several of the training schools which have been established since.

[7] See William W. Wattenberg and James Balistrieri, "Automobile Theft: A 'Favored Group' Delinquency," *American Journal of Sociology*, Vol. 57, p. 575 et seq., 1952, a study which deals with car thefts committed by adolescents in Detroit, Michigan, in 1948.

[8] See Erwin Schepses, "Puerto Rican Delinquent Boys in New York City," *Social Service Review*, March 1949, p. 51 seq.; Martin B. Dworkis (Editor) *The Impact of Puerto Rican Migration on Governmental Services in New York City*, New York University Press, 1957, p. 54 seq.

such as probation officers' reports, evaluations by the court clinic and professional personnel at Youth House (detention center in New York City), social histories compiled after the boy's arrival at the Training School; an evaluation by the Training School psychiatrist; results of intelligence, achievement, and personality tests; reports of social workers, teachers, house parents, and other staff members working with the boys; summaries of reviews held by classification committees; notes of aftercare workers on a boy's parole adjustment, and, finally, the application for discharge and the reason given.

## "Pure" and "Mixed" Auto Theft Groups

When we studied the boys involved in auto theft we soon found it was necessary to divide them into two groups. Twenty-two of the boys never engaged in any delinquent activity but stealing automobiles, and 59 had committed antisocial acts of various nature in addition to stealing cars. It will be shown that these two groups—the "pure" and the "mixed"—differed from each other in many respects.

We have already indicated that race appeared to be an important factor in the cases studied by us. More than half of the boys were white, about one-third Negro, and the rest Puerto Ricans. Within the "pure" group of 22 boys the percentage of white boys was even higher. There we found 13 white boys (59.1 per cent), 7 Negro boys (31.8 per cent), and only 2 Puerto Ricans (9.1 per cent). The "mixed" group had 31 white boys (52.5 per cent), 22 Negroes (37.3 per cent), and 6 Puerto Ricans (10.2 per cent). The control group, as mentioned above, contained 40.6 per cent whites, 44.8 per cent Negroes, and 14.6 per cent Puerto Ricans. The difference in racial composition is not quite so striking as in the Detroit group dealt with by Wattenberg and Balistrieri [9] where 230 out of 260 arrested for auto theft were white (88.5 per cent) and only 30 nonwhite (11.5 per cent). But then we were dealing with a younger group than the one studied in Detroit. Wattenberg and Balistrieri have pointed out that the boys they studied tended to be older, rarely below 14.[10]

Why white boys steal more cars than nonwhites cannot be explained without an attempt at evaluating this phenomenon as a whole. The explanation of the Detroit police quoted by Wattenberg and Balistrieri that Negro boys would arouse suspicion sitting behind a wheel and

[9] p. 576 l.c.
[10] p. 577 l.c.

therefore refrain from stealing automobiles, being afraid of arrest, is obviously too superficial to satisfy our curiosity. We will return to this question later.

## Age at Time of First Court Appearance, Intelligence, and Reading Ability

We have reliable data on the ages of our boys at the time of their first court appearance, their intelligence, and their reading ability. The boys of the "pure" group, as a rule, started their delinquent career considerably later than boys who had either committed other offenses in addition to auto thefts or had not been involved in car stealing at all. Boys in the "pure" group, with rare exceptions, are over 14 years old when they appear for the first time in court. We found that about one-third of the boys in the "mixed" group as well as those in the control group were known to the Children's Court before they were 14. Twelve boys in the "mixed" and 15 in the control group were under 12 years old at the time of their first court appearance.

The boys in the "pure" group are not only older, but are also more intelligent than their nonspecialized or non-car-stealing contemporaries. In our sample less than 10 per cent of the boys in the "pure" group were mentally deficient or of borderline intelligence, and 50 per cent were of average mental endowment. Close to 30 per cent of the boys in the "mixed" group as well as in the control group, had I.Q.'s below 80, placing them in the borderline or mentally deficient category, and only about 40 per cent in both groups, "mixed" and control, tested average.

As far as reading is concerned, the well-known retardation of delinquent boys in this field [11] was noticeable in all three groups. Still, 50 per cent of the "pure" group could read above 6th grade. The comparable figures for the "mixed" group and the control group were 32.2 per cent and 28.4 per cent, respectively. On the other hand, there were only 4 nonreaders out of 22 (18.2 per cent) among the "pure" group who read below 3rd grade, while the "mixed" group had 18 out of 59 (30.5 per cent), and the control group 30 out of 81 (37 per cent).

---

[11] See e.g., Sheldon and Eleanor Glueck, *Unraveling Juvenile Delinquency*, The Commonwealth Fund, New York, 1950, p. 140.

## Social Background

A few words should be given about the background of the boys. The broad ethnic groupings have been mentioned before. At this point, we want to answer the question (1) whether the economic situation of the original and the control groups or their families showed any marked differences, and (2) whether family compositions—especially the absence of a parent—played an important part. Our material indicates that the families of those involved in car theft enjoyed much greater economic security than those of the control group, and that those in the "pure" car theft group apparently came largely from what may be called a middle-class background. Nine of the "pure" group (more than 40 per cent) had families which led a comfortable existence, with money to spend on luxuries after the basic needs like rent, food, clothing, and utilities had been taken care of. For 10 of the "pure" group (45 per cent), the economic background was described as fair, meaning that the necessities just mentioned could be paid for but that there was nothing left for luxuries. Only one family in this group depended on public assistance. Both the "mixed" and the control groups had 22 per cent public assistance cases. Aside from this, families in the "mixed" group were somewhat better off than those in the control group, with about 65 per cent comfortable or fair economic situations in the "mixed" compared with a little over 40 per cent in the control group.

It would be desirable to describe the emotional climate of the homes of the boys but in attempting to do this we are confronted with the difficulties which intangibles always present. At best, we have some subjective reactions on the part of family members and agency representatives. We, therefore, limit our evaluations to whether a home was complete or broken by the absence of one or both parents.

The "pure" group came from 13 intact (59 per cent), and 9 broken homes (41 per cent). The "mixed" group showed 25 intact (42.4 per cent) and 34 broken homes (57.6 per cent), and the control group 30 intact (37 per cent) and 51 broken homes (63 per cent). Thus it can be stated again that those in the car theft group—especially the "pure" group—came from a more secure background than the control group.

# Why Boys Steal Cars

An examination of the offenses committed and the possible motivations shows we are dealing with only two large groups of car-theft types. In the overwhelming majority of cases, the reason for stealing a car seemed to be to have a good time.[12] Only in 8 of the cases studied was the car used as a means of escape from an intolerable situation in the delinquent's own home or in an institution. It is noteworthy that we did not encounter a single case where the stolen car was used in connection with another crime—a holdup for instance.

In the great majority of cases the boys acted with at least one companion—frequently with more than one. Wattenberg and Balistrieri [13] emphasize that the boys they studied had better relations with peers than other delinquents.

Emphasis on the ability to relate with peers, in a sense, begs the question since car theft is a group offense. Only in 4 of the cases, did we have definite information that the young offender stole the car alone. Those were instances where the car was used to flee from a home or an institution. Girls were participants in car thefts in only 4 cases. Since we are dealing with a very young age group this is not surprising. In one instance we had 3 boys with 3 girls engaging in a wild escapade with several stolen cars, ending in an assault on a gas station attendant. The 3 boys were committed to the Training School. All 3 boys, interestingly, were discharged from aftercare supervision on the basis of a satisfactory community adjustment.

Attempts have been made to find a common denominator for car thefts by adolescents. These attempts have not been successful. Wattenberg and Balistrieri [14] speak in somewhat general terms of a lax family

[12] See Teeters and Reinemann, *loc. cit.*, p. 135, 517; Wedekind, *loc. cit.*, p. 444. It is interesting to note that a committee studying the *Uniform Crime Reports* of the Federal Bureau of Investigation debated the question whether car thefts should continue to be included in those reports, inasmuch as "joyriding," which comprises a very substantial portion of the auto thefts, "is presumably not an offense of such an inherently criminal nature as to appropriately be used for the purpose of a criminal index" (see p. 28 of the Special Issue of the *Uniform Crime Reports* published in December 1958). It was, however, decided to retain the car thefts in these reports, largely because of their economic significance. It has also been pointed out that, from the point of view of the delinquent himself, car theft is a very serious offense as it shows a disturbing disregard for the property rights of others (see J. Richard Perlman, "Delinquency Prevention: The Size of the Problem," *The Annals* of The American Academy of Political and Social Sciences, March 1959, pp. 1, 5, 6).

[13] *Loc. cit.*, p. 577.
[14] *Loc. cit.*, p. 579.

structure and of "permissive upbringing" which produces a personality type with little moral courage and a potential for engaging in antisocial behavior. Dr. Gibbens [15] finds that those involved in auto theft come, as a rule, from middle-class or working-class homes where the mother plays the dominant role and the father is more or less in the background. These boys, they point out, would fight against identification with the female sex and try to assert their masculinity by the aggressive act of stealing a car. Though this may be true in some instances, it has been demonstrated in the French study mentioned earlier that there is actually an infinite variety of constellations which may be considered as explanations of car thefts.[16] This is confirmed by our case material. We have boys from families ruled by an authoritative father "with an iron hand," and others from homes where the father figure was insignificant or completely missing. We have members of various cultural groups. We have boys coming from economically secure or even affluent homes, and others who did not know anything but the severest economic deprivation throughout their young lives.

A few examples may suffice to demonstrate the possible varieties:

*Salvatore,* one of 16 children born to illiterate parents, natives of Italy. Father has court record, and so do some of Salvatore's older brothers. Salvatore begins to steal cars at the age of 13, always with others. Dull-normal intelligence, reading at 4th grade level. Apparently a case of a mentally-limited boy reacting to a substandard environment. Hostile, poor adjustment at Training School. Discharged after commitment to correction for another car theft.

*George,* a Negro boy, out-of-wedlock child, rejected by mother, lived with putative father, a somewhat limited well-meaning man, and a "stepmother" who is described as good-natured and carefree. George has average intelligence, does not present a school problem. Steals with a companion who is suspected of being a homosexual. Apparently a case where sexual drives may have played an important part. This boy made a good adjustment under aftercare.

*Sam,* a boy of Polish Jewish descent, whose family was killed by the Nazis. Lived in D.P. camps as a young boy until he was adopted by an elderly orthodox Jewish couple and came to the United States. High standards in the home. Sam is of average intelligence. He was first apprehended in a burglary, referred to a private agency for treatment. Then began to steal cars and was committed to the Training School. Conforming adjustment, described as shrewd and calculating with little awareness of ethical standards. Did poorly on parole;

---

[15] *Loc. cit.,* p. 264.

[16] Parrott, Ribettes, and Mabille, *loc. cit.,* p. 673. The 12 case sketches presented by these writers are highly instructive.

worked only a short time. Then he stole a car and had a serious accident as a result of which he had to walk on crutches for several months. After that he settled down, worked steadily, and was finally discharged on the basis of satisfactory community adjustment.

Here, we are obviously dealing with one of those products of war and postwar experiences, a boy who through the struggle for survival has become completely self-centered and lives practically by the law of the jungle as long as he believes that he does not have to face the consequences of antisocial acts. That he expresses this attitude by committing car thefts is probably accidental.

*Henry,* the only son of parents of German descent. Father intelligent, commercial draftsman, good provider. Mother, a high school graduate, described as tense and neurotic. Secure economic situation, high standards. Boy committed to Training School after first court appearance for car theft, at his own request. Told court about "home difficulties." Of superior intelligence, he made an excellent adjustment at the Training School. When released, he refused to return to his family and was placed in a residential center, operated by aftercare staff. Finally discharged on the basis of satisfactory adjustment. At that time he still lived away from home. Here, we have undoubtedly a case of adolescent rebellion.

To repeat, car theft is a phenomenon which may result from any number of factors. So far as the immediate impulse to steal a car is concerned, we are dealing, on the other hand, with certain characteristics which show up again and again. Parrot, Ribettes, and Mabille have dealt at length with the fascination the car exerts on most persons of the Western countries, and in particular on adolescents.[17] Associated with the feeling of power instilled by mastering an automobile there is the domination of the "Goddess Speed"—to quote the French authors again[18]—intoxicating people who otherwise are quite mature and sensible. The restlessness which is a characteristic of the adolescent, his desire to move from one place to another one, is reflected in numerous car thefts. The erotic element must not be neglected. The car may be stolen to impress girls or to provide an opportunity for sexual intercourse.

There is a significantly higher percentage of white boys among those engaged in auto theft than among delinquent boys not involved in car theft, particularly among the "pure" group. This may be explained by the fact that those involved in auto theft in the main also come from

[17] *Loc. cit.,* p. 667. See also Dr. L. Hyman Weiland, "The Psychological Significance of Hot Rods and Automobile Driving to Adolescent Males," *Psychiatric Quarterly Supplement,* Volume 31, Part 2, p. 261.
[18] *Loc. cit.,* p. 666.

families which have better economic standards than the families of the control group. In New York City, perhaps as much as anywhere else in the United States, the white population is on the whole in a considerably better economic situation than Negroes and Puerto Ricans. It may be assumed, therefore, that young white boys of middle-class origin are more exposed to the use of cars within their family than children growing up in a proletarian environment. They are more car-conscious and in all probability learn much earlier how to drive a car than other boys.

## Adjustment at the Institution

It remains to be seen how the boys in the various groups reacted to treatment at the Training School and how they adjusted after return to the community. It is recognized that an evaluation of a boy's adjustment within the institution is somewhat questionable. Reports submitted by staff members working with him, such as cottage parents, teachers, shop instructors, and work group supervisors, are bound to be subjective. Moreover, it is practically impossible for a large number of people to evaluate behavior in exactly the same way. What may seem acceptable behavior to one staff member may be considered a serious deviation by another.

We generally call a boy's adjustment *good* if he cooperates with the staff in all his assignments and does not present a discipline problem. A *fair* adjustment may be described as conformity without noticeable enthusiasm and with occasional breaches of discipline. The adjustment of a boy who is uncooperative, resentful, and in frequent disciplinary difficulties is called *poor*.

We found that the same number of auto-theft boys and control group boys—31—made a good adjustment. Twenty-three of the boys involved in auto theft and 29 control group boys were in the fair category, and 14 auto-theft boys and 17 control group boys were in the poor group. The "pure" group comprised 12 boys who made a good adjustment, 2 who made a fair adjustment, and 5 who made a poor adjustment. In addition, there were a number of boys in each group who ran away from the institution or failed to return from weekend home visits and were discharged from the Training School's active count for one reason or another. There were 13 car-theft boys in this group—a rather high percentage (16 per cent)—and only 4 control group cases (less than 5 per cent). Of the 13 boys arrested for auto theft, 7 had again been involved in car thefts when they were apprehended. In 2 more cases, the record indicates "grand larceny" which may very well have been the theft of an automobile. All in all, it can be said that the nature of the offense which brought a boy to the Training School did not have any great bearing on his institutional adjustment.

## Postrelease Adjustment

The information we have on a boy's community adjustment after he left the Training School is more revealing.

The reasons for discharging a boy from aftercare are, in general, (1) a good community adjustment, at least 1 year after the boy has completed his 16th year; (2) commitment to a correctional institution; or (3) placement on probation to an adult or adolescent court. Other reasons for discharge such as enlistment in the armed forces, whereabouts unknown, removal from the State of New York, are of little significance numerically. So far as the three main reasons are concerned, our control group seems to have fared a little better than those involved in auto theft. Twenty-five of the control group (30.9 per cent) were discharged with a good adjustment, while only 21 of the car-theft group (25.9 per cent) terminated their contact with the Training School with a good adjustment. On the other hand, 31 control group boys (38.3 per cent) came into conflict with the law again after they had left the Training School. Twenty of them were committed to correctional institutions for adults; 9 were placed on probation to adult courts; and 2 were committed to training schools of other states. Among the auto-theft group we find 46 boys (56.8 per cent) who came into conflict with the law: 34 commitments to correctional institutions; 11 placements on probation; and 1 commitment to a hospital which specializes in the treatment of young drug addicts (Riverside Hospital in New York City). The picture, however, becomes somewhat more favorable if we look, once again, at the "pure" auto-theft boys as a separate group. Ten of them had good adjustments (45.5 per cent) and 10 (also 45.5 per cent) came into conflict with the law again and were committed to correctional institutions or placed on probation.

It is interesting to note that no less than 6 of the 10 boys in the "pure" car-theft group discharged for commitment to a correctional institution or for placement on probation, were involved again in car theft. One was adjudged a youthful offender (the offense committed by him does not appear in our record material). One boy was sent to prison for committing a homicide as a result of a drunken argument at a party. One was found with a knife in his possession, and another one was

## BOYS WHO STEAL CARS

### COMPARISON OF 81 BOYS COMMITTED ON AUTO THEFT CHARGES WITH A CONTROL GROUP OF 81 BOYS COMMITTED ON CHARGES OTHER THAN AUTO THEFT

| | (A) "Pure" Group | | (B) "Mixed" Group | | (A) Plus (B) | | Control Group | |
|---|---|---|---|---|---|---|---|---|
| | No. | Per Cent | No. | Per Cent | No. | Per Cent | No. | Per Cent |
| Total | 22 | 100.0 | 59 | 100.0 | 81 | 100.0 | 81 | 100.0 |
| Race | | | | | | | | |
| White | 13 | 59.1 | 31 | 52.5 | 44 | 54.3 | 33 | 40.6 |
| Negro | 7 | 31.8 | 22 | 37.3 | 29 | 35.8 | 36 | 44.8 |
| Puerto Rican | 2 | 9.1 | 6 | 10.2 | 8 | 9.9 | 12 | 14.6 |
| Age First Time in Court | | | | | | | | |
| 14 and over | 20 | 90.9 | 31 | 52.6 | 51 | 62.9 | 43 | 53.0 |
| Under 14 | 2 | 9.1 | 28 | 47.4 | 30 | 37.1 | 38 | 47.0 |
| Intelligence | | | | | | | | |
| Mental deficient or borderline | 2 | 9.1 | 17 | 28.8 | 19 | 23.5 | 25 | 30.9 |
| Dull normal | 9 | 40.9 | 20 | 33.9 | 29 | 35.8 | 21 | 25.9 |
| Average or above | 11 | 50.0 | 22 | 37.3 | 33 | 40.7 | 35 | 43.2 |
| Reading ability | | | | | | | | |
| Below 3rd grade | 4 | 18.2 | 18 | 30.5 | 22 | 27.2 | 30 | 37.0 |
| 3rd to 6th grade inclusive | 7 | 31.8 | 22 | 37.3 | 29 | 35.8 | 28 | 34.6 |
| Above 6th grade | 11 | 50.0 | 19 | 32.2 | 30 | 37.0 | 23 | 28.4 |
| Economic Background | | | | | | | | |
| Comfortable | 9 | 40.9 | 10 | 16.9 | 19 | 23.5 | 9 | 11.1 |
| Fair | 10 | 45.5 | 28 | 47.4 | 38 | 46.9 | 24 | 29.6 |
| Marginal | 2 | 9.1 | 8 | 13.6 | 10 | 12.3 | 28 | 34.6 |
| Public assistance | 1 | 4.5 | 13 | 22.1 | 14 | 17.3 | 18 | 22.2 |
| No information | — | — | — | — | — | — | 2 | 2.5 |
| Home | | | | | | | | |
| Intact | 13 | 59.0 | 25 | 42.5 | 38 | 46.9 | 30 | 37.0 |
| Broken | 9 | 41.0 | 34 | 57.5 | 43 | 53.1 | 51 | 63.0 |
| Institution Adjustment | | | | | | | | |
| Good | 12 | 54.5 | 19 | 32.2 | 31 | 38.3 | 31 | 38.3 |
| Fair | 2 | 9.1 | 21 | 35.6 | 23 | 28.4 | 29 | 35.8 |
| Poor | 5 | 22.7 | 9 | 15.3 | 14 | 17.3 | 17 | 21.0 |
| Ran away from training school | 3 | 13.7 | 10 | 16.9 | 13 | 16.0 | 4 | 4.9 |
| Discharge | | | | | | | | |
| With good adjustment | 10 | 45.5 | 11 | 18.6 | 21 | 25.9 | 25 | 30.9 |
| With poor adjustment 1 | 10 | 45.5 | 36 | 61.0 | 46 | 56.8 | 31 | 38.3 |
| Others 2 | 2 | 9.0 | 12 | 20.4 | 14 | 17.3 | 17 | 21.0 |

1 Commitment to correctional institutions or other training schools or placement on probation.
2 Enlistment in Armed Forces, whereabouts unknown, removal from New York State, commitment vacated. Eight boys in the control group (9.8 per cent) were still on parole to the aftercare department at the completion of this paper.

convicted of extorting money from a school boy. Only in the latter case did we see a definite indication of a boy embarking on a criminal career. The homicide case and the possession-of-a-knife case may very well have been accidental. The others apparently had not yet achieved the necessary maturity to abandon delinquent activity which, as stated before, is largely a manifestation of turbulent adolescence.

The table on page 218 gives a condensed picture of the statistical material presented in this paper.

## Conclusions

Our findings may be summarized as follows:

1. In evaluating the very young boy (between 12 and 16) arrested for auto theft we have to distinguish between the boy who commits no offense except car theft, and the one who combines auto theft with other delinquent activities, e.g., stealing, assault, vandalism, sexual misconduct.

2. Statistically significant characteristics distinguishing boys arrested for auto theft from other delinquent boys are particularly pronounced with the "pure" group. Such characteristics are:

(a) Prevalence of white over Negro and Puerto Rican boys.

(b) Onset of delinquent behavior at a later age.

(c) Fewer very dull boys.

(d) Fewer illiterate boys.

(e) Homes with better economic circumstances.

(f) Fewer broken homes.

3. In the great majority of cases, thefts are committed by groups of boys for the purpose of joy rides. Occasionally stolen cars are used for the purpose of escapes from homes or institutions. There were no car thefts committed in connection with other offenses, e.g., holdups.

4. The adjustment of a boy within a training school seems to have no relationship to the offense which brought him to the institution. Boys involved in car theft show a tendency to escape by stealing a car again.

5. Those in the "pure" auto-theft group may have a slightly better chance to make a satisfactory community adjustment after treatment at a training school than delinquents of the "mixed" type or those engaged in delinquent activities other than car thefts. If a boy in the "pure" auto-theft group gets into difficulty again, it will, in the majority of cases, be because of car theft.

# 19. Juvenile Vandalism

## Marshall B. Clinard and Andrew L. Wade

Clinard holds the degree of Doctor of Philosophy from the University of Chicago and is Professor of Sociology at the University of Wisconsin. He has held a Fulbright Research Professorship in Sweden, went to India in 1958 on an urban community development program sponsored by the Ford Foundation and the Government of India, and returned to India in 1962 as a Ford Foundation consultant on urban community development and for research on a grant from the Institute of Public Administration. He is the author of *The Black Market: A Study of White Collar Crime, Sociology of Deviant Behavior,* and numerous articles.

Wade received the Master of Arts degree from the University of Oregon and is an Assistant Probation Officer with the San Diego California County Probation Office.

Vandalism is here proposed as an example of the typological approach to juvenile delinquency. By vandalism is meant the deliberate defacement, mutilation or destruction of private or public property by a juvenile or group of juveniles not having immediate or direct ownership in the property so abused. Although a common type of property offense among adolescent boys, the term itself is a relatively recent one, having come into official use as applied to delinquency only since the late thirties. What is here defined as vandalism is often included in such designations of delinquent activity as "malicious mischief," "acts of carelessness or mischief," "willful and wanton misconduct," "destructiveness," "disorderly conduct," "incorrigibility," or even "assault." Communities utilizing the categories employed by the United States Children's Bureau for reporting juvenile court statistics have included vandalism offenses in the statistical unit "act of carelessness or mischief." However, a number of municipal, county and state agencies are now using the term "vandalism" as a category to describe this distinct type of property offense.

Marshall B. Clinard and Andrew L. Wade, "Toward the Delineation of Vandalism as a Sub-Type in Juvenile Delinquency," *Journal of Criminal Law, Criminology and Police Science,* 48 (January-February, 1958), excerpts from pp. 494, 497-499. Reprinted with permission of the publishers of the *Journal.*

## Some Characteristics of Vandalism

The available statistics on juvenile court referrals reported annually to the United States Children's Bureau indicate that property destruction is a common offense among adolescent boys. The cost to the American public of this deliberate damage is probably greater than the combined costs of other forms of juvenile property offenses. The cost of an offense is not the only way to measure seriousness. Research has shown that attitudes toward respect for property are not always the same and that any concept of property rights is to a considerable extent fluid and conditional.[5] Actually a violation of property rights is not, of itself, necessarily serious. Its seriousness is dependent on such factors as the relationship of the owner to the offender, the danger of punishment for the offender, the likelihood of real injury to the owner, the kind of property involved, and the value of the property. Studies attempting to measure the relative seriousness of this offense have shown that vandalism ranks low in order of seriousness when compared with other typical juvenile offenses and that within the general designation of "vandalism" there are different types of property destruction, each with its relative degree of seriousness.[6]

## Dimensions in a Typology of Vandalism

Providing there is not serious injury to property, the American public tends to view pranks with a kind of careless tolerance, probably because most American males were once participants in this kind of activity. There are, however, certain implied limits to juvenile vandalism growing out of ambiguous definitions of the roles and status of children in contemporary society. The destructiveness of very young children is often excused with the rationalization that they have not yet matured to a responsible understanding of property rights and its value. Much of the damage by this group is probably accidental, hence more readily excusable. Furthermore, most of this vandalism seems to grow out of

[5] Cf. John C. Eberhart, "Attitudes Toward Property: A Genetic Study by the Paired-Comparisons Rating of Offenses," *Jour. of Genet. Psychol.*, 60 (March 1942), 3-25.

[6] See Mervin A. Durea, "An Experimental Study of Attitudes Toward Juvenile Delinquency," *Jour. of Appl. Psychol.*, 17 (1933), 522-534; and Edwin Powers and Helen Witmer, *An Experiment in the Prevention of Delinquency* (New York: Columbia University Press, 1951), pp. 329-332.

random play-group activity. In its beginning stages this activity is inherently neither recreational nor delinquent. Later it may be defined as one or the other, depending upon whether the culmination of the activity is acceptable or unacceptable to the community. With younger children vandalism is not, therefore, necesssarily malicious; rather it is more often destructive play motivated largely by curiosity.[28]

The adolescent, on the other hand, is generally held morally culpable for his destructiveness. More often than not, his vandalism is considered deliberate and malicious even by the juvenile, as a fourteen year old boy has stated:

> Well, my parents came over to Gene's. I told my father we'd go over to the (drugstore). . . . Went over to the apartment house where cars were parked . . . wanted to "split tires" and did . . . meanness, I guess,—get an urge to do it—start with one and keep on doing it. . . . Well, it didn't matter, any car would do. . . . Teenagers are different from adults, feel urge to do something ornery. . . . I didn't know the people, of course, just something mean to do . . . everybody does something mean.[29]

How severely the teenager is censured is often dependent on the nature of the damage and the property vandalized. Community tolerance limits of various types of property destruction also appear to be affected by whether it occurs in a rural or urban area. As Ellingston has suggested, to overturn a farm wagon or an outhouse on Halloween may be regarded as permissible skylarking, but to overturn a truck in the urban community is labelled destruction of property.[30]

These normative aspects are important in the assessment of the meaning of vandalism to the community. It is commonplace for the community to overlook certain forms of vandalism on Halloween. But even within this institutionalized setting the norms are undergoing change and less destructive behavior is approved than formerly.[31] The social situation in which the offense takes place is another important dimension. Although the society may not have a well-structured and consistent set

[28] A. H. Maslow, "A Comparative Approach to the Problem of Destructiveness," *Psychiatry,* 5 (November 1942), p. 520.

[29] This and subsequent undesignated interviews were obtained as part of a research project on teen-age vandalism financed through a research fellowship by Community Studies, Inc., Kansas City, Missouri.

[30] *Protecting Our Children from Criminal Careers* (New York: Prentice-Hall, Inc., 1948), pp. 197f.

[31] *Cf.* Ralph and Adelin Linton, *Halloween: Through Twenty Centuries* (New York: Henry Schuman, 1950). In Great Britain, the Guy Fawkes Day Celebration (November 5th) is an institutionalized occasion for college-boy pranks; students let off "steam" mainly by setting bonfires.

of norms relative to property destruction, within the society certain groups or members of particular social classes, may be accorded a well-defined field in which to indulge in vandalism. One British writer has stated:

> . . . the party of public schoolboys who damage property during the course of a "rag" are behaving very differently from the street corner gang who smash street lamps or shop windows "just for the fun of it," or to work off their aggression. The mores of the Public School community allow and even encourage such explosively expressive behavior and the scholars' participation in its restricted setting, whereas the casual destructiveness of promiscuous gangs has no such social approval to sustain it.[32]

Often there is a certain flavor of spontaneity present indicating the type of criminal behavior characterized by Reckless as "behavior of the moment" in response to certain situations.[33] Much teen-age vandalism appears to be of this kind; it is extemporaneous behavior, adventitious and fortuitous in character, an outgrowth of the restless and exuberant nature of the adolescent boy.

> In the evening, between five or six, we was out to ——— Center (this center had been burned) messin' around. We was gonna play some ball. It was gettin' too dark for that, so one of us suggested to go in; so we went in. . . . Climbed up on the rest room roof. See, it used to be a school, that's where the exits outside from the restrooms were. We climbed up on there and went in through the window. . . . Well, first we went up and we thought we'd see what the Teen Town room looked like. Went up there, it wasn't bothered or burnt too much—floor was a little weak, dirty. Then we come back downstairs—we was gonna go in the art room but we couldn't get in there, the floor, it was burnt through. There was, oh, about an eighth of an inch of wood left. So we couldn't get in there. Uh—we just went messin' around. Started throwin' rocks. . . . From what we heard they was gonna tear the building down, build one the full length of the lot down there. . . . About in there an hour; just went around —throw one or two (rocks) . . . pretty soon we were going like mad. . . . While we were doing it we didn't think nothing about doing it because, like I say, what we heard they was going to tear the whole building down and I didn't think they would save them (windows)—big percentage of them were cracked and discolored, anyway. . . . What we was doing there would be about three of us

---

[32] John Barron Mays, *Growing Up in the City* (Liverpool: University of Liverpool Press, 1954), pp. 18f.

[33] Reckless, *op. cit.*, p. 73. [Walter C. Reckless, *The Crime Problem* (2nd edition) New York: Appleton-Century-Crofts, Inc., 1955.]

outside and three of us inside and we would have wars, throwing rocks back and forth at each other. . . . I guess anybody likes to get in trouble once in a while . . . not actually go out to look for trouble, but I mean at the time we thought it was fun until the police came; that was all.

On the other hand, the differential social expectations as to the roles of boys and girls are important in the inhibition of destructive behavior by girls. Since American culture does not place the same inhibitions on the boy's outward expression of his feelings, positive or negative, as it does on that of girls, the male youth, as one author has suggested, often appears to feel it essential to be self-directive in order to be considered masculine and acceptable to his peers.[34] Participation in vandalism is one way of meeting these needs for autonomy and peer group acceptance.

Fundamentally related is the frustration felt by the adolescent in a culture in which his role and status lack a well-defined normative structure. Moreover, there is little consensus on values and no consistency in adult behavior which might serve as guideposts. This absence of dominant and clearly defined norms, coupled with the factor of peer group loyalty with its attendant norms and values, results in conflict between the adolescent and adult authority figures, usually his parents and teachers. The consequence is behavior often termed delinquent by the adult world, while the adolescent defines it in terms of conformity to peer group expectations.[35]

This difference in the definition of behavior is true of vandalism. Whereas the adult world thinks of the teen-age vandal as a delinquent, the vandal may often have an entirely different self-conception. His self image is frequently that of a prankster:

> We did all kinds of dirty tricks for fun. We'd see a sign, "Please keep the street clean," but we'd tear it down and say, "We don't feel like keeping it clean." One day we put a can of glue in the engine of a man's car. We would always tear things down. That would make us laugh and feel good, to have so many jokes.[36]

> One time . . . four or five of us boys went to an apartment just being built, took a whole wall of cement down. We took a chisel and

---

[34] See Aileen Schoeppe, "Sex Differences in Adolescent Socialization," *Jour. of Soc. Psychol.,* 38 (November 1953), 175-185.

[35] For a criticism of the view that adolescent culture is in conflict with its adult counterpart, see Frederick Elkin and William A. Westley, "The Myth of Adolescent Culture," *Amer. Sociol. Rev.,* 20 (December 1955), 680-684.

[36] Frederic M. Thrasher, *The Gang* (2nd Edition; Chicago: University of Chicago Press, 1936), pp. 94f.

knocked down hundreds of cinder blocks, just mischievous. We went to old houses, broke windows. . . . In one house we found a big victrola. We threw it down the stairs, we pushed down the bannister, we broke the chandelier. We didn't steal anything, just broke things. . . . I had to do it so they wouldn't call me chicken.[37]

The fact that often nothing is stolen during such vandalism tends to re-enforce the vandal's conception of himself as merely a prankster and not a delinquent. Some writers have pointed this out as a distinguishing characteristic of the vandal when compared with other property offenders, assuming that since nothing is taken vandalism has a non-utilitarian function. However, these acts often do have a real meaning and utility for the participants, even though the reasons for participation are not expressed. Property destruction appears to function for the adolescent as a protest against his ill-defined role and ambiguous status in the social structure. Although role frustration is basic to this protest, the nature of the frustration differs as to the position of the vandal in the social structure as implied in this statement by a sixteen year old delinquent.

Well, he accused us of stealing some stuff out of his joint. He didn't come right out and say it was us, but the way he talked he made it sound like it—particularly us. . . . Yeah, we was kidding him about an old rifle he had in there, about ninety years old, and he wanted fifteen dollars for it and the stock on it was all cracked up and everything. And we kept kidding his mother—she's in there (the store) with him—and we kept kidding her, and old Gay (the store owner), himself, come over there and started raising the devil, blowing off steam and everything. We didn't like it too well. We left and came back later. . . . I told him (his companion) let's go down and break those windows. He said OK and we went down there and picked up some rocks along the way. We got down there and stood in front of the place till there weren't any cars very close to it and we threw the rocks and ran. . . . I guess you gotta get into something once in a while or you don't live right out there. It didn't seem like then that it would amount to this much.

## Summary

It has been pointed out that more concentration of research on types of delinquency is needed. Rather than grouping all kinds of delinquen-

[37] Benjamin Fine, *1,000,000 Delinquents* (New York: World Publishing Company, 1955), pp. 36f.

cies and delinquents into a heterogeneous category designated as "juvenile delinquents" and comparing this with an equally omnibus one labeled "juvenile non-delinquents," efforts should be directed toward a fuller understanding of the act itself and the kind of juvenile who predominantly commits this type of offense. The findings of such typological comparisons could conceivably be of help in the formulation of more specific theories of delinquent behavior and social control.

Vandalism has certain dimensions, specifically the community's definition of the act and its tolerance limits when property destruction occurs. Also of importance is the social setting in which the offense takes place. Whether or not there is a well-defined field in which vandalism is a permissible act has much to do with its occurrence and direction. Not only is it an important delinquency, judging from community reaction and financial cost, but vandalism is also illustrative of what has been called "behavior of the moment" in response to certain situations.

Research on vandalism has been largely explorative and descriptive without a unifying frame of reference and testable hypotheses. Consequently, it is proposed that property destruction be examined within a sociological framework of adolescent behavior. From this perspective vandalism is seen as one expression of the frustration felt by teen-age boys in their attempts to achieve autonomy and a satisfying self-conception in a culture where the adolescent's role and status lack a normative structure.

# 20.    Sex Offenses of Adolescents

## Albert J. Reiss

The author received the degree of Doctor of Philosophy from the University of Chicago in 1949. He has taught in several Universities: State University of Iowa, University of Wisconsin, and University of Michigan. He is co-author of *Reader in Urban Sociology, Social Characteristics of Urban and Rural Communities,* and *Community Life and Social Policy.* He is the author of *Cities and Societies.* Contributions to professional journals include a number of articles on juvenile delinquency.

Selections from Albert J. Reiss, "Sex Offenses: The Marginal Status of the Adolescent," reprinted from a symposium, "Sex Offenses," *Law and Contemporary Problems* 25, No. 2 (Spring 1960), 309-316, 318, and 322-324, by permission from the author and *Law and Contemporary Problems,* published by the Duke University School of Law, Durham, North Carolina. Copyright, 1960, by Duke University.

# Introduction *

Adolescence is not a highly institutionalized position in American society.[1] It is a transitional status between childhood and adulthood, but it is less institutionalized than either of the two age-based status positions that it borders and connects. The adolescent is a marginal person who is no longer accorded the privileged status of the child, nor as yet many of the rights and responsibilities of the adult.

The relatively low degree of institutionalization of adolescence as a status position and the marginal position of the adolescent in terms of role expectations in American society are reflected in the fact that most of the norms governing adolescent behavior do not have adolescent behavior patterns as their reference point. Rather, the norms and expectations governing adolescent behavior have either child or adult behavior patterns as their reference point. The exhortations of parents and other adults admonish the adolescent either to "behave like a grown-up" or to "quit behaving like a child." They rarely encourage him to "behave like an adolescent." There are, then, no highly institutionalized expectations of how one is to behave like an adolescent, in the sense that achievement of these status expectations is a positive transitional link with the adult status.

This article is an attempt to show that the failure to accord adolescence a distinct status position that is closely integrated with the larger structure of American society and the resulting minimum institutionalization of norms for governing adolescent behavior has several very important implications for defining and sanctioning the sexual conduct of adolescents in our society:

1. The perception of adolescent sex offenders as neither children nor adults tends to (a) encourage considerable variation in definition of their sexual offenses; (b) lead to preferential treatment and differential adjudication of their cases of sexual behavior on the basis of age, sex, socioeconomic status, and jurisdictional considerations; and (c) obscure the degree to which they are denied the due process of law.

2. The age-based status reference point for evaluating adolescent sexual offenses is a factor in the sanctions applied to their deviation.

* The writer gratefully acknowledges his obligation to Clark E. Vincent for helpful comment and criticism.
[1] Throughout this article, the sociological concept of adolescent is used interchangeably with the legal concept of juvenile. The context should make clear whether the concept is used primarily in the specialized sense of one discipline or the other.

When adolescent sex offenders are viewed as "not adult," they are generally overprotected and absolved from moral responsibility for their behavior, thereby weakening the moral integration of the total society. When they are viewed as "not children," there often is a tendency to deal more punitively with them than with adults who commit similar sex offenses.

3. The sexual behavior of adolescents is primarily peer-organized and peer-controlled. As such, it reflects the attempt by adolescents to achieve a compromise between being encouraged to behave like adults and being denied the rights and privileges of that status. An examination of the peer-organized basis for adolescent sexual conduct provides a normative basis for evaluating their behavior in relation to the larger social structure in which they are held accountable for their behavior.

## The Effect of Adolescent Status on Dealing with Sexual Conduct

What acts committed by adolescents will be defined as violations of sexual conduct norms? And how will his status as "not child" and "not adult" encourage variability in the definition of an adolescent's sexual conduct as a sex offense?

Despite some variation in the legal codes from state to state in our society, the statutes define the acts for which violators are classified as adult sex offenders. But the problem is not as simple for defining the juvenile as a sex offender. Most juvenile court statutes not only define the violation of all criminal statutory codes as sufficient ground for a finding of delinquency, but also hold that if the child is growing up in a situation inimical to his welfare, he or she may be adjudicated a delinquent. For all practical purposes, then, the definition of a juvenile sex offender rests with the standards followed in each juvenile jurisdiction.[2] The statutes, in fact, prescribe that the finding be that the child is a delinquent person, and not a specific type of offender.

Going beyond the immediate jurisdiction of the court to the legal

[2] Appeal from the decisions rendered by a juvenile court are relatively rare, and particularly so for cases involving violations of sexual conduct norms. The relatively low rate of appeal from the decisions of a juvenile court itself reflects a social definition of the adolescent as a person whose best interest is protected by the court, so that the traditional safeguards for civil rights are unnecessary. This position needs careful examination, since many juveniles and their families are unaware of their legal rights in a juvenile hearing. The personnel in most juvenile jurisdictions make no attempt to apprise juveniles of their rights and, in fact, often express obvious resentment when the juvenile is represented by counsel.

institutions for the care and treatment of juvenile offenders, one finds that still other standards may be applied in defining what is a sex offense. Reaching out into the social environment of juveniles, one quickly finds further variation in what is a sex offense, depending upon the status environment of the juvenile's family, his adolescent peers, and the institutional organizations within the community. There is no question but that in any of these contexts—the family, peer group and community, including the organizations administering justice—all forms of sex activity, including nocturnal emissions, may be prima facie evidence of the violation of sexual norms, so that negative sanctions may be invoked against the person engaging in the behavior.

The governing statutes are phrased in such general and inclusive terms that *any* sexual act or conduct can be defined as a delinquent offense. The omnibus provision for "immoral conduct or behavior" can be construed to cover all deviations from sexual conduct norms. The body of legal opinion and decision for delinquent acts similarly reflects considerable ambiguity as to what sexual conduct is to be defined as a violation and what is permitted sexual behavior for adolescents. Juveniles who are held to be guilty of a sex offense often are not charged with a specific sex conduct violation. The categories of "ungovernability," "loitering," "immoral or indecent conduct," "runaway," and similar designations frequently are the preferred charges, particularly if the court has a policy to avoid stigmatizing an individual with a sex offense. The terms "sex offense" and "sex offender" are not clearly defined, then, for adolescents in legal codes or in the adjudication of cases involving the violation of sexual conduct norms.

Most forms of behavioral deviation from norms or legal codes are linked with other forms of behavioral deviation, at least for a substantial proportion of all known deviators. For this reason, a person classified as a violator of legal or other conduct norms governing sexual behavior also may usually be classified as violator of other legal conduct norms. An adolescent boy or girl who is arrested for stealing almost always has also violated sexual conduct norms, and the reverse is usually the case as well. In behavioral terms, then, it is not particularly meaningful to define a person as a sex offender. This, of course, is true of most other delinquency classificatory terms as well. One technically violates the sexual conduct norm through behavior and thereby commits a *delinquent* offense. The term sex offender should perhaps signify no more nor less than this. Certainly, it should not imply that this is the only major kind of delinquent activity the person has committed. To classify a person as a sex offender may only serve to develop self and public definitions of the person as a sex offender.

The term sex offender, of course, is very ambiguous since it does not specify the specific kind of behavior that is used as the basis for charging a violation. But even if one employs specific behavioral definitions—as, for example, by designating the person as an exhibitionist or an unwed mother—the charge usually would not exhaust the sexual conduct violations for which the person could be charged. As Kinsey and others have shown, total sexual outlet is derived from a variety of types of sexual behavior,[3] almost any one of which could in the case of many adolescents be used to charge conduct violation. Although there is difficulty in classifying a person as a type of offender when an act of sexual behavior violates a conduct norm, the simple cumulation of such acts as a basis for classifying a person as a specific type of offender (e.g., persistence) involves one in even greater difficulty. Not only is it difficult to secure accurate and reliable statistics on violation of sexual conduct norms for adolescents charged with a sex offense, but, as Kinsey observes, the frequency distribution is continuous for any kind of sexual behavior; any cutting point chosen on that curve, therefore, is arbitrary.[4]

The status of adolescent is an apparent factor in the application of adult sex norms to their conduct. The prescribed form of sexual behavior in American society is that of heterosexual coition in private surroundings between partners in a monogamous marriage. The legal norms, however, specifically prohibit adolescents to marry without the consent of parents. Unless this condition is met, therefore, heterosexual coition is proscribed for an adolescent. This example is instructive in that the norms do not specifically prohibit young persons from engaging in heterosexual coition; the limitation rather arises for adolescents because of difficulty in satisfying the conditions for marriage. Adolescents lack both the privilege and opportunities for self-determination of their marital status and thereby for their heterosexual behavior that culminates in sexual intercourse. It is not surprising, therefore, that for adolescents, petting to orgasm becomes a functional equivalent to coition.

Adolescents themselves set standards for what is a violation of their sexual codes. The standards in these adolescent codes vary considerably according to the social status position of the adolescent and his family in the larger society. A comparison of the prescribed heterosexual coition patterns of middle- and lower-status boys and girls may illustrate this variability. Among the lower-status white adolescent boys in our society,

---

[3] Alfred C. Kinsey, Wardell B. Pomeroy & Clyde E. Martin, *Sexual Behavior in the Human Male passim* (1948) [hereinafter cited as *Kinsey Male Report*]; Alfred C. Kinsey, Wardell B. Pomeroy, Clyde E. Martin & Paul H. Gebhard, *Sexual Behavior in the Human Female passim* (1953) [hereinafter cited as *Kinsey Female Report*].

[4] *Kinsey Male Report* 199.

premarital heterosexual intercourse is prescribed to secure status within the group, while it is not necessary to secure status within most middle-peer status groups, even though it does confer some status.

Heterosexual behavior with prostitutes is not very common among adolescents up to the age of fifteen, although it is more common after that age. For adolescent boys, however, intercourse with female prostitutes comprises only a relatively small proportion of their total sexual outlet. Premarital sexual intercourse apart from organized prostitution is far more common among boys than is intercourse with prostitutes.

Among young lower-status adolescent boys, perhaps the most common mode of heterosexual intercourse is the "gang-shag" or "gang-bang." A gang of boys usually knows one or more girls who are easy "pick-ups" for the group who will consent to serial intercourse with the members of the gang. To understand this behavior, several peer normative factors need to be taken into account. First of all, the girl in the "gang-bang" almost always is one who gives her consent. She is not being sexually exploited in any sense of forcible rape. In fact, when she consents to being picked up, she understands that she is to be a partner in heterosexual coition. Lower-status boys clearly distinguish between "putting it to a girl" (she consents) and "making a girl" (she does not consent). Few lower-status boys, particularly delinquent boys, will "make a girl," although almost all frequently engage in heterosexual intercourse and most have at least participated in a gang-bang. Most lower-status adolescent boys express the view: "Why should I *make* a girl when I can get all I want without it." The opportunities for heterosexual coition with consent are ever present to lower-status boys, so that they negatively sanction forcible rape. This is not to say that some adolescent girls are not forcibly raped by an adolescent boy or even a gang, but the proportion who are is, without doubt, very small.

The girl who consents to sexual intercourse with the gang loses her reputation as a "nice girl," and they no longer regard her as a possible partner in a marriage relationship.[5] Her status becomes that of a prostitute. Similarly, a girl who consents to sexual intercourse with a number of boys, even if the acts are separate and private, risks her reputation as a partner in marriage. The status of an "easy mark" in sexual intercourse sharply reduces her life chances for marriage, at least among the lower-status boys who are acquainted with her. As a consequence, sexual behavior becomes her only competitive claim to masculine attention. This

[5] See, e.g., Whyte, A Slum Sex Code, 49 Am. J. Sociology 24 (1943). Investigation since Whyte's original statement of this sex code discloses that this might more appropriately be called the sex code of low-status persons in American society, whether or not they dwell in slums.

very loss of status as "marriageable," with the substitute status as "easy-to-get," gradually forces the girl either to withdraw altogether from the competitive struggle for the attentions of boys or to bargain increasingly the only thing she has—*i.e.*, sexual favors.[6]

The adolescent girl faced with the status dilemma described above is likely to adopt one of two solutions to the problem. One of these is the "steady date," which includes the "understanding" that he has sexual access to her and she is guaranteed a steady date—she does not have to compete with other girls for a date. Under these circumstances, the girl can defend her behavior in terms of romantic love ideals. Many middle- and upper-status girls undertake heterosexual coitus under these circumstances, since it protects their status within the group. They are "in love," "going steady," and "intend to be married"; *ergo,* if coition is a private act between two who are as married, it can be permitted. The other major alternative is some form of prostitution, either in organized prostitution or through the acquisition of a status or reputation as a "pick-up" or "easy-to-get" girl. The major risk a girl encounters in either solution is that of pregnancy, while in the case of prostitution, she also runs a fairly high risk of venereal infection.

It is not so much the sexual act of coition that brings the girl to the attention of legal authorities as it is either of these consequences of the act—premarital pregnancy or venereal infection. The couple is seldom caught in the act of coition. Since girls are more likely than boys to be defined as the carriers of venereal infection, a girl who is picked up by police or juvenile authorities is almost always given a physical examination to determine whether she has had sexual intercourse, now has a venereal infection, or is pregnant. This is particularly true for runaway girls. Boys seldom are given as complete a physical examination for venereal infection as are girls. Even less often are they questioned as to their sex experiences. There is a great variation among jurisdictions in this respect, however. Personnel in some are more likely than in others to learn about the sexual deviation of girls. The life chances of a girl before police and juvenile authorities, therefore, are more favorable to defini- tion as a sex delinquent than are the life chances of the boy.

A number of other factors are important in the greater relative fre- quency with which girls, as compared with boys, are defined as sex offenders. Many policemen come from lower-status social origins. In their youth, many of them, therefore, shared the sex patterns of the lower-status boys and accepted the norm that deviation in heterosexual intercourse is permissible. So long as the boys do not forcibly rape a

[6] See James F. Coleman, *Social Structures and Social Climates in High Schools* chs. 3 and 4 ( 1959 ).

girl, or so long as the girl's parents or others do not file a complaint, the police are generally accepting of this form of sexual deviation. They may make a concerted effort to limit the opportunities for deviation, since that is expected of them in their work role, but they seldom arrest on discovery. Discovery in the act of intercourse is difficult, so that evidence is almost always obtained by confession or circumstances.

Adolescent boys come to the attention of the court as heterosexual sex offenders usually only when the morality of the girl's family is offended. The most common form of complaint is for the family to define coition as "rape" of their daughter. Research evidence shows that in most cases, the boy is not a rapist in any technical sense that force or coercion was used. The act occurred through common consent. The complaint arises because the girl, under family pressure, charges that she did not consent. Although many complaints arise in this way, it does not follow, of course, that some delinquent boys gangs do not forcibly rape a young girl nor that boys individually do not engage in such acts; it is rather to emphasize that available evidence strongly indicates that most heterosexual coition between adolescents occurs through mutual consent. The girl has a reputation. She is sought out or picked up. She knows what is expected of her, consents, and services one or more boys. No money is exchanged.

Middle-status boys do not prescribe premarital intercourse, and certainly not at as early an age as do lower-status boys. Experience in heterosexual coition confers status, however. The middle-status white adolescent boy assumes no obligation for premarital pregnancy, and marriage under these circumstances is to be avoided. The preservation of a middle-status boy's reputation is more important than the preservation of the reputation of the girl, particularly if she is of lower social status. Community organizations will strive to preserve his reputation, even at the expense of the reputation of the girl.

It has been suggested that a major difference between lower- and middle-status adolescents in respect to premarital intercourse is that lower-status girls commonly enter into the relationship by perceiving it as fun morality—"if it's fun, it's good"—while middle-status girls see it as one involving love morality—"it's good because we're in love." [7]

Status within a peer group is a very important factor determining whether an adolescent girl will engage in coition with boys. Courtship patterns in American society require that girls use a variety of means to attract males as dates or potential marriage partners when in competition with other girls for these boys. One of the competitive ad-

[7] Vincent, *Ego Involvement in Sexual Relations: Implications for Research on Illegitimacy*, 65 Am. J. Sociology 287 (1959).

vantages a girl has available to her is her sexual attractiveness to males. Yet, the male norms prescribing the ideal marriage mate require that the girl one marries cannot have a reputation among other males as being sexually immoral. A girl's competitive advantage, therefore, is easily lost if she gains the reputation that she will enter into a sexual liaison with a boy if she is dated. Recent research shows that the adolescent girl who fails to acquire status within a conforming adolescent peer group of girls is at a competitive disadvantage in securing dates with boys, since dating is largely controlled by peer groups of boys and of girls who enter into "diplomatic relations" with one another. The failure to acquire status within a peer group of girls forces a girl to date by herself rather than "double date," to use more overt means of sexual attractiveness to get a date, or to withdraw from dating competition altogether. The use of any means to get dates other than those controlled by the peer group of girls results in her further exclusion from the peer society and leads to a definition of her as "sexually loose." Girls often communicate such definitions to groups of boys before the boys have formed a similar evaluation of the girl. An adolescent girl's status as being sexually immoral, therefore, often arises among girls rather than among boys.[8] Having acquired such an unfavorable definition then further deprives a girl of using conventional dating attributes as a means for getting the attention of boys in competition with other girls. Gradually, her only means for getting a date, therefore, is her reputation of ease of sexual access. She progressively is forced to resort to the use of this means if she hopes to attract boys as dates, and her behavior must conform to the boy's expectations once she gets the date.

The single most important reason, perhaps, why most adolescents who engage in premarital coition are not defined as delinquents is the difficulty in detecting couples in the act of violation and obtaining evidence of coition. For the most part, adolescent violators have a strong social status investment in not being discovered. This renders detection even more difficult. Violators, therefore, seldom come to the attention of the police or juvenile officials unless a girl involved in heterosexual coition, or her family, enters a formal complaint. Interrogation then is the principal means for determining whether the accused boy or boys are guilty of the offense. In some jurisdictions, even a lie-detector then is used on the boy, without any regard for his consent, in an effort to determine whether or not the behavior was as charged. Middle-status families generally will not risk the reputation of their daughter by bringing heterosexual violations to the attention of the police and courts, while

[8] See Coleman, *op. cit. supra* note 6, chs. 3 and 4.

lower-status families are less likely to see such a risk for their daughter. The lower-status family, in fact, sometimes sees formal complaint as necessary to protect the status reputation of their daughter. The effect of these status differences in the discovery and reporting of sexual violations is that the lower-status boy or girl is more likely to come to the attention of the police and courts as a sex violator than is the middle-status adolescent.

Many Americans, particularly at the lower-social-status levels, still condemn masturbation. Nowhere is this condemnation more apparent than in the codes governing sex behavior in institutions for adolescents. Masturbation is usually severely condemned within these institutions, and punishment is administered for its practice. At one such institution, a state training school for boys, the writer recently discovered that boys were physically punished if caught in the act of masturbation. Repeated violation resulted in confinement to the disciplinary dormitory of the institution. Such administrative policies within institutions to which delinquents are committed by the court or in which delinquents are held in detention by the court appears only to heighten the ingenuity of adolescents to seek more clandestine modes of sexual outlet. Among other consequences, the policy may only serve to exacerbate the problem of controlling homosexual practices in these single-sex institutions.

Recently, research has shown that the social definition of the sexual relationship between an adult male and an adolescent boy is in many cases erroneous. The homosexual act in a large proportion of cases occurs within a prostitute-client set of expectations, where the adolescent boy is the prostitute and the adult male is the client. From the standpoint of the lower-status delinquent boy who usually gets involved in this sexual relationship, the act is an instrumental one in which the boy seeks adult males, particularly fellators, to minimize the risk in making money. A brief description of the way this behavior is organized in a number of metropolitan areas may serve as an illustration of what is involved in the relationship.[21]

Adolescent boys in delinquent gangs quite commonly seek out older males—"queers"—to perform mouth-genital fellatio in exchange for money. These boys, however, have no conception of themselves as

[21] Investigation discloses it is quite common among career-oriented delinquents in such large metropolitan areas as Chicago, Los Angeles, New York, and Washington, D.C., and smaller ones such as Nashville, Tenn. It is observed in smaller cities that attract large numbers of adult male homosexuals, such as the resort city of Hot Springs, Ark.

homosexual, although they view the fellator as a "gay" or "queer boy." The relationship, however, is quite clearly defined and prescribed as a part of the culture of career-oriented delinquents. There are a number of elements in this definition. Peer-hustling of "queers" is defined as an acceptable substitute for "legitimate" delinquent earnings (theft, for example) when one cannot afford to risk being caught. The "peer-queer" sexual transaction of mouth-genital fellation provides "easy money" for the delinquent boy at very low risk of being caught.

The delinquent boy often is inducted into this form of hustling by his older peers. He learns how contacts are to be made and where they are easily effected. Above all, he learns the norms and sanctions attached to the relationship. There are several such norms. He learns first of all that the sexual transaction with a "queer" must occur solely as a means of making money, that the relationship should be restricted to mouth-genital fellatio, that it must be affectively neutral, and that violence must not be used against the "queer" if he conforms to these expectations. For many career-oriented delinquent boys, then, hustling of "queers" is permitted. For other delinquent gangs, the practice becomes one of "queer-baiting," to roll the "queer" for his money, since he fears legal recourse to charge he has been robbed. In either case, the adolescent boy exploits adult males in the homosexual transaction, if exploitation is a meaningful term in this context.

The point to be made about legal sanctions in this context is that in many instances, the sexual transactions between adult males and adolescent boys arise precisely because both parties are outside the law. The laws of our society and the mores of the public define both delinquents and adults who engage in homosexual practices as deviators and restrict their opportunities to pursue their respective goals. Under these circumstances, it is not surprising to learn that the adult male who engages in homosexual acts and the delinquent pursue a mutually instrumental relationship.

In a fairly large number of cases involving an adult male and an adolescent boy in a sexual transaction, it is questionable whether the adult male seduces the adolescent boy. There are, of course, cases in which such seduction occurs. These cases of seduction, however, do not appear to involve large numbers of adolescent boys—certainly not to the point where the boys in the long run become involved in homosexual practices. Most of the delinquent boys who become involved in the "peer-queer" relationship described above do not continue the practices after adolescence. A small proportion of them undertake hustling careers,[22] but most assume the typical lower-status adult male role of

[22] See Ross, *The Hustler in Chicago*, 1 *J. Student Research* 13 (1959).

husband and father. The relationship never was defined by the boy as one in which he was in the social roles of either homosexual or prostitute.

## 21.  Narcotics Use among Juveniles

Isidor Chein

> The author is Professor of Psychology and a senior staff member of the Research Center for Human Relations at New York University. This article concerns a number of studies of narcotics use supported in part by the U.S. Public Health Service. Dr. Chein's articles have appeared in numerous publications.

When our group at New York University and others started investigating juvenile drug use in 1952 at the request of the United States Public Health Service, we were exploring a virtually unknown territory. Available information was for the most part unsystematic or unreliable or both. This condition largely determined the design of our studies: it was necessary to obtain, first, a bird's eye view of *each* of the many aspects of drug use among juveniles before pursuing detailed investigations of any one. At present we have completed the collection of data in a number of studies. In these studies we have attempted to analyze:

a. The characteristics of neighborhoods in Manhattan, Brooklyn, and the Bronx in which heroin use by male adolescents has the widest prevalence;

b. The relationship between the rates of drug use in various neighborhoods and the rates of other delinquent activity;

c. The home life and other behavioral and attitudinal characteristics of one hundred heroin users and one hundred nonusers;

d. The role that the delinquent street gang plays in heroin activity; and

e. The prevailing information and attitudes toward drugs and drug use among about one thousand young boys, about thirteen or fourteen years old, who live in three neighborhoods differing in known incidence of heroin use.

In the last-mentioned study, in addition to items about drug information and attitudes, we also inquired about certain general attitudes and

Isidor Chein, "Narcotics Use among Juveniles," *Social Work*, 1 (April, 1956), pp. 50-60. Reprinted with permission of the National Association of Social Workers.

value systems held by these boys, and certain specific attitudes toward police, parents, etc., that we hope will help to establish some of the psychological context within which these boys hold their beliefs about and their attitudes toward narcotics.

The first four of these studies are essentially complete and the fifth is now in its final stages [in 1956]. During most of this period we had the benefit of close contact with the psychiatric and clinical psychological study of juvenile drug users and a control group which was conducted by Donald Gerard and Conan Kornetsky. We have also collected the data and are now in the midst of a more intensive analysis of family relations in a group of users and controls; we are also conducting a six-month follow-up study of 30 boys released from Riverside Hospital; and, since all of the preceding involves only boys, we are planning to collect comparable information about a series of female cases.

## Where Does Juvenile Drug Use Flourish?

Our first study sought to determine some of the characteristics of neighborhoods with high drug incidence. The first step was to collect the names and addresses of boys between the ages of sixteen and twenty-one who had in the four-year period from 1949 through 1952 come to the attention of some official agency in the city in connection with narcotics. Our primary sources of cases were the courts and municipal hospitals in the three boroughs of Manhattan, Brooklyn, and the Bronx. Drug incidence in the two remaining boroughs of New York City was negligible during that period. From the courts we obtained not only the names of boys who had appeared on a drug charge, but also of others who had been apprehended on other criminal charges and, upon medical examination, proved to be drug users. We pruned the list, eliminating duplicate references to young men whose names came up more than once. We thus arrived at a list of 1,844 boys who were involved with the use, possession, and/or sale of drugs. There were, on the average, more than five hundred new cases a year from 1950 onward. We distributed the addresses by the census tract divisions (areas of from four to six square city blocks) of the 1950 census, and calculated census tract rates of drug use. The 1950 census also gave much information about each census tract, such as median income, educational level, and so on. We were then in a position to describe the relative characteristics of the neighborhoods in which youthful drug use flourished and those in which drug incidence was low.

Briefly, our findings from this study were these: in each of the boroughs, drug use among adolescent males is mainly concentrated in a small number of census tracts (three-quarters of the cases in 15 per cent of the tracts). These tracts constitute the most underprivileged, crowded, and dilapidated areas in the city. The next step involved an analysis of the relationship between neighborhood characteristics and drug rate *within* the area of high incidence of narcotics use. This analysis supported the first findings; that is, even when we looked only within the epidemic areas in each of the three boroughs, drug use was highest where income and education were lowest and where there was the greatest breakdown of normal family living arrangements.

## Other Forms of Delinquency and Drug Use

The second study consisted of an analysis of a sample of court charges other than narcotics violations lodged against boys in the same age group as in the first study. We also covered the same time period but for practical reasons limited this study to the Borough of Manhattan.

Our data show that all the neighborhoods where drug use has spread in "epidemic" proportions are located in very high delinquency areas. However, there are areas of equally high delinquency rates where drug use has not spread to any comparable degree. Those areas which are high in both drug use and other forms of delinquency are economically and socially the most deprived areas in the city. Those areas that are high in delinquency but low in drug use are substantially less deprived.

There was a general rise in total delinquency from 1949 to 1952. This borough-wide rise in delinquency can, however, be accounted for entirely by an increase in lesser violations—misdemeanors and summary offenses. There was no year-to-year change in the number of felonies. The sharp increase in lesser violations along with no change in the number of more serious ones held true in both the high drug-use neighborhoods and those with less drug activity. The only difference we found between the high and low drug-use areas was that the percentage of delinquencies probably motivated by profit was substantially greater in areas of high drug use than elsewhere in the borough—in other words, that where drug use was epidemic, the pattern of juvenile crime tended to shift to activities that could yield ready cash. This trend was especially strong in 1951 and 1952, the period when drug use had reached peak levels in these neighborhoods.

As one would expect, only some adolescents in even the areas of highest incidence took to drugs; by far the highest proportion of known users in any census tract was 10 per cent of the adolescents.

## Comparison of Backgrounds

Our third study explored further into family characteristics and personal experiences which might distinguish users from nonusers who lived in relatively high-use areas. We interviewed 200 boys at great length. The original design called for four groups of 50 cases each, but some of the cases had to be shifted from the cells to which they were originally allocated when additional information was accumulated. As a result, we had one group of 59 who were otherwise delinquent before they became users, one group of 50 delinquents who had not ·become users, one group of 41 users who were not delinquents before they took to drugs, and a fourth group of 50 boys who were neither delinquent nor users. The four groups were matched as closely as possible for incidence of drug use in neighborhoods of residence and on a number of other variables ( age, ethnic origin).

One of the questions that concerned us was whether environmental deprivation is as characteristic among drug users as it has been proven to be among delinquents. In our study of the four groups (delinquent versus nondelinquent, and users versus nonusers) we secured such rough indices of economic deprivation as the family being dependent on outside financial help, low occupational status of the chief breadwinner, and poor housing facilities. We also obtained such rough indices of deficient family atmosphere as poor family cohesion, psychosocial pathology in the family, and many traumatic experiences.

A comparison of delinquents and nondelinquents showed, as one would expect by now, that the delinquents are significantly more deprived than nondelinquents on both types of indices. This greater deprivation in the background of delinquents obtains when we compare drug users who were not previously delinquent with those who were; and the greater deprivation of delinquents also holds when we consider only nonusers. These differences, moreover, are still found when we consider the Negroes, the Spanish-speaking group, and the remaining whites separately.

However, when we compare users and nonusers, we find no differences between them in the white and Spanish-speaking groups. Though the delinquents as a group were the most deprived, there was no difference in this respect between those boys who were users and those who were not. Similarly, for the white and Spanish-speaking nondelinquents: there was no evident difference in deprivation between the users and nonusers. But we do find differences among Negroes that are related to drug use: Negro users (both delinquent and nondelinquent) come from economically more deprived homes than comparable Negro nonusers.

Thus we may conclude that (within the relatively narrow range of variation found in areas of drug use) gross differences in environmental deprivation within the home do not appear to play a significant role in the etiology of drug use among white and Spanish-speaking youths over and beyond their role as a factor in delinquency. Environmental factors that do play a special role in drug use would have to be along lines other than those that are associated with delinquency. Among the Negroes, the pattern is not too clear, but factors related to economic deprivation may be playing a special role in the etiology of drug use. This is in line with a finding reported above from the first two studies —namely, that the neighborhoods which are high in both delinquency and drug rates are more deprived than areas which are equally high in delinquency, but low in drug rate. The neighborhoods which are high in both tend to be Negro neighborhoods.

## Heroin Users

From the 100 heroin users in our sample we learned a great deal about the heroin involvement and practice among adolescents in New York. Almost all had smoked marijuana prior to trying heroin—a sequence almost universal until a few years ago. (There is some more recent evidence that some beginners may now start with heroin without the intervening step.) Only 10 per cent actively sought the first opportunity. The typical introduction to heroin was either in a group setting or at the initiative of a youthful friend. Contrary to popular belief, in almost all cases the novice does not get his first shot from an adult pusher. The vast majority were regularly on heroin within a year, at a median age of sixteen. The age of sixteen appears to be the most vulnerable age for those prone to drugs: if offered heroin at this age, they are more likely to try, they are more likely to have a positive reaction, and they subsequently make less effort to break the habit. Once regularly on the drug, 85 per cent took at least one dose daily, a majority taking it twice a day or more. Almost all "mainlined," that is, took the drug intravenously. The habit is expensive, the median outlay being about $35 a week and ranging to more than $70 a week.

There appears to be a difference between those boys who had been delinquent prior to using heroin and those who had not, and there are substantial numbers of both types. Those who had been delinquent tend to be "social users" more often, take the drug in order to belong, to "be down," and for the pleasure of it. Drug use seems to be, so to say, just another way of being delinquent. This conclusion is also supported by the fact that we experienced great difficulty in locating delinquents in the very high drug-use areas who were not also drug users—that is, where drug use is widespread, the delinquency pattern apparently comes to include it. By contrast, those who were not delinquent before they became users come from somewhat higher economic levels and appear to be more psychologically disturbed. Drugs seem to play a supportive role for them—they do not take them for the "kicks" as much as for the sense of being better able to cope with their problems. It is necessary to add that this distinction between the delinquent and nondelinquent users, which we are reasonably convinced embodies a basic core of truth, is nevertheless saved from being a gross oversimplification only by the semantic ambiguities inherent in the concept of delinquency.

Many users expect little from life and society and they value refinement and an easy and comfortable life. At the same time they do not appear capable of exploiting the opportunities available to them in their environment. Their social values and attitudes fall into a syndrome which could be called the *cat* culture.

Asked to check a true or false list of attitude statements, the majority of a supplementary sample of users for whom the prior relationship to delinquency was, unfortunately, not determined checked the following as true:

> Most policemen can be paid off.
> The police often pick on people for no good reason.
> You're a fool if you believe what most people try to tell you.
> The thing to do is to live for today rather than to try to plan for tomorrow.
> The way things look for the future, most people would be better off if they were never born.
> Everybody is just out for himself. Nobody really cares about anybody else.

They checked the following as *not* true:

> Most policemen treat people of all races the same.
> I am sure that most of my friends would stand by me no matter what kind of trouble I got into.

And they checked that, more than almost anything else in the world, they would like very much to:

> Always be doing a lot of new and exciting things—never to be bored.

Be able to get other people to do what you want.
Be able to take things easy and not have to work hard.

A majority of the controls gave the opposite responses to all eleven items.

The presence of antisocial gangs and individuals in the neighborhood and the "cat-culture" they have created constitute a threat to those adolescent boys who want to avoid trouble with the police and make something of themselves. The control group protected themselves by using more discrimination in selecting friends, by dissociating themselves determinedly from those who were heading for trouble, and by forming a subculture of "squares" which differed in activities, interests, and aspirations from the "cat-culture" which surrounded them. The value-system of the control boys is more rooted in reality and more oriented to the future. They manage to find opportunities for expanding their horizons, and they utilize more fully the limited resources at their disposal in both school and community.

We expect to know more about the nature of the relationship between pro- or antidrug attitudes and the general system of social values and attitudes when our analysis of the fifth study is completed.


## Drug Use in Street Gangs

But we have not yet described the fourth. In this study, conducted in cooperation with the New York City Youth Board, we obtained information about the drug-use patterns of 18 antisocial street gangs in the city from reports of group workers who are in close contact with the gangs. From this study we have learned that, contrary to widespread belief, drug use is not by any means necessarily tied up with gang activities. In some of the clubs there is no drug use at all, in others less than half the membership take drugs, in only two clubs were more than 65 per cent of the members also users. Only occasional heroin use is approved by the bulk of club members; habitual use of heroin is generally disapproved and addicts lose their leadership status.

The common belief that street gangs are the centers of organized drug selling activity is evidently another myth. In fact, there appears to be no organized selling activity in any of the clubs.

The allegation that street gangs are a major source of recruitment into drug use has not been substantiated. We know that within the club there are not only no efforts to recruit users, but there are often active efforts to discourage habitual heroin use.

Finally, certain differences seem to be apparent in the life style of users and nonusers in the clubs: users are more likely to go along on gang-planned robberies and burglaries as well as "lineups" and other forms of sexual delinquency, but they are less likely to participate in club-sponsored social and sports activities or in gang fights.

In general, it appears that the street gang is like the neighborhood itself, an area in which juvenile drug use occurs. The gang in itself does not seem to be a special causative factor. If there is a special problem of drug use in the street gangs, it is mainly because street gangs are likely to bring together a high concentration of otherwise personally and socially maladjusted boys. With respect to these boys, there appear to be two developmental stages in which the gang seems to assume different roles related to drug use. In the adolescent stage (roughly under the age of eighteen) the street culture favors "acting out" on a gang basis. Rumbles, fights, hell-raising, competitive sports are an appropriate expression for this age. Even if the gang includes a large proportion of anxious, inadequately functioning boys (of the type we would consider prone to drug use), the activities of the gang offer a measure of shared status, a measure of security and a sense of belonging. The boys do not have to face life alone—the group protects them. Escape into drugs is not necessary as yet.

But as the group grows older, two things happen. Sports, hell-raising, and gang fights become "kid stuff" and are given up. In the normal course of events, the youthful preoccupations are replaced by more individual concerns about work, future, a "steady" girl, and so on. If most of the gang members are healthy enough to face these new personal needs and engage in the new activities appropriate for their age, the availability of drugs will not attract their interest.

But for those gang members who are too disturbed emotionally to face the future as adults, the passing of adolescent hell-raising leaves emptiness, boredom, apathy, and restless anxiety. In a gang where there are many such disturbed members, the lone user will soon find companions, and cliques of users will grow quickly. Enmeshed in the pattern of activities revolving around the purchase, sale, and use of drugs and the delinquent efforts to get money to meet the exorbitant cost of heroin, the young users can comfortably forget about girls, careers, status, and recognition in the society at large. Their sexual drive is diminished, they maintain a sense of belonging in the limited world of the addict, they remain children forever.

## Attitudes, Values, and Drug Information

The fifth study represents, apart from its intrinsic theoretical interest, a research bridge to an action program of prevention. Any such program must deal with youngsters who are approaching but who have not yet reached the age when drug use typically starts. Partly for this reason and partly for reasons that have to do with sampling problems, we focused in this study on eighth-graders. The municipal and parochial school systems of the city assisted us in administering drug information and attitude questionnaires to about one thousand boys—the entire eighth grade—in three selected neighborhoods of low socioeconomic status. One of these neighborhoods had the highest drug rate in the city; the second had a somewhat lower drug rate; and the third had very little drug activity at all until recently. In general, we find that boys from the neighborhood in which drug use is most widely prevalent hold the most tolerant attitudes toward drugs and drug users, but at the same time are least likely to possess correct information about drugs and their consequences. These are the same boys who, according to their own report, pick up most of their drug information from the street, about half of them knowing at least one heroin user personally.

Two categories of boys were especially uninformed on almost all questions, even in comparison to the general low level of information held by all groups. These are the adjustment class boys in Harlem [1] and the Puerto Rican boys on the Lower East Side. There was not a single item among the 15 we asked to which a majority knew the correct answer—not even the easiest item on the test, namely that it is against the law to give away drugs. Only 40 per cent in these two groups gave the correct answer to this.

It is of interest to note that these two groups of boys have the most favorable attitudes toward drug use and heroin users. One-third of them agree with the statement, "Heroin is not as bad for a person as some people say. They make too big a fuss about it." Twenty per cent indicate that they believe that users can get along better on their own than nonusers. The very groups of boys who reveal a gross lack of even rudimentary information about drugs contain substantial numbers who profess favorable attitudes to drugs and to drug users.

Our questionnaire allows us to look further into the boys' value systems and attitudes about other topics. As one might expect in a group of problem youngsters in a high delinquency neighborhood, the adjust-

[1] These particular adjustment classes contain only Negro boys.

ment class boys have very negative attitudes toward the police. A large majority of them, in contrast to our other groups, highly value the enjoyment of life by "having lots of thrills and taking chances." These boys think of themselves as lucky; most feel that nothing can stop them once they really make up their minds to do something and that you should live for today rather than try to plan for tomorrow. Yet they are pessimistic and distrustful. Half believe that, the way things look for the future, most people would be better off if they were never born. Nearly as many agree with the thought that there is not much chance that people will really do anything to make this a better world to live in.

All these studies have concerned themselves with the social environment of the juvenile drug users. We have learned that the social pattern of using narcotics is highly concentrated in the most deprived areas of the city; that it is associated with the type of delinquency producing ready cash; that the pattern of using drugs spreads within the peer-group and apparently is meaningful in the context of the social reality in which the boys live; that the users (and nonusing delinquents) live in a special defiant and escapist subculture side by side with the other subculture of "squares" who want to lift themselves out of their depriving environment. This last and other findings point to a selective factor in the personality of the drug-prone youths.

## Personality of the Young Addict

Psychiatric research into the personality of young addicts—and especially the study of addicts and controls by Donald Gerard and Conan Kornetsky—suggests that juvenile addicts are seriously disturbed emotionally, a large proportion suffering from overt or incipient schizophrenia. There appears to exist among the juvenile addicts a pattern of symptoms which clinicians in various parts of the country continue to confirm: (1) dysphoria, i.e., a characteristic mood verging on depression and involving feelings of futility and expectations of failure; (2) problems of sexual identification evidenced by manifest sexual psychopathology and/or difficulties in assuming a masculine role; and (3) disturbances of interpersonal relations, characterized by inability to enter prolonged, close, or friendly relationships with either peers or adults. Furthermore, addicts typically have a low tolerance of anxiety and frustration, and are eager to use "props" and supports of any kind whenever available. Opiates are particularly effective for addicts as anxiety-reducing and tranquility-producing agents.

In the broadest terms, the potential male addict may be described as suffering from a weak ego structure, weak superego functioning, and inadequate masculine identification. In addition, the typical young addict's attitude characteristically involves a lack of a realistic middle-class orientation and a distrust of major institutions.

## Factors Conducive to Addiction-Prone Personalities

Our more recent study of the family background was designed to test our predictions that the family background of addicts would contain specified kinds of factors conducive to the development of these three personality characteristics and two social attitudes. Two groups of families—30 families of users and 29 of controls—were interviewed by social workers on details of family life and history.

The analysis of the findings of this study confirms our predictions that addicts come from a home environment with features conducive to the development of the type of personality structure and attitudes found in these young people.

As to what we have called ego-damaging factors, almost all the 30 addicts came from families where there was a disturbed relationship between the parents as evidenced by separation, divorce, overt hostility, or lack of warmth and mutual interest. Furthermore, most of these parents either over-indulged or harshly frustrated the boys as children. Most of the parents of our addicts had unrealistically low (though sometimes they had unrealistically high) ambitions for the boy. What they wanted for him as an adult was usually inappropriate to their objective family circumstances or the ability of the youngster.

In relation to factors we have considered as leading to inadequate superego functioning, we found that the addicts experienced very frequently, and much more often than the controls, cool or hostile parent figures, weak parent-child relationships, lack of clarity as to the way in which disciplinary policies were established, and vague or inconsistent parental standards for the boy.

In relation to the third personality characteristic, there were many things about the family background of the addicts that would interfere with the normal development of feelings of masculine identification. In almost half of the cases, the father-figure was absent from the home during the early childhood period, and in many other cases when a father was present, he was cool or hostile in his attitude to the boy. The general pattern was of a weak relationship (the father having very little to do with his son), open hostility, or no relationship at all because of a broken home.

As for items related to our prediction that the parents of our addict subjects would be much less realistically middle-class oriented people, this was especially true in relation to their attitudes toward the future of their sons. Though the control families were also living in very poor neighborhoods, and were very often members of socially and economically deprived minority groups, the latter parents were able to encourage their sons to plan on the basis of their abilities and to make realistic use of the limited opportunities open to them. Not so the parents of the addicts.

Finally, with regard to the general life attitudes of many of the addicts' parents that would tend to make for pessimism and distrust on the part of the youngsters, these parents were frequently distrustful of authority figures such as teachers and social workers. They tended to entertain low aspirations for the boy and a pessimistic outlook toward their own future.

In summary, the findings of this study clearly suggest that the pathologic personality characteristics of the addict are consistent outgrowths of the disturbed pattern of family relationships to which he has been exposed.

## Theoretical Overview

We have, of course, struck only the highlights of our various studies, but, even so, the very variety of data must be quite confusing at first reading. Perhaps it may be helpful if we were to review, in admittedly oversimplified form, how the picture adds up to us.

Forms of behavior like delinquency and drug addiction—and, for that matter, any other form of behavior—do not take place in a vacuum. They are carried out in a physical and social context which plays an important role in determining their likelihood of occurrence and the specific forms that they take.

Obviously, for example, no one would take narcotics if there were none available to be taken. This is a basic fact even though it is extremely difficult to hold it in balanced perspective. For one thing, it dangles before us the tantalizing objective of eliminating narcotics addiction by making narcotics unavailable. This objective is so tantalizingly real that it makes it difficult to bear in mind various complicating factors. For instance: (1) the fact that reduced supply without a corresponding reduction in demand raises the market value of narcotics and, hence, places an additional premium on smuggling and also puts increased pressure on the addict so that he must increase his own criminal activities to be able to support his habit; and (2) the fact that law enforcement is effective in controlling behavior only to the extent that its sanctions are stronger, more certain, and more immediate than the potential rewards of violating the law. But, more fundamentally, the basic fact is that a supply of narcotics is simply a necessary condition for taking them and not an impelling force. Hence, eliminating the necessary condition would not in itself eliminate the impelling forces and these would continue to have some kind of consequence even though they could no longer lead to drug addiction. If we were to go into this matter further, therefore, we would have to face up to the question, if the channel to addiction were irrevocably closed, into what other channels would the unaltered impelling forces push the individual —and would these alternatives be preferable to addiction?

Now, it is not our purpose to evaluate the law-enforcement approach, but merely to illustrate that the environment does influence behavior and that even when some aspects of this role are obvious, they are not necessarily simple. We have, however, digressed from our main purpose which was to give our interpretation of the available information about the determinants of drug use. Let us return to this.

## Breeding Ground

There are segments of communities in which there is a relative breakdown in the fabric of human relationships. The individual has no real roots in a permanent community. His position is such that he experiences himself as standing essentially alone against the rest of the world. The fellow human beings with whom he comes into contact are compelled by force of circumstances, if not by personal predilection, to scrabble around, each for his own needs—and he does not have the security of knowing that, should he need their support, he can rely upon them for this. He shares in the common dreams of a good life, however he may interpret the latter, but the bleak circumstances of his situation give him no realistic expectations of ever being able to achieve it, and he is confronted by an "endlessness of days." There does not appear to be any real point in working toward a brighter future, only in seizing upon the pleasures of the moment. The standards of behavior which are so highly valued by other segments of society have, at best, only negative significance for him—for living up to them can only protect him from an additional burden of trouble rather than provide him with the missing satisfactions of living. Perhaps there are also constructive possibilities open to a person in such an environment; but almost everyone whom he meets is in a like situation to his own, and their communicated perceptions and the observable events of their lives only reinforce his view of human society and of his own future—that is, the constructive possibilities, if they exist, are not easy to see.

This is the kind of environment which is the breeding ground of delinquency and crime, alcoholism, drug addiction when drugs are widely available, and a variety of other antisocial and socially maladaptive behavior. Such an environment can, no doubt, come into being in a variety of ways. In New York City, it is associated with the triad of neighborhood characteristics already mentioned—widespread poverty, low level of education, and high proportion of broken families and other deviant family arrangements—and with a large number of other related characteristics that are brought out in our analysis of the neighborhood data. Also, we should not forget that where antisocial behavior becomes widespread, a new norm tends to emerge which is not only consistent with the prevailing atmosphere but which also makes such behavior acceptable and even desirable.

The prevailing atmosphere of degenerated interpersonal relationships that characterize the neighborhood can be markedly counteracted by one's experiences in a cohesive family group. Such experience can give one a sense of human solidarity, a feeling of belonging, respect for the integrity and value of the individual human being, and the long-range motivation of things worth living for. But in the kind of environment that we have been describing, the family itself is especially vulnerable as is evidenced by the high proportion of abnormal family arrangements in the high use areas.

Even in the best residential areas, poor family relationships in the early life experience of a person can go pretty far toward creating an atmosphere of degenerated interpersonal relationships such as that described as characteristic of our deteriorated neighborhoods—that is, a lack of security in one's fellow human beings, a sense of everyone's being out for himself, a sense of futility, of not really belonging, and so on. Now, place such a disrupted family in the midst of such a deteriorated neighborhood and the effect must be immeasurably enhanced. It is precisely from such disrupted families in such deteriorated neighborhoods that the bulk of our delinquents and drug users come.

Yet, after all, a person is still a being who is more or less capable of resisting the pressures of his environment, of responding differentially to its various aspects, and of helping to shape it to his own ends. We do not mean to imply that the environment played no role in making him what he is. The history of a person's interactions with the environment that go into shaping his personality, however, involves not merely the order of environmental conditions that we have described, but also many more subtle and more or less idiosyncratic events occurring in a particular order in time in an infinite series of epigenetic cycles. It is as a net product of such a history that an individual stands, at any given period of time, more or less against his immediate environment and also more or less vulnerable to it.

Now, there are some individuals who, on the one hand, do not have strong internalized restraints and who, on the other hand, have various neurotic and other needs such as an accumulated fund of hostility against man and society, an urge to maintain a sense of personal integrity in the face of society at large, a desire to share in the social goods that seem to be denied to them, a need to conform to the behavior standards of the deviant social circles in which they move, and so on—such individuals are inclined to act in what we regard as an antisocial manner. If these needs are strong enough, and the inner restraints weak enough, such people will become delinquents and criminals in the best of environments. Suppose, however, that the balance of needs and restraints is not essentially different than in the average member of our society. Place a person with such needs in an environment which is favorable and conducive to antisocial behavior—an environment such as we have described—and he too is likely to become a delinquent. The stronger the needs and the more conducive the environment to delinquency, the more certain does eventual delinquency and crime become.

If drugs become available on a large scale—in the highest drug-use area of the city, 45 per cent of the eighth-grade boys indicated they knew one or more heroin users personally, close to 40 per cent claimed to have actually seen someone taking heroin, and 10 per cent said that they themselves have already had the opportunity to try it out—with such easy access to drugs, a new wide-open channel of delinquent activity becomes available. And many try it out although not all of them become addicted. In fact, our study of juvenile gangs brought out the existence of regular "weekend" users who have not developed increased tolerance and need or withdrawal symptoms after several years of use. Addiction apparently depends not merely on continued use, but also on psychological and perhaps physiological predisposition. This is not to gainsay the possibility that there may be some limit of prolonged use beyond which everyone would become addicted—and, of course, the frequency and size of intake are undoubtedly a factor.

Many of the delinquents who experiment with heroin do, of course, become addicted. There are other addicts, however, who have not responded to the delinquency-producing vectors of their environment by becoming delinquent, but who nevertheless display personality patterns that are in close harmony with the social atmosphere of their neighborhoods. These are the unaggressive, withdrawn, dysphoric individuals who even at best would find it difficult to relate to other people. In an environment which fully justifies a pessimistic outlook and in which it is at best difficult to establish wholesome interpersonal relationships, they are totally lost souls. To them, narcotic drugs like heroin offer a quick and royal route to meeting the challenge of living. Heroin and its related subculture gives them a sense of well-being and of social acceptability and participation. If the price is a terrible one to pay—and, as our data indicate, it is one of which they are likely to be all too imperfectly aware—the pseudo-rewards, especially in the "honeymoon stage," are far more glittering than anything else their environment offers them. Given heroin, these young people are doomed.

## Rehabilitation and Prevention

This, then, is the interpretation of juvenile narcotics use that we offer. Our studies, however, were not simply academically motivated. If so much of our initial efforts were oriented toward elucidating and explaining the phenomena, it was at least in part because we had to understand the nature of the problem before we could hope to offer any worth-while ideas that might contribute to doing something about it.

During the past year, our thinking has moved in the direction of the problem of rehabilitation and prevention. We are now in the midst of a follow-up study of 30 boys released from Riverside Hospital and we hope to gain much practical insight into their problems and the role of the community in the posthospitalization period.

As for prevention, we have come to the conclusion that it is not feasible to conceive of worth-while community action programs with a narrowly defined goal of preventing drug use. We perceive drug use among juveniles as one symptom among many and we envisage a program aimed at helping personally damaged and environmentally deprived youths to grow up into healthy adults—and that means *not* users, *not* delinquents, *not* mental patients, *not* recluses. But this is a topic for another paper.

## 22.   The Metropolis and Juvenile Delinquency among Negroes

# Mozell Hill

The author, with the Ph.D. degree from the University of Chicago, is Professor of Education, Teachers College, Columbia University. He has taught in England and at the University of Nigeria and has been a consultant to the Federal Security Agency and the U.S. Public Health Service. He has had various articles published on problems of delinquency.

This discussion will view juvenile delinquency as "a way of life" in urban living.[1] The main emphasis will be on the deviant behavior of minority youth, particularly Negroes, living in segregated communities, culturally isolated "islands," as it were, located in heterogeneous, multigroup, metropolitan areas of the United States. The central purpose of this approach is to disclose the nature and peculiar cultural components of the social relationships between individuals and groups in racial and cultural minority (segregated) communities of standard metropolitan areas.

Recognizing, of course, that moral values provide the basis for all interpersonal and intergroup actions, this discussion will not, however, concern itself with moralistic and legalistic views of the complex phenomena of deviant behavior among Negro youth. The foibles inherent in moral and legal definitional modes of thinking about the problem lead the analysts to a reliance upon selected, inaccurate, and frequently distorted statistical data for "facts." As a consequence, many studies do little more than compound and "refine" quantitative errors of judgment about the alarming increase in deviant and nonconforming behavior of young people.

Juvenile delinquency among Negroes, whether in metropolitan areas, small market-town cities, or in the open country, must be viewed within the context of the overall social system in which it exists. In fact, there appears to be at least one single criterion, social status, that poignantly

Mozell Hill, "The Metropolis and Juvenile Delinquency among Negroes," *Journal of Negro Education*, 28 (Summer, 1959), pp. 277-285. Reprinted with permission of the publishers of the *Journal*.

[1] See Louis Wirth, "Urbanism as a Way of Life," *American Journal of Sociology*. 44:1-24, July 1938.

distinguishes delinquent and nondelinquent behavior—a criterion of rights, privileges, prestige, social power and authority, and norms (rules and regulations). The status system of any community including its subsystems—neighborhoods, families, schools, churches, voluntary associations—mirrors the variations in patterns of interpersonal and intergroup relations. Thus, from at least one important point of view, juvenile delinquency becomes "a way of life," a subcultural system of interpersonal relations for achieving social status.[2]

In this connection, Merton has suggested that juvenile delinquency, like any other form of deviant conduct, is little more than a symptom of an individual's or a group's lack of conformity to "culturally prescribed aspirations and socially structured means of achieving them"—a symptom of anomie.[3] What Merton has indicated here is that modern urban living places persons and groups under tremendous social stress—stress upon money, appearances, belongingness, popularity, acceptability, and other features of pragmatic success. Whenever a status system of any community arranges its members in such a way that certain segments are limited and even denied avenues for "social success," the system will be characterized by varying degrees of anomie (social normlessness).

It is well known, and has been demonstrated repeatedly in scientific studies, editorials, essays, and even in popular fiction, that most Negroes, along with Puerto Ricans, Mexicans, Japanese-Americans, and other readily distinguishable minority groups are afforded the least opportunities to attain the minimum promises of American democracy; their educational opportunities are limited through segregation; they are ofttimes the last hired and the first fired, thus diminishing an equitable share in economic and business activities. They are unwelcome in many situations and are often encouraged and even threatened to isolate themselves from the religious life of the community; indeed, too many Negroes have been culturally starved as a result of segregation, and are emotionally frustrated as a result of these deprivations.

It is little wonder, then, that minority groups, and lower-class Negroes in particular, have been forced into deviant conduct—petty stealing,

---

[2] For a detailed and penetrating analysis of social status and behavioral differentials among young people, see A. B. Hollingshead, *Elmtown's Youth*. New York: John Wiley and Sons, Inc. 1949.

[3] *Anomie.* A theory of deviant behavior which focuses attention upon pathological behavior as it arises from discrepancies between cultural norms, goals and objectives, and approved modes of access to them. See Emile Durkheim's *Suicide*, translated by J. A. Spaulding and George Simpson. Glencoe, Illinois: The Free Press, 1951; also Robert K. Merton's *Social Theory and Social Structure*. Glencoe, Illinois: The Free Press, 1957, Chapts. 4 and 5.

cheating, lying, vice, and even organized crime as "a way of life." Deviant conduct, therefore, might be approached as a nonconforming means of survival in a segregated, presumably hostile, society. Economically deprived, culturally starved, and emotionally frustrated, many Negro youths have established ingenious means and channels of achieving social status that are manifested in both covert and overt delinquent patterns.

## "The Exploding Metropolis" and the Negro Community

Perhaps the most powerful, yet the most silent and imperceptibly revolutionary aspect of the American city is the highly mobile character of individuals and families. Migrations from rural to urban centers and both horizontal and vertical social mobility have been the main determinants in the changing behavior of all segments of the American population; however, the dynamics of Negro life and culture have been the most uneven, dramatic, and productive of social problems. For the past one hundred years, Negroes, along with other racial and cultural minorities including "poor whites" have been on the move in ever-increasing numbers from South to North, from East to West, and from lower status to higher status, into the great metropolitan centers of the nation.

On January 1, 1958, more than one hundred million Americans were living in some two hundred "standard metropolitan areas." [4] These "exploding" areas are neither distinct political areas nor socially and economically isolated units. They not only touch each other, they also interpenetrate. For example, metropolitan New York includes some twenty-two counties and over six hundred political units.

The percentage of minorities living in metropolitan regions has been increasing since the turn of the century. The migration from rural to urban areas has been most dramatic in recent years. The influx of Negroes to the great metropolitan areas was unprecedented in volume. Between 1940 and 1950, more than three million Negroes migrated from the farm into the city. By 1950, approximately three-fifths of the Negro populations was living in cities, compared with two-fifths in 1930, and less than one-fifth in 1920.

The distribution and redistribution of Negroes (residential mobility)

[4] Standard metropolitan areas of the United States embrace the old central city, suburbs, and even the open country—exurbia. See Donald J. Bogue, *The Structure of the Metropolitan Community*. Ann Arbor: University of Michigan Press, 1949; Rupert B. Vance and Sara Smith, "Metropolitan Dominance and Integration" in Vance and Demerath (eds.) *The Urban South*, Chapel Hill: University of North Carolina Press, 1955.

within metropolitan areas are producing strange and unanticipated patterns of social relations. For example, today in the typical metropolis, less than six out of every ten residents are living in the old central city; on the other hand, almost nine out of every ten Negroes are segregated and restricted to the old central city. In fact, Negroes are rapidly becoming a central-city phenomenon, along with Puerto Ricans, Mexicans, Chinese, and Japanese-Americans. In contrast, the white population, especially second and third generation foreign-borns and native white stocks are moving, sometimes in panic, to the outskirts of town, leaving the slums to minority and underprivileged groups. Between 1940 and 1950 the population of standard metropolitan areas increased 29.7 per cent, while the percentage increase in the central city was only 9.6 per cent. But paradoxically, the Negro population in central city increased almost seventy per cent. As a case in point, central-city sections of New York City contain a larger number of Negroes than all but five Southern states: Alabama, Georgia, Louisiana, Mississippi, and South Carolina.

## The Negro Community

Studies of the life and culture of Negroes on the American scene reveal that every metropolis North, South, East, or West, contains one, two, three, or several subcommunities and/or neighborhoods whose population is predominantly Negro. In general, these physical units are but cultural "islands" segregated—and in some instances almost completely isolated—from the overall structures of the metropolis.

Perhaps the greatest error in thinking about these Negro communities is to stereotype them. The belief that they are homogeneous owing to their racial composition is a fallacy, for Negro neighborhoods run the gamut from closed to open, small to large, cohesive to loose, and from central city to suburbia, and on into exurbia. Moreover, they can be characterized as heterogeneous in respect to every index and indicator employed by social scientists to measure social differentiation: level of income, type of occupation, style of living, level of aspiration, degree of frustration, cultural norm, amount of education, and so on.

In addition to physical deterioration, the only difference from other residential units manifested by the urban Negro community is reflected in its "reference group behavior" and "status-role conceptions"[5] which

[5] For a critical discussion of these concepts, see Muzafer Sherif, *Group Relations at the Cross Roads*. New York: Harper Bros., 1955. This volume contains a series of insightful essays by leading psychologists, psychiatrists, sociologists and anthro-

Negroes are forced to learn. Yet these differences are sufficient to give it a unique character (for analytical purposes only). Thus the behavior of Negroes in the metropolis stems from at least three common components.

1. A *segregated minority group* of individuals who are forced to share and organize their life experiences, the result of which produces

2. A *segregated minority group* that develops the capacity for compulsive identification—an ever-deepening empathy and "recipathy" with those who share their deprivations and frustrations, and ending in

3. A *selfconscious, segregated minority group* that circulates a wide variety of ingroup symbols, legends, and myths among its members; symbols that are goal directed, "collective representations," as it were, that become pragmatic variations of the "American Dream," the promise of success, happiness, self-fulfillment, equal opportunity, justice, survival, and freedom.

## Juvenile Delinquency Subcultures in Metropolitan Negro Communities

At least three distinct subcultural modes of delinquent behavior are manifested by Negro youth in metropolitan areas: (1) criminal patterns, (2) conflict patterns, and (3) retreatist patterns.[6] Moreover, the incidence, types and rates of deviant conduct vary with the peculiar nature (social structure) of the Negro community. Segregated Negro communities might be classified, for the sake of convenience and at the risk of oversimplification, into a four-fold typology:

1. *The transitory segregated Negro communities,* composed chiefly of migrant Negroes who are forced to live in segregated communities, but do not feel that they are a part of it.

2. *The involuntary yet planned segregated Negro communities* in which most residents get hemmed in by customary housing patterns, planned land-use patterns (zoning), gerrymandering, and the like.

---

pologists that will prove helpful to those who wish to probe deeper into the problem of group relations.

[6] See Albert K. Cohen, *Delinquent Boys.* Glencoe, Illinois: The Free Press, 1955, Chapt. 2; Frederic M. Thrasher, *The Gang.* Chicago: The University of Chicago Press, 1936; Richard Cloward and Lloyd E. Ohlin, "Types of Delinquent Subcultures." Unpublished manuscript. New York School of Social Work, Columbia University, December 1958.

3. *The residual (hard core) segregated Negro community* in which much voluntary separation takes place. Individuals and families are too old and apathetic to become mobile; many have few skills, low education, and little orientation and motivation for competitive life in the city.

4. *The underworld segregated Negro communities* that are highly organized in which people loaf on street corners and in bars, where they maintain a tight communication system and scrutinize behavior on the basis of personal control. Here demoralization is sometimes rife and most of the people are broken in spirit.

What has been indicated earlier should be reiterated: the only unique quality of deviant conduct in the so-called Negro community must be analyzed within the context of reference group behavior and expectational role conceptions of individuals and groups.

The discriminating forces guiding and controlling Negro youths' acceptance of criminal subcultural patterns as a way of life result from learned feelings that the underworld makes accessible and sanctions. These represent to Negro youth ready and meaningful culture channels and operational means of achieving success goals. Many of these youth are taught systematically that one should be on the lookout for the "successful lead" that will move them from down-and-outers to persons of means. Thus they learn very early states of readiness and routine practices of crime: theft, fraud, and racketeering. The subculture of the underworld even demands for survival social learnings of its young people that reward those who acquire mastery of the techniques and subcultural criminal orientation; attitudes of hostility and distrust—seeking out the "suckers"—their natural enemies or victims.

If a young, thoughtful, resourceful person is to become an accepted and respected member of the criminal world, he must become a "right guy"; he must develop the "right connections"; that is, he must join up with all of the other "right guys" and develop a sense of loyalty, honesty, and trustworthiness in the subculture of the underworld.

Another pattern of delinquency among Negroes in metropolitan areas is one of social conflict. Juveniles in conflict with the legitimate means and values of society generally develop a moral order of their own usually expressed in delinquent gangs. Isolated from the mainstream of society, conflicting juveniles become deviants that some label "boopers." These youth act with a compensating arrogance; they fight with weapons, chiefly against other gangs, to win respect or recognition.

Delinquent gangs in metropolitan areas are guided by a motivation to win and defend the "rep" of both their individual members and the total group. This means that each member of the gang must have "heart"; he cannot "chicken out," no matter what force the opposition might employ. Indeed, everyone outside of the gang represents the opposition—parents, teachers, ministers, social workers, juvenile judges, and above all, policemen—"coppers." The juvenile delinquent gang members view themselves as completely isolated from the adult world which they consider as "weaks" and saturated with "squares," "phonies," and hypocrites.

Among Negro juvenile delinquents in the "exploding metropolis" perhaps the dominant manifestation of deviant conduct takes the form of retreat. These youths are emotionally frustrated and carry deep psychological scars of oppression.[7] Moreover, they have given up—"the 'American Dream' is for white folks." It provides little promise or hope for them. Within the retreatist patterns many urban Negro youths acquire an obsession for sensory and expressive experiences; they are in continuous and unrelenting pursuit of a thrill—the "kick." "We are a bunch of 'cool cats.'" Every "cat" must have a "kick." As "cool cats" they take to alcohol, marijuana cigarettes, drugs (dope), tranquilizers, exciting sexual experiences, "hot jazz," "cool jazz," and varying combinations of these and other stimulants. This reflects the feelings and the informal differential associations of an increasingly larger number of adolescent Negroes caught in the web of urban life.

One of the dangers of such depressed states of mind and extreme retreatist view is that a juvenile delinquent feels that in order to be a "cool cat" he or she must "get a hustle"—a lucrative racket. However, the "cool cat" rejects violence and force, and prefers manipulation, persuasion, outwitting, or "conning." Thus he begs, borrows, steals, or engages in "con" games. To be successful, the "cat" must have finesse, demeanor, good taste—the aesthetics of "coolness." For example, the "cool cat" retreatist in most cases exhibits highly developed and sophisticated tastes in clothing, hair styles, unruffled manners, colorful and discriminating vocabulary, and ritualized gestures. Above all, the "cool cat" is oriented to the "world of cats," and keeps his associations with the "world of squares," at the irreducible minimum. He is constantly at work developing a "hustle" to achieve more and more "kicks."

[7] Some social psychologists and psychiatrists emphasize that delinquent behavior among urban Negro youth is but a symptom of an oppression psychosis. See Abram Kardiner and Lionel Onesey, The Mark of Oppression. New York: W. W. Norton & Company, 1951.

# Etiology and Sources of Juvenile Delinquency: Social Disorganization or Anomie?

The popular notion that because of segregation Negro communities are inevitably disorganized is inaccurate and limited. In fact, only those segregated neighborhoods that are in rapid transition—either deteriorating toward complete blight or in process of "planned" relocation of families—exhibit an increase in the social isolation of individuals and corresponding breakdown in social cohesion. Such communities are characterized by varying degrees of personal demoralization and social disorganization. Moreover, these segregated cultural islands are composed of disproportionate numbers of permanently unemployables, hardened prostitutes, drug addicts, alcoholics, beggars, vagrants, and homeless men. The composition of the typically socially-disorganized population reveals a preponderance of females over males, sometimes as high a ratio as eight to one; the age structure shows a bulging of the age groups between fifteen and forty-four, with a shrinkage in the number of children and old people. Finally, the per cent of married persons is comparatively low except for common law unions many of which are temporary, weak, and unstable.

It is difficult and sometimes well-nigh impossible to rehabilitate people or to establish delinquency controls in such blighted areas. Perhaps the only hope for these tragic individuals that are captured inside of the irreversible processes of social disorganization is to remove them from these segregated ghettos into planned relocation centers under the supervision of persons trained and skilled in community organization.

In general, Negro community life in most metropolitan areas is highly organized. Organization in and of itself is not a deterrent of deviant conduct. In fact, many institutional structures are so well organized that they defy rehabilitation and guided redirection. Many delinquent gangs are tightly integrated. They are generally led by youth who have exceptional leadership abilities—young people who are able to take the initiative. The members of urban gangs are inventive, courageous, and energetic; they display loyalty and are good followers, showing a willingness to make great sacrifices. From the point of view of social cohesion, they are quite superior to most middle-class Negro children.[8] Nowhere else in the Negro community are group solidarity, mutual assistance, and the communal spirit as strong as in most delinquent

[8] See E. Franklin Frazier, *Black Bourgeoisie*. Glencoe, Illinois: The Free Press, 1930.

gangs. Accordingly, it is neither the lack of organization nor the degree of disorganization that poses the greatest threat to society. Rather, it is the values, moral codes, reference group behavior, and self-images and conceptions that produce the high incidence of juvenile delinquency among metropolitan youth.

The etiology of juvenile delinquency in the Negro community becomes clearer when one looks into the problems faced by youth in the modern city. Young people, and especially minority groups, are confronted with both psychological and cultural limitations with respect to the avenues of access to the goals and promises of democracy. At the same time, practically every adolescent growing up in the city is unable, and quite understandably unwilling, to revise his or her aspirations downward.

Shaw,[9] Sutherland,[10] Whyte,[11] Kobrin,[12] and others have demonstrated in their studies that delinquent behavior increases differentially among ethnic and racial groups, depending upon the group's position in the social structure. They stress the discriminating force of such factors as age, sex, social class, ethnic group, race, kinship, and the type of area in which the individual grows up.

The fundamental causes for the increasing rate of juvenile delinquency among Negroes, as compared with native and foreign-born white groups as well as other minorities, stem from the systematic and persistent segregation of Negroes into so-called "natural areas" of the metropolis.[13] Whenever any group is segregated from the rest of the community by custom and law, the segregated individuals will intensify their in-group actions and create formal and informal structures that may or may not be compatible with the overall society. Segregation tends to knit individuals into closer webs of social relationships based upon special language symbols, sentiments, legends and myths. Moreover, segregated groups learn above everything else to distrust, question, and ofttimes reject the values of the larger community.

But segregation also creates slum behavior. Negroes who live in

[9] Clifford Shaw et al., Delinquency Areas. Chicago: University of Chicago Press, 1930.

[10] Edwin H. Sutherland, Principles of Criminology. (4th ed.) Philadelphia, Pa.: J. B. Lippincott Co., 1947.

[11] William F. Whyte, Street Corner Society. (2nd ed.) Chicago: University of Chicago Press, 1955.

[12] Solomon Kobrin. "The Conflict of Values in Delinquency Areas," American Sociological Review, 16:657-668, 1951.

[13] Many social planners have attempted to extend this concept of "natural areas" into programs of urban renewal and slum clearance; they are guided by a dangerous separatist view—to keep ethnic and racial groups homogeneous. See Louis Wirth, The Ghetto. Chicago: University of Chicago Press, 1929.

blighted areas suffer deeply from discrimination, rejection, and lack of integration into the society. Juvenile delinquency among them is generated by this lack of integration rather than by processes of social disorganization. An increase in juvenile delinquency is likely to occur most frequently when and where aspirations of youth persist under conditions of limited and prescribed opportunities. Under such circumstances, access to the success-goals by legitimate means is seldom available to Negro youth in cities. They do not have opportunities for internalization of acceptable and respectable norms of conduct.

On the other hand, illegal means are readily accessible in most metropolitan areas, especially in the neglected, poorly-schooled, and poorly-policed sections. Thus, unwittingly, too many Negro youth, motivated by an effort of conformity to the norms and goals of a society to which they aspire but do not belong, begin to manifest behavior patterns that deviate from the standards of the total society.

## Summary

The emphasis in this discussion is upon juvenile delinquency as a way of life. The overall effort has been to highlight the unique cultural components of the social relationships of Negro youth living in segregated communities in metropolitan areas. A list of tentatively conclusive, categorical statements follows.

1. Juvenile delinquency among Negroes does not emerge from racial factors; it is a way of life—survival techniques that must be viewed as part and parcel of the overall social system in which they inhere.

2. Juvenile delinquency is but symptomatic of an individual's or a group's lack of conformity to culturally desired aspirations and the socially-structured means of attaining them.

3. Juvenile delinquency among Negroes is accentuated by the rapidity of social change, population shifts, social mobility, and "explosions" within the metropolis.

4. The Negro community, like all other communities, is a very heterogeneous, complex, and multidimensional phenomenon.

5. Juvenile delinquency among Negroes is patterned into a variety of modes of behavior: criminal, social, conflict, and escape.

6. Juvenile delinquency in the Negro community is more of an expression of *anomie* (normlessness) than of social disorganization.

7. The etiology of juvenile delinquency in the metropolitan Negro community rests primarily on the culturally and socially limited channels to "success" accorded to Negroes.

8. Perhaps the most signally poignant condition explaining the increasing rates of deviant conduct among Negroes evolves out of segregation and lack of integration of the various social and cultural components within the Negro community.

9. Juvenile delinquency cannot be controlled simply by dealing with symptoms and factors of social disorganization. Delinquency control must be brought within the structural framework of the rapidly changing metropolis.

10. Future studies of juvenile delinquency among Negroes in metropolitan areas must break with conventional approaches, such as factor analyses and ecological methods, and begin to view deviant conduct of segregated minority groups situationally and from structural-functional perspectives, *i.e.*, within the context of reference group, status-rule behavior, and the self images of individual and groups possessing minority group consciousness.

SECTION VI

# Individual and Group Programs of Prevention and Treatment

**E**FFORTS to prevent delinquency or to rehabilitate delinquents tend to fall into two types. In one, the individual delinquent is central, and the procedure is carried out by psychiatrists, psychologists, and social workers. In the other, groups of children or youths are central, and the program is carried out by group workers with a background of training in applied social science; for example, social workers, recreation specialists, or teachers. Sometimes the two approaches are combined and delinquents receive individual therapy at the same time that they are members of groups involved in a preventive or rehabilitative program.

In Article 23, Chwast sets forth the issues created for the therapist by conflicts in values that confront him, a major conflict arising from the middle-class orientation of the typical therapist and the lower-class orientation of the typical delinquent. Other conflicts are also examined.

Famous among community programs is the Chicago Area Project, which has furnished a basic pattern for many community projects in cities other than Chicago. Sparked by the late Clifford R. Shaw, its philosophy and procedures were based on preceding studies of the ecology of delinquency areas and the development of delinquent attitudes and behavior among boys. Article 24 discusses the underlying philosophy and the problems met and solved, and gives a present-day evaluation of the work of the Project. A key part of the program was the involvement of local adults in the rehabilitation of their own neighborhoods and their personal assumption of leadership roles in the work with youth.

A type of group work that has developed rapidly since 1950 is the assignment of a group worker (street or detached worker) to a specific boys' gang with which he works intensively, meeting them on street corners or in whatever store or vacant building they use as a hangout. The program has gone through a period of trial and error. Recently, various evaluations have been made of the program and its degree of success in preventing delinquency or guiding gangs into nondelinquent behavior. Article 25 first describes in detail a detached worker program as carried out in Boston, and then gives an objective evaluation of the impact of the project.

## 23.  Value Conflicts in Treating Delinquents

### Jacob Chwast

The author, a psychologist with the Ph.D. degree from New York University, is Director of the Consultation Service of the Educational Alliance. He was formerly Supervising Psychologist and Director of Information, Planning, and Training in the Juvenile Aid Bureau, New York City Police Department, and in all had more than fifteen years experience in the field of juvenile police work. He has acted as consultant to various organizations and is a frequent contributor to professional journals.

In recent years, the problem of values has become a critical issue in psychotherapy, casework, and counseling.* Values—goal-oriented attitudes arising out of personal and social experiences leading to judg-

Jacob Chwast, "Value Conflicts in Treating Delinquents," *Children*, 6 (May-June, 1959), 95-100. Reprinted by permission.

* The author presents the views expressed in this article as his own and not necessarily as those of the agency with which he is connected. [At the time of publication, Dr. Chwast was with the Youth Division, Police Department, City of New York.]

ments of behavior as being right or wrong, desirable or undesirable—permeate all human relationships. They are crucial in the treatment relationship.

No matter how one approaches treatment objectives—whether directly, rather indirectly, or passively—the values of the therapist, consciously or unconsciously held, become operative influences in the treatment process. In treating juvenile delinquents, whether in a court, institution, or nonauthoritative setting, values are of the essence, since the client's antisocial behavior runs counter to the values of the community as expressed in its laws, and often to the less formally defined values embodied in social and moral codes.

Treatment can scarcely move forward constructively if there is no coming to grips with value conflicts, not only in recognizing them when they occur but also in finding ways of dealing with them. This necessitates an understanding of the values operative in the lives of the delinquent, on one hand, and of the therapist, on the other, as well as some clarification of goals.

## Sources of Values

Of course, values are not spontaneously generated; they are generated from the individual's own experiences and those of the group in which he is reared.

Probably the most potent value-bearing influence affecting the individual is what has been referred to by the Gluecks as "the under the roof culture"—the family.[1] Parental attitudes toward life and society begin very early to shape the goals, ideals, attitudes, and values of the child. In the family are fused various degrees (or distortions) of cultural, national, racial, and religious standards which in many ways govern the family members' expectations. While individual families differ, various subgroups within our social structure exhibit differences in attitudes toward property, chastity, and expressions of feeling and other types of behavior. Because many delinquents come from lower socioeconomic groups, the therapist in working with them must fully appreciate that the prevailing attitudes toward schools, jobs, religion, recreation, friends, sex, personal hygiene, clothing, adults, and authority vary considerably between underprivileged and well-to-do neighborhoods.

[1] Glueck, Sheldon and Eleanor: *Unraveling Juvenile Delinquency.* Commonwealth Fund, New York, 1950.

As opposed to the middle-class orientation toward long-range planning and the deferment of immediate gratifications in attaining goals, values in lower socio-economic groups are apt to emphasize short-term objectives.[2] For many persons of lower socio-economic status, the struggle for survival dictates emphasis on success in meeting immediate stresses in living without looking toward a rather abstract future. An understanding of this makes it easier to appreciate, although not to condone, such attitudes among delinquents of low socio-economic status as "It's all right to take it if you don't get caught" and "It's all right to walk off with it if it's unattached." Such attitudes are reinforced in underprivileged groups by a low capacity to gratify desires created and constantly stimulated through the general culture's omnipresent advertising apparatus and other culture vectors.

[  A recognition of the existence of value conflicts will help little unless the therapist has a clear conception of both the ultimate and immediate goals of treatment. He has to be clear about the relation of immediate to ultimate goals when such concrete questions arise as: What does a boy wear for a job interview? Should a boy who expects to be a truck-driver finish high school? Or how should a girl act on her first date?

## Conflicts in Goals

The problem becomes even more acute when it calls for a resolution of value conflicts within the therapist's (or the agency's) own conception of the purposes of treatment. For instance, practitioners have observed among some delinquents that the giving up of delinquent behavior may be followed by compulsiveness, phobias, and other neurotic or psychosomatic symptoms. This happened to Harold, a 14-year-old boy, who had been involved in several minor thefts and fights. Initially he had appeared independent and hostile, and spoke with but a slight speech impediment, but after 2 years of intensive psychotherapy, during which he discontinued his antisocial behavior, he developed a pronounced facial twitch, stammered embarrassingly, and became somewhat hypochondriacal.

[  With some delinquents, giving up a gang affiliation may mean surrendering their only human contacts. For example, Earl, a peripheral member of a gang, became so isolated and self-absorbed in the 8

[2] Davis, Allison: *Social Class Differences upon Learning.* Harvard University Press, Cambridge, 1952.

months after he dropped the gang that serious concern was aroused about what had been accomplished in treatment. Since the boy was marginal, intellectually, emotionally, and socially, the gang's tolerance of him had been one of his few ties to reality. Treatment did not seem to be successful in replacing this with any stronger tie.

Such situations confront the therapist with the necessity of making very delicate decisions. How can he resolve such symptom-exchange complications? What issues must he carefully weigh in the balance? Assuming that the therapist can foresee eventualities like this, the course of action he follows cannot be prescribed automatically. It seems evident, however, that the therapist must measure his estimate of the amount of personal damage to the patient or client that might result against the potential social damage. In any case, I believe that in regard to delinquents the important criterion is the degree to which antisocial behavior is diminished.[3]

## Some Treatment Problems

From the point of view of treatment, the problem of values makes itself felt in two ways. On the one hand, the therapist must be able to sort out the confusions and contradictions of the differing standards facing each client. Unless he can do this, he may gravely impair the progress of treatment by misinterpreting the significance of the client's reactions. Thus, for example, he might mistakenly regard a young delinquent who maintains his hostility toward middle-class authoritative adults, including the therapist, as sick and therefore requiring intensive psychotherapy and fail to perceive his sound emotional and intellectual resources.

On the other hand, and probably of much greater significance in the dynamics of treatment, are the values explicitly or implicitly accepted by the therapist and reflected in his techniques. In this connection, it becomes essential that the therapist recognize the ways in which his value system may differ from the delinquent's because of differences in background, orientation, and life experiences.

Since many professional workers have middle-class orientations and living patterns, they tend to act in conscious or unconscious accordance with middle-class values. Indeed, even for the most competent professionals, class values that become merged with living styles achieve

[3] Chwast, Jacob: "Realistic Goal-Setting in Treating Delinquents," *Journal of the Association for Psychiatric Treatment of Offenders,* September 1958.

such potency as ideals and status symbols that looking at them with objectivity is extremely difficult. This suggests that often the therapist's middle-class values are built into the determination of treatment goals. While such goals may be appropriate for youngsters who come from a cultural background similar to the therapist's, they may not all be appropriate for a young person from a different socio-economic background.

However, in conceiving *long-range* goals the clash in values between the middle-class therapist and the delinquent of low socio-economic status may not create much real difficulty. After all, both the therapist and client generally accept the notion that therapy is intended to help the delinquent. Furthermore, since long-range goals are projected into the future, the delinquent tends not to become too concerned about them. Characteristically he is more concerned with meeting immediate problems. Goal disparities become much more acute in relation to the short-range day by day objectives which develop in treatment.

A value problem arose for a therapist who was treating Connie, a physically matured, 17-year-old delinquent girl, when Connie announced that she was about to marry a sailor whom she had known only 2 weeks and who was scheduled to ship out soon. In the light of the girl's obvious charm and intelligence, and the shortness of the acquaintance, the step seemed tragic to the therapist, but from Connie's point of view it seemed to be the best way to escape from a near psychotic mother and a sadistic, sexually forward stepfather. Actually the marriage worked out well.

## Examining Assumptions

An examination of some traditional assumptions regarding treatment methods seems warranted. Time-honored practices in regard to confidentiality of information, recordkeeping, environmental manipulation, and sharing information with the client, for instance, may require modification in treating juvenile delinquents. In a New York agency which works with gangs, recognition of the need for some changes has resulted in the establishment of explicit criteria for guiding workers in reporting to the police such dangers as the use of narcotics, possession of firearms, and impending or actual gang battles. The need for immediate action in relation to a client being brought before the court might also require a prompt decision by the worker, without consultation with the client, on release of information to the authorities.

In the therapist are merged all of the value pressures forced upon the treatment relationship from the outside. If he is in an agency he not only brings to the therapeutic relationship his own set of values, but he also mediates the values of the agency's director, and board, and the community. For example, when a young delinquent acts out his conflicts aggressively in the agency's office or waiting room by loud yelling, banging away at an expensive typewriter, tinkering with the dictating machine, pocketing small objects, or disarranging pictures and shelves, the therapist's own attitude might be well attuned to the youngster's treatment needs, but the agency's administrator might not appreciate the therapeutic necessities and insist upon limitations which would circumscribe the therapeutic possibilities. In handling such a dilemma, the therapist had best be clear about the respective apportionments of permissiveness and of limit setting in treatment.

Agencies dealing with delinquents should be prepared for actional possibilities so that too much limit setting does not occur. The techniques developed by Redl and Wineman in an institution for seriously disturbed delinquents could be examined profitably in this regard.[4] The worker would also do well to anticipate acting out on the delinquent's part and, to the extent possible at the level of the therapeutic relationship, let the client know what is and what' is not allowed before he actually does any damage. When Joe stole a dictating machine from the agency's office as a declaration of independence in the face of a deepening of his relationship with the therapist, the agency's administrator took a rather dim view of the therapist's assertion that progress was being made.

It seems clear that the view that the therapist must see himself functioning as a professional solely on behalf of his client needs some modification. For instance, if the therapist realizes that a client's strong destructive or self-destructive drives are fairly close to enactment, should he not let some other qualified persons, at school, in a recreational agency, or elsewhere, know so that preventive measures might be taken? Surely, a boy with overwhelming psychosexual difficulties could be steered away from such sexually stimulating situations as being left alone with a much younger girl or cast in a role certain to inflame his sexual fantasies. Certainly, departures from rigid confidentiality, even when strictly in the client's own interests, should be based on a prior understanding with the client, whenever possible. But when not possible, and the client or the community needs protection, what then? A reconceptualization of some formal ethical principles may be neces-

<hr/>

[4] Redl, Fritz; Wineman, David: *Controls from Within.* Free Press, Glencoe, Ill., 1951.

sary, with the resulting hypotheses subjected to validation. The recently issued report of the National Social Welfare Assembly's ad hoc committee on confidentiality is a stride in this direction.[5] [See *Children*, September-October 1958, page 195.]

## A Look at Techniques

Orthodox treatment techniques, which flow from assumptions that may be valid for middle- and upper-class clients, seem also to require alteration to be effective for socially and economically depressed persons. Such techniques as remaining passive and not becoming involved in the client's day to day problems have been derived from these assumptions, as have such practices as keeping interviews to tight time limits and insisting that all interviews be held in the office. In working with a delinquent, such practices often result in loss of the client to treatment.

When Julian told his therapist that he was going out directly to steal an airplane, he would undoubtedly have either successfully flown away or killed himself trying if the therapist had not hastily trailed him to an airport and physically grappled with him beside the cockpit. Incidentally, this experience turned out to be the beginning of Julian's real involvement in treatment.

The delinquent most frequently is an especially resistant client, not merely because of inner motivations but also because of his immediately pressing concrete problems such as court appearance, physical danger, or the necessity to find a job. Such problems cannot await a detached, time-consuming, verbalistic approach. Moreover, talking to the therapist can to him seem too much like "squealing." Then too, the words of the therapist, unless artfully selected in language the delinquent understands, can sometimes increase his mistrust and confusion.

Another difficulty in treatment may arise because of a failure to realize that what middle-class, college-trained practitioners consider to be ordinary logic is not so perceived by many disadvantaged persons. This is not necessarily due to a lack of intelligence, but rather to a loss of interest when cause and effect relationships become complicated by numerous intervening variables. The threat of immediate demands is too great to permit such persons the luxury or anxiety of waiting for some future benefit.

Treatment of such clients is not an unalloyed, antiseptic process. The

[5] National Social Welfare Assembly, New York: *Confidentiality in Social Service to Individuals*, 1958.

therapist working with delinquents invariably runs up against situations in which he must put himself out to a considerable degree. He must be prepared for a string of latenesses or broken appointments, calls from or to lawyers and probation or parole officers, appearances in court, visits to prison, efforts to help the client get a job or into a special school, and emergency calls at any hour.

Unfortunately, many trained therapists avoid working with adolescents, and particularly with delinquent adolescents. Low salaries and poor advancement possibilities in such work may be partly to blame, but so is a human tendency to prefer regularity, security, and comfort, which results in a sloughing off of the less desirable and less conforming (to treatment requirements) patient.

It is strange how often the same delinquent is regarded differently in different settings. Martin, who had been referred to an authoritative agency as a "psychopathic personality" requiring institutionalization, is a case in point. Further psychological and psychiatric examination indicated that the boy was reacting violently to a very difficult home situation and did not have anything like the degree of pathology indicated in the referring agency's diagnosis. He improved markedly in 3 months of intensive treatment in another agency. In the past 5 years he has committed no further delinquencies and is now a respected, self-supporting member of society.

In commenting upon the recruitment of staff to work with such delinquents and their families, Overton has said, "Often the workers with greater experience, whom it was most important to attract, saw this assignment as beneath their professional dignity. It was disappointing that they ran away. . . ."[6]

Experienced therapists seem to be ceding this area to the newcomers to treatment and consequently the less competent.


## Clarifying Responsibility

Because of the antisocial nature of the delinquent's behavior outside of the treatment setting, the therapist must at times face up to his own responsibility in regard to the possible consequences of such actions. What turns the balance to allow, or require, the therapist to call in other authorities—the probation officer, the parole office, or the police? What about the therapist's dilemma in handling aggressive behavior which occurs in his presence?

[6] Overton, Alice: *Aggressive Casework*. In "Reaching the Unreached." New York City Youth Board, New York, 1952. (Revised 1957.)

Suppose a delinquent in treatment steals the therapist's fountain pen, or a towering 6-foot teenager loudly threatens a much frailer therapist with physical abuse? Does the therapist have to take it? And if he does not, can the line of demarcation between punishing and setting limits be clearly distinguished?

These questions are not easy to answer. A great deal depends upon the role which the agency sees itself performing in the community. Certainly, however, a concern for other important matters such as an agency's public esteem can add heavy burdens to the therapist trying to treat the delinquent creatively.

Nevertheless, in the actual treatment relationship, the therapist must be in a position to perceive whether his own response is based upon his misinterpretation of the situation because of his own anxieties or whether the situation presents a real danger. If the latter, then active intervention by the therapist, with the help of others, if needed, would seem necessary in instances in which the client himself, the therapist, the agency, or the community might be hurt. Failure to intervene may sometimes constitute an abdication of responsibility and lead to an inevitable failure in treatment.

When, as sometimes happens, the therapist receives a phone call that his delinquent client is getting drunk or threatening to get even with someone, the therapist ought to be able to move out toward the client at a moment's notice. It many cases treatment of the delinquent has to take place not only anywhere but also anytime. Therefore, agency treatment programming should be planned to assure continuous availability. Acting out, precipitated by the frequent crises in the delinquent's life, does not respect time schedules.

The question of what constitutes professional and citizen responsibility calls for much clarification—a task requiring considerable willingness, creativity, and mutuality on the part of all parties involved in the treatment of delinquents. Therapists must think this through not only individually and in their professional groups and agencies, but also with representatives of the bench, bar, law enforcement agencies, and the community at large.

The professional's conscience has probably had to wrestle more with descrying and allocating his responsibilities than with any other single problem. Yet any solution is apt to leave him feeling uneasy. To whom is a professional treatment person loyal and responsible? To his profession? His agency? The community? The client? Himself? He must, of course, be loyal and responsible to all, but the distribution and proportions of priorities need a basic spelling out.

How to do this is not easy to say. Clearly, however, each individual practitioner cannot avoid responsibility for his own actions. The sight of two or more experts testifying in contradiction to one another on the mental status of an offender can reflect not only on the validity of the data presented but also on the dignity of the adversaries and their professions. Such a situation, and others equally unfortunate, arise partly from disparities in role perception within the profession. More research on the role perception of therapists is needed. With more facts professional schools, community councils, and interdisciplinary organizations could join in developing sound guides for individual practitioners and agencies.

Similarly, agency responsibility requires clarification. An "agonizing reappraisal" of agency policies is called for to allow for more fluidities in treatment practice. The increasing effort in many places to "reach out" to the client is a move in the right direction. This sometimes requires teamwork, for one worker alone cannot always be effective in an acute crisis.

## Agency Practices

An example of the effectiveness of quick "team action" in a social agency is afforded in the case of 13-year-old Ellen, who ran away from home. If the agency supervisor had not talked to her father, the psychologist to her girl friend, and another agency worker to a relative—all at the same time—it might not have been possible for Ellen to go back home the next day as she did. The case of 14-year-old Joan affords another example. Joan's splenetic father would have needlessly taken her into court on a charge of ungovernability, if several agency workers had not teamed up to speak to father, daughter, and stepmother, and if one worker had not accompanied them home. Dealing instantly with these crises prevented them from further aggravating difficult family relationships.

Since the delinquent is almost always an "unwilling" client, it seems hard to justify, on a basis other than the agency's and the worker's convenience, a rigid insistence upon client voluntariness, office interviews exclusively and only in the daytime, tight time limits for appointments, and noninvolvement with the client's day to day affairs. These practices fit nicely into the middle-class pattern of living. The delinquent does not have such a pattern and if expected to follow one may rebel against the agency.

Many treatment agencies will not accept delinquents for treatment. Some even drop hitherto nondelinquent clients from their caseloads if they become delinquent while under treatment, although this is not now so common as in the past. Referring primarily to delinquents, Bloch and Flynn conclude that: "It is necessary to face the fact that the great majority of voluntary agencies dealing with family and children's problems have intake policies which turn away many of these children. . . ." [7] Public agencies cannot exercise such discretion.

Voluntary agencies, of course, have the right to define their function. Still the policies of many treatment agencies indicate why they are not more effective in meeting the area of social need exposed in delinquency. Their view of a client's repeated failure to appear for appointments as proof of therapeutic inaccessibility is not convincing in the face of the experience of other agencies in working with "hard-to-reach" families.[8]

Clearly many value decisions affecting the treatment relationship lie beyond the therapist. As already mentioned, the agency might impose limitations upon the therapist, reflecting limitations imposed by the community. If the therapist's and agency's responsibility for safeguarding the community is accepted as a basic premise, some questions, with a reverse emphasis, might also properly be asked: How much will the community have to allow for in treatment? What tolerances should it provide? The answers can surely be defined more clearly, specifically, and scientifically.

Such specification requires considerable discussion of agency policy and practice on the basis of staff experience. It also requires carefully designed research. This might include: investigations of the types of antisocial reactions arising during the treatment process, correlating treatment dynamics with behavioral sequences; controlled assessment of the amount of damage to other persons and property wrought by delinquents who are undergoing treatment in comparison with their productivity and positive contributions to others; efforts to determine the effectiveness of different treatment approaches with different types of delinquents. We might then proceed to determine the implications of our findings for legislation, court procedures, police handling, and professional and citizen responsibility.

## Value Similarities

While the stress in this paper has been upon the effects of value conflict in treatment, it is equally important to understand the similarities of values between the delinquent and therapist.

[7] Bloch, Herbert A., Flynn, Frank T.: *Delinquency: the Juvenile Offender in America Today.* Random House, New York, 1956.

[8] New York City Youth Board, New York: *Reaching the Unreached.* 1952. (Revised 1957.)

The sociologist Kobrin has indicated that delinquents generally are affected by "a duality of conduct norms rather than by the dominance of either a conventional or a criminal culture," [9] and maintains that no segment of our subculture places a positive value on delinquency per se. Cohen,[10] on the other hand, holds that the delinquent's subculture is essentially in opposition to the values of the dominant middle class.

The therapist does not need to resolve these differences in theory in order to recognize points not only where his delinquent client's values differ from those of the dominant culture, but also where they are the same, as in loyalty to one's family and friends, the need to work for a living, and the right to fulfill oneself. Such similarities in values afford tremendous support for the furtherance of treatment objectives since, in a sense, they provide a common operating base between therapist and client.

Unfortunately delinquents often share some or many of the values of the therapist, yet act in ways which are in contradiction to them. Their value systems, including those values which are directly opposed to the community's, seem to be poorly integrated and unstable, and hence they are confused and conflicted about how to behave.

One of the objectives of the therapist is to help the delinquent hang on to, and indeed augment, those aspects of social conformity and self-control which can be used in keeping him from getting into trouble. I believe that this can be accomplished while helping the individual to fulfill his rights to self-expression and self-realization within the framework of a democratic conception of living.[11]

[9] Kobrin, Solomon: "The Conflict in Values in Delinquency Areas. *American Sociological Review,* October 1951.
[10] Cohen, Albert K.: *Delinquent Boys.* Free Press, Glencoe, Ill., 1955.
[11] Chwast, Jacob: "The Significance of Control in the Treatment of the Antisocial Person." *Archives of Criminal Psychodynamics,* Vol. 2, No. 4, Fall 1957.

# 24. The Chicago Area Project—A 25-Year Assessment

## Solomon Kobrin

The author holds the M.A. degree from the University of Chicago. He is a supervising sociologist on the staff of the Illinois Institute for Juvenile Research, Chicago, and has worked intensively with the Chicago Area Project. In 1951-53 he was Project Director of a study of juvenile drug addiction, sponsored by the National Institute for Mental Health. He has taught sociology at Roosevelt University and the Illinois Masonic Hospital of Nursing Education, is active in various professional associations, and has contributed articles to professional journals.

The Chicago Area Project shares with other delinquency prevention programs the difficulty of measuring its success in a simple and direct manner. At bottom this difficulty rests on the fact that such programs, as efforts to intervene in the life of a person, a group, or a community, cannot by their very nature constitute more than a subsidiary element in changing the fundamental and sweeping forces which create the problems of groups and of persons or which shape human personality. Declines in rates of delinquents—the only conclusive way to evaluate a delinquency prevention—may reflect influences unconnected with those of organized programs and are difficult to define and measure.[1]

For two reasons the simple and satisfying laboratory model of the controlled experiment is difficult to achieve in measuring the effects of a program. First, it is virtually impossible to find groups which are identical in all major respects save that of participation in a given program. Second, there exists a widespread and understandable reluctance to deny to systematically selected segments of homogeneous groups the putative benefits of programs, a procedure which does produce an approximation to a control group.[2]

The present assessment of the Chicago Area Project will have to rest, therefore, on an appraisal of its experience in carrying out procedures assumed by its founders and supporters to be relevant to the reduction of delinquency. To this end, the theory of delinquency causation underlying the Area Project program will be presented. This will be followed by a description of the procedures regarded as essential to the modification of conditions which produce delinquency. Finally, the adaptations and modifications of these procedures will be described and evaluated.

Solomon Kobrin, "The Chicago Area Project—A 25-Year Assessment," *Annals of the American Academy of Political and Social Science*, 322 (March, 1959), 20-29. Reprinted with permission of the Academy.

[1] For example, rates of delinquents among nationality groups whose children at one time figured prominently in juvenile court statistics declined as these groups improved their economic and social position and moved out of neighborhoods of high rates of delinquents. See Clifford R. Shaw and Henry D. McKay, *Juvenile Delinquency and Urban Areas* (Chicago: University of Chicago Press, 1942), pp. 151-57.

[2] See Edwin Powers and Helen Witmer, *An Experiment in the Prevention of Delinquency* (New York: Columbia University Press, 1951), as a distinguished and solitary example of one program which, in the interest of advancing knowledge, denied hypothesized benefits of a program to a control group.

## Conception of the Delinquency Problem

A distinctive feature of the Area Project program is that at its inception it attempted explicitly to relate its procedures in a logical manner to sociological postulates and to the findings of sociological research in delinquency. Under the leadership of the late Clifford R. Shaw, founder of the Area Project and its director during virtually all of its existence, a series of studies completed between 1929 and 1933 brought to the investigation of this problem two heretofore neglected viewpoints: the ecological and the socio-psychological. The first was concerned with the epidemiology of delinquency in the large city; the second with the social experience of the delinquent boy in the setting of his family, his play group, and his neighborhood.[3]

With respect to the first problem, it was found that certain areas of the large city produced a disproportionately large number of the delinquents. The high rate areas were characterized as "delinquency areas" and subsequently an effort was made to define their major social features. In the American city of the period, the populations of these communities were made up of predominantly recent migrants from the rural areas of the Old World. As a group they occupied the least desirable status in the economic, political, and social hierarchies of the metropolitan society and in many ways showed an acute awareness of their position. Their efforts to adapt their social institutions to the urban industrial order were at the most only partly successful. The generation of immigrants, in their colonies in the decaying heart of the city, adapted with moderate success only those institutions which preserved customary forms of religious practice, mutual aid, and sociability.

However, the immigrant generation was notably unable to preserve the authority of the old institutions, including the family, in the eyes of the rising generation and was quickly confronted with a problem of

---

[3] Studies in the first category include Clifford R. Shaw and others, *Delinquency Areas* (Chicago: University of Chicago Press, 1929); certain sections of Clifford R. Shaw and Henry D. McKay, *Social Factors in Juvenile Delinquency* (Washington: U.S. Government Printing Office, 1931); and a final volume in which the geographic distribution of rates of delinquents in a number of American cities was analyzed in great detail, Clifford R. Shaw and Henry D. McKay, *Juvenile Delinquency and Urban Areas*. While the last volume was published a decade after the earlier ones much of its data were available to the authors at the time of the founding of the Area Project. Studies of the social experience of delinquent boys include Clifford R. Shaw, *The Jack-roller* (Chicago: University of Chicago Press, 1930); Clifford R. Shaw, *The Natural History of a Delinquent Career* (Chicago: University of Chicago Press, 1931); and Clifford R. Shaw, Henry D. McKay, and James F. McDonald, *Brothers in Crime* (Chicago: University of Chicago Press, 1938).

conflict with their children. Disruption of cross-generational control produced the conditions for the emergence of a variant species of youth subculture in these communities marked by a tradition of sophisticated delinquency. At the same time this tradition was sustained and fostered by the anonymity of much of the population of slum areas, by the presence of a young adult element which engaged in crime both as an occupation and a way of life, and by the extraordinary harshness of the competitive struggle which arises when the controls of social usage decay. The distribution of official delinquents pointed firmly to the conclusion that the high-rate areas constituted the locus of the city's delinquency problem, both as to number of delinquents and seriousness of offenses.

## The Delinquent as a Person

With respect to the second problem, these investigations suggested that, given the conditions of social life in the delinquency areas, delinquency in most cases was the product of the simple and direct processes of social learning. Where growing boys are alienated from the institutions of their parents and are confronted with a vital tradition of delinquency among their peers, they engage in delinquent activity as part of their groping for a place in the only social groups available to them. From investigations of the type reported in The Jack-roller, Natural History of a Delinquent Career, and Brothers in Crime, the conclusion was drawn that with significant frequency, delinquency in the slum areas of our cities reflects the strivings of boys in a social rather than an antisocial direction. These studies focused attention on the paradoxical fact that no matter how destructive or morally shocking, delinquency may often represent the efforts of the person to find and vindicate his status as a human being, rather than an abdication of his humanity or an intrinsic incapacity to experience human sentiment.

This view formed something of a contrast to notions of human nature and delinquency which were, and still are, somewhat more widely accepted. These beliefs, which generally represent delinquent conduct as a manifestation of pathology or malfunction of personality, rest implicitly on an image of man as quick to lose his distinctively human capacities under adverse conditions. The image implied in the Area Project conception of the delinquency problem is that man tends always to organize his behavior in the service of his human identity. To what extent this view is supported by the research of Shaw and his associates, and to what extent the research proceeded from this view is, of course, a difficult question to answer. The fact remains, however, that from the beginning the Area Project program rested on a conception of human nature which was optimistic concerning the prevention of delinquency and the rehabilitation of the delinquent. Delinquency was regarded as, for the most part, a reversible accident of the person's social experience.

Thus, the theory on which the Area Project program is based is that, taken in its most general aspect, delinquency as a problem in the modern metropolis is principally a product of the breakdown of the machinery of spontaneous social control. The breakdown is precipitated by the cataclysmic pace of social change to which migrants from a peasant or rural background are subjected when they enter the city. In its more specific aspects, delinquency was seen as adaptive behavior on the part of the male children of rural migrants acting as members of adolescent peer groups in their efforts to find their way to meaningful and respected adult roles essentially unaided by the older generation and under the influence of criminal models for whom the inner city areas furnish a haven.

## Socialization and Community Action

Research in the problem of delinquency formed one of two major sources of suggestion for the Area Project program. The second was furnished by what may best be regarded as a set of sociological postulates concerning, first, the processes by which persons come under the influence and control of social groups and take over their values; and, second, those affecting communal or collective action in the solution of social problems.

It is a commonplace of sociological observation that the source of control of conduct for the person lies in his natural social world. The rules and values having validity for the person are those which affect his daily nurturance, his place in primary groups, and his self-development. He is responsive as a person within the web of relationships in which his daily existence as a human being is embedded.

The inference seemed unavoidable, therefore, that to succeed delinquency prevention activities must somehow first become activities of the adults constituting the natural social world of the youngster. Or, put another way, a delinquency prevention program could hardly hope to be effective unless and until the aims of such a program became the aims of the local populations. Thus, an indispensable preliminary task of delinquency prevention is to discover effective methods of inducing residents of the disadvantaged city areas to take up the cause of prevention in a serious manner. The disposition of the founders of the Area Project was to regard this element of the program as so indispensable that if these populations proved unable to act in relation to the problem, the prevention of delinquency was a lost cause.

A second postulation concerned the problem of developing collective action toward delinquency. Here another commonplace of sociological observation suggested that people support and participate only in those enterprises in which they have a meaningful role. The organized activity of people everywhere flows in the channels of institutions and organizations indigenous to their cultural traditions and to the system of social relationships which defines their social groups. Consequently one could not expect people to devote their energies to enterprises which form part of the social systems of groups in which they have no membership. The relevance of this observation is that there had always existed an expectation that people residing in the high delinquency rate areas could somehow be induced to support the welfare agencies established there. A basic assumption of the Area Project program was that under prevailing conditions it was illusory to expect this to happen.

Thus, in view of the primacy of the local social life in the socialization and control of the young person, all effort, it was felt, should be devoted to helping residents of high delinquency rate areas to take constructive action toward the problem. The interest of the wider society in winning the rising generation of these communities to orderliness and conformity had first to become a vital interest of the local society.

## Organization of the Delinquency Area

A final assumption necessary to the rationale of the Area Project program had to do with the social and institutional organization of the high delinquency rate neighborhood and with the related issue of the capacity of residents of these areas to organize and administer local welfare programs. It was observed that despite the real disorder and confusion of the delinquency area, there existed a core of organized communal life centering mainly in religious, economic, and political activity. Because the function of the slum area is to house the flow of impoverished newcomers and to furnish a haven of residence for the multitudes who, for various reasons, live at the edge of respectability, the nucleus of institutional order actually present is sometimes difficult to discern. There seemed further to be strong evidence that the residents most active in these local institutions were, in terms of interest, motivation, and capacity, on their way up the social class ladder. With respect to these elements of the population it was assumed, therefore, that they represented forces of considerable strength for initiating delinquency prevention activities.[4] There being no evidence of a deficiency of intelligence among them, it was taken for granted that with proper guidance and encouragement they could learn how to organize and administer local welfare programs.

In summary it may be said, then, that the Area Project program regards as indispensable to the success of welfare activity in general and delinquency prevention in particular the participation of those who form a significant part of the social world of the recipients of help. This is seen not as a prescription or a panacea, but as a condition for progress in finding a solution. The program has remained experimental in the sense that it has continued to explore the question: What kind of participation is necessary on the part of which kinds of persons in terms of social role in the local society? But it has rested firmly and consistently on the conviction that no solution of a basic and lasting character is possible in the absence of such participation.

## Procedures in Neighborhood Organization

It follows that the basic procedure in the program is the development of local welfare organization among residents of high delinquency rate neighborhoods. This undertaking called for skill in the organizer in identifying the residents holding key positions of influence and the ability to arouse their interest in youth welfare activities. The first phase requires a knowledge of the local society; the second a capacity for sympathetic identification with the local resident. Knowledge of the local society implies familiarity with its culture and history, in the case of ethnic groups; with the local institutions; with the structure of power through which decisions are made and executed; and with the conflicts and cleavages which orient and align the population.

Initial organization in several of Chicago's delinquency areas was undertaken by sociologists employed jointly by the Behavior Research Fund, now dissolved, the Chicago Area Project, and the Illinois Institute for Juvenile Research. The Institute, an agency of state government,

---

[4] It should be observed in passing that some of the economic and political leadership of these communities did not always fit philistine specifications of respectability, and that on this score the Area Project program came under criticism during its early days.

until recently has furnished a major share of the salaries of the staff engaged in this program.[5]

It became quickly evident, however, that, for cogent reasons, the employment of qualified local residents offered advantages in the establishment of such programs. In the first place the indigenous worker usually possessed a natural knowledge of the local society. Second, he was hampered by none of the barriers to communications with residents for whom the nonresident, especially those identified with "welfare" enterprise, tended to be an object of suspicion and hostility. Third, his employment was a demonstration of sincere confidence in the capacity of the area resident for work of this sort. Fourth, he was more likely than the nonresident to have access to the neighborhood's delinquent boys and therefore to be more effective in redirecting their conduct. Fifth, his employment represented a prime means of initiating the education of the local population in the mysteries of conducting the welfare enterprise. Hence, virtually from the first, one of the most distinctive features of Area Project procedure was the employment, in appropriate categories and under the tutelage of staff sociologists of the Institute, of local residents to aid in the organization of the approximately dozen community or civic "committees" which were established in Chicago over the course of two decades.[6]

A second major procedural feature of the Area Project program is represented by efforts to preserve the independence of the neighborhood groups after they become established as functioning units. This turned out to be mainly an exercise in self restraint, for the easier and in many ways more natural course would have been to maintain a close supervision and control of their activities. However, since it was the aim of the program to foster the development of knowledge and competence in the conduct of youth welfare activities and to encourage among residents of delinquency areas confidence in their own capacities to act with respect to their problems, the policy was followed of insisting upon a formal, structural autonomy of the organization. The problem in this connection was to maintain full support and help without rendering the independence of the group an empty formality.

[5] A recent reorganization of these services shifted much of this staff to the administrative jurisdiction of the Illinois Youth Commission.

[6] Sharp question has been raised by leaders of the social work profession regarding the competence of such persons, whose qualifications rested on assets of character and personal trait rather than on formal training and education. Leaders of the Area Project have always encouraged talented workers in this field to obtain as much training in the group work and social work fields as they could. However, they have regarded the talent for this work as the primary value.

## Maintaining Autonomy

Three devices were found to be useful in dealing with this problem. First, neighborhood groups either exercised the power of veto in the assignment of Area Project staff to function as their executives; or, more frequently, nominated a qualified local resident as their executive who was then employed as an Area Project staff member. Second, staff members were required to function as representatives and spokesmen of the local groups rather than as representatives of the Area Project central office or of the Sociology Department of the Institute for Juvenile Research. This served to foster an identification of the worker with the point of view and the needs of the local group. Third, policy decisions of neighborhood groups which appeared to Area Project staff to be unsound were nonetheless accepted and acted upon by them. Since staff members exercised much informal influence with the groups to which they were assigned, this problem arose infrequently. However, when it did arise, the autonomy of the neighborhood group was scrupulously respected.

These, then, are the procedural principles of the Area Project program: development of youth welfare organizations among residents of delinquency areas; employment of so-called indigenous workers wherever possible; and the fostering and preservation of the independence of these groups.

## Types of Neighborhood Groups

Before moving to an evaluation of the Area Project as a delinquency prevention program, some indication ought to be made of the specific activities and forms of organization found among these neighborhood groups. The founders of the Area Project were always mindful of variety in the forms of social life and of the necessity, therefore, of adapting the approach to problems of organization as well as the content of program to conditions existing in each work location. In consequence each neighborhood organization within the Area Project differs somewhat from the others in both these respects.

Generally these differences are related to the patterns of social organization existing in their areas of operation and to the degree of unity and co-ordination among local institutions. On this axis, delinquency areas may be classified as structured and stable, structured but unstable, and unstructured and unstable.[7]

In the structured and stable communities, Area Project neighborhood organizations reflect a direct expansion in interests and functions of established neighborhood institutions. In some cases in this category, the dominant local church sponsors the organization, encouraging influential lay leaders to assume responsibility in the development of its program. However, there are few urban neighborhoods in which a single institution exercises complete dominance of the life of the residents. The more usual case in this class is represented by the local organization in which a number of important neighborhood institutions participate. These may include one or more churches, local political bodies, businessmen's groups, and lodges and fraternal groups. However, the representation is always informal, and membership belongs to participating persons as individuals. This informal mode of representation has come to be preferred, probably because it permits the inclusion of important groups which are not formally constituted. Such, for example, are extended kinship groups, friendship cliques, and aggregations of persons temporarily unified around specific problems or issues. In unstructured or unstable communities the member usually represents only himself.

## Reasons for Joining Groups

Differences of this order among Area Project groups seem also to be accompanied by differences in motivation for participation. Members of all Area Project groups share a responsiveness to slogans of youth welfare. However, members of groups operating in the relatively well-organized neighborhoods tend to find in this activity a means for realizing their aspiration for upward mobility. A related need is served in those communities where the framework of institutional life fails to furnish a satisfactory place for certain age or sex groups. In these situations young adults and women, for example, may find in the Area Project neighborhood organization a means of gaining recognition.

The second major motivation is found most frequently in communities with few or no organizations (unstructured), and in those that have no

---

[7] These terms are relative. From the vantage point of an orderly and integrated middle-class residential community the structured and stable delinquency area might appear to be both excessively disorderly in terms of delinquency, crime, and other social problems and excessively controlled and dominated by religious or political organizations.

fixed pattern of integration of the activities of organizations which may exist (unstable). Here the dominant motives for participation in the Area Project group are, first, a simple concern with the tragedies attending youthful law violation; and second, a desire to break down social isolation through organized contact with neighbors. These constitute the motivations most frequently sanctioned in official representations of Area Project doctrine because they are most apt to evoke a positive response to promotional appeals.

## Variety in Program Content

Area Project neighborhood organizations all include, with varying emphasis and elaboration, three elements in their programs. The first is the sponsorship of a standard kind of recreation program for the children of the neighborhood, including in some instances programs of summer camping of considerable scope. Such recreation programs are likely to have two distinctive features: the use of residents, usually active members of the Area Project group, as volunteers assisting in carrying on the recreation program; and the improvisation of store-front locations or unused space in churches, police stations, and even basements of homes for recreational use.

The second element of the program is represented by campaigns for community improvement. These are usually concerned with such issues as school improvement, sanitation, traffic safety, physical conservation, and law enforcement.

The third element of the program is reflected in the activity directed to the delinquent child, gangs of boys involved in delinquency, and, in some cases, adult offenders returning to the neighborhood from penal institutions. The activity includes helping police and juvenile court personnel develop plans for the supervision of delinquent youngsters; visiting boys committed to training schools and reformatories; working with boys' gangs in the informal settings of the neighborhood; and assisting adult parolees in their problems of returning to the community.

Specific program content in each of the local groups varies in relation to a number of factors. Among these are the facilities available for recreation or camping; the character and intensity of problems of safety, physical maintenance, or law enforcement in the area; and the staff's ability to arouse enthusiasm and effort from the leaders of the local organization in carrying on direct work with delinquents. Some groups are committed to an extensive program of recreation, including the development and operation of summer camps. Others, located in neighborhoods well equipped with such facilities, carry on no recreation work at all.[8] Some have labored strenuously in programs of neighborhood conservation; others have not concerned themselves with such issues. All have been continuously encouraged and helped by state employed Area Project staff to maintain direct work with delinquent children and with street gangs, and with virtually no exception all local groups have done so.

## Achievements of the Area Project

The achievements of the Area Project may best be assessed in relation to its theory of delinquency causation in the social setting of the high-rate neighborhoods. In this theory, delinquency is regarded as a product of a local milieu (a) in which adult residents do little or nothing in an organized public way to mobilize their resources in behalf of the welfare of the youth of the area; (b) in which the relative isolation of the adolescent male group, common throughout urban society, becomes at its extreme an absolute isolation with a consequent absolute loss of adult control; and (c) in which the formal agencies of correction and reformation fail to enlist the collaboration of persons and groups influential in the local society. Leaders of the Area Project assume that progress in the prevention of delinquency cannot be expected until these three problems are well on their way to solution. Since progress in the solution of these problems comes only slowly, permanent declines in delinquency are not expected even after years of effort.

First among the accomplishments claimed by the Area Project is its demonstration of the feasibility of creating youth welfare organizations among residents of delinquency areas. Even in the most unlikely localities capable persons of good will have responded to the challenge of responsibility and have, with help and guidance, operated neighborhood programs. On the whole these organizations have exhibited vitality and stability and have come to represent centers of local opinion regarding issues which concern the welfare of the young. Above all, they have justified the assumption made by Clifford Shaw and his associates that persons residing in these localities have the capacity to take hold of such problems and contribute to their solution.

The Area Project has made an equally distinctive contribution respect-

[8] Contrary to popular impression those of our big city neighborhoods which have been centers of social problems, including delinquency, for many decades sometimes acquire more than a just share of recreational facilities. This has resulted, quite simply, from their long-time status as objects of society's solicitude and philanthropy.

ing the problem of the isolation of the male adolescent in the delinquency area. From the beginning it called attention to the fact that the recreational and character-building agencies in these areas were unable, through their established programs, to modify the conduct of boys caught up in gang delinquency. In all probability the Area Project was the first organized program in the United States to use workers to establish direct and personal contact with the "unreached" boys to help them find their way back to acceptable norms of conduct. The adoption of this pattern in many cities during recent years may be regarded as in part, at least, a contribution of the Area Project to the development of working methods in the delinquency prevention field. At the same time, it should be indicated that from the viewpoint of Area Project assumptions and procedures such work, to be effective, must be carried on as an integral part of a more general program sponsored by residents of the locality.

Finally, the Area Project has pioneered in exploring the problem of tempering the impersonality of the machinery which an urban society erects to control and correct the wayward child. Leaders of the Area Project have tended to regard the procedures of juvenile courts, school systems, police departments, probation and parole systems, training schools, and reformatories as inescapably bureaucratic. That is, the procedures of these organizations tend to become set ways of dealing with persons as members of categories. While it is both rational and efficient as a way of processing human problems, of doing something about and hence disposing of cases, this mode of operating results in serious loss of control of the conduct of the young person. The young person in particular is regarded as responsive mainly to the expectations of his primary groups. Thus, to enhance the effectiveness of the corrective agencies of society, it is necessary to enlist the disciplining power of such groups. This is a difficult and complex undertaking, since the customary primary groups for the child, namely family and peers, are often, in the disorder of the delinquency area, unable or undisposed to exercise the needed discipline.

However, it has been found that in no area is the disorder so unmitigated as to be devoid of persons, whether residents or staff employees of the local organization or both, who staunchly represent the values of conformity, many of whom have or can gain the trust of the wayward. Such relationships capture the essential element of the primary group. The Area Project effort has been to discover an effective pattern through which the good offices of these persons may be used by teachers, police, social workers, and court officials to formulate and execute for the supervision of delinquent children jointly conceived plans designed to meet the specific problems and needs of the person. In this exploration the Area Project has found that there are natural primary relationships with delinquents which may be used effectively for delinquency prevention and that they are best utilized in collaboration with the agencies having formal responsibility for the welfare of the children and the protection of the community.

## Concluding Observations

In all probability these achievements have reduced delinquency in the program areas, as any substantial improvement in the social climate of a community must. However, the extent of the reduction is not subject to precise measurement. The effects of improvement in the environment of children are diffuse, cumulative, and intertwined with trends and forces which have their origin outside of programs of this character. In the final analysis, therefore, the Area Project program must rest its case on logical and analytic grounds.

No assessment of this program can be complete without defining its historically unique character. The genius of its founder, Clifford Shaw, lay in his sharp perception of delinquency as human behavior and in his sense of the naturalness or inevitability of violative activity in the youngster who, whether singly or in groups, is neglected, despised, or ignored as a person. This is the spirit which has animated the Area Project program and which has made it distinctive among delinquency prevention programs. This image of the delinquent and this notion of the delinquency-making process have led to the program's insistence on centering the operation within the milieu directly productive of delinquency, upon drawing into the operation as many as possible of the persons involved in the basic socializing experiences of youngsters, and upon dealing with delinquents or incipient delinquents as persons worthy of consideration and respect.

Not uncommonly, programs of prevention, whatever their initial intention or resolve, understandably tend to move away from direct contact with the delinquent and his milieu. Distance is achieved by interposing institutional forms between workers and delinquents, as in programs of formal and official treatment, or by dealing with the delinquent as a person arbitrarily abstracted from his social environment, as in programs based on individual therapy. This kind of evolution is comprehensible in the former type of retreat because the delinquent arouses anger and resentment in the law-abiding person, who consequently is hard put to form a sympathetic identification with him. Retreat from the milieu of the delinquent is even more understandable, for nothing would seem more unrewarding than to attempt to put aright the social disorder of the delinquency area.

It may well be that in perspective the Area Project's distinctive contribution to delinquency prevention as a field of practice and technique will be seen in its development of a method designed to keep preventional work focused upon its proper object, the delinquent as a person in his milieu. Central to this method is not only a view of the problem which stubbornly refuses to uncouple the delinquent from the social world which has created him, but a set of procedures which have demonstrated a capacity to draw into the preventional process itself the inhabitants of this world.

## 25.   The Impact of a "Total-Community" Delinquency Control Project

## Walter B. Miller

The author's biography is given with Article 5.

## The Midcity Project: Methods and Client Population

The Midcity Project conducted a delinquency control program in a lower-class district of Boston between the years 1954 and 1957. A major objective of the Project was to inhibit or reduce the amount of illegal activity engaged in by resident adolescents. Project methods derived from a "total community" philosophy which has become increasingly popular in recent years, and currently forms the basis of several large-scale delinquency control programs.[1] On the assumption that delinquent

Walter B. Miller, "The Impact of a 'Total-Community' Delinquency Control Project," *Social Problems*, 10 (Fall, 1962), 168-191. Reprinted with permission of the Society for the Study of Social Problems and the author.

[1] The principal current example is the extensive "Mobilization for Youth" project now underway in the Lower East Side of Manhattan. Present plans call for over 30 separate "action" programs in four major areas of work, education, community, and group service. The project is reported in detail in "A Proposal for the Prevention and Control of Delinquency by Expanding Opportunities," New York City: Mobilization for Youth, Inc. (December, 1961), and in brief in "Report on Juvenile Delinquency," Washington: Hearings of the Subcommittee on Appropriations, 1960, pp. 113-116.

behavior by urban lower-class adolescents, whatever their personality characteristics, is in some significant degree facilitated by or actualized through certain structural features of the community, the Project executed "action" programs directed at three of the societal units seen to figure importantly in the genesis and perpetuation of delinquent behavior—the community, the family, and the gang.

The community program involved two major efforts: 1) the development and strengthening of local citizens' groups so as to enable them to take direct action in regard to local problems, including delinquency, and 2) an attempt to secure cooperation between those professional agencies whose operations in the community in some way involved adolescents (e.g., settlement houses, churches, schools, psychiatric and medical clinics, police, courts and probation departments, corrections and parole departments). A major short-term objective was to increase the possibility of concerted action both among the professional agencies themselves and between the professionals and the citizens' groups. The ultimate objective of these organizational efforts was to focus a variety of diffuse and uncoordinated efforts on problems of youth and delinquency in a single community so as to bring about more effective processes of prevention and control.[2]

Work with families was conducted within the framework of a "chronic-problem-family" approach; a group of families with histories of repeated and long-term utilization of public welfare services were located and subjected to a special and intensive program of psychiatrically-oriented casework.[3]

Work with gangs, the major effort of the Project, was based on the detached worker or area worker approach utilized by the New York Youth Board and similar projects.[4] An adult worker is assigned to an area, group, or groups with a mandate to contact, establish relations with, and attempt to change resident gangs. The application of this method by the Midcity Project incorporated three features not generally included in earlier programs: 1) All workers were professionally trained, with degrees in case work, group work, or both; 2) Each worker but one devoted primary attention to a single group, maintaining recurrent and intensive contact with group members over an ex-

---

[2] See Lester Houston and Lena DiCicco, "Community Development in a Boston District," on file United Community Services of Boston, 1956.

[3] See David M. Austin, "The Special Youth Program Approach to Chronic Problem Families," *Community Organization Papers*, New York City: Columbia University Press, 1958. Also, Joan Zilbach, "Work with Chronic Problem Families: A Five Year Appraisal," Boston: on file Judge Baker Guidance Center, 1962.

[4] A brief description of the background of this method appears on p. 406 of Walter B. Miller, "The Impact of a Community Group Work Program on Delinquent Corner Groups," *The Social Service Review*, 31 (December, 1957), pp. 390-406.

tended time period; 3) Psychiatric consultation was made available on a regular basis, so that workers were in a pcsition to utilize methods and perspectives of psychodynamic psychiatry in addition to the group dynamics and recreational approaches in which they had been trained.

Between June 1954 and May 1957, seven project field workers (five men, two women) maintained contact with approximately 400 youngsters between the ages of 12 and 21, comprising the membership of some 21 corner gangs. Seven of these, totaling 205 members, were subjected to intensive attention. Workers contacted their groups on an average of 3.5 times a week; contact periods averaged about 5 or 6 hours; total duration of contact ranged from 10 to 34 months. Four of the intensive service groups were white males (Catholic, largely Irish, some Italians and Canadian French); one was negro male, one white female, and one negro female. All groups "hung out" in contiguous neighborhoods of a single district of Midcity—a fairly typical lower-class "inner-city" community.[5]

The average size of male groups was 30, and of female 9. All intensive service groups, as well as most of the other known groups, were "locality-based" rather than "emergent" or "situationally organized" groups.[6] This meant that the groups were indigenous, self-formed, and

[5] The term "lower class" is used in this paper to refer to that sector of the population in the lowest educational and occupational categories. For the purposes of Project statistical analyses, those census tracts in Midcity were designated as "lower class" in which 50% or more of the adult residents had failed to finish high school, and 60% or more of resident males pursued occupations in the bottom five occupational categories delineated by the 1950 United States Census. Nineteen of the 21 census tracts in Midcity were designated "lower class" by these criteria. Within lower class, three levels were distinguished. "Lower-class 3" included census tracts with 80% or more of adult males in the bottom five occupational categories and 70% or more of the adults in the "high-school non-completion" category; "Lower-class 2" included tracts with 70-80% males in low occupations and 60-70% adults not having completed high school; "Lower-class 1," 60-70% low occupation males, 50-60% high school non-completion. Of the 6,500 adolescents in Midcity, 17.5% lived in Lower-class 3 tracts; 53.1% in Lower-class 2, and 20.4% in Lower-class 1. The remaining 8.8% were designated "middle class." Project gangs derived primarily from Lower-class 2 and 3 areas; studied gangs comprised approximately 16% of the adolescent (13-19) Lower-class 2 and 3 population of the study area—roughly 30% of the males and 4% of the females.

[6] Beyond this crude distinction between "locality-based" gangs and "other" types, a more systematic typology of Midcity gangs cannot be presented here. Karl Holton also distinguishes a locality-based gang ("area gang") as one type in Los Angeles County, and includes a classic brief description which applies without modification to the Midcity type. Karl Holton, "Juvenile Gangs in the Los Angeles Area," in Hearings of the Subcommittee on Juvenile Delinquency, 86th Congress, Part 5, Washington, D.C.: (November, 1960), pp. 886-888. The importance of the "locality-based" typological distinction in this context is to emphasize the fact that Project gangs were not "emergent" groups organized in response to some common activity interest such as athletics, or formed around a single influential "magnetic" youngster, or organized under the influence of recreational or social work personnel. The gang structure pre-

inheritors of a gang tradition which in some cases extended back for fifty years or more. This kind of gang system in important respects resembled certain African age-class systems in that a new "class" or corner-group unit was formed every two or three years, recruiting from like-aged boys residing in the vicinity of the central "hanging" locale.[7] Thus the total corner aggregate in relatively stable residential areas generally consisted of three to five age-graded male groups, each maintaining a sense of allegiance to their corner and/or traditional gang name, and at the same time maintaining a clear sense of identity as a particular age-graded unit within the larger grouping.

Girls groups, for the most part, achieved their identity primarily through their relations with specific boys' units, which were both larger and more solidary. Each locality aggregate thus included several female groups, generally bearing a feminized version of the male group name (Bandits-Bandettes; Kings-Queens).

## Action Methods with Corner Gangs

The methods used by Project workers encompassed a wide range of techniques and entailed work on many levels with many kinds of groups, agencies and organizations.[8] Workers conceptualized the process

---

existed the Project, was coordinate with and systematically related to the kinship structure, and was "multi-functional" and "versatile" in that it served as a staging base for a wide range of activities and served a wide range of functions, both practical and psychological, for its members.

[7] The age-class system of Midcity closely resembles that of the Otoro of Central Sudan as described by Asmarom Legesse, "[Some East African Age-] Class Systems," Special Paper, Graduate School of Education, Harvard University, May 1961 and S. F. Nadel, The Nuba, London: Oxford University Press, 1947, pp. 132-146. The Otoro age-class system, "one of the simplest . . . in eastern Africa" is in operation between the ages of 11 and 26 (in contrast to other systems which operate during the total life span), and comprises five classes formed at three-year intervals (Class I, 11-14; II, 14-17; III, 17-20; IV, 20-23; V, 23-26). The Midcity system, while less formalized, operates roughly between the ages of 12 and 23, and generally comprises four classes with new classes forming every two to four years, depending on the size of the available recruitment pool, density of population, and other factors. (Class I [Midgets] 12-14; II [Juniors] 14-16; III [Intermediates] 16-19; IV [Seniors] 19-22.) Otoro age classes, like Midcity's, are "multi-functional" in that they form the basis of athletic teams, work groups, and other types of associational unit.

[8] Project "action" methods have been described briefly in several published papers; David M. Austin, "Goals for Gang Workers," Social Work, 2 (October 1957), pp. 43-50; Ethel Ackley and Beverly Fliegel, "A Social Work Approach to Street-Corner Girls," Social Work, 5 (October 1960), pp. 27-36; Walter B. Miller, "The Impact of a Community Group Work Program on Delinquent Corner Groups," op. cit.; and "Preventive Work with Street-Corner Groups: Boston Delinquency Project," The Annals of the American Academy of Political and Social Science, 322 (March 1959), pp. 97-106, and in detail in one unpublished report, David Kantor and Lester

of working with the groups as a series of sequential phases, on the model of individual psychotherapy. Three major phases were delineated— roughly, relationship establishment, behavior modification, and termination. In practice workers found it difficult to conduct operations according to the planned "phase" sequence, and techniques seen as primarily appropriate to one phase were often used during another. There was, however, sufficiently close adherence to the phase concept as to make it possible to consider specific techniques as primarily associated with a given phase.

*Phase I: Contact and Relationship Establishment.* During this phase workers sought out and located resident corner gangs and established an acceptable role-identity. Neither the location of the groups nor the establishment of a viable basis for a continued relationship entailed particular difficulties.[9] This phase included considerable "testing" of the workers; the youngsters put on display a wide range of their customary behavior, with particular stress on violative forms—watching the worker closely to see whether his reactions and evaluative responses fell within an acceptable range. The workers, for their part, had to evince sufficient familiarity with and control over the basic subcultural system of lower class adolescents and its component skills as to merit the respect of the groups, and the right to continued association.

A major objective in gaining entree to the groups was to establish what workers called a "relationship." Influenced in part by concepts derived from individual psychotherapy, Project staff felt that the establishment of close and meaningful relationships with group members was a major device for effecting behavior change, and was in fact a necessary precondition of all other direct service methods. The workers' conception of a "good" relationship was complex, but can be described briefly as a situation in which both worker and group defined themselves as contained within a common orbit whose major conditions were mutual trust, mutual affection, and maintenance of reciprocal obligations. The workers in fact succeeded in establishing and maintaining relationships of just this type. Considering the fact that these alliances had to bridge both age (adult-adolescent) and social status (lower class-middle class) differences, they were achieved and maintained with a surprising degree of success.[10]

---

Houston, *Methods of Working with Street Corner Youth*, 1959, mimeo, 227 pp., on file Harvard Student Volunteers Project.

[9] Extensive discussion of the specific techniques of contact, role-identity establishment and relationship maintenance is included in Kantor and Houston, *ibid.*

[10] Research methods for categorizing worker-group relationships according to intensity and intimacy will be cited in future reports.

*Phase II: Behavior Modification via Mutual Activity Involvement.* The behavior modification phase made the greatest demands on the skills, resourcefulness, and energy of the workers. Workers engaged in a wide variety of activities with and in behalf of their groups. The bulk of these activities, however, centered around three major kinds of effort: 1) Organizing groups and using these as the basis of involvement in organized activities; 2) Serving as intermediary between group members and adult institutions; 3) Utilizing techniques of direct influence.

The workers devoted considerable effort to changing group relational systems from the informal type of the street gang to the formal type of the club or athletic team, and involving the groups so reorganized in a range of activities such as club meetings, athletic contests, dances, and fund-raising dinners. In most cases this effort was highly successful. Clubs formed from the corner groups met regularly, adopted constitutions, carried out extensive and effective club activities. Athletic teams moved from cellar positions to championships in city athletic leagues. One group grossed close to a thousand dollars at a fund-raising dance.

Project use of the "organized group and planned activities" method was buttressed by rationale which included at least five premises. 1) The experience of learning to operate in the "rule-governed" atmosphere of the formal club would, it was felt, increase the group members' ability to conduct collective activities in an orderly and law-abiding fashion. 2) The influence of the more lawfully-oriented leaders would be increased, since authority-roles in clubs or teams would be allocated on different bases from those in the corner gang. 3) The need for the clubs to rely heavily on the adult worker for advice and facilitation would place him in a strategic position to influence group behavior. 4) The need for clubs to maintain harmonious relations with local adults such as settlement house personnel and dance hall owners in order to carry out their activity program, as well as the increasing visibility of the organized group, would put a premium on maintaining a public reputation as non-troublesome, and thus inhibit behavior which would jeopardize this objective. 5) Active and extensive involvement in lawful and adult-approved recreational activities would, it was felt, substantially curtail both time and energy potentially available for unlawful activity. This devil-finds-work premise was taken as self-evidently valid, and was reinforced by the idleness-boredom explanation frequently forwarded by group members themselves—"We get in trouble because there's nuthin to do around here." On these grounds as well as others, the use of this method appeared amply justified.[11]

[11] Further elaboration of the rationale behind the "group-organization-and-activity" method, as well as some additional detail on its operation, is contained in David

In performing the role of intermediary, workers proceeded on the premise that gang members were essentially isolated within their own adolescent slum world and were either denied, or lacked the ability to seek out, "access" to major adult institutions. This blocked access, it was felt, prevented the youngsters from seeking prestige through "legitimate" channels, forcing them instead to resort to "illegitimate" forms of achievement such as thievery, fighting, and prostitution. On this assumption, the Project aimed deliberately to open up channels of access to adult institutions—particularly in the areas of education and employment.

In the world of work, Project workers arranged appointments with employment agencies, drove group members to job interviews, counseled them as to proper demeanor as job applicants and as employees, urged wavering workers not to quit their jobs. Workers also contacted business firms and urged them to hire group members. In the area of education, workers attempted to solidify the often tenuous bonds between group members and the schools. They visited teachers, acted to discourage truancy, and worked assiduously—through means ranging from subtle persuasion to vigorous argument—to discourage the practice of dropping-out of school at or before the legally-permissible age. Workers arranged meetings with school personnel and attempted to acquaint teachers and other school staff with the special problems of corner youngsters. Every effort was made to arrange scholarships (generally athletic) for those group members for whom college seemed a possibility.

Workers also acted as go-between for their youngsters and a variety of other institutions. They arranged for lawyers in the event of court appearances, and interceded with judges, probation officers, correctional officials and parole personnel. They obtained the use of the recreational facilities and meeting places in settlement houses and gyms which would not have considered admitting the rough and troublesome gang members in the absence of a responsible adult sponsor. They persuaded local storekeepers and businessmen to aid the groups in their money-raising efforts. They arranged for the use or rental of dance halls, and solicited radio stations to provide locally-famous disc-jockeys to conduct record hops. They organized meetings between gang members and local policemen during which both sides were given the opportunity to air their mutual grievances.

During later stages of the Project, workers brought together the clubs of the corner gangs and the adult organizations formed by the

Austin, "Goals for Gang Workers," *op. cit.*, p. 49, and Walter B. Miller, *The Place of the Organized Club in Corner-Group Work Method*, Boston: on file Special Youth Program, mimeo, 7 pp. (November, 1956).

Project's Community Organization program, and gang members and community adults served together on joint committees working in the area of community improvement. One such committee exerted sufficient pressure on municipal authorities to obtain a $60,000 allocation for the improvement of a local ball field; another committee instituted an annual "Sports Night" during which most of the community's gangs—some of whom were active gang-fighting enemies—attended a large banquet in which city officials and well-known sports figures made speeches and presented awards for meritorious athletic achievement.

Thus, as a consequence of the workers' activities, gang members gained access to a wide variety of legitimate adult institutions and organizations—schools, business establishments, settlement houses, municipal athletic leagues, public recreational facilities, guidance services, health facilities, municipal governmental agencies, citizens groups, and others. It could no longer be said that the groups were isolated, in any practical sense, from the world of legitimate opportunity.[12]

While Project methods placed major stress on changing environmental conditions through organization, activity involvement, and opening channels of access, workers were also committed to the use of methods designed to induce personality change. The training of most workers had involved exposure to the principles of, and some practice in the techniques of, psychodynamic psychotherapy, and serious consideration was given to the possibility of attempting some form of direct application of psychotherapeutic principles, or techniques based on "insight" therapy. After much discussion workers decided that the use of techniques appropriate to the controlled therapist-patient situation would not be practicable in the open and multi-cliented arena of the corner gang world, and arrangements were made to utilize this approach through indirect rather than direct means.

Psychodynamic methods and individual treatment approaches were utilized in two ways. First, a contract was made with a well-known

---

[12] Project research data made it possible to determine the relative amount of worker effort devoted to various types of activity. The frequency of 12 different kinds of activity engaged in by workers toward or in behalf of group members ("worker functions") was tabulated for all 7 workers. Of 9958 recorded worker functions, 3878 were executed in connection with 22 organizations or agencies. Of these "institutionally-oriented" functions, workers acted in the capacity of "intermediary" for group members 768 times (19.8%), making "intermediation" the second most frequent type of "institutionally-oriented" worker function. The most frequent function was the exercise of "direct influence" (28.7%), to be discussed in the next section. Thus about one-half of all institutionally-oriented worker activity involved two functions—acting as intermediary and engaging in direct influence efforts. Of the 768 intermediary functions, 466 (60.7%) were exercised in connection with 6 kinds of organizations or groups—business organizations, schools, social welfare agencies, families, and other gangs.

child-psychiatry clinic, and workers consulted with psychodynamically trained psychiatrists on a regular basis. During these sessions the psychiatrists analyzed individual cases on the basis of detailed case summaries, and recommended procedures for the workers to execute. In this way the actual operating policies of the workers were directly influenced by the diagnostic concepts and therapeutic procedures of psychodynamic psychiatry. Second, in cases where the workers or the psychiatric consultants felt that more direct or intensive therapy for group members or their families was indicated, arrangements were made to refer these cases either to the psychiatric clinic or to local casework or family-service agencies.

Another type of direct influence technique utilized by the workers was "group-dynamics"—a method which combined approaches of both psychodynamic and small-group theory. As adult advisors during club meetings, during informal bull-sessions, and in some instances during specially-arranged group-therapy sessions, workers employed the specific techniques of persuasion and influence developed out of the group-dynamics approach (indirect suggestion, non-directive leadership, permissive group guidance, collective reinforcement). Sessions based on the group-therapy model were generally geared to specific emergent situations—such as an episode of sexual misbehavior among the girls or an upsurge of racial sentiment among the boys.[13]

The direct-influence technique which operated most consistently, however, was simply the continued presence with the group of a law-abiding, middle-class-oriented adult who provided active support for a particular value position. This value stance was communicated to the youngsters through two principal devices—advice and exemplification. The worker served as counsellor, advisor, mentor in a wide range of specific issues, problems and areas of behavioral choice as these emerged in the course of daily life. Should I continue school or drop-out? Can we refrain from retaliatory attack and still maintain our honor? How does one approach girls? How does one handle an overly-romantic boy? Should I start a pimping operation? In all these issues and many more— sometimes broached by the worker, more frequently by the youngsters —the workers put their support—often subtle but nonetheless consistent —behind the law-abiding versus the law-violating choice, and, to a lesser extent, the middle-class-oriented over the lower-class-oriented course of action in regard to long-term issues such as education, occupation, and family life.[14]

[13] A description of the use of group-dynamics techniques by Project workers is included in A. Paul Hare, "Group Dynamics as a Technique for Reducing Intergroup Tensions," Cambridge: Harvard University, unpublished paper, 1957, pp. 14-22.
[14] For the frequency of use of "direct influence" techniques, see footnote 12.

But the continued association of worker and group engaged a mechanism of influence which proved in many ways more potent than advice and counsel. The fact of constant association, and the fact that workers became increasingly accepted and admired, meant that they were in a particularly strategic position to serve as a "role-model," or object of emulation. A strong case can be made for the influencive potency of this device. Adolescents, as they move towards adult status, are often pictured as highly sensitive to, and in search of, models of estimable adult behavior, and to be particularly susceptible to emulation of an adult who plays an important role in their lives, and whom they respect and admire. It appeared, in fact, that gang members were considerably more impressed by what the workers *were* than by what they said or did. The youngsters were particularly aware that the workers were college people, that they were responsible spouses and parents in stable mother-father families, that they were conscientious workers under circumstances which afforded maximum opportunities for goofing-off. The workers' statuses as college people, "good" family people, and responsible workers constituted an implicit endorsement of these statuses, and the course of action they implied.

In some instances the admiration of group members for their worker approached hero-worship. One group set up a kind of shrine to their worker after his departure; on a shelf in the corner store where they hung out they placed his photograph, the athletic trophies they had won under his aegis, and a scrap-book containing accounts of the many activities they had shared together. Visitors who knew the worker were importuned to relay to him a vital message—"Tell him we're keepin' our noses clean. . . ."

*Phase III: Termination.* Since the Project was set up on a three-year "demonstration" basis, the date of final contact was known well in advance. Due largely to the influence of psychodynamic concepts, workers were very much concerned about the possibly harmful effects of "termination," and formulated careful and extensive plans for effecting disengagement from their groups. During the termination phase the workers' efforts centered around three major areas; scheduling a gradual reduction in the frequency of contact and "services" so as to avoid an abrupt cut-off; preparing the groups emotionally for the idea of termination by probing for and discussing feelings of "desertion" anger and loss; and arranging for community agencies to assume as many as possible of the services workers had provided for the groups (e.g., recreational involvement, counseling, meeting places for the clubs).

Despite some difficult moments for both workers and group members (one worker's car was stolen during the tearful farewell banquet tendered him by his group the night before he was to leave for a new job in another city; group members explained this as a symbolic way of saying "Don't leave Midcity!"), termination was effected quite successfully; workers moved off to other involvements and the groups reassumed their workerless position within the community.

In sum, then, the methods used in the Project's attempt to inhibit delinquent behavior were based on a sophisticated rationale, utilized both sociocultural and psychological concepts and methods, encompassed an unusually wide range of practice techniques, and were executed with care, diligence and energy by competent and professionally trained workers. It was impossible, of course, to execute all planned programs and methods as fully or as extensively as might have been desired, but in overall perspective the execution of the Project showed an unusually close degree of adherence to its ambitious and comprehensive plan of operation.[15] What, then, was the impact of these efforts on delinquent behavior?

## THE IMPACT OF PROJECT EFFORTS

The Midcity Project was originally instituted in response to a community perception that uncontrolled gang violence was rampant in Midcity. Once the furor attending its inception had abated, the Project was reconceptualized as a "demonstration" project in community delinquency control.[16] This meant that in addition to setting up methods for effecting changes in its client population, the Project also assumed responsibility for testing the efficacy of these methods. The task of evaluating project effectiveness was assigned to a social science research staff which operated in conjunction with the action program.[17] Since

15 A previous report, "Preventive Work with Street-Corner Groups: Boston Delinquency Project," *op. cit.*, p. 106, cited certain factors which made it difficult to execute some project methods as fully as might have been desired. With greater perspective, derived both from the passage of time and increased knowledge of the experience of other projects, it would now appear that the Midcity Project was relatively less impeded in this regard than many similar projects, especially in regard to difficulties with police, courts, and schools, and that from a comparative viewpoint the Project was able to proceed relatively freely to effect most of its major methods.

16 Events attending the inception of the Midcity Project are cited in "The Impact of a Community Group Work Program on Delinquent Corner Groups," *op. cit.*, and in Walter B. Miller, "Inter-Institutional Conflict as a Major Impediment to Delinquency Prevention," *Human Organization*, 17 (Fall 1958), pp. 20-23.

17 Research methods were complex, utilizing a wide range of techniques and approaches. A major distinction was made between "evaluative" (measurement of impact) and "informational" (ethnographic description and analysis) research. No detailed account of research methods has been published, but brief descriptions appear in "The Impact of a Community Group Work Program on Delinquent Corner Groups,"

the major effort of the Project was its work with gangs, the evaluative aspect of the research design focused on the gang program, and took as a major concern the impact of group-directed methods on the behavior of target gangs. However, since the focal "client" population of the group-work program (gang members) was a subpopulation of the larger client population of the overall project ("trouble"-prone Midcity adolescents), measures of change in the gangs also constituted a test of the totality of control measures utilized by the Project, including its community organization and family-service programs.

The broad question—"Did the Project have any impact on the behavior of the groups it worked with?"—has, in effect, already been answered. The above description of Project methods shows that workers became actively and intensively involved in the lives and activities of the groups. It is hardly conceivable that relatively small groups of adolescents could experience daily association with an adult—especially an adult committed to the task of changing their behavior—without undergoing some substantial modification. But the fundamental *raison d'etre* of the Project was not that of demonstrating the possibility of establishing close relationships with gangs, or of organizing them into clubs, or of increasing their involvement in recreational activities, or of providing them with access to occupational or educational opportunities, or of forming citizens' organizations, or of increasing inter-agency cooperation. These objectives, estimable as they might be, were pursued not as ends in themselves but as means to a further and more fundamental end —the inhibition and control of criminal behavior. The substantial effects of the Project on non-violative forms of behavior will be reported elsewhere; this paper addresses itself to a central and critical measure—the impact of the Project on specifically violative behavior.[18]

The principal question of the evaluative research was phrased as follows: *Was there a significant measurable inhibition of law-violating or morally-disapproved behavior as a consequence of Project efforts?* For purposes of research procedure this question was broken down into two

---

*op. cit.*, pp. 392-396, and "Preventive Work with Street-Corner Groups: Boston Delinquency Project," *op. cit.*, pp. 99-100, *passim*. A somewhat more detailed description of one kind of content analysis method used in an earlier pilot study, and modified for use in the larger study, appears in Walter B. Miller, Hildred Geertz and Henry S. G. Cutter, "Aggression in a Boys' Street-Corner Group," *Psychiatry*, 24 (November 1961), pp. 284-285.

[18] Detailed analyses of changes in "non-violative" forms of behavior (e.g., frequency of recreational activities, trends in "evaluatively neutral" behaviors) as well as more generalized "change-process" analyses (e.g., "structural" changes in groups— factions, leadership; overall patterning of change and relations between changes in violative and non-violative patterns) will appear in Walter B. Miller, *City Gangs: An Experiment in Changing Gang Behavior*, John Wiley and Sons, in preparation.

component questions: 1) To what extent was there a measurable reduction in the actual or expected frequency of violative behavior by Project group members during or after the period of Project contact? and 2) To what extent could observed changes in violative behavior be attributed to Project activity rather than to other possible "causative" factors such as maturation or police activity? [19] Firm affirmative answers to the first question would necessarily have to precede attempts to answer further questions such as "Which methods were most effective?"; the value of describing what the workers did in order to reduce delinquency would evidently depend on whether it could be shown that delinquency had in fact been reduced.

Following sections will report three separate measures of change in patterns of violative behavior. These are: 1) Disapproved forms of customary behavior; 2) Illegal behavior; 3) Court appearance rates. These three sets of measures represent different methods of analysis, different orders of specificity, and were derived from different sources. The implications of this for achieved results will be discussed later.

TRENDS IN DISAPPROVED BEHAVIOR

A central form of "violative" behavior is that which violates specific legal statutes (e.g., theft, armed assault). Also important, however, is behavior which violates "moral" norms or ethical standards. Concern with such behavior is of interest in its own right (Was there a reduction in morally-violative behavior?) as well as in relation to illegal behavior. (Were developments in the areas of illegal and immoral behavior related or independent?). The relationship between immoral and illegal behavior is highly complex; most behavior which violates legal norms also violates moral norms (overtime parking is one example of an exception), but much immoral behavior seldom results in legal action (homosexual intimacy between women; failure to attempt to rescue a drowning stranger).

Designating specific forms of behavior as "illegal" presents a relatively simple task, since detailed and fairly explicit criminal codes are available; designating behavior as "immoral" is far more difficult, both because of the multiplicity of moral codes in American society, and because many important moral norms are not explicitly codified.[20] In

---

[19] The "study population" toward which these questions were directed was the 205 members of the seven corner gangs subjected to "intensive service" by workers. (See pp. 169-170.) Unless otherwise specified, the term "Project Groups" will be used to refer to this population.

[20] A brief discussion of the complexities of the "multiple-moral-norm" system of the United States is contained in William C. Kvaraceus, Walter B. Miller, et al.,

addressing the question—"Did the Project bring about a decrease in morally-violative behavior?," at least four sets of moral codes are of relevance—those of middle class adults, of middle class adolescents, of lower class adults, and of lower class adolescents.[21] While there are large areas of concordance among these sets, there are also important areas of noncorrespondence. The method employed in this area was as follows:

A major source of data for Project research was a large population of "behavior sequences" engaged in by group members during the study period. These were derived from a variety of sources, the principal source being the detailed descriptive daily field reports of the workers.[22] All recorded behavioral events involving group members were extracted from the records and typed on separate data cards. These cards were coded, and filed in chronological order under 65 separate categories of behavior such as drinking behavior, sexual behavior, and theft. A total of 100,000 behavior sequences was recorded, coded, and filed.

Fourteen of the 65 behavior categories were selected for the purpose of analyzing trends in immoral behavior.[23] These were: theft, assault, drinking, sex, mating, work, education, religion, and involvement with courts, police, corrections, social welfare, family, and other gangs. Seventy-five thousand behavioral sequences were included under these fourteen categories.

A separate set of evaluative standards, based primarily on the workers' own values, was developed for each of the fourteen areas. The workers as individuals were essentially oriented to the value system of middle class adults, but due largely to their training in social work, they espoused an "easier" or more permissive version of these standards. In addition, as a result of their experiences in the lower class community, their standards had been further modified to accommodate in some de-

---

*Delinquent Behavior: Culture and the Individual*, Washington: National Education Association of the United States, 1959, pp. 46-49.

[21] This four-type distinction is very gross; a range of subsystems could be delineated within each of the four cited "systems."

[22] 8870 pages of typescript records were subjected to coding. Of these, 6600 pages were self-recorded field reports by workers; 690 pages were worker reports to the Project Director; 640 were field reports and interviews by research staff; 150 were tape-recorded transcriptions of group interaction. A brief description of the principles of the data-coding system, based on the concept of the "object-oriented-behavior-sequence," is included in Ernest Lilienstein, James Short, *et al.*, "Procedural Notes for the Coding of Detached Worker Interviews," Chicago: University of Chicago Youth Studies Program (February 1962), pp. 2-7.

[23] These 14 were selected because they included the largest numbers of recorded events, and because they represented a range of behaviors along the dimension "high violative potential" (theft, assault) through "low violative potential" (church, family-oriented behavior).

gree those of the adolescent gangs. The workers' standards thus comprised an easier baseline against which to measure change since they were considerably less rigid than those which would be applied by most middle class adults.

Listings were drawn up for each of the fourteen areas which designated as "approved" or "disapproved" about 25 specific forms of behavior per area. A distinction was made between "actions" (behavioral events observed to occur) and "sentiments" (attitudes or intentions).[24] Designations were based on three kinds of information: evaluative statements made by the workers concerning particular areas of behavior; attitudes or actions workers had supported or opposed in actual situations; and an attitude questionnaire administered to each worker. Preliminary listings were submitted to the workers to see if the items did in fact reflect the evaluative standards they felt themselves to espouse; there was high agreement with the listings; in a few instances of disagreement modifications were made.

A total of 14,471 actions and sentiments were categorized as "approved," "disapproved," or "evaluatively-neutral." While these data made possible detailed and extensive analysis of differential patterns of behavior change in various areas and on different levels, the primary question for the most general purposes of impact measurement was phrased as—"Was there a significant reduction in the relative frequency of *disapproved actions* during the period of worker contact?" With some qualifications, the answer was "No."

Each worker's term of contact was divided into three equal phases, and the relative frequency of disapproved actions during the first and third phase was compared.[25] During the full study period, the 205 members of the seven intensive analysis groups engaged in 4518 approved or disapproved actions. During the initial phase, 785 of 1604 actions (48.9%) were disapproved; during the final phase, 613 of 1364 (44.9%)—a reduction of only 4%.

Of the fourteen behavior areas, only one ("school-oriented behavior") showed a statistically significant reduction in disapproved actions. Of the remaining 13, ten showed decreases in disapproved actions, one no change, and two (church- and social-agency-oriented behavior) showed

[24] Examples of approved and disapproved actions and sentiments in the area of drinking are as follows: *Approved action;* "refusal to buy or accept liquor": *disapproved action;* "getting drunk, going on a drinking spree": *approved sentiment;* "stated intention to discontinue or reduce frequency of drinking": *disapproved sentiment;* "bragging of one's drinking prowess."

[25] Selected findings in regard only to disapproved actions are reported here. Future reports will present and analyze trends in both actions and sentiments, and in approved, disapproved and evaluatively-neutral forms, and the relations among these.

increases. Of the seven analysis groups, only one (white, male, younger, higher social status) showed a statistically significant reduction. Of the remaining six, five showed decreases in disapproved actions, one no change, and one (white, male, older, lower social status) an increase.[26]

The unexpected degree of stability over time in the ratio of approved to disapproved actions is all the more noteworthy in view of the fact that one might have expected the area of moral behavior to have felt the most direct impact of the workers' presence. One clue to the stability of the change figures lies in the fact that there was a good correspondence between the degree of change in disapproved actions and the social status of the group; in general, the lower the group's social status, the smaller the reduction in disapproved actions.[27]

TRENDS IN ILLEGAL ACTS

The central question to be asked of a delinquency control program is—"Does it control delinquency?" One direct way of approaching this question is to focus on that "target" population most directly exposed to program action methods and ask "Was there a decrease in the frequency of crimes committed by the target population during the period of the program?" Under most circumstances this is difficult to answer, owing to the necessity of relying on records collected by police, courts, or other "official" agencies. The drawbacks of utilizing official incidence statistics as a measure of the actual occurrence of criminal behavior have frequently been pointed out; among these is the very complex process of selectivity which governs the conversion of committed crimes into official statistics; many crimes are never officially detected; many of those detected do not result in an official arrest; many arrests do not eventuate in court action, and so on. At each stage of the conversion process, there is a multiplicity of factors relatively independent of the

---

[26] Chi-square was used to test significance. For all fourteen behavior areas for all seven groups, chi-square was 4.57 (one d.f.), which was significant between the .02 and .05 level. However, almost all the "change" variance was accounted for by the single area which showed a significant reduction (chi-square for "school" was 14.32, significant beyond the .01 level). The other 13 behavior areas, accounting for 91.6% of the evaluated actions, showed a reduction of only 2.3%. Chi-square was 1.52 (one d.f.) which fails of significance. Chi-square for the one significant change group (Junior Outlaws) was 9.21, significant at the .01 level. However, omitting the one "significant change" behavior area (school) from consideration, chi-square for the remaining 90% of Junior Outlaws behavior areas was 3.19—which fails of significance at the .05 level.

[27] Rank-difference correlation between "reduction in disapproved actions" and "lower social status" was −.82. The fact that this kind of association (the lower the social status the less change) appeared frequently in analyses of specific forms of behavior attests to the strength of the influence of group social status on patterns of delinquency and vulnerability to change efforts.

commission of the crime itself which determines whether or not a crime will be officially recorded, and in what form.

The Midcity Project was able to a large extent to overcome this difficulty by the nature of its base data. Because of their intimate daily association with gang members, workers were in a position both to observe crimes directly, and to receive reports of crimes shortly after they occurred. The great majority of these never appeared in official records.[28]

The research question in the area of illegal behavior was phrased: "Was there a significant decrease in the frequency of statute violations committed by Project group members during the period of worker contact?" As in the case of disapproved actions, the answer was, with some qualifications, "No." Methods and results were as follows.

Every statute-violating act committed by a Project group member during the course of the contact period was recorded on an individual record form. While the bulk of recorded acts were derived from the workers' field reports, information was obtained from all available sources, including official records. Very few of the crimes recorded by official agencies were not also recorded by the Project; many of the crimes recorded by the Project did not appear in official records. During the course of the Project, a total of 1005 legally violative acts was recorded for members of the seven intensive analysis groups. Eighty-three per cent of the 205 Project group members had committed at least one illegal act; 90% of the 150 males had been so involved. These figures alone show that the Project did not prevent crime, and there had been no expectation that it would. But did it "control" or "inhibit" crime?

Offenses were classified under eleven categories: theft, assault, alcohol violations, sex offenses, trespassing, disorderly conduct, truancy, vandalism, gambling violations, and "other" (e.g., strewing tacks on street, killing cats).[29] Each worker's term of contact was divided into three

[28] The availability to the Project of both official and unofficial statistics on crime frequency made it possible to derive "conversion ratios" showing the proportion of crimes recorded by official agencies to those recorded by the Project. These ratios will be reported in greater detail in *City Gangs, op. cit.*; in brief, ratios of "Project-recorded" to "court-appeared" offenses were as follows. For all categories of offense for both sexes, 15% of known crimes resulted in court action. For males only this ratio was 16%; fewer than 1% of recorded female crimes were court processed. The highest ratio was in the case of theft-type offenses by males; about 25% were court processed. About 10% of male drinking and assaultive offenses resulted in court appearance.

[29] Determination of illegality was based on the offense classifications of the Massachusetts Penal Code. The complexities of definition of the various offense categories cannot be detailed here, but most categories represent higher level generality definitions than those of the code. For example, the category "theft" is used here to include all forms of unlawful appropriation of property, thus subsuming the more

equal phases, and the frequency of offenses during the initial and final phase was compared.

Seven hundred and fifty-two of the 1005 offenses were committed during the initial and final phases. Of these, 394 occurred during the initial phase, and 358 during the final—a reduction of 9.1%. Considering males only, however, 614 male crimes accounting for 81.6% of all offenses showed an *increase* of 1.3% between initial and final phases. In order to localize areas of greater and lesser change, a distinction was made between "major" and "minor" types of offense, in which theft, assault, and alcohol offenses, accounting for 70.5% of all male offenses, were categorized as "major." On these major offenses the male groups showed an increase of 11.2%—the older male groups showing an increase of 4.7%, and the younger an increase of 21.8%.

In sum, then, it could not be said that there was any significant reduction in the frequency of known crimes during the course of the Project. The modest decrease shown by the total sample was accounted for largely by the girls and by minor offenses; major offenses by boys, in contrast, increased in frequency during the course of the Project, and major offenses by younger boys increased most of all.[30]

TRENDS IN COURT APPEARANCES

The third major index to Project impact was based on court appearance statistics. The principal research question in this area was phrased: "Did the Project effect any decrease in the frequency with which Project group members appeared in court in connection with crimes?"[31] The use of court-appearance data made it possible to amplify and strengthen

---

than 30 distinctions of the Penal code, e.g., robbery, armed, unarmed; larceny, grand, petty; burglary, etc.). Non-theft auto violations are included under "other" since so few were recorded; similarly, narcotics violations, a major form of crime from a "seriousness" point of view, are included under "other" since virtually no instances were recorded.

[30] None of these changes proved significant on the basis of chi-square. Chi-square for the largest change, the increase of 21.8% for the younger males, was 3.32, which is just below the .05 level. More detailed analyses of these trends, broken down according to type of offense, sex, age, etc., will be presented in *City Gangs, op. cit.*

[31] Phrasing the question in this way was one of the devices used to accommodate the difficulties in using statistics compiled by official agencies. This phrasing takes the court appearance itself as an essentially independent index of impact; it does not assume any systematic connection between frequency of court appearance and frequency of criminal behavior. Having separate measures of Project-recorded and court-processed crimes (See footnote 28) makes possible separate computations of these ratios. Further, since court-appeared crime rather than committed crime can be seen, from one perspective, as the more serious social problem, Project impact on the likelihood of appearance itself can be taken as one relatively independent measure of effectiveness.

the measurement of impact in three major ways. 1) It permitted a considerable time-extension. Previous sections describe trends which occurred during the actual period of worker contact. Sound determination of impact makes it necessary to know how these "during" trends related to trends both preceding and following the contact period. Post-contact trends become particularly important in light of the "negligible change" findings of the "during-contact" period, which raises the possibility that the real impact of the Project may have occurred following the workers' departure, as a kind of delayed reaction response. 2) The data were compiled by agencies which were essentially independent of the Project. Although the Project made every attempt to recognize, accommodate to, and correct for the possibility of in-project bias,[32] exclusive reliance on data collected primarily by those in the employ of the Project would admit the possibility that the objectives or values of Project staff would in some way prejudice results. Despite some contact between Project and court personnel, the operations of the courts were essentially independent of those of the Project, and the likelihood that the various courts in which group members appeared would be influenced in any consistent way by Project values or objectives was extremely small. 3) It made possible the application of time-trend measures to groups other than those taken by the Project as objects of change. The inclusion of a control population as part of the basic evaluative design was of vital importance. Despite the detail obtainable through the continued and intimate contact of group and worker, it would have been difficult to know, without a control population, the extent to which the experience of Project group members during the contact period was a response to worker influence rather than a variety of other possible influencing factors.

Court-appearance data were processed in three different ways. The first made these data directly comparable with the other "during-contact" measures by asking—"Was there a significant decrease in the frequency with which Project group members appeared in court in connection with crimes during the contact period?" The second exploited the time-extension potentialities of the data by asking—"How did the frequency of court appearance during the contact period compare with frequency preceding and following this period?" The third utilized a control population and asked—"Did the court-appearance experience of gang members worked with by a delinquency control project for various periods between the ages of 14 and 19 differ significantly from the experience of similar gang members not so worked with?"

[32] The technical and methodological devices for accommodating to or correcting for the possibility of in-project bias will be detailed in future reporting.

*Contact Period Trends:* Names of the 205 members of the Project's intensive contact groups were submitted to the state's central criminal records division. Court appearance records were returned for all group members with court experience. These records contained full court appearance and correctional commitment data for the 16 year period from 1945 to 1961—at which time older group members averaged 23 years of age, and younger, 21. It was thus possible to process the full sample as an age cohort in regard to court experience between the ages of 7 and 23, and including the period of Project contact. Each appearance in court on a new count for all male group members was tabulated.[33] "During-contact" appearance trends were analyzed in the same fashion as disapproved and illegal actions. The contact term for each group was divided into three equal phases, and the frequency of appearances during the initial and final phase was compared.

Trends in court-appeared offenses were essentially the same as trends in illegal actions. Group members appeared in court in connection with 144 offenses during the contact period. Fifty-one appearances occurred during the initial period and 48 during the final—a decrease of 5.8%. However, categorizing offenses as "major" and "minor" as was done in the case of illegal actions showed that for major offenses (theft, assault, alcohol), 31 appearances occurred during the initial phase and 35 during the final—an increase of 12.9%.[34] There was, therefore, no significant decrease in the frequency with which group members appeared in court during the term of worker contact. Neither the slight decrease in all-offense trends nor the increase in major offense trends proved statistically significant. The fact that these "during-contact" court appearance trends, involving 155 offenses, closely paralleled illegal act trends, involving 1005 offenses, served to corroborate both sets of trends, and to reinforce the finding of "negligible change" in legally-violative behavior for the period of worker contact.

*Before-During-After Trends: Project Groups:* In order to place the "during-contact" offense trends in a broader time-perspective, it was necessary to compare them to rates preceding and following the contact period. Since group members were of different ages during the contact

---

[33] Out of 145 "during-contact" court appearances, only one involved a girl. Since 155 illegal acts involved females, this supports the frequently reported finding that females are far less likely to be subjected to official processing for crimes than males. All following figures, therefore, refer to males only.

[34] Neither of these changes was statistically significant, testing with chi-square and Fisher's Exact Test. The three "major" offenses showed differing trends—with "theft" showing some decrease (23 to 19), "assault" remaining about the same (5 to 6), and "alcohol" showing a considerable increase (3 to 10). "Minor" crimes decreased from 20 to 13. These trends will be reported and analyzed more fully in future reports.

period, data were processed so as to make it possible to compare the court experience of the several groups at equivalent age periods. The average age of each group was determined, and the number of court appearances per group for each six month period between the ages of 7 and 23 was tabulated. One set of results is shown in Table I. The fre-

TABLE I

NUMBER OF COURT APPEARANCES PER YEAR*: AGES 7-23

PROJECT AND CONTROL GROUPS

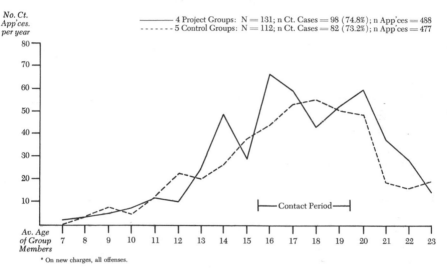

No. Ct.
App'ces.
per year

————— 4 Project Groups: N = 131; n Ct. Cases = 98 (74.8%); n App'ces = 488
- - - - - - 5 Control Groups: N = 112; n Ct. Cases = 82 (73.2%); n App'ces = 477

Contact Period

Av. Age of Group Members    7   8   9   10   11   12   13   14   15   16   17   18   19   20   21   22   23

* On new charges, all offenses.

quency curve of yearly court appearances resembled a normal distribution curve, skewed to the right. Appearance frequency increased gradually between the ages of 7 and 16, maintained a high level between 16 and 20, and dropped off quite rapidly after 20.

The period of maximum frequency of court appearances coincided, in general, with the period of worker contact. Although no single group remained in contact with a worker during the full period between ages 16 and 20, each of the groups experienced contact for periods ranging from one to two and a half years during this period. It could not be said, then, that frequency of court appearance during the contact period was appreciably lower than during the pre-contact period; on the contrary, groups achieved a peak of appearance frequency during the period of Project service efforts.

Another way of describing these trends is by examining appearance frequency by six month periods. During the six months preceding contact there were 21 appearances; during the first six months of contact there were 29, and during the last, 27. In the six months following termination appearances rose to 39, dropped to 20 for the next six months, and rose to 39 for the next. Thus, 18 months after project termination, appearance frequency was at its highest point for the total adolescent period.

The yearly appearance curve (Table I) does, however, show two rather prominent dips—one at age 15, the other at 18. The dip at 15 could not have been related to the Project, since contact had not yet begun. The dip at 18, however, occurred at a time when each of the three older groups was in contact with workers, and thus admits the possibility of worker influence.[35] It is also possible that the post-twenty decline may have represented a delayed-action effect. Thus, looking at the period of worker contact as one phase within the overall period of adolescence, it would appear that the presence of the workers did not inhibit the frequency of court appearances, but that a dip in appearance frequency at age 18 and a drop in frequency after age 20 may have been related to the workers' efforts.

*Comparison of Project and Control Group Trends:* Extending the examination of offense trends from the during-contact period to "before" and "after" periods, while furnishing important additional information, also raised additional questions. Was it just coincidental that the 16 to 19 peak in court appearances occurred during the contact period— or could the presence of the workers have been in some way responsible? Was the sharp decline in frequency of appearances after age 20 a delayed action result of worker effort? To clarify these questions it was necessary to examine the court appearance experience of a control population—a set of corner gangs as similar as possible to Project gangs, but who had *not* been worked with by the Project. The indexes reported so far have provided information as to whether significant change occurred, but have been inconclusive as to the all-important question of cause-and-effect (To what extent were observed trends related to the workers' efforts?). The use of a control population entailed certain risks—primarily the possibility that service and control populations might not be adequately matched in some respects—but the unique potency of the control method as a device for furnishing evidence in the vital area of "cause" outweighed these risks.

[35] This "dip" phenomenon—a lowering of the frequency of violative behavior during the "middle" phase of worker contact—was also noted in connection with a somewhat different kind of processing of illegal acts reported in "Preventive Work with Street-Corner Groups: Boston Delinquency Project," *op. cit.*, p. 100. Currently available data make it possible to amplify and modify the interpretation presented in the earlier paper.

Each of the Project's seven intensive service groups was matched with a somewhat smaller number of members of similarly organized corner gangs of similar age, sex, ethnic status, and social status. Most of these groups hung out in the same district as did Project groups, and their existence and membership had been ascertained during the course of the Project. Since the total membership of the Control groups was not known as fully as that of Project groups, it was necessary in some instances to match one Project group with two Control groups of similar status characteristics. By this process, a population comprising 172 members of 11 corner gangs was selected to serve as a control population for the 205 members of the seven project gangs. Court appearance data on Control groups were obtained, and the groups were processed as an age cohort in the same manner as Project groups.

The court appearance frequency curves for Project and Control groups are very similar (See Table I). If the two dips in the Project curve are

TABLE II

NUMBER OF INDIVIDUALS APPEARING IN COURT PER YEAR*: AGES 7-23

PROJECT AND CONTROL GROUPS

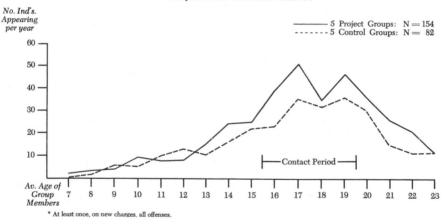

———— 5 Project Groups: N = 154
- - - - - 5 Control Groups: N = 82

* At least once, on new charges, all offenses.

eliminated by joining the peaks at 14, 16 and 20, the shape of the two curves becomes almost identical. Both curves show a gradual rise from ages 7 to 16 or 17, maintain a high level to age 20, and drop rapidly between 20 and 23. Table II compares Project and Control groups according to the number of *individuals* per year per group to appear in court, rather than according to the number of *appearances* per year per group. On this basis, the similarity between Project and Control curves becomes even more marked. The dip at age 14 in the Project appearance curve (Table I) flattens out, and both Project and Control groups show a dip at age 18, making the Project and Control curves virtually identical.[36]

The unusual degree of similarity between the court appearance curves of Project and Control groups constitutes the single most powerful piece of evidence on Project impact obtained by the research. The fact that a group of similar gangs not worked with by the Project showed an almost identical decrease in court appearance frequency between ages 20 and 23 removes any reasonable basis for attributing the post-20 decline of Project groups to worker efforts. Indeed, the high degree of overall similarity in court appearance experience between "served" and "unserved" groups makes it most difficult to claim that anything done by the Project had any significant influence on the likelihood of court appearance.

Project and Control groups show equally striking similarities in regard to three additional measures—the proportion of individuals who had appeared in court by age 23, the proportion who had re-appeared, and the number of appearances per individual. Of 131 members of four male Project groups, 98, or 74.8%, had appeared in court at least once by age 23. The fact that 75% of the members of gangs worked with by social workers had nevertheless appeared in court by age 23 would in itself appear to indicate very limited Project impact. This finding, however, still admits the possibility that appearance frequency might have been even higher in the absence of the workers, or conversely, that the high figure was in some way a consequence of the workers' efforts. Both of these possibilities are weakened by the Control cohort figures. Of 112 members of five male groups *not* worked with by the Project, 82, or 73.2%, had appeared in court by age 23—almost exactly the same percentage shown by Project groups.[37]

[36] The implications of these court-appearance frequency trends transcend their utility as a technique for "controlling" for worker influence. One implication will be cited in footnote 43; more detailed interpretation and analysis, with special attention to the relative influence of worker activity and subcultural forces on the shape of the curves will be included in *City Gangs, op. cit.* Also included will be greater detail on the process of locating, selecting, matching and processing the control population.

[37] The finding of negligible difference in court appearance frequency between Project and Control groups parallels the findings of the Cambridge-Somerville Youth Study—one of the few delinquency control projects to report findings of careful evaluative research (Edwin Powers and Helen Witmer, *An Experiment in the Prevention of Delinquency*, New York: Columbia University Press, 1951). It was found that 29.5% of a 325 boy treatment group had appeared in court by the time the oldest boys were 21, as compared with 28.3% of a 325 boy control group (p. 326). Despite differences in methods (Cambridge-Somerville used primarily individually-focused counseling) and client populations (Cambridge-Somerville boys were less delinquent), the degree of similarity between the two projects in treatment and control outcomes is striking.

The possibility still remains that Project group members, once having appeared in court, would be less likely than Control members to *reappear*. This was not the case. Of 98 members of Project groups who appeared in court at least once, 72, or 73.5%, appeared at least once again; of 82 Control group members who appeared at least once, 61, or 74.3%, appeared at least once more. A further possibility exists that while similar proportions of *individuals* might have appeared in court, Project group members might have made fewer *appearances* per individual. However, Project and Control groups were also similar in this respect. Ninety-eight Project members who appeared in court between the ages of 7 and 23 appeared 488 times, or 5.0 appearances per individual. Eighty-two Control males appeared 447 times, or 5.4 appearances per individual. These figures, while not as close to identity as the outcome figures, fail to show a statistically significant difference. The unusual degree of closeness in all these court appearance measures for male Project and Control groups provides a firm basis for concluding that Project impact on the likelihood of court appearance was negligible.

### SUMMARY OF "IMPACT" FINDINGS

It is now possible to provide a definite answer to the principal evaluative research question—"Was there a significant measurable inhibition of law-violating or morally-disapproved behavior as a consequence of Project efforts?" The answer, with little necessary qualification, is "No." All major measures of violative behavior—disapproved actions, illegal actions, during-contact court appearances, before-during-after appearances, and Project-Control group appearances—provide consistent support for a finding of "Negligible impact."

There was a modest decrease, during the period of worker contact, in the frequency of disapproved actions in 14 areas of behavior—but much of this reduction was due to a decrease in a single area—school-oriented behavior. The overall change in the other 13 areas was only −2.3%.[38] The total number of illegal actions engaged in by group members also decreased slightly, though not significantly, during the course of the Project. Most of this reduction, however, was accounted for by minor offenses; major offenses showed a slight increase. Similarly, while there was a small decrease in the frequency of all categories of court-appeared offenses, major offenses showed an increase. Examining the

---

[38] It is possible that the decrease in disapproved school-oriented actions was due largely to a decrease in the frequency of truancy brought about by the fact that many of the earlier period truants had, by Project termination, passed the age at which school attendance was compulsory, thus ending their truancy. This possibility will be tested as part of a detailed analysis of change trends in each behavior area.

group members' court-appearance trends between the ages 7 and 23 showed that court appearances were most frequent during the age-period when Project workers were with the groups. The possibility that a pronounced decrease in court-appearance frequency after age 20 represented a delayed response to the Project was weakened by the fact that a similar decline occurred in the case of a set of similar gangs not worked with by the Project, and which, in fact, showed extremely similar court appearance trends both before, during, and after the age period during which Project groups were in contact with workers.

The fact that the various measures of impact are mutually consistent increases confidence in the overall "negligible impact" finding. Not only do the several indexes delineate similar trends in regard to the direction and magnitude of change (e.g., "during-period" change in disapproved actions, −4.0%; in illegal actions, −9.1%; in court appearance frequency, −5.8%), but also show a high degree of internal consistency in other respects. For example, the rank position of the five male groups in the degree of reduction in violative behavior shown by the three major indexes was very similar.[39]

Two previous papers reporting impact findings of the Midcity Project conveyed the impression of a limited but definite reduction in delinquency.[40] Why does the present report support a different conclusion? In the first place, present findings are based on new data not available in 1957 and '59, as well as on more extensive analysis of data then available. Both previous papers stated that reported results were preliminary, and cited the possibility of modification by future analysis.[41] Second, present data focus more directly on the specific experience of a specific target population; some of the previous impact findings were based on less focused indexes of general community trends, in which the behavior of the Project's target groups was not as directly distinguishable. Third, the "before" and "after" time extension made possible by the use of court data show some previously reported trends to have been relatively temporary fluctuations. Fourth, the use of a control population made it possible to anchor results more firmly by show-

[39] Rank-difference correlation coefficients were as follows: disapproved acts and illegal acts +.80; disapproved acts and court appearances +.87; illegal acts and court appearances, +.97. Even with the small N of 5, the good correspondence between disapproved acts and court appearances is impressive, since the data for the two rank series were derived from completely independent sources.

[40] "The Impact of a Community Group Work Program on Delinquent Corner Groups," op. cit., pp. 390-406, and "Preventive Work with Street-Corner Groups: Boston Delinquency Project," op. cit., pp. 97-106.

[41] It is similarly possible that some of the results cited here will be modified in the final Project report, especially in areas where more extensive internal analysis will enable fuller interpretations of reported trends.

ing that important observed trends were common to both Project and non-Project groups, thus making possible a better determination of the extent to which "during" Project variation was in fact related to the workers' efforts.

## The Efficacy of Project Control Methods

Which of the Project's methods were "tested" by the "negligible impact" findings? This complex question can be addressed only briefly here. It is evident that it was those methods which were most extensively employed or successfully executed which were shown most directly to have been least effective in inhibiting delinquency. Fifteen separate methods or techniques were cited earlier in connection with the three major programs (Community Organization, Family Service, Gang Work) of the Midcity Project. Of these, seven could be designated as extensively employed or successfully executed: establishment of district citizens' council; locating and contacting adolescent corner gangs; establishing relationships with gang members; effecting formal organization and involvement in organized recreational activity; provision of access to adult institutions; provision of adult role-model. It is to these seven methods that the "negligible impact" finding applies most directly. Of these, "recreation" is already recognized quite widely to be of limited effectiveness as an exclusive method; "relationship" is still seen in many quarters as quite effective; "adult role-model" was also found, by the Cambridge-Somerville Project, to have had little effect. Of two aspects of "access-provision"—enabling youngsters to avail themselves of existing opportunities, and altering larger societal institutions so as to create new opportunities—the Project achieved the former but exerted limited systematic effort in regard to the latter, so that this aspect of access-provision was only minimally tested.

Six methods could be characterized as less extensively employed or implemented with only moderate success: formation of citizens' groups; coordination of efforts of youth groups and adult citizens' groups; coordination of family-service agencies; treatment of "chronic problem" families; psychodynamic counseling and therapy; group dynamics. Some of these programs continued beyond the Project's three year demonstration period, but there is as yet no evidence available that any of these have had an impact on delinquency substantially different from that of the "best-tested" methods.

Two final methods—effecting concerted effort between citizens' groups and professional agencies, and coordinating the varied efforts of professional agencies themselves—were implemented only minimally. It is to these methods, then, that the "negligible impact" finding has least applicability. However, this failure of effectuation, especially in the area of inter-agency-cooperation, was achieved only after extensive expenditure of effort, which might suggest that the cost of implementing this type of method, whose potential impact on delinquency is as yet undetermined, might not be commensurate with the degree of delinquency-reduction it could perhaps produce.

In addition, granting that some of the Project's methods were tested less fully than others, the fact that all 15 (and others) were applied concurrently and in concert also constituted a test of the "synergism" concept—that the simultaneous and concerted application of multiple and diverse programs on different levels will produce an impact greater than the summed impact of the component programs. Thus the total-community-multiple-programs approach, as executed by the Midcity Project, also fell within the category of methods best tested by the finding of "negligible impact."

In evaluating the significance of these "negligible impact" findings three considerations should be borne in mind. The first concerns the scope and nature of the question to which "negligible impact" is an answer, the second the level on which the answer is presented, and the third the value of the Project to delinquency control as a larger enterprise.

The phrasing of the principal evaluative research question tests the effectiveness of the Project against a single and central criterion—the measurable inhibition of explicitly violative behavior of a designated target population. The Project had considerable impact in other areas. To cite only two of these; the establishment of the control project and the spread of knowledge as to its existence had a calming effect on the adult community. Pre-Project gang activities in Midcity had activated a sense of fear among many adults, and a feeling of helplessness in the face of actual and potential violence. Simple knowledge of the existence of the Project served to alleviate the community's sense of threat, in that there was now an established locus of responsibility for gang crime. The fact that *something* was being done was in itself important quite independent of the possible effectiveness of what was being done.

The Project was also instrumental in establishing new delinquency-control organizations, and left the community a legacy of organizations and programs which it had either brought into being or taken primary responsibility for. Among these were the District Community Council organized by Project staff, the project for providing direct service to "chronic problem" families, an annual sports award dinner for the youth of the community, and a permanent program of area work administered by the municipal government. The organizational plan of this latter enterprise was drawn up before Project termination, so that the municipal delinquency control bureau, once established, was able to extend the general approach of the Project to the entire municipal area.[42] While the value of these organized enterprises must also be measured against the same "impact on delinquency" criterion which was applied to the Project, it is clear that their existence was one tangible product of the Project.

A second consideration concerns the "level" of the reported findings. Data presented in connection with each of the major indexes to impact are at the most gross analytical level—that is, they neither specify nor analyze systematically the internal variation of the reported trends in three important respects—variations among the several groups, variations among the several behavior areas, and finer fluctuations over time. The finding of "negligible impact" encompasses, most accurately, *all* analyzed forms of behavior of *all* analyzed groups for extended periods. Internal analyses not reported here show that some groups showed considerable change in some areas, and that some areas showed considerable change for some groups. Further, while initial and final levels of violative behavior in many instances showed little difference, a good deal of turbulence or fluctuation characterized intervening periods. The flat "negligible impact" statement, then, by concealing a considerable degree of internal variability, obscures the fact that there was differential vulnerability to change in different areas and for different groups. Fuller analyses of these variations, along with the methods associated with greater and lesser vulnerability, will furnish specific policy guides to more and less strategic points of intervention.

A final consideration concerns the "value" of the Project in the face of its "negligible inhibition of delinquent behavior" outcome. There can be an important distinction, obscured by the term "evaluation" between the "effect" of an enterprise and its "value." The Midcity Project was established to test the possible effectiveness of its several approaches. These were in fact tested, and the Project was thus successful in the achievement of its "demonstration" objective. The evaluation model used here, based on multiple indexes to change, and using the "behavioral event" as a primary unit of analysis, can be applied in other instances where the impact of a specific change enterprise is at issue. Even more important, perhaps, is the fact that the process of gathering and analyzing the great bulk of data necessary to furnish a sound answer to the question of impact also produced a large volume of information of direct relevance to basic theoretical questions as to the origins of gangs and of

[42] See D. Austin, "Recommendations for a Municipal Program of Delinquency Prevention," mimeo, 7 pp., United Community Services of Boston, 1957.

gang delinquency. These findings also bear directly on a further question of considerable importance—"Why did the Project have so little impact on delinquency?"—a question to be addressed in some detail in future reports.[43]

[43] Factors accounting for the limited impact of Project efforts will be treated in detail in *City Gangs, op. cit.* The explanatory analysis will forward the thesis that culturally-derived incentives for engaging in violative behavior were far stronger than any counterpressures the Project could bring to bear. This explanation will derive from a general theory of gang delinquency whose central proposition, to be expanded at length, will be that patterned involvement in violative behavior by gangs of the Midcity type occurs where four cultural "conditions" exist concurrently—*maleness, adolescence, urban residence,* and *low-skill laboring class status.* Each of these conditions is conceptualized as a particular type of subcultural system—each, of whose "demanded" sets of behavior, taken separately, contribute some element of the motivation for engagement in gang delinquency, and whose concerted operation produces a subcultural milieu which furnishes strong and consistent support for customary involvement in criminal behavior. Data on "impact" presented here document the influence of two of these conditions—age status and social status. Court-appearance frequency trends (Tables I and II) would appear to indicate that the single most important determinant of the frequency of that order of criminal behavior which eventuated in court appearance for Midcity male gangs was *age,* or more specifically, movement through a series of age-based subcultural stages. Commission of criminal acts of given types and frequency appeared as a required concomitant of passing through the successive age-stages of adolescence and a prerequisite to the assumption of adult status. The influence of these age-class demands, on the basis of this and other evidence, would appear to exceed that of other factors—including conditions of the family, school, neighborhood or job world; police arrest policies, sentencing, confinement, probation and parole policies, and others. Data on *social status* (e.g., footnote 27, *passim*) along with much additional data not reported here, indicate a systematic relationship between social status *within* the lower class, and delinquency. 1. Within the 21 gang sample of the Midcity study, crime was both more prevalent and more serious among those whose social status, measured by occupational and educational indexes, was lowest. 2. Relatively small differences in status were associated with relatively large differences in patterned behavior; as lower status levels were approached, delinquency incidence increased exponentially rather than linearly; this indicates the necessity of making refined intra-class distinctions when analyzing the social "location" of criminal behavior. 3. Groups of lower social status showed the least reduction in violative forms of behavior; this lower vulnerability to change efforts would indicate that violative behavior was more entrenched, and thus more central to the subcultural system.

# Police, Courts, and Probation

THREE important and related agencies that deal officially with juvenile delinquents are the police, the juvenile court, and the probation agency. The police apprehend the delinquent, and in three cases out of four handle him without reference to court or probation. One case out of four is referred to the juvenile court, and of this group about a fourth are placed on probation. (Almost half of the court cases are dismissed or otherwise disposed of without further supervision.) These three agencies are the key ones for the majority of delinquents. Conflicting opinions as to the functions of each and their relationship to each other and to other agencies remain unresolved. The following articles attempt to redefine functions and clarify relationships.

Police are often publicly criticized for their treatment of juvenile delinquents; they are also often criticized for well-meaning efforts to help children by organizing recreational programs or attempting to carry out social-work functions. Article 26 discusses issues regarding the proper functions of police when dealing with delinquents and defines the duties of police and of special juvenile units.

Article 27, after a brief statement on the history and present legal status of the juvenile court, plunges into one of the most critical issues regarding the court—the conflict between the social-agency image and the legal image of the juvenile court. In accordance with the first image, courts and their retinue of clinicians and social workers focus attention on the child's personality and regard him as a client to be treated; the second image calls for strict attention to legal regulations and safeguards. Many courts practice some combination of the two concepts, which are, however, opposed to each other in many respects.

In Article 28 probation as a form of casework is supported, regardless of the dilemma of the probation officer in fitting together social work and authoritarian roles.

## 26.  Police and Children

Lynn D. Swanson

> The author is Consultant on Specialized Police Services for Children of the U.S. Children's Bureau. He has authored publications of the Children's Bureau and articles published in various professional journals.

More than one million boys and girls come to the attention of the police each year. Some come because of parental neglect and abuse. More for violations of local, state, and federal statutes. The majority of these boys and girls are between the ages of 10-17.

Each one of these million young citizens represents a person in a certain stage of immaturity. Many are reaching for independence and adult status. These are children who usually have unmet needs. The police officer in his brief but important contact with a child can be of assistance in seeing that the child's initial needs are met.

In the last two decades, police have moved toward protective and more understanding handling of delinquent and neglected children. This development has not been uniform and has grown, more or less, in topsy-like way. As a result, guidelines for police in handling cases involving children are needed.

The importance of these basic guidelines is enhanced when the im-

Lynn D. Swanson, "Police and Children," *The Police Chief*, 25 (June, 1958), 18, 20, 22, 24, 26. Reprinted with permission of the International Association of Chiefs of Police.

portance of police dispositions as they affect the lives of children is considered. Current statistics available to the Children's Bureau indicate that only one-quarter of the juveniles contacted by the police are referred to court; the remaining three-quarters involve other types of disposition. Even here great variations in practice exist. Some police departments refer all cases to court, regardless of need. Others refer only a small percentage of children.

These variations may be due to differences in law or administrative policy. Some police departments require that all children coming to the attention of the department be referred immediately to the specialized police unit assigned to work with children. Others want these special units to process for disposition those children initially dealt with by other police units. Still others expect the police generalist to assume more responsibility and discretion in dealing with cases of individual children and to refer only those children to the specialized youth unit when they are uncertain as to how to proceed.

Police as well as other agencies seem to be in general agreement with respect to the importance of the decisions made by police each day as they affect the lives of individual children. Even the most casual contact with a child by the police can have a profound influence upon the child's life. "When an officer (police) knows something about the reasons for different types of behavior and something about the reactions of people under such circumstances, he can carry out his responsibility without causing an increase in the individual's problem of living in a satisfactory manner. In children's cases, it is particularly true that a police officer's way of handling the situation may make a great difference." [1] What the police officer does or fails to do may have a lasting effect not only upon the future plans for the child but upon his attitude toward treatment personnel and respect toward authority.

The respect and consideration for this authority by children may be greatly influenced by the approach the police officer may choose to use. This approach may be positive and understanding or it may be negative and indifferent. Different approaches to different children by police within the same department oftentimes confuse the child's concept of police authority and engenders in him misunderstanding about the overall treatment plans proposed for him.

All citizens, adults as well as children, are entitled to be dealt with with consideration and deliberation. It is just as important for the police to deal with the hardened and sophisticated youth in an individualized

[1] *The Role of the Police in Mental Health.* Public Health Service Pub. No. 360, Washington 25, D.C. U.S. Department of Health, Education and Welfare, 1954. 5 pp. (p. 1).

and understanding manner as it is for them to do so with the naive and bewildered child. The police approach should be firm and fair, but flexible enough to meet the variety of problems and needs of different children. How the police handle children in these situations may determine to some extent not only the attitude of the child but of the public toward all police activities.

## Traditional Role of Police

Bruce Smith states, "the policeman's art, then, consists in applying a multitude of laws and ordinances in such degree or proportion and in such manner that the greatest degree of social protection will be assured." [2]

Thus, the police function is one of authority. He suppresses crime, apprehends offenders, and preserves the public peace. He protects the rights of the individual. He sets the tone of law enforcement for the area he patrols. The police officer is cognizant of the demands made of him by citizens and by his superiors toward the enforcement of existing statutes. The action he takes in an individual case depends upon these and the many other variables arising out of individual and community needs in each case. Each day police officers observe numerous violations of law without taking any official action in all cases. These include jaywalking, hitchhiking, illegal parking, merchants' wares blocking sidewalks, discarding trash in streets and many others. He doesn't arrest every traffic violator or every child involved in a petty violation. If he enforced the law to the letter and arrested every violator, he wouldn't have time for other essential police activities, such as traffic control and patrolling. In addition, courts and other agencies involved would be sorely over-taxed. Perhaps, however, if the police enforced all of the archaic laws on the statute books, something might be done about their repeal.

Law enforcement functions as they relate to all citizens are, for the most part, clearly established by law. When the police officer stops a driver in a speeding car or apprehends a person criminally involved in a robbery, his role to the violator should be essentially the same regardless of the age of the offender. His function is to ascertain the facts, record the evidence, find material witnesses, and prepare the case for prosecution. The officer must know the specific law involved and the evidence needed by the prosecution to bring the case to court. He is expected

[2] Bruce Smith: *Police Systems in the United States.* New York, Harper, 1949, p. 20.

to use good judgment, to be discreet, objective, and thorough in discharging these duties. He must not permit the severity of the offense or the physical condition of the victim to interfere with his objectivity in the investigation and disposition of the case. He should be professional in his approach and avail himself of all the scientific tools possible. These include modus operandi, fundamental methods of disarming persons, identification, fingerprinting, crime laboratory services and uniform crime reporting.

In the apprehending process or in the detaining of suspects, the police officer should safeguard the public and himself. When necessary, he may have to protect the suspect from the public.

There are few, if any, differences in the traditional and appropriate police processes of investigation between cases of children and adults. One difference may arise in those states which have laws regulating places of detention or prohibiting the taking of fingerprints or pictures of juveniles without court order. However, these laws do not materially change the basic role of police in the processes of apprehension, investigation, and disposition. Furthermore, as much discretion, if not more, is practiced by the police in cases affecting juveniles as in adults.

Although the police officer is expected to apply traditional processes of investigation to all citizens, he should take into consideration the immaturity of children and youth. This accounts for differences in the approach an officer uses in interviewing and the setting for the interview, since the manner of approach may have a direct effect upon the child in his relationship to his peers as well as his attitude toward the officer.

The need for a different approach in relation to children and youth led to a specialization in this aspect of police work. In 1905 at Portland, Oregon, a policewoman was assigned to preventive-protective work with girls. At Los Angeles, California, the police department juvenile bureau was initiated in 1909. Since then, in cities of over 25,000 population, a large number of police departments have established separate units or appointed a specialist for work with children. The growth of these units has been rapid and unfortunately somewhat haphazard without too much thought given to their function and relationship to the rest of the department and other community agencies working with children.

By law the role of the police, with respect to crime and delinquency, is specific and limited. Nevertheless it is an important role. Too often the community and some of the police administrations have expected the police to take a primary or major role in building character and developing in children the desirable ideals essential to growing children in a community. However, it is with respect to this activity that the police specialized units dealing with children appear to have gone beyond an appropriate police role. In some communities, these special units have appropriately involved themselves in community planning by working with other related agencies and individuals and pointing out undesirable community conditions contributing to delinquency as well as other program needs. In other communities, these units, under the guise of "crime prevention," have taken on activities that have been a subject of controversy, often duplicating other programs, such as recreational activities, camps, ranches, operation of foster home care, informal police supervision and other types of group work programs for children.

Today, police administrations are beginning to take a new look at their activities in relation to children. They recognize the need that any specialization in this area must become an integral part of the department. They recognize more and more that an effective program in this area must include the participation of every police officer, not only those assigned to specialized youth units. In fact, the Committee on Juvenile Delinquency, International Association of Chiefs of Police, has recommended that all police officers, from the plainclothesman to the patrolman, be involved in the appropriate police program to children.

Many questions arise when police take on organized recreational activities as a departmental function. First, recreation is a full-time profession requiring specialized training and skills. This training is not and cannot be given through ordinary police training programs. Secondly, the expending of public funds by two governmental agencies (recreation department and police) to carry out similar programs is not sound. Third, there is no one cause of delinquency, and no one program can cure delinquency. A recreational activity can help meet part of a child's needs but it should not be regarded as being "the deterrent" to delinquency.

Recreation programs should be broad and not based upon the idea of "crime prevention" or focused on or established for a particular group. Many law enforcement officers themselves have questioned the involvement of police in recreation, boys' clubs, informal police supervision, and other such activities. Often feelings develop between these specialized units and the other members of the department. Questions are asked, such as, "are these police officers or are they recreation workers, social workers, or probation officers?" People already working in these various fields ask the same questions. At times other police officers have referred to the juvenile unit as the "cream puff brigade," or "the boy scout troop." When this happens, strained working relationships develop which seriously hamper the effectiveness of the police program in this area. However, this should not preclude individual police officers, as citizens, from participating in voluntary recreational activities.

Another problem area is the involvement of police in "probation services." This usually involves supervision of a child on a continuing basis for a definite or indefinite period. It is likened to a casework treatment service by social agencies. Again, as in the case of recreation programs, police are not trained for this type of service. Moreover, other agencies have been given the responsibility for providing these services. This so-called "voluntary" supervision is subject to abuses by police, and therefore is open to question the same as "unofficial probation" practiced by some courts. Police and probation officers have specific roles with respect to children. They must work together as a team for the benefit of the child and the community. It is not possible for a police officer to be both a probation officer and a police officer. Such a dual role cannot help but lead to ineffective service in both areas.

Thus, specialization of police working with children creates many problems within the department as well as outside the department. It raises questions of function and problems of coordination between the specialist and the generalist as well as other specialists, such as in the traffic and detective divisions. In practice, the great majority of juvenile cases are investigated initially by officers other than the members of the juvenile unit. If such investigations were all referred to the juvenile unit it would, in order to meet the workload, become the largest division of the police department. Such a result would be neither feasible nor sound. In practice, juvenile units are relatively small in relation to the rest of the department. It is neither possible nor sound to expect these special youth officers to deal with each juvenile at the initial contact with police. Therefore, the officer who makes the initial contact with the juvenile has an important role to play in the police program as it relates to children and youth. He must, therefore, be prepared by training and fitness to discharge this role.

Police involvement in recreational programs is often thought to be justified on the basis that it promotes good public relations. Through such programs they are able to show the children that "police are human." Good public relations and gaining of respect of children can better be secured by good, progressive, scientific law enforcement procedures coupled with a professional attitude and due respect for the rights and dignity of the individual—both child and adult.

Police training does not provide knowledge and skills necessary for them to become probation officers. When a governmental service, like probation, is seriously hampered by a lack of personnel, this should not be regarded as an excuse for the automatic entry of police to this field. Instead, it is the police department's, as well as other community agencies' responsibility, to continuously bring this to the attention of the public as an essential community need. They should work hand in hand toward the ultimate improvement of probation services. Probation services by police are inappropriate for many of the same reasons as discussed in recreation.

Summer camps and boys' ranches established by and under police supervision are not legitimate police functions either. The entrance of the police officer in the foster care field is equally as questionable.

## Appropriate Functions for Police

V. A. Leonard states, "The work of the patrol force really includes all police functions, therefore, the more effective the patrol division, the less need there is for the other more specialized operating divisions." [3] Patrolling is a traditional function. The information and statistics evaluated by the central records system can be used in determining the placement of personnel which by the use of selective enforcement can help repress delinquent acts by juveniles. They are in the most feasible position to investigate and dispose of juvenile cases at the time and place where these offenses most often occur. In addition, when members of the patrol force become cognizant of community conditions which may be contributing to the delinquency of children, this information should be brought to the attention of the appropriate persons and agencies.

The police officer investigating an offense reportedly committed by a juvenile must first determine the validity of the complaint and ascertain whether the juvenile was involved. He should use the scientific tools of crime detection available to him. He should accept responsibility for preparing a "social evaluation" of the child. The "social evaluation" should not be regarded as a social history but rather it should include the officer's observation of factors having social significance. Oftentimes, the police officer is the first person in an official capacity to enter a home. What he hears or observes can be of considerable help in determining what action he should take. Dispositions of children coming to the attention of the police should be based upon all the facts of the case, including the seriousness of the offense, the social factors revealed, the

---

[3] International City Managers Association: *Municipal Police Administration*, 4th Edition, Chicago: International City Managers Association, 1954, p. 255.

protection of the community, the legal requirements of police, and the previous police experience with the juvenile. Police officers should be permitted to warn and release the child and then make a record for the future use of police, courts, and related agencies.

Police should have the power to refer to detention any juvenile who in their appraisal may possibly endanger himself or the community; or to assure court appearance of the child.

They should have the responsibility for referring to court any juvenile on the basis of such criteria as the seriousness of the offense, the attitude of the parents, child, and complainant as well as any community feeling.

Police should refer a juvenile to agencies, other than the juvenile court, when in their opinion an available community service can be of assistance to the child and his family and when there is no need for official court action.

The police role in the overall community-wide prevention of delinquency program includes the reporting of statistical data and other related information, representation in coordinating agencies, assisting in the development of the community-wide program and carrying out the delegated police role in the plan.

## The Role of the Police Generalist

The police generalist investigating complaints about children should have available to him three dispositions; warn and release, referral to the juvenile court, or referral to the special police unit assigned to juveniles.

If he warns and releases the child, a record of his disposition should be kept for the future use of the police, courts, and other agencies. No record should be kept of minor contacts, such as boys playing ball in the street.

When an officer refers the child to the juvenile court, he should include information that will substantiate a petition in court as well as other pertinent social information.

When an officer is uncertain as to police disposition, other than referral to court or to warn and release, he should be able to request assistance from the special police unit dealing with juveniles.

Community conditions that need correcting should be brought to the attention of the special police unit by the generalist.

Thus, the police generalist has an important and responsible role in relation to children. In fact, in a recent address to a group of juvenile officers, W. Cleon Skousen, Chief of Police, Salt Lake City, Utah, said,

"We must not allow other officers to get the feeling that only the Juvenile Bureau can handle juveniles." Chief Skousen goes on to say, "The juvenile problem belongs to the entire department. That's the point I want to make, and we as juvenile specialists do not want specialization to get out of control or become a cult. Keep pushing it back to the entire department. We are like the scientific laboratory, the patrols are not helping us, we are helping them." [4]

## Role of the Special Unit or Officer

The role of this unit should primarily be one of consultation to other police officers in matters of dealing with cases of children and youth.

Bruce Smith states, "Youthful crime is too common and too widespread to be handled by any small select corps of specialists. . . . The dissemination of sound doctrines to the rank and file should be the particular task of the juvenile specialist in police work." [5]

Thus, one of the initial responsibilities of this unit should be the development of a manual to be issued to all police officers as an aid in their contacts and dispositions of juveniles.

This unit would have the responsibility for disseminating knowledge about juveniles to the entire department through in-service and recruit training programs.

The police specialist must be able to interpret to the public the objectives and functions of this unit. He should receive referrals from other police officers in those cases needing more facts and social information before a sound police disposition can be made. He would be helpful to other officers when there is some question concerning the detention of a juvenile.

When an unusual situation arises during the hours the special unit is not in operation, some provisions should be made to enable the officer to contact the unit for consultation.

The police specialist would assume responsibility for all referrals to agencies, other than the juvenile court. He would act in a liaison capacity between the police department and these other agencies.

The special unit should screen and have the responsibility for disposing of juvenile cases referred to them by other police officers. When

---

[4] *Proceedings* of the Eighth Annual Conference California State Juvenile Officers Association and the First Annual Conference, International Juvenile Officers' Association, Oakland, March 1957, pp. 47-48.

[5] *Youth and Crime,* edited by Frank J. Cohen, Proceedings of the Law Enforcement Institute held at New York University. New York, International Universities Press, 1957. 271 pp. (p. 170).

processing and filing the recorded dispositions of children made by other police officers, an occasional review of these cases should be made by the unit in order that the police administration may determine whether the departmental program to children is being effectively carried out. This review may also indicate needs in the training program of the department.

The juvenile unit should be the liaison unit between the police department and the prevention-oriented agencies, such as community welfare councils. The juvenile unit should bring statistical data and other information about the needs of children to the attention of these agencies usually obtained through their authoritative role in the community.

## Training of Police Specialists

The police generalist as well as the specialist must receive the training necessary to being effective law enforcement officers. This should include some basic training in working with children and youth. In addition, members of the special unit should receive additional training to adequately carry out the appropriate and specific functions delegated to the unit. This training should include a basic understanding of human behavior, including causes of delinquent behavior as well as how to handle it. The specialist must have a working knowledge of community resources and agencies as well as the services that they provide with their operating methods. Such specialized training will not only prepare them to more effectively carry out their activities to individual children, but it will prepare them to actively participate in the department training program as well.

## Summary

Total police specialization to children is not feasible. The police generalist should be given more discretion and responsibility in his contacts with children. With this responsibility, he should receive more training and knowledge about human behavior than police are generally receiving today.

The police specialist with children should have the responsibility for coordinating police activities in relation to children among the various units and divisions as well as to serve in a liaison capacity between other governmental and community groups. His training should be based upon an academic curriculum which will prepare him to adequately discharge the appropriate functions of this special unit. When the appropriate police activities with children have been determined, along with the necessary training requirements, police departments will have less need to resort to such activities as recreation, boys' clubs, or camps in order to effect good public relations. Instead, the just rewards to those of us in police work will be forthcoming when we apply courteous, courageous, and professional standards in our handling of the million-plus children coming to the attention of the police each year.

## 27.  The Juvenile Court: Contradictory Orientations in Processing Offenders

### H. Warren Dunham

> The author holds the degree of Doctor of Philosophy from the University of Chicago, 1941, and is Professor of Sociology at Wayne State University. He has been a Fulbright Scholar to The Netherlands, is co-author of *Mental Disorders in Urban Areas*, author of *Homeless Men and Their Habitats—A Research Planning Report*, and contributor to professional journals.

Depending on one's historical perspective, the juvenile court has had either a short or long span of existence. Its history has been short when one attempts to survey the numerous tribunals which have been directed to the task of securing justice for men under some system of law. On the other hand, in the light of the earliest legal attempt to define the juvenile delinquent, it has had a relatively long history, covering more than a fourth of this period. From the latter perspective, sufficient time has elapsed to justify a closer, more critical look at what the juvenile court is, what it does, and what it has accomplished.

In this analysis, there are five central objectives. First, the history of the juvenile court and the interacting social forces that have produced it will briefly be considered. Second, the image of the juvenile court that has developed from the implementation of reformistic ideals will be portrayed. Third, another image of the juvenile court, as derived

H. Warren Dunham, "The Juvenile Court: Contradictory Orientations in Processing Offenders." Reprinted from a symposium, "Sentencing," *Law and Contemporary Problems*, 23, No. 3 (Summer, 1958), 508-527, by permission from the author and *Law and Contemporary Problems*, published by the Duke University School of Law, Durham, North Carolina. Copyright, 1958, by Duke University.

from the traditional view of the law, will be constructed. Fourth, some of the consequences and problems that have resulted from the conflict of these two images will be discussed. And finally, some opportunities will be suggested for the juvenile court today. Such an analysis, it is felt, will illuminate not only what the juvenile court is, what it does, what it has accomplished, but perhaps where it is going.

## I. Events and Forces Forming the Juvenile Court

The historical origin of the juvenile court is, no doubt, sufficiently familiar to the readers of this symposium to warrant but a brief recapitulation. While the first law defining juvenile delinquency was passed by the Illinois legislature in April 1899,[1] and the juvenile court itself began functioning in June of that year, its founding had been amply anticipated by certain legalistic precedents in equity and criminal law. More specifically, from the English courts of chancery or equity, the principle of *parens patriae* had evolved in the case of *Eyre v. Shaftsbury* in 1772.[2] This principle, which enabled the court to act in lieu of parents who were deemed unwilling or unable to perform their proper parental functions, paved the way for the juvenile court to assume jurisdiction of dependent and neglected children. Even before this decision, however, the doctrine that the state under certain conditions had to act as a protector of minors had long been a part of the common law.[3]

But it is in dealing with delinquent children that the criminal law origins of the juvenile court are of significance. It had long been an accepted principle of the common law that a child under seven years of age could not commit a criminal act because he could not have *mens rea*, a guilty mind.[4] From here, it was logical next to question the responsibility of children above seven years of age, and in so doing, the juvenile court law has been regarded merely as extending the application of a common-law principle.

Another development anticipating the juvenile court was the inauguration of probation as a device for dealing with offenders. This practice, initiated in Boston in 1841,[5] which included from the beginning adult as well as juvenile offenders, early highlighted some of the special protections that a child needed when brought before a court of law.

[1] Ill. Laws 1899, p. 131.
[2] P. Wms. 103, 24 Eng. Rep. 659 (Ch. 1722).
[3] See H. H. Lou, Juvenile Courts in the United States 3 (1927).
[4] See Rollin M. Perkins, Criminal Law 729-32 (1957).
[5] See Helen D. Pigeon, Probation and Parole in Theory and Practice 85 (1942).

One other development which paved the way for the juvenile court was the establishment of special institutions for confining child offenders. The first institution for juvenile delinquents, the House of Refuge, in New York City, opened on January 1, 1825, and by 1860, sixteen of such institutions had been opened in the United States.[6] These responded to the need long-felt by the reform element in American society that a child who had been convicted of violating a law should not be confined with hardened adult criminals in jails and penitentiaries, where, it was believed, only further demoralization and corruption could ensue. Even so, up to the first quarter of the twentieth century, children were still being punished by incarceration in institutions designed for adults.

Thus, it is seen that early legal precedents, the development of probation, and the establishment of special institutions for juvenile offenders anticipated the first juvenile court in Illinois, which was to become the prototype for legal tribunals dealing with children whose behavior or situation indicated positive state intervention. The concept of the juvenile court spread quickly and was favorably received throughout the country. Indeed, by 1923, all states, with the exception of Connecticut and Wyoming, had enacted legislation defining a juvenile delinquent and establishing a special court for hearing children's cases; and by the early 1940's, even the two hold-out states had come into compliance with this trend.

While these historical events define the establishment of the juvenile court, in a broader cultural sense, it can be regarded as the product of such social forces as our humanitarianism, on the one hand, and the growth of cities, on the other. The force of humanitarianism is well symbolized in the personalities of those women, Jane Addams and Julia Lathrop in Illinois, who agitated for the first juvenile court law. The high principles and unselfish motives which fired these women played a positive role in giving to the juvenile court, from its inception, the stamp of a social agency for dealing with a maladjusted child, rather than that of a punitive court attempting to exact retribution.

The rapid growth of cities, which characterized not only the United States, but the world in the nineteenth century, was also a significant factor. In 1800, there was no city with a population of 100,000 in the United States, but by 1900, there were thirty-seven.[7] This urbanization

---

[6] See N. K. TEETERS AND J. O. REINEMAN, The Challenge of Delinquency 429-47 (1950).

[7] See U.S. Dep't of State, Census Office, Second Census of the United States (1801); U.S. Dep't of Commerce, Bureau of the Census, Statistical Abstract of the United States (1957).

was a product of the factory system plus improvements in agricultural technology. The cities grew not so much through natural increase, as through vast movements of people thereto from rural areas and from various European countries seeking jobs, opportunities, and a new life.

Most of these European migrants faced new and untested situations in the slum environments of our large cities. Their children, often caught in the conflict between European peasant values and the values reflected in American institutions, responded in delinquent ways and began to flood the jails, reformatories, and courts. Their parents, handicapped by language difficulties, were unable to comprehend or cope with these situations, and this tended to foster certain unforeseen functions of the emerging juvenile court, such as aiding the process of immigrant family adjustment, serving as an educational agency in American values, and often protecting the child from demoralizing home situations.

A. DEFINITIONS

Some difficulty has been experienced in determining exactly what the juvenile court is and what a juvenile delinquent is. The difficulty in defining the juvenile court stems from the fact that it is usually attached to a probate or county court and is generally of limited jurisdiction. Thus, while each state now has a juvenile court, its organization and the policies governing it vary markedly throughout the country. While most large cities have a court presided over by a special judge that is devoted exclusively to the processing of cases involving children, many rural counties merely have the probate judge change hats when hearing children's cases. In some jurisdictions, the juvenile court judge is appointed; in many other jurisdictions, he is an elected official. A few judges have looked upon the juvenile court judgeship as a career; others have seen it merely as a step in an upward political climb. Some judges take a human, personal interest in the children brought before them; others merely handle the cases within the framework of the law. Some juvenile courts, particularly those in large cities, have a staff of trained professionals, probation officers, social workers, psychologists, statisticians; others have hardly any. In some juvenile courts, the probation officers are trained social workers; in others, their professional training is minimal. In some juvenile courts, these professionals are under civil service and have tenure; in others, they are largely personal and political appointments. Some juvenile courts work closely with the numerous social agencies dealing with children; others have little or no contact with such agencies.

Three types of juvenile courts which have emerged in the various states have been identified. First, in most counties, other courts have jurisdiction over juvenile cases as well, and when hearing such cases they are referred to as juvenile courts. Second, there are some juvenile courts which are separate and divorced completely from other courts; these are usually found in counties with large cities. Finally, some juvenile courts are tied to special courts that handle selected social-problem cases, such as divorce and truancy, although there also has been a tendency to place such social-problem cases in juvenile courts which have an independent organization—a practice that has engendered certain support for a so-called family court.

A recent survey shows that in some forty states, jurisdiction is over-lapping between the general criminal and juvenile courts. It is noted that the provision for alternate authority is related to the seriousness of the offense and/or the maturity of the child-defendant. The interpretive remarks on this matter are most relevant: [8]

> Practice belies the motives which have supported the child welfare movement, revealing the limitations of our humanitarianism. More specifically, it points up the emphasis which our legal system continues to place upon incapacitation and deterrence—the protection of the public even at the expense of the child. In part, it may reflect too, the feeling that a fuller and more careful hearing should be given to serious cases than the juvenile court ordinarily provides.

When one turns to the definition of a juvenile delinquent, there is not so much variation as in the case of the juvenile court. All states have laws which, although varying in wording, show a common core of agreement in this regard. Thus, a child is uniformly considered delinquent if he acts in such a way as to violate a local ordinance or state law. In addition, most states further include such acts or conditions as "habitual truancy from school," "knowingly associating with thieves, vicious or immoral persons," "incorrigibility," "beyond control of parent or guardian," and "growing up in idleness and crime." These are only a few of the thirty-four items commonly found in the laws defining juvenile delinquency in the several states.[9]

In general, state laws defining delinquency have moved from the specific to the generic. Accordingly, the legislation that established the juvenile court in Illinois defined a delinquent as "any child under the age of sixteen years who has violated any law of the state or any

---

[8] Tappan, *Children and Youth in the Criminal Court*, 261 Annals 128, 132 (1947).
[9] See FREDERICK B. SUSSMAN, Law of Juvenile Delinquency: The Laws of the Forty-Eight States 20 (1950).

city or village ordinance." [10] This concise statement contrasts markedly with the later New York legislation which defines a delinquent as: [11]

> . . . a child over seven and under sixteen years of age (a) who violates any law of . . . this state or any ordinance of the city of New York, or who commits any act which if committed by an adult would be an offense punishable otherwise than by death or life imprisonment; (b) who is incorrigible, ungovernable, or habitually disobedient and beyond the control of his parents, guardian, custodian or other lawful authority; (c) who is habitually truant; (d) who without just cause and without the consent of his parent, guardian or other custodian deserts his home or place of abode; (e) who engages in any occupation which is in violation of the law; (f) who begs or solicits alms or money in public places; (g) who associates with immoral or vicious persons; (h) who frequents any place the maintenance of which is in violation of law; (i) who habitually uses obscene or profane language; or (j) who so deports himself as wilfully to injure or endanger the morals or health of himself or others.

Another observable trend has been the strengthening of the role of the juvenile court by assuring it wider jurisdiction over children's cases and by emphasizing that the child is not on trial for a specific crime. But some decisions contain language to the effect that the child's constitutional rights are to be assured through right of appeal—even though this right is seldom exercised in the juvenile court; [12] and this matter has provided one of the principal foci for criticism of the juvenile court. Some judges and lawyers have maintained that the juvenile court in operation practically subverts the "due process" clause of the constitution in its zeal to apply the doctrine of *parens patriae.*

In addition to the generally diffuse manner in which they define delinquency, state laws differ markedly with respect to fixing the maximum legal age of a delinquent, varying from sixteen to twenty-one, with seventeen being the most common.

In summary, then, it should be noted that juvenile delinquency is a broad generic term which embraces many diverse forms of antisocial behavior of the child and which is defined somewhat differently in the various states, even though a converging tendency may be observed in the various laws.

It is only to be expected that these differences in court organization and in the definition of delinquency have made for wide variations

---

[10] Ill. Laws 1899, p. 137.

[11] N.Y.C. Dom. Rel. Ct. Act § 2(15).

[12] Herbert A. Bloch & Frank T. Flynn, Delinquency: The Juvenile Offender in America Today 353 (1956).

in juvenile court policies and practices. Some juvenile courts are rigid, others are flexible; some are authoritarian, others are permissive; some are dictatorial, others are democratic. These contrasts are reflected in the number of cases heard unofficially in comparison with those heard officially, as well as in the use of various dispositions and the differences among juvenile court judges in the use of the dispositions available to them. But above all, they are reflected by the dominance of the image, as either a legal or social agency, that the juvenile court has of itself.

## II.  The Social-Agency Image of the Court

Juvenile courts in the United States run the gamut from the authoritarian legalistic tribunal at one extreme to the permissive, social-agency type of organization at the other. While there is no one juvenile court which coincides completely with either of these idealized poles, it could probably be demonstrated that those which are an adjunct to another court correspond more closely to the legalistic image and those which have a completely independent organization, with a full-time judge, tend to adhere to the social-agency image. In this part, an attempt will be made to delineate the ideal social-agency image of the juvenile court. In so doing, those influences that were crucial in molding this image, the general character of this image, and some of its unanticipated consequences will be identified.

In the social-agency image, the purposes of the juvenile court are to understand the child, to diagnose his difficulty, to treat his condition, and to fit him back into the community. These purposes are held, to a greater or lesser degree, by the personnel that constitutes the juvenile court organization. More difficult, however, is the unraveling of all the tangible and intangible influences that have gone into constructing this social-agency image. In this connection, five influences have been selected which, in the judgment of the writer, have been primarily responsible for the evolution of this image and for its development at the expense of the juvenile court's more legalistic role. These are and have been: (1) the aggressive social-work orientation of the United States Children's Bureau; (2) the broadening jurisdiction of the juvenile court to include not only neglected and dependent children, but all matters of a legal nature involving children; (3) the gradual professionalization of social work; (4) various court decisions involving delinquency; and (5) the growing prospects of treatment through the increased acceptance by social workers of psychoanalysis, which has provided techniques for getting at the roots of conflict which supposedly produce delinquency. While each one of these influences has played its specific role, it would be quite difficult to assess their respective weights. It is sufficient merely to note that collectively they interacted and mutually reinforced an image of the juvenile court as a social-agency institution of independent status.

Thirteen years after the first juvenile court was established in Illinois, the Children's Bureau was created and lodged in the United States Department of Labor.[13] The appointment of Julia Lathrop, an early proponent of the first juvenile court law, as its first head was a significant factor in enabling the emerging profession of social work to exercise a powerful influence over the development of the juvenile court. This influence has been reflected in the collection of statistics, the development of model juvenile court laws, the promulgation of standards for measuring juvenile court operation, the initiation of studies of juvenile court cases, the encouragement of juvenile courts to institute treatment services, the calling of national conferences of practicing professionals dealing with the problem, the emphasis on the need of probation officers with case-work training, and the attempts to construct educational and experience standards for those persons who would enter juvenile court work. All of these efforts and others have helped so to orient the juvenile court as to enable it to construct an image of itself as a social-work agency, designed primarily to meet the needs of the child. When Julia Lathrop left the Bureau in 1921, the high standards which she had set and the high ideals of child care and welfare for which she strived were carried forward by the distinguished social workers that followed her—Grace Abbott, 1921-33, Katherine Lenroot, 1934-51, and Martha Eliot, 1951-56.

In short, the Children's Bureau, during its comparatively short history, has been most successful in shaping the image of the juvenile court as an agency for seeking the welfare of the child. Its failures, if they may be so termed, have been primarily of a negative nature— that is, it has failed to recognize that high ideals without sufficient knowledge are not enough, with the consequence that the social-agency image, which is at present the dominant image, has led to certain unanticipated consequences and unresolved dilemmas which have often placed the child in situations that are harmful rather than helpful to him. One commentator probably had these matters in mind when he noted that "the plight of the youngster has been increased by the deprivation of these [public hearings, trial by jury, right of appeal]

[13] 37 STAT. 79 (1912), 42 U.S.C. § 191 (1952); 37 STAT. 737 (1913), 5 U.S.S., § 616 (1952).

and other ordinary elements of due process that are assured in the criminal court." [14]

The second influence, the broadening jurisdiction of the juvenile court, was a natural outgrowth of the reform spirit which dominated its founding. This helped, again, to emphasize the often-quoted characteristic of the juvenile court—that the child before it is not being tried for a crime, but rather that the court is acting in lieu of the parent and, as a benevolent one, by inquiring into the development and circumstances surrounding his maladjustment in order to determine the course of action that will best meet his needs and insure his continued welfare. This tendency of the juvenile court to deal with all cases involving children, however, has resulted in an obscuring and sloughing over of the differences between the delinquent and the dependent or neglected child and in a dealing with every child as if he were maladjusted or presented some kind of a problem. Social workers, in fact, in their conception of juvenile courts, unwittingly reflect this obscuring tendency: [15]

> The purpose of the juvenile court is not to inflict a penalty on a child but to save him from further delinquency and from neglect. Its success, therefore, depends upon a comprehensive understanding of all significant aspects of the case.
>
> . . . If treatment is to be directed to causes and adapted to the needs of the individual, the child himself must be studied—his physical condition, his mental capacities, his personality and the driving forces of his conduct.

It seems only too clear. The purpose of the juvenile court is not to determine whether the child has committed any act for which he should be held; rather it is to get at the causes of his misbehavior in order that he can be given treatment appropriate to his needs.

The growth and establishment of social-work practice on a professional level has been a third influence that has helped to strengthen the social-agency image of the juvenile court. During the forty years following the birth of the juvenile court, the growth of social work was rapid. In the colleges and universities, social work, often lodged in sociology departments, gradually broke away to form independent departments; in some universities, it emerged as a full-fledged, degree-granting graduate professional school. The professional organizations for social workers kept pace. The American Association of Social Workers, an out-

---

[14] Tappan, *supra* note 8, at 130.

[15] K. F. LENROOT AND E. O. LUNDBERG, Juvenile Courts at Work—A Study of the Organization and Method of Ten Courts 88, 94 (U.S. Children's Bureau, Dep't of Labor Pub. No. 141, 1925).

growth of the National Social Workers Exchange, was founded in 1921, the American Association of Medical Social Workers in 1918, the National Association of School of Social Workers in 1919, the American Association of Psychiatric Social Workers in 1926, the American Association of Group Workers in 1946, and the Social Work Research Group in 1949. Within the last three years, all of these groups have joined to form the National Association of Social Workers. These professional organizations not only have helped to support the hands of those strategically-placed workers in the Children's Bureau, but also have served as pressure groups in various communities to bring about the appointment of the type of juvenile court personnel that would strengthen the social-agency image of the court.

The fourth influence here—certain court decisions—have also helped to move the juvenile court toward a social-agency image. The constitutionality of the legislation creating the juvenile court was quick to be tested. In one of the earliest of these cases, *Commonwealth v. Fisher,* the defendant attacked the juvenile court and its procedures, claiming that he had been deprived thereby of certain of his constitutional rights. The court stated in part: [16]

> The last reason to be noticed why the act should be declared unconstitutional is that it denies the appellant a trial by jury. Here again is the fallacy that he was tried by the court . . . and no act of the legislature can deny this right to any citizen, young or old, minor or adult, if he is to be tried for a crime against the commonwealth. But there was no trial for any crime here, and the act is operative only when there is to be no trial. The very purpose of the act is to prevent a trial. . . .

And so it went. Decision after decision helped to mold an image of the juvenile court that departed farther and farther from traditional legal principles. At the time, various criticisms were leveled at these decisions. One charge was "socialism"; another, more reasoned, was that they were merely in keeping with a certain popular support that the new laws enjoyed. In any event, these decisions provided solid support for interpreting the laws to the end of converting the juvenile court into a kind of social agency.

Perhaps, the most outstanding influence impelling the juvenile court towards its social-agency self-image has been the early recognition that a child brought before the court must be treated for his problem, rather than be punished for his crime. This attitude supposedly opened the door for "scientific justice," where the child before the juvenile court would be studied in a total fashion—biological, psychological and

[16] Commonwealth v. Fisher, 213 Pa. 48, 53, 62 Atl. 198, 200 (1905).

sociological; a diagnostic judgment made; and a treatment prescribed which would meet unfulfilled needs, secure his protection, and insure his return to social and psychological health. Thus, individualization of treatment was to be achieved in the juvenile court by the convergence of the enthusiastic support of reformers, the scientific advances in psychology and psychiatry, and the dominant individualistic theme of our culture.

With this initial treatment-orientation, the medical analogy was quick to appear in the literature, aided and abetted particularly by the development of psychoanalysis, with its varieties and the application of its insights into the delinquent child.[17] From the study of neuroses and their emotional manifestations, it was, then, but a short jump to the viewing of delinquent behavior as a symptom of some underlying emotional conflict.[18] When this occurred, it followed that each case must be studied carefully and completely to reach the source of the conflict in the child's personality that could account for the "acting-out" —even though socially-disapproved—behavior, and adequate provisions, psychiatric and/or case-work, made for its correction. As the doctor restores the physically-sick child to health, so it was urged, would the clinical team of psychiatrist, psychologist, and social worker restore the delinquent child to behavioral health, where those unpleasant "acting-out" symptoms would disappear.

As has been pointed out above, this treatment viewpoint has been present from the very beginning, despite the fact that no technique for treating delinquent behavior had been adequately formulated and tested. Even today, with the many advances of the basic sciences, such techniques are but imperfectly understood and do not, as many sophisticated therapists have recognized, meet expectations.[19] In study after study, this fact has been demonstrated. The fact remains, however, that during the fifty-nine years since the founding of the juvenile court, the clamor concerning the need for treatment, nature of treatment, correct treatment procedure, and treatment facilities has continued to fill the pages of the professional journals, newspaper supplements, and professional lectures on delinquency to various community groups.

[17] See, e.g., A. Aichhorn, *Wayward Youth* (1935).

[18] It should be emphasized that the claim is not advanced that delinquency is *never* the outgrowth of some emotional condition. It cannot, however, *explain* all delinquent behavior, as some of the uncritical adherents of the medical analogy seem to imply. The sole purpose here is to show the manner in which "treatment" philosophy has molded the social agency image of the juvenile court.

[19] See Peck, *Why Does a Young Delinquent Resist Treatment?*, The Child, Nov. 1951, p. 35; Lippman, *Treatment of Juvenile Delinquents*, in National Conference of Social Work, Proceedings 317 (1945).

While treatment has been discussed here primarily in terms of the application of psychiatric and case-work techniques, the inference should not be drawn that these are the only activities regarded as treatment by the juvenile court. The fact of the matter is that under the impact of the treatment philosophy held by professionals, every action that the juvenile court takes is regarded as "treatment." Whether the juvenile court sends the child to the reformatory or the clinic, places him on probation or in a foster home, dismisses him with a lecture or without a lecture—all is rationalized as treatment, especially by those professionals who have a deep need to view the juvenile court as an agency for treatment and never for punishment of the child.

The social-agency image of the juvenile court has had a dynamic quality—that is, it has been growing and expanding since the birth of the juvenile court in Illinois—and it is reflected in annual reports of various juvenile courts, in numerous publications of the Children's Bureau, in certain court decisions, and in many articles in professional and semiprofessional social-work journals. For example, here is a statement from an annual report of 1925: [20]

> Or as the statute now reads, "The court from time to time may adjourn the hearing and inquire into the habits, surroundings, conditions and tendencies of the child so as to enable the court to render such order or judgment as shall best conserve the welfare of the child and carry out the objects of this act." As a result of this enactment the justices have been enabled to scrap once and for all the old legal trial of children with its absurd and obsolete limitations of testimony and to inquire into the causes of the children's neglect or delinquency untrammelled by narrow rules of evidence.

It is significant to note that the writer has no difficulty in considering delinquency and neglect together and is perfectly willing to throw out the "narrow rules of evidence" and the "absurd and obsolete limitations of testimony" in order to get at the "real causes" of the child's difficulty. It is difficult to refrain from observing, however, that it seems extremely relevant, if only in the interest of fair play, to establish the fact as to whether or not the child committed a particular act that would make him delinquent under the existing statute.

In this same report, the judge writes of the future of the court: [21]

> We prefer to think of it as a definite arm of the government engaged in the task of protecting and correcting the handicapped children of the community and of supervising their social adjustments, but

[20] Children's Court of the City of New York, Ann. Rep. 16 (1925).
[21] Id. at 31.

not extending its functions over matters which could be administered by other departments of state or even by semi-public agencies without invoking judicial action. . . . Even now the court is seeking to treat every case, in which its assistance is invoked, to the end that the cause of the disease or disorder complained of may be removed and that its patients may be restored to perfect moral health. As time goes on its facilities for helping its patients and of achieving their social adjustments will be developed and improved. . . . In short the court of tomorrow, as we picture it, will resemble in many respects the ideal which we are struggling, more or less imperfectly, to obtain today. It will administer the law faithfully and conscientiously but at the same time its emphasis will be laid more and more on the exercise of social justice by which alone the children who come before it may be readjusted, safeguarded and developed into future assets for the State.

This judge, only too clearly, has been willing to have his legal training modified or supplemented, as the case may be, by certain conceptions and values derived from a social-work point of view.

Perhaps, no clearer formulation of this social-agency image of the juvenile court is provided than a statement by the Wayne County Juvenile Court made over fifteen years ago: [22]

The average citizen thinks of the Juvenile Court in terms of a criminal court for young boys and girls, and believes that the Detention Home is a jail to which these boys and girls are sentenced. These misconceptions overlook the great progress which society has made in the past one hundred years in dealing with delinquent children. For it is as recent as that, that children of tender years who violated the criminal laws were locked up in the same jails, were tried by the same prosecutors and judges, and in many cases received the same punishment, as hardened adult criminals. Often the punishment consisted of many years' imprisonment, and even, in a few instances, death. The protest by socially-minded people against this treatment by the criminal courts of juvenile offenders on the same basis as adult offenders, resulted in the Juvenile Court movement. Progressive people realized that the administration of social justice, at least so far as children are concerned, should not be based on theories of retribution and revenge, but rather on the principles of reformation and correction. They felt that children, by the very reason of their immature years, cannot and should not be held as strictly accountable for their acts as are adults.

The Juvenile Court is the outcome of this agitation for social justice for children. It is the first legal tribunal where the law works side

[22] The Wayne County Juvenile Court 1-2 (n.d.).

by side with the sciences which deal with human behavior. The Court adopted the social case-work method, by which the child is treated individually in relation to his whole environment. It is in this procedure that the Juvenile Court differs from the criminal courts, where an accused person is sought to be convicted of and punished for having committed a particular crime. The juvenile delinquents who are brought before the Juvenile Court are not regarded as criminals, irrespective of the misconduct or offense with which they are charged. They are considered to be boys and girls who have become maladjusted and, perhaps through no fault of their own, have expressed their normal feelings and emotions in delinquent ways. The Court recognizes that these children need its special care, protection and understanding; and through proper supervision and guidance, it endeavors to divert the forces of delinquent behavior into normal and satisfactory channels.

This statement, which appears to be largely for public-relations purposes, epitomizes the spirit and aspirations of the juvenile court set in a social-agency framework. It goes almost without saying that there will be great disparity between actual practice and this pollyanna view of what the juvenile court aspires to be.

Within this social-agency framework, the juvenile court ideally should function in the following manner: A complaint would be made to the juvenile court's intake desk by the police, a social agency, a neighbor, a parent, or a socially-minded citizen. If the behavior difficulty could not be resolved with the complainant, process would issue and the child would be brought in. The child and its parents would be questioned by a social worker, and if the child could be released to its parents, this would be done; otherwise, the child would be held at a detention home pending a thorough social study of the case. In this latter event, the child himself would be variously viewed as maladjusted, having a problem, in trouble, or an example of need frustration or a type of "acting out" behavior. A social worker then would be assigned to the case to make the required social study.

Preliminary study of the case might indicate to the worker that the child's difficulty was not very deep-seated and that the case could be handled unofficially with a preliminary hearing and dismissed to the best interests of the child and others who were involved. On the other hand, preliminary inquiry might indicate the need for a complete social study; and, if so, the study would continue and might include thorough physical, psychiatric, and psychological examinations, as well as a thorough developmental picture of the child in his family and/or other social situation. The social investigation would logically lead to some diagnostic formulation involving the nature of the problem and the probable roots of the difficulty. On the basis of this formulation, some plan of treatment would be outlined which, of course, might include "institutional treatment." At this point, again, a decision would be made as to whether the case could be handled unofficially and recommended treatment carried out by the juvenile court clinic, child-guidance agency, a family agency, or a private psychiatrist, or whether the case should be handled officially and brought before the juvenile court judge, with the understanding that he would see that the recommended treatment was carried out. In either case, treatment would continue if the subject proved willing to accept it. If, however, he did not, more stringent measures would probably be recommended; in fact, the plan might include any one of the several dispositions, euphemistically called "treatments," that have been traditionally open to the juvenile court judge—namely, dismissal, supervised probation, foster-home placement, or institutional commitment. The juvenile court might also insist that the child be given psychiatric treatment by some independent agency. At this point, social-work supervisors, now termed probation officers, would take over and follow the child through the prescribed course. In the ideal social-agency-type juvenile court, however, the great majority of the cases would tend to be handled "unofficially."

As the juvenile court has moved in the direction of perfecting its social-agency image, several unforeseen consequences have emerged. For example, court decisions have helped mold this image as, one after another, they have affirmed that private hearings, the introduction of social-study material, the absence of a defense attorney, and the lack of trial by jury do not constitute a denial of due process because the child is not being tried for a crime. Accordingly, those legal safeguards which have been the cornerstone of Anglo-Saxon jurisprudence for centuries are not available to the child in the juvenile court because he is considered not to be responsible for his act up to a specified age, depending upon the state law, but rather is regarded as "having a problem." The disposition of the child in the juvenile court is, thus, almost entirely dependent upon the wisdom of the judge.

Another consequence of this emerging social-agency image of the juvenile court has been an attempt, particularly noticeable in the first six postwar years, to hold parents responsible for the delinquent acts of their child. The underlying reasoning is this: Social workers, via their varieties of psychoanalytic orientations, have regarded the home as the fundamental source of the love and security necessary to shape the child into a mature adult. When the child is not given this love and security, he experiences a feeling of frustration and unfulfilled needs, which leads to distorted and ambivalent reactions to one or both parents, and some resultant deep-seated conflict or splintering of his ego. The parents, in turn, owing to their own inadequacies or because of the emotional state of the child, are able to provide nothing but the most erratic and inconsistent discipline and supervision. In such a family atmosphere, accordingly, the child may begin to "act out" his conflicts in delinquent ways. Now, this all-too-brief statement of the asserted psychological roots of delinquency in the family setting has been sold to certain juvenile court judges, with the result that schools for parents have been started, and parents have been summoned into juvenile court and, in some instances, given jail sentences because they have, from this perspective, been adjudged responsible for the delinquencies of their child.[23]

Another consequence of the juvenile court's assumption of the role of a social-work agency is that the original differences among the conditions of dependency, neglect, and delinquency have gradually become obscure, and the juvenile court has approached each child as a young person who has a problem and needs help, regardless of his basic condition. It is but a step from this obfuscation to the general notion that the underlying cause of these diverse conditions is the same, despite the lack of evidence to support such a position.

A final consequence of this adherence to a social-agency orientation by the juvenile court—and perhaps the most telling one—is the moral confusion it occasions in both the child and his parents. In the popular mind, a court is an instrument for securing justice between persons and for securing the rights of the person charged with a specific criminal act by the state. When, however, the juvenile court fails directly to advert to the fact that a particular illegal act has been committed by the child and, in its zeal to "treat" the child, completely glosses over this matter, the final disposition of the child's case is very likely to seem to him confusing and even unjust. And his parents, in turn, will reflect this confusion, because on their social level, they cannot very easily accept the view that the child by virtue of his behavior is "sick" and needs "treatment," but rather are committed to the view that the court is there for justice and for punishing a person who has done something that is wrong.

[23] Space does not permit consideration of this problem in greater detail. The statutes have generally given judges authority to proceed against a parent or other adult where it can be shown that he has directly contributed to the delinquency of the child. See Teeters and Reinemann, op. cit. supra note 6, at 200-06.

One critic perceives this situation very clearly when he notes the lack of understanding of parents as to the function of a psychiatric clinic to which the juvenile court referred their children's cases. He points out that when cases brought before the juvenile court on charges of incorrigibility were referred to the clinic, the parents and the child considered the clinic action a part of the punishment for the offense instead of a means of treatment.[24] Moreover, this attitude on the part of the child and his parents will continue to exist and plague the "treatment" process, because it will generally be impossible for the juvenile court to convey its "scientific" orientation to people whose morality is framed exclusively in terms of right and wrong.

It is also cogent to inquire how far we can carry certain theories of treatment of criminal behavior, on both juvenile and adult levels, without undermining the concept of legal responsibility; for it should be clear that a popular acceptance of the idea that no one is responsible for what he does would lead to chaos. Here, confusion is attributable to the deterministic character of science—the attempt to explain given behavior by isolating the interrelated factors antecedent to it—under which the doctrine of scientific responsibility replaces that of legal responsibility.[25] So, when the juvenile court attempts to help the child by "treating" his "disorder," it is literally using the child to collect data to substantiate certain theories of child behavior and to foist on him some inadequately-tested notions about treatment of juvenile misconduct, while, at the same time, chipping away at the concept of legal responsibility.

## III. The Legal Image of the Court

It has been observed that the true social-agency image of the juvenile court tends to emerge only in those few highly-organized, independent juvenile courts to be found in large cities. The juvenile court as established by law in the great majority of states, however, is a part of a court of general jurisdiction and, as such, is part of a county court system. With such legal status, therefore, one can well appreciate the furious character of the conflict that has been occasioned by efforts to convert the juvenile court into a type of social agency, with traditional legal procedures de-emphasized or eliminated and various treatments

---

[24] O'Keefe, *Mental Hygiene Facilities for the Juvenile Delinquent,* Federal Probation, June 1948, pp. 31-35.

[25] See Green, *The Concept of Responsibility,* 33 J. Crim. L. & Criminology 392-94 (1943).

introduced in order "to cure" the child. The conflict has, in fact, been continuous and, in recent years, it has become even sharper as various studies have indicated both that many basic legal rights are being denied the child and his parents and that there may be a great gap between conception and execution of successful treatment of a "maladjusted" child. Thus, it has been observed that "measured by any reasonable standards the juvenile courts have failed to live up to the high expectations held by the early reformers." [26]

The conventional response to such observations has been that the juvenile court fails precisely because the community cannot or is unwilling to provide the necessary resources and facilities to do a first-rate job. Statements to the effect that there are not enough properly-trained probation officers, the judge is only part-time and has failed to grasp the juvenile court idea, detention facilities are inadequate, there are not sufficient treatment facilities in the juvenile court or community there is a need for more psychiatric time, the people comprising the community must be educated to the function of the juvenile court, and the salary scale is inadequate are to be found scattered throughout the literature. While any one or all of these shortcomings may exist with respect to any particular juvenile court, however, there is no evidence convincingly to show that if these defects were remedied, juvenile courts in general would be able to do a better job in preventing recidivism in children who had once been found to be delinquent. In fact, much of the evidence appears to be exactly to the contrary.[27] Even so, ameliorative measures might still be justified on the ground that the juvenile court would be able to perform its social-control function more adequately and more humanely.

What, then, are some of the central issues in this conflict between the social-agency and the legalistic orientations of the juvenile court?

First, the problem of the extent of jurisdiction of the juvenile court has been debated on two fronts: what relationship does it bear to other courts; and what type of cases should legitimately come before it? The problem of the relationship of the juvenile court to other courts was considered in the often-quoted case of *People v. Lattimore*. There,

---

[26] BLOCH AND FLYNN, *op. cit. supra* note 12, at 317.

[27] See W. HEALY AND A. BRONNER, Treatment and What Happened Afterward (1939); E. POWERS AND H. WITMER, An Experiment in the Prevention of Juvenile Delinquency: The Cambridge Somerville Youth Study (1951); Dunham and Knauer, *The Juvenile Court and Its Relation to Adult Criminality*, 32 Social Forces 290 (1954); Diana, *Is Casework in Probation Necessary?*, Focus, Jan. 1955, p. 1; Adamson and Dunham, *Clinical Treatment of Male Juvenile Delinquency: A Case Study in Effort and Result*, 21 Am. Socio. Rev. 312 (1956); R. W. England, *What Is Responsible for Satisfactory Probation and Post Probation Outcome?*, 47 J. Crim. L., C. & P.S. 667 (1957).

the Illinois Supreme Court reviewed and affirmed the criminal court conviction of the defendant while she was still a ward of the juvenile court, upholding the lower court's jurisdiction in these words: [28]

> The Juvenile Court is a court of limited jurisdiction. The legislature is without authority to confer upon an inferior court the power to stay a court created by the constitution from proceeding with the trial of a cause jurisdiction of which is expressly granted to it by the constitution. . . . It was not intended by the legislature that the juvenile court should be made a haven of refuge where a delinquent child of the age recognized by law as capable of committing a crime should be immune from punishment of violating the criminal laws of the state, committed by such child subsequent to his or her being declared a delinquent child.

The problem is still widely-debated, however, and generally arises in one form or another when a child of juvenile-court age commits a capital offense. One solution has been to make the juvenile court independent by creating state-wide juvenile courts systems, as has been done in Connecticut, Rhode Island, and Utah. But it will take more time to determine where this system has improved the administration of juvenile justice.[29]

With respect to the types of cases that should come before it, there has been a tendency throughout its history for the juvenile court to assume jurisdiction over most cases involving children—often, it is asserted, more than it could satisfactorily handle. Thus, adoption, unmarried mothers, mother's pension, and sometimes divorce cases have been lodged in the juvenile court, as it has extended its aegis over cases of dependency and neglect as well as delinquency. As noted above, this tends to confuse the juvenile court's function.

The practice of handling cases unofficially is another matter about which much controversy has raged over the years. This practice is extremely variable among juvenile courts, as certain juvenile courts handle no cases unofficially, while others may handle the bulk of their cases in this manner. The arguments advanced in support of the practice is that it is in keeping with the juvenile court's basic treatment philosophy; it keeps the child from having a court record; it enables professional opinion other than that of the judge to influence the case; and it saves the time and energy of the judge for the more serious cases. On the other hand, it is argued that the practice conduces inefficiency in that it diverts judicial attention to cases that should be handled by other agencies; it weakens the juvenile court's authority in

---

[28] People v. Lattimore, 119 N.E. 275, 362 Ill. 206 (1935).
[29] See Rubin, *State Juvenile Court: A New Standard,* Focus, July 1951, p. 103.

the more serious cases; and it confuses any criteria which attempt to distinguish between court and noncourt cases and discourages other agencies from developing and devoting their resources to the prevention of delinquency. It almost goes without saying that the practice makes meaningless any attempt to report statistical comparisons between communities as to the frequency of delinquency.

Another problem confronting every juvenile court judge is that of balancing the welfare of the child, in accordance with the juvenile court's basic philosophy, against the protection of the community. This issue has not been articulated very clearly in the past, but recently it has received greater attention as it has been brought more sharply into focus.[30] While it might be argued, in the spirit of Adam Smith's economic theory, that securing the welfare of the child will insure best the welfare of the community, this is not likely to have much appeal to those persons who have been injured in some fashion by the acts of a child. They may demand retribution and even revenge, which to them is justice. In fact, it is extremely doubtful that the aims of protecting and securing the welfare of the child can ever be completely realized until a sizable majority of the people in any community understands and accepts the basic philosophy of the juvenile court. This widespread lack of public rapport accounts for the perennial charge that the juvenile court is "coddling young criminals." Even if the necessary public understanding were brought about, however, the issue would still have to be faced as to how to deal most effectively with delinquent behavior in achieving both the welfare of the community and that of the child.

Another problem, as yet not adequately explored, concerns the limitations of individualized treatment within an authoritative court setting. While it has been accepted by many enlightened persons that punishment per se secures no beneficial results to the person or to the community, it is also becoming increasingly clear that our treatment techniques do not accomplish what we would like. In this area, however, our knowledge is quite deficient. We cannot well distinguish between those cases that might benefit from some form of psychotherapy and those cases that will not. Nor can we distinguish between those cases in which delinquency will, in any event, be arrested and those in which help is needed. Then, too, no matter what "treatment" disposition the court may use—probation, foster home-placement, referral to a treatment clinic, or commitment to an institution—the fact remains

[30] See Standards for Specialized Courts Dealing with Children 2 (U.S. Children's Bureau, Dep't of Health, Education, and Welfare Pub. No. 346, 1954).

that it is likely to be viewed by the child and his parents as punishment and not treatment, although these devices probably afford a more individualized and progressive scheme of punishment than various kinds of treatment per se. There is, finally, some doubt as to the validity of one assumption of treatment philosophy seldom mentioned in the literature—the assumption that the child facing the therapist is either not thinking or, if he is, he is freely entering into cooperation with the therapist to achieve a cure. With delinquents, nothing could be farther from reality. For quite often, the delinquent "patient" is not only thinking, but thinking of how he can beat this "rap"; and in trying to do so, he will not hesitate to attempt to manipulate the therapist, who will have to be steeped in a knowledge of the delinquent's world if he is not to be duped.

These issues must all be resolved if the juvenile court is to fulfill a valid legal function.[31] Ideally, the juvenile court would be independent of other courts, with its jurisdiction carefully defined by law. The law would, for the guidance of the juvenile court, carefully and precisely define the specific acts for which a child could be held as a delinquent. At the intake desk, a complaint would be registered with the appropriate evidence to support the contention that an act of delinquency had been committed. The gathering of such evidence would be primarily a police task, in which assistance might perhaps be rendered by a probation officer of the juvenile court. The probation officer, the police, and the juvenile court referee would decide whether or not the evidence was sufficient to warrant a delinquency petition. If not, the child would be dismissed with a warm, friendly attitude; if the evidence was sufficient, however, the child would be held either in the custody of his parents or guardian or in a detention home for a juvenile court appearance.

When brought before the juvenile court, after a very short detention period, the first task of the judge would be to inform the child and his parents of all their legal rights according to law, particularly their right to legal counsel and appeal. The judge would then hear the evidence and find whether or not the child had committed a delinquent act. The judge, before determining the disposition of the case, would then confer with those professional members of his staff who had worked on the case to determine if some consensus had been reached among them as to which available disposition would serve best to secure both the welfare of the child and protection for the community. He would then pronounce the disposition that had been decided in con-

---

[31] In constructing this legal image, the focus here is primarily on delinquency cases and excludes other kinds of cases handled by juvenile courts.

sultation. Such dispositions even though mild and humane, would bear a punishment and not a treatment label. The atmosphere of the juvenile court at all times would be formal, dignified, and authoritative. The judge, as representative of community authority, would always attempt to impress the child and his parents with the gravity of the situation and the consequences that would likely ensue if such act or acts were repeated. Such a juvenile court would have no facility for clinical treatment of the child, for it would be recognized that treatment can be carried on only when a case is not being adjudicated. Nor would it indulge in the unofficial handling of cases. For it should be clear that if no delinquent act has been committed, the taking of any action with reference to the child is a violation of his rights, unless the child and/or his parents request help—and in that event, he and/or they would be referred to the most appropriate available agency.

## IV. Conflict of Images—A New Opportunity

The proponents of these two images—the social-agency and the legalistic—which have here been delineated have been engaged in ideological battle over the juvenile court during its sixty years of existence. To be sure, the social-agency image has been the more dominant and aggressive, although in recent years, the balance has swung back somewhat toward the legalistic image.[32] The conflict of these images, however, still clearly appears in juvenile court attitudes and the decisions of the various judges as they seek to cope with the cases before them. A slight ironical twist may be seen when an eminent judge describes the juvenile court as comparable to a hospital or clinic where the "sick" patient is diagnosed, hospitalized, treated, and discharged,[33] while a well-known social worker states that the juvenile court is first a court where legal responsibility is established specifically by law with respect to certain behavior and conditions of children and adults.[34]

The clash of these two images in the history of the juvenile court

[32] See, e.g., PAUL W. TAPPAN, Comparative Survey on Juvenile Delinquency (1952); Killian, The Juvenile Court as an Institution, 261 ANNALS 89 (1949). Over thirty years ago, Eliot saw the need to separate judicial and treatment functions. See Eliot, The Project Problem Method Applied in Indeterminate Sentence, Probation, and Other Re-educational Treatment, in THE CHILD, THE CLINIC AND THE COURT 102 (1925).

[33] P. W. Alexander, Of Juvenile Court Justice and Judges, in NPPA YEARBOOK 187, 192 (1947).

[34] ALICE SCOTT NUTT, The Juvenile Court and the Public Welfare Agency in the Child Welfare Program (U.S. Children's Bureau, Dep't of Health, Education, and Welfare Pub. No. 327, 1949).

has been of crucial significance, because it tends to force a re-examination of all theories concerning the etiology of delinquent behavior, as well as theories concerning the most effective ways of handling delinquents to produce the desired results. It has brought the juvenile court to what one critic, drawing an analogy from the field of mechanics, has termed "dead center," where no force can move it either way and it slowly grinds to a dead stop! [35] Whether "dead center" or some other phrase best describes the present situation of the juvenile court, however, is beside the point; the fact still remains that the juvenile court has not demonstrated the accomplishments which would justify the faith of its founders. But the present situation of the juvenile court might well afford a unique opportunity—that is, the opportunity to sponsor and encourage scientific research inquiries to answer some of the pressing questions that this clash of images has produced. Both the spirit and tradition of the juvenile court make it possible to do this.

Lack of space limits a detailed discussion here, and so only a few problems suitable for research can be suggested. There is a great need to determine how the juvenile court can be made most effective, both as an instrument of social control in the community and as an instrument for arresting delinquent behavior in youth. Let us consider this experiment: We hear from many sources that a delinquent child needs psychological treatment and not punishment. Therefore, let us set up a well-equipped clinic, with the best-qualified personnel that it is possible to obtain, even at the expense of paying them salaries somewhat higher than the prevailing scales in the community. When such a clinic is established, from the signed complaints coming to the juvenile court, one child would go to the clinic for appropriate treatment and one would go to the juvenile court, which would function exclusively as a legal tribunal, using the dispositions available to it. The clinic would only take enough cases to insure an adequately-sized sample, previously agreed upon. Two to three years after treatment, a follow-up study would be made on both juvenile court and clinic cases, primarily to determine if the subjects still continued their delinquent behavior or were in any way dependent problems for the community. The writer strongly suspects that there would be no significant differences in outcome between the juvenile court and clinic cases because of the almost universally-overlooked fact that clinic treatment may be useful in only certain types of cases. If the clinic succeeded with certain kinds of cases, they might be hidden in the figures and would be balanced by those cases in which a favorable adjustment would have been effected

[35] McCrea, *Juvenile Courts and Juvenile Probation*, 3 N.P.P.A.J. 385 (1957).

regardless of the disposition made. This suggests that successfully treated cases are those that would recover if nothing were done.

There is need also to determine the relative merits of the different disposals available to the juvenile court and the kind of cases that might respond most appropriately to each. Similarly, there is need to determine, if possible, the significance of the impact of the court experience upon the child: Will it be more crucial to certain children coming from some segments of society than to other children from other segments? In evaluating each study, a two-faceted standard would be employed: does the child continue his antisocial behavior as an adult; and/or does the child continue to have a socially-unacceptable dependent status as an adult?

These research suggestions are only a few of the tacks that the juvenile court might pursue to help ease itself from its present static position. Research might also promote the divestiture of the built-in egocentric protective mechanisms that are found in certain juvenile courts and direct attention once again to the problem of the child and the task of transforming the juvenile court into an effective agency for the social control of youth.

There would hardly seem to be any dispute among professionals in the criminological field that a philosophy of treatment and reformation is of a morally higher order than is a philosophy of punishment; there is less certainty, however, about the views of the general public on this matter. But regardless of public attitudes, the question of how far and under what circumstances the reward-penalty system of a society can be modified is most crucial. For it would seem that in any kind of social structure, there will always be certain persons who cannot and will not be accommodated. Some of these persons will be so-called criminals, and the central sociological task is to discover, if possible, what their minimum number should be and then to determine the best social arrangements to keep their number at this level. With respect to juvenile delinquents, this probably represents the "hard core" which fails to respond to any therapeutic approach.

The juvenile court, most markedly of all our agencies for handling socially-aberrant individuals, has adhered to the philosophy of treatment and reformation, with the lofty ideal of safeguarding, almost at any cost, the welfare of the child. While this ideal is eminently praiseworthy and expressive of the humanitarian quality of American culture, the question can, however, and should be raised as to whether the existing social-agency-type juvenile court has succeeded in creating the most appropriate conditions for arresting a child's misconduct and for providing him with those personality strengths that will enable him to adjust to the community in a socially acceptable manner. This is a question, it is submitted, that merits the most careful and thoughtful examination.

In this paper an attempt has been made to portray two idealized conceptions of the juvenile court—the social-agency and the legalistic—the nature of the conflict between them, and the resultant state of rigidity into which it has become frozen. While the social-agency image has been the most dominant and aggressive, the legalistic image still remains with us in many juvenile courts, hidden in the traditions of the criminal law. The future of the juvenile court hinges upon our capacity to analyze carefully the issues in this conflict in order that we may devise the type of institutional procedure—in conformity with our existing knowledge—that will best insure both protection for the community and essential personality strengths for our youth.


# 28.   Probation: Case Work

## Richard A. Chappell

> The author was Chief of Probation, Administrative Office of the United States Courts, at the time he wrote this material. After twenty-five years with the federal probation service, he resigned and accepted a teaching position at the Walter F. George School of Law at Mercer University, his alma mater. He later became a member and then chairman of the U.S. Board of Parole. He has served the federal government on special assignments. He is an active member of various professional organizations and has published *Decisions Interpreting the Federal Probation Act.*

One attempting to discuss the subject of case work in probation comes head on against the problem of definitions. There are different concepts about the meaning, scope, and function of case work. With developments in the fields of psychology and psychiatry, both of which have made their contributions to case work, there has been a shift of emphasis in case work from the "furnishing of services" to "counseling." There remains some disagreement among case workers, however, about the nature and function of the case-work process, and there is much

Richard A. Chappell, "Probation: Case Work and Current Status," pp. 384-92 from *Contemporary Correction,* by Paul W. Tappan, editor. Copyright, 1951. McGraw-Hill Book Company, Inc. Used by permission.

ignorance and many misconceptions in the mind of the public about social case work.

One impediment to an extension of case work has been the jargon used by those who write and talk about it. This jargon, much of which has been borrowed from the fields of sociology, psychology, and psychiatry, is not understood by the layman. What case work needs is an Abraham Lincoln or Franklin Roosevelt to express its concepts in simple, understandable English.

Probation also has different meanings to different persons. Probation officers themselves have varying concepts about their duties, methods, and techniques. Probation means one thing to the probationer and something else to the judge, the probation officer, and to the man in the street. Following are some of the varying interpretations and concepts about probation.

1. *Probation is a device to escape punishment.* The man in the street sometimes believes that probation is merely a device whereby a guilty offender escapes deserved punishment. Many persons sincerely believe that justice should be meted out with complete impartiality—that "justice should be blind." They reason that if the law has been violated, the penalties provided in the statutes should be invoked to the fullest extent, regardless of the circumstances surrounding the violation or the motives for the offense. Even a few judges lean to this view and treat alike all offenders, regardless of age, intelligence, and economic and social status. Those who hold to this view usually accept the theory that "every man is captain of his own soul." They contend that every citizen lives under an implied agreement to live up to the social contract to "keep the peace." Any violation of this social contract should be followed by an imposition of the penalties prescribed in the criminal laws.

2. *Probation is leniency.* Another concept of probation is that it is pure leniency, dictated primarily by sympathy for the unfortunate offender and a desire to relieve him from the contaminating influences and stigma of imprisonment. Some judges grant probation out of sympathy alone, but they do a disservice to the process of probation. It is admitted that probation is a more lenient form of treatment than imprisonment, but it should not be granted by the heart alone, but rather by the head and heart. Society is neither protected nor the recipient benefited by the grant of probation only because of sympathy when all the circumstances do not point to it as the best disposition of the case.

3. *Probation is punishment.* Still others look upon probation as punishment. They point out that probation throws around the recipient many anxieties and restrictions of movement. The probationer is required

to comply with certain conditions laid down by the court, some of which may be difficult to keep. It requires that, if he is capable of doing so, the probationer work at some honest vocation, support those for whom he has legal responsibility, and report his work activities and leisure-time pursuits. Those who think of probation as punishment point out that the probationer suffers embarrassment because of his probation status. It should be understood that there are punitive and disciplinary aspects to probation but that they are incidental and should not be the primary objective of the process.

4. *Probation is a policing device.* Another view is that probation is primarily a policing device and that the function of the probation officer is to "watch and wait" for a violation of probation. He is sort of a "psychological policeman" to whom is entrusted the task of seeing to it that the probationer "proves" himself. When a violation occurs, the probation officer returns the probationer to the court for sentence. It is admitted that the probation officer has a responsibility to report violations to the court, but this function, though necessary, is secondary to the more important one of helping the probationer become a law-abiding and successful member of the community.

The weakness of this point of view is that it overlooks the fact that persons on probation need help, counsel, and guidance. They have shown themselves to be inadequate or disinclined to keep the laws. Unless something is done to bolster them or change their attitudes, they may be expected to repeat their offenses. There is no magic in the term "probation." It neither inspires nor frightens persons into conformity. Neither will force and pressure from a diligent supervising officer make the weak strong. The police approach may be useful with that unusual offender who is smart enough to count the cost of his acts, but it has little value for most probationers.

5. *Probation is treatment.* Finally, there are those who look upon probation as a method of treatment whose main objectives are the protection of society and the rehabilitation of the offender. By reclaiming the offender to useful citizenship, society is protected. Usually there is no conflict between these two objectives, provided suitable persons are selected for probation and suitable measures are taken to assist the probationer in changing his patterns of conduct, modifying his attitudes, setting new goals, and embarking upon a plan of living that will conform to society's expectations.

Most persons who have studied the methods and practices of successful probation services agree that the probation process is based primarily on case work skills, methods, and practices. It involves a knowledge of personality and behavior and the skill to assist persons in their efforts to seek solutions for their own problems, whether they are of health, emotional instability, educational limitations, unemployment, family relationships, or economic difficulty.

## Case Work in an Authoritarian Setting

There are those who contend that case work cannot function in an authoritarian setting. Those who uphold this view realize that probationers are persons in trouble who need counsel, support, and help. They propose, however, that such services should be supplied by a nonauthoritarian case work agency and that probationers should be referred by the probation officer to such agencies for help. This view is shared by many workers in the child welfare field. There are many who would change the character of the juvenile court from an agency equipped with the machinery for diagnosis and treatment to one with purely legal authority. The court would be stripped of all functions except the determination of legal questions and referral of a youngster to a correctional institution or a case-work agency for treatment.

The prime argument against the use of case work in an authoritarian relationship is that case work is a unique personal relationship that can be useful only if the client seeks help voluntarily and is entirely free at all times to choose between continuation and termination of the relationship.

Is it not true that most of life's situations involve authority? The parent-child, teacher-child, and employer-worker relationships do. While the worker may quit his job and seek employment elsewhere, is this alternative always a convenient one? Would he escape authority by changing "bosses"? The patient must follow the doctor's orders, and the relief client is expected to follow the suggestions of the worker or find himself "cut off the rolls." In the same way, the soldier is subject to military regulations. It is the manner in which the authority is used that determines whether it is irksome and intolerable, or unobtrusive and constructive.

Although a probationer comes involuntarily to the probation office, it may develop that he will have no objection to the relationship. As a matter of fact, he may find growth and satisfaction in it. The number of probationers who voluntarily continue to maintain contact with former supervising officers after the termination of probation bears testimony to this.

The probation officer has a responsibility to fulfill and must use authority occasionally and take on a police role in the event of a serious violation of probation, but this policing function should be kept in the background and be used as sparingly as conditions permit. Moreover, the authority can be made impersonal. In interpreting the relationship between the probation officer and the probationer and in defining the limits within which they operate, the officer does not say, "If you violate, I will return you to the court for sentence." Such a statement would create a barrier that would preclude effective case work, since it makes use of threat and force and attempts to obtain conformance through fear. This is hardly an ennobling motivation. Out of sight of the probation officer and on his own, the probationer may react to this treatment with an attitude of "try and stop me."

On the other hand, if it is the situation and not the officer as a person that makes the demands, authority can be accepted more easily. The probation officer at the outset puts it this way: "You have broken the law that was made for the protection of all members of society, including you, and you have been held accountable in court for your acts. Because the court believes that you can profit from this experience and live according to the rules in the future, you have been granted probation. This affords you an opportunity to avoid the more unpleasant consequencies of imprisonment and to prove to yourself and others that you can conform in the future. The court has assigned me the task of assisting you in every possible way by rendering what services I can to help you make good on probation and be a law-abiding citizen. The primary responsibility for succeeding, however, is yours. Should you for any reason violate any of the terms of your probation, you do it on your own responsibility and it will be my duty to present the full facts to the court."

In this way the probationer sees that both he and the probation officer are under certain legal and authoritative obligations. He accepts authority as a part of the framework of counseling and realizes that "making good" becomes a joint effort, and that the probation officer is primarily a helpful person rather than one who will quickly assert his authority.

On the subject of case work in an authoritarian setting, Ben Meeker has said: [1]

> The assertion is sometimes made that the methods of casework cannot be applied in the authoritative setting of probation. Experience has shown otherwise. Authority per se does not preclude casework. All casework is *authorized*. The authority of the child welfare worker may differ from that of a probation officer in degree but hardly

[1] Ben Meeker, "Probation Is Casework," *Federal Probation,* June, 1948, p. 53.

in kind. The clients of both are seldom so from choice. Yet casework
is basic in the treatment of problem children. So is it in the treatment
of problem adults—those willful, aggressive, disturbed, irresponsible,
and almost always immature members of society who find themselves
in conflict with its laws. To use authority wisely is of course essential,
and helping the probationer accept the realities of his special status
on probation is a *casework* problem.

On the same subject of the use of authority with the delinquent, Kenneth Pray wrote: [2]

It is peculiarly true of the delinquent that social readjustment
must be founded upon the recognition and acceptance of the inherent, rightful, essential social authority that underlies social living.
He has rejected or violated that authority in the past. He has to learn
anew, through painful experience, that those limits, like his own
capacities, are inviolable and that his real satisfactions are to be
found only within them. It is obvious that he cannot learn the values
of these standards to him unless they are actually upheld in practice
and constitute the framework against which he struggles and with
which he must ultimately come to terms by his own will if he is to
resume free, independent life in the community. To assume, therefore,
that social casework with delinquents must be separated from authority, must be divorced from all external limitations upon conduct, is
to rob the service of its most important dynamic and to frustrate, in
advance, its primary objective.

Since social casework, in its true philosophy and in every area of its
practice, inherently involves not only the sufferance but the conscious, deliberate utilization of a fixed framework of limiting conditions with opportunities for free choice and judgment within those
fixed limits, and since the probation and parole function inherently
rests upon the same combination of freedom and authority, we are
justified, then, in concluding that the two are not only compatible
with each other—they are one and the same thing.

Although case-work techniques are essential, they are utilized fully
in too few probation departments, both adult and juvenile. Very few
probation workers are drawn from the ranks of trained and experienced
social workers because appointing authorities have not sought personnel
with this kind of background.

Some probation officers who have had no formal case-work training,
but who possess an understanding of human behavior and are well
grounded in psychology, sociology, economics, and related subjects,

[2] Kenneth L. M. Pray, "The Principles of Social Casework as Applied to Probation
and Parole," *Federal Probation,* April-June, 1945, p. 17.

with good over-all perspectives and suitable personalities, have been successful in the probation field. With training in case-work methods and fieldwork practice under competent supervision, however, they would have been even more skilled and more helpful to persons in trouble.

*Personnel Selection.* The efficacy and success of probation, like any other enterprise, depends upon the ability and qualifications of the persons who serve in the field. To be successful, a probation service must have well-trained and capable probation officers who are selected and retained on a basis of merit and who are adequately compensated. Probation officers must understand their own attitudes, emotions, and feelings. Prejudices and biases often are difficult to overcome completely, but if recognized and understood by the officer, they need not interfere with his work. If an officer is prejudiced against a particular race or sect or intolerant of those who commit particular offenses or who exhibit distasteful personal traits, he should be conscious of these prejudices and not let them militate against effective work. It is important that probation officers occasionally take stock of their attitudes and feelings and learn to look at themselves objectively.

One of the principal'problems in probation work today is the lack of trained personnel and, even more serious, the lack of recognition that probation work requires highly developed skills and training. The Federal courts and many state probation jurisdictions recognize these needs and have set up minimum standards of qualifications for probation officers. We are not far removed, however, from the notion that anyone can be a probation officer and no particular knowledge, character, personality, or training is necessary.

The formal training of a probation officer *is* important. The Federal Probation Service, for example, has the following standards of qualifications for appointments of probation officers,' recommended by the Judicial Conference of the United States.

1. Exemplary character;
2. Good health and vigor;
3. An age at the time of appointment within the range of 24-45 years inclusive;
4. A liberal education of not less than collegiate grade, evidenced by a bachelor's degree (B.A. or B.S.) from a college of recognized standing or its equivalent;
5. Experience in personnel work for the welfare of others of not less than 2 years, or 2 years of specific training for welfare work (a) in a school of social service of recognized standing, or (b) in a professional course of a college or university of recognized standing.

It is generally recognized that the most successful probation officers also must have a broad understanding and knowledge of psychology, sociology, and social case work.

*In-Service Training.* Some jurisdictions have endeavored to meet the need for better trained and more understanding personnel by establishing regular in-service training programs. These programs are conducted by trained leaders who, through group-discussion methods, demonstrate success in developing better insight into behavior problems and methods of dealing with people. More of this type of in-service training is needed. It best serves its purpose when regular meetings are held frequently for probation personnel in local communities. Small discussion groups under competent leadership are very stimulating, and much is being accomplished in this way toward developing real case-work skills in the probation field.

## Case-Work Methods and Probation

The probation officer uses case-work techniques throughout the two important areas of his work, namely, study and treatment. It is impossible to say where "study" ends and "treatment" begins. Treatment begins with the initial interview with the offender during the period of study and study continues through the period of treatment—supervision on probation.

*The Presentence Investigation.* The study process is commonly referred to as the "presentence investigation." It is the "social investigation" or "social diagnosis" of the case worker and includes the social history, diagnosis, prognosis, and plan of treatment.

The presentence-investigation report serves several purposes. The primary and immediate purpose is to inform the court about the offender's past; his surroundings, habits, accomplishments, and failures; his emotional, mental, and physical make-up; and his goals and attitudes. From all these facts which have been obtained from those who have dealt with the offender and from the offender himself, the officer attempts to discover the person's ambitions, drives, and needs. He examines the factors underlying the offense and draws conclusions about the causes of the difficulty and the probable course that will be followed by the offender in the future.

In conducting and compiling a presentence investigation, the probation officer uses the personal approach of the case worker. He is careful to make a painstaking and systematic inquiry into the life circumstances of the offender. He omits no source of information—either documented or personal—which may shed light on the person's past or which will assist in the evaluation of the worth of the person and his capacity to profit from a plan of probationary treatment. The probation officer makes use of all the accepted tools of the case worker in making a social investigation—court and police records, educational data, marital information, etc. He is careful to verify all important data and he avoids interpretations based on unverified information. He also considers the reaction of the person to his present difficulties and his plans to overcome them.

If the court is to impose a sentence which will fit the needs of the offender and meet the demands of society, the judge must know the offender and his background. A complete, well-prepared report informs the court about the man who stands before him for sentence. With the knowledge of the offender's past he will be in a position to predict with some degree of accuracy the course that the offender will probably follow in the future. The judge will have learned by experience the chances of an offender's reacting favorably to the type of guidance and counseling that the probation officer is able to give, having in mind the assets and liabilities of the social setting, the family, and the resources of the community.

The most important tool the probation officer has in the investigation and treatment of the offender is the interview. Without skills in recognized counseling methods he cannot succeed as a probation officer.

*Supervision.* Case-work treatment takes place during the period of probation supervision. "Supervision" is the convenient term for the definite period imposed by the court during which the offender is required to maintain contact with the probation officer. Admittedly, the term has in it the elements of authority, as pointed out earlier, and sets the structure within which both the probation officer, as the supervisor, and the probationer, as the one to be supervised, must work out their relationship.

Nevertheless, there are those in the field of social work who still contend, as pointed out earlier, that case-work principles cannot be applied in this authoritarian setting. In actual practice the effectiveness and success of probation is closely related to the extent to which the principles of case work are applied. There must be respect for the individual, understanding of the motivation for his behavior, and a recognition that all forms of behavior which may be encountered are human responses to a given set of circumstances and have some meaning and relationship to the individual's total personality structure.

While many forms of behavior may not be socially acceptable and therefore must be controlled, they are not to be condemned as being beyond the realm of natural response for the particular individual at the particular time. Therefore, one of the first principles of case work applied to probation supervision is that each offender is an individual, differing in many respects from other individuals, with needs, wants, and desires that have resulted from his particular development.

A second case-work principle which is applied in probation supervision is that any fundamental change in attitude, behavior, and goal can be made only by the individual himself. In an authoritarian setting, he may conform for a time to the rules because of fear of consequences, of being deprived of his liberty, and he may therefore "mark time" by diligently trying to stay out of trouble until his probation period has been "successfully" terminated. This type of remote control, however, produces no real change in his basic behavior patterns. No amount of persuasion, coercion, cajoling, or wielding "the big stick" will effect any basic changes. Those in probation work must recognize this case-work principle. The individual may be helped to seek more satisfying and acceptable goals and to reorient himself if he wishes and can accept this kind of help, but the decisions must be made by him, and the action which he takes toward achieving these new goals must be his. Even in the matter of employment, it is often found that the job which has been obtained *for* the probationer through considerable effort is one of which he tires and quits in a very short time. The probationer, therefore, must fully participate in, if not actually initiate, all plans in his own behalf. The officer cannot impose standards of behavior nor do for the other person; he can only try to help him do for himself.

These principles do not relieve the probation officer of all responsibility for the probationer. They do relieve him of the impossible task of trying to order the lives of numerous other persons who come under his brief care; but in a much deeper sense, they increase his responsibility. He must have understanding of human behavior, accept the probationer as he is with any limitations he might have, and let him feel that he can come to him at any time with his problems and needs. In this way the probationer can make constructive use of his contacts with the probation officer and receive help in reorienting his life. It is much easier to give advice, to say you may do this, you may not do that, to encourage, exhort, praise, and condemn, than it is to create a setting in which the individual can truly feel free to work out solutions to his problems.

In the initial stages of the supervision period, and particularly during the first interview, the meaning of probation and the role of the probation officer is defined for the probationer. Frequently, the court experience through which he has just passed is very disturbing emotionally. He feels helpless, apprehensive, and confused. A certain amount of relaxation and relief accompanies the realization that he has been released on probation. He is generally receptive at this time to the interpretation which the probation officer can give him of the meaning of the probation relationship. At the same time, the probationer's emotional state may prevent him from assimilating or hearing another "lecture" at this point, and therefore a good approach is one which recognizes that the court experience has been a disturbing one. This permits the new probationer to express some of his feelings about it. In addition to outlining the authoritarian conditions of probation and showing the probationer the setting and limitations within which he and the probation officer must work, an effort is made to help him accept supervision and understand that, within the limits outlined, the probationer will have an opportunity to use his contacts with the probation officer to gain greater insight and work toward the solution of some of his problems.

The probation officer must decide, after a complete evaluation of each case, which of his probationers can respond to, and make use of, a nondirective type of counseling, and learn which cases, either because of limited intelligence, lack of insight, or resistance to the entire authoritarian setting, must be handled on a more directive and environmental basis. It is true that the authoritarian setting itself may prove to be a barrier to the nondirective approach in many cases. This certainly would not be true in all. Much depends on the skill and understanding of the probation officer and the opportunities which he is able to give the probationer to express his feelings and to assume the initiative in discussing his problems. Perhaps the greatest successes in probation are achieved with those probationers who are capable of making use of this type of nondirective counseling because they work out a more satisfying adjustment for themselves and in the process are able to resolve some of their more pressing conflicts. As indicated above, this technique may be limited to a comparatively small percentage of the total case load.

Even in those cases where the nondirective approach is not the main emphasis, an effort is made by the probation officer to help each probationer gain some insight into his own strengths and weaknesses. The interpretation of his problems, needs, goals, etc., must be handled carefully and only on a level which the probationer can understand and use. Even with the group with whom the officer has assumed a directive type of relationship, the probationer is encouraged to solve his own problems in his own way. The officer does not attempt to impose his own plan and his own standards on the probationer because, as a case worker, he recognizes the futility of such an approach. Instead, he tries to help the probationer arrive at his own decisions and formulate his own plans.

Any probation case load includes persons of limited abilities and resources who are incapable of making any basic changes either in their goals or in their environments. With this group the probation officer's approach may be one of manipulating the environment and supplying services which will bring about external changes and enable the probationer to achieve a better adjustment. Particularly with this group, the probation officer must call upon the assistance of other community agencies when their help is indicated. Often comparatively little can be accomplished through environmental changes. When this is so, an effort is made to help the probationer live within the limitations of his environment and capabilities, making the most of those resources available to him.

It is unfortunately a fact that recognized counseling methods are not as widely used in probation work as is desirable. In the first place, probation work has not advanced to the point where there are enough officers qualified academically and trained in the use of counseling techniques. Moreover, because counseling is time-consuming and the probation case load in most courts is high, many officers qualifying in counseling techniques have too little opportunity to use them. Case loads of 100, or even 200 in some courts, must be reduced to 40 or 50 per officer.

One realistic approach to the problem of excessive case loads is the classification of cases into three or four groups. Attention then can be given to them in accordance with individual needs and the ability of the probationer to benefit from more intensive treatment.

SECTION **VIII**

# Training Schools and the Public School

A SMALL percentage of boys and girls who are adjudicated delinquent by the juvenile court are committed to training schools. Although they are few in number, they are regarded as representative of "hard core" delinquents. The traditional philosophy for their treatment was strict discipline and severe punishment. Currently, the philosophy is swinging toward rehabilitation.

The first four articles deal with various aspects of training schools, most of which have been only moderately successful in converting juvenile delinquents into legal and social conformers. The articles selected emphasize rehabilitative aspects against the realistic limitations of a training school. Most discussions of training schools are concerned with the official aspects of staff and organization. However, the informal set of relationships and modes of interaction that prevail among the boys or girls in the schools often are more effective in determining behavior than are the formal procedures. Article 29 analyzes the social structure typical of boys' training schools.

Article 30 asks, "How can the correctional school correct?" and brings out the kinds of relationship between staff and boys that are necessary for rehabilitation.

In Article 31, a psychiatrist sets forth the theory that the entire training school is the therapist, and outlines the therapeutic process that may take place with an individual, simply through institutional living. The article is a paper that was presented at the Berkshire International Forum at Canaan, New York, under the auspices of Berkshire Industrial Farm, with participation of the United Nations Secretariat.

The articles listed above apply to the typical training school for the average type of delinquent. The next two articles in the series deal with extremes—the psychologically disturbed delinquent and the one unusually amenable to rehabilitation. In Article 32, Dr. Gerstle describes the creation in California of special institutions for emotionally disturbed delinquents. Other states are beginning to develop similar programs. In contrast, Article 33 discusses the origin of camps for delinquent boys and then presents a general discussion of the policies and practices considered desirable by specialists in this field and of the types of boys most likely to benefit from the camp program.

The average period of time that delinquents remain in a training school is about nine months for boys and a year for girls. With release comes readjustment to family, school, and community. Some of the special problems of the mutual readjustment of school and delinquent to each other are discussed in Article No. 34.

## 29. The Social Structure of a Correctional Institution

Gordon H. Barker and W. Thomas Adams

Barker has the Ph.D. degree in Sociology from Northwestern University and is Professor and Chairman of the Department of Sociology at the University of Colorado. He is active in state welfare organizations and has published various articles in professional journals.

Adams, who holds the M.A. degree in Sociology from the University of Colorado, is Project Coordinator, Juvenile Delinquency Project of the Western Interstate Commission for Higher Education in Boulder. He was formerly Director of the Lookout Mountain School for Boys in Colorado. He is the author of a number of articles on delinquency.

Every social grouping develops patterns of interrelationships that have significance for the members of those groupings. These patterns are sometimes called the social structure and such a structure exists in every assemblage of persons which is more than temporary.

The social structure of an institution which handles more than one hundred boys in a special capacity has a very definite effect on the population of that institution. On occasion this effect may be negative. In fact, there are many important ways in which this social structure may clearly create problems which can be detected through an analysis of the culture patterns that develop among the boys who reside in such institutions as Reformatories, State Industrial Schools, and Orphanages. This paper attempts to analyze this effect of the social structure in a boy's Industrial School which houses two hundred boys or more.

Groupings in general vary according to many factors and the effects of these groupings are subject to scrutiny by trained personnel as well as by lay persons. For example, the impact of the family grouping with its emphasis on intense interaction between the parent figures through the male and female role and mother-father roles and their children is very different from that pattern in a community grouping where the roles are more diversified and less personal and intense. The child in the family structure is affected by the intensity and emotional attachments in the interaction. His learning is very different from the learning that occurs in a broader and more impersonal social structure such as a public school system. The social structure of the community is broad and general for the most part and the roles are less distinct. The learning or socialization that occurs in community living is again different from that which exists in the family or the school. The interplay between individuals has a vast range.[2]

The social structure of an institution which is geared toward re-education of delinquent boys is indeed of a vast range. The major aspects

Gordon H. Barker and W. Thomas Adams, "The Social Structure of a Correctional Institution," *Journal of Criminal Law, Criminology and Police Science*, 49 (January-February, 1959), 417-422. Reprinted with permission of the publishers of the *Journal*.

[2] The differential stake in conformity in the individuals within a given community can account for a varying tendency to become committed to an anti-social way of life. See, Social Disorganization and Stake in Conformity: Complementary Factors in the Predatory Behavior of Hoodlums, by Jackson Toby, this Journal, *48*, 12-17. (May-June, 1957.)

of the structure are centered around an authoritarian system of adult personnel playing the role of the supervisor and the educator of the child. The boy is expected to accept a pattern of submission to the dominance of the adult. He is expected to defer to the demands and decisions and directives of the adult figures. These adults are different from parents because the child is not expected to identify himself emotionally with them as he would with his mother or father. Identification and emotional attachment do not exist for him in this adult-leader situation. His response in learning and development is different from the family life that he has had prior to his commitment to the institution. His learning is based on his ability to conform to the requirements of the personnel in charge. There is very little in the way of idealization and emulation between the authoritarian personnel and the child in the school. The many aspects of contact are different and almost indescribable in the family setting, whereas in the institution, the contact tends to be linear and categoric with litte variation in quality.

Another major difference is the existence of a homogeneity in terms of sex. The student population is composed of boys entirely in a special age grouping. The adult personnel is composed of both men and women. The impact of the male population is very different from that of the social structure of the community in which the boy lived prior to his commitment. The very definite problems with sexual matters and identification of this age group are naturally different from those of the broader culture outside. The institutional structure has a profound impact in that at best it is but a substitute, albeit an inadequate substitute of necessity.

## Culture Patterns Reveal Institutional Problems [3]

Many problems develop in institutional living, some of which are easily detected through the culture patterns that spring up among the boys. A culture pattern is a way of doing something which is distinct and can be observed as a real and persistent expression over a period of time. The culture patterns that seem to indicate the most important problems are usually those dealing with sexual identifications and

[3] For a comprehensive development of the subject of culture patterns, institutional patterns and problems viewed from various approaches, see the following: Delinquent Boys by ALBERT COHEN, The Free Press, 1955; Teenage Gangs, by KRAMER AND KARR, Henry Holt, 1953, with special reference to pages 208-240; The Juvenile Offender: Perspective and Readings by CLYDE VEDDER, Doubleday, 1954; My Six Convicts by DONALD WILSON, Rinehart and Co., 1948.

anxieties, mother-feminine relationships, father-masculine compulsiveness expressions, big-shotism, personal status discontent, cynicism of unfulfilled dreams, racial-ethnic conflicts, and the aggressiveness and hostility arrangements among the boys. Each of these expressions will be analyzed later.

One thing stands out clearly in the relations of the existing culture patterns. This problem of relationships is called polarity. Issues tend to become polarized in extremes very easily in the institutional structure. The barriers between the children and the adults are frequently very rigid and the social distance is acute. Polarity often occurs between ethnic or racial groups with an intense amount of negative feelings developing. There are strong polarities in regard to sexual manifestations. The boys with problems over sexual identification often find themselves alienated from the others through various culture patterns that develop.

Polarity means the absence of good communication lines for the most part. Acceptance of another individual is often impeded by the effect of rigidity of ideas and interaction. Once a person becomes categorized, he often finds that his entire actions are judged in terms of the limited perception of his category that has developed. Polarization often means a reaction by the institutional personnel that becomes entrenched against a particular child or group of children. The possibility of learning or modification is endangered.

In order to break down the barrier in communication that develops through the polarization of issues, a member of the adult personnel must have extraordinary skills and a vast perspective about the total institution. It is difficult for the personnel, for example, to help a child work through a feeling of being considered a bully. The label or concept circulates throughout the institution and thus persons react to the child as if he were expressing his aggressiveness and dominance in all phases of his group living. To effect a change in this situation, the adult person must understand the nature of the interaction of the child with his peers, the feelings he has toward adult-child relationships, his own self-concept, and many other factors. Frequently, institutions reinforce bad self-concepts and behavior patterns by making them seem synonymous with the child in every action he portrays.

The boys outside correctional institutions are not confronted with the same kinds of problems that boys within the gates face. The structure of the institution has many important functions in this regard. For example, a boy in school may have an acute disagreement with a boy next to him and have an impending fight scheduled later in the day. This may become lost in the larger community when the boys leave the schools and have the freedom to go with those whom they choose and where they choose. The freedom of movement is very different for a boy in the larger community structure from what it is for the boy in the institution. If conflicts develop along very personal lines in which there is a desire to engage in fighting, the boys are kept in close association and the tight social structure produces intensity of response. The boys do not have the freedom to get out of the impact of the situation they create when there is a flare-up of hostility. Some courses of action seem to demand immediate attention with little ability to alter the situation. Relationships have a tendency to move under greater stress and tension in a closed structure such as an institution than they do in the broader social systems of the public schools and the neighborhoods.

The behavior problems of the institutional child permeate the closer situational living more intricately than they possibly would in the public school. The boys are forced to live with the problems in all phases of their lives in closed institutions.

The culture patterns of the children in the correctional institutions often are diagnostic of the problems that are created and manifested among the boys.[4] When there is an ability to gain insight from the culture patterns as to the important issues and problems to be dealt with in the institution, the staff that is trained to handle such problems is at a great advantage. Some of these culture patterns are now discussed at length.

## "Big Shotism" as a Culture Pattern

In almost all groupings, power-status hierarchies develop. There is no exception in an Industrial School. The function of the "big-shot" is deeply significant to the entire social structure of the institution. The person who achieves a position of power and dominance over the other boys is the big-shot. There seem to be two distinct types of power leaders. The one is the boy who achieves his position through brute force. He is able physically to best anyone who counters him. He usually has a cluster of lieutenants who administer his feelings and force throughout the groupings that exist. He solicits favors from others and takes things from them without having to worry about the effects of being detected

---

[4] For a study of the dynamic relationship between the informal social structure of a prison community and the formal social structure, see: *Group Dynamics in the Prison Community* by MORRIS G. CALDWELL, this Journal, *46*, 648-657 (Jan.-Feb. 1956).

by the administration. The other boys are afraid to resist in any way. The power arrangement here is very important because a shift in power means a great deal to the entire functioning of the population of the school. There is an intense interplay between the minority groups and the position of the big-shot. Often the size and strength of the minority ethnic group determine which person will be the big-shot.

A very significant thing develops in many institutions. There tend to be very high rates of delinquency among various ethnic groups which seem to have low status positions in the dominant culture. In the southern part of the United States, there are high rates of crime and delinquency among Negroes. There are also high rates in large urban areas. The population of Negroes in some state institutions is frequently very high. In the southwestern and western states, the rates of delinquency are very high among the Spanish-American and Mexican-American children. In some state institutions in these areas, the population of the institution is the reverse of the regular population because the Spanish-Americans are the minority group in these states as a rule. With the tables turned, there are often needs to retaliate against the members of the institutions who are non-Spanish. The reaction is often hostile and aggressive.

Shifts in institutional population often influence patterns of interaction. For instance, if the big-shots and power leaders in a company assignment follow an ethnic line and they are removed either through parole or isolation due to misconduct, the status hierarchy is changed and the new groups begin to vie for power and control. Vengeance and seeking of retribution often provoke a battle between the groups. The symbols and ways of doing things indicate the particular problems that are responses to the problems of ethnic or racial conflicts. When a person in charge is aware of the expressions of prejudice and racial hatred and their effects in the status hierarchy and the total institution, he has an enormously useful insight that he can implement professionally for the purpose of controlling situations.

The second type of leader that often develops in the institution is the so-called charismatic leader. This person holds the groups in his power through their emotional attachment to him. He does not have to apply a strong-arm method of control. He still dictates the events and can have control of the persons with whom he deals and he tends to be the real decision-maker among the boys, but his control is through their identification with his appeal as a strong person. His control is often very tenuous due to the impact of the institutional structure because he finds himself constantly being judged by both the boys and the administrators. Any wrong move that would deflect his character means a problem for him in terms of his mastery of the others around him. There are fewer charismatic leaders than big-shots in institutions for correction.

## Sexual Identification as a Culture Pattern [5]

Perhaps the most important cluster of culture patterns exist in the area of sexual identification and dilemma. There are many expressions of these problems in the institutional structure. The boys who come to industrial schools are usually in the prepuberty or puberty stage and have a sufficient amount of anxiety about their new sexual role. There are times when they wish to experiment with the new surges in their bodies and the new emotional states that exist for them. The contagion of a large group of boys frequently arouses exaggerated responses. The past training and socialization of the boys means a good deal also in the manner in which the new energies and interests are expressed. There are several striking culture patterns that develop and an analysis of them is very much needed.

In recent studies and observations, there appears to be a large number of children who come to the correctional institutions who were living with their mothers only. Many of the boys have been deserted by their fathers at a very early age and thus the boys have grown up with their mothers. In other cases there are family relationships which indicate that the boys have had a very poor relationship with their fathers due to some form of personal disorganization that the fathers have experienced, such as alcoholism, imprisonment, mental illness, physical incompetence and long records of unemployment and others. Thus the end result is that the fathers have not been good role models for the boys and they have thus failed to assist their children in formulating male role requirements in the culture and internalizing the social skills to play the male role adequately.

Thus a boy may come to the school with a good deal of anxiety about his role position and the needed skills to handle himself properly or, in some cases, he may come with the need to understand what the expectations of the culture are for him as a young man and an eventual male adult. Coupled with this failure to experience this very essential identification and idealization with the adult male figure in the form of the father is the fact that most of these boys have been forced to learn almost exclusively from female figures. Many have mothers who are

---

[5] For a sociologist's approach to the subject of sexual identification and sex rules, see Family, Socialization and Integration Processes, by PARSONS AND BALES, The Free Press, 1955, pages 91 and following.

dominant in their attachment to the child. The over-identification with the feminine figure and the feeling that the mother is the only one who can give warmth and support combine to produce a dependency on the female figure. The anxieties here are very keen. The child also experiences the pressures in his socialization of the compulsion to express his masculinity when he reaches this pre-adolescent and adolescent age. The demands are clear in the culture that he should play the male role and not do anything that would subject him to being called a sissy or too much like a girl. With his identification with the mother and the lack of internalization of male role requirements, he often experiences a good deal of anxiety. Then, his age also indicates that he is developing biologically with a surgence of new sexual energy. The dilemma is often very great. If he is left with his peer group as the instructor, he often feels a need to overreact and prove how very tough and masculine he really is and thus his behavior becomes anti-social because he frequently confuses masculinity with being tough and bad and hard. Much delinquency is precisely an expression of this very personal masculine protest.

The culture patterns that develop in the school indicate how very important the above problems are to the boy and how the institutional structure nurtures the growth of such problems and channels the expressions. One of these problems is noticed in what the boys express as "calling down someone's mother." The boy will find out the name of the mother or the sister of another boy and will then proceed to call that boy by his mother's first name. He will also tell the boy that he has "had the boy's mother or that he is going to have her" when he gets out. He calls the boy's mother a prostitute and talks about her sexuality. The boy who is being "called down" becomes angry and retaliates in some manner. There are times when the "calling down of the mother" becomes very intense and tempers flare. The need of a boy to express hostility, sexuality, and defamation in this culture pattern is understandable in the light of the above analysis. The anxiety over a need for sexual release is one facet. The hostility toward the female figure and mother figure because of the over-identification and the sanctions against such dependency is another facet. The internalized anger and the need to hurt and antagonize is still another.[6]

If a deeper psycho-analytical approach were used, the problem could be explained in terms of an unresolved oedipal stage. The ten-

[6] The Aggressive Child by REDL AND WINEMAN, The Free Press, 1957, includes two books by these authors: Children Who Hate and Controls from Within, Chapter 3 in the former, and Chapters 1 and 2, pages 281-393 in the latter. These passages point up the significance of programs and institutions in the lives of delinquents as well as the development of aggressions and antagonisms.

sion that exists in institutional group living is increased by the existence of this particular culture pattern and the dynamics that exist in the boys which find expression through the form of sexuality and hostility.

## Polarity as a Variation of Sexual Identification

Another variation of the problem of sexuality and dilemma can be noted in a polarity that springs up among the boys. When a boy indicates that he is probably possessed with too many feminine traits and has failed to demonstrate his ultra masculine compulsiveness, he finds himself in a conflict situation. The boys who fall in the category of being feminine, weak, and cowards are called by various names. They may be called "fruits" or "crackouts" or "chickens." They are resented and attacked by the other boys who see themselves as the tough and strong boys. There is a definite polarity that exists between these groups. Social relationships follow these lines in great part. There is also a vague feeling that the matter of legality and conformity to the institution's rules are associated with being the "crackout" or the "fruit."

The failure to have had a significant identification and emotional attachment with the father in early childhood produces many problems for these boys who come to industrial schools. There is resentment and belligerence toward the male figure because of the desertion and alienation that has existed between the child and his father. The above discussion indicates the effects of the over-identification with the female figure and the reaction formations that develop. There are also culture patterns that exist which clearly indicate the further problems that the boys have with their male identification anxieties. Again the aspect of polarity is very important. The males with whom the boys would identify are the adult personnel in the institution. These might be teachers, the shop attendants, the administrators, the clinical and social service personnel and others. If a boy identifies with one of the male personnel, the other boys begin to tell him that this man "is your daddy." Such a statement is said with resentment and anger, and to be told that one of the employees is "your daddy" is a negative and destructive thing. Further dynamics of the situation are very involved. In the first place the boy may feel that the male figures have been desertive and often objectionable people in his past life. There is some resentment. A boy feels he should not trust a man because of the past experiences of desertion and hatred from the father. Again, if he does identify with the male, he is aligning himself with the adult authoritarian structure of the institution and such a process holds much negative sanction among the boys. Then the sexuality angle develops because if a boy tells another boy that a particular male figure in the institution is "your daddy," the ultimate meaning is that this man must be having sexual relations with the mother of that boy. The emotional dynamite here is vast. The tension is again increased when such a culture pattern has an important place in the lives of these children.

A further aspect of the problem of polarity in the institutional social structure appears. There is reason to believe that in some institutions some boys are actually strengthened in their delinquent adjustments. The dynamics involved here are very intense and subtle. Many boys come to a correctional institution with some very deep personal anger and hostility toward their worlds and significant people in them. They have often been brutalized to the point where they manifest a hardened exterior with a very deeply embedded cynicism and anger toward the parent figures and the broader social systems. They often react against the dominant value structure and develop the feeling that anything that is valuable and acceptable for the dominant culture is wrong for them and vice versa. The boy becomes polarized in regard to the feeling that he cannot become a significant figure in the culture around him and thus he develops a feeling of alienation from the culture. If he has been brutalized through vindictive and cruel punishment or observation of very distraught parent figures, he frequently develops strong feelings of cynicism and hostility and further alienates himself from the world around him. He frequently begins to strike out aggressively against legalized norms and the people whose function it is to administer control in the culture. He begins to feel that he cannot possibly accept legitimate standards because a compromise would mean weakness or laying himself open to be hurt further in his relations with people who he feels are so very different from him. If an institution has within it a structure of punishment and discipline that is largely corporal and vindictive and prolonged punishment, the chances are that the boy who functions with alienated feelings and deep hostility will be further reinforced in these feelings and become a dangerous or potentially explosive individual. Some institutions insure the world of having murderers and destructive criminals and delinquents through their treatment program if it is one that deals with conflicts through abuse and terror and irrational retribution. The real movement of the individual in this situation seems to be further alienation from the dominant culture. The alienation is colored with hostility and rigorous cynicism. The world is cruel and the only way to cope with it is by being more cruel and strong. This description is frequently too real in too many cases of children who become brutalized and express their dismay and anger through the most atrocious behavior patterns.

## Culture Patterns Which Emphasize Weak and Negative Aspects of the Child

Another culture pattern that exists in the institutional structure refers to the problem of self-concept and the fact that people do act in terms of the way they deeply feel about themselves. When a boy comes to the school, he is accepted into the group of boys either with ease or with varying amounts of difficulty. He is scrutinized by the boys and then is evaluated by them in terms of his abilities and toughness and the factors of confidence among the boys and the polarity with the administrative staff. He is also viewed as an individual. Unfortunately, the boys tend to select the physically maladjusted or psychologically inhibiting aspects of the other children and then to use them further to strengthen any negative feelings that the boy might have about himself. If he has a number of pimples on his face, he is referred to as "pimples." If he has a limp in his walk, he is referred to as the "crip" or "popo." If he has scars on his face or body, he is called "scars." If he is overweight, he is called "blimp." If he is underweight, he is called "boney." There are many of these negative nicknames that are given to the boys. Very rarely is there a positive one. There seem to be strong indications that the boys are attempting to deride the fellow students, apparently in the belief that it heightens their own status to do so.

Most of the boys who are sent to industrial schools have fairly negative self-concepts. They see themselves as being very worthless and bad individuals. The institutional structure often creates a psychological situation which reinforces these negative self-concepts. The manner in which a person feels about himself is very meaningful in terms of his behavior in specific situations.

Most of the boys who come to correctional institutions are boys who are not able to accept the responsibility of their behavior. They do not have the internalized controls that are necessary for them to realize and accept the consequences of their behavior. Many are consistently excusing themselves and trying to find means of escape from any personal responsibility. As a result, persons who are working with them in various problem areas must always be consistent and fair in their dealings. Any mistake they might make is a means of escape from responsibility for the boy. If he is accused of stealing a pen from a desk drawer and he really took some paper clips, he immediately feels that he was "framed" because he did not take the pen at all. He feels that he is being unjustly accused because he did not take the pen. He cannot generalize to the larger act of theft and see his responsibility for that behavior. There are many of these experiences in the every-day lives of these children which point out their inability to accept responsibility for their behavior and their intense means of finding ways which will eliminate their having to accept any responsibility.

A correctional institution is a very complicated place with many events occurring every day. Every interpersonal relation that develops is important in the total structure of social interaction. The culture patterns that exist are often very good indicators of the individual and group problems that exist. These culture patterns need to be thoroughly understood and dealt with by the staff that is trained to rehabilitate the children. A diagnosis can be developed from the effects of the patterns that develop in the institution and this diagnosis can be effective in therapy.

## 30. How Can the Correctional School Correct?

### Charles H. Shireman

The author is Assistant Professor of Delinquency Control and Corrections, School of Social Service Administration, University of Chicago. He has the degree of Master of Social Work from the School of Social Welfare, University of California (Los Angeles). He spent four years with the Welfare Council of Metropolitan Chicago as Director of the Hyde Park Youth Project and as Consultant on Delinquency to the Council; four years as consultant on child welfare to the U.S. High Commission to Germany, U.S. State Department; and seven years with the King County Juvenile Court, Seattle, the last three as Supervisor of Probation. He has engaged in various research projects, as consultant, staff member, or director of survey teams. He has published various articles on phases of juvenile delinquency.

Probably all of us who have anything to do with the care of young people in correctional schools have been asked accusingly, "You say

Charles H. Shireman, "How Can the Correctional School Correct?" *Crime and Delinquency*, 6 (1960), 267-274. Reprinted with permission of the National Council on Crime and Delinquency.

you want to help me, but what good is it going to do to keep me locked up for months at a time?" And most of us would admit that occasionally we have a disquieting and guilt-producing fear that we can't answer the question satisfactorily.

We are convinced—or at least we hope—that institutional care *will* help, but we cannot always say exactly *how*. In many cases, too, we see youths leaving the correctional school and fear that we have failed with them; often, we don't honestly know why.

In recent years we have done much to eliminate faulty practices; now, we should know precisely what we may expect the correctional school to accomplish, how it can do this—and what it cannot do.

We now generally agree that our task—at least in theory—is to re-educate and rehabilitate, rather than to provide mere incarceration or retributive punishment. For a long time we have assured the general public, legislators, and one another that this is the cornerstone of our policy. Yet we are not quite clear ourselves about what the institution can actually do in the way of re-education and rehabilitation.

What should the correctional school do for its charges? It is surprising how frequently one still hears the view, from institutional personnel as well as from interested citizens, that what delinquent youth needs is punishment as a deterrent—and more severe punishment if the deterrent doesn't seem at first to deter.

Another group thinks our primary goal is to provide more individual therapy. The extreme proponents of this view see the correctional school as a sort of holding center where children are housed and cared for while they wait for their treatment hours. Daily life in the institution is important, but largely as an adjunct to individual therapy.

From another discouraged group—perhaps the fastest growing of all —comes the suspicion that the correctional institution has in fact little to offer in the way of rehabilitation. At best, some say, such an institution can protect youngsters for a time from injuring themselves or the public. It may hold them until, in at least a few cases, the natural process of maturation brings greater stability. The supporters of this theory hope that, if a child is kept "on ice" for a few months or years, somehow he or his environment may change for the better before he is released.

None of these theories is very frequently set forth in scholarly papers. Usually they are not stated formally at all; they are, however, implied in the actions of many persons who are actually doing the job in the institution, or who are determining the job others shall do.

Many of us would not agree with any of these approaches, or would say that each of them plays a part in a much more complicated whole. But as long as we fail to clarify the goals we do set for ourselves, as long as we fail to state exactly what sort of experience we think the institution should provide its wards, we are tremendously handicapped.

This handicap is particularly obvious where staff training is concerned. Most of us believe that staff training programs are necessary—but some of us have seen even conscientiously planned programs fail. One reason for such failure is that staff training programs often do not have a precise definition of the institution's task to work on.[1] We intend our training program to give our staff a deeper understanding of the personalities of our charges, but we make it so broad that it scarcely seems to apply to practice. Indeed, until we decide much more precisely what we are trying to do for our wards, we are obligated either to make our program broad and theoretical, or to concentrate on a day-by-day functioning on the job.

This writer is sure that the institution's task cannot be summed up by such short phrases as "deterrent treatment" or "individual psychotherapy," or "protective care." Neither does he think, indeed, that he himself can describe the institution's task fully. He doubts whether we have yet applied to institutions enough of our knowledge of the human personality for anyone to be able to do this. However, some of the experiences which the correctional school can provide do stand out as particularly important.

## A Healthy Experience with Authority

One of our goals should certainly be to give the institutional ward a healthy relationship with authority figures. Rebellion against authority, whether of the parent, the school, or society in general, is one of the most common elements in the personality of delinquent youth. Case studies show that this rebellion tends to come about as a quite natural result of embittering experience. Parents, or others who have represented authority to the child, may have taught him to fear, hate, or despise authority and the persons who exercise it. Such people may have been hostile, inconsistent, or weak in their treatment of the child or may have rejected or misunderstood him. The youth to whom authority has been so represented throughout his formative years will carry over his attitudes into other situations. This has frequently been

---

[1] This is not always true, however. See, for example: Alex C. Sherrifs and Mary Duren, "The Los Guilicos Project" and "Increasing the Effectiveness of Correctional Institution Staff," *California Youth Authority Quarterly*, Fall, 1950, pp. 7-21, and Winter, 1950, pp. 3-20. Many of the ideas in this paper were stimulated by these articles on an imaginative in-service training program.

at the root of his antisocial behavior. When such a boy comes to the institution he will not interpret a rule or a command in the way in which (we hope) it is given. He automatically resents it and, depending on the nature of his experience with authority in the past, may either struggle against it or evade it.

Our task, therefore, is to help the young person understand through experience that authority can be exercised firmly but fairly, with sympathetic regard for his welfare and with respect for him as a worthwhile person, entitled to have his wishes and rights considered. We can't do this merely by "reasoning" with a youngster. Words aren't enough. He must learn by living with authority that *is* firm, fair, and based on the conviction that the institutional ward remains a human being—one extraordinarily sensitive to the abuse of authority and to being "kicked around."

To provide such an environment is perhaps the most difficult task the institution faces. It must be staffed by personnel who can learn to exercise the proper authority and who can continue to do so even though, as the maxim has it, "power corrupts." They must be so richly mature and so well provided with helpful supervision that they use their power only in the interests of their job of personality reconstruction, never for their own satisfaction.

Every staff member must make a constant, conscientiously honest scrutiny of his own use of authority. We must carefully analyze every order we give, every regulation we enforce. We must understand how our order is going to appear to the ward, and what are our motives in giving it. Is it actually necessary to the welfare of the ward or of the group? If so, does the ward understand this? If he does not, can we explain it to him so that he will see its necessity? Does the ward reject our order because of the *manner* in which we gave it? Have we shown him that we respect him and his wishes and have taken them into consideration as much as possible? Or are we looking for the easy way out and enforcing an unnecessary or senseless order or one calculated to meet our own need for recognition or power? Are we being honest with the boy? Are we being careful that he sees that we are being honest with him?

In short, is the ward's experience with authority in the institution a corrective one? Will it give a new, healthier concept of the nature of authority? Or will it further embitter him, further convince him that authority is something to evade, to struggle against, and to hate?

## Use of Limits

Proper limits upon youngsters' behavior can be of value to them. By setting such limits, we can provide an environment simple enough for a youngster to master; in mastering this simple society he may gain confidence and learn techniques for mastering the more complicated world outside the institution. For the adolescent must, in his normal life, make a great many difficult choices between right and wrong, between short-term desires and long-term values and between socially approved and antisocial behavior. His mother and father can no longer make decisions for him. He is becoming an independent person, and at the same time he is becoming aware of urges and temptations that he was only vaguely aware of before.

Many youngsters, because of faulty endowment or damaging life experience, are simply not capable of accepting this responsibility. They cannot cope with the freedom of choice and the variety of temptations that adolescence brings. They are not "grown up" enough to postpone immediate satisfaction in favor of the ethically right, or the socially acceptable, or even of long-term personal gain.

The institution may serve at least some of these young people like the sanitarium which provides rest care for t.b. victims. Such care protects the patient against the demands that life makes upon his energies. All his strength can be devoted to the fight against his disease.

By the same token, the correctional school ward may need protection against many of the demands of life. He may need to have some of the most difficult decisions made for him by the limits the institution sets on his behavior; then he can use all his moral and psychological strength to solve a smaller number of problems. He will still have to make decisions on questions of right and wrong and conformance or nonconformance, but the decisions will be fewer, and their results more immediate and more clear. He may thus gain confidence by learning to master these small problems successfully and may begin to discover his own strengths and to see the possibility of gaining satisfaction from self-control and social conformity. Ultimately he may come to appreciate the value of right for right's sake.

Obviously the limits set by the institution must not be too narrow. If the youngster is to learn to make choices, he must have some room to choose. He must have the opportunity to learn from trial and error; his initiative must not be stifled. Too much restriction leads to "institutionalization"—the creation of persons unable to live outside the sheltering walls of the institution. But in the proper use of limits upon behavior we may have another tool for the reconstruction of personality.

## Socially Acceptable Achievement

Another valuable experience that we can give our wards is that of achievement of a goal that society approves. Many youngsters rarely, if ever, have known the feeling of self-confidence and social approval that such achievement brings. Unsure that they are loved and wanted at home, entering school unprepared or ill-equipped and gaining from it only a sense of failure, personal inadequacy, and social rejection, and seeing no way open to them to function successfully as conforming adults, they have sometimes turned to antisocial activities, partially as a means of showing themselves and others that they are capable, adult, and virile. Auto theft, bullying aggression, or demonstration of sexual prowess are ways of gaining a sort of recognition and feeling of personal accomplishment they cannot otherwise get.

There are many ways in which the correctional school can help its wards to gain this feeling of personal achievement. Sports programs, assignment of tasks or functions with which recognition is associated, shop and trade programs are all possibilities. The academic school program, also, can do something even more important than teaching the "three R's." It can give the youngster a chance to start work at a level at which he can be successful, and stimulate him to move forward at a pace which challenges without defeating. With such a program, many youngsters may for the first time in their lives see school as something other than a baffling series of frustrations marking them as failures. Success breeds success, and the boy may begin to think of himself as one who is capable of functioning successfully in society instead of as the eternal "dummy."

A prerequisite of such a program is, of course, sound diagnosis of each boy's *strengths* as well as of his limitations. Our clinical studies must seek the positives in the youngster's personality to help us determine what we can build upon. All too often we may search through these studies and find detailed analysis of a youngster's failures and weaknesses but little recognition of his strengths.

## Peer Relationships

Many of the young people who come to us have never been able to get along with others of their own age. Some have drawn into themselves and have, to varying degrees, become social isolates. Others have become very aggressive in their attempt to force people to recognize and accept them. But the basic trouble with many of the children is that they are lonely or unhappy, or unsure that they are loved and liked by others. We may be able to do little about whatever it is that caused the trouble originally. But we may very well be able to provide our wards with an environment that will at least help them to begin to achieve social acceptance in their own age group.

The social pressures of group life may do much to help. Many young people are adaptable enough to learn from their fellows in a group that tends to enforce codes of social living. They begin to understand some of the elements of successful group membership: mutual tolerance, ability to cooperate, and ability to live with others without losing their own identity.

But we are treading on dangerous ground here. We dare not merely throw a boy into a group and trust that the experience will be beneficial. Other youngsters can be cruel, both physically and in less tangible ways. The boy who becomes a member of a poorly supervised group may be made to feel more inadequate than ever, or may be driven to try to solve his problem by becoming even more bullyingly aggressive.

We must, therefore, see that the youngsters do not go beyond reasonable limits in their treatment of each other. Our wards, who are usually deeply disturbed youngsters who have not solved their own problems, tend to be angry and resentful at the world and to "take out" their feelings on anyone they can. They should never be permitted, for example, to administer punishment to others. How can we possibly expect them to think objectively of the needs of the one to be punished, as they would have to do in order to administer punishment that would help rather than harm the recipient?

However, supervision must not only restrict; it must be positive, too. Wise counseling can provide encouragement and advice to the timid, and friendly caution to the overaggressive. Some of our wards simply do not know the fundamentals of getting along in a group. Often we can help them to understand that they can best win the liking of others by showing that they like others, or we can show them the results of their own boastful or bullying behavior.

Proper activity programs can also help in the teaching of group citizenship. Sports, group games, and other recreation are often thought of only as rather unimportant ways of permitting youngsters an occasional good time, or as a sort of indulging or pampering of our wards. But, as some other countries have come to realize sooner than we, such activities can actually provide valuable training. Activities should be varied enough to give as much opportunity as possible for everyone to participate; they should provide a healthy group experience which exploits the potentialities of each child and helps him find his place in the group. Such programs can teach our wards to be cooperating citizens of society by actually functioning as citizens of a small group. It is most unfortunate that often our recreation and sports programs are unplanned and only incidental to the institution's main program. Actually, they should be considered a major resource for correctional work: they should be planned just as carefully as our academic training and should be led by personnel possessing qualifications just as high as those of our academic teachers.

Another problem is that the boys in an institution tend to form a complex of unofficial, sometimes little-recognized subgroups whose goals and identifications are different from those of the institution's staff. Such groups often determine the institution's impact upon the individdual. We cannot eliminate these cliques and friendship groups, although all too often we tend either to try to do so or to ignore them. We must, however, constantly seek ways of penetrating them. Perhaps we can learn from the work of the street gang workers, who have recently been functioning in so creative a way in some cities. We may be able to apply the same techniques to our problem in the institution. We may be able to do much through the right type of adult effort to meet such groups on their own ground, to identify with some of their goals in a legitimate manner. We must seek the friendly acceptance of such groups, and try to develop shared goals and interests with them, and to build bridges between them and the administration.

## Relationship with an Older Adult

Almost all adolescents pass through a stage of hero-worship of an older acquaintance or associate. They will imitate this person's mannerisms, ways of speaking, and attitudes and will frequently want to choose the same career. As they are leaving childhood they seize upon this figure as the representation of the kind of adult they hope to become. Of course, it is vitally important to society that the man whom the adolescent chooses to imitate and follow be the right kind of person.

In the case of the normal, healthy youngster this "hero" may be a school teacher, an athletic coach, a recreation leader, an employer, or some other person capable of wielding a powerful influence for good. But the youngster who grows up in an antisocial environment, or who has a hard time getting along with people who seem to him to represent either an authority which he resents or a society that has been hostile and has rejected him, may choose someone quite different. This may be a gang leader, a criminal, or some other strongly antisocial figure.

In the correctional school we should try to give as many of our wards as possible a chance to find desirable models. We can't force a young person to choose us in this way. But if we respect the youngsters in our charge, and show our understanding of and interest in them, we will often find ourselves playing this role. If we can represent true social values to our charges we will provide them with one of life's best educational experiences.

## Moral Values

It is not unreasonable to hope that our wards will leave the institution with a strengthened sense of the value of "right for right's sake"—with a desire to avoid delinquent behavior not only because it might bring punishment but because it is wrong. But although we may hope that ideas of basic honesty and respect for the rights of others will gain some ground, we certainly cannot be sure that this will happen.

Youngsters learn from their experience of life. And many of them have learned, from their families and neighborhoods, that it is simply not practical to live by doing what is right for its own sake. We can't combat this lesson from life by lectures. But we can combat it to some degree by giving our charges a different, more positive experience of life. Do we wish our youngsters to learn respect for the rights of others? All right: let us show them that others respect their rights. Do we want them to gain some concept of basic honesty? Then let us be sure that they see that we are honest with them. In a fair number of years of experience the writer can remember very few cases in which it was either ethically or, in the long run, practically desirable to lie to a youngster. But he can, unfortunately, remember a great many cases in which a lie has been told.

Here, then, is another experience that the correctional school must strive to give young persons in its care—a living lesson in social ethics, learnt through being on the receiving end of ethical behavior.

## The Role of Counseling

Thus far we have spoken almost entirely of the rehabilitative possibilities of wisely controlled group-living. We have made very little mention of the role of individual counseling. However, such counseling is probably the indispensable "other half" of the experience we should offer youth under our care.

Without individual counseling, our wards are quite liable to misinterpret the experience they are undergoing, for they will interpret it in terms of their own pasts. Those whose experience has been that adults in authority over them are hostile, selfish, and inconsistent will expect all authority to be of this nature. Consequently, they will automatically fear and hate any person, or rule, or regulation which symbolizes authority.

In the institution we wish to use authority only as a way to help the child and to teach him how to fit into society and to be happy. With the best intentions, we impose upon him rules and regulations that are carefully planned for his welfare. But he doesn't see them that way. Since his life has taught him that all authority is hateful, he sees us just as so many additions to the long line of persons who have been "kicking him around."

Individualized counseling can help many youngsters to see for the first time that their present experience with authority is different from their past experience. Frequently it can help them to see that they are uselessly rebelling against something that no longer exists. Sometimes a youngster comes to realize this when the counselor helps him to think back over past unhappy experiences, talk about them, come to understand them better, and come to see the difference between past relationships with authority and present ones. In other cases, close examination of an unhappy past may be neither wise nor possible. The counselor may restrict himself to helping the youngster analyze and understand the experience he is having at the moment. But in either event the counselor must help the youngsters to see that they must revise their ideas about the attitudes of people in authority over them. Only then can they profit from the new experience we are trying to offer them, for only then can they understand it.

Counseling is just as necessary to help us attain all the institution's other goals. None of our efforts can be constructive unless the ward understands them in the manner in which they are meant. All of them are liable to misinterpretation unless the ward, through patient and skillful counseling, learns to evaluate them correctly.

This writer, like most others in the field, has been baffled by many cases. Youngsters with whom he has worked hardest have sometimes failed most miserably. Others who had shown few indications of successful adjustment have made tremendous progress. We are still at the pioneering stage in our profession. There is much that we do not see, or see only vaguely, and much of what we do see we do not understand.

We are still groping with poorly formed tools to reach "shores dimly seen." But we are learning constantly. One way to advance is surely by the constant and painstaking analysis of the experience we offer our wards, and the way in which they assimilate it.

## 31.  The Institution as Therapist

### George E. Gardner

The author, a psychiatrist, is Director of the Judge Baker Guidance Center in Boston. He has had wide experience in teaching, the practice of psychiatry, as a consultant, and as editor of the *American Journal of Orthopsychiatry*. His writings have appeared in numerous professional publications.

It is accurate, I believe, to state that the community expects the institution to change the individual delinquent. It expects it to return him to the community a law-abiding citizen, with social, educational, and occupational aims and attitudes consistent with those expected from, demanded of, and expressed by the majority of youngsters of comparable age. The changes that it expects, then, are not changes such as the acquirement of specific skills or educational accomplishments, save in relation to the rudiments of interpersonal relationships.

In this context of our expectations we can, for purposes of discussion, consider the institution as a whole as a psychotherapeutic unit and proceed as if we regarded it as a therapist. I am not unmindful of the fact that an institution is a group of people, each with his or her own assets and shortcomings as a person giving treatment, but I am sure that you will allow me this excursion into a modified anthropomorphism so that I may stress the importance of attitudes and principles.

Let us proceed clinically in this institutional analogy and outline: First of all, the chief complaint; secondly, the therapeutic goal; and, finally, the therapeutic process as it evolves.

1. The chief complaint. I think it is a fair estimate that in 90 per cent of delinquency cases the community's chief complaint is that the child is hostile and aggressive. Hostility and aggressiveness are apparent in that these children break and enter, steal other people's property, as-

George E. Gardner, "The Institution as Therapist," *The Child*, 16 (January, 1952), 70-72, U.S. Department of Health, Education and Welfare, Washington, D.C.

sault and damage, refuse to go to school, and resent the authority of the community and the home. Such is the chief complaint of society. It is manifest and vocal and it is expressed in the application of certain corrective and punishing restraints.

But the "chief complaint" of the child himself—the one in which the therapist-institution is primarily concerned—although parallel, is by no means so apparent and clear. It is for the most part hidden and covert. But long-continued psychotherapy of individual delinquents has repeatedly given us data relative to these latent concepts, drives, and attitudes, and I shall cite them briefly.

The majority of our studies would indicate that the chief and nuclear personality defects in these boys and girls are brought about by their concept of the external world and the human beings in it, and their concept of self. The delinquent's concept of the external world is a world that is at all points aggressive, destructive, and primitive. By this I mean that for hundreds of "reasons" based on adverse interpersonal experiences of an extremely harsh—and at times almost psychopathological—nature, the delinquent's concept of the human beings in the world is that they are definitely not human in the sense that we believe them to be.

We need not go into the complex, highly charged emotional experiences in the early lives of these children that have led to the formulation of this concept. Suffice it to say that in their eyes, although they do not realize it, human beings have in great abundance the attributes, the attitudes, and the methods of operation of the predatory animal. Through their experience, delinquents in their earliest and predelinquent years have become highly sensitized to the expressed, and particularly the unexpressed, hostility of which all human beings are capable; and they have, on the other hand, been deprived of those corrective emotional experiences that modify this sensitivity in the homes where children are genuinely wanted and unconditionally loved.

It is difficult for you and me to entertain a concept of a human being (every human being) as (as one delinquent adolescent revealed to me) a cobra that sways into a position to strike when any other animal (meaning himself) comes near. But it is not difficult for us to envisage what lack of warmth this boy, or ourselves, would reasonably expect from human beings if such was our concept of them—or, in turn, how much warmth could reasonably be expected of us in our dealing with such humans. Nor is it difficult for us to appreciate the difficulty such an individual has in identifying with adults, and the seeming ease with which he can identify with other persons, the major aspects of whose concepts are similar to his own.

I assure you that this is not an extraordinary or unexpected unconscious concept that this boy holds. It can be duplicated as typical of the nuclear human-being concept in case after case. This is the chief complaint of the delinquent himself, rarely recognized without guidance, voiced only under the stimulus of a treatment relationship, but nonetheless operative in his behavior with deadly and disabling repetitiveness.

Concomitant with this, and equally disabling in its behavioral expression, is the delinquent's own concept of self—again usually unconscious and unexpressed save in the treatment setting. His nuclear concept of himself is that he too is a hostile, aggressive, predatory animal, driven by urges he does not completely understand to wrest from this environment of humans whatever he can—either through mutilative or destructive methods or by a process of leechlike osmosis—or by both methods.

How he arrives at such a concept of self we in psychiatry are only now beginning to envision dimly; but we are convinced that this is a very prevalent concept, that it is due to development faults or arrests in what usually is orderly personality growth, and that it is just at this point (in relation to the concept of self) that the elements common to delinquent behavior and neurotic behavior are beginning to become apparent. It probably goes without saying, in this connection, that punishing an individual who has this self-concept not only will not alter the concept itself, but on the contrary will go far in confirming within the child the very attitude which is the motivation and source of power for his antisocial behavior. With such a concept of self, too, it is not difficult to explain the almost total lack of self-respect which is noted in our delinquents.

The presence of self-respect necessitates the internal concept of oneself as a worth-while human being together with the frequent demonstration of respect externally on the part of others acting like human beings. Unfortunately, we do too little at the present time to break this cycle of concept relationships by a treatment "attack" on the nuclear ingredients of both.

2. The therapeutic aim. Such is the "chief complaint"—the child's disabling concept of his external world of humans. It is our fundamental hypothesis that this is so. The therapeutic aim or treatment goal is to alter these concepts as speedily as we can in all cases, and as thoroughly as is necessary in the individual case.

The means by which these changes can be effected are varied, and none of them are easy. It would be fine, of course, if every delinquent were to be treated individually by a skilled psychotherapist. But you and I know this to be a practical impossibility. At the present time we can get but an approximation to this type of program, and in the majority of instances cannot get it at all. And this, for a number of reasons, is perhaps particularly true in respect to boys and girls who are remanded to correctional institutions.

However, it is apparent to me that the institution itself—its collective personnel—can go far in initiating these changes in concepts that seem to be so necessary. Whether or not the institution has enough specialized personnel, the institution itself can forward this psychotherapeutic process, and can and should do so, with an understanding of—and a conscious use of—some basic principles and steps in the treatment process that seem to operate in all psychotherapy—individual, group, or institutional. Let us look at the institution as therapist.

3. The institution-therapist. There are at least four well-definable steps in the psychotherapeutic process—any psychotherapeutic process —and the institution can orient and outline its total program, and particularly its over-all treatment philosophy, in respect to them.

(a) There is, first of all, the establishment of the optimal treatment relationship—the positive transference relationship, if you will. This positive relationship is, in its very essence, a noncombative and nonaggressive relationship. It is accepting and permissive, but not to the stage of unlimited freedom of individual expression and license that arouses a feeling of guilt. It is permissiveness broadly drawn, but fairly and consistently drawn, and the limits thereto are set at a point to control the child's own instinctual drives, which he himself fears, and to control the aggressiveness of his associated colleagues and superiors, which he also fears. If the child is to alter his concepts of himself and others at all, such changes will only take place in a milieu—an institution, if you will —of such security and noncombativeness. Education and growth just will not take place save in the presence of security feelings.

(b) The second stage in the therapeutic process is the revelation or exposure of unconscious or only dimly conscious impulses, drives, and needs that govern our behavior with other human beings—those of equal status and those of authoritative or supervisory status above us. It might be thought that a cognizance of such impulses and of their efficacious or disabling effects upon our interpersonal relationships could be brought about only through long intensive individual psychotherapy, and of course to a certain degree and in certain respects this is undoubtedly true. However, I submit that great numbers of individuals to whom a psychoanalytic procedure is not available—by the very fact of continued inevitable contacts with other people in groups—do arrive at an appreciable degree of insight as to their own underlying motives. Surely institutional living does no less—and perhaps can do more than ordinary life contacts, through its general and specific programs—to bring these impulses to self-attention. It is in the experience of all of us doing individual therapy with delinquents—though too infrequently—that youngsters have returned to us from institutions where individual work is at a minimum—to be amazed at the beneficial insights they have arrived at through group living in a correctional institution.

(c) A third element in the therapeutic process is technically referred to as confrontation and interpretation of our behavioral patterns. It is a making clear to us repeatedly of just what we seem to be trying to do. This, too, goes on apace in institutional living, whether we are aware of it or not. It is done wittingly or unwittingly by the child's associates at all times, and it is done by housemasters and teachers and administrators as an integral part of their jobs. The institution as a whole is a confronting and an interpretative agent, and all directing personnel within it should be aware of their opportunities to forward this aspect of the total institutional treatment process. As I suggested above, however, none of these broader educational elements of institution life will have a beneficial effect unless done in a nonaggressive relationship motivated by the desire to help.

(d) Finally, in the treatment process, comes the inevitable stage when trial and error learning must emerge—when the individual child will make the first tentative attempts to change his behavior through a modification of his previous concept of self and others. The institution in its programs—educational, social, athletic, vocational, and so forth, provides (or should provide) numerous opportunities for such trials, and its personnel should be alert to the initial endeavors of the child in change. Here in abundance are the need for and the opportunities for the application of those genuinely therapeutic devices of suggestion, advice, encouragement, sympathy at the time of failure, approval, prestige citation through work or house assignments—all these and many more whose value we are inclined at times to minimize. The institution can make for changes in self-concepts as noted above, and it also has ample opportunity to provide suitable outlets for the feelings that are expressed in trial behavior, and to guide those feelings.

Such, then, is the institution in its totality as a therapeutic unit, as the psychiatrist might view it. The chief complaints of the delinquent boy or girl are disabling concepts of self and human beings as a whole; the therapeutic aim is to change these concepts to the extent that both concepts include values truly human. The therapist is "the institution treating"—treating through all of the constructive personal relationships and through all of the activities that it is able to offer. And regardless of the presence of the highly skilled individual or group psychotherapists that we so sorely need, treatment success will only be assured when the institution is genuinely treatment-oriented.

## 32.  The California Youth Authority Psychiatric Treatment Program, Its Historical Significance and Philosophy

Mark Lewis Gerstle

> The author is Chief Psychiatrist to the Youth Authority, State of California.

For many years the problem of dealing with emotionally disturbed teen-aged delinquents has confronted California courts, probation departments, the Youth Authority, Department of Mental Hygiene and many private agencies. Many different committees have been established through the years to study this problem, which in 1955 became so critical that judges in some of the larger counties communicated with members of the Legislature in order to get a legislative policy with regard to it.

Representatives of the California State Senate and Assembly met with representatives of the 11 western states under the auspices of the Council of State Governments and learned that the same serious problems exist in these states.

In the 1956 Census of Special Problem Cases, the Youth Authority reported that about 17 per cent of the persons admitted to the Youth Authority could be classified as "special problem delinquents" who, because of emotional disturbance, could not be expected to benefit from the existing correctional and rehabilitation program. Such wards of the state, although relatively few in number, create a tremendous impact. They occupy a kind of institutional "no man's land" since there appears to be no proper place for them in regular mental hospitals or in existing institutions for the mentally deficient. They require more efforts to rehabilitate and a greater amount of staff time. More important, many adult criminals come from among them. It is clear that psychiatric care and treatment is seriously needed for them.

At the 1956 legislative session the matter was referred to the Assem-

Mark Lewis Gerstle, "The California Youth Authority Psychiatric Treatment Program," *California Medicine,* 92 (1960), 277-279. Reprinted by permission of the California Medical Association and the author.

bly Interim Committee on Social Welfare under the chairmanship of the Honorable Bruce F. Allen, Assemblyman. On June 22, 1956, this committee called together a group representing the courts, probation departments, the Department of Mental Hygiene, the Youth Authority and the Department of Corrections to discuss the problem. From the testimony given by all persons present it was decided that the Youth Authority should address itself to this problem. By resolution, the committee requested the Youth Authority to do the staff work necessary to meet the problem, including the drafting of legislation and the preparation of plans for appropriate buildings and staff at Youth Authority institutions.

An amendment to the Welfare and Institutions Code was passed by the 1957 Legislature which provides that the Youth Authority shall also accept "a person committed to it . . . if he is a borderline psychotic or borderline mentally deficient case, if he is a sex deviate unless he is of a type whose presence in the community under parole supervision would present a menace to the public welfare, or if he suffers from a primary behavior disorder."

In August of 1957 a development committee for Psychiatric Treatment Units was organized within the Youth Authority to develop the program. In the original proposal by the agency, Psychiatric Treatment Units were to be placed in each of the existing Youth Authority facilities. However, the Legislature, recognizing the vast extent of the problem, the lack of precedent and the problems involved in organization and procurement of buildings and professional personnel, was careful to authorize the establishment of the Psychiatric Treatment Units on a staggered basis providing sufficient time for the development of plans, procedures, and training. The units were initially authorized at Preston School of Industry and Los Guilucos School for Girls, with the third Psychiatric Treatment Unit to begin operation after July 1, 1959, at the Fred C. Nelles School for Boys.

## Concepts of Treatment and Psychotherapy

Although all psychotherapy is treatment, all treatment is not psychotherapy. This distinction is of more than academic value. The warm-hearted solicitude, encouragement and understanding of a house-mother, for instance, is often invaluable. No one can say that her endeavor on behalf of one of her charges is not treatment, yet this cannot be called psychotherapy in any accurate sense. Another way of putting this, is to state that not everything that is helpful is treatment, although certainly all treatment must be helpful.

## Objectives and Rationale of Psychotherapy

Psychotherapy as carried out in the Youth Authority gives the patient carte blanche to say anything that comes into his mind which will, to the best of his ability, express his feelings. It is our firm conviction that, with such freedom encouraged, the chances of such a patient's acting out these aggressions and resistance are less than they would be if he were not given the opportunity of such expression. In other words, the permissiveness of the therapeutic relationship between patient and therapist is a safety valve and the fact that the patient can and will, if properly encouraged and guided, give vent to any and all antisocial, disrupting contra-mores ideas and feelings will go a long way to relieve pent-up tensions, disruptive aggressions, confusion and anxiety.

To pursue this thought a bit further, the erroneous but far too prevalent notion that psychotherapy and the administrations of a therapist tend to diminish the need for discipline and self-control must be once and for all abandoned. On the contrary, one of the most important and vital roles psychotherapy can play is to gradually bring about greater control and reduce the compulsive irresistible urges and obsessional factors so that the patient can adapt himself better to his environment in the institution, on parole, and eventually in the outside world where he will again take his place. There will be less need to "act out" and a better chance for him to feel that he is a member of society, and that, as such, he must conform to its prescribed ethics. He acquires respect for other human beings with whom he will always have to deal. To the extent that these goals are attained, he will then learn to incorporate within himself the feeling that he "belongs"—that he no longer is an outcast, that he has a place under the sun, and that, without servility and without demanding inappropriate or exorbitant solicitude, he can respect and be respected.

Every effort in therapy is directed toward inculcating self-esteem without enough of which a human being either retreats into despair, depression and apathy, or, in order to spare himself the conscious pain of his inadequacies, proceeds to overcompensate, thus becoming an antisocial, lawless, aggressive menace to society, which is the core of the delinquency pattern.

It is necessary to be just as concerned about the status and needs of the troubled child as about the troublesome one. Of course, greater clinical acumen is needed for recognition of the former in order to bring him to treatment.


## Psychotherapy Can Save Money

It is expensive to care for the sick regardless of the nature of the symptoms or the disease. Every good hospital in the United States operates in the red even with the aid of usually generous endowments. This is particularly true in large teaching hospitals and those affiliated with a medical school or center. Since, from the clinician's point of view, all the wards of the state with whom we deal are disturbed and also emotionally unstable, as well as usually infantile or immature, they are in this sense sick. The expense, great though it is and will continue to be, can be looked upon as a stitch in time. Money spent now on these children may prove to be the most economical investment the taxpayer could make. The rehabilitation, partial or complete, of one of these children can be expected to pay handsome dividends through saving money that would otherwise go to paying for the damage and the expense of custody that usually follow uncorrected and neglected delinquency.


## Participation in the Research Program

The central office, with the assistance of the Chief of Medical Services, the Consulting Clinical Psychologist and the Chief of the Research Program, aided by the professional staff of each institution, has entered into various research endeavors, some of which are in the category of "pure research" and some of which will be more practical and, therefore, more directly helpful in helping us to deal more efficiently with the Psychiatric Treatment Program.

Good "treatment" can be properly regarded as anything which has a tendency to help the recipient to deal with his anxieties and tribulations.

"Treatment" includes environmental as well as personal impacts. It is clear, therefore, that every locale and every person in the California Youth Authority will have an effect on the wards of the state with whom the Youth Authority deals. The range of such impact is unlimited. It includes such diverse matters as the type of clothing insisted upon, the size, shape and color of the dormitory or room; the convenience and efficiency of the showers and lavatories; the appearance, quantity and quality of the food; the tone of voice in which a gardener or janitor says,

"Good morning"; and, of course, the friendliness and warmth in even the briefest encounter between the ward of the state and every member of the staff. Actually, the ward's initial commitment to the California Youth Authority, followed by a sojourn in a juvenile hall, are also significant but since these are not properly within the control of the California Youth Authority they will not receive any more than this cursory mention. The ward's first actual experience in the California Youth Authority begins at one of the two reception centers. The weeks that he spends there add up to the beginning of a continuum which progresses from the center to the institution, to parole and, finally, to his release to society.

## Integration of Treatment and Custody

One of the most important efforts has been that of integrating "treatment" with custody. As was predictable, these two disciplines can never be expected to completely fuse. There will always be areas of difference of emphasis—there will always be people who stress one aspect of our total responsibility at the expense of the other. Hence constant watch must be kept to hold such hampering differences to a minimum. One hostile or unduly skeptical staff member can greatly diminish the over-all morale of his institution. It is my belief that the task of integration rests more on the Psychiatric Treatment Units than it does on the administrative staff, since the former are trained to understand differences or different points of view and are, therefore, better equipped to reconcile them. It is a great source of satisfaction that such efforts have been proceeding more satisfactorily than we had any reason to hope. The Psychiatric Treatment Units welcome the administrative staffs' participation in their conferences and classifications meetings.

By and large, a remarkable degree of cooperation, mutual understanding and "team play" seems to permeate our institutions. Exceptions, of course, there are; but they are not numerous and, when detected, they are dealt with forthrightly, not in a spirit of rivalry, but with a deep-rooted wish and conviction that all that is necessary is to understand. With mutual understanding comes respect for the attitude and point of view of others, even though these may materially differ from one's own.

In the California Youth Authority schools, institutions and camps that do not have Psychiatric Treatment Units, "treatment" is also of the greatest importance. Counseling, guidance, support, and instruction are all therapeutic. It may be said at this time that it is extremely important who does what to whom—just as important and in some cases more so than what or how he does it. Many staff members are making invaluable contributions to the "treatment" and rehabilitation of their charges, and it is impossible to evaluate these services in terms of their relative importance. It is important, however, for everyone who is doing a good job in this effort to realize it. No one is so broad-shouldered or secure that he does not need the repetitious confirmation of recognition and unsolicited commendation, and it is here that the professional and more experienced members of the Psychiatric Treatment Units can and must play the role of the reassuring and appreciative "father-figure." In general, the stature of any staff member will be in inverse proportion to the amount of encouragement and support he is apt to need and benefit from. This, I think, is a clue to how such efforts should be directed and to whom.

It may be advisable to state that for all intents and purposes "therapy" includes the connotation of psychotherapy; *treatment* can be thought of as broader and more comprehensive. Treatment is, therefore, no prerogative of the medical profession. Hence, it is being lavishly and continuously used by everyone regardless of varying philosophies, disciplines and training. Treatment is largely confined to attempts to deal realistically with conscious material, as brought out verbally by the persons with whom we are dealing. In contradistinction, therapy, and particularly psychotherapy, must take into account motivations which are largely unconscious, and although interpretations on this level are often not clinically indicated, the accomplished therapist can never afford to lose sight of them. They make up the core of his understanding, thereby furthering significantly his useful and meaningful therapy.

## Indoctrination of the Indoctrinators

The indoctrination of the indoctrinators can, therefore, be seen to be an essential; hence it is proper to give time to it. Regularly scheduled meetings and interviews help in the indoctrination, but the effort must go further. It must comprise every single encounter, with the youths themselves and with other members of the staff, in the hallway, in the dining room and in the meetings which take place after hours. For some of these golden opportunities, unofficial, sporadic and spontaneous as they are, may often prove to be the beam of light shining into the darkness of misunderstanding.

## 33.   Camps for Delinquent Boys

## George  H.  Weber

> The author is Director of the Berkshire Farm Institute for Training
> and Research, which opened in 1962 to offer training to persons plan-
> ning to work in the juvenile delinquency field and to carry on re-
> search. He was formerly Chief of the Technical Aid Branch of the
> Delinquency Service Division of the U.S. Children's Bureau. Prior
> to joining the Children's Bureau he was Director of the Division
> of Diagnosis and Treatment of the Youth Conservation Commission,
> State of Minnesota. In addition to publications of the Children's
> Bureau, numerous articles in the field of delinquency are to his credit.

In recent years camps have become increasingly prominent as a way
of helping delinquent boys who must be removed from the community. There are now approximately 50 county, state, and federal camps
providing some measure of training and treatment to a considerable
number of boys, and several states are planning to begin a camp program or increase the number they already have. But a clear statement
of the principles and techniques necessary for the effective operation
of a camp has not yet been developed. Further, the place of a camp in
a network of services for delinquents is far from clear. There are even
differences of opinion as to the need for such camps and as to their
character, if they are to be developed.

This publication is concerned with the planning and operating of
camps, and suggests the lines along which camp programs might be
developed and administered. It does not attempt to measure the effectiveness of current programs, nor offer a critique of their past and present operations. Such evaluations are currently being made in several
states. These will deal with such topics as the extent to which camp
programs have helped the boys who have participated in them. Although
this material touches on such questions, it is not primarily concerned
with them.

Camps for delinquent youth have generally been patterned on the
camps of the Civilian Conservation Corps that were established and

George H. Weber, *Camps for Delinquent Boys, A Guide to Planning,* Children's
Bureau Publication No. 385, U.S. Government Printing Office, Washington, D.C.,
1960, Chapter 1. Reprinted by permission.

operated between 1933 and 1943 [1]  as part of a program to conserve natural resources while providing employment and vocational training. Prior to this, camps had been developed by Los Angeles County, Calif., in 1931 and 1932, to take care of transient youth until arrangements could be made to send them to their legal residences.[2] In 1935 the State of California passed legislation establishing forestry camps to care for delinquent boys.[3] To some extent, the entire movement has been influenced by the European work camps for adolescents.[4]

But organized camping for young people is much older than this. A camp functioning as part of a school program was established in 1861.[5] This, like other camps in that period, emphasized an orderly program of "character building" activities under the supervision of model adults. Today, there are countless summer camps that offer children enjoyable and healthful surroundings.[6] In addition there are many specialized camps. Some of these emphasize therapeutic camping to help the children improve their emotional health.[7] Others stress an educational program to help children with their learning.[8] Still other camps

[1] For reports of this program see: Holland, Kenneth and Hill, Frank E. *Youth in the Civilian Conservation Corps,* Washington: American Council on Education, 1942, 263 pp.; Lorwin, Lewis L. *Youth Work Programs,* Washington: American Council on Education, 1941, 195 pp.; and Wirth, Conrad. *Civilian Conservation Corps Program of the United States Department of the Interior, March 1933 to June 30, 1943,* A Report to Harold L. Ickes, January 1944.

[2] Close, O. H.: "California Camps for Delinquents" in *Social Correctives for Delinquency,* National Probation and Parole Association Yearbook for 1945, New York: National Probation and Parole Association, 328 pp. (pp. 136-147). For other forerunners of the Civilian Conservation Corps, see *The Civilian Conservation Corps,* Washington: American Council on Education, 1940, 23 pp. (pp. 3-4).

[3] See Close, O. H. *op. cit.,* p. 136.

[4] Several European nations had had experience with labor camps for youth prior to the establishment of the Civilian Conservation Corps. Kenneth Holland studied their programs and reported on this in his *Youth in European Labor Camps,* Washington: American Council on Education, 1939, 303 pp.

[5] Ward, Carlos Edgar. *Organized Camping and Progressive Education,* Copyrighted 1935 by C. E. Ward, Galax, Va., 180 pp. (p. 4).

[6] For the philosophy and description of these programs, see Joy, Barbara E. *Annotated Bibliography on Camping,* Martinsville, Ind.: The American Camping Association, 1955, 34 pp.

[7] For a review of the therapeutic camping movement as well as specialized articles in this field, see McNeil, Elton E. (issue editor) "Therapeutic Camping for Disturbed Youth," *Journal of Social Issues,* vol. 13, No. 1, 1957, 63 pp.

[8] For illustrations of these programs, see "Camping and Outdoor Education in California" in *Bulletin of the California State Department of Education,* California State Department of Education, vol. XXI, No. 3, March 1952, 49 pp.; Clarke, James M.: *Public School Camping,* Stanford: Stanford University Press, 1951, 184 pp.; and Thurston, Lee M. *Community School Camps,* Lansing, Mich. Department of Public Instruction, 39 pp.

offer summer employment to boys.[9] Even some training schools for delinquent youth operate a summer camp program to give the boys an outing and constructive employment.[10]

## Types of Camps

### CURRENT PROGRAMS

Against this diverse background, two general categories of camps for delinquents can be seen—those that are primarily oriented toward work and those that have an educational emphasis.[11] Many camps have programs that are mixed in character and all strive to provide a helpful experience for the delinquent children in their care.

The work programs are largely designed to help the older adolescent boys learn how to meet the demands of full-time employment. In addition, there is usually some off-duty program in education and some counseling, and an attempt is made to provide the boys with a positive living experience that includes recreation and religious activities. These programs view the adolescents as sufficiently stable and advanced in their development to face the demands of the world of work and society generally. Consequently, the work program is gauged to the normal pressures and conflicts of life in the world of work. The heavy emphasis on work is based to some extent on the belief that these boys would gain little from further education, at least at this particular point in their life. Generally, such camps aim to teach the boys good work

[9] For discussions of some of these programs see a number of articles in *The American Child*, vol. 41, No. 3, May 1959, 24 pp.; for example: Clark, Kenneth: "Some Questions Concerning Youth Work Camps," pp. 5-7; Fried, Antoinette: "Day Camp," pp. 8-12; Gatlin, Curtis: "Youth Work Camps—Opportunities for Young Workers," pp. 1-4; and Harris, Virginia B.: "Youth for Service," pp. 17-21.

[10] The Utah State Industrial School and the Idaho Industrial Training School have such programs.

[11] The statement of Harold Butterfield, *Institutions for Rehabilitation and Treatment of Juvenile Delinquency*, Hearing before the Subcommittee to Investigate Juvenile Delinquency of the Committee on the Judiciary, United States Senate, 85th Congress, 2d session, Pursuant to S. Res. 237, Washington, Government Printing Office, 1958, 78 pp. (p. 11), gives a brief description of both types of programs. New York City Youth Board: "Report and Recommendations of Ad Hoc Committee on Work Camps," 21 pp. (mimeo. c. 1957), reviews a considerable number of the current state programs. Sherman, B. F. (editor): "Guide for Juvenile Camps, Ranches, or Homes," Sacramento, Calif.: Department of Youth Authority, 52 pp. (mimeo. c. 1954); and "State of California Forestry Honor Camp Program," Sacramento: State of California, 1956, 26 pp. (mimeo.) describes the principles upon which the California camp programs are based.

habits and attitudes. Emphasis is placed on being able to accept and use supervision and to relate satisfactorily to one's peers.

The camps with an educational orientation usually have broader programs that include, in addition to education, some conservation work and some counseling and, like the work camps, they provide the boys with activities and personal contacts that are supportive and helpful to them. The extent of the educational program is largely determined by the boy's educational level and the mandatory school attendance laws.

LIMITATIONS IN CURRENT PROGRAMS

The camps emphasizing work enlist the interests and energies of the boys in the conservation of natural resources. This has the advantage of cooperating in a long-range conservation program. But the training which conservation work gives the boys is not extensive nor particularly varied, and the occupational outlook in the field is not wide. Moreover, the fact that the camp often separates the boys from urban associations and opportunities may be detrimental in preparing them for private employment in an urban setting.

These camps hope to help the boys develop good work habits through participation in conservation work. But developing positive work attitudes and habits is a complex undertaking and depends upon the total camp program as much as on the work done. The positive relationships between the work supervisors and the boys, and the extent to which negative attitudes about work are modified through counseling, are as important as the work itself.

The camps which have a full educational program and combine this with a positive work experience, recreational and religious activities, and some counseling, usually have boys of mandatory school age in their population. These camps, like the camps that emphasize a work program, use a planned approach in working with the delinquent. They appeal to his sense of wanting to do well. At the same time, the camp staff let the boys know that misbehavior in the camp will not be tolerated. These firm requirements are coupled with friendly support and encouragement. The numerous educational and vocational activities generally contribute to a full program and it is believed that constructive camp experience provides the boy with the necessary corrective for his delinquency.

This essentially environmental approach of the two types of camps is limited, because the counseling techniques and other personal contacts that accompany it frequently fail to meet the basic problems at the root of the delinquency and are usually restricted to surface problems that arise in a boy's adjustment to the camp. This is true not only of the counseling that is done informally about the camp but also in many cases of much of the counseling that is given when the boy comes to a counselor to discuss a problem.

In practice, the camps are often characterized by diverse aims and methods. On the one hand, they emphasize conservation work and education; on the other hand, they try to be an institution of treatment. In some instances counseling is stressed. However, its practice is often limited to a type of positive supervision in which the boys are guided in their daily program and given some help in planning for the future. Although there have been some notable efforts to resolve this conflict by making work and education an integral part of a total treatment program, there is a great difference between these two orientations. Efforts have also been made to use a more thorough counseling approach. However, the gap between a deliberate, common sense approach and an approach that attempts to deal with the underlying factors of a delinquent's problems has not been bridged. As a result, camp programs have tended to be uneven, with certain aspects being over-emphasized while others are de-emphasized or neglected. This is one of the reasons why camps have appeared to some persons alternately as a panacea for accomplishing conservation work and as a facility struggling to assume a treatment function.

This does not mean that work, education, and treatment are incompatible. The difficulty is due to a variety of things: failure to spell out the various objectives of the camps and develop the relationships among the several goals; failure to specify the appropriate means to achieve these objectives; inadequate funds to actually develop programs as they have been planned; and poor administrative direction, and coordination and control of the programs.

FUTURE POLICY

In considering the lines along which camps may be developed, it is necessary to reconcile the various points of view about the purpose of the program. Should the program be considered a temporary arrangement to cope with the overcrowding in training schools? Or should full programs be developed to treat delinquent children? Should the program emphasize conservation work or vocational education? Or should it emphasize the treatment of boys who are in need of help? It would be unrealistic to deny the emergencies created by overcrowded training schools or to belittle the attempts being made to provide improved care for some of these boys in a camp. It is also impossible to ignore the obstacles that stand in the way of developing a fuller program in some camps, because of the camp's commitment for conservation work. Still other obstacles stand in the way of needed improvement, such as difficulties in gaining adequate appropriations to increase the size and quality of the camp staff, or the need for a larger and more technically effective parent agency or administrative organization which would give planning and general direction to the individual camps.

These problems notwithstanding, camps for delinquent boys have undoubtedly captured the interest and enthusiasm of the people who administer them or are closely associated with them. Today, a discussion of camps for delinquent boys will usually be a consideration of which needs of delinquent children can be served best by which type of camp or, to put it more broadly, what types of delinquents can be served best by what kind of camps.[12]

## A Conception of a Camp

Considerable diversity is possible among camps. However, they usually have a number of characteristic features: location in a conservation area such as a forest or wildlife reserve; a physical plant with minimal security measures; a small number of boys, preferably no more than 50 to 60; an informal and relaxed relationship among the staff and boys; and a variety of conservation work projects that are an integral part of a broader treatment program.

The camp program aims to return the delinquent youth to the community sufficiently improved in his social and personal adjustment to function in a socially constructive way. Consequently, the program must be broad enough to include the services necessary for the treatment of delinquent children. For this the camp must have:

1. The help of a diagnostic service which screens the boys and sends those to camp whose particular needs can best be served in such a facility.

[12] *Institutions Serving Delinquent Children—Guides and Goals.* Children's Bureau Publication No. 360. Washington, D.C.: U.S. Government Printing Office, 1957, 119 pp. (p. 10), indicates that the stimulus for a specialized program in camping must be supplied by the unique contribution that such a program offers for the treatment of delinquents. The importance of adequate diagnostic evaluation of a youth's difficulties prior to placement in a particular institution is discussed by 'Gula, Martin: *Child-Caring Institutions,* Children's Bureau Publication No. 368. Washington, D.C.: U.S. Government Printing Office, 1958, 27 pp. (pp. 5-7).

2. An administrative person or unit to organize, direct, and coordinate the camp's activities and to create a generally positive camp routine and atmosphere.

3. Health services that include preventive measures, health maintenance, and medical care.

4. A counseling program designed to meet the individual needs of the boys, and arrangements for specialized psychiatric or psychological consultation on special problems that the boys present.

5. A recreational program that is geared to meet the delinquents' need for group participation and personal expression, and that provides a choice of activities that have some carry-over value for the boys after they leave the camp.

6. A work program that interests and challenges the boys but does not exploit them, that gives them a fair remuneration for their work, and that has some carry-over value for employment in private life.

7. Religious activities to serve the spiritual needs of the boys.

8. An educational program that is appropriate to the age, interests, and future needs of the boys and which meets the state educational requirements.

9. Access to an adequate aftercare program for the boys.[13]

10. Casework, clinical, and related services available to the boys' families. This service will help the parents with their problems so that they can provide the boy with a healthier setting in which to live upon his return. Generally, these services will not be provided under camp auspices.

11. An evaluation program to clearly delineate the treatment processes and assess their effectiveness.

Such a program is designed to help the boy develop socially constructive interests and abilities, to relate himself to others more sincerely and responsibly, to view his life situations more openly and less defensively, and to gain a greater measure of self-direction and self-discipline.

The objectives of a camp set the general character of its program. The specific characteristics of the program, however, must vary with the needs of the particular boys concerned. The first question then, in considering what a program should be, is: Who shall participate in the program, how many and what type of boys?

In order to develop and maintain a relaxed setting, with comfortable relations among the staff and the boys, the camp must be kept small. Coordinating the program and focusing it on the boys are simplified when the group is small. For this reason camps should be limited to 50 or 60 youths. Actual practice generally follows this pattern. Even where

[13] For the various arrangements whereby aftercare can be provided, see: *Guides and Goals,* op. cit. (pp. 115-116).

this is not the case, administrators and people having firsthand experience with camps have recommended that a camp accommodate no more than 60 boys. Camps smaller than 50 boys may be desirable, but they have greater difficulty maintaining the various specialized services that are needed for their operation.

Deciding what kinds of boys can profit most from a camp placement and what methods are best suited for selecting such boys is difficult. No organized research has yet been done on how different kinds of boys respond to various types of camps. The information that has been accumulated, however, may yield some guides and provide material that can be tested through research. But until more research has been done on who benefits significantly from a camp assignment, any criteria must be used tentatively and with care.

## What Group to Serve?

Camps can serve delinquent boys in various phases of adolescence and on various levels of adjustment. However, the boys in a given camp should be in about the same phase of development and the same level of adjustment or it will be difficult to work out a program that will be helpful to all of them, or a pattern of leadership and counseling to which they will all respond. In a state's diversified program several kinds of camps are conceivable; for example, camps for relatively well adjusted boys in early, middle, or late adolescence, or camps for any one or two of these groups, such as middle and late adolescence, etc.

The ideas of "developmental phase" and "adjustment" are difficult subjects and will not be discussed at length. It is important to note, however, that "developmental phase" includes not only the age of the boys, but also their physical and mental maturity as well as their level of emotional and social development, and that "adjustment" includes their degree of disturbance or stability and their adaptability. The boys in early adolescence, as a rule, will be considerably less well developed than the more mature boys and will have different needs. Similarly the boys who are relatively well adjusted will have different needs than those who are seriously maladjusted.

PROGRAM NEEDS

*Education*—Since the younger children as well as those in middle adolescence will require schoolwork, for this age group a bona fide education program must be established and boys must be selected who are sufficiently intelligent (dull normal and above) to participate in it. Academic work may not be required for the older adolescents who are beyond the mandatory school age, particularly if they are not interested in formal study and have very little aptitude for it. But the older adolescents' needs must not be overlooked; they should have some kind of vocational or prevocational training.

Boys who will attend school and those who will not should be placed in separate programs. There is a strong tendency for the nonschool program to detract from the school program and lower the boys' interest in it, and under some circumstances the school program may have a similar effect on the nonschool activities.

*Recreation*—Boys in their early adolescence, because of their smallness, more childlike interests, and tendencies to become frustrated easily, should have special recreation outlets. The recreation programs should provide the activities required for that age group and also have sufficient flexibility to take care of fluctuations in the boys' behavior. Boys in later adolescence will occasionally slip back to early interests and behavior and a recreation program for older adolescents should be prepared to meet this. Given this adaptable type of program, a few boys who are less mature than most of the group can still be considered for placement. However, mixing boys of different levels of maturity must be considered carefully because the boys themselves place a high value on what they consider their sophistication and may refuse to accept activities that they feel are beneath them.

The boys need activities that have carry-over value to the community—activities that will help integrate them into various desirable groups. Also, the boys need assistance in developing simple hobbies— things they can do by themselves. Since some of them will be living independently after they leave camp, they need to be interested in activities that will not make them delinquency prone.

*Work*—Work also must be gauged to the boys' level of maturity. The more mature boys can work the greater part of the day, the younger boys can not. In either case, the work group is especially important to all adolescents, though perhaps more so to the older adolescents than to those who are just beginning to develop. In selecting boys for camp, it is important to know whether a boy is interested in affiliating with a group and able to draw some of his feelings of security from the group, or whether his primary source of security comes from dependence on an affectionate adult. In the latter case, a boy 16 to 18 years of age might have a difficult time in a camp for boys of his age because the group would probably expect him to strive for independence. A younger boy with the same characteristics might have little difficulty in a camp for younger boys because the younger group would be more apt to accept strivings for a dependency relationship.

It is important that the work in camp be organized in a manner to prepare the boys for work outside the camp. Consequently, stress should be placed on helping the boys develop constructive work attitudes and habits. Emphasis should be placed on helping them develop a positive relationship with people on the job, with the "boss" and the peer group.

Attention must also be given to helping the boy seek employment: how to read a want ad; how to make and sustain contact with an employment office; how to fill out an application form; how to prepare for an interview. Once on the job, the boy has to be prepared to get to work on time. Perhaps certain camp practices, like rotating who gets the boys up in the morning, might prepare them for future responsibilities. The boys also need help in budgeting money, and in how to use their future salaries to meet their various obligations and interests.

## RELATIONSHIP NEEDS

The younger children, because they are still close to their early childhood, are usually able to accept boys who are even less mature. But boys in middle and later adolescence, who are striving to put their dependency needs behind them and be independent, may not respond well to requests for support and help from more immature boys. The younger boys will also need adult relationships that offer personal attention, time, concern, support and encouragement, to an extent that is not true of the older boys.

## PHYSICAL CONDITION

The boys in camp will have health needs, some of which may require the attention of a physician or a dentist or possibly even of a hospital. Camps located in a conservation area may be a considerable distance from a community having these services and the time required to travel this distance may be dangerous to the health of the boys. For this reason boys should not be accepted in such camps unless they are in good health and able to participate in the camp's recreation and work activities.

## INTELLIGENCE LEVEL

If the camp operates a school, the boys admitted should have at least the minimum intelligence necessary to participate in the program. This usually means that boys who are dull normal in intelligence or above can be considered for a camp assignment. If the camp does not have a school, boys whose intelligence is borderline may also be considered.

## PREFERENCE FOR CAMP

Boys being considered for a camp placement should have a preference for a camp assignment. If the boys have this interest, they will involve themselves in the program and gain the greatest value from it. If the number who need this care is greater than the number of camp billets available, it may be possible to use the boys' desires to go to a camp as a basis for deciding whether this or some other type of placement should be made.

## LEVEL OF ADJUSTMENT

It is conceivable that the particular program needs of various types of delinquent boys on various levels of adjustment could be delineated, and a number of special camps created to treat their particular problems. This publication deals primarily with the overall problems of camps for delinquent youth, but the sections on counseling and staff refer specifically to camps for delinquents who are adaptive [14] and relatively normal, but whose behavior requires that they be removed from the community and given some help in working out their problems. Such boys need short-term supportive treatment that will help them to develop a greater mastery of themselves and to establish a more normal pattern of behavior. This group of delinquents also needs assistance in meeting the young adult responsibilities the community expects of youth who are interested in employment. Their relationships to others, especially to people in positions of authority, need improvement as does their ability to persevere and see their efforts through to a point of accomplishment. They also need opportunities to identify themselves with responsible adults and "learn by doing."

[14] For a fuller discussion of this concept, see: Jenkins, Richard L.: "Adaptive and Maladaptive Delinquents," *The Nervous Child*, vol. 11, No. 1, October 1955 (pp. 9-12); and Brancale, Ralph: "Problems of Classification," *National Probation and Parole Association Journal*, vol. 1, No. 2, October 1955 (pp. 118-125).

Typically, the adaptive delinquents' efforts at adjustment appear reasonable and plausible in terms of their particular situation and the expectations of the community. These efforts are often carried out in a manner which shows that the boys are not highly vindictive or emotionally disturbed—though their behavior may be aggressive, bold, and assertive. However, the boys' reliance on antisocial ways of handling whatever problems are facing them and the associated agitating events indicate their need for help. Also, the degree of anxiety present, the emotional lability, and the difficulty these boys have in controlling and modifying their ideas and actions are disruptive to their attempts to conform.

Consequently, the boys' level of adjustment, as well as their developmental level, makes particular program demands. Educational placement, recreational activities, work assignments, and relationship needs should be considered from the standpoint of the boys' adjustment. Negative attitudes, stemming from a disappointing school experience, may be expressed by the boys in the camp's educational program.

Though some may have been participants in organized recreational activities, most of the boys will need help in adjusting themselves to group recreation. Others will need help in developing skills in activities that only involve themselves. Work may be a new experience to many. A low regard for work as well as negative attitudes toward it should be anticipated. Many boys will have significant problems that are of concern to themselves—problems they will need to discuss and work through with someone skilled in such work. Since attitudes, feelings, and impulsive modes of adaptation arise in the treatment of delinquents in a camp, the various program people should be sensitive, observant, versatile, and consistent. The boys may be venturesome and press the limits of these activities and so need effective guidance, counseling, group direction, and control. Yet, they will generally be socially responsive and receptive.

Boys with severely incapacitating tendencies that make it impossible for them to participate in the camp's program should not be mixed with adaptive delinquent boys. This includes strongly hostile or sadistic boys, boys who are unusually passive and dependent, boys who are pleasure-oriented in the extreme and lacking in controls over their impulses, and those who are very withdrawn or highly anxious and fearful. It also includes boys who characteristically run from situations that make them tense, boys who have tendencies to set fires, are active homosexuals, or who have strong latent homosexual tendencies.

The boy being considered for a camp of this type should have some ability to get along in a relatively well structured group, and a desire to achieve some socially approved goals. He should have at least a fair capacity to form and sustain interpersonal relationships and to identify himself with constructive group and adult leadership.

## The Selection Process

The selection of boys for the camp should be guided by the information contained in the social study, psychological tests, and psychiatric interviews if such service is available. These tools should be examined to determine how they can make their greatest contribution to the selection process; for example, what psychological test findings reflect the extent of a boy's hostility and what findings indicate something about his controls. Such a study should also aim to provide the camp with information that will be helpful in grouping the boys into different living and activity units. Thought must also be given to the preparation of reports. These must be written in a manner that makes their content most useful to the people in camp.

Lastly, such studies should be tied into the evaluation program of the camp. They can provide data about the youth's background and personality prior to a camp placement. Some of these measures applied after a camp experience may show changes that have taken place as a result of the camp program.

## 34.    Getting the Returnee Back to School

### Samuel M. Greenstone

The author holds the B.A. degree from the College of the City of New York and is counselor in charge of Placement of Children from Institutions for the Board of Education of New York City. He has also had experience as Educational and Vocational Counselor for the Board of Education, New York City.

A counselor charged with the responsibility of effecting school placement for children returning from institutions is often in the position

Samuel M. Greenstone, "Getting the Returnee Back to School," *Crime and Delinquency,* 7 (1961), 249-54. Reprinted with the permission of the National Council on Crime and Delinquency.

of a matchmaker trying to bring together two people with an active dislike for each other.

> Many teachers are unwilling to accept returnees from institutions into their classes or . . . are often cold and hostile to the returning student.[1]
> In the cases studied by us, almost two-thirds of the boys had a history of truancy, and in more than half of the cases . . . the boys were absent from school without excuse for at least half of the total school period preceding their admission to the Training School.[2]

Fortunately, mutual repugnance is not always the case. Many children return to the community with some understanding of the forces contributing to their delinquency and with a strong desire to "make good." In addition, there are many teachers who welcome the opportunity to assist in their rehabilitation. When both parties have a positive feeling toward each other, the matchmaker's role is simple and rewarding.

But all children returning from institutions—regardless of whether they want school or the school wants them—must go to school if they are the right age, physically fit, and of sound mind. The New York City Board of Education, though cognizant of the difficulties involved in the returnee's absorption into the school system, is determined that he shall not be denied the education that is his due. In conjunction with the institutions to which children are committed, machinery has been set up to reduce these difficulties to a minimum. The machinery is far from perfect; procedures are constantly modified when it becomes apparent that a change will result in more successful transition from institution to public school. Let us take a look at this machinery, examine some of the points at which it falters, and see what is being done to achieve smoother operation.

## Machinery for Transition

Before a New York City boy or girl (henceforward, for the sake of convenience, we shall refer to returnees as boys) is released from an institution, the progress committee of the institution reviews the findings and reports of all personnel who have had major contact with the

---

[1] William C. Kvaraceus, *Delinquent Behavior*, Washington, D.C., National Education Association, 1959, Vol. 2, p. 279.

[2] Erwin Schepses, "The Academic School Experience of the Training School Student," *Federal Probation*, June, 1955, p. 47.

boy during his stay. If the committee decides to release him and recommends further schooling, a form (which we shall call the school form) is sent to the New York City branch of the institution, where it is turned over to the youth parole worker responsible for the boy's aftercare. The school form contains a record of the boy's scholastic achievement at the institution and a brief summary of his adjustment there.

When the boy arrives in the city, his youth parole worker informs the counselor who has been assigned by the New York City Board of Education to supervise school placement of returnees; this counselor arranges to meet with both the youth parole worker and the returnee. Parents of returnees are welcome, but few attend these meetings. The interview, which usually takes place about a week after it is requested, is a two-stage affair. In stage one, involving the youth parole worker and the counselor only, the counselor reviews the school form, and the worker goes into the boy's background, reports on his own work with the boy, and makes recommendations. The boy is then introduced to the counselor (stage two) and his educational and vocational goals are discussed. Eventually, a school and a course are agreed upon. The worker receives from the counselor a directive addressed to the principal of the school selected and then escorts the boy there. At the school the directive is presented to the principal or his delegate, who greets the boy and assures him of interest and support from school personnel. The boy is then given a program in keeping with his educational plan and achievement level and soon becomes absorbed into the life of the school.

## "Bugs" in the Machinery

That is the way things are supposed to happen. Now let us examine the blocks to smooth operation, why they exist, and what is being done to overcome them.

The first serious breakdown in the machinery comes when there is a lapse of time between the boy's release and his placement in school. There may be various reasons for this delay: (1) the boy may have been released for employment; (2) he may deliberately avoid the placement interview; (3) the youth parole worker may be new to his caseload and may need time to "catch up"; (4) the placement counselor may feel that the boy is not ready for school placement; and (5) institutional releases may be so numerous at that time of the year that the placement office cannot keep up with them.

If, prior to release, the boy has indicated to institution personnel that he intends to seek employment, the school form is not sent to the New York office. However, if the boy cannot find work, or does find a job and cannot hold it, he may decide that he wants to go to school; or, having failed to find employment and content to hang around the streets, he may be picked up by an attendance officer or a member of the Youth Squad and be obliged to go, "creeping like a snail, unwillingly to school." In either case, the necessary school form is then requested from the institution and the placement machinery is set in motion.

At a time when unemployment is a national problem, the institution boy looking for work is at a disadvantage, and it can be readily understood how the above situation can arise. However, institutions maintain contact with agencies dedicated to finding work for young people, and every effort is made to help the boy who is seriously entering the job market.

To better conditions in this area even more, one of the largest institutions is planning a program of pre-vocational guidance, which will give not only occupational information about entering jobs, but training in such basics as filling out applications, grooming for and handling the job interview, on-the-job grooming, proper use of the telephone, and so forth. Boys from culturally deprived families need this kind of preparation as urgently as the sub-deb needs her finishing school.

A school-age returnee not motivated for school often "gets sick" on the day of the interview. A series of illnesses, messages misinterpreted or unreceived ("I thought the appointment was for *next* Thursday!") can effectively block school placement for a long time. If, while the boy is parrying attempts to place him, his worker leaves or is transferred and his replacement takes a while to become thoroughly acquainted with his caseload, an artful dodger may go unplaced for months.

Occasionally the counselor does not feel that regular school is in order for the boy. It then becomes necessary either to offer some other type of schooling or to establish the returnee's fitness for conventional school. Special school requires special screening by the service to which the boy is referred; clearance for conventional school usually involves a psychiatric evaluation. In any event, there will be a time loss.

Should psychiatric evaluation be necessary, it has been agreed that institution personnel may be employed—a procedure recently adopted by New York in the interests of expediency. Previously, dubious school risks were referred to the Board of Education's Bureau of Child Guidance; but the Bureau, frequently called upon for more urgent services, could rarely give an immediate appraisal of a returnee. And so, long delays were often the rule. In contrast to this, the institution psychiatrist is available almost on demand.

The three last-mentioned causes of delay—an unwilling client, turn-over in agency personnel, and screening by the placement counselor—can be considerably reduced if the counselor interviews the prospective returnee while he is still at the institution. While the boy is away, the school is selected and the directive to the principal is mailed to the New York office, where it is ready and waiting when the boy arrives in the city. His worker, new or old, can then escort him to school without any waste of time.

If screening for a special service is necessary, it is done before the boy's release so that whatever part of the school system he is destined for will be known before he hits the city. There is no necessity for a long period of mounting anger while the boy hangs around waiting to find out what will happen to him.

Of course, there are practical considerations which stand in the way of interviewing *all* boys before they are released, but the number has been increasing dramatically. In 1959, about thirty boys were so interviewed; in 1960, over 170. We hope that even more can be seen before their release this year.

To return to the prerelease interview procedure, which helps in still another way: A large number of children are released late in June or during July and August, and in September the opening of school finds so many unplaced, waiting children that, despite the Board of Education's valiant attempt, it is almost impossible to enter them all before school begins. Last year, however, about forty returnees were seen during the summer and so the September crush was alleviated by that number.

The watchdog role of the Bureau of Attendance has been another means of reducing the delay in school placement. By requesting that institutions notify them of any boy who is out of school more than ten days after his release, the Bureau can assume the responsibility of following through until he is put on a school register.

On occasion, placement machinery bogs down during the interview itself, where the interpretation of a boy's behavior by an institution-oriented worker sometimes proves unsatisfactory to a school-oriented counselor. Very often, the institution is interested merely in returning a boy to school and the community. And, although it may not necessarily believe he will make a satisfactory adjustment, the institution would nevertheless like to give the boy an opportunity to try. If, however, the counselor has any suspicion that the applicant may be dangerous to others or that he may need the kind of attention not available in a public school, it is inadvisable to admit him until the suspicion has been allayed. In such cases, a psychiatric evaluation is generally demanded.

The heart of the interview, of course, is that part conducted with the returnee, who is usually somewhat overwhelmed by the situation. The counselor's first task is to relax him sufficiently so that he can think clearly about the business at hand. Most problems arising during the interview concern the school and course the boy wants. Sometimes his goals are unrealistic in terms of his natural endowments and he must be directed toward an educational and vocational goal in keeping with them; sometimes what he wants is unavailable because admission to certain courses is made only after qualifying examinations are passed and these exams have been given long before the interview takes place; sometimes there is just no room in the preferred course.

A vocational sequence starts with the beginning of the tenth year in the New York vocational high schools. A boy who has gone beyond the ninth year at a training school cannot be placed in the tenth year of a vocational course. He frequently prefers a school which gives him the prestige of a higher grade placement, though he cannot get the trade training he would like.

Both these trouble sources are being attacked. The placement counselor sends the institutions a list of examination schools with dates of the exams. Some institutions make arrangements to transport aspirants for examination schools to the scene of the exams when they are given. Boys from these institutions then lose none of the opportunities that other New York City students enjoy.

The matter of admitting a boy into a vocational school at a grade level compatible with his achievement is being met by introducing into the institutions curricula which run parallel to public school courses. For this purpose, the placement counselor has arranged for training school personnel to visit those New York City schools which offer courses in demand by their boys. Their plan is to organize institution courses in such a way that a boy pursuing one of them at a training school will be able to step into the same course, at the same level, upon admission to a public school.

Another "bug" that sometimes develops in the placement machinery is the school itself. Aftercare workers still report that, upon his arrival at school, their boy, instead of a word of encouragement and a program, received a dead-fish handshake and a warning to the tune of: "We've got a good school and we want to keep it that way. Remember, one false move and out you go!" Fortunately, this sort of "welcome" is on the way out. Most school administrators today are guidance minded; if they question the appropriateness of assigning a particular returnee to their school, they do it after the boy has been civilly received and when he is well out of earshot, by telephoning the placement counselor.

The public school's concern about the returnee is often justifiable—especially when it does not receive the boy's complete school record. Often the boy's last school has not forwarded his scholastic records to the institution where he was committed. Comes placement time and the boy's new school finds itself at a loss to program him with only his training school records on hand. They put in a call for his past public school records, and, while waiting for them, program the returnee as best they can. When the records finally come through, the school may find itself in the odious position of ousting a boy from classes to which he is adjusting and putting him into ones which are more "appropriate" in light of the new information.

In view of the possibility of such situations, the school placement counselor is always available to public school personnel, who can call on him to expedite the transfer of records. Then, too, bi-pronged pressure—one prod from institutions, the other from the Board of Education—is being brought to bear on those schools discharging children to institutions so that they make sure to forward all the necessary records.

## Why Not Let Them Go?

Sometimes, the Board of Education's insistence on school placement for poorly motivated returnees is challenged. Why force a boy to go to school if he doesn't want to and if his school experience has always been unhappy? Why not permit him to find a job, earn some money, and let him enjoy the grown-up feeling that going to work will give? Then, too, teachers sometimes claim that if several boys from institutions are returned to the same school, they fuse into a nucleus of hard-core delinquency. We also hear the objection that, since most returnees either drop out of school or are sent back to institutions in short order, it is wasteful to give them all the time and energy they require at the expense of those students who have never exhibited delinquent behavior and could benefit from the services showered on the returnees.

The answer to these queries is always the same: The school *must* accept the returnee because that is its responsibility to the community and, if for no other reason, because the returnee is entitled to all the education and guidance every other child gets. Perhaps even more important is putting the returnee on register, as school attendance may be the community's last opportunity to effect desirable changes in attitudes. "In all cultures, education is designed to change the lives of students in accordance with objectives and standards of society." [3] A child is sent to an institution because he has departed from the norms of societal behavior. At the institution he presumably acquires some understanding of his problem, substituting new values for old and taking his first steps toward acceptable social behavior.

True, return to the community carries with it a period of parole, during which the returnee's behavior is observed and directed by a youth parole worker. But no worker is able to see his boy for several hours five days every week. Moreover, a boy who leaves an institution and does *not* go to school is faced with the same community forces which may originally have encouraged his delinquency. Through its daily supervision and guidance of teachers, counselors, and administrative personnel, the school can support the youth parole worker and supplement the unavoidable paucity of his visits; it can deepen the roots and strengthen the tendrils of growth that made their appearance in the institutional greenhouse. No other community resource is so rich in opportunities to channel youthful energy into socially desirable activity. Guidance is a continuous process, and the school's job is to pick up where the institution left off.

That the returnee is not long for school, that he is a certain dropout, has been accepted almost as an axiom. However, a follow-up of returnees placed in school from September, 1959, to June, 1960, revealed that 45 per cent dropped out during the year. In the same period, the dropout rate among high school pupils throughout the city was considerably less. But one high school lost exactly the same percentage of its tenth-year pupils (the tenth year is the grade to which most high school returnees go) and one even more—49 per cent. Four returnees were graduated at the end of the school year. That's not many—but it's four.

An evaluation of our placement program revealed that all high schools did not have the same holding power over returnees; some were unable to hold a single returnee for an entire school year while others held them all.

The schools with the highest retention ratings did not come by them without reason. The first ingredient of their success was an attitude that reflected the guidance mindedness of the administration. This was apparent in the principal's approach to children with problems and per-

[3] E. G. Williamson, "The Meaning of Communication in Counseling," *Personnel and Guidance Journal,* Sept., 1959.

colated through the dean and counselors to the entire faculty. The personnel selected for key positions were guidance-trained and were allotted adequate time to perform that function.

The returnee was welcomed, *warmly* welcomed, by the dean and was given the clear understanding that if ever anything troubled him he was free to come in and talk things over. He was persuaded of the reality of the open-door policy.

A youngster who presented a discipline problem was assumed to be a troubled youngster, and it was the school's job to find out what the trouble was. In the school which seemed to do most for the returnee, the counselor was allowed to deal with any problem once it was discovered. If a change of class was necessary, he arranged the transfer; if a short program was needed (so that a boy could hold an afternoon job), he gave it.

If the returnee wanted to leave school for full-time employment, he had to be interviewed first by his counselor, and the reason for dropping out was gone over thoroughly. Often, the boy was helped over some temporary hurdle and his plans were changed. There was a definite, determined effort on the counselor's part to keep the boy in school. The returnee knew he was wanted.

There is no doubt that getting the returnee back to school is a king-sized task, and it presents king-sized problems; but the 55 per cent who remained in school after their first year and the four who earned a diploma make the effort worth while. When these boys "make good" the school has really done a job of salvaging human resources. All that is needed is for the school to understand that returnees really want to rise above their past and for returnees to understand that the school really wants to help them do it.

# Prediction and Future Experiences

I T IS now well established that delinquent behavior does not suddenly appear in the experiences of a child. Sometimes a delinquent act may seem completely out of character with the previous behavior of a peer group or an individual—the massive vandalism by an otherwise seemingly normal peer group or the multiple murder committed by a previously well-behaved boy. Close investigation shows, however, that in case after case, preceding behavior and attitudes favorable to the commission of the crime have been operative. Only the overt aspect of the criminal act has come suddenly. In other instances, persistent delinquency of a less serious character has seemed almost like an inborn trait—although psychologists and sociologists now know that there are no "born criminals." Somewhere in the child's experiences, the bent toward delinquent behavior begins to develop. Why and when and by what process of development are questions that various research projects are designed to answer. The research has not given definite answers but progress is being made. Instead of discarding the results of this research as useless because they do not unequivocally identify why, when, and how delinquency develops, they may be regarded as a step into the research of the future.

One line of effort has been to devise prediction tests and scales that will foretell during preadolescent years which children will develop into serious delinquents in the mid-teen peak years of delinquency. Among the many attempts at prediction, three stand out as most significant. Since the 1950's, Monachesi and his associates have worked with an inventory of neurotic and psychotic factors as exhibited in mild form in normal people. They have found distinctions between delinquent and nondelinquent children and some progress has been made in identifying children who will later become delinquent.[1]

A second approach to prediction has been through the Kvaraceus delinquency scale, called the KD Delinquency Proneness Scale and Check List. The scale consists of multiple choice items, known to differentiate between delinquent and nondelinquent children, which children are asked to check. The check list, designed for teachers or other adults to check for each child, covers personal, environmental, and school factors. Experimentation with the scale shows that it differentiates to some extent between known delinquent and nondelinquent children. The scale and check list have not been used in the attempt to predict future delinquency of young children.[2]

The third major attempt to devise a prediction instrument for juvenile delinquency has been made by the research team of Sheldon and Eleanor Glueck, the latest in a number of approaches they have made toward prediction in the field of criminology. Called the Glueck Social Prediction Table for Identifying Potential Delinquents, the instrument involves only five questions, all related to parent-child relationships. Each reply is weighted, and the sum of the weights constitutes the prediction score, which for an individual

[1] Clara Kanun and Elio D. Monachesi, "Delinquency and the Validating Scales of the Minnesota Multiphasic Personality Inventory," *Journal of Criminal Law, Criminology and Police Science,* 50 (1960), 525-534; Starke R. Hathaway and Monachesi, *Analyzing and Predicting Juvenile Delinquency with the MMPI,* University of Minnesota Press, Minneapolis, Minn., 1953; Hathaway, "The Personalities of Predelinquent Boys," *Journal of Criminal Law, Criminology and Police Science,* 48 (1957), 148-163; Hathaway, Monachesi, and Lawrence A. Young, "Delinquency Rates and Personality," *Journal of Criminal Law, Criminology and Police Science,* 50 (1960), 433-440.

[2] W. C. Kvaraceus, *The Community and the Delinquent,* World Book Company, Yonkers-on-Hudson, New York, 1954, pp. 139-154; Kvaraceus, "Forecasting Juvenile Delinquency," *Journal of Education,* 138 (April, 1956), 1-43; Joseph K. Balogh and Charles J. Rumage, *Juvenile Delinquency Proneness, A Study of the Kvaraceus Scale,* Annals of American Sociology, Public Affairs Press, Washington, D.C., 1956.

child may then be compared with a master table to determine the chances out of one hundred that the child will become delinquent at a future date. The choice of items, the weights, and the master table are taken from their comparative study of five hundred delinquent and five hundred nondelinquent boys, published under the title, *Unraveling Juvenile Delinquency*. The items, the weights and the score classes are given in Tables A and B.

*TABLE A* *

FIVE FACTORS COMPRISING SOCIAL PREDICTION TABLE WITH
"DELINQUENCY SCORE" OF EACH SUBCATEGORY

|  | Score [weight] |
| --- | --- |
| Discipline of boy by father |  |
| Overstrict or erratic | 72.5 |
| Lax | 59.8 |
| Firm but kindly | 9.3 |
| Supervision of boy by mother |  |
| Unsuitable | 83.2 |
| Fair | 57.5 |
| Suitable | 9.9 |
| Affection of father for boy |  |
| Indifferent or hostile | 75.9 |
| Warm (including overprotective) | 33.8 |
| Affection of mother for boy |  |
| Indifferent or hostile | 86.2 |
| Warm (including overprotective) | 43.1 |
| Cohesiveness of family |  |
| Unintegrated | 96.9 |
| Some elements of cohesion | 61.3 |
| Cohesive | 20.6 |

\* Source: Eleanor T. Glueck, "Spotting Potential Delinquents: Can It Be Done?" *Federal Probation*, 20 (September, 1956), 7-13.

The instrument has been severely criticized on several counts. It rests solely on parent-child relationships and is thought by the Gluecks to be predictable at the early age of six years. Later social experiences of the child, including the important peer group influences, are therefore ignored. The Gluecks tend to divide the scores at a mid-point with scores higher than this point showing more inclination to delinquency than to nondelinquency, and scores lower than this point showing the reverse tendency. Actually, the

## TABLE B †

LIKELIHOOD OF PERSISTENT DELINQUENCY

(Derived from status on five interpersonal family factors)

| | Likelihood of persistent delinquency | |
| Score Class | Percentage of delinquencies occurring in this score class | Likelihood of delinquency |
| --- | --- | --- |
| Under 200 | 8.2 | Negligible |
| 200-249 | 37.0 | Low |
| 250-299 | 63.5 | More than an even chance |
| 300 and over | 89.2 | High |

† Same source as Table A.

middle scores have low predictability value, so that a large percentage of middle-score children labelled delinquency prone actually belong in the nondelinquency group and vice versa, with a large proportion of potentially delinquent children arbitrarily placed by their scores in the nondelinquency group.

In the course of testing, various classifications of children and youth have been used in different studies, for example, aggressive children and neurotic children in addition to delinquent children. There is the possibility therefore that the instrument predicts the probability of some sort of deviant attitudes or conduct when family relationships are unfavorable, but does not specifically select out future delinquents.

The instrument has been applied retrospectively to youth with past or present delinquency records, by subjective judgment of the early parent-child relationships involved in the rating table. A high percentage of correct predictions appear; however, no control group has been used in these studies to determine how many nondelinquent youths might also have had unfavorable family relationships.

Two long-term projects to test the instrument are under way in which the prediction table was applied to children six years of age with later evaluation of their conduct at intervals of time. The Gluecks expect a final evaluation of the predictive values of the instrument to be possible when the subjects reach the age of seventeen, which will be about 1963 for the earlier of the two studies.

From time to time the Gluecks report on the progress of the project. Article 35, published in 1960, reports on both retrospective studies and current studies up to that time.

Article 36 does not contain a predictive scale but affords an objective view of some of the future experiences of children who are referred to clinics by juvenile courts. The study in question uses three groups of subjects in St. Louis who, as children during certain years in the 1920's, were respectively juvenile court cases, nondelinquents in conflict with the mores, and nonclinic nondelinquents. Thirty years later, they were studied with reference to mortality, mobility, and criminality. Clear relationships were found between childhood deviancy and adult criminal behavior.

## 35. Efforts to Identify Delinquents

### Eleanor Touroff Glueck

> The author, who holds the degree of Doctor of Education, is Research Associate in the Harvard Law School. She and her husband, Sheldon Glueck, have carried out and published the results of many extensive research projects in the field of delinquency and crime. *Unraveling Juvenile Delinquency* (1950) was followed by many articles and three books drawing totally or in large part upon data assembled for *Unraveling Juvenile Delinquency: Physique and Delinquency, Predicting Delinquency and Crime,* and *Family Environment and Delinquency.*

In *Federal Probation* (September 1956) appeared an article by the writer entitled, "Spotting Potential Delinquents: Can It Be Done?" In this article a description was given of what is now called the *Glueck Social Prediction Table for Identifying Potential Delinquents,* and the findings of several retrospective applications of this Table were briefly summarized. As the device approaches validation, interest in it is becoming greater and, although experimentation must continue, this seems an appropriate time to summarize the efforts to check it, espe-

Eleanor Touroff Glueck, "Efforts to Identify Delinquents," *Federal Probation,* 24 (June 1960), 49-56. Reprinted with permission of the publisher.

cially as the chapter in *Predicting Delinquency and Crime* [1] entitled "Checkings of Table Identifying Potential Delinquents" was prepared at an earlier stage and does not, therefore, incorporate the most recent attempts to check the Table.

The purpose of the predictive instrument is to distinguish at school entrance those children who are and those *who are not* in danger of developing into persistent offenders. (It is equally important to identify the latter, especially in high-delinquency areas). Its purpose is also to distinguish delinquents from pseudo-delinquents and nondelinquents among those manifesting difficulties.

The Table, first published in *Unraveling Juvenile Delinquency* [2] derives from a comparison of five hundred persistent delinquents and five hundred nondelinquents matched by age, intelligence, ethnic origin and residence in depressed areas of Boston.

The Social Prediction Table, which is one of four predictive instruments based on the findings of *Unraveling Juvenile Delinquency* [3] comprises five factors in the family background (Affection of Mother for Boy, Affection of Father for Boy, Discipline of Boy by Father, Supervision of Boy by Mother, Family Cohesiveness), found in *Unraveling Juvenile Delinquency* markedly to differentiate delinquents from nondelinquents. As it was learned in *Unraveling Juvenile Delinquency* that half the delinquents had shown their first overt signs of antisocial behavior before age 8, and 90 per cent at 10 or younger, it was necessary to limit the selection of differentiative factors to those clearly operative in a child's life prior to the time he might evidence the earliest signs of maladaptive behavior. (The interested reader is asked to refer to *Unraveling Juvenile Delinquency*, Chapter XX, pps. 259, 260, and to *Predicting Delinquency and Crime*, Chapter II, pps. 23-31, for a description of the method of constructing the Table.)

A predictive table, is, strictly speaking, only an "experience" table until it has been successfully applied to other samples of cases. For this reason, checkings on many and varied samples need to be made. During the period of the earliest efforts to check the device, attention was largely focused on determining the extent to which it would have

[1] Sheldon and Eleanor Glueck, *Predicting Delinquency and Crime.* Cambridge, Mass.: Harvard University Press, 1959 (with an *Introduction* by the Chief Justice of the United States, the Honorable Earl Warren). Chapter X, pps. 127 *et seq.*

[2] Sheldon and Eleanor Glueck, New York, The Commonwealth Fund, 1950: Harvard University Press, Cambridge, Mass., Chapter XX, pp. 258 *et seq.*

[3] A second predictive device grew out of differences in the character structure of delinquents and nondelinquents (*ibid.*, pp. 263, 264), a third from the temperamental differences between them (*ibid.*, pp. 264, 265), and a fourth from differences in their response to certain intelligence tests (only recently published in *Predicting Delinquency and Crime*, p. 239).

been possible by retrospective application of the Table to already ad-judicated delinquents and also to nondelinquents, to have correctly identified them at age 5 or 6 as the persistent offenders or the non-offenders they actually turned out to be.

The wisdom of ascertaining to what extent the predictive cluster (derived from the comparison of 500 persistent offenders in Boston and 500 matched nondelinquents) is present in many and varied samples of cases should be self-evident. The search for "causes" of delinquency (by which is here meant *persisting* antisocial behavior) may be narrowed, should the predictive cluster of factors be found present in great measure in other samples of already persistent offenders and in nonoffenders differing from the original sample in age, ethnic origin, intelligence level (and so on). Their far greater presence in delinquents and their far lesser presence in nondelinquents should lend confidence to their significance for a clearer understanding of certain aspects of the causation of delinquency.

## Retrospective Studies Previously Reported in Federal Probation Quarterly

The first retrospective study was undertaken in 1952 by Black and Glick of the Jewish Board of Guardians on 100 delinquent boys at the Hawthorne-Cedar Knolls School.[4] The second, also in 1952, was made by Richard E. Thompson,[5] candidate for Honors at Harvard University, Department of Social Relations, on 100 boys originally encompassed in the well-known Cambridge-Somerville Youth Study.[6]

The third checkup on cases other than the ones on which the Table was based, was made in 1953 by the New Jersey State Department of Institutions and Agencies, on 51 parolees;[7] the fourth, in 1956, by clinicians of the Douglas A. Thom Clinic for Children in Boston on 57 "antisocial" young children.[8] A fifth check by Thompson, also made

---

[4] Bertram J. Black and Selma J. Glick, "Predicted vs. Actual Outcome for De-linquent Boys," New York, Jewish Board of Guardians, 1952.

[5] Richard E. Thompson, "A Validation of the Glueck Social Prediction Scale for Proneness to Delinquency," *Journal of Criminal Law, Criminology and Police Science*, November-December 1952.

[6] Edwin Powers and Helen Witmer, *An Experiment in the Prediction of Delinquency*, New York: Columbia University Press, 1951.

[7] "Predicting Juvenile Delinquency," *Research Bulletin* No. 124, April 1955, published by State Department of Institutions and Agencies, Trenton, N.J.

[8] Eveoleen N. Rexford, M.D., Maxwell Schleifer, and Suzanne T. Van Amerongen, M.D., "A Follow-up of a Psychiatric Study of 57 Antisocial Young Children," *Mental Hygiene*, April 1956, pp. 196-214.

in 1957, comprised 50 boys who had appeared in the Boston Juvenile Court in 1950 and 50 girls committed by the Boston Juvenile Court to the care of the Massachusetts Youth Service Board during 1954-55.[9]

In addition to these already published studies, two as yet unpublished "retrospective" efforts, one in 1957 by Selma J. Glick and Catherine Donnell applied the Table to 150 unmarried mothers,[10] and another in 1957 by Glick, to 81 boys from upper-income families ($7,500 a year and over).[11]

This completes the roster of *retrospective* applications of the five-factor Social Prediction Table as reported in the article "Spotting Potential Delinquents: Can It Be Done?"

In most of these inquiries, it was found that in 9 out of 10 instances the offenders involved would have been correctly identified at age 6 as potentially persistent offenders; and in the few remaining investigations a slightly lesser result was derived. It is of particular significance that in the first of the two studies by Thompson (see f.5 for reference), it was ascertained that true *nondelinquents*, even though evidencing behavioral difficulties in school (thought by teachers and clinicians to be prodromal of delinquency), were correctly identified by the Table in 91.3 per cent of instances. (This is in contrast with 58.7 per cent, 53.5 per cent, and 56.9 per cent of correct predictions by three clinicians charged with selecting boys for the Cambridge-Somerville Youth Study.) It is to be noted also that in the study of unmarried mothers (the first application of the Table to girls) evidence began to suggest that the predictive instrument might be applicable to girls as well as boys.

## Prospective Studies Reported in Federal Probation Quarterly

In addition to a resumé of retrospective studies, the writer made brief mention of two ongoing projects of a different nature, in which the identification of true delinquents and true nondelinquents was being attempted before clear evidence of their status was apparent—one, an investigation set up in 1953 by the New York City Youth Board in

---

[9] Richard E. Thompson, "Further Validation of Glueck Social Prediction Table for Identifying Potential Delinquents," *Journal of Criminal Law Criminology, and Police Science,* Volume 48, No. 2, July-August 1957.

[10] Selma J. Glick and Catherine Donnell, "Background Factors in 150 Cases of Jewish Unmarried Mothers," presented in part in the *Jewish Social Service Quarterly,* Volume XXX, No. 2, Winter 1953. The Section on Prediction was omitted from the printed paper.

[11] Letter, May 31, 1956.

two public schools in very high delinquency areas where the Table was being applied to all first-grade boys shortly after school entrance, that is, roughly at age 6; the other called the Maximum Benefits Project initiated in 1954 under the auspices of the Commissioners' Youth Council of the District of Columbia in two elementary schools in very high delinquency areas and including girls as well as boys (179 children) already manifesting severe behavioral difficulties in school.

In the New York City Youth Board inquiry the objective is to determine whether and to what extent the Social Prediction Table, if applied even before clear signs of antisocial behavior, will serve to distinguish on the basis of *subsequent* evidence, the true delinquents in a high delinquency area from the nondelinquents; while in the Maximum Benefits Project the purpose (among others) is to determine whether the Social Prediction Table, if applied to children reported by teachers as already showing evidences of severe behavioral difficulties, will correctly differentiate, as determined by subsequent followup, the potential delinquents from the pseudodelinquents. Both inquiries are still in process and will, it is hoped, continue until the subjects are 17. A brief resumé of the findings to date follows.

## Further Retrospective Studies in the United States

Subsequent to the appearance of "Spotting Potential Delinquents: Can It Be Done?" several other retrospective checkings of the Social Prediction Table have been made—one at the Thom Clinic in Boston where Dr. Virginia Clower applied the Table in 1956 to 100 boys "chosen at random for a wide variety of behavior and emotional difficulties" who had been referred to the Clinic during 1953 and 1954. The results showed that of 31 boys in this group who had been diagnosed by the clinicians as "antisocial characters," all "without exception" were placed by the Prediction Table in the group having a high likelihood of persistent delinquency. And in 1957, the Clinic, continuing its experimental application of the Social Prediction Table, again reported a consistently high degree of correlation between the clinical diagnoses and the rating by the Social Prediction Table:

> "Our impression is that the Scale almost invariably gives high scores to the child with aggressive, destructive behavior problems, whether these problems are seen in an individual with an antisocial character formation, neurosis or psychosis. The work we have done so

far suggests a positive correlation between the ability of the child to manage aggression and his score on the Glueck scales. That is, the less tendency to act out aggressive impulses, the lower the score." [12]

In 1957, Selma J. Glick applied the Prediction Table to a small group of boys who were independently diagnosed by the clinical staff of the Jewish Board of Guardians as true delinquents on intake into the Clinic and she found that the Table itself, "without psychiatric and psychological studies of the children, would have properly identified the same cases." [13]

Still another retrospective study completed since the publication of "Spotting Potential Delinquents" encompasses 28 inmates of Sing Sing Prison who had been juvenile offenders. In this were involved a team of researchers at the Post-Graduate Center for Psychiatric Research headed by Bernard Glueck, Jr., M.D.,[14] and the findings presented at the Third International Congress of Criminology in London (1955) by Mrs. Isa Brandon. The prisoners included rapists, men committing sexual assaults, heterosexual pedophiles, homosexual pedophiles, and nonsexual offenders. Coauthored by Bernard Glueck, Jr., M.D., and Mrs. Brandon, the report stated that regardless of offense, 71 per cent of the men would have been correctly identified by the Social Prediction Table in their early years as headed for criminal careers; and that 90 per cent of the "nonsexual" offenders would have been correctly identified.[15]

Also during 1957, the South Shore Courts Clinic of Quincy, Massachusetts, which was set up by the Massachusetts State Department of Mental Health and charged with the study and diagnosis of children referred by the local Juvenile Court, applied the Table to 50 young offenders in an effort to determine its usefulness to clinicians. The results of the pilot study were sufficiently encouraging to the project director, B. R. Hutcheson, M.D., and to the research director, J. I. Hurwitz, Ph.D., to suggest the possibility that the Table may be of aid in differentiating between true delinquents and accidental offenders.

The above constitutes a brief resumé of American retrospective studies applying the Social Prediction Table that have come directly to the writer's attention.

[12] Letter from Dr. Eveoleen N. Rexford, Director, Douglas A. Thom Clinic for Child Guidance, dated May 16, 1957.

[13] Letter, May 17, 1957.

[14] Now professor of psychiatry in the Medical School of the University of Minnesota.

[15] Unpublished paper presented at the Third International Congress of Criminology, London, September 1955.

In addition to the actual applications of the Table, diverse inquiries about it reflecting widespread interest have come, for example, from police departments (notably the Juvenile Aid Bureau of the New York City Police Department); from school systems in different parts of the United States, including Rochester, Denver, Los Angeles, and Tacoma; from school counselors; family service societies; youth authorities, notably the Southern Reception Center for Children of the State of California; from institutions for young children, including schools for retarded children; from child guidance clinics; from mental hospitals; from Community Chests and Councils; Governor's Committees on Children and Youth; child psychiatrists, psychologists, pediatricians, ministers; and more recently, from a nursery school training center.

## Retrospective Studies in Foreign Countries

Some checkings of the Social Prediction Table have been attempted also in foreign countries, notably in Japan and France. A third is in the planning stage in Belgium.

In addition have come expressions of earnest interest in a means for early differentiation between potential delinquents and true nondelinquents from England, Holland, Germany, Sweden, India, Israel, Australia, New Zealand, Uruguay and other South American countries. And worldwide interest is reflected in a resolution presented and passed at the Third International Congress of Criminology held in London in September 1955:

> Because of the close relationship between recidivism and early delinquency, it is advisable to encourage the development and use of prognostic devices, including predictive tables in the prediction of early delinquency. . . . That an indispensable aspect of any improved prognostic technique is the validation of the predictive methods on samples of cases other than those on which they were developed in order to transform them as far as possible into effective instruments for prognosis.[16]

It is noted in the Program of the Third International Penal and Penitentiary Congress of the Spanish American countries, which is to

---

[16] See *Summary of Proceedings,* Third International Congress of Criminology, Bedford College, London, September 12-18, 1955, 251 pp., published by the British Organizing Committee on behalf of the International Society for Criminology, 1957. The resolution was adopted by a vote of 260 to 10 (see pp. 222-223. Conclusion of Section IV).

be held in Lisbon in the summer of 1960, that the Fifth Section is to be devoted to *"Pronostics Criminologiques:"*

> Le choix de ce sujet dérive de la décision adoptée par le II^e Congrès pénal et pénitentiaire de Sao-Paulo qui recommandait comme sujet de travail du prochain Congrès l'étude de l'examen médico-psychiatrique, psychologique et social des délinquants, spécialement en ce qui concerne les délinquants par habitude.[17]

(a) *Japan.* Japanese interest in a means for the early identification of potential delinquents is especially keen, and is manifested not only by the recent organization of a Criminology Study Society within the Ministry of Justice, a major effort of which is devoted to prediction studies, but also by the publication of a two-hundred page book in Japanese by a public prosecutor and a psychiatrist, entitled *Introduction to the Glueck Prediction Method.*[18]

The first of the Japanese attempts to apply the Social Prediction Table was made by Tokuhiro Tatezawa, probation officer of the Yokohama Family Court, on 30 delinquents appearing before a juvenile court in Morioka, Japan, and a control group of 30 nondelinquent boys from a public school in the same neighborhood.[19]

The application of the Table appears to have been successful because 87 per cent of the delinquents and 92 per cent of the nondelinquents were correctly identified by the Social Prediction Table. This first retrospective Japanese checking assumes particular significance in the light of the marked cultural differences between Japanese and American delinquents and nondelinquents:

> This prediction study revealed that the factors used in the Gluecks' prediction table show rather high predictive power when applied to the Japanese juvenile cases which have their own cultural and social background.[20]

Subsequently, other inquiries were made in Japan, and some are still under way:

> Our Criminology Study Society has been successfully carrying out a series of studies for the validation of Glueck Social Prediction Scales. A Progress Report on one of these studies revealed that the Social

---

[17] For Program, see *Revue de Science Criminelle et de Droit Pénal Comparé,* Paris, Octobre-Décembre 1959, Nouvelle Série, Numéro 4, p. 915.

[18] Haruo Abe and Kokichi Higuchi, Tokyo, Ichiryusha Publishing Company, 1959.

[19] Tokuhiro Tatezawa, "A Study of Prediction of Juvenile Delinquency," mimeographed by Ministry of Justice, Japan, 1956, and distributed by the Criminology Study Society.

[20] *Ibid.,* p. 30.

Prediction Scale would have successfully detected 92 per cent of 70 persistently delinquent juveniles, had it been applied to these cases as early as when they were nine years of age.[21]

(b) *France*. An ongoing study in Strasbourg, France, was initiated in 1958 by Professor Jacques Léauté of the Institut de Science Criminelle of the Faculty of Law of the University of Strasbourg, and is being carried on in cooperation with M. Didier Ansieu (Professor of Psychology and Head of the Institut Psycho-Pedagogie of the University of Strasbourg), Dr. René Oberlé (psychologist at the Centre d'Observation of the Juvenile Court in Strasbourg), and Dr. Berge (Head of the Institut Psycho-Pedagogie of the Lycée Claude Bernard, Paris). They made a pilot study in 1958, applying the Social Prediction Table to 46 delinquents at the Centre d'Observation de Délinquants Juvénile in Strasbourg and found that 91.4 per cent of these boys would have been correctly identified as potential delinquents had the prediction table been applied to them at the age of 6. It is of special interest that the psychologist, M. Oberlé, who was charged with the details of the study, was initially skeptical of the ability of the Prediction Table to identify the delinquents and is now convinced of its usefulness.

Encouraged by the result of the pilot project, Professor Léauté and his coworkers applied the Table early in 1959 to two additional groups of offenders totalling 203 boys, one group being already adjudicated delinquents and the other, though never arrested, was brought before the juvenile court by their parents on complaint of incorrigibility. Of the 140 delinquents in the first group, 89.9 per cent would have been correctly predicted as potential delinquents at age six; while of the 63 boys in the second group, almost all were identified as potential delinquents.

A comparison of the findings regarding the incidence of the five predictive factors among the French delinquents and predelinquents, as compared with the 500 delinquents of *Unraveling Juvenile Delinquency* (on the basis of which cases the Social Prediction Table was constructed), is of interest:

In *Unraveling Juvenile Delinquency*, 27.9 per cent of the mothers of the delinquents were found to be indifferent or hostile to the boys as compared with 46.4 per cent of the French delinquents and 49.2 per cent of the French predelinquents; as regards *Affection of Father*, 59.8 per cent of the fathers of our delinquents of *Unraveling* were found

[21] Letter from Haruo Abe, Public Prosecutor, Ministry of Justice, November 21, 1958. Additional studies have been reported (all confirmatory) since the completion of this article.

to be indifferent or hostile to them, as compared with 75 per cent of the fathers of the French delinquents and 69.8 per cent of the fathers of the French predelinquents; as regards *Supervision by Mother,* it was unsuitable in 93 per cent of the cases of 500 delinquents of *Unraveling,* as compared with 95.7 per cent of the French delinquents and 93.7 per cent of the French predelinquents; in regard to *Discipline by Father,* it was other than firm and kindly in 94.3 per cent of the 500 delinquents of *Unraveling* as compared with 100 per cent of the French delinquents and 98.4 per cent of the French predelinquents; finally, as regards *Family Cohesiveness,* the family was not completely cohesive in 84 per cent of instances among the 500 delinquents of *Unraveling Juvenile Delinquency* as compared with 95.7 per cent of the French delinquents and 98.4 per cent of the French predelinquents.[22]

(c) *Interest in Other Foreign Countries.* A study to test the usefulness of the Table is now being formulated in Brussels by Professor Aimée Racine of the University of Brussels, director of the Centre d'Etude de la Délinquance Juvénile [23] with a subsidy from the Belgian Ministry of Justice. This study has the support of the Secretary-General of the Ministry, M. Paul Cornil, and of M. DeCant, Public Prosecutor, as well as of the Ministry of Public Health (especially of its Conseil Supérieur de la Famille, the Chairman of which was, until recently, Professor Fernand Collin of the Law Faculty of Louvain University, and who is largely responsible for initiating interest in a prediction validation project in Belgium).

It is our intention to prepare a motion to be submitted to the Conseil Supérieur, in which we request the Government to give first priority to the study of the detection of possible delinquency among Belgian youth.[24]

There are other significant evidences of interest in foreign countries in the early identification of potential delinquents which might be mentioned. For example, in Holland, Professor Willem Nagel of the

[22] Findings reported to Professor and Mrs. Sheldon Glueck in July 1958 in Strasbourg, and in June 1959 in Paris by Professor Léauté and some of his coworkers and supplemented by a letter from Professor Léauté, February 25, 1960. As regards the incorrigible boys, in accordance with Article 375 of the French Civil Code (September 1, 1945), a parent or guardian may, if a child is unmanageable, request the judge of the juvenile court to examine into the situation. Article 376 requests that the judge make an investigation and that he may for this purpose order that a child be held in an observation center (already adjudicated delinquents may also be held in such a center). The incorrigibles are regarded as predelinquents and the results of the application of the Social Prediction Table have indeed proved them to be such.

[23] 49, rue du Châtelain, Bruxelles 5, Belgique.

[24] Letter, January 28, 1958.

Criminological Institute of the University of Leiden has been charged with, and has recently completed, the preparation of a report to the Dutch Ministry of Justice on the possible uses of prediction tables in Holland. This is a complete survey of predictive theories and devices, including a description of the Glueck Prediction Tables. The Dutch Ministry of Justice is now engaged in determining next steps in the application of such devices.

In Germany, Judge Wolf Middendorff of Freiburg/Breisgau has prepared a Report for the German Ministry of Justice on American and European Prediction Studies, in which considerable space is given to the Social Prediction Table. This is now in process of publication. In India, Mr. D. V. Kulkarni, Chief Inspector of the Certified Schools in Bombay, and Mr. Chinnea Doraiswami, Deputy Inspector General of Prisons and Correctional Schools of India, have each expressed the hope that they might develop some experimental applications of the Social Prediction Table. From New Zealand, Mr. Henry Field, professor of educational psychology of Canterbury University College in Christchurch, wrote in February 1957:

> I am satisfied that this work of prediction is of fundamental importance and that it points the way to successful measures of prophylaxis and prevention.

In July 1956, a report on juvenile delinquency in Australia, prepared by the Advisory Committee to the Honorable Chief Secretary of Victoria [25] indicates that "research in this field should be undertaken in Victoria with the objective of ascertaining the extent to which, and the manner in which, these methods may be properly used here."

These are a few illustrations of the far-flung interest in a means for identifying delinquents and for experimenting with the Social Prediction Table.

## Projects Directed Toward the Identification of Potential Delinquents

I return now to two ongoing experiments in which the Social Prediction Table has been applied:

(1) by the New York City Youth Board to 224 boys in the first grade of two schools in high delinquency areas of New York City, in advance

[25] Report of Juvenile Delinquency Advisory Committee to The Honorable A. G. Rylah, M.L.A., Chief Secretary of Victoria, The Honorable Mr. Justice John V. Barry of the Supreme Court of Victoria (Chairman); Printed at Melbourne, July 17, 1956, 96 pp. See p. 32 *et seq., Prediction Studies.*

of, or without knowledge of, any overt signs of antisocial behavior, in order to determine the extent of ultimate agreement between predicted and actual delinquency or nondelinquency.

(2) by the Maximum Benefits Project, to 179 boys and girls in all grades of two elementary schools in high-delinquency areas in the District of Columbia referred to the Project staff by teachers as manifesting severe behavioral difficulties. Among the questions raised in this inquiry is the extent to which the behavioral symptoms are indeed prodromal of future delinquency according to the Prediction Table when checked against the later behavior of the children.

Both inquiries are still in progress and it is hoped will continue until the youngsters are 17. Meanwhile, the New York City Youth Board [26] has briefly reported in January 1960 that "followup" data covering a 7-year period is available on 223 of the initial sample of 224 boys who are now 12½ to 13 years old and scattered in 89 different schools: Of 186 boys predicted at school entrance as *nondelinquents*, 176, or 94.6 per cent are still *nondelinquent*; of 37 boys predicted as delinquents, 13 are already adjudicated delinquents and 4 more are "unofficial" offenders, a total of 46 per cent; of 191 boys who are still nondelinquents, regardless of how predicted, 176, or 89.7 per cent, had been correctly predicted as nondelinquents; of 27 boys already delinquents, 17, or 63 per cent, had been correctly predicted as delinquents.

In considering these interim results, it should be kept in mind that the boys are only now approaching the peak years of delinquency and arrest. It is essential that the followup continue until they are 17, since it was found in *Unraveling Juvenile Delinquency* [27] that about half of the 500 Boston delinquents did not make their first court appearance until they were between 13 and 16 years old.

As regards the Maximum Benefits Project, a preliminary report issued in 1958 states that "The Glueck criteria . . . have proven in our opinion to be a very effective predictive device." [28]

In a later interim report it is stated that of 58 children already having police or court records 4 years after the beginning of the study, 57 had been previously identified by the Social Prediction Table as potential delinquents.

And a more recent summary of the Project made in preparation for the 1960 White House Conference on Children and Youth now stresses

[26] 79 Madison Avenue, New York City.
[27] *Unraveling Juvenile Delinquency*, Appendix A, p. 294.
[28] Emory F. Hodges, M.D., C. Downing Tait, Jr., M.D., and Nina B. Trevvett, "Preliminary Report of the Maximum Benefits Project," made to the Eugene and Agnes E. Meyer Foundation; Commissioners' Youth Council, 1145 19th Street N.W., Washington, D.C., September 1958 (mimeographed), p. 18.

that "The Glueck Scores, in conjunction with the teacher referrals, appear to be effective tools in the identification of potential delinquents":

> Since the average child still has 5.9 years to go before reaching 18, and since the incidence of juvenile court appearances increases in the teenage group, we are inclined to think the percentage will draw near expected levels.[29]

## General Trend of Findings

The accumulated evidence thus far gathered from "retrospective" and "prospective" studies both in the United States and in foreign countries all seems to be tending in the same direction. A total of 18 inquiries in which the Social Prediction Table has been applied, are all suggestive of its usefulness. The studies include four samples of nondelinquents (the latter incorporated into the first of the two investigations by Thompson in 1954, in the New York City Youth Board study, in the Maximum Benefits Project, and in the first of the Japanese inquiries); three studies include girls (the second Thompson study, the study by Glick and Donnell of 150 unmarried mothers, and the Maximum Benefits Project).

The results thus far indicate that regardless of ethnic origin, color, religion, intelligence level, residence in urban or rural areas, economic level, or even sex, the predictive cluster is equally potent, not only on American but on Japanese and French samplings.

The Table has to date been applied to some 1,600 young children and adolescents—preponderantly males—in three American States (Massachusetts, New Jersey, and New York) and the District of Columbia, and in two foreign countries (Japan and France), each time with highly encouraging results. This does not mean that Professor Sheldon Glueck and I, who are responsible for the construction of this device based on 500 delinquents and 500 matched nondelinquents of *Unraveling Juvenile Delinquency*, are satisfied that it is beyond the stage of testing. We urge that checkings continue and that careful record be kept of the work done.

The instrument appears to hold promise not only for the identification of emotionally healthy potential delinquents, but also for the identification of neurotic, psychotic, or psychopathic children who are likely to give overt expression to their conflicts in aggressive behavior.

[29] Emory F. Hodges, M.D., C. Downing Tait, Jr., M.D., and Nina B. Trevvett, "Four Years of Work with Problem Children in Elementary Schools," Maximum Benefits Project (mimeographed 1959). Address as in footnote, p. 438.

Some gleanings of the capacity of the Table to identify this latter group of potential delinquents come from the experiments with it in the Thom Clinic by Rexford, Van Amerongen and Schleifer; [30] by Glick at the Jewish Board of Guardians; and in the study of 28 cases at Sing Sing Prison.

The Table also holds promise of distinguishing among children already manifesting behavior difficulties, those who are and who are not likely to develop into persistent offenders.

## Resolution of Difficulties in Applying Tables

A pioneer venture must to some extent proceed by trial and error, and the one of checking even a carefully constructed predictive device is no exception. Difficulties have emerged in the course of the experimental use of the Social Prediction Table that could not have been fully anticipated, and this has provided an invaluable opportunity to find ways of coping with them.

A device of this kind, the use of which is in part at least based on observational skills and the capacity to make judgments on data gathered from home interviews as well as from already recorded data in the files of social agencies, police, probation departments and other repositories of information about children and their families, is naturally subject to pitfalls. It has become abundantly clear that the difficulties stem from variations in the training and experience of those applying the Tables (psychiatrists, social workers, psychologists and others) as well as from occasional inadequacies in data. Questions have arisen, for example, as to the particular subcategory of one or another of the five factors into which to place a case. Likewise, there have at times emerged disagreements among different investigators in the same inquiry about the rating of some factors, especially affection of parents for a child which psychoanalytically oriented observers interpret in accordance with Freudian depth psychology and others on the basis of *surface* manifestations of parental affection. In addition to the difficulties encountered in the rating of parental affection, is the rating of Discipline by Father (as well as Affection of Father) in instances in which the father or a father-substitute had never been a part of the family group, or left the home before the child was 3 years of age. Still another

---

[30] See Eveoleen N. Rexford, "Antisocial Young Children and Their Families," reprinted from *Dynamic Psychopathology in Childhood*. Edited by Lucie Jessner and Eleanor Pavenstedt, M.D., Grune and Stratton, Inc., 1959, pp. 186-220. See especially pp. 197-200.

difficulty relates to the assessment of Family Cohesiveness in instances in which children were reared solely by the mother or mother-substitute.

These and similar considerations led us to investigate the possibility that the rating of one or another of the five factors could be dispensed with in instances in which the data appeared insufficient for purposes of making an accurate judgment, or was altogether lacking. This was accomplished with the aid of the Research Bureau of the Harvard Business School (which had on punch cards for each of the thousand cases of *Unraveling Juvenile Delinquency* the five factors comprising the original Table). Correlations were systematically pursued between the total scores for the Five Factors (Affection of Mother for Boy, Affection of Father for Boy, Supervision by Mother, Discipline by Father, and Family Cohesiveness) and every possible combination of 4, 3, and 2 factors, eliminating those combinations in which the Coefficient of Correlation was less than .90. Actually, the coefficients were found to range from .932 in a Table made up of two factors to .987 in a table made up of four factors. (The interested reader is invited to examine *Predicting Delinquency and Crime,* Appendix B, Tables IX-1 to IX-1e, pp. 233 to 235, for all possible combinations of four and fewer factors that nevertheless retain a very high predictive potential. These shortened prediction tables were completed just in time to be added to the galley proof of *Predicting Delinquency and Crime.*)

In instances in which the Five-Factor Table cannot be used, one or another of the shorter Tables should meet any problem reflected in the course of the validation efforts, except those arising from lack of sufficient training in gathering and interpreting the needed data. Some illustrations of how the shortened prediction Table would meet the problems that have been revealed in the course of attempts to check the Social Prediction Table against various samples of cases might be helpful. For example, the inconsistency of ratings of Affection of Mother or Affection of Father by workers of differing "persuasions" has been eliminated by confining the scoring in certain instances to the three remaining factors (Supervision by Mother, Discipline by Father, and Family Cohesiveness). The Coefficient of Correlation between the Three-Factor Total Scores and the Total Scores for the Five Factors is .961. To those who may conclude that the elimination of these factors implies that they are not potent in the etiology of delinquency, the writer wishes to emphasize that this is not the case; for these two factors were found in *Unraveling Juvenile Delinquency* markedly to differentiate delinquents from nondelinquents; it is rather to be stressed that the remaining three factors reflect parental affection and it is for this reason that the fewer number of factors have been found in the original sample to be as potent as the greater number in differentiating between persistent delinquents and true nondelinquents.

The problem of rating Discipline by Father in a situation in which he has not been part of the family group since a child was 3 years old is met in turn by the use of a Two-Factor Table (Supervision by Mother, Family Cohesiveness), the Coefficient of Correlation between the Total Scores for the Two Factors being .932 in the cases included in *Unraveling Juvenile Delinquency*. And the rating of Family Cohesiveness in instances in which one of the parents, usually the father or a father-substitute has not been an integral part of the family group since the child in question was 3 years of age, is now met by considering the relationship between mother and children as "cohesive" if the ties between them are close and warm, rather than rating such a situation as having only some elements of cohesiveness by reason of a father's absence. Our attention was particularly directed to this clarification because in both the Youth Board and the Maximum Benefits Projects this kind of family pattern, rarely present in the cases of *Unraveling Juvenile Delinquency*, emerged in a particular ethnic group that had not been there included.

By reducing the burden of data-gathering and increasing the accuracy of the rating of cases, the Social Prediction Table becomes more usable and more efficient. Certainly, nonpsychiatric workers should not encounter difficulties in the rating of Supervision by Mother, Discipline by Father, and Family Cohesiveness.[31]

The New York City Youth Board has already corrected errors of rating resulting from the first two difficulties, but must yet give consideration to the third; and the Maximum Benefits Project is now in process of rerating cases to take account of all three of the above-mentioned difficulties.

It is clear that the accuracy of the predictive device is being sharpened and it is to be hoped that experimentation by the Youth Board and the Maximum Benefits Project will continue to the advantage of those who may ultimately wish to apply the Social Prediction Table. There is still much to learn, however, and many difficulties to be resolved in connection with any large-scale use of this or any other device for the identification of potential delinquents.

There are additional problems that would follow the general acceptance of this device as a means for differentiating soon after school entrance among those children who are not and those who are likely

---

[31] Definitions of terms appear in Appendix B, pp. 245 *et seq.* of *Predicting Delinquency and Crime*.

to develop into persistent offenders unless suitable measures of intervention are applied. Among them might be mentioned the wisdom of using such devices at all. In this connection, the interested reader is asked to consult *Predicting Delinquency and Crime*, Chapter XII, "Some Objections to Predictive Devices," as a means of orientation in the pros and cons.

Still another basic issue has to do with meeting the challenge of "doing something" following the identification of potential delinquents. The way points to the early treatment of families and children by the constituted agencies of society when the interpersonal relations between the parents and a particular child make him vulnerable to delinquency. The rationale for such intervention is embraced in the already accepted philosophy of "reaching out" casework and poses only the problem of the *stage at which* this "reaching out" is to be initiated, *i.e., after* signs of antisocial behavior have become clearly evident or *in advance* of them.

Beyond this is the need for a new profession of "family educators" drawn from among psychiatrists, social workers, psychologists, ministers, pediatricians, public health nurses, teachers and others whose first task it would be to explore *methods* of reeducating the families of children found to be vulnerable to delinquency. Despite the many forms that delinquency may take and the many "types" of delinquents, the common denominator is aggressive antisocial behavior and it is to the prevention and control of this that family educators must direct themselves.

[Editor's Note. Just before this book went to press an article appeared giving the results of the testing by the New York City Youth Board of boys at age six, when these boys had reached the age of sixteen.[32] In the final analysis, the predictive factors in the scale were reduced from the original five to three: supervision of boy by mother, discipline of boy by mother, and cohesiveness of family. All reference to the father and to affection were omitted. Score classes were reduced from four to three: low probability of future delinquency, almost even chance for delinquency or nondelinquency, and high probability for delinquency. Of the 240 boys who had reached age sixteen, forty had exhibited delinquent behavior (one of whom could not be rated), and 200 had no record

[32] Maude M. Craig and Selma J. Glick, "Ten Years' Experience with the Glueck Social Prediction Table," *Crime and Delinquency*, 9 (July, 1963), 249-261.

of delinquency. For the purpose of the study the delinquency category included serious offenders and persistent minor delinquents, apparently as classified by the research staff (the article is not clear on this point). The results follow:

Of 193 boys who, at age six, made scores below 140, indicating low probability of delinquency, 7 or 3.6 were classified as delinquent at age sixteen and 186 or 96.4 per cent were nondelinquent.

Of 19 boys who, at age six, made scores between 140 and 200, indicating even chances of future delinquency or nondelinquency, 9 or 47.3 per cent were delinquent at age sixteen, and 10 or 52.7 per cent nondelinquent.

Of 27 boys who, at age six, made scores of 200 or over, indicating future delinquency, 23 or 85.2 per cent were delinquent at age sixteen, and 4 or 14.8 per cent were nondelinquent.

The authors of the article conclude that the specific factors included in the test, if allowed to persist, will tend to produce delinquency, but that "six years' exposure to deleterious home situations does not necessarily predestine a youngster to delinquency."]

## 36. Mortality, Mobility and Crime: Problem Children Thirty Years Later

### Lee N. Robins and Patricia O'Neal

Lee Robins, Ph.D., is Research Associate Professor of Sociology and Patricia O'Neal, M.D., is Associate Professor of Psychology at the Washington University School of Medicine. Both are active in research and have many published articles to their credit. The research of which this article is a part has been supported by the Foundations' Fund for Research in Psychiatry and the U.S. Public Health Service. The article was presented at the Annual Meeting of the American Sociological Society, Washington, D.C., in 1957.

Lee N. Robins and Patricia O'Neal, "Mortality, Mobility and Crime: Problem Children Thirty Years Later," *American Sociological Review*, 23 (April, 1958), 162-71. Reprinted by permission of the American Sociological Association and the authors.

## Introduction

Studies in social problems have centered on a variety of phenomena of the American scene, including juvenile delinquency, crime, divorce, alcoholism, and mental illness. While in the last fifteen years attention has been focused on the multiple background variables related to a given social problem, as the Gluecks [1] relate genetic, social, and psychological predictors to criminality, little attention has been given to the multiplicity of social problems occurring within defined segments of society. While older studies in urban ecology [2] have assigned multiple social problems to slum areas, implicitly suggesting that inhabitants of these areas are socially maladjusted in a variety of ways, few efforts have been made to examine the range of social problems found in a given group of individuals.

A study now in progress is concerned with the occurrence of deviant social behavior in adults with a history of childhood behavior problems. The rate of occurrence of various expressions of social deviance, including not only criminal behavior, but also failure to achieve satisfactory employment status, transiency, alcoholism, mental illness, unstable marital relations, inadequacy as parents, and social isolation, is being investigated and contrasted with the rate of occurrence of these phenomena among a control group of adults without serious childhood behavior problems.

While this study is not yet complete, there are already striking indications that these various kinds of social deviance occur in the group with a history of childhood behavior problems and are relatively rare among those with normal childhood behavior. It would follow then that diverse expressions of social deviance are related to a common nexus of social and psychiatric variables identifiable in the childhood experience of socially deviant individuals. This study will attempt in its later phases to explore the relative contribution of social and psychiatric factors to the occurrence of social deviance or acceptable social adjustment in the adult life of individuals who had serious behavior problems in childhood. The present paper presents findings concerning three areas related to the social deviance as adults of individuals who had behavior problems as children: rate and cause of death, geographic

---

[1] Sheldon and Eleanor Glueck, *Unraveling Juvenile Delinquency*, Cambridge: Harvard University Press, 1950; *Physique and Delinquency*, New York: Harper Brothers, 1956.

[2] E.g., Harvey Zorbaugh, *The Gold Coast and the Slum*, Chicago: University of Chicago Press, 1929.

mobility, and criminality. The persistence of serious behavior problems into the adult life of these subjects encourages speculation about the degree to which major social problems in America may be the contribution of a relatively restricted segment of the population, distinguished by a total and life-long failure to fulfill conventional norms.

## Methods

The subjects of the study reported in part in this paper are, first, the patient group, a consecutive series of 524 persons seen as children at the St. Louis Municipal Psychiatric Clinic between 1924 and 1929. Their records as children describe a broad spectrum of behavioral and emotional disturbance. These former patients are being located 30 years later and personally interviewed with the aid of a standardized questionnaire designed to evaluate many aspects of their social adjustment and psychiatric status. Public records are being searched for objective evidence of their school achievement, arrest and prison history, mental hospitalization, Armed Services records, Veterans Administration records, social service contacts, and cause of death. Their current social and psychiatric status, as revealed through interview and public records, is then related to their childhood behavior problems and childhood social environment, as recorded in the detailed records of the St. Louis Municipal Psychiatric Clinic, the St. Louis Juvenile Court, records of social agencies interested in the family during the childhood of the patient, and school records.

At the same time, the patient group is being compared with a control group, 100 subjects selected from the St. Louis Public School records, located, interviewed, and checked through the public records in the same manner as the patient group, to discover to what extent childhood behavior problems are associated with an adult adjustment different from that found in a group without serious behavior problems in childhood.

The patient group includes every patient seen at the Clinic within the specified period who met the following criteria: age under 18 years at first clinic contact; Caucasian race; I.Q. not less than 80 (Stanford-Binet); referral because of problem behavior (patients seen as part of a school survey, for placement, or for vocational advice were omitted).

The control group was randomly selected from the records of the St. Louis Public Schools to match the patient group with respect to sex, race, and year of birth. In order to match the socio-economic background of the patients as closely as possible, home addresses were used to provide a match for neighborhood. This was done by finding the census tract in which each patient lived at time of referral, grouping tracts by their median monthly rental as reported in the 1930 Census, and setting up tract quotas met by the control subjects' last home address in public school. The matching of home neighborhoods seemed to be the best available means of matching socio-economic status since, on the one hand, information about the occupation of the father was erratically reported in the public school records and, on the other, the incidence of fatherless and dependent families was so high in the patient group that quotas based on the father's occupation would fail to represent a large proportion of the patient group. Since children in the St. Louis public schools were routinely given only group intelligence tests while patients had been given individual tests, no precise matching of intelligence quotients was possible. To eliminate mentally deficient children from the control series, as they had been eliminated from the patient series, a minimum score of 80 on the group intelligence test was required. The control subjects were also required to show no obvious behavior disturbances as indicated by repeating school years, their transfer to a correctional institution, or excessive absences.

At the present time, information as to whether subjects are alive or dead is available for 92 per cent of the total group. Exact current addresses are known for 85 per cent of the subjects.[3] Checking of coroner's records and of police records in the St. Louis area has been completed. Approximately 330 subjects have been interviewed.

Since the location of subjects and record checking are approaching completion, findings will be presented concerning: (1) how many patients and control subjects have survived 30 years, (2) where they now live, and (3) how many have adult police records. While findings must be considered tentative until the study is finished, these particular aspects of the study are so nearly complete that it is highly improbable that later information will materially change the conclusions.

## Description of the Patient Group as Children

The patient group is predominantly male (73 per cent). The median age at first clinic contact was 13 years. The social background was predominantly laboring class, but 25 per cent of the children came from white-collar families and 7 per cent from professional or executive families. The chief problems for which patients were seen were theft, incorrigibility, learning problems, sexual activity, and "nervousness."

---

[3] Geographic areas in which subjects live are known for an additional 6 per cent for whom no precise address is available. These will be included in studying geographic mobility.

The patients fell into three behavior problem categories, as indicated in Table 1. Group 1, the juvenile delinquents, are defined as children who

TABLE 1

DESIGNATION OF CHILDHOOD BEHAVIOR PROBLEM GROUPS

| Group | Juvenile Court at Time of Referral | Behavior in Conflict with Mores * | Other Behavior Problems † |
|---|---|---|---|
| Group 1 N = 194 (37% of patient group) Males: 80% | Yes | Yes | In some cases |
| Group 2 N = 206 (40% of patient group) Males: 68% | No | Yes | In some cases |
| Group 3 N = 124 (23% of patient group) Males: 68% | No | No | Yes |

* Including theft, truancy, running away, assault, vandalism, incorrigibility, sexual misbehavior, use of alcohol, forgery.

† Including learning disabilities, tics, seclusiveness, fears, sleep disturbance, eating problems, speech defects.

had a Juvenile Court hearing before or at the time of referral (37 per cent of the patient group). Group 2 is composed of non-delinquents who showed behavior in conflict with the social mores (40 per cent of the patient group), including children who had shown behavior similar to that for which Group 1 had been charged in Juvenile Court—theft, running away, truancy, assault, destruction of property, incorrigibility, and sexual misbehavior. At the time of referral, this behavior had not yet involved the child in an official Juvenile Court hearing. Some Group 2 children were pre-delinquents who later had Juvenile Court appearances; others showed this behavior in a less severe or less public form than Group 1 children, or perhaps had more protection from Court action through family or social agency intervention. Group 3 consists of non-delinquents whose behavior problems were not conflicts with social mores (23 per cent of the Clinic population); included here were difficulties in attention and learning and neurotic traits such as tics, nightmares, tantrums, stuttering, and unusual fears.

While only Group 1 patients had had Juvenile Court hearings at the time of referral, some members of Groups 2 and 3 had already had a "police brush," that is, an arrest and dismissal without an official court hearing.[4] By age 18, 14 per cent of Group 2 and two per cent of Group 3 had become Juvenile Court cases (Table 2). Twenty-six per cent of Group 2 and eleven per cent of Group 3 had police brushes but no Juvenile Court appearances as children. Among the 100 control subjects, only one ever had a Juvenile Court record, and only five had juvenile police brushes. In Groups 2 and 3 and the control group, boys had more juvenile police troubles than girls.[5] As might therefore be expected, Group 1, consisting only of Juvenile Court cases, contained fewer girls than Groups 2 or 3 (20 as against 32 per cent).

## Results

*Mortality:* Information as to whether subjects are now alive is available for 92 per cent of the total group, 98 per cent of the controls, and 91 per cent of the patients. Among the control subjects, nine per cent have died during the 30-year follow-up interval (Table 3), as compared with 13 per cent of the patients. While not a statistically significant difference, it is interesting that the excess patient deaths are confined to men and are accounted for by homicides, which occurred only in male ex-juvenile delinquent patients (six cases), suicides (two cases), and death from acute alcoholism (two cases). The homicide victims included three shot by the police in line of duty, one justifiable homicide, one murdered, assailant unknown, and one killed in a gang feud at the age of 16. One of the suicides was an alcoholic, the other a drug addict. Apparently deaths unrelated to problem behavior do not vary between patient and control groups.

*Geographic Mobility:* The patient and control subjects, all residents of the Greater St. Louis area 30 years ago, have now dispersed as far as Iran and Japan. Most of them (58 per cent of the patient group and 76 per cent of the control group), however, are now located in the St. Louis area (Table 4). The patients' greater dispersion is accounted for

---

[4] Information about juvenile offenses was obtained from Clinic, Juvenile Court, and police records.

[5] Significance of differences was in all cases tested by Chi Square using the Yates correction for all cells in which the expected frequency was 5 or less. All differences are significant at the .05 level unless specifically stated otherwise. In this case, the difference between boys and girls in proportion having juvenile police troubles was significant in Group 2. In Group 2 and the control group, there were too few cases of juvenile police troubles to give a statistically significant difference in the rates for boys and girls, but the same trend of more juvenile police difficulties for boys may be seen.

## TABLE 2

### JUVENILE POLICE TROUBLES IN PATIENT GROUPS AND CONTROL SUBJECTS

| | Total Patient Group | Patients — Group 1 Court Hearing by Date of Referral | | | Patients — Group 2 Behavior in Conflict with Mores | | | Patients — Group 3 Other Behavior Problems | | | Control Subjects | | |
|---|---|---|---|---|---|---|---|---|---|---|---|---|---|
| | | M | F | T | M | F | T | M | F | T | M | F | T |
| Juvenile court before clinic | 37% | 100% | 100% | 100% | 17% | 8% | 14% | 2% | 2% | 2% | 1%† | .... | 1%† |
| Juvenile court only after clinic | 6 | .... | .... | .... | 31 | 17 | 26 | 14 | 5 | 11 | 7 | .... | 5 |
| Juvenile police brushes only ‡ | 13 | .... | .... | .... | 52* | 75* | 60 | | | | | | |
| No juvenile police trouble | 44 | .... | .... | .... | | | | 84 | 93 | 87 | 92 | 100 | 94 |
| N's: | 100% 525 | 100% 156 | 100% 38 | 100% 194 | 100% 141 | 100% 65 | 100% 206 | 100% 84 | 100% 40 | 100% 124 | 100% 70 | 100% 30 | 100% 100 |

† Juvenile Court at any time, since control subjects did not attend the Clinic.
‡ Arrests without Court proceedings.
* P < .02 for significance of difference between starred groups.

## TABLE 3

### CAUSE OF DEATH

(*Based on those for whom information is available*)

| Cause of Death | Patients | | | Control Subjects | | |
|---|---|---|---|---|---|---|
| | Male | Female | Total | Male | Female | Total |
| War | 1% | . . . | 1% | 1% | . . . | 1% |
| Accidents | 3 | 1% | 3 | 2 | 3% | 2 |
| Homicide | 2 | . . . | 1 | . . . | . . . | . . . |
| Suicide | 1 | . . . | * | . . . | . . . | . . . |
| Natural causes | 5 | 7 | 6 | 6 | 7 | 6 |
| Cause not known | 2 | 1 | 2 | . . . | . . . | . . . |
| Still alive | 86 | 91 | 87 | 91 | 90 | 91 |
| | 100% | 100% | 100% | 100% | 100% | 100% |
| | N = 361 | N = 116 | N = 477 | N = 69 | N = 29 | N = 98 |

* Less than 1%.

## TABLE 4

### REGIONS TO WHICH SUBJECTS HAVE MOVED

(*Based on those so far located*)

| | Patients | | | Control Subjects | | |
|---|---|---|---|---|---|---|
| | Male | Female | Total | Male | Female | Total |
| Now in St. Louis | 62% | 48% | 58% † | 71% | 89% | 76% † |
| Out of St. Louis | | | | | | |
|   Mid-West | 14 | 24 | 17 * | 4 | . . . | 3 * |
|   West Coast | 12 | 13 | 12 † | 6 | 7 | 6 † |
|   East Coast | 5 | 2 | 4 | 6 | . . . | 4 |
|   All other U.S. | 6 | 12 | 8 | 12 | 4 | 10 |
|     (North, South, West) | | | | | | |
|   Foreign | 1 | 1 | 1 | 1 | . . . | 1 |
| | 100% | 100% | 100% | 100% | 100% | 100% |
| | N = 347 | N = 121 | N = 468 | N = 70 | N = 27 | N = 97 |

† P < .05.
* P < .01.

by their higher rate of migration to other parts of the Middle West and to the West Coast. Since other regions have drawn no higher proportion of patients than control subjects, it appears that these two areas (and in particular Chicago and Los Angeles) exercise a special attraction for the patients.

The difference in geographic mobility between patient and control groups is probably considerably greater than these figures indicate. Subjects are asked during interview to name the cities in which they have lived and their number of addresses in the last ten years. A review of interviews so far analyzed shows that of 34 patients now living in St. Louis, 47 per cent have previously lived elsewhere since they have been adult, but of 16 control subjects now living in St. Louis only one has ever lived elsewhere (P < .01). Therefore, it seems that not only are fewer patients than control subjects now in the St. Louis area, but fewer of the patients than control subjects now in St. Louis have resided there continuously throughout their adult lives. Among patients interviewed, 46 per cent have had four or more addresses in the last ten years; among the control subjects only 18 per cent have moved this often. Not only do patients move from one town to another more than control subjects, but they change address more often within a given city.

Sex of the subject appears related to mobility differently for patient and control groups. Among control subjects, no significant difference between men and women in the rate of moving from St. Louis was found, although the rate for women is somewhat lower. Among patients, more women than men have left St. Louis (P < .01). The control subjects fit the expected patterns of a lower mobility rate for women. An investigation of the reasons for the high mobility of the female patients must await further analysis of the interviews.

*Adult Arrests:* At the present time, police records of the City of St. Louis, St. Louis County, and the Sheriff's Office have been checked for all subjects. Police records in other cities in which subjects have lived have not yet been systematically checked. During the interview, subjects are asked for the names of all cities in which they have lived. When the interviews are completed, police departments in every city in which any subject has lived will be contacted for information. As reported above, more control than patient subjects have spent their entire adult life in St. Louis. Consequently, the police records of control subjects must be considered more complete than those of the patients. The data presented here will therefore underestimate the adult police records of the patients as compared with the control subjects; the reported differences must therefore be considered minimal.

Adult police records were evaluated in the following ways: (1)

whether there existed any police record, defined as any arrest [6] for non-traffic reasons or three or more traffic violations; (2) whether this record included non-traffic arrests; (3) whether the subject had repeated non-traffic arrests (defined as three or more); and (4) whether the subject had served any time in prison.

It was found that patients exceeded control subjects with respect to all four measures of adult criminality (Table 5). Forty-seven per

TABLE 5

ADULT POLICE RECORDS

|  | Patients | | Control Subjects | |
| --- | --- | --- | --- | --- |
| Any non-traffic arrest | 44% | .. | 11% | .. |
| 3 or more non-traffic arrests | .. | 24% | .. | 3% |
| 1 or 2 non-traffic arrests | .. | 20 | .. | 8 |
| Prison term served | .. | 16 | .. | 1 |
| Arrests without imprisonment | .. | 28 | .. | 10 |
| Traffic arrests only (3 or more) | 3 | .. | 5 | .. |
| No adult arrests | 53 | .. | 84 | .. |
|  | 100% | .. | 100% | .. |
|  | N * = 486 | .. | N * = 97 | .. |

* N's exclude those known to have died, been institutionalized, or permanently out of St. Louis before age 25.

P < .001 for all comparisons of patients and control subjects except for traffic arrests, where no significant differences were found.

cent of the patients had a police record as compared with 16 per cent of the control subjects. Among patients, 44 per cent had a non-traffic arrest, 24 per cent had been arrested at least three times, and 16 per cent had served time in prison. Among the control subjects, 11 per cent had a non-traffic arrest, 3 per cent had been arrested at least three times, and one per cent had served time in prison.

What is the meaning of the high rate of repeated arrests and prison sentences in the patient group? Obviously, the fact that there are more offenders in the patient group means that there will be also more multiple offenders and more individuals with prison experience. We wondered whether the rate of multiple offenses and prison experience was high enough to mean that the patient group not only included more individuals with adult records, but that these individuals with police records included a disproportionate number of chronic offenders

[6] The definition of police record used here involves *arrests* only, not convictions. In many cases, patients were repeatedly arrested on suspicion and then released.

and offenders whose crimes were serious enough to lead to imprison-ment. To test this possibility, the incidence of multiple arrests and prison sentences in patients was compared with that in control subjects, holding the variable of total number of offenders constant (Table 6).

## TABLE 6

Proportion of Offenders with Multiple Arrests and Imprisonment

|  | Patient Offenders | Control Offenders |
|---|---|---|
| (A)  Number of non-traffic arrests | | |
| 3 or more | 55% | 27% |
| 1 or 2 | 45 | 73 |
|  | 100% | 100% |
| (B)  Prison record | | |
| Prison | 38% * | 9% * |
| No prison | 62 | 91 |
|  | 100% | 100% |
|  | N = 211 | N = 11 |

\* > .05 < .10 for significance of difference between starred groups.

Findings are not clear-cut because the small number of offenders from the control group limits statistical treatment. Inspection of the results strongly suggests, however, that patient offenders have a higher rate both of multiple arrests and of prison terms than control offenders. Differences between the number of patient and control offenders going to prison would be statistically significant had the small number of control offenders not required the use of an adjustment of the Chi-Square value.

It was found that the groups to which the patients had been assigned on the basis of their childhood behavior problems were related to their adult police difficulties. With respect to all four measures (exist-ence of police record, occurrence of non-traffic arrests, number of arrests, and time served), Group 1, the ex-juvenile delinquents, had the highest rate, and differed significantly from both other patient groups and from the control group (Table 7). Group 2 had a signifi-cantly higher rate than Group 3 and the control group with respect to all four measures, but Group 3 did not differ significantly from the control group with respect to any of these measures.

When we investigated whether differences in the number with multiple arrests and prison records in the three behavior problem groups merely reflected the higher rate of offenders, or whether offenders from one

## TABLE 7

RELATION OF CHILDHOOD BEHAVIOR PROBLEM GROUP TO ADULT ARRESTS

| | | | *Patients* | | | | | *Control Subjects* | |
|---|---|---|---|---|---|---|---|---|---|
| | *Group 1* | | *Group 2* | | *Group 3* | | | | |
| Any non-traffic arrests | 60% | | 43% | | 20% | | | 11% | |
| 3 or more | | 38% | | 20% | | 9% | | | 3% |
| 1 or 2 | | 22 | | 23 | | 11 | | | 8 |
| Prison | | 28 | | 13 | | 6 | | | 1 |
| No prison | | 32 | | 30 | | 14 | | | 10 |
| Traffic only | 2 | | 4 | | 3 | | | 5 | |
| None | 38 | | 53 | | 77 | | | 84 | |
| | 100% | | 100% | | 100% | | | 100% | |
| | N * = 176 | | N * = 191 | | N * = 119 | | | N * = 97 | |

* N's exclude those known to have died, been institutionalized, or permanently out of St. Louis before age 25.

P < .001 for all comparisons among Groups 1, 2, and 3; between Group 1 and control subjects; between Group 2 and control subjects, except for traffic arrests, where no significant difference was found.

group tended to be more serious offenders than those from another, we found that Group 1 offenders are significantly more serious offenders (as measured by the proportion going to prison) than control offenders (Table 8). Differences between Group 2 and Group 3 offenders disappeared. Again, we are handicapped statistically by the small number of offenders among the control subjects. Although there are no

## TABLE 8

FREQUENCY OF ARREST AND IMPRISONMENT
IN CHILDHOOD BEHAVIOR PROBLEM GROUPS FOR OFFENDERS ONLY

| | *Group 1 Offenders* N = 105 | *Group 2 Offenders* N = 82 | *Group 3 Offenders* N = 24 | *Control Group Offenders* N = 11 |
|---|---|---|---|---|
| Number of non-traffic arrests | | | | |
| 3 or more | 63% | 48% | 46% | 27% |
| 1 or 2 | 37 | 52 | 54 | 73 |
| | 100% | 100% | 100% | 100% |
| Prison record | | | | |
| Prison | 46% ° | 30% | 29% | 9% ° |
| No prison | 54 | 70 | 71 | 91 |
| | 100% | 100% | 100% | 100% |

° Difference between starred groups is significant at the .05 level.

## TABLE 9

### Relation of Any Juvenile Police History and Sex to Adult Police Records

| | Patients | | | | | | Control Subjects | | | | | |
| --- | --- | --- | --- | --- | --- | --- | --- | --- | --- | --- | --- | --- |
| | Juvenile Court | | Juvenile Police Brush Only | | None | | Juvenile Court | | Juvenile Police Brush Only | | None | |
| | M | F | M | F | M | F | M | F | M | F | M | F |
| Adult police record | 71% | 39% | 63% | 45% | 35% | 12% | 100% | .... | 50% | .... | 13% | 3% |
| No adult police record | 29 | 61 | 37 | 55 | 65 | 88 | .... | .... | 50 | .... | 87 | 97 |
| N's * = | 100% 173 | 100% 36 | 100% 48 | 100% 11 | 100% 138 | 100% 82 | 100% 1 | .... | 100% 6 | .... | 100% 61 | 100% 30 |

* N's exclude subjects known to have died, been institutionalized, or left the St. Louis area before the age of 25. Male patients with any juvenile police troubles differed from those with none. P < .001.

statistically significant differences between Group 2 or Group 3 patients and the control subjects, inspection suggests that even in these groups, patients had a disproportionate number of serious offenders.

It was noted earlier that the three behavior problem groups to which patients had been assigned differed not only in the kind of behavior displayed, in which Groups 1 and 2 resembled each other and differed from Group 3, but also in the proportion with police difficulties as juveniles and in the proportion of males. All Group 1 patients had had Juvenile Court experience, and Group 1 also had the highest proportion of males. It is well known from other studies [7] and substantiated by this one (Table 9), that juvenile offenders have a high rate of recidivism and that men experience more police difficulties than women. The question remains whether childhood behavior problems in themselves, when sex differences and juvenile police difficulties are controlled, are related to adult criminality.

To examine the relation of childhood behavior to adult police records, patients with no history of juvenile police troubles (neither delinquency nor a "police brush") are compared with control-subjects without juvenile police troubles (Table 10). A higher proportion of pa-

## TABLE 10

### RELATION OF CHILDHOOD BEHAVIOR PROBLEMS TO ADULT ARRESTS IN SUBJECTS WITHOUT JUVENILE POLICE TROUBLES

| | Group 2 Behavior in Conflict with Mores | | | Group 3 Other Behavior Problems | | | Control Subjects | | |
|---|---|---|---|---|---|---|---|---|---|
| | M | F | T | M | F | T | M | F | T |
| Adult arrests | 38% | 13% | 28% * | 27% | ... | 18% | 18% | 3% | 14% * |
| No adult police record | 62 | 87 | 72 | 73 | 100 | 82 | 82 | 97 | 86 |
| | 100% | 100% | 100% | 100% | 100% | 100% | 100% | 100% | 100% |
| | N = 66 | N = 45 | N = 111 | N = 67 | N = 35 | N = 102 | N = 65 | N = 30 | N = 95 |

* Difference between starred groups is significant at the .02 level.

tients than control subjects (23 and 14 per cent, respectively) were again found to have been arrested as adults—a not quite significant difference. However, when patients without juvenile police troubles are divided according to the nature of their childhood behavior prob-

[7] Sheldon and Eleanor Glueck, *Juvenile Delinquents Grown Up*, New York: The Commonwealth Fund, 1940; Edward Schwartz, "Statistics of Juvenile Delinquency in the United States," *Annals of the American Academy of Political and Social Science*, 261 (January, 1949), pp. 9-20; *Uniform Crime Reports for the United States*, U.S. Department of Justice, Federal Bureau of Investigation, Annual Bulletin, 27, 1956.

lems, Group 2 patients, those whose childhood behavior problems were conflicts with the mores, have significantly more members arrested as adults than control subjects. Behavior problems in childhood which involve conflicts with the mores are therefore associated with an excess of adult police offenders even in the absence of police troubles in childhood.

## Discussion

In evaluating these results, it should be remembered that the subjects are drawn from a special population. Coming from a single geographic locality at the time of original referral to the Clinic, the subjects were also largely of lower-class background. The contrast in mobility between patients and control subjects might be less striking in a less stable community than St. Louis. To the extent, however, that the Clinic patients can be regarded as typical of seriously disturbed children and the control subjects typical of children without serious behavior problems, our findings suggest that children who are sufficiently disturbed to be referred to a child guidance clinic grow into adults who not only are highly mobile but who contribute a disproportionate share to serious social problems—violent death by homicide and suicide and crime.

Other papers to be published [8] indicate that this same group contributes disproportionately also to the mental hospital population, to the divorce rate, and to the breeding of a second generation of disturbed offspring. Our findings suggest, first, that these phenomena may occur with a significant incidence in a relatively circumscribed segment of the population distinguished by a life-long failure to conform to the social mores, and second, that diverse social problems may be anchored in similar social and psychiatric conditions. Although there may be psychiatrically normal criminals who pursue crime as a profession while leading stable, well-organized lives in other areas, it seems probable that criminal activities are more frequently only one expression of a grossly disturbed life pattern of which transiency, violence, and unstable family relations as well as crime, are typical. Further analysis of the interviews will permit an exploration of the points at which psychiatric

[8] P. O'Neal and L. Robins, "The Relation of Childhood Behavior Problems to Adult Psychiatric Status," *American Journal of Psychiatry* . . . [114 (1958), 961-69]; "The Marital Status of Adults Who Had Childhood Behavior Problems" . . . [Published as "Marital History of Former Problem Children," *Social Problems*, 5 (1958), 347-58.]

disease and social background are intermeshed in the development of social problems.

Of equal or perhaps greater interest than the finding that childhood behavior problems signal a high probability of adult difficulties, is the fact that many earlier patients are well adjusted as adults. Even the former juvenile delinquents, who rank first in the proportion of adults with criminal offenses, include 38 per cent who have reached a median age of 43 years without an adult police record. The interviews now being conducted are structured to investigate factors which protect over one-third of this most disfavored group from adult crime. It is hoped that this study will suggest reasons for the diverse careers of similarly disturbed children.

# Correlation of This Book with Juvenile Delinquency Texts
*(The reader should use the index to locate short discussions of*

| Text chs. | Barron, *The Juvenile in Delinquent Society* Knopf, 1954 | Bloch and Flynn, *Delinquency* Randon House, 1956 | Carr, *Delinquency Control* Harper, 1950 | Cavan, *Juvenile Delinquency* Lippincott, 1962 |
|---|---|---|---|---|
| | | RELATED ARTICLES | | |
| 1 | 17–22 | 2, 3 | — | 4 |
| 2 | 2, 3 | 1, 17–22 | 4, 10, 12, 13 | 2, 3 |
| 3 | 1 | 4, 13 | 1, 2, 3, 5, 6, 22, 36 | 1 |
| 4 | 5, 6 | — | 1 | — |
| 5 | 4 | — | — | 11 |
| 6 | — | — | 11, 17–21 | 17, 22 |
| 7 | 11 | 11 | 7, 8, 9, 14, 15, 35 | 5, 7, 8, 9 |
| 8 | 14, 15 | 5–10, 12, 14–17 | — | 6, 10 |
| 9 | 7, 8, 10, 17, 21 | — | 35 | — |
| 10 | 16 | 26 | 26, 27 | 14, 15 |
| 11 | — | — | 23, 28–34 | — |
| 12 | 5, 6, 9, 12, 13 | 27 | 14, 15 | 18, 19 |
| 13 | — | 27 | 5, 6, 22, 24, 25 | 20, 21 |
| 14 | 26 | 27, 28 | 7, 8, 9, 24, 25 | 12, 13, 17 |
| 15 | 27 | 29–34 | — | 16, 34 |
| 16 | 29–33 | — | — | 24 |
| 17 | 28, 34 | 23, 24, 25, 35, 36 | — | 23, 25, 35 |
| 18 | 23, 24, 25, 35, 36 | | — | — |
| 19 | | | — | 26 |
| 20 | | | — | — |
| 21 | | | — | 27 |
| 22 | | | — | 28 |
| 23 | | | 16, 34 | — |
| 24 | | | — | 29, 30 |
| 25 | | | 35, 36 | 31, 32, 33 |
| 26 | | | | 36 |
| 27 | | | | |
| 28 | | | | |
| 29 | | | | |
| 30 | | | | |

*any specific subject.*)

| Neumeyer, *Juvenile Delinquency in Modern Society* Van Nostrand, 1961 | Robison, *Juvenile Delinquency* Holt, 1960 | Shulman, *Juvenile Delinquency in American Society* Harper, 1961 | Tappan, *Juvenile Delinquency* McGraw-Hill, 1949 |
|---|---|---|---|
| **IN *Readings* BOOK** | | | |
| 2, 3 | 2 | — | 2, 3, 17–21 |
| 1 | 1, 36 | 2, 3, 18–21 | 1 |
| — | 3 | 1 | 4 |
| 4, 9, 10 | — | — | 5–10 |
| 11, 35 | — | 4, 12, 13 | 11 |
| 12, 18–21, 36 | 11, 35 | — | — |
| 14, 15 | 5–10, 12, 13 | — | 5–9, 12–15, 17 |
| 7, 8, 17 | 14, 15 | 5–9 | 27 |
| 16 | 7, 8, 17–21 | 22 | 27 |
| 5, 6, 22 | 16, 34 | — | — |
| — | 22 | 7, 8 | — |
| 13 | 2, 4 | — | 28 |
| 26 | 26 | — | 23, 24, 25 |
| 27, 28–34 | 27 | 11 | — |
| 16, 23–25 | — | — | 29–33 |
|  | 28 | 14, 15 | 16 |
|  | 23 | 12 | 26, 35, 36 |
|  | — | 10, 17 |  |
|  | — | 20 |  |
|  | 29 | 21 |  |
|  | — | 26 |  |
|  | 30 | 27, 28 |  |
|  | — | — |  |
|  | 31, 32, 33 | 29–34 |  |
|  | — | 23 |  |
|  | 24 | 24, 25 |  |
|  | 34 | 16, 34 |  |
|  | 17, 25 | 24, 35, 36 |  |
|  |  | — |  |

# Index

**463**